Psalms

Volume 2

TEACH THE TEXT COMMENTARY SERIES

John H. Walton
Old Testament General Editor

Mark L. Strauss
New Testament General Editor

Old Testament Volumes

Exodus .... T. Desmond Alexander

Leviticus and Numbers .... Joe M. Sprinkle

Joshua .... Kenneth A. Mathews

Judges and Ruth .... Kenneth C. Way

1 & 2 Samuel .... Robert B. Chisholm Jr.

Ezra, Nehemiah, and Esther ....Douglas J. E. Nykolaishen
and Andrew J. Schmutzer

Job .... Daniel J. Estes

Psalms, two volumes .... C. Hassell Bullock

Ecclesiastes and Song of Songs .... Edward M. Curtis

Jeremiah and Lamentations .... J. Daniel Hays

Daniel .... Ronald W. Pierce

New Testament Volumes

Matthew .... Jeannine K. Brown

Mark .... Grant R. Osborne

Luke .... R. T. France

Acts .... David E. Garland

Romans .... C. Marvin Pate

1 Corinthians .... Preben Vang

2 Corinthians .... Moyer V. Hubbard

James, 1 & 2 Peter, and Jude .... Jim Samra

Revelation .... J. Scott Duvall

Visit the series website at www.teachthetextseries.com.

TEACH the TEXT
COMMENTARY SERIES

Psalms

Volume 2
Psalms 73–150

C. Hassell Bullock

Mark L. Strauss and John H. Walton
GENERAL EDITORS

BakerBooks

a division of Baker Publishing Group
Grand Rapids, Michigan

Published by Baker Books
a division of Baker Publishing Group
PO Box 6287, Grand Rapids, MI 49516–6287
www.bakerbooks.com

Printed in the United States of America

Library of Congress Cataloging-in-Publication Data
Bullock, C. Hassell.
    Psalms / C. Hassell Bullock ; Mark L. Strauss and John H. Walton, general editors ; illustrating the text, Kevin and Sherry Harney, associate editors ; Donald C. Porter, contributing author.
        pages cm. — (Teach the text commentary)
    Includes bibliographical references and index.
    ISBN 978-0-8010-9197-1 (cloth : v. 1)
    ISBN 978-0-8010-9239-8 (paper : v. 2)
    1. Bible. Psalms—Commentaries. I. Strauss, Mark L., 1959– editor. II. Walton, John H., 1952– editor. III. Title.
BS1430.53.P725 2015
223'.207—dc23   2014044252

In keeping with biblical principles of creation stewardship, Baker Publishing Group advocates the responsible use of our natural resources. As a member of the Green Press Initiative, our company uses recycled paper when possible. The text paper of this book is composed in part of post-consumer waste.

17   18   19   20   21   22   23   7   6   5   4   3   2   1

Contents

List of Sidebars   ix
Welcome to the Teach the Text
   Commentary Series   xi
Introduction to the Teach the Text
   Commentary Series   xiii
Preface   xv
Abbreviations   xvii

Psalm 73 1
   "Earth Has Nothing I Desire besides
   You"
Psalm 74 9
   "Remember the Nation You Purchased
   Long Ago"
Psalm 75 18
   "We Praise You, God, We Praise You,
   for Your Name Is Near"
Psalm 76 24
   "Surely the Wrath of Man Shall Praise
   Thee"
Psalm 77 32
   "Your Path Led through the Sea, . . .
   Though Your Footprints Were Not
   Seen"
Psalm 78 39
   "He Sent the Ark of His Might into
   Captivity, His Splendor into the Hands
   of the Enemy"
Psalm 79 51
   "Then We Your People, the Sheep of
   Your Pasture, Will Praise You Forever"

Psalm 80 59
   "Make Your Face Shine on Us, That
   We May Be Saved"
Psalm 81 67
   "If My People Would Only Listen to
   Me"
Psalm 82 75
   "Rise Up, O God, Judge the Earth"
Additional Insights 81
   The Meaning of "Gods" in Psalm 82
Psalm 83 83
   "O God, Do Not Remain Silent; Do
   Not Turn a Deaf Ear, Do Not Stand
   Aloof, O God"
Psalm 84 90
   "How Lovely Is Your Dwelling Place,
   Lord Almighty!"
Psalm 85 98
   "Righteousness and Peace Kiss Each
   Other"
Psalm 86 105
   "Give Me an Undivided Heart, That I
   May Fear Your Name"
Additional Insights 111
   David, the Prototype of the "Poor and
   Needy"
Psalm 87 112
   "The Lord Will Write in the Register
   of the Peoples: 'This One Was Born in
   Zion'"
Psalm 88 119
   "Darkness Is My Closest Friend"

Psalm 89.................................... 125
"I Will Sing of the Lord's Great Love
Forever"

Psalm 90.................................... 134
"Lord, You Have Been Our Dwelling
Place throughout All Generations"

Psalm 91.................................... 141
"I Will Say of the Lord, 'He Is My
Refuge and My Fortress, My God, in
Whom I Trust'"

Psalm 92.................................... 150
"I Sing for Joy at What Your Hands
Have Done"

Psalm 93.................................... 157
"The Lord Reigns, He Is Robed in
Majesty"

Psalm 94.................................... 164
"The Lord Knows All Human Plans;
He Knows That They Are Futile"

Psalm 95.................................... 170
"Come, Let Us Sing for Joy to the
Lord"

Psalm 96.................................... 177
"Sing to the Lord a New Song"

Psalm 97.................................... 184
"The Lord Reigns, Let the Earth Be
Glad"

Psalm 98.................................... 191
"Sing to the Lord a New Song, for He
Has Done Marvelous Things"

Psalm 99.................................... 197
"The Lord Our God Is Holy"

Psalm 100.................................. 204
"Shout for Joy to the Lord, All the
Earth"

Additional Insights 212
Why the Universal Perspective in the
Wake of the Exile?

Psalm 101.................................. 214
"I Will Conduct the Affairs of My
House with a Blameless Heart"

Psalm 102.................................. 220
"The Heavens . . . Will Perish, but You
Remain"

Psalm 103.................................. 227
"The Lord Is Compassionate and
Gracious, Slow to Anger, Abounding
in Love"

Psalm 104.................................. 234
"I Will Sing Praise to My God as Long
as I Live"

Additional Insights 245
The Hallelujahs of Books 4 and 5

Psalm 105.................................. 248
"He Remembered His Holy Promise
Given to His Servant Abraham"

Psalm 106.................................. 256
"We Have Sinned, Even as Our
Ancestors Did"

Psalm 107.................................. 266
"Let the Redeemed of the Lord Tell
Their Story"

Psalm 108.................................. 275
"I Will Awaken the Dawn"

Psalm 109.................................. 282
"He Stands at the Right Hand of the
Needy, to Save Their Lives"

Additional Insights 290
A Hypothesis on Psalm 109

Psalm 110.................................. 292
"The Lord Says to My Lord: 'Sit at
My Right Hand Until I Make Your
Enemies a Footstool'"

Additional Insights 299
The Priest-King Ruler Model

Psalm 111.................................. 301
"Glorious and Majestic Are His
Deeds, and His Righteousness Endures
Forever"

Psalm 112.................................. 308
"Blessed Are Those Who Fear the
Lord, Who Find Great Delight in His
Commands"

Psalm 113.................................. 315
"Who Is like the Lord Our God, the
One Who Sits Enthroned on High?"

Additional Insights 322
The Egyptian Hallel (Psalms 113–18)

Psalm 114.................................. 324
"Tremble, Earth, at the Presence of the
Lord"

Psalm 115.. 330
"Those Who Make [Idols] Will Be like
Them"
Psalm 116.. 337
"Return to Your Rest, My Soul, for the
LORD Has Been Good to You"
Psalm 117.. 344
"Great Is His Love toward Us"
Psalm 118.. 348
"Give Thanks to the LORD, for He Is
Good; His Love Endures Forever"
Psalm 119.. 357
"I Have Hidden Your Word in My
Heart That I Might Not Sin against
You"
Psalm 120.. 372
"I Am for Peace; but . . . They Are for
War"
Additional Insights 378
Songs of Ascents, the Pilgrim Psalter
(Psalms 120–34)
Psalm 121.. 381
"My Help Comes from the LORD, the
Maker of Heaven and Earth"
Psalm 122.. 388
"I Rejoiced with Those Who Said to
Me, 'Let Us Go to the House of the
LORD'"
Psalm 123.. 395
"Have Mercy on Us, LORD, Have
Mercy on Us"
Psalm 124.. 400
"We Have Escaped like a Bird from the
Fowler's Snare"
Psalm 125.. 406
"Those Who Trust in the LORD Are
like Mount Zion, Which Cannot Be
Shaken"
Psalm 126.. 412
"The LORD Has Done Great Things for
Us, and We Are Filled with Joy"
Psalm 127.. 419
"Unless the LORD Builds the House, the
Builders Labor in Vain"
Psalm 128.. 426
"Blessed Are All Who Fear the LORD,
Who Walk in Obedience to Him"

Psalm 129.. 432
"They Have Greatly Oppressed
Me . . . , but They Have Not Gained
the Victory over Me"
Psalm 130.. 438
"I Wait for the LORD, My Whole Being
Waits"
Psalm 131.. 444
"Like a Weaned Child I Am Content"
Psalm 132.. 450
"I Will Not Enter My House or Go to
My Bed . . . Till I Find a Place for the
LORD"
Psalm 133.. 459
"How Good and Pleasant It Is When
God's People Live Together in Unity!"
Psalm 134.. 465
"Praise the LORD, All You Servants
of the LORD Who Minister . . . in the
House of the LORD"
Psalm 135.. 469
"I Know That the LORD Is Great, That
Our Lord Is Greater Than All Gods"
Psalm 136.. 479
"Give Thanks to the LORD . . . Who
Alone Does Great Wonders, His Love
Endures Forever"
Psalm 137.. 486
"By the Rivers of Babylon We Sat and
Wept When We Remembered Zion"
Psalm 138.. 492
"Do Not Abandon the Works of Your
Hands"
Additional Insights 501
The Model of Historical
Double-Tracking
Psalm 139.. 503
"You Have Searched Me, LORD, and
You Know Me"
Psalm 140.. 512
"I Say to the LORD, 'You Are My God'"
Psalm 141.. 518
"Do Not Let My Heart Be Drawn to
What Is Evil So That I Take Part in
Wicked Deeds"

Psalm 142............................ 525
"There Is No One at My Right Hand;
No One Is Concerned for Me"

Psalm 143............................ 532
"Let the Morning Bring Me Word of
Your Unfailing Love"

Psalm 144............................ 538
"Blessed Is the People Whose God Is
the LORD"

Psalm 145............................ 547
"Great Is the LORD and Most Worthy
of Praise; His Greatness No One Can
Fathom"

Psalm 146............................ 555
"Blessed Are Those Whose Help Is the
God of Jacob, Whose Hope Is in the
LORD Their God"

Psalm 147............................ 562
"The LORD Delights in Those Who
Fear Him, Who Put Their Hope in His
Unfailing Love"

Psalm 148............................ 569
"Praise the LORD from the Heavens. . . .
Praise the LORD from the Earth"

Psalm 149............................ 577
"May the Praise of God Be . . . a
Double-Edged Sword in Their Hands"

Psalm 150............................ 585
"Let Everything That Has Breath
Praise the LORD"

Notes   593
Bibliography   608
Contributors   614
Index   615

List of Sidebars

Vows   28
The Shepherd Theme of Psalms
   77–80   33
Realignment from Rachel to
   Leah   41
Does God Deceive?   45
The Covenant Formula   54
Psalm 83 and the Asaph
   Collection   84
The Temple in Book 3   91
Names of God in Psalm 84   92
Three Musical Instruments   151
The Palm and the Cedar   153
"The LORD Reigns": Psalms of the
   Heavenly King   159

Ranking the Severity of Wrongs   230
The Thirteen Attributes of God   304
The Song of Hannah and Psalm
   113   318
Reading Psalm 119   358
Ten Words for "Law" in Psalm
   119   359
The Broom Bush   374
The Names Israel and Judah   407
History and Liturgy in Code
   Language   451
The Poplar Tree   488
A Pictogram of Worship   528
Number Symbolism   589

Welcome to the Teach the Text Commentary Series

Why another commentary series? That was the question the general editors posed when Baker Books asked us to produce this series. Is there something that we can offer to pastors and teachers that is not currently being offered by other commentary series, or that can be offered in a more helpful way? After carefully researching the needs of pastors who teach the text on a weekly basis, we concluded that yes, more can be done; the Teach the Text Commentary Series (TTCS) is carefully designed to fill an important gap.

The technicality of modern commentaries often overwhelms readers with details that are tangential to the main purpose of the text. Discussions of source and redaction criticism, as well as detailed surveys of secondary literature, seem far removed from preaching and teaching the Word. Rather than wade through technical discussions, pastors often turn to devotional commentaries, which may contain exegetical weaknesses, misuse the Greek and Hebrew languages, and lack hermeneutical sophistication. There is a need for a commentary that utilizes the best of biblical scholarship but also presents the material in a clear, concise, attractive, and user-friendly format.

This commentary is designed for that purpose—to provide a ready reference for the exposition of the biblical text, giving easy access to information that a pastor needs to communicate the text effectively. To that end, the commentary is divided into carefully selected preaching units (with carefully regulated word counts both in the passage as a whole and in each subsection). Pastors and teachers engaged in weekly preparation thus know that they will be reading approximately the same amount of material on a week-by-week basis.

Each passage begins with a concise summary of the central message, or "Big Idea," of the passage and a list of its main themes. This is followed by a more detailed interpretation of the text, including the literary context of the passage, historical background material, and interpretive insights. While drawing on the best of biblical scholarship, this material is clear, concise, and to the point. Technical material is kept to a minimum, with endnotes pointing the reader to more detailed discussion and additional resources.

A second major focus of this commentary is on the preaching and teaching process itself. Few commentaries today help the pastor/teacher move from the meaning of the text to its effective communication. Our goal is to bridge this gap. In addition to interpreting the text in the "Understanding the Text" section, each unit contains a "Teaching the Text" section and an "Illustrating the Text" section. The teaching section points to the key theological themes of the passage and ways to communicate these themes to today's audiences. The illustration section provides ideas and examples for retaining the interest of hearers and connecting the message to daily life.

The creative format of this commentary arises from our belief that the Bible is not just a record of God's dealings in the past but is the living Word of God, "alive and active" and "sharper than any double-edged sword" (Heb. 4:12). Our prayer is that this commentary will help to unleash that transforming power for the glory of God.

The General Editors

Introduction to the Teach the Text Commentary Series

This series is designed to provide a ready reference for teaching the biblical text, giving easy access to information that is needed to communicate a passage effectively. To that end, the commentary is carefully divided into units that are faithful to the biblical authors' ideas and of an appropriate length for teaching or preaching.

The following standard sections are offered in each unit.

1. *Big Idea*. For each unit the commentary identifies the primary theme, or "Big Idea," that drives both the passage and the commentary.
2. *Key Themes*. Together with the Big Idea, the commentary addresses in bullet-point fashion the key ideas presented in the passage.
3. *Understanding the Text*. This section focuses on the exegesis of the text and includes several sections.
   a. The Text in Context. Here the author gives a brief explanation of how the unit fits into the flow of the text around it, including reference to the rhetorical strategy of the book and the unit's contribution to the purpose of the book.
   b. Outline/Structure. For some literary genres (e.g., epistles), a brief exegetical outline may be provided to guide the reader through the structure and flow of the passage.

c. Historical and Cultural Background. This section addresses historical and cultural background information that may illuminate a verse or passage.

d. Interpretive Insights. This section provides information needed for a clear understanding of the passage. The intention of the author is to be highly selective and concise rather than exhaustive and expansive.

e. Theological Insights. In this very brief section the commentary identifies a few carefully selected theological insights about the passage.

4. *Teaching the Text*. Under this second main heading the commentary offers guidance for teaching the text. In this section the author lays out the main themes and applications of the passage. These are linked carefully to the Big Idea and are represented in the Key Themes.

5. *Illustrating the Text*. At this point in the commentary the writers partner with a team of pastor/teachers to provide suggestions for relevant and contemporary illustrations from current culture, entertainment, history, the Bible, news, literature, ethics, biography, daily life, medicine, and over forty other categories. They are designed to spark creative thinking for preachers and teachers and to help them design illustrations that bring alive the passage's key themes and message.

Preface

This preface is intended not so much to celebrate the end of the writing of this commentary as to exult in the joy of discovering over and over again the riches of the Psalms. Indeed, the deeper I have delved into the Psalms in this second volume, the richer the experience has become. The treasures of the Psalter are endless, and this work would never have seen the light of day without the myriad of studies on the Psalms that have been written over the last two millennia and for which I am inexpressibly grateful. When the Psalms are part of our spiritual life, they are absorbed into the fibers of our souls. They will walk us through the valley, will direct our eyes to the hills where our help comes from, will steady our hearts when the arrows by day and the terrors by night are making havoc all around us. Indeed, we ought to wear the Psalms like a garment, and when we do, they will not grow threadbare—quite the opposite. The Spirit will reweave their fabric with each new reading.

But the Psalms also have a unique emotive power because their spiritual insights are a mirror that draws out of our souls those things we cannot or would not otherwise see in our souls and express with our lips. When we look into that mirror, we see our circumstances, emotions, actions and reactions, hope and despair, and God illumines our souls from the glow of the psalmists' faith, whose embers have been collected from the passionate spirits of individuals like us.

One of my life's greatest honors has been writing this commentary. It has not only increased exponentially my understanding of the Psalms, but I have personally experienced again and again their shaping power, bringing the contours of my worldview more in line with that of the psalmists who are confident of the Lord's love and faithfulness to reshape his people and his world. To all who have had a part in commissioning me to this task and facilitating its completion, I express my deepest gratitude. And to the Lord, maker of heaven and earth and redeemer of our souls, I offer the Psalter's own quintessential word of praise, "Hallelujah!" *Soli Deo Gloria!*

C. Hassell Bullock
January 23, 2017
Wheaton, Illinois

Abbreviations

Old Testament

Gen.	Genesis	2 Chron.	2 Chronicles	Dan.	Daniel
Exod.	Exodus	Ezra	Ezra	Hosea	Hosea
Lev.	Leviticus	Neh.	Nehemiah	Joel	Joel
Num.	Numbers	Esther	Esther	Amos	Amos
Deut.	Deuteronomy	Job	Job	Obad.	Obadiah
Josh.	Joshua	Ps(s).	Psalm(s)	Jon.	Jonah
Judg.	Judges	Prov.	Proverbs	Mic.	Micah
Ruth	Ruth	Eccles.	Ecclesiastes	Nah.	Nahum
1 Sam.	1 Samuel	Song	Song of Songs	Hab.	Habakkuk
2 Sam.	2 Samuel	Isa.	Isaiah	Zeph.	Zephaniah
1 Kings	1 Kings	Jer.	Jeremiah	Hag.	Haggai
2 Kings	2 Kings	Lam.	Lamentations	Zech.	Zechariah
1 Chron.	1 Chronicles	Ezek.	Ezekiel	Mal.	Malachi

New Testament

Matt.	Matthew	Eph.	Ephesians	Heb.	Hebrews
Mark	Mark	Phil.	Philippians	James	James
Luke	Luke	Col.	Colossians	1 Pet.	1 Peter
John	John	1 Thess.	1 Thessalonians	2 Pet.	2 Peter
Acts	Acts	2 Thess.	2 Thessalonians	1 John	1 John
Rom.	Romans	1 Tim.	1 Timothy	2 John	2 John
1 Cor.	1 Corinthians	2 Tim.	2 Timothy	3 John	3 John
2 Cor.	2 Corinthians	Titus	Titus	Jude	Jude
Gal.	Galatians	Philem.	Philemon	Rev.	Revelation

General

ca.	*circa*, about	lit.	literally
cf.	*confer*, compare	no(s).	number(s)
chap(s).	chapter(s)	p(p).	page(s)
e.g.	for example	pass.	passive
esp.	especially	pl.	plural
et al.	and others	ptc.	participle
etc.	and the rest	sg.	singular
Heb.	Hebrew	v(v).	verse(s)
i.e.	that is	//	parallel

Ancient Versions

LXX	Septuagint	MT	Masoretic Text

Modern Versions

ASV	American Standard Version	NIV	New International Version
ESV	English Standard Version	NJPS	*The Tanakh: The Holy Scriptures; The New JPS Translation according to the Traditional Hebrew Text* (2nd ed.; 2000)
HCSB	Holman Christian Standard Bible		
JB	The Jerusalem Bible		
JPS	*The Tanakh: The Holy Scriptures* (1917)	NKJV	New King James Version
		NLT	New Living Translation
KJV	King James Version	NRSV	New Revised Standard Version
NASB	New American Standard Bible		
		RSV	Revised Standard Version
NET	New English Translation		

Apocrypha and Septuagint

1 Macc.	1 Maccabees

Mishnah and Talmud

b.	Babylonian Talmud	*y.*	Jerusalem Talmud
m.	Mishnah		

Secondary Sources

ANET	James B. Pritchard, ed. *Ancient Near Eastern Texts Relating to the Old Testament*. 3rd ed. Princeton, NJ: Princeton University Press, 1969.
NIDB	Katharine Doob Sakenfeld, ed. *The New Interpreter's Dictionary of the Bible*. 5 vols. Nashville: Abingdon, 2009.
NIDOTTE	Willem VanGemeren, ed. *New International Dictionary of Old Testament Theology and Exegesis*. 5 vols. Grand Rapids: Zondervan, 1997.

"Earth Has Nothing
I Desire besides You"

Big Idea

When the prosperity of the wicked causes our faith to waver, God is still the only one who matters.

Key Themes

- Envy of evildoers is ultimately conquered only by the incomparable reality of God's presence.
- Sometimes we talk too much about the problem and too little about its resolution.

Understanding the Text

The Psalter contains twelve Asaph psalms (Pss. 50; 73–83),[1] and this group of eleven (Pss. 73–83) introduces Book 3. The Asaph psalms elude our system of classification, with some scholars preferring the wisdom psalm category,[2] others the individual lament, or the psalm of trust, and the list goes on. The subject matter, as well as the vocabulary, tends to place them in the wisdom column, even though the definition of wisdom psalms is still under discussion (while the so-called wisdom psalms can be classified under more than one category, with the lists varying from one scholar to another, the following gives a typical list by book: Book 1: Pss. 32; 34; 37; Book 2: Ps. 49; Book 3: Ps. 73; Book 4: none; Book 5: Pss. 112; 127; 128; 133).[3] I would prefer to speak about a wisdom way of conceptualizing the world rather than a wisdom literary category of psalms, even though we will use the category of wisdom psalms as a convenience. That means the writers of ancient Israel were free to move in and out of this mode of thought without being confined to a particular style of composition, which had not yet been clearly delineated. In the case of Psalm 73, it seems that the wisdom vocabulary (see the list based on Scott's wisdom glossary)[4] and the topic of concern point in the direction of wisdom thought. Further, the fact that Psalm 72 is dedicated to Solomon, known for his wisdom (1 Kings 3), associates Psalm 73, in both history and thought, with the wisdom tradition.

The Text in Context

The subject of this psalm connects it to Psalms 37 and 49, and particularly to Job. Hossfeld and Zenger call attention to the fact that the psalmist claims innocence as does Job (Ps. 73:13; Job 13:18; 16:17; etc.); they both have some type of "vision of God" (Ps. 73:17; Job 38:1; 42:5); and the profile of the wicked given in Psalm 73:4–12 is closely related to the sketch in Job 21:7–34.[5] Moreover, Walter Brueggemann and Patrick Miller note that the verb "will perish" in 73:27 recalls the same verb in Psalm 1:6 (NIV: "leads to destruction") to indicate that Psalm 73 is intended to be the introduction to Book 3 of the Psalter, as Psalm 1 was the introduction to Book 1.[6]

Outline/Structure

The poem is divided into three parts by the use of the adverb "surely" (*'ak*):

1. "Surely"—the problem and resulting crisis (73:1–12)
2. "Surely"—the jealousy and resulting perplexity (73:13–17)
3. "Surely"—the resolution and the reality of God (73:18–28)

Historical and Cultural Background

Psalm 73 begins Book 3, and with it a new perspective on Israel's life and world. Asaph was one of David's Levitical directors (1 Chron. 25:1), and a further hint of that is the phrase "my portion" (Ps. 73:26), alluding to the fact that the Levites did not receive a landed inheritance, but Yahweh was their "portion" (Num. 18:20 ESV). That perspective has shaped the psalmist's theological viewpoint generally, as he has come to recognize that Yahweh is his only possession: "Whom have I in heaven but you?" (73:25a).

Quite likely the prophetic elements and the strong sense of history that characterize this collection of Asaph psalms (Pss. 73–83) were in part the criteria for their inclusion in Book 3, especially as the initial psalms.[7] See "The Structure and Composition of the Psalter" in the introduction in volume 1.

Interpretive Insights

Title *A psalm of Asaph.* The divine name in the Asaph psalms is overwhelmingly *'elohim* (God). See the sidebar "The Divine Names in Psalm 50" in the unit on Psalm 50, and "The Divine Names and the Elohistic Psalter" in the unit on Psalms 42–43.[8]

73:1 *Surely God is good to Israel.* The adverb "surely" (*'ak*, "surely, truly") occurs in three places, marking the beginning of the psalm's three parts (73:1, 13, 18). The emendation of the clause "God is good *to Israel*" (*l'yisra'el*) to

"God is good to the *upright*" (*lᵉyashar 'el*; see RSV, NRSV) has no textual support and is unnecessary, particularly in view of the fact that the psalm is placed in the lead position of Book 3, which is about Israel's tragic history and the ostensible failure of the Davidic covenant (see Ps. 89). Thus, the editor, by the inclusion and placement of the poems of Book 3, is addressing the theological implications of a new era. The rhetorical voice[9] of Book 3 offers reassurance to Israel, exiled by a prosperous and arrogant nation whom they are tempted to envy (73:3). Despite the catastrophic proportions of Israel's humiliating condition that are brought to our attention in 74:4–8, the psalmist's witness is positive: "Surely God is good to Israel" (73:1). Already the editor of Book 3, by placing Psalm 73 in first place in the book, has begun to offset the depressing dimensions of Psalm 89.

pure in heart. Psalm 24:4 applies the term "pure heart" to those who reject idolatry.

73:2 *my feet had almost slipped*. This is a metaphor describing the confusion in the suppliant's mind regarding the problem he is about to address. This clause is parallel to the second clause, "I had nearly lost my foothold." See 40:2.

73:3 *For I envied the arrogant*. Now the psalmist begins to describe the problem, and it begins with his own envy of the "arrogant" (also 5:5). On the historical level, the "arrogant" were probably prosperous and wicked individuals whom the psalmist knew. On the rhetorical level—that is, the way the editor is adapting the psalm—the "arrogant" are likely the Babylonians.

when I saw. Parallel to "I envied," this verb suggests that the suppliant was jealous of the prosperity (or "peace/well-being") of the wicked. See Genesis 30:1 as another example of envy.

73:4 *They have no struggles*. The word for "struggles" is literally "chains," perhaps a metaphor describing the chain of physical maladies that lead to death[10] (see Isa. 58:6). The NIV translates the Hebrew phrase meaning "to their death" (*lᵉmotam*) as an older form of "to them"—that is, "*They have no struggles*" (see also the NIV footnote).[11]

healthy. The Hebrew word means "fat" (cf. Hab. 1:16; NIV: "choicest food"), which was a sign of prosperity, often unlawfully gained.

73:5 *They are free from common human burdens*. That is, they do not experience the troubles that strike other human beings. Two words for "human/humankind" (*'enosh* and *'adam*) occur in the two parallel lines: "They are not in trouble as other men; Neither are they plagued like other men" (ASV). While the two terms sometimes carry different nuances (see 90:3), here they function as synonyms.

73:6 *pride is their necklace . . . with violence*. The second half of the sentence further explains that their "pride" was serviced by "violence." That is, they used violence as a way to guard their pride, or to save face.

73:7 *From their callous hearts comes iniquity.* The Hebrew (MT) reads literally, "Their eyes stand out from fat" (see the NIV footnote). The suppliant further explains: literally, "The chambers of [their] heart overflow [with fat]" (NIV: "Their evil imaginations have no limits").

73:8 *They scoff.* This verb, which occurs only here, contextually seems to indicate mockery, or perhaps even slander ("and speak with malice"; "they threaten oppression").

73:9 *Their mouths lay claim to heaven, and their tongues take possession of the earth.* The NIV renders the second clause as synonymously parallel to the thought of the first clause, but the Hebrew verb for "lay claim" means "to set," and the sense would be, literally, "They set their mouths in heaven" (so presumptuous is their speech), giving a complementary parallelism to the second clause, literally, "Their tongue walks through the earth" (the latter clause suggesting arrogant speech) (so ESV). Their hypocritical posture is in view.

73:10 *Therefore their people turn to them and drink up waters in abundance.* Literally, "Therefore his people return here; they drink up abundant waters." Sometimes we can translate the words of the text while its meaning remains obscure. That is the case with this rather opaque verse. The idea seems to be that they are so envious of the wicked and their prosperity that they come to them and drink up their words voraciously, just as the psalmist was at first inclined to do (73:3).

73:11 *They say, "How would God know? Does the Most High know anything?"* The two questions are rhetorical, the first expecting the answer "There is no way he could know!" and the second, "The Most High knows nothing!" They illustrate the arrogance of the wicked. See 2 Samuel 14:17 for a counterstatement. Note that "the Most High" (*'elyon*), used contemptibly here, occurs at the end of the Asaph collection in a prayer that God would make the nations recognize that Yahweh is "the Most High" (83:18).

73:13 *Surely in vain I have kept my heart pure.* The righteous wonder if right living has any benefit. It is a contrast between the "wicked" who enjoy success and acclaim (73:10–12) and the righteous. This same sentiment is expressed in 15:2.

washed my hands in innocence. We may take this both literally (he was a Levite) and metaphorically. See also 26:6.

73:14 *All day long I have been afflicted.* It is difficult to know whether this was physical or emotional suffering—perhaps both.

73:15 *your children.* The suppliant is concerned about his own generation, saying that he has not introduced unnecessary doubts into their minds by talking too much about the issue.

73:17 *till I entered the sanctuary of God.* Literally, "until I came to the sanctuaries of God." The plural noun is not unusual in reference to the sanctuary and most likely refers to the Jerusalem temple (the LXX and Syriac have the singular). Anderson calls it a "plural of amplification or intensity."[12] See also 84:1, "How lovely is your dwelling place" (lit., pl., "dwelling places"). We are not told what happened in the sanctuary, whether the speaker received a priestly pronouncement or a prophetic oracle or experienced a theophany. The important thing is that "then I understood their final destiny."

73:18 *Surely you place them on slippery ground.* Note that "surely" (*'ak*) again introduces a new part in the psalm (73:18–28). God puts the wicked into a situation ("slippery ground") that assures their ruin.

73:19 *How suddenly are they destroyed.* Literally, "How they are brought into desolation in a moment!" The word "how" (*'ek*) expresses distress and is used at the beginning of a lamentation (Jer. 9:19 [9:18 MT]).[13] The suddenness of their fate indicates the certain and strategic judgment of God.

73:20 *when one awakes.* The ephemeral nature of the wicked is the idea. Elsewhere in the Psalter, God's dealing with evil is described as "awakening from sleep" (Pss. 35:23; 44:23; 59:4–5; 78:65–66).

73:22 *I was senseless and ignorant.* Now that he sees the bigger picture, the suppliant confesses that his envy of the wicked and the anxiety he felt were all "senseless" (see also 92:6).

73:24 *afterward you will take me into glory.* The preposition "into" does not occur in the phrase, although the single noun may still be used adverbially (an adverbial accusative), and "into glory" (*kabod*) could mean "honor,"[14] but here it seems to transcend the earthly experience. Anderson believes that the author "may represent a tentative venture to go beyond the then current beliefs. . . . If this was the case, then it is understandable why the Psalmist remained content that God was his portion forever (v. 26) without giving a more definite shape to his hope."[15] See "Additional Insights: The Afterlife and Immortality in the Old Testament," following the unit on Psalm 49.

73:25 *Whom have I in heaven but you?* This is the high point of faith in the psalm. Now the reality of God's presence (73:23) has become his greatest confidence and his strongest longing (73:26). See "Teaching the Text."

73:26 *my portion.* In its literal sense this refers to the landed inheritance of the Israelites. Asaph being a Levite, he is probably now acknowledging, in a way that rises out of experience, that the Lord himself was his inheritance ("portion"; see Num. 18:20 ESV; Ps. 16:5).

73:28 *it is good to be near God.* This verse, and especially this clause, sums up the suppliant's faith, composed of his awareness that he is always with God, who supports him, guides him, and takes him to glory (see comments on 73:24), and that God is his ultimate desire (73:25). For that reason he will tell of God's deeds, which are either God's redemptive works in history or his redemptive works in the suppliant's own life. But in the order of faith, these two confessions belong together.

Theological Insights

This psalm is in the top rubric of theological reflections in the Psalter. Theodicy is the substance of the psalmist's opening reflections and a problem that had the potential of disarming his faith, but this worshiper found a resolution in the sanctuary (73:17). While we do not know the precise form of the problem, we definitely know the end product, a faith focused on God alone (73:25), who is always there and "grips" (*'ḥz*; NIV: "hold") the psalmist with his right hand, "guides" with his counsel, and "takes" him to "glory" (73:23–24). That sequence of verbs spans the scope of faith ("heaven" and "earth"), leaving nothing untouched, and eventuates in a faith that finds God to be the psalmist's all in all (73:25). The "senseless" anxiety of the suppliant, which had no higher quality than beastly instinct (73:22), was transformed into an ascendant faith that sees the whole of life in view of God, who is, to use Jesus's term for the kingdom, the "pearl of great price" (see Matt. 13:45–46). So having begun with the problem of God's justice, the psalmist has discovered that the problem is resolved in the reality of God's presence, for God is everything.

Teaching the Text

Psalm 73 gives us a textual framework for our sermon/lesson, three occurrences of the word "surely" (*'ak*; 73:1, 13, and 18). They are the pegs on which our poet hangs his ideas (see "Outline/Structure"). Thus we might begin by suggesting, as does Anderson,[16] that the first "surely" (73:1) revolves around not theodicy per se but the survival of faith. If there is not some kind of justice behind this God-made universe, then whom can we trust? While justice is the real issue, the problem of envy, which introduces the psalm (73:2–12), is certainly ancillary. Gregory the Great insightfully observes that the real solution to the problem of envy is love (see "Illustrating the Text"). Envy is wishing we possessed the gifts and accomplishments of others, essentially depriving them of those assets. But we cannot envy those whom we truly love. Love causes us to hope and strive for the best gifts and accomplishments for those we love. Loving parents want their children to exceed their own accomplishments, to stand on their shoulders, and when they do, it is as if the parents have achieved those goals themselves.

While injustice and the envy it spawns may lead us to reexamine our faith, this psalm teaches us that divine justice is really intended to lead us to trust

God (73:23–25), to make our whole life the answer to the psalmist's rhetorical question, "Whom have I in heaven but you?" (73:25a). The question is tinged with desperation, but more than that, with the finality of absolute trust.

That quandary brings us to the second "surely" of the psalm (73:13), an angle of faith that the Psalms describe so well and so often, especially if we, like the psalmist, have tried to follow the path of obedience and encountered the obstacle of doubt (73:13–14). We could, of course, allow the passionate dimensions of the problem to create a garrulous reaction, and as a result, we could "betray" our generation and the next by talking too much about the problem and too little about the solution (73:15). One of the temptations of scholars and saints alike—these two categories are too often distinctly separate—is that academia and culture have a way of "glorifying" the problem, and examining and presenting it in its multiple dimensions (which we ought to do), but giving too little attention to the solution. The psalmist's strategy, however, was to talk less and worship more (73:17–19). That drove him, as it should us, into the sanctuary (73:23), where our spirits can be renewed by a power we cannot fully describe, but nevertheless a power we know is present and real (73:23–24). At this turning point of faith (73:17) we begin to discover, or rediscover, the truth that dominates the last movement of the psalm.

That leads us to the third "surely" of the psalm (73:18), that when the injustice in the world sends a seismic rumble through the foundations of our faith, the truth of the psalm is that God is still the only one who matters. It follows then that envy of evildoers is only assuaged by the reality of God's presence (73:25b). In fact, the Psalms are replete with declarations and long-ings to be in the sanctuary, where God is. And God is always the key, just as he is here in this psalm. The suppliant's earthly experience ("When my heart was grieved . . . You hold me by my right hand," 73:21a, 23b) was merely the worldly tether held at the other end by his heavenly God: "Whom have I in heaven but you?" (73:25a). And the marvelous truth is that God and God alone is all the psalmist needs, and all he needs and all he desires have become one and the same: "And earth has nothing I desire besides you" (73:25b). "Thy will be done on earth as it is in heaven" is not only a prayer for the coming of God's kingdom in the world but a prayer for its coming in our hearts.

Illustrating the Text

Love makes the good deeds of others our own.

Church Fathers: Gregory the Great. The psalmist was tempted to envy the prosperity of the wicked (73:3). While this is not the kind of thing we should envy, when envy is turned instead toward people who are good and do good things, it reminds us that a very important ingredient is missing from our spiritual profile—love. Love makes the good deeds of others our own, while envy denies them to others and to ourselves. Parents can understand this truth because when they truly love their children, they look on their children's accomplishments as if they were their own. Gregory the Great explicates this mystery:

> The good things of others which these people cannot have, they would be making their own if they but loved them. For, indeed, all are knit together in faith, just as the various members of one body, though having their different functions, are yet constituted one by mutual concord.
>
> In fact, those things are ours which we love in others, even if we cannot imitate them, and what is loved in ourselves becomes the possession of those who love it. Wherefore, let the envious consider how efficacious is charity, which renders the works of another's labour our own, without any labour on our part.[17]

Anxiety is sometimes a sin.

Quote: C. S. Lewis. The psalmist describes his anxiety as beastly (73:22), suggesting that it is not appropriate, at least in the context of faith, for us humans to be possessed by such a faithless emotion. To be anxious belongs to our sinful nature, for it is the counter position to trust, trusting the God who holds us by our right hand. Lewis wrote to an American friend: "I am also very conscious (and was especially so while praying of you during your workless time) that anxiety is not only a pain which we must ask God to assuage but also a weakness we must ask Him to pardon—for He's told us take no care for the morrow."[18] Paul admonished the Philippian church, "Do not be anxious about anything, but in every situation, by prayer and petition, with thanksgiving, present your requests to God. And the peace of God, which transcends all understanding, will guard your hearts and your minds in Christ Jesus" (Phil. 4:6–7).

"Remember the Nation You Purchased Long Ago"

Big Idea

Our questions, even when they go unanswered, are ultimately resolved in the reality of God.

Key Themes

- The "perpetual" sense of the kingdom's decline is an ongoing sense of God's people.
- In biblical theology, God is both subject and "victim" of disaster.

Understanding the Text

Psalm 74 is a community lament, generated by a national crisis that resulted in the destruction of the temple. The crisis is the background of Psalm 89, with its reflection on the ostensible failure of the Davidic covenant, and this psalm is the capstone of the collection of psalms contained in Book 3 (Pss. 73–89). In Psalm 74 we are likely hearing the historical voice of the Psalter, as the "Asaph" poet tells the story of the fall of Jerusalem and the destruction of the temple by the Babylonians in 586 BC.

The Text in Context

Psalm 73 opened Book 3 with a crisis of personal faith, applied in the context of Book 3 to the national crisis created by the Babylonian invasions of Judah in the early sixth century. It is thus quite appropriate that Psalm 74 should exploit the historical situation by describing the invasion as it centered on the destruction of the temple (74:4–8). Hossfeld and Zenger propose that Psalms 74; 75; and 76 form a "compositional arc," sharing three themes: God as the saving judge (74:12; 75:2, 4; 76:8–9), divine wrath (74:1; 75:8; 76:7), and the theology of the divine name (74:7, 10, 18, 21; 75:1; 76:1).[1] Psalm 73 draws the hermeneutical horizon of these three psalms by raising the question of God's justice and drawing attention to the temple, the place where divine justice can be understood, or at least dealt with in the larger context.

Outline/Structure

Psalm 74 falls into three parts, the first bounded by the interrogative "why?" and the second taking the form of a hymn celebrating the kingdom of God. The third is a series of petitions framed by "remember" (74:18a and 22b) and "do not forget" (74:19b and 23a).[2]

1. Prayer bounded by "why?" (74:1–11)
   a. The first boundary, a prayer (74:1–9)
      i. "O God, *why* have you rejected us forever?" (74:1)
      ii. "*Remember*" your relationship to Israel, and "turn your steps" to "these everlasting ruins" (74:2–3)
      iii. Description of the destruction of the temple (74:4–7)
      iv. Reflection on the enemies' detestable destruction (74:8–9)
   b. The second boundary, a prayer (74:10–11)
      i. "How long" will the enemy mock God? (74:10)
      ii. "*Why*" does God not act? (74:11)
2. God's kingship and kingdom (74:12–17)
   a. Affirmation of God as King (74:12)
   b. Prayer affirming God's kingdom and creation (74:13–17)
3. Prayer bounded by "remember" and "do not forget" (74:18–23)
   a. "*Remember* how the enemy has mocked you" (74:18)
   b. "Do not hand over the life of your dove" (74:19a)
   c. "*Do not forget* the lives of your afflicted" (74:19b)
   d. "Have regard for your covenant" (74:20)
   e. "Do not let the oppressed retreat in disgrace" (74:21a)
   f. "May the poor and needy praise your name" (74:21b)
   g. "Rise up, O God, and defend your cause" (74:22a)
   h. "*Remember* how fools mock you" (74:22b)
   i. "*Do not ignore* ["forget"] the clamor of your adversaries" (74:23)

Historical and Cultural Background

The destruction of the temple (74:3–7) positions this psalm sometime after 586 BC, when Nebuchadnezzar captured Jerusalem and burned the temple (2 Kings 25), perhaps soon after the tragedy since the details seem fresh in the psalmist's mind. Psalm 74 may have been used as a lament on other occasions, for example, the desecration of the temple by Antiochus Epiphanes in 167 BC and the destruction of the Herodian temple by Titus in AD 70. The reference to other worship places in the land is made with no word of condemnation, leading some to suggest they were merely places of prayer.[3]

With the psalmist's concern being the temple and not pagan worship, verse 8b may simply report the fact of their destruction without comment.

Interpretive Insights

Title maskil. A *maskil* (from *skl*, "to instruct," or "to be skilled") may teach a moral lesson[4] or relate to skillful and artistic style[5] (see the comments on the title for Ps. 32). Among the Asaph psalms, only Psalms 74 and 78 have the term *maskil* in the title, suggesting that their purpose was to draw a lesson from the historical tragedies of Israel's past.[6]

74:1 *O God, why have you rejected us forever?* The use of *'elohim* ("God") characterizes the Elohistic Psalter (see the sidebar "The Divine Names and the Elohistic Psalter" in the unit on Pss. 42–43). The interrogative "why?" used twice in this verse, forms an *inclusio* to part 1 of the psalm (74:1 and 11). The verb "rejected" (*znh*) is used in the exilic literature to refer to Yahweh's rejection of Israel, which implies an abandonment of the covenant he himself made with them,[7] thus presenting the theological conflict: Yahweh has chosen Israel and then rejected them.

Why does your anger smolder against the sheep of your pasture? The expression "your anger smolder" (lit., "your nose smoke") suggests the image of an angry person who is breathing so hard that it seems almost as though his nose is smoking. And since Israel is metaphorically the "sheep" of Yahweh's pasture,[8] that makes the question all the more insistent.

74:2 *the nation you purchased long ago.* Literally, "your congregation you purchased of old." See, for example, Exodus 12:3; 16:1 (ESV) for Israel as Yahweh's "congregation." (See "Theological Insights" for the "you" [God] of the psalm.)

the people of your inheritance, whom you redeemed. Two verbs and one noun allude to Exodus 15:13 ("redeem"), 16 ("purchase"; NIV: "bought"), and 17 ("inheritance"). The verb "purchased" is common to commercial law, while "redeemed" is common to family law and refers to a person buying the freedom of a relative who has fallen into poverty resulting in enslavement. The noun "inheritance" alludes to the land of Canaan.[9]

Mount Zion, where you dwelt. The use of duplicate terms from the Song of the Sea ("the people you have redeemed," "in your strength you will guide them to your holy dwelling," Exod. 15:13; and "you will bring them in and plant them on the mountain of your inheritance," Exod. 15:17), and following the same order of that text, the psalmist may be alluding to the similar circumstances that Israel faced then (Egyptian bondage) and now (Babylonian exile), and by so doing implanting in the psalm and in the hearts of his compatriots the hope of a miraculous deliverance from exile comparable to that from Egypt (see Jer. 16:14–15; see also "Additional Insights: The Model of Historical Double-Tracking" following the unit on Ps. 138). The verb "you dwelt" may carry the nuance of "you used to dwell," and thus the petition of verse 3 would follow naturally: "[Now] turn your steps [again] toward these everlasting ruins."

74:3 *everlasting ruins.* This expression, though a difficult one, is generally understood as "ruins," and the modifier "everlasting" may be used hyperbolically to mean they have been that way for some time and will probably remain ruins.[10]

74:4 *Your foes roared.* The verb is used of the roar of a lion. Verses 4–9 describe the destruction Israel's enemies carried out in the temple (2 Kings 24:13). Note that the suppliant understands the devastation to be directed against Yahweh himself ("*your* foes," "*your* sanctuary," "the dwelling place of *your* Name"; Ps. 74:4, 7). According to Kings, the burning of the temple (2 Kings 25:9) took place one month after the Babylonians breached the walls of Jerusalem (2 Kings 25:2–12).

74:7 *They burned your sanctuary.* See 89:39 for a statement that implies that the destruction of Jerusalem represents damage to the reputation of David, the Lord's "servant."

74:8 *We will crush them completely!* The verb "we will crush" occurs only here in the Hebrew Bible and seems to carry the sense of "destroy."[11]

every place where God was worshiped. In spite of King Josiah's reform that removed the local sanctuaries (2 Kings 23:7–8), evidently many of them still existed at the time of the exile.

74:9 *no signs from God; no prophets are left.* The central statement is "no prophets are left," and on either side of this Hebrew verbless clause is a description of the lack of prophetic activity. This clause is a hint of the prophetic content of the Asaph psalms, for which they are known.[12]

74:10 *How long . . . your name forever?* Both the interrogative phrase and the object "your name" belong to both halves of the verse, which reads literally, "How long, O God, will the enemy insult [your name], [how long] will the foe revile your name forever?"

74:11–12 *your hand, your right hand?* In the Hebrew, "your hand" and "your right [hand]" are a hendiadys, meaning, "your right hand."

from the folds of your garment. The imagery is that God has hidden his right hand in his robe, an imagery of inactivity.[13] There is a wordplay on the word "midst" (*qereb*) in verses 11 and 12. In verse 11b God has his hand in the "midst" (*qereb*) of his bosom (NIV: "*folds* of your garment"), withholding his help, but in verse 12 the psalmist remembers the olden days when God was performing his saving deeds "in the midst [*qereb*] of the earth" (see ESV), the opposite of his present inactivity (see also Exod. 8:22 ESV [8:18 MT]).

74:13–17 Verses 13–17 enumerate the saving deeds mentioned in verse 12. They are concentrated in Yahweh's mighty acts surrounding the exodus (Exod. 15:2–13). In 74:13, 14, 15, and 17 the independent Hebrew pronoun "you" precedes the seven finite verbs, putting emphasis upon the subject, who is Yahweh.[14] Note also the double occurrence in Hebrew of "to you" (74:16a). If we put "it was you" before each of the seven verbs, the force of the grammar becomes apparent, although it might not be quite as beautiful as the NIV's fourfold use of "it was you" (74:13–17).

74:13–14 *split open the sea.* The verb (root *prr*) connotes dissolution of a solid mass.[15]

the heads of the monster . . . the heads of Leviathan. This could allude to the multiple-headed sea monster of the Ugaritic texts (ca. 1300 BC) called Litan, whom the sea god, Baal, defeated. However, it could also be a mythical symbol of Egypt (Ps. 87:4; Isa. 30:7).[16]

74:16–17 *all the boundaries of the earth . . . summer and winter.* These verses probably allude to Genesis 8:22.[17] Genesis 1 may be the general background. God has built "boundaries" in the order of creation, as Psalm 104:9 suggests, so that everything operates sequentially. "Winter" is the rainy season that begins in the autumn and softens the ground so that it can be plowed and planted.

74:18 *Remember.* This verb occurs three times, the first with a very positive usage, referring to God's election of Israel (74:3), and the other two instances in reference to the enemies' mockery of God (74:18a, 22b). The verb frames part 3 of the psalm (74:18–23) along with its negative expression "do not forget" (74:19b, 23a). See "Outline/Structure," above.

foolish people. A term from wisdom thought that pits the "foolish" against the "wise." Their wisdom consisted in part of their recognition of the order of the universe. Note the use of the covenant name "LORD," as compared to "God" (*'elohim*) in verse 10, where the same verb ("defiled"; NIV: "reviled") and noun ("your name") occur.

74:19–20 *Do not hand over the life of your dove to wild beasts.* This is likely a reference to Israel, with the sense "Do not allow the nations to destroy your people Israel." There may be allusions to the Noah story here, even though "dove" (*tor*) is a different word from "dove" in Genesis 8 (*yonah*). The covenant would then be the Noachian covenant, and "have regard" (or "look") would imply that God ought to look into the covenant he made as a reminder of his promises.

74:22 *Rise up, O God.* This is the call for Yahweh to rise up and defend himself from his adversaries, an exact duplication of Numbers 10:35, except for "God" (*'elohim*) instead of Yahweh.

defend your cause. In other instances the psalmists ask Yahweh to "defend *my* cause" (119:154; cf. 35:1; 43:1), but here the pronoun references God. It is reminiscent of the phrase "for your sake" or "for the sake of your name," where the referent is Yahweh rather than the psalmist.[18]

remember. The occurrence of this verb here and in verse 2 provides a virtual *inclusio* for the psalm. God's people's cause is God's cause too.

74:23 *the uproar of your enemies, which rises continually.* The abrupt close of the psalm prompts Goldingay to remark that the psalm stops rather than finishes, achieving no closure, as the people's experience had achieved no closure.[19]

Theological Insights

As is generally true in the Psalms, the literary clues of this psalm also point the reader to its theology. One of those is the personal pronoun "you" for addressing God, God being front and center in the psalm, making him the subject and object of the prayer. The destruction has been done to "*your* congregation" (74:2 ESV); Israel is the "sheep of *your* pasture" (74:1), "the nation *you* purchased"; "*your* inheritance, whom *you* redeemed"; "Mount Zion, where *you* dwelt" (74:2). Moreover, the explicit pronoun "you" occurs seven times in verses 13–17 and is reinforced by two occurrences of "to you" (see the comments on 74:13–17).

God, the "you" of the psalm, is the actor (e.g., 74:1), and he is also the victim. The poet does not recount the story in the third person, as he could have done, but in the second person "you" (74:4–7), which makes the offense much more acute. And more than that, God's foes ("*your* foes," 74:4) set their destructive sights on "the place where *you* met with us" (lit., "*your* appointed place"). And the weight of the offense reaches colossal proportions when it is against the King of the world, "*you* who split open the sea" and created the universe (74:12–17)—the offense was against "you," God! That is, the Creator God becomes the offended God (74:18–23).

Teaching the Text

"Why?" and "How long?" are the two questions that sound louder than all others in the Psalms, and for good reason: human tragedy continues to generate these questions in every age. Psalm 74 asks both of them (74:10, 11a). They are particularly created by the evil events and persons of human history, and we have known them as well as those sad victims of Nebuchadnezzar's destruction of Jerusalem in 586 BC. Such names as 9/11, Boston Marathon, Sandy Hook, the Paris massacre, San Bernardino, and so many others trigger our awful memories. These events modulate these questions into a still higher key.

The rubble of Jerusalem's destruction at the hands of the Babylonians in 586 BC is strewn throughout this psalm. But thankfully that is not the theme of the psalm. Rather the theme is God, and it is developed in an interesting way: God is both the subject and object of history.

First, God is the *subject* of history. That is, this world is about God, and if we miss that point, we miss the meaning of Scripture altogether. That's the note of Genesis 1:1: "In the beginning God created the heavens and the earth." The reason the modern world is so devoid of hope is that men and women no longer perceive God as the subject of history, that God is both the Subject and the Verb. We have lost our perspective. The psalmist recognized that malady in his own world: as subject, God has "rejected" Israel (74:1); "but *you*, O God, are my king from of old; *you* bring salvation upon the earth" (74:12, author's translation). And our suppliant's review of history has the same effect: "It was *you* who split open the sea by your power" (74:13a); "it was *you* who crushed the heads of Leviathan" (74:14a; also 15 and 16). While we may feel uneasy saying that God causes the tragic events of our world, it was not difficult for the psalmist. Whether he viewed God as the subject (cause) of the tragic events or believed that God merely permitted them to happen is a question we won't argue here, because the psalm is intent on informing us that God is in charge of the universe, and however he initiates and accomplishes the events of history, and for whatever reason, his sovereign rule in the universe is a basic premise of the psalm (see "Teaching the Text" and "Illustrating the Text" in the unit on Ps. 53).

Our second point is even more challenging, but it is demanded by the text: God is also the *object* of history. The psalmist writes, "They burned *your* sanctuary to the ground; they defiled the dwelling place of *your* Name" (74:7). It was *his* sanctuary that the Babylonians burned down, and it was the dwelling place of *his* name that they defiled (see also 78:60–61). This, of course, raises the question of how the sovereign God can be both the subject and the object of history. While it is a topic that is no stranger to the Hebrew Bible, the New Testament works this out for us much more clearly, and it secures God's sovereignty by presenting the doctrine of Christ's *willing* sacrifice on the cross (Matt. 26:39; Phil. 2:5–8; Heb. 12:2). That is, Christ was not a victim of sin's ravages by accident, but he was a willing victim and was so, in fact, says John, from the beginning of history: "the Lamb who was slain from the creation of the world" (Rev. 13:8). That certainly makes our victimization by intentional and random events of our personal history easier to understand and hopefully endure—God identifies with us in our victimization. As Christopher J. H. Wright says, lament is a reflection of God's grief, what we might call the human reflex of divine sorrow (see "Illustrating the Text" in the unit on Ps. 79).[20] And, as Calvin taught us, the church, as did ancient Israel, must always see itself with bent back, overflowing tears, among these "everlasting ruins," while it never forgets that God created this world for its happiness (see "Illustrating the Text").

Illustrating the Text

The church must see itself with bent back and overflowing tears, among these "everlasting ruins."

Church History: This psalm raises a question that the church, by virtue of its antagonistic posture toward this evil world, must ask in every age: "How long will the enemy mock you, God? Will the foe revile your name forever?" (74:10). While the church's normal stance should not be confrontational, one cannot eliminate altogether an element of antagonism in the church's strategy. The "everlasting" destruction (74:3) that the forces of evil have caused to the kingdom of God are visible in every age. So the image, often attributed to Calvin, of the church making a pilgrimage through this evil world with bent back and flowing tears (a Jeremianic figure; see Jer. 9:1) is one that we cannot escape, indeed one that we dare not try to escape. When the church, at the sight of the "everlasting ruins," ceases to cry "How long?" (74:9, 10), then it will have lost its vision of redemption that causes it to cry out, "Rise up, O God, and defend your cause" (74:22). Selderhuis observes that Calvin held these two images in balance and believed that God had created the world for humankind's happiness:

> Calvin's anthropology, or view of the human condition, was as dark as his view of the world! One needs, however, to ask how much light there actually was in Calvin's time. How much cause for optimism was there really? Calvin's time was one of high infant mortality and great political and social uncertainty. Europe was ready to buckle under a refugee crisis, poverty and threats of religious wars. It is no wonder that Calvin was so gloomy at times. What is remarkable, in fact, is that he still had a lot to say about the goodness of this life. What else could he have done? He believed that God had created the world with no other goal than the happiness of humanity.[21]

Intimacy with God means we can ask the hard questions.

Story: Psalm 74 sounds like a protest against God, and it is, but there is another way to look at the tone of this psalm. It is only those who have an intimate relationship with God, like Moses, who can ask the hard questions without offending the opposite party. Wolpe tells the story of a revered rabbi's prayer on Yom Kippur, the Day of Atonement. The exact moment of sunset had arrived, and tradition has it that the service must begin precisely at that moment. So the rabbi hesitated for a moment while the congregation uneasily waited for him to begin, and these were his opening words: "Dear God, we come before You this year, as we do every year, to ask Your forgiveness. But in this past year, I have caused no death, I have brought no plagues upon the world, no earthquakes, no floods. I have made no women widows, no children orphans. God, You have done these things, not me! Perhaps You should be asking forgiveness from me." The rabbi then paused, and in a softer, submissive voice, he continued, "But since You are God, and I am only Levi Yitzhak, *Yisgadal v'yiskadah sh'mei rabah* ["Magnified and sanctified is Your Name"]." And so the service began.[22]

"We Praise You, God, We Praise You, for Your Name Is Near"

Big Idea

Justice is part of the infrastructure of the world, and God takes a personal hand in dispensing it.

Key Themes

- God amends our distorted system of justice by bringing one down and elevating another, all according to his standard.
- There is an appointed time for God's equitable judgment.

Understanding the Text

As a response to the prayer of 74:22, that God arise and defend his cause, especially in a world where God himself is the object of mockery, Psalm 75 affirms God's justice, humbling one and exalting another, all by his equitable standard (75:2b). Because the psalm begins with the first common plural ("we"), it may fall into the classification of a community thanksgiving.

The Text in Context

Hannah's Song in 1 Samuel 2:1–10 emphasizes God's humbling and elevating work of grace and alludes to the "columns" (75:3; NIV: "pillars") on which God has set the earth (1 Sam. 2:8).[1] The Song of Mary (the Magnificat) in Luke 1:46–55 is its New Testament counterpart.

Outline/Structure

The psalm breaks down into three parts. After the voice of the community resounds God's praise in the introductory verse, we hear God's voice in part 1, the psalmist's in part 2, and both the psalmist's and God's voices in part 3.

Introduction: Community praise of God (75:1)
1. God's voice of judgment (75:2–5)
   a. God's appointed time for equitable judgment (75:2)
   b. God's support of justice, the cosmic substructure of the earth (75:3)
   c. God's warning to the arrogant (75:4–5)
2. The psalmist's voice affirming God as Judge and Vindicator (75:6–8)
   a. A disclaimer of human success (75:6)
   b. God as Judge (75:7)
   c. God as Vindicator (75:8)
3. The psalmist's vow of praise and God's final affirmation of justice (75:9–10)
   a. Psalmist's vow of praise (75:9)
   b. God's final affirmation of justice (75:10)

Historical and Cultural Background

Since Book 3 has its orientation toward the Babylonian exile of the early sixth century BC, Psalm 75 affirms the God of justice who sets the ethical standard of the world (75:6, 7) and makes sure the wicked are punished and the righteous are rewarded (75:10). It is a psalm vindicating the God of history, even in the face of conflicting circumstances.

Two common metaphors become vehicles of the psalmist's message: "horns" (75:4, 5, 10) and "wine" (75:8), both from the fauna and flora of Israel's world. Cattle were a vital part of life, and everyone understood the bull's horns as a symbol of strength, with their raising and lowering as expressions of challenge and defeat, respectively. "Foaming wine" (75:8) suggests the fermenting process. Sometimes wine was mixed with spices to augment its effect (Song 8:2), while the "dregs" were the sediment that settled to the bottom of the vessel.[2] In some instances wine is a pleasant metaphor, but here, especially with the descriptor "dregs," it becomes a metaphor of judgment.

Interpretive Insights

Title *To the tune of "Do Not Destroy."* The titles of Psalms 57 and 59 also contain this phrase, generally understood as a tune name.

A psalm of Asaph. See comments on the title of Psalm 73.

75:1 *We praise you, God.* The perfect form of the verb here expresses something the psalmist is doing as he speaks.

for your Name is near. "Name" is another word for God, and this phrase gives the reason for praising.

people tell. In good liturgical style, the verse begins with the congregational plural verb ("we praise") and ends with the inclusive plural ("they") to include the whole community (also Isa. 42:24).[3] "Your wonderful deeds" usually refers to God's works of creation (e.g., Ps. 136:4), judgment, and redemption (e.g., 26:7; 71:17; 75:1; 78:4, 11).[4]

75:2 *You say, "I choose the appointed time."* Now the speaker is God, and the NIV adds "you say," and also "who says" in verse 10, to indicate a change of speaker. "Appointed time" (or "place," Josh. 8:14; Ps. 74:4) is used of (1) a mutually agreed-upon time or place (Amos 3:3), (2) the religious festivals (Exod. 23:15; Lev. 23:2), or (3) an appointed time of judgment (Hab. 2:3). Here it carries the last meaning.

equity. This noun is used adverbially, as in 58:1, and means "justly."

75:3 *quake.* The verb literally means "to move back and forth," a metaphor describing the awesome effect on the earth when God appears as Judge (46:6). Even if the earth should reel and rock, God is still in control.[5]

it is I who hold its pillars firm. Literally, "I established its pillars." As the earth is melting, God speaks this word of reassurance, that he established the earth's "pillars," implying stability rather than insecurity.[6]

75:4 *I say.* The speaker is the psalmist again, addressing his words to the wicked.

75:5 *Do not lift your horns against heaven.* Horned animals lift their heads to challenge their opponents and lower them when they are not in a challenger mode (see Job 16:15; NIV has "brow" rather than "horn," as the Hebrew text reads). "Against heaven" is literally "on high" (ESV)—that is, do not challenge heaven (God).

do not speak so defiantly. The metaphor is continued here, with the phrase "so defiantly" literally being "arrogant [outstretched] neck" (see Ps. 31:18).

75:6 *No one . . . from the desert can exalt themselves.* One of the problems with this verse is that it does not have a subject. The NIV has supplied "no one." The contrast is between the wicked, who speak and act arrogantly, as if they were in charge of the world, and God, who on the contrary is really in charge.[7]

75:8 *a cup.* The cup of God's wrath (Jer. 25:15).

its very dregs. The "dregs" ("the leftovers") are the elements that sink to the bottom of the wine. The metaphor means they have drunk every last drop of the cup, dregs and all.

75:9 *I will declare.* Note the speaker has changed from "we" of verse 1 to "I," who is likely a member or representative of the congregation. The psalmist makes a vow to "declare forever" that God is in control of the world, and he will pour the wicked a cup of wine that their intemperate appetite will devour to the last drop, even though it is a cup of destruction. Singing God's praises in acknowledgment of his justice is a witness to his true nature.

75:10 *I will cut off the horns of all the wicked.* God's voice announces in summary fashion the ethical system endorsed by the psalm, that he dispenses justice properly. The verse picks up the metaphor of the bull's horns in verses 4 and 5, which were God's warning to the wicked (75:2–5). The Asaph psalms, in prophetic fashion, often record God's direct words (cf. Ps. 50).

Theological Insights

This poem is an excellent representative of the theology of justice. Justice is part of the infrastructure of the universe, supported by God, who "holds its pillars firm" (75:3). More than the infrastructure, it is the fabric of a moral world, where God, even against the moral realities of the social order, amends the system, bringing one down and elevating another, all according to God's standard of justice that flows from his own nature (75:7, 10). God does not impose a standard of justice that is alien to himself but uses a standard that represents who he himself is. Thus, when the earth as we know it sways back and forth in the uncertain rhythm of injustice, God is its stability. The psalmist does not go beyond this theoretical affirmation, but it is deep and confident. Whether this reeling and rocking is merely a metaphor for the struggle of justice against injustice or a metaphor for a world in the throes of divine judgment, it is certain that justice underlies the system, whatever its perceived outcome. Haggai 2:6 predicts that God will shake the created order to pieces, and only the enduring elements will remain. The writer to the Hebrews cites Haggai to say that this is an eschatological event, and what remains is a "kingdom that cannot be shaken" (Heb. 12:26–28).

Teaching the Text

The topic of justice and its opposite is easy to preach and teach, at least in theory. It is much more difficult to lay out the theory alongside its practical applications, because so many injustices get in the way of the theory that God is just. Sometimes we too easily and too quickly fall into the mind-set that our best recourse is to explain the final adjudication as becoming reality in the world to come. That is and must continue to be a great comfort to those who have suffered injustice, whether at the hands of human offenders or at the seemingly random hand of nature. Either one poses a steep challenge to the preacher and teacher.

Two realities brought the system of justice into some fitting form for our psalmist, a form that he could live with, and hopefully these can also refine our understanding of this critical doctrine of Scripture. First is the suppliant's witness that God himself has spoken regarding an appointed time when he will judge equitably (75:2). Since the Psalms are not inclined to speak of the world to come, we must assume that God is speaking of this world rather than the world to come. So, that may help us live with—not accept—the inequities and wait for God's appointed time. Luther recognized that God sometimes hides his justice, even though it is very real: "God hides his power in weakness, his wisdom in folly, his goodness in severity, his justice in sins, his mercy in anger."[8] Many of us in our own lifetimes have seen the arrogant brought down, but we have also seen the humble exalted. These are God's amendments of the system of justice as it operates in our distorted world.

The second reality that our psalmist puts forward is that, while justice may seem inequitable to our perception, God will indeed mete out his justice (75:2). And again, God speaks in the psalm to confirm that he fulfills these appointments: "I will cut off the horns of all the wicked, but the horns of the righteous will be lifted up" (75:10). The fact that we hear God's voice affirming both of these realities underlies the trust that the psalmist has in God's promises. In Psalm 74 the promises took the form of the covenant (74:20), and here in Psalm 75 they assume the form of God's direct words, which we did not hear in Psalm 74. The psalmist pledges to "declare this forever" and "sing praise to the God of Jacob" (75:9), and we can join him. In the meantime, God's management of the system of justice is such that he can bring one person down and exalt another, and the psalmist is so confident of this truth that he announces he "will declare this forever" (75:9a).

Of course, our psalm does not deal with those instances when justice is a mystery and there is no explanation for it within human reason, such as Job's suffering although he was innocent, at least innocent of the charges made by his friends. While these occasions do not satisfy our human urgency to understand life's inequities, they nevertheless drive us into the mystery of God, where we are left with no options but to trust him. And this too is grace.

Illustrating the Text

Is injustice an argument against or for God?

Quote: *Mere Christianity*, by C. S. Lewis. One of the arguments often brought against the existence of God, or at least a just God, is that there is so much injustice in the world. Lewis acknowledges that when he was an agnostic, this too was one of his arguments: "My argument against God was that the universe seemed so cruel and unjust. But how had I got this idea of just and unjust? A man does not call a line crooked unless he has some idea of a straight line. What was I comparing this universe with when I called it unjust?"[9] It is the teaching of psalms such as this one that has established the Judeo-Christian belief that God is just, and that he is so concerned about justice that he amends our human system and "brings one down" and "exalts another" (75:7).

Cushions in the pews—and cushions in the sermons too?

True Story: God's word of judgment is an integral part of the prophetic message of the Hebrew Bible, and the New Testament has its counterpart in the Revelation of John. It is not the word we like to hear, but it is a word we must hear if we truly believe God is a God of justice. At the end of World War II an exchange student arrived in Ann Arbor, Michigan, from Europe. He attended church services for several Sundays and expressed his astonishment to the director of the university's student religious association that many churches had cushions. Then he added, "I observed that the sermons had cushions in them, too."[10]

"Surely the Wrath of Man Shall Praise Thee"

Big Idea

God's sovereignty is decisively established in the transmutation of the world's wrath into God's praises.

Key Themes

- Though human wrath is intended to disavow God, by divine sovereign grace it instead furthers God's kingdom.
- God is portrayed as the one who is known, radiant, awesome, and feared.

Understanding the Text

Traditionally Psalm 76 is classified as a Zion song, along with Psalms 46; 47; 48; 84; 87; 122; 125; 126; and 132. This subgenre is, like the hymn, normally composed of an introduction proclaiming God's praise, a main section giving reasons for praising God, and a conclusion calling for a response to God's majesty.[1]

The Text in Context

Psalms 46–48 share subject matter and language with this psalm, although the position of Psalm 76 in Book 3 is largely determined by its relationship to Psalms 72–75.[2]

Outline/Structure

In terms of content, Psalm 76 falls into four strophes, as outlined below, each describing God with a passive participle (Niphal) (the participles are italicized in the outline). Strophe 1 (76:1–3) is about God in the third-person singular ("God who is *known*"); strophe 2 (76:4–6) is spoken directly to God in the second-person singular ("You [God] are *radiant* with *light*"); strophe 3 (76:7–10) is also spoken to God in the second-person singular ("you [God] who are feared"); and strophe 4 (76:11–12) is, like the first, about God ("the God who is feared/awesome") and addressed to the congregation.

1. The God *who is known* (ptc. *noda'*, 76:1–3)
   a. The declaration (76:1)
   b. The evidence (76:2–3)
      i. His sanctuary in Zion (76:2)
      ii. His destruction of weapons of war (76:3)
2. The God *who is light* (ptc. *na'or*, 76:4–6)
   a. The declaration (76:4a)
   b. The evidence (76:4b–6)
      i. His majesty in nature (76:4b)
      ii. His victory in war (76:5–6)
3. The God *who is awesome* (ptc. *nora'*, 76:7–10)
   a. The declaration (76:7)
   b. The evidence (76:8–10)
      i. The earth's awe-filled silence at God's judgment (76:8)
      ii. God's deliverance of the earth's afflicted ones (76:9)
      iii. The general rule that humankind's wrath will praise God (76:10)
4. The God *who is feared* (76:11–12)
   a. Make vows, fulfill them, and bring gifts to the One who is feared (noun, *mora'*, 76:11)
   b. The rulers of the earth are *afraid of* him (pass. ptc. *nora'*, 76:12)

Historical and Cultural Background

The background for this psalm is traditionally thought to be the invasion by Sennacherib in 701 BC (2 Kings 18–19 // Isa. 36–37). While that connection is not explicit, the references to events in Israel's history, particularly to saving events like the exodus, are most often allusive in the Psalms. As a matter of style they are recalled with indirect references. The Septuagint has made the connection explicit with its title "For the Assyrian."

Interpretive Insights

Title *A song.* The Septuagint adds "for the Assyrian," which is generally interpreted as a reference to Sennacherib, who invaded Judah in 701 BC.

76:1 *God is renowned in Judah.* This is the first ("known," *noda'*, 76:2 MT; NIV: "renowned") of four passive participles that describe God (also 76:4, 7, 12). Presenting "Judah" (southern kingdom) and "Israel" (northern kingdom) in parallel lines suggests that both political entities are God-worshipers, an interesting note in this section of the Psalter (Elohistic Psalter) that was adapted for use in the northern kingdom. If the psalm reflects Sennacherib's invasion, then "is renowned" may be a recognition that Judah is really the legitimate place of worship (note "in Salem" and "in Zion" in v. 2), yet Israel also recognizes, especially after their fall and Judah's deliverance from Sennacherib, that "his [Yahweh's] name is great."

76:2 *Salem.* Salem is an older name for Jerusalem or Zion (Gen. 14:18). See the sidebar "(Mount) Zion" in the unit on Psalm 48.

dwelling place. God's dwelling place in Zion (see also 26:8) sets Judah apart, but it is more a distinction of honor than favoritism. Isaiah 31:4 describes the Lord coming to Zion as a lion, which is the imagery here.

76:3 *There.* This verse explains why God is "renowned [known] in Judah." "There" (*shammah*, 76:4 MT) is an allusion either to Judah/Israel or to Jerusalem, a reminder of God's defensive protection of his people. It is reminiscent of Ezekiel's name for the city, "THE LORD IS THERE" (*YHWH shammah*, Ezek. 48:35).

he broke the flashing arrows. The "arrows" (lit., "bow[s] of lightning") are called "flashing" because they resemble fire as they fly through the air[3] (see 2 Kings 19:32 // Isa. 37:33).

the shields and the swords, the weapons of war. Literally, "shield and sword, and war." The "and" before "war" is appositional, giving us this sense: "There he broke the flashing arrow, shield, and sword—that is, war."

76:4 *You are radiant with light.* This is the second passive participle ("radiant," *na'or*, 76:5 MT) that describes God. Note also that the grammatical person changes from the third singular ("God") to the second singular ("You [God] are radiant").

more majestic than mountains rich with game. "Majestic" describes Yahweh's name in 8:1. "Mountains rich with game" is literally "mountains of prey."

76:5 *they sleep their last sleep.* While the historical background must remain uncertain, it sounds like a description of death such as that suffered by the Assyrian army during the night (2 Kings 19:35; see also Nah. 3:18).

not one of the warriors can lift his hands. The NIV reproduces the sense of the statement. The literal reading is quite descriptive: "All the warriors could not find their hands" (either because they were incapacitated or dead, or perhaps an allusion to the practice of cutting off the hands of battle casualties). The traditional view is that this is a description of the 185,000 soldiers whom the angel of the Lord slew during the night, after which Sennacherib withdrew his army to Nineveh (2 Kings 19:35–36).

76:6 *both horse and chariot lie still.* An allusion to the crossing of the Red Sea is here applied to this military situation (Exod. 15:1, 21).

76:7 *It is you alone who are to be feared.* This is the third occurrence of a passive participle ("feared," *nora'*, 76:8 MT) describing God. The "you" is emphatic, and the NIV has represented that with "it is you alone."

76:8 *the land feared and was quiet.* Silence is the response of awe—in this case, awe of God's judgment.

76:9 *when you, God, rose up to judge, to save all the afflicted.* This is one of the best statements on the purpose of divine judgment in the Psalms: to save the "afflicted" (the righteous; ESV: "humble"). Calvin comments, "The design of the passage is to show that it is impossible for God to forsake the afflicted and innocent, as it is impossible for him to deny himself."[4] It is part of God's nature to "humble himself," and forsaking the "afflicted," who are "humble" in life's circumstances and in the eyes of the world, would be to forsake his own self-humbling nature.

of the land. The Hebrew word *'erets* (76:10 MT) can be translated "land" or "earth," and in view of the universal term "mankind" (*'adam*) in 76:10a (76:11a MT), the broader term "earth" seems a better fit here. On that basis, Goldingay draws the conclusion, elsewhere attested in the Psalms, that "Yahweh's action on Israel's behalf, at a moment such as the Red Sea deliverance, the victories of David, or the defeat of Assyria, is undertaken not merely for the benefit of Israel but also for the benefit of the whole world."[5]

76:10 *Surely your wrath against mankind brings you praise.* The memorable phrasing of this verse in the KJV, "Surely the wrath of man shall praise thee," captures the sense of the verse very well. Strangely, and without any apparent justification, the NIV turns the subject around and makes it God's wrath rather than humankind's. The point seems rather to be humanity's wrath against God, not God's against humanity.

the survivors of your wrath are restrained. The only thing that seems certain about this difficult half verse is that it must be related in some way to the first half. The verb translated "restrain" also means "gird on," so that the image is that of God clothing himself with wrath (Isa. 59:17, "He put on the garments of vengeance"), and the object is "the remainder [NIV: "survivors"] of wrath(s)," giving us something like "You gird yourself with the rest of wrath(s)," perhaps suggesting that when the wrath of humankind praises God, there are still remnants of human wrath, which God then restrains. That is, in general the wrath of humankind praises God, but the remnants that do not God restrains so that they cause him no harm, even though that is the purpose of human wrath.

76:11 *Make vows.* Making vows was a way to demonstrate one's devotion (fear of God). The imperative is addressed either to the suppliant's audience (perhaps in the temple) or to the nations, who should bring their votive gifts to God (see 76:12).

the One to be feared. Since they are making vows and bringing gifts, this is awe, not fright.

76:12 *He breaks the spirit of rulers.* The verb for "breaks" is used of cutting off grapes in preparation for the treading of the winepress and here gives the picture of "snipping" off the spirits of rulers, a figure of divine vengeance.

This is an example of a truncated metaphor, where a verb or noun is enough to suggest the whole picture of the phenomenon represented in the author's mind.

he is feared by the kings of the earth. This is the fourth occurrence of the passive participle ("feared," *nora'*, 76:13 MT) describing God, and in parallel with the notion of worship in 76:11, the "kings of the earth" are paying homage to God.

Theological Insights

This psalm proclaims a dimension of God's sovereignty that has been verbalized memorably in the translation of the KJV: "Surely the wrath of man shall praise thee" (76:10a). Most English translations agree with the KJV in making "the wrath of man" the subject of the sentence.

The point of the declaration is that human wrath, intended to disavow God's sovereign majesty, has the opposite effect—it acknowledges God and his control over the world, and in effect furthers his kingdom. Spurgeon says, "The wrath of man shall not only be overcome but rendered subservient to thy glory."[6] This truth is borne out in another way in the Psalter with the explanation that evil has an innate boomerang capacity—it hits its target but then rebounds on its perpetrators (see 7:15, 16; 9:15, 16; 54:5). Parallel to this image are the descriptions of the work of evildoers who set a net to capture their prey and then fall into the pit themselves (35:8); and God turns the words of slanderers against themselves (64:8). The question is whether the capacity for the reversal of evil is in the nature of evil itself or in the nature of God—most likely both, although the Psalms are most explicit on God's power to reverse any condition or circumstance.

Teaching the Text

It is quite a homiletical luxury when a psalm gives the preacher or teacher the outline of the sermon/lesson. Psalm 76 is such a case, where we see the underpinning of four passive participles that describe God (vv. 1, 4, 7, 12). Because we want to be faithful to the text, when the text offers us an outline of this clarity, we should take advantage of it (see "Outline/Structure"). Of course, this does not rule out other valid ways to outline our message. In this instance, however, the content of the poem flows out of these participial notations.

First, God is "known" (NIV: "renowned," 76:1) by his people because he has chosen to reveal himself to them. His presence in the sanctuary and his overpowering of the instruments of war attest to his revelation of greatness. When we put together the four elements of verses 1–3, (a) the knowledge of God (76:1), (b) his presence ("his tent," *sukko*, 76:2a [76:3a MT]), (c) Jerusalem ("Salem," 76:2a; cf. Gen. 14; the ancient name of Jerusalem), and (d) the abolition of war (76:3; cf. Isa. 2:4), we have a picture of God's reign of peace. And peace cannot come apart from the knowledge of God "in Judah" (76:1), which means the biblical revelation.[7] It is quite remarkable, and most reassuring, that when God is known, and where God is known, there is peace. The knowledge of God is more than a state of mind; it is a condition of the soul, and that applies to our personal lives, our community of faith, our nation, and our world. The extent to which we know God determines the extent and quality of our peace.

Second, God is "light" (NIV: "radiant with light," 76:4) in the sense that he is the Creator of light (Gen. 1:3–5), and the "darkness" of this world, which the psalmist presents under the imagery of war, "has not overcome it" (John 1:5). We may point out that in the Psalter a favorite image of God is "light" (e.g., Ps. 27:1), and the conflict between light and darkness is a parable of the ongoing struggle between good and evil (Ps. 139:11–12), a battle that the God of light will certainly win. Indeed, God's powerful disarming of the weapons of war in verse 3 is illustrated in verses 4–6, where the warriors cannot even wield their weapons.[8] The fact, then, that God is "light" is, as with the first descriptor ("known"), a statement about God's person as he relates to his creation. It reminds us of the creation of light in Genesis 1, and also the psalmist's declaration that in him is no darkness at all (Ps. 139:12; see 1 John 1:5). Once the state of peace combines with the condition of light, the world becomes the paradise of God.

Third, God is "awesome" (NIV: "to be feared," 76:7), evidenced in the pall of silence his judgment casts over the world (76:8), his deliverance of the "afflicted" (76:9), and, not least, the amazing truth that he causes the wrath of humans to praise him (see the comments on 76:10, and "Theological Insights"). Although the pall of silence in verse 8 follows God's judgment, Habakkuk calls attention to the pall of silence that follows God's acts of grace (Hab. 2:20), and Chaim Potok reminds us that we can listen to these silences (see "Illustrating the Text"). At the same time, there is a more mysterious transaction of God's power that occurs when he turns the acts of evil men and women into his good purposes. I think immediately of the Sunday after 9/11 when churches were filled with people who were trying to make sense of one of America's greatest tragedies. The evil perpetrators intended the disaster to be divine judgment on America, but many believers were praying that God would cause the "wrath of men to praise him," even though the accomplishment of that thought seemed impossible. Yet we still hope and wait for that. Indeed, this is one of the Psalter's most beautiful expressions of God's sovereignty, and this is an appropriate point to stress the biblical doctrine that all human opposition must ultimately become subservient to the sovereign God (Phil. 2:10–11). MacDonald's lovely metaphor of God's sovereign grace expresses this truth so beautifully, that God, in his sovereign grace, chains our sins "like galley-slaves to the rowing-benches of the gospel-ship" (see "Illustrating the Text"). This means that our lives, even our sins, are engaged by our sovereign God as his servants to accomplish his gracious will. This does not mean that God authorizes our sins or that he assigns suffering *so that* he might demonstrate his sovereign grace (although he certainly may do the latter). Rather, he conscripts them for his service.

Fourth, God is "feared" by the rulers of the world (76:11–12), evidenced in the fact that he removes rulers at his will and causes them to fear him. While the two participles for "feared" (76:7, 12) are the same, they have different nuances. The first occurrence, in verse 7, carries the sense of awe, nudging up to a "saving" fear, while the use in verse 12 is a repelling fear, a you-better-watch-out fear. Yet, even the fear of God that repels can have a redeeming effect, and that may be suggested by verse 11, which pictures "all the neighboring lands" bringing gifts to "the One to be feared." If so, the redemption of the nations is in view.

While we do not normally end our sermon/lesson on a word of judgment, we may stress that such a concluding word calls for the loud affirmation of faith in the God who is known in judgment *and* grace. They are not mutually exclusive. The message of this psalm is the word of sovereign grace: "If God is for us, who can be against us?" (Rom. 8:31).

Illustrating the Text

God chains our sins to the rowing benches of the gospel ship.

Literature: *Thomas Wingfold, Curate*, by George MacDonald. In biblical theology the great challenge to God's sovereignty is human sin, the story of which begins in Genesis 3. The Psalms articulate the problem, and they are not short on solutions. One of them is the retroactive quality of sin. In MacDonald's novel *Thomas Wingfold, Curate*, the curate says about our sins that Christ "takes our sins on himself, and while he drives them out of us with a whip of scorpions he will yet make them work his ends. He defeats our sins, makes them prisoners, forces them into the service of good, chains them like galley-slaves to the rowing-benches of the gospel-ship."[9]

The silences of judgment and grace

Literature: *The Chosen*, by Chaim Potok. Sometimes silence becomes the most effective language of communication. Our psalmist hears God's voice in judgment (76:8–9), and the pall of silence represents the reverberation of God's voice. Habakkuk speaks of another kind of silence, the silence of awe that follows the revelation of God's holiness: "The LORD is in his holy temple; let all the earth be silent before him" (Hab. 2:20). In Potok's novel *The Chosen*, Reuven, one of the main characters, tells his Hasidic friend Danny a story about the tzaddik (the leader of a Hasidic group): "The tzaddik sits in absolute silence, saying nothing, and all his followers listen attentively." Though Reuven intends the story to be humorous, his Hasidic friend Danny responds, "There's more truth to that than you realize. You can listen to silence, Reuven. I've begun to realize that you can listen to silence and learn from it. It has a quality and a dimension all its own. It talks to me sometimes. I feel myself alive in it. It talks. And I can hear it."[10] We are silenced not only by God's acts of judgment (Ps. 76:8) but also by his acts of grace (Hab. 2:20), and we meditate on God in those awesome silences.

"Your Path Led through the Sea, . . . Though Your Footprints Were Not Seen"

Big Idea

When we cannot discern God's presence with us in times of adversity, we must be aware that, while his "footprints" may not be visible, he is still walking with us.

Key Themes

- God's ways lead through the sanctuary.
- Even though God leads his people and leaves no footprints, he nevertheless has his surrogate shepherds like David.

Understanding the Text

Judging from the first-person singular (77:1–6, 10–12), this psalm is most likely an individual lament, although if verses 1–3 are read as a crisis in the past tense and verses 14–15 as thanksgiving for deliverance, it could be viewed as a corporate psalm of thanksgiving.[1]

The Text in Context

Book 3 (Pss. 73–89) is oriented to the fall of Jerusalem (586 BC) and the Babylonian exile, so Psalm 73 opens on that political landscape. Although the crisis of that psalm is personal, it can also be viewed as national, just as the perspective of Psalm 77 is personal but placed by the editor(s) to imply a national crisis of justice. It is not surprising, then, that following Psalm 73, virtually the first scan of the literary camera captures the destruction of the temple, definitely a national crisis (74:4–8).

The Shepherd Theme of Psalms 77–80

The Lord is Israel's Shepherd, who led them out of Egypt through the Red Sea and will now punish their enemies and restore them. This theme was evidently intended to bring comfort and assurance to the exiles.

Psalm 77	"You led your people [through the Red Sea] like a flock by the hand of Moses and Aaron" (77:20).
Psalm 78	"But he brought his people out like a flock [out of Egypt]; he led them like sheep through the wilderness. He guided them safely, so they were unafraid" (78:52–53a). "He chose David his servant and took him from the sheep pens; from tending the sheep he brought him to be the shepherd of his people Jacob, of Israel his inheritance. And David shepherded them with integrity of heart; with skillful hands he led them" (78:70–72).
Psalm 79	When God has avenged Israel's enemies, "then we your people, the sheep of your pasture, will praise you forever" (79:13).
Psalm 80	In anticipation of God's deliverance (from exile), the psalmist prays: "Hear us, Shepherd of Israel, you who lead Joseph like a flock" (80:1).

With its concern for divine justice, Psalm 73 draws a "hermeneutical horizon" and sets the stage for the "compositional arc" of Psalms 74–76, as Hossfeld and Zenger call it.[2] Psalm 74 closes with the challenge that God should "rise up" and "defend" his cause (74:22), and Psalm 75 follows with the assurance that he will do precisely that (75:2–5), while Psalm 76 acclaims God's sovereign rule of the world that includes saving "the afflicted" (76:9) and causing humankind's wrath to praise him (76:10). In a world where Israel has been humiliated by exile and God's covenant with David has ostensibly failed (Ps. 89), this quadruplet of poems lays a foundation of encouragement and hope.

Psalms 77–80 form a group of psalms that is held together by the theme of shepherd (see the sidebar). The function of this theme and this minicollection of psalms is to provide the comfort of God as Israel's Shepherd, especially through this era of humiliation and soul-searching. Even though the editor(s) of the book knows that Israel's fortunes now lie in ruins, God still guides, and he guides them through the exile even though his "footprints" are not seen.

Outline/Structure

Verses 1–9 are a lament, with verses 7–9 giving its gist, and verses 10–20 stating the psalmist's counter way of answering the sixfold questions of verses 7–9:

1. The lament (77:1–9)
   a. Lament proper (77:1–6)
   b. Six questions rising from the lament (77:7–9)

2. The resolution (77:10–20)
   a. Remembering God's right-hand miracles (77:10–12)
   b. Remembering God's miracles displayed among the peoples (77:13–15)
   c. Remembering nature's reaction and God's trackless path of deliverance from Egypt (77:16–19)
   d. Remembering God's surrogate shepherds (77:20)

Historical and Cultural Background

As we have already noted, the historical crucible in which Book 3 was composed was the Babylonian exile of the sixth century BC. Some of the psalms in this book may have originated in an earlier period and been adapted in various ways to address the circumstance of the exilic and postexilic periods. One of the ways the exiles found their orientation again was through remembering the past, especially Yahweh's great acts of deliverance associated with the exodus from Egypt, the crossing of the Red Sea, and the giving of the law on Sinai (Exod. 15:11–18). This remembering was part of the theological scrutiny that constituted the exilic and postexilic mind, as it tried to figure out what had gone so terribly wrong in the relationship between Israel and Yahweh.[3]

Interpretive Insights

Title *For Jeduthun.* See the titles of Psalms 39 and 62. Jeduthun was a senior temple musician in David and Solomon's era (1 Chron. 16:41–42; 2 Chron. 5:12).[4]

77:2 *at night I stretched out untiring hands.* The verb translated "stretched out" can also mean "to drip" (2 Sam. 14:14; NIV: "spilled") and in that sense connotes the "dripping" of sweat from the hands.

77:3 *I meditated.* This verb carries the nuance of a bitter spirit. The NIV's translation is also possible, but in the context of his troubled spirit, "I pleaded" seems preferable (102, title).[5] The sense of the second half of the verse may be, "I pleaded with all my strength until I was exhausted."

77:4 *You kept my eyes from closing.* The psalmist accuses God of depriving him of sleep.

77:5 *I thought about the former days.* The verb translated "thought" means to "ponder" (see 73:16 NASB), in this case the former days of God's miraculous works (77:10–12).

the years of long ago. See Deuteronomy 32:7.

77:6 *I remembered my songs in the night.* The thought of God's miraculous works in the past has now given way to the suppliant's lamentive song in the night that wonders if God has forgotten him (77:7–9). Verses 7–9 may be a reflection on Exodus 34:6–7.[6]

77:7 *Will the Lord reject forever?* The verb "reject" (*znh*) carries the nuance of abhorrence.

77:8 *Has his unfailing love vanished forever?* This is another way to ask if God has forsaken his covenant with Israel, "his unfailing love" (*hesed*) being a synonym for "covenant."

77:10 *the years when the Most High stretched out his right hand.* The "right hand" of the Most High recalls Exodus 15:6–12, where the term "right hand" occurs three times.

77:11 *the deeds of the* LORD . . . *your miracles of long ago.* "Deeds" and "miracles" (see Exod. 10:2) are synonyms and allude to the great saving events of history, like the exodus, the Red Sea, and the crossing of the Jordan.

77:13 *Your ways, God, are holy.* Literally, "Your way(s), God, is *in holiness.*" The NIV assumes the prepositional phrase to be adverbial, describing the way God conducts his works, "in a holy manner." See "Theological Insights" for an alternative (and in my view, preferable) interpretation. From this point to the end of the psalm the writer contemplates the wonderful works of God that he mentioned in verses 11 and 12.

What god is as great as our God? The question anticipates the answer, "No god is great like our God." It alludes to the Song of the Sea (Exod. 15:11). See the sidebar "Yahweh and Other Gods in the Psalter" in the unit on Psalm 7.

77:14–20 These verses provide a brief history of God's mighty acts at the exodus and Red Sea that in effect answer the question of verse 13b, "What god is as great as our God?"

77:14 *you display your power among the peoples.* An allusion to Exodus 15:13–14.

77:15 *descendants of Jacob and Joseph.* The reference may suggest that the psalm was used among the northern tribes, since Jacob and Joseph are names for the northern kingdom (see the sidebar "The Divine Names" in the unit on Ps. 4 for a discussion of the Elohistic Psalter and the northern kingdom). It is not unusual to take a psalm from an earlier period and adapt it to later historical circumstances such as the exile.

77:16 *The waters saw you, God, the waters saw you and writhed.* The repetition of the clause "the waters saw you" is stylistic and intensifies the idea of the verse. It alludes to the miracle at the Red Sea and is similar to 114:3, 7.

77:18 *Your thunder was heard in the whirlwind.* More literally, "the sound of your rolling thunder," suggesting the sound of a rolling wheel. Also 18:14.
your lightning lit up the world. See verse 17c. Also Exodus 19:16–19.

77:19 *Your path led through the sea, . . . though your footprints were not seen.* See "Teaching the Text."

77:20 *You led your people like a flock.* The picture is the Lord as Shepherd of Israel, not of the individual psalmist, as in 23:1. Moses and Aaron were God's shepherding agents (see the sidebar).

Theological Insights

The centrality of the sanctuary in Israel's life is a recurring theme in the Psalter. Already Book 3 has introduced the theme (73:16–17; 74:1–9), so it is not surprising to find it here again in the prepositional phrase "in the sanctuary" (lit., "holy place," 77:13). The NIV's rendering of the phrase as "holy" ("Your ways, God, are holy") is possible (see the comments on 77:13) and is found in other English translations (e.g., RSV, ESV, NJPS), but the KJV and ASV, following the Septuagint, translate, "Thy way, O God, is *in the sanctuary*." The preference for this translation may be further supported by the observation that God's "ways" form an *inclusio* for this section (77:13–19): first God's way is "in the *sanctuary*" (77:13), and at the end of the section, God's way ("path") is in "the *sea*," through which he led Israel (77:19). Another reason is that the Song of Moses, on which Psalm 77 reflects, depicts the sanctuary as Yahweh's destination once he has brought Israel through the Red Sea (Exod. 15:13b, 17b).

The psalmist is saying that all God's ways, in some strangely wonderful design, pass through or into his sanctuary. Or we might put it differently: we understand God's ways only when we see them in the context of worship. That seems to be the sense of 73:16–17: everything must be explained ultimately in terms of God's will and God's ways. They are the fixed reference point, the standard by which everything else is measured. It was such a personal thing for the writer of Psalm 84 that he described the ways to the "courts of the Lord" as being in the hearts of those who trust in the Lord (84:2, 4–5). Though expressed in different terms, Paul's declaration in Romans 8:28 aims in that same direction: "We know that in all things God works for the good of those who love him, who have been called according to his purpose." That is, God has a unique way of making the evil designs a part of his story. The Joseph story bears witness to this truth. God took the brothers' evil plan and wove it into his story in such a way that he turned evil into good, and by their evil plan, transmuted by God into a plan of saving grace, God saved the Israelites from famine and spared them for his future purposes.

Teaching the Text

A metaphor is a shorthand way to describe an event, truth, or idea, and it can open up vistas of thought that attach to the metaphor in enlightening ways. Psalm 77:19 describes God's leading Israel through the Red Sea and attaches the beautiful metaphor, "though your footprints were not seen." Here the preacher/teacher has the opportunity to read out of this metaphor an important message of Scripture.

First, we may draw attention to the plethora of questions about life in 77:7–9, the kind of interrogation that causes us to look for God's "footprints"—that is, evidence of God's action in life and history. The clear footprints of God in human history are rare, a reality that Lew Wallace notes in his novel *Ben-Hur*: "When God walks the earth, his steps are often centuries apart."[7] In a sermon on Habakkuk, Donald G. Miller says: "When our lot falls between the steps, we are tempted to think that God has ceased walking the earth; or to grow impatient and to wish he would hurry. . . . If only his foot would fall once more! He dwelt in the midst of the years, 'between the footsteps of the Almighty.'"[8] The perspective of succeeding generations is more likely to give clarity that contemporary generations do not have. But our psalmist makes the point that even though we do not see clear evidence of God's presence, he is nevertheless there.

Second, we may make the observation that the psalmist follows these questions with his resolve to "remember the deeds of the LORD" (77:11), and the most amazing was Israel's miraculous deliverance at the Red Sea. As miraculous as it was, God's "footprints," like God himself, were not seen. When we find ourselves in the midst of life's adversities that threaten our well-being, we must look at the wider circumstances and the virtual effects of God's presence after he has led us through the maze of our circumstances, and then we can acknowledge God's unseen "footprints" (see "Seeing is not believing" in "Illustrating the Text" in this unit; see also "God's work is perceptible only to those who believe" in "Illustrating the Text" in the unit on Ps. 53). The eyes of faith penetrate beyond the mundane circumstances of our lives to the real presence of God. And we should not forget that sometimes our faith is assisted—God be praised!—by his shepherds like David, who refract our lenses of faith.

Illustrating the Text

Seeing is not believing.

Literature: *The Princess and the Goblin*, by George MacDonald. MacDonald tells the story of Princess Irene, who visits her great-grandmother in the attic room of the princess's house. The great-grandmother is a symbol of spiritual things, maybe even a symbol of God in MacDonald's thought. The princess takes her friend Curdie with her. In the attic the princess cuddles up in her great-grandmother's lap, looks at the beautiful fire burning in the fireplace, notices a lovely chandelier hanging from the ceiling—just the most lavish of furnishings. But Curdie can't see any of these things; he sees only an old room with a tub and a heap of musty straw, a withered apple, and a ray of sunlight coming through a hole in the middle of the roof. The great-grandmother is not discouraged by Curdie's failure to see, even though the princess desperately wants her friend to see what she sees. But the grandmother does not want to show herself to him at that point. "Seeing is not believing—it is only seeing," MacDonald writes.[9]

Psalm 77 can release a troubled soul.

Biography: John Bunyan. Bunyan was troubled in his soul about his sins much like Luther was, and after two years of turmoil the questions of Psalm 77:7–9 came rolling into his mind.[10] Bunyan's release, like Luther's, had the effect not only of personal peace but of blessing to the world with his *Pilgrim's Progress* and many other writings. God's forgiving grace always makes our cup run over.

"He Sent the Ark of His Might into Captivity, His Splendor into the Hands of the Enemy"

Big Idea

Disobedience to God's will is always a threatening danger in the ongoing history of God's people.

Key Themes

- There is an easily permeable line between authentic faith and hypocrisy.
- God's response to disobedience is, not surprisingly, grace.
- When recipients of grace demand more grace, they turn grace into merit.

Understanding the Text

Second in length in the Psalter to Psalm 119, Psalm 78, along with Psalms 105; 106; and 136, is a historical psalm, differing from others in this category in that it is a reflection on history, not merely a rehearsal of historical events.[1] In the title the psalm is called a *maskil*; the didactic nature of the poem supports the view that this technical term alludes to the "teaching" mode (see the comments on the title for Ps. 74), and the voice of the psalm is that of a teacher who instructs the people of God.

Although the psalm's date of composition is debatable, the safest guess is that it falls somewhere between David (ca. 931 BC) and the Babylonian exile, the latter being nowhere mentioned in the psalm.

The Text in Context

Psalm 77:11 pledges to remember the Lord's deeds of the past, and Psalm 78 fulfills that pledge. Canonically it overlaps with Exodus to Joshua in its historical survey (see "Interpretive Insights").[2]

Calling the Asaph psalmist a prophet, Matthew quotes Psalm 78:2 to say that Jesus fulfilled this prophecy in his use of parables (Matt. 13:34–35). In John's Gospel, Jesus quotes Psalm 78:24 to identify the true manna as being he himself, the Bread of Life (John 6:3–40, esp. 6:31).

Outline/Structure

Note ideas of part 1 that are repeated or amplified in part 2.

Invitation and introduction (78:1–8): To explain the purpose of rehearsing Israel's history—that future generations might trust God and distinguish themselves from their ancestors' disobedience

Part 1 (78:9–39)
- a. Preface: Centers on *"they forgot"* (78:9–11) (compare 78:40–42)
- b. God's redemption of Israel (78:12–14)
- c. God's provision for his people (78:15–16)
- d. God's judgment on Israel (78:17–33)
- e. God's love for Israel in spite of their rebellion (78:34–39)

Part 2 (78:40–72)
- a. Preface: Centers on *"they did not remember"* (78:40–42)
- b. God's redemption of Israel amplified (78:43–53)
- c. God's provision for his people amplified (78:54–55)
- d. God's judgment on Israel amplified (78:56–64)
- e. God's love for Israel in spite of their rebellion amplified (78:65–72)

Historical and Cultural Background

The historical span of this psalm stretches from the time of Moses to David, with a strong focus on Egypt and the wilderness, selectively spanning five centuries of Israel's history. The "parable" and "hidden things" (78:2) of the psalm are two different but related aspects: first of all, the story of God's mighty deeds in Israel's history, and second, the "mystery" (riddle) of the historical shift from the central tribe of "Ephraim," the Rachel side of Jacob's family, to the tribe of Judah, the Leah side of the family, a change we would not expect, given Rachel's favored status in the patriarchal story (Gen. 29:18). See the sidebar "Realignment from Rachel to Leah." For the historical record of the events of this psalm, see table 2.

Interpretive Insights

Title maskil. See the introduction to "Understanding the Text," above.

of Asaph. See the introduction to "Understanding the Text" in the unit on Psalm 73.

78:1 *My people, hear my teaching; listen*. This invitation has a parallel in 49:1 and a similar one in 50:7, each time addressing Israel directly and calling them to "listen." See also Deuteronomy 32:1. "My teaching" is literally "my law," in the sense of "instruction."

78:2 *parable*. Here the "parable" is a story.

hidden things. Literally, "riddles." These can be complex questions or "mysteries" that must be explained. Here they likely include the historical reality of God's transfer of favor from a Rachel (Benjamin) to a Leah (Judah) tribe (78:67–72).

78:3 *things we have heard and known*. For this practice of intergenerational instruction, see also Exodus 10:2 and Deuteronomy 6:7.

78:4 *praiseworthy deeds*. Elsewhere in the Psalms this noun is translated "praises," but here the parallel lines support the NIV's "praiseworthy deeds."

78:5 *statutes*. The word is "testimony" ('*edut*), which in other contexts refers to the stone tablets of the Torah (Exod. 31:18; 32:15; 34:29) and here alludes to them. It is parallel with "law," and Israel's instructions were to obey it and teach it to their children.

78:7 *their trust*. While "trust" carries the sense of "confidence," the two ideas overlap, since "trust" requires a high degree of "confidence." The Israelites hold tenaciously to God, and do not forget his great deeds. In other contexts this word means stubborn stupidity or foolhardiness (e.g., 49:13) and implies confidence in the wrong thing.

would not forget. This is the hope of the psalmist for future generations, and in part 1 he expresses that with a chain of negative assertions, summing up the tragic reality of verse 11a, "They *forgot* what he had done":

Realignment from Rachel to Leah

Psalm 78 deals with the transfer of Israel's chosen line from Benjamin, Rachel's son, to Judah, Leah's son—that is from Saul to David—which was both the crux of political conflict and a theological quandary.

The Rachel and Leah Tribes

Rachel Tribes	Leah Tribes
*Dan	Reuben
*Naphtali	Simeon
Joseph	Levi
Benjamin	Judah
	+Gad
	+Asher
	Issachar
	Zebulun

* Sons of Bilhah (Rachel's maid)
+ Sons of Zilpah (Leah's maid)

"whose hearts *were not loyal* to God" (78:8b)

"whose spirits *were not faithful* to him" (78:8c)

"they *did not keep* God's covenant" (78:10a)

"they *did not believe in God* or trust in his deliverance" (78:22)

"they *did not believe*" (78:32b)

78:8 *whose hearts were not loyal to God.* This explains Israel's spiritual nature throughout history and makes evident the need for this psalm.

78:9–11 *The men of Ephraim.* Here begins the story of Ephraim, a name used for Israel. He and Manasseh were Joseph's two sons. The occasion could be nonspecific or specific. Some suggestions are (1) the capture of the ark by the Philistines (1 Sam. 4); (2) the death of Saul on Mount Gilboa (1 Sam. 31), which facilitated the transfer of power from the tribe of Benjamin (Saul) to the tribe of Judah (David); and (3) the fall of Samaria to the Assyrians in 722 BC (2 Kings 17). Since verse 9 is connected to verse 67, where the shift of divine favor from the Rachel tribe of Benjamin to the Leah tribe of Judah becomes the focus, Mount Gilboa is preferable, although the nonspecific understanding is possible. The real problem was Israel's failure to keep the covenant (78:10), which was equivalent to forgetting God's great deeds (78:11).

78:12–16 The locations of this story are Egypt and the wilderness (see table 2).

78:12 *Zoan.* Zoan = Tanis (LXX), located in the northeast Nile Delta.

78:13 *made the water stand up like a wall.* See Exodus 14:21–22. "Wall" is the dammed-up waters (Exod. 15:8; cf. Josh. 3:13, 16).

78:15 *as abundant as the seas.* The Hebrew uses the plural form of the noun *tᵉhom*, which designates the "deep" in Genesis 1:2, perhaps alluding to the abundance of the waters (so NIV). The incident is water from the rock (Exod. 17:1–7).

78:17–20 These verses describe Israel's response to God's gracious deeds.

78:18 *put God to the test.* While Exodus 15:25 and 16:4 speak of God testing Israel, our psalmist makes the observation, also made in Exodus 17:2 and Numbers 14:22, that Israel tested God, and this became a pattern of behavior (Num. 14:22: Israel tested God "ten times"). This state of affairs was a reversal of what it should have been. The verb "tested" also occurs in verses 41 and 56. When God "tests" an individual, generally the purpose is to determine whether that person will be faithful to a particular cause or directive. When individuals "test" God, it carries the tone of challenge to God's character and power. Here Israel's testing God was for the purpose of contesting his will or his power to provide food in the wilderness. Either motive involved them in "rebelling . . . against the Most High" (78:17), because they were not trusting Yahweh's covenant commitment to Israel (78:22).

78:19 *They spoke against God.* While the people spoke against Moses (Exod. 16:2–3), their complaint in reality was against God (Exod. 16:7–8; 17:7).

78:21–31 The anger of God frames this section (78:21 and 31) and is attested in Numbers 11:1–3.

78:22 *they did not believe in God.* "Believe" is parallel to "trust" in the second half of the verse and suggests obeying God's commandments and believing his promises (see Deut. 9:23).

78:23 *Yet he gave a command.* The verse begins with an adversative conjunction rendered here as "yet," distinguishing God's action from Israel's. His commanding the "skies" (lit., "clouds") depicts a God who controls the world and who would take such drastic action for his people, even though they had behaved so skeptically.

doors of the heavens. The only time this expression occurs in the Old Testament, it implies that the manna mentioned in the following verse was God's gift.

78:24 *manna.* Some explain this as a natural phenomenon,³ but the text views it as miraculous.

grain of heaven. Compare 105:40, "bread of heaven."

78:25 *bread of angels.* Literally, "bread of the mighty." The NIV leans on the Septuagint for "bread of angels." The superlative terms "the grain of heaven" (78:24) and "the bread of angels" allude to the Source of the gift and its miraculous delivery.

78:27–28 *He rained meat down on them.* See table 2.

78:30–31 *he put to death the sturdiest among them.* The story in Numbers 11 is that they were struck with a plague. Whether the sickness came through the meat itself or directly from divine displeasure is not clear. Their desire became their own undoing. Verse 31 is a paraphrase of Numbers 11:33.

78:32–43 The spiritual configuration of the wilderness era is a repeating line of sin, punishment, repentance, and forgiveness, which makes God's love and patience all the more impressive. Note the pattern in table 1.

Table 1. The Pattern of Israel's Sin and God's Patience in Psalm 78:32–72

Israel's Action	God's Action
"They kept on sinning . . . they did not believe" (78:32)	"So he ended their days in futility" (78:33)
"They eagerly turned to him again. They remembered that God was their Rock. . . . Their hearts were not loyal to him" (78:34–37)	"Yet he was merciful; he forgave their iniquities and did not destroy them. . . . He remembered that they were but flesh" (78:38–39)
"They rebelled against him in the wilderness. . . . They put God to the test" (78:40–41)	"He redeemed them from the oppressor, . . . he displayed his signs in Egypt. . . . He brought his people out like a flock. . . . He drove out nations before them and allotted their lands to them as an inheritance" (78:42–55)

Israel's Action	God's Action
"But they put God to the test and rebelled against the Most High; they did not keep his statutes. . . . They aroused his jealousy with their idols" (78:56–58)	"He rejected Israel completely. He abandoned the tabernacle of Shiloh. . . . He gave his people over to the sword" (78:59–64)
	God's action in spite of Israel's rebellion: "Then the Lord awoke as from sleep. . . . He beat back his enemies. . . . He chose the tribe of Judah, Mount Zion. . . . He chose David his servant" (78:65–72)

Note also the pattern of "*they* remembered" or "did not remember" and "*he* remembered": "*they* [Israel] remembered that God was their Rock, that God Most High was their Redeemer" (78:35); "*he* [God] remembered that they were but flesh" (78:39); "*they* did not remember his power" (78:42a) or the plagues of Egypt (78:44–51).

78:36 *flatter . . . lying to him.* When the verb "flatter" appears in a religious context, it generally refers to Yahweh's deceptiveness (e.g., 1 Kings 22:20–22; Jer. 20:7), but it can also suggest human deceptiveness (e.g., Judg. 14:15; 16:5; Job 31:9).[4] See the sidebar "Does God Deceive?" Israel's deceptive behavior was virtually *lying* to God. While verse 35 seems to be a moment of faith, verse 36 implies that it was hypocritical.

78:37–39 *Yet he was merciful.* God still loved Israel in spite of what they had done. Although he had redeemed them, they would not trust him; and although he punished them for their unbelief, they were not repentant. "But they had the gall to pretend they were. And still he loved them!"[5]

78:40–41 *rebelled . . . grieved . . . put God to the test; they vexed.* This fourfold pattern of antagonism and rebellion was intended by the psalmist, and it was a historical pattern ("again and again," 78:41). One is reminded of the stylistic pattern in the accounts in Judges and Kings that emphasizes the recurring cycles of unbelief (e.g., Judg. 3:11–12; 3:30–4:1; 1 Kings 15:25–26, 31–32).

78:42–43 *signs . . . wonders.* The two words occur together in Deuteronomy (e.g., Deut. 4:34; 6:22; 7:19) and refer to the miracles God performed to bring Israel out of Egypt.

78:44–55 The language of these verses reflects heavily the language of Exodus 7–13. First, verses 44–51 focus on the signs and wonders in Egypt; then, verses 52–55 summarize the Lord's leading Israel from Egypt to Canaan. Yet the author takes liberty with the vocabulary of the Exodus narrative and in verse 46 mentions the "grasshopper" (*hasil* [also 1 Kings 8:37], evidently a synonym for "locust," *'arbeh*, the more common word for the species). Our author uses selective vocabulary in verses 47 and 48, where he refers to the more specific "vines" and "sycamore-figs" instead of the

Obviously 78:36 refers to Israel's attempt to "flatter" God, which is a subtle way to try to deceive God and to make him believe something false ("lying to him with their tongues"). This motive in human beings is no surprise, but, as noted (see the comments on 78:36), the verb is sometimes used of God, giving the impression that God also engages in deceit. Obviously, the problem for the reader is that the language about God's deceiving individuals is contrary to the ethic God imposes on us human beings, and if we are to pattern our lives after God ("Be holy because I, the LORD your God, am holy," Lev. 19:2), then we have a double standard. This question belongs to a much larger discussion of Old Testament ethics, but this particular occurrence demands a brief comment. The idea that God may deceive his human subjects can be explained several ways: (1) it is merely an accommodation to human emotions and language (anthropopathism); but the stories in 1 Kings 22:20–22 and Jeremiah 4:10 put God in a suspicious and disparaging light; (2) the Old Testament sometimes expresses what God permits in terms of what God commands, which is essentially another "accommodation" theory; (3) it is one of Scripture's ways of expressing the mystery of God's control over evil (W. B. Greene Jr.); that is, it is not a maligning of God's character but a statement about the mystery of his work. While none of these "explanations" may be altogether convincing, all three of them obviously attempt to protect God's character and reputation. Yet, the third option, it seems to me, does more, for it assumes that there are some things about God we cannot understand. Greene's proposal has merit.

general "all the vegetation of the field" (NIV: "everything growing in the fields") and "every tree" of the Exodus narrative (Exod. 9:22, 25), and he uses a different word for "lightning" (*reshapim*, rather than *'esh* [lit., "fire"], as in Exod. 9:23).

78:51 *firstfruits of manhood.* This is a term used of Jacob's firstborn, Reuben (Gen. 49:3), implying the manliness of the male progenitor. While the order of the plagues in this psalm and Psalm 105 differs from that of the Exodus narrative, the death of the firstborn is last in all three lists, implying its final and decisive effect.

78:54 *his holy land.* Since the noun is simply "his holiness," it could be his holy mountain (Zion), but "border" suggests the land of Israel generally, parallel to "the hill country" in the second half of the verse, and verse 55 definitely refers to Joshua's conquest of the land.

78:55 *allotted.* The verbs translated "allotted" (lit., "caused to fall" [see Josh. 17:5 ESV], implies casting lots) and "settled" are causative verbs, suggesting that, rather than being mere chance, God is very much in control of these developments.

78:57 *faulty bow.* Something was inherently wrong either with the bow or with its user.

78:58 *high places . . . idols.* This verse brings the reader into the period of the judges, when idolatry clearly became a problem. See Judges 2:10–19 for the historical cycle.

78:60 *He abandoned the tabernacle of Shiloh.* Joshua 18:1 records the erection of the tabernacle at Shiloh, the first "permanent" place for the tabernacle. The story of 1 Samuel 4 is focused on the capture of the ark by the Philistines, with no mention of the tabernacle, but it is quite probable that when the Philistines captured the ark, they also destroyed the tabernacle (as implied by Jer. 7:12–15).

78:61 *He sent the ark of his might into captivity.* The ESV renders the clause quite literally, "[He] delivered his power to captivity," which is evidently based on a similar expression in 132:8 ("the ark of your strength," ESV). The NIV's "ark" does not appear in the Hebrew text.

his splendor into the hands of the enemy. The phrase "his splendor" may mean "Israel," but the stronger implication is that it is Yahweh himself, represented by the ark, who goes into captivity. Since the ark represented Yahweh's presence, this is likely the way Israel would have understood the incident. Note that Yahweh is the subject of the action.

78:65–72 Here is "amazing grace," demonstrated in the fact that in spite of all Israel had done, God still loved them. The last word is not theirs or that of their enemies, but it is God's, and it is a word of love. See Psalm 44:23 for God's sleeping.

78:65 *as a warrior wakes from the stupor of wine.* This bold metaphor depicts God's reaction to their tragic history, especially as represented by the capture of his own "glory" (the ark), as a man who wakes from his drunken stupor and takes violent defensive action.[6] Verse 66 further describes God's combative mode, followed by his radical change in leadership, the choice of David, which represented a shift from the Rachel to the Leah line of Jacob's family (78:70–72). While this change may seem abrupt, it is an outgrowth of Yahweh's long frustration with Israel's disobedience and his love that will not give up on them (see Hosea 11).

78:66 *He beat back his enemies.* This is a summary of Israel's victories under Samuel, Saul, and David (1 Sam. 5 onward).

78:68 *he chose the tribe of Judah.* The prophecy of Genesis 49:8–10 predicted this transfer of leadership to Judah.

78:71–72 *David shepherded them with integrity of heart; with skillful hands.* See 1 Samuel 16:11. While the "shepherd" theme is a play on words, it is more than that, for David's "shepherding" experience was an expression of both his genuine character ("with integrity of heart") and his capable leadership ("with skillful hands").

Table 2. Historical Places and Events in Psalm 78

Historical Place or Event	Psalm 78	Location in Old Testament
Mount Gilboa	78:9	1 Sam. 31
Crossing of the Red Sea	78:13a	Exod. 14:21–31
Water stood up like a wall	78:13b	Exod. 14:21–22
Cloud by day and fire by night	78:14	Exod. 13:21–22, etc.
Water from the rock	78:15–16	Exod. 17
Manna	78:18–25	Exod. 16
Complained against the LORD	78:19	Num. 11:1
Meat (quail)	78:27–29	Exod. 16
Fire broke out	78:21	Num. 11:1–3
Anger of God	78:31	Num. 11:33
They tested God	78:41	Exod. 17:2; Num. 14:22
Signs and wonders in Zoan	78:43	Exod. 7–13
River into blood	78:44	Exod. 7:14–21
Flies	78:45a	Exod. 8:20–32
Frogs	78:45b	Exod. 8:1–15
Locusts	78:46	Exod. 10:3–20
Hail, thunder, and lightning	78:47–48	Exod. 9:13–35
"Destroying angels"	78:49	Exod. 14:19
Death of the firstborn	78:51	Exod. 11
Exodus from Egypt	78:52–53a	Exod. 12:31–42
Drowning of Pharaoh's army	78:53b	Exod. 14:27–28
Conquest of the land	78:54–55	Josh. 1–12
High places	78:58	Judges; 1–2 Kings, etc.
Capture of ark and destruction of Shiloh	78:60–62	1 Sam. 4
David as shepherd	78:70–72	1 Sam. 16:1–13

Theological Insights

Psalm 78 is all about God's grace and Israel's disobedience, a lesson that applies to all believers, however far advanced they may be in their spiritual formation. In this sense, no biblical writer gives a better perspective on the biblical faith, both Old Testament and New; he thus provides us with a model as well as a warning. Israel's ever-changing loyalty to their God was to be disavowed. Even when they had seeming moments of sincere faith (78:35), they were quickly exposed as hypocritical (78:36–37), illustrating the sad reality that the line separating authentic faith and hypocrisy is all too thin and permeable.

Regrettably, an offshoot of such a faith is the diminishing quality of grace in the eyes of its objects. God performed miracles in his people's sight, and their response was ingratitude—"They sinned still more against him" (78:17

RSV), and they met God's grace of giving with a demand for more (78:20), which meant that they were treating God's favor as though it were no longer grace, since grace is a free gift and never the object of demand.[7]

Teaching the Text

Psychologically all of us fall somewhere along the spectrum between an inferiority and a superiority complex. The Bible, being a good study of human personality and behavior, opens with the story of humanity's attempt to become like God, leading to the other end of the spectrum, "They realized they were naked" (Gen. 3:7b), stripped of all human dignity. A sense of superiority always has a strong tinge of disingenuousness. The next part of that story symbolically presents the long and conflicting chronicle of biblical theology, constituted by the paltry human effort to fix the problem ("They sewed fig leaves together and made coverings for themselves," Gen. 3:7c), and the magnanimity of grace ("The LORD God made garments of skin for Adam and his wife and clothed them," Gen. 3:21).

We may also think of Israel's story on a spectrum from human to divine effort. As Israel's story, Psalm 78 highlights the human-effort end of that spectrum; and as God's story, it shines its light on the mystery of the divine-effort end of the spectrum (grace). As Weiser remarks, "History remains a mystery which God has reserved to himself and in which only those participate who submit to him in faith and obedience."[8] Hidden in the mystery of God's shift of power and favor from the Rachel side of Jacob's family to the less-favored Leah side of his family (see "Historical and Cultural Background") is God's liberty to dispense his grace to whomever he chooses and his strategic eternal plan to humble himself for the work of redemption. In fact, the opening reference to "hidden things" in 78:2 should make us wonder if the writer of the psalm consciously intended to connect the mystery of the transition from the Rachel to the Leah line with the mystery of God's condescension, even delivering the "ark of his might into captivity, his splendor into the hands of the enemy" (78:61). It is the mystery of the Suffering Servant, or, as we Christians say, the "Suffering God": "Yet it was the LORD's will to crush him and cause him to suffer, and though the LORD makes his life an offering for sin, he will see his offspring and prolong his days, and the will of the LORD will prosper in his hand" (Isa. 53:10).

The climax of our psalm (78:60–72) is the long description of God's response to Israel's disobedience (see "Outline/Structure"), which included an act of self-humiliation—that is, delivering "his power to captivity, his glory to the hand of the foe" (78:61 ESV). But this suggests that God's action went beyond self-humiliation—it involved the mystery that Paul spoke about: "And being found in appearance as a man, he humbled himself by becoming obedient to death—even death on a cross!" (Phil. 2:8). What looked like defeat for Israel and for God was in effect Yahweh's act of self-humiliation and suffering for his people's sake; as C. S. Lewis's Christ character Aslan says, "I will see to it that the worst falls upon myself" (see "Illustrating the Text"). Out of the crucible of humiliation and suffering came the victory. In fact, one of the boldest God metaphors of the Psalms describes it thus: "Then the Lord awoke as from sleep. . . . He beat back his enemies" (78:65a, 66a). Likewise, in the New Testament it was in the crucible of Calvary that Christ suffered for the world's sins, and out of that dark mystery of self-humiliation he brought salvation to the world: "For you know the grace of our Lord Jesus Christ, that though he was rich, yet for your sake he became poor, so that you through his poverty might become rich" (2 Cor. 8:9).

In practical terms, the doctrine of God's self-humiliation (condescension) reminds us that our humanity is God's gift stamped with his image and is so special that God took upon himself our humanity to redeem us. G. K. Chesterton says, "Christianity is the only religion on earth that has felt that omnipotence made God incomplete" (see "Illustrating the Text"). This truth also can contribute to the cure of the symptoms and spiritual malady of our inferiority: God loved us that much![9]

On the other hand, the sin of pride (superiority) at the opposite end of the spectrum can find a cure in the marvelous doctrine of God's condescension in Jesus Christ. Our human frailty that God assumed in Christ is the only posture in which we can receive the grace of divine love. Indeed, the foundational principles of God's kingdom are constituted by the doctrine of humiliation, for the kingdom of heaven belongs to the "poor in spirit," the mourners over their sin "will be comforted," and the meek "will inherit the earth" (Matt. 5:3–5). And these principles of God's kingdom are a reflection of his mysterious nature that expresses itself in his condescension and suffering for our redemption.

Illustrating the Text

In redemption God sees that the worst falls on himself.

Children's Book: *The Magician's Nephew*, **by C. S. Lewis.** In this book from the Chronicles of Narnia series, Aslan describes the presence of evil in the world:

> "You see, friend," [Aslan] said, "that before the new, clean world I gave you is seven hours old, a force of evil has already entered it; waked and brought hither by this Son of Adam." The Beasts, even Strawberry, all turned their eyes on Digory till he felt that he wished the ground would swallow him up. "But do not be cast down," said Aslan, still speaking to the Beasts. "Evil will come

of that evil, but it is still a long way off, and I will see to it that the worst falls upon myself. In the meantime, let us take such order that for many hundred years yet this shall be a merry land in a merry world. And as Adam's race has done the harm, Adam's race shall help to heal it."[10]

When God has his back to the wall

Quote: *Orthodoxy*, by G. K. Chesterton. Chesterton speaks of Christ's condescension and suffering:

> That a good man may have his back to the wall is no more than we knew already; but that God could have his back to the wall is a boast for all insurgents for ever. Christianity is the only religion on earth that has felt that omnipotence made God incomplete. Christianity alone has felt that God, to be wholly God, must have been a rebel as well as a king. Alone of all creeds, Christianity has added courage to the virtues of the Creator. For the only courage worth calling courage must necessarily mean that the soul passes a breaking point—and does not break.[11]

Weiser speaks to this theological mystery also: "In the eyes of men God forgoes all his power in order to show that he is the Lord; this is perhaps his providence's most puzzling and most incomprehensible mystery."[12]

The worship of oneself

Literature: *The Maiden's Bequest*, by George MacDonald. In this novel, MacDonald describes an arrogant medical student in the class with the main character, Alec Forbes, in this way: "[Patrick] Beauchamp was no great favorite even in his own set, though there were many who would follow his lead at his fests; for there is one kind of religion in which the more devoted a man is, the fewer proselytes he makes; it is the worship of himself."[13] However sincere Israel's repentant moments may have been (78:34–35), they turned quickly into pretense as Israel "flatter[ed] him [Yahweh] with their mouths, lying to him with their tongues" (78:36). It was, like Patrick Beauchamp's religion, self-worship.

"Then We Your People, the Sheep of Your Pasture, Will Praise You Forever"

Big Idea

God is affected by the actions of those who do not know him, as well as by the actions of those who do.

Key Themes

- We deal with our sins for our own sake, but for God's too, because they affect him.
- Faith's laments end in hope—even when our questions are unanswered.
- Hope is our guidance system that directs us into the future of God's promises.

Understanding the Text

This community lament lets us peer into the mind-set of the early postexilic community as they begin the agonizing process of analyzing their spiritual state, as well as the political and social dimensions of this devastated community. As we have observed, Book 3 is an anthology on the fall of Jerusalem and the end of the Davidic dynasty. In this psalm David is nowhere to be seen, but for a moment we get a hopeful glimpse of the community's repentant heart and their dependence on the character of God rather than their own (79:9). At this point, the community's moral conscience may not have begun the intense self-reflection about the exile's causes, such as we see in Ezekiel (Ezek. 18:2, 25; 33:10, 17, 20; see also Zech. 1:2–6), and in that climate the people had turned their attention naturally to Yahweh's character rather than their own (see especially Ezek. 18:10), and their confession of sin in verses 8–10 may be more a face-saving move in light of the nations' mockery of their faith (79:10).

The Text in Context

This psalm stands linguistically and substantively in direct relationship to Psalm 74, but the purpose of these two psalms is quite different. While they share some covenant terms (see table 1), Psalm 74 makes no confession of sin as does Psalm 79 (79:9), and details about the destruction of the temple (74:4–8) are missing from Psalm 79. While the appeal of Psalm 74 to Yahweh is based on exodus and creation theology (this is what you [God] did! 74:13–17), Psalm 79 appeals to Yahweh's character as the basis of his action and positions Israel's desperation in the act of repentance (this is who you are! 79:9). An interesting observation of the religious climate comes into view in Psalm 74 with the advice that there is no prophet present (74:9), and the psalmist appeals generally to Yahweh's covenant (esp. 74:20). In comparison, Psalm 79 goes beyond Yahweh's acts and appeals to his character (79:9). In the sum of things, the differences are subtle, but God's character is primary to his acts.

Psalm 79:2–3 is quoted in 1 Maccabees 7:17 to affirm that the prophecy has been fulfilled.

Table 1. Shared Vocabulary between Psalms 74 and 79

Term	Psalm 74	Psalm 79
"Inheritance" (land of Israel)	74:2	79:1
"(Your) temple/sanctuary"	74:3: "sanctuary" (*qodesh*) 74:7: "your sanctuary" (*miqdasheka*) "sanctuary [NIV: "dwelling place"] of your Name" (*mishkan-sheᵉmeka*)	79:1: "your holy temple" (*hekal qodsheka*)
"(Your) name"	74:7	79:6, 9
"Sheep of your pasture"	74:1	79:13
"Defile"	74:7 (*hll*)	79:1 (*tm'*)
"Why?"	74:1, 11	79:10
"How long?"	74:10 (*'ad-matay*)	79:5 (*'ad-mah*)
"Contempt/mockery"	74:22: "mockery" (NIV: "how fools mock you" = noun, *herpatᵉka*)	79:4: "contempt" (*herpah*)

Outline/Structure

In all three sections of the poem the movement is from "the nations" (79:1, 6, 10) to the faith community "we/us" (79:4, 8, 13).[1] Yet God stands at the theological center of the psalm (79:10–13).

1. The lament (79:1–4)
2. The question and prayer of vindication (79:5–9)

3. The resolution (79:10–13)
   a. The reverse taunt (79:10a)
   b. Informing the nations (79:10b)
   c. Prayer of intercession for the prisoners (79:11)
   d. Prayer of vengeance on the neighbors (79:12)
   e. Prayer of praise (79:13)

Historical and Cultural Background

Since the psalm does not refer explicitly to the temple's destruction, just to its defilement (79:1), the incident could be the Babylonian invasion of 597 BC, which, according to the addendum to Jeremiah (Jer. 52:28–30), involved the largest number of exiles of the three Babylonian deportations,[2] in addition to the removal of temple treasures (2 Kings 24:8–17). Just the trafficking of foreigners in the temple would have been enough to defile it. Others prefer the fall of Jerusalem in 586 BC (e.g., Tate).[3]

Interpretive Insights

79:1 *defiled your holy temple.* See "Historical and Cultural Background."
rubble. It is possible that Jerusalem could be in ruins and the temple still be intact.

79:2 *your servants.* This one phrase is a window into Israel's self-image at the time, either as an acknowledgment of their obedience to their Master or as a reminder that they ought to be obedient.
your own people. This is literally "faithful ones." The NIV's rendering of this phrase has obscured the particular idea of covenant loyalty.

79:3 *there is no one to bury the dead.* This was in itself a tragedy, for it prevented the dead from being gathered to their ancestors. We do not know whether this was thought to have some effect on their existence in Sheol, or whether it is just human decency that is the concern here.

79:4 *our neighbors.* The Edomites, Moabites, and Ammonites. See Ezekiel 25; 36:1–15, and Obadiah, which is about the Edomites' unbrotherly exploitation of Judah on the occasion of the Babylonian destruction of Jerusalem. Most of this verse is found in 44:13, suggesting the dependence of the psalm on other psalms (compare also 79:11 and 102:20).

79:5 *How long, Lord?* The middle question, "Will you be angry forever?" is the sense of the rhetorical questions on either side of it. It was God's displeasure that was Israel's greatest burden to bear. See 13:1; 80:4; 89:46.

79:7 *for they have devoured Jacob.* The second reason the Lord should punish the nations is what they have done to Israel, the first being what they have done to God. The nations exceeded the task Yahweh gave them to do against Israel (Zech. 1:15), so their excessive violence was justifiably punishable.

79:8 *hold against us . . . may your mercy come quickly.* Since the psalmist confesses the present generation's own sins in verse 9, "against us" seems to imply a past generation. He prays against the principle that God will hold the sins of the fathers against the "third and fourth generation," trusting divine grace promised to a "thousand generations of those who love" God and keep his commandments (Exod. 20:5–6; Lam. 5:7). God's grace far exceeds the nations' overexercised assignment to punish Israel for their sins, and by the psalmist's petition, grace should "come quickly."

for we are in desperate need. The urgent reason for the Lord's intervention is introduced here in verse 8b with "for" (*ki*, "because"), constituted by what the nations have done to Israel and its effect on them. This desperation includes the political, social, and theological dimensions of Judah's tragedy.

79:9 *God our Savior.* Literally, "God of our salvation," a slightly different nuance than the NIV, since "Savior" is an appellation that stresses his identity, while "salvation" puts the emphasis on his activity. While the difference is subtle, it is God's actions ("help us" and "deliver us") that the psalmist prays for.

forgive our sins. It is very clear that "salvation" here carries the meaning of deliverance from sin, not merely deliverance from a political or personal crisis (see Jer. 31:34). Psalm 78:38 recalls that God has done precisely that in the past, and now the writer of Psalm 79 prays this prayer for his generation.

for your name's sake. See the sidebar, "For His Name's Sake," in the unit on Psalm 23. Appealing to God's name was equivalent to invoking his presence. Deuteronomy has a strong "Name" theology (e.g., Deut. 12:5, 11, 21).

The Covenant Formula

God formalizes his relationship with his people with a covenant formula, summarized as "I will be your God, and you will be my people, and I will dwell in your midst." It occurs in the Pentateuch (e.g., Lev. 26:11–12), and then pretty much becomes implicit in the Former and Latter Prophets until we approach the exilic prophets Jeremiah and Ezekiel and the postexilic prophet Zechariah. These three prophets viewed the age that was opening before Israel as a renewal or even a repetition of the great era that witnessed the exodus from Egypt, when God constituted the people of Israel as God's people (Jer. 7:23; 11:4; 24:7; 30:22; 31:33; 32:38; Ezek. 11:20; 14:11; 36:28; 37:23, 27; Zech. 8:8). It would not be inaccurate, in fact, to say that the prophets were engaged in the prescription and description of all three aspects of the covenant formula: how Yahweh sought to be Israel's God (part 1), how Israel became or failed to become Yahweh's people (part 2), and how Yahweh sought to be with them (part 3).

79:10 *Where is their God?* This is the nations' taunt of Israel (also 115:2), whereas in 42:3 it is the taunt of individuals.

79:11 *groans of the prisoners.* This prayer comes from the community that did not go into exile, but they are "prisoners" nevertheless, both politically and emotionally.

79:12 *Pay back . . . our neighbors seven times.* "Seven times" is used to describe a more than ample measure (Lev. 26:18, etc.).

79:13 *sheep of your pasture.* See Psalm 100:3. Note the terms applied to Israel: "your servants" (79:2), "your people" (79:2, 13), and "the sheep of your pasture" (79:13). The psalm closes with this tender prayer of confession that recalls the second part of the covenant formula ("You shall be my people"; see the sidebar) and pledges their perpetual praise.

Theological Insights

It may seem strange to ask God to do something for us *for his sake* rather than for ours, but this is precisely what the writer of this psalm does (79:9). On the one hand, this theological principle is articulated by Ezekiel, with God as the initiating subject ("But for the sake of my name I did what would keep it from being profaned in the eyes of the nations in whose sight I had brought them out [of Egypt]," Ezek. 20:14), but here it is the psalmist who makes this request. The character of God is the object, and the will of God is the purpose. When we pray the Lord's Prayer and ask, "Hallowed be thy name. . . . Thy will be done, on earth as it is in heaven," we tap into the mystery of this phrase, "for your name's sake" (Ps. 79:9). It is a phrase of *admission* that God's character and will are primary, and a phrase of *submission* to God's will. The underlying assumption of this phrase is that when God does what is in the best interests of his own character and will, that is synonymous with doing what is in our best interests (see the sidebar "For His Name's Sake" in the unit on Ps. 23).

This is tied into the prayer of forgiveness for sins, which implies that our forgiven hearts and holy life are in God's best interests, and thus in ours. That not only puts us right with ourselves but makes us right with God, and not only removes the grief of disobedience from our own minds but pleases God because our will has become aligned with his. This kind of radical transformation is possible only when God's radical power of forgiveness sets the process in order. Given our self-centered orientation, forgiveness is an unnatural progression because it means giving up something of ourselves, or, as Thielicke says, putting ourselves in the offender's place, and that requires a divine transaction (see "Illustrating the Text" in the unit on Ps. 144).[4] Forgiving our enemies is also subsumed under that category.

Teaching the Text

This psalm is one whose foundational theological assumptions can provide a sermon/lesson that certainly highlights one aspect of the spiritual instruction of this poem. Hermeneutically, however, we must be aware that assumptions are written between the lines, and we have to be careful that we read them accurately—but they are readable!

The three centers of attention in the psalm are God, the nations, and Israel. The pronouns "you/your" (God), "we/us/our" (Israel), and "they" (the nations), as well as the nouns, are instructive. Thus, using those as a guide, we can structure a sermon/lesson on the underlying assumptions of the psalmist. As sovereign and free as God is, he does not go unaffected by human actions. The reason may be found in the fact that God created us in his image, and that means he is forever connected with us human beings in a way that affects his own being—when his image is disrespected, God is disrespected. A human analogy—not a perfect one, of course—is the father and mother who are connected to their children in such a way that the children's actions and attitudes affect the parents in profound ways (see "Remember whose daughter or son you are" in "Illustrating the Text" in the unit on Ps. 44).

So moving from that beginning observation, we may make the first point, that God is affected by the actions of the nations (79:1, 6, 10), who "do not acknowledge" and worship God (79:6). Even though this poem does not deal with God's grief over the nations that do not acknowledge him, the fact that they are belligerent against God's people assumes that reality, so much so that a note of reminder to God was quite appropriate. Reminding God of one's problems and the problems of the world is a typical feature of biblical prayer, so frequent that we may safely conclude that our prayers too can appropriately contain such notes of reminder—without malice, of course, and with humility, to be sure—reminding God of what his opponents have done, even bending the exclamation point into a question mark, as our psalmist does in verse 10.

Second, God is concerned about the actions perpetrated against his people (79:4, 12), and it is in that confidence that the suppliant prays. This is basically a prayer balanced on the poles of "you/your" (God) and "we/us/our" (Israel). Those two perspectives are not kept separate but are intertwined, bearing the message of the inseparable relationship between God and his people—as goes God's reputation, so goes Israel's, and as goes Israel's, so goes God's (79:9). Christopher J. H. Wright has wisely observed that lament in the Psalms "is all hurled at God, not by his enemies but *by those who loved and trusted him most*" (see "Illustrating the Text").

Third, God is affected by the sins of our ancestors (79:8), and, of course, we do not go unaffected by them either. However their sins and failures have misshaped us, we can, and ought to, ask God to minimize their effect on our lives. This is different from 106:6, where the psalmist admits, "We have sinned, even as our ancestors did" (see the comments on 106:6–7). And we certainly ought not to fall into the "sour grapes" error by faulting our fathers and mothers (Jer. 31:29–30; Ezek. 18:2)—our own sins are the problem! Here the suppliant puts distance between Israel and their ancestors, not mentioning that there is a generational limit on their punishment. We may assume God's love that he shows to a "thousand generations of those who love [him] and keep [his] commandments" (Exod. 20:6) is the principle behind the psalmist's prayer.

Fourth—and here comes the hard one—God is *affected by our sins* (79:9). Regardless of how animated we become about the first three points, we have to come to the spiritual posture where we are convicted of our own sins and lay them before the God who forgives. As David confessed, "Against you, you only, have I sinned and done what is evil in your sight" (51:4). The emotional tone and content of this psalm are closely related to Psalm 74, both using the tender term for Israel, "the sheep of your pasture" (74:1; 79:13), which assumes God's tender care. As difficult as it is to confess our sins against God, it becomes much easier when we recognize that we are his "people" and the "sheep" of his pasture, objects of his tender care, and that will change our whole perspective from a life of lament to a life of praise (79:13).

Illustrating the Text

God gives us the words to fill in our complaint forms, as well as our thank-you notes.

Quote: **Christopher J. H. Wright.** Wright insists, and quite correctly, that the biblical laments are most appropriate on the lips of God's faithful servants:

> The point we should notice (possibly to our surprise) is that it [lament] is all hurled at God, not by his enemies but *by those who loved and trusted him most*. It seems, indeed, that it is precisely those who have the closest relationship with God who feel most at liberty to pour out their pain and protest to God—without fear of reproach. Lament is not only allowed in the Bible; it is abundantly modeled for us. God seems to want to give us as many words with which to fill in our complaint forms as to write our thank-you notes. Perhaps this is because whatever amount of lament the world causes us to express is a drop in the ocean compared to the grief in the heart of God himself at the totality of suffering that only God can comprehend.[5]

But we should also remember that, as a rule, the psalmic laments lead to hope.

Our misery and praise can sing to God in harmony.

True Story: An inquirer wrote John Newton a letter, saying that he was more disposed to cry "Misery" than "Hallelujah," and Newton wrote him back and said, "Why not both together? When the treble is praise and heart humiliation for the bass, the melody is pleasant and the harmony is good."[6] The editor of Book 5 combines two lament psalms (Pss. 57 and 60) to form Psalm 108 and, in combination, turns them into a psalm of thanksgiving for the new era of restoration that is about to occur (see "Understanding the Text" in the unit on Ps. 108).

Buy a field.

Bible: Jeremiah 32. Hope is an ingredient of life that is absolutely necessary for our well-being. When there is no prospect of tomorrow, life becomes unbearable. The writer to the Hebrews calls hope "an anchor for the soul" (Heb. 6:19). That metaphor seems so appropriate because hope gives our lives stability. It is the inner certainty that what you cannot yet see is already within your grasp. M. A. C. Warren has called it "faith on tiptoe."[7] The prophet Jeremiah provides one of the most dramatic illustrations of hope in the entire Bible when the Lord instructs him to buy a field (Jer. 32). The story takes place under hopeless circumstances. First, when the Babylonians launch their military campaign against Judah, King Zedekiah puts Jeremiah in prison so the prophet cannot spread his demoralizing message that encourages the Judeans to surrender to the Babylonians so they will be spared (588/587 BC). Second, the Babylonians have already taken control of the town of Anathoth where the field Jeremiah buys is located (32:25). Jeremiah transacts his business in a way that neglects no legal detail. He pays the purchase price, signs the deed, seals it, gets witnesses, and deposits both copies of the transaction with his scribe Baruch (32:9–12a). Then, in the presence of the Jews who are sitting in the court of the guard where Jeremiah is held prisoner, this prophet instructs Baruch to deposit the deeds in an earthenware vessel to await the time of the fulfillment of God's word. The final verse of his instructions to Baruch (32:15) states the thing they are hoping for, the return of Judean life to normalcy: "Houses, fields and vineyards will again be bought in this land" (see also 31:5). Jeremiah's purchase of the field in territory that is already in enemy hands is a sign of hope.

"Make Your Face Shine on Us, That We May Be Saved"

Big Idea

Our Shepherd God sometimes feeds us with the "bread of tears," but never as our adversary—he is always our Shepherd.

Key Themes

- God planted the vine (Israel), and he can protect it as well.
- We cling to the God who causes our tears.

Understanding the Text

This community lament arises out of an unnamed situation where the nation has suffered a devastating crisis—no fault of its own, it would seem—and, with the tender imagery of Yahweh as "Shepherd," prays for restoration.

The Text in Context

Psalm 79 ends with God's people confessing, "[We are] the sheep of your pasture" (79:13), and, like hand in glove, Psalm 80 begins with a prayer to the "Shepherd of Israel," intended as a continuation of the spirit of Psalm 79. The links with Psalm 89 are also significant (see table 1).

Table 1. Affinities of Psalms 80 and 89

Psalm 80	Psalm 89
"The son of man you have strengthened [NIV: "raised up"] for yourself" (80:17b, author's translation)	David my servant, whom "my hand will strengthen" (89:21)
The vine's (country's) "branches reached as far as the Sea, its shoots as far as the River" (the extent of Israel's kingdom) (80:11)	"I will set his [David's] hand over the sea, his right hand over the rivers" (the extent of David's kingdom) (89:25)

Psalm 80	Psalm 89
"Why have you broken down its [the country's] walls so that all who pass by pick its grapes?" (80:12)	"You have broken through all his [the king's] walls. . . . All who pass by have plundered him" (89:40–41a)
"You have made us [the people] an object of derision to our neighbors" (80:6a)	"He [the king] has become the scorn of his neighbors" (89:41b)

Note: These parallels are given and discussed briefly by Hill, "Son of Man," 266–67.

Outline/Structure

This is a beautifully structured poem, with a refrain that marks off the three parts (80:3, 7, 19). The refrain augments its effect on each occurrence by adding another name for God (80:3, "God"; 80:7, "God Almighty" ["God of Hosts"]; 80:19, "Yahweh God Almighty" [ESV: "Lord God of hosts"]), using the tetragrammaton (*YHWH*, "Lord") in the final refrain.

1. Prayer for restoration (80:1–3)
   a. Prayer to the *Shepherd* of Israel (80:1–2)
   b. Refrain (80:3)
2. Lament over their present condition of devastation (80:4–7)
   a. Lament (80:4–6)
   b. Refrain (80:7)
3. Israel's story and present crisis (80:8–19)
   a. Prayer to the *Vinedresser* of Israel (80:8–13)
   b. A prayer for God's return (80:14–15)
   c. Lament continued (80:16–17)
   d. Vow to faithfulness (80:18)
   e. Refrain (80:19)

Historical and Cultural Background

Taking a cue from the superscription of the Septuagint that adds "a psalm concerning the Assyrian," some scholars have proposed the decade of the Assyrian crisis that led to the fall of the northern kingdom as the historical occasion for Psalm 80 (732–722 BC).[1] While this psalm was not likely written in the context of the Babylonian exile, Book 3 certainly uses it in that context, which is the editorial backdrop of the collection. Thus its unnamed crisis, whatever it was, has been called into play as the cause for lamenting the destruction of Jerusalem and the temple and the fall of the Davidic dynasty. If the historical occasion of the psalm was related to the fall of the northern kingdom, as might well be the case, this reuse for Judah's national disaster seems quite natural.

Interpretive Insights

Title *Lilies of the Covenant.* The Masoretes placed a disjunctive accent after "lilies," either leaving the next word, "testimony" (*'edut*; NIV: "covenant"), standing alone (as NRSV and ESV) or joining it to the following noun: "testimony of Asaph. A psalm." "Lilies" seems to be the name of the tune and is given also to the titles of Psalms 45 and 69 (Ps. 60 has a variant).

80:1 *Shepherd of Israel.* Although this is the only occurrence of this phrase in the Hebrew Bible, the idea is nevertheless known in the Psalms and elsewhere (see "The Text in Context").

Joseph. "Joseph" may be a general term for all of Israel. In verse 2 the two sons of Joseph are positioned on either side of Benjamin, one of the southern tribes. Thus we have the inclusive terms of the kingdom of Israel, Joseph and Ephraim (sometimes listed as Ephraim and Manasseh, Joseph's sons) and Benjamin (southern tribes). The emphasis is on the Rachel tribes (Joseph and Benjamin), quite in contrast to the shift to the Leah tribe of Judah drawn out in Psalm 78. Jacob's blessing of Joseph and his sons includes the term "shepherd" (Gen. 48:15), giving an ancient precedent for the "Shepherd of Israel."

80:2 *before Ephraim, Benjamin and Manasseh.* The NIV and other translations connect verse 2 to the preceding verse and make these three names (see Num. 2:18–22) the effective object of "shine forth." Observing the end of the sentence as marked by the Masoretes, others make them the effective object of the verb "stir up" (e.g., ESV). The latter option would imply that the prayer asks God to "awaken" and show his might to Israel, which fits the context well.

80:3 *Restore us.* The psalmist's prayer is to "restore us" to the condition of the people prior to the crisis they have suffered.

make your face shine on us, that we may be saved. See "Outline/Structure." Israel's deliverance in this time of political devastation (80:5–6, 12–13, 16) will be a result of God's blessing, expressed by this excerpt from the priestly benediction (80:3b; see Num. 6:24–26). The verb "shine" connotes, at least symbolically, God's presence that dwells between the "cherubim" of the ark (Exod. 25:19–21; 1 Kings 6:26–28; Ps. 99:1).

80:4 *How long, LORD God Almighty, will your anger smolder against the prayers of your people?* The supplicant considers the anger of God to be in direct conflict with the prayers of his people, which is to say that God does not regard their prayers. The imagery of God's "smoking" anger presents the picture of smoke so thick that it obscures God's face and prevents Israel's prayers from reaching him.[2] The NIV consistently translates the Hebrew for "hosts" (see, e.g., ESV, NRSV) as "Almighty," which is an arbitrary choice.

80:5 *You have fed them with the bread of tears.* With shepherding imagery, the supplicant says Yahweh has fed them with a diet of tears, quite the opposite of what they would expect the "Shepherd of Israel" to do. "Bread of tears" occurs only here in the Old Testament (but see the idea in 42:3).

by the bowlful. The noun rendered "bowlful" means "a third" (of some larger measure) and has become the name of a vessel (Isa. 40:12 [NIV: "basket"]; compare our "quart" = a "quarter" of a gallon).[3]

80:6 *object of derision to our neighbors.* This theme occurs in 79:4, 12, where it evidently alludes to the Edomites, Moabites, and Ammonites. See Jeremiah 15:10 for the use of the word "derision/contention."

mock us. Hebrew has "them," but other versions, including the Septuagint, have "us," which fits the national lament better. Psalm 79:4 has the same expression, where "us" (Israel) is definitely the object of the scorn.

80:7–13 *You transplanted a vine from Egypt.* The metaphor changes from "shepherd" (God) to "vine" (Israel) and composes a beautiful allegory of Israel's history, from Egypt to the monarchical period, making specific mention of the conquest (80:8b) and including the latest crisis ("Why have you broken down its walls?"; 80:12a). The boundaries of the country, "as far as the Sea" and "as far as the River" (from the Mediterranean to the Euphrates; 80:11), suggest the time of David and Solomon as a measurement of Israel's great success in the land. The picture has affinities with Isaiah's Song of the Vineyard (Isa. 5:1–7; see also Jer. 2:21), particularly the preparation of the land for Israel's occupation (Ps. 80:9a; Isa. 5:2). Yet the stunning picture of a beautiful vine that covers the mountains and climbs the "mighty cedars" (lit., "the cedars of *God* [*'el*]," Ps. 80:10 [80:11 MT]) is the poem's own literary charm. With verses 12–13 the metaphor shifts slightly from that of the vine to a lovely vineyard, whose "walls" have been breached and its grapes plucked by everyone who passes by (80:12).[4] Moreover, the wild boar and large birds (*ziz*; the NIV has "insects" for this uncertain word) devour their share of the vineyard (80:13 [80:14 MT]).

80:14 *Return to us.* The Hebrew lacks the prepositional phrase "to us." The prayer is that God will "turn around / repent" and turn his attention from his heavenly throne to the earthly vine.

Look down from heaven and see! Perhaps the petition also implies the distance the psalmist feels from God and the humiliation the people have suffered.

80:15 *the root your right hand has planted.* Note that the thought of verse 14 carries over to verse 15. This Hebrew word for "root" occurs only here and seems to mean "sapling," which, because it was planted by God's "right hand," is both precious and strong.

the son you have raised up. Since the metaphor is a vine, the term "son" obviously means "sapling" and is parallel to "root" in the first half of the verse.

80:16 *Your vine is cut down, it is burned with fire.* The verbs portend an unnamed devastating event, describing the destruction "by fire," which was common in most military conquests.

80:17 *the man at your right hand.* Since "Benjamin" means "son of (your) right hand," this could be a play on words, especially since Benjamin has already been mentioned. Or it may simply refer to the king, who can be described as sitting at God's right hand (see 110:1). The country as a whole is the object of God's wrath, especially since the "vine" is a metaphor for Israel. While some commentators interpret this figure as the king, such a dual meaning, people and king, would not be unusual, since the king represented the people.

the son of man you have raised up for yourself. While the terms "man" (*'ish*) and "son of man" (*ben-'adam*) normally refer to individuals, the symbolic language of the psalm makes allowance for these terms as references to Israel. The NIV's rendering of the verb in the clause as "raised up" is possible but not preferable, because it really means "to make strong," and in 89:21 it is used to say the Lord will "strengthen" the king.

Even though this psalm is not quoted in the New Testament, there are messianic overtones in the terms "the man at your right hand" and "the son of man you have raised up for yourself." The Targum, though from the third or fourth century AD, likely preserves a much older messianic tradition by interpreting "son of man" as "king messiah."[5]

80:18 *Then we will not turn away.* The verb (*nasog*) is either a first common plural ("*we* will not turn away," and so NIV and most English translations) or a third singular perfect (Niphal, "*he* has not turned back from you"; the Hebrew forms are identical). If it is "he," it likely references the king, but since the verb of 18b is clearly first common plural, "*we* will call," the verb in the first half of the sentence should be parsed the same way ("*we* will not turn away"). So it is a statement not in defense of the king's faithfulness but as a vow of Israel's faithfulness. In 53:3 the same verb has the nuance of apostate behavior ("fall away"; NIV: "turned away").

revive us, and we will call on your name. "Revive us" (lit., "make us live") carries a similar sense to the third line of the refrain ("that we may be saved"). The destruction has been so extensive that the country is effectively dead. The effect of this revival will be that Israel will worship the Lord ("call on your name") with its inclusive dimensions of devotion and praise.

80:19 Lord *God Almighty.* The presence of the tetragrammaton (*YHWH*, "Lord") is not unusual in the Asaph psalms, which are a part of the Elohistic Psalter (Pss. 42–83), but generally it is purposely placed. Here it not only represents the climax of the poem but is essentially the Levitical stamp of approval on this collection.

Theological Insights

There are ample paradoxes in the biblical faith, one of which is a feature of this poem: that we must cling to the God who causes our tears. The God of Scripture also embraces pain and suffers humiliation (Ps. 78), and that, according to the New Testament (e.g., Phil. 2), is integral to his plan of redemption. Never confessing any fault on Israel's part, Psalm 80 views God as the cause of Israel's present trouble, even though he deserves the title of "Shepherd of Israel" (80:1) and in fulfilling that office feeds them "with the bread of tears" (80:5).

The dark valleys that our sins have burrowed out for us mean that we cannot escape them and that we need someone to walk through them with us. While this psalm does not bring out that aspect of the paradox, it does identify the fact that the "Shepherd of Israel" sometimes leads them, and us, into the valley of tears (compare 23:4, "valley of the shadow of death" [see NIV note]) and makes Israel an object of derision. Even in the presence of their enemies (80:6; cf. 23:5) the Lord sets a banquet table before them. Somewhere in their hearts they know that God's anger is an instrument of restoration as it is also of humiliation, for when the mask of opposition is removed, "goodness and mercy" (23:6 ESV) will pursue the sheep safely into the fold. So they can pray for deliverance to their Shepherd (see refrain, "restore us") and ask him to "look down from heaven and see! Watch over this vine" (80:14b–c).

This dilemma, which is real for people of faith as well as people with no faith at all, is only meaningful if, says Weiser, "adversity and deliverance are not understood as exclusive antitheses, but as having their ultimate unity in God's character."[6] In fact, the verb of verse 14c, "watch over," carries the dual meaning of an encounter with God as affliction and as deliverance and reminds us that our "momentary affliction" may have a connection with the "educational purpose of the divine economy of salvation."[7] Paul turns the kind of trust that underlies this psalm into a promise: "For our light affliction, which is but for a moment, worketh for us a far more exceeding and eternal weight of glory" (2 Cor. 4:17 KJV).

Teaching the Text

Preparing a sermon/lesson on Psalm 80, especially the "bread of tears" idea in verse 5, will be emotionally and intellectually challenging, but very helpful, because sometimes the people of God, as in this psalm, need to hear this lesson expounded. In those situations when we shed "tears by the keg" (Tate's phrase; see the comments on 80:5), some of us have asked the question, "Is God angry with me?" And it is a legitimate as well as a therapeutic question. We might develop this message by first acknowledging that divine anger is a valid response to those situations that defy God's goodness and love. Even believers can be angry and not sin (Eph. 4:26).

Second, the challenge for us is explaining our adversities in the light of God's love. It is true that the hand of the "Shepherd of Israel" who led "Joseph like a flock" also "fed them" with the "bread of tears" (80:1, 5). This psalm operates in the same spiritual climate as Psalm 23, where the Lord does not prevent the enemies from assailing the psalmist, but he prepares a table for the psalmist in their presence. When the long-range perspective can finally be seen—"goodness and mercy" come behind us ("follow")—even though our lives are often "pursued" by the adversities that generate the "tears by the bowlful" (80:5), it is "goodness and mercy" (the identity of our pursuers is important) that "pursue" us to the house of God, where we want and ought to be. François Mauriac reminds us that we do not know the worth of a single tear (see "Illustrating the Text").

We might even bring into our message Paul's kaleidoscopic picture of the beautiful design for our lives that God constructs out of all the jigsaw pieces of our personal and corporate worlds (Rom. 8:28). Of course, the question we must ask is whether God is trying to get our attention about something that is genuinely wrong in our lives, and nobody can answer that question except the person concerned. Or does our tearful situation configure a plan that, once the larger plan is in view, will reveal the refinement of soul that makes us pleasing in God's sight? That, as Augustine suggests, is the "hidden hand of [God's] healing art" at work (see "Illustrating the Text"). Another alternative (a Joban alternative, in fact) is this: Does God want to put our genuine faith on display to show that there are still those who worship God for no ulterior motive—he is God and deserves our worship (see Job 1–2)? Finally, Ecclesiastes 7:14 admonishes us to be happy when the times are conducive to happiness, and when the bad times come, to remember that "God has made the one as well as the other." Qoheleth's advice is not that we should surrender to our circumstances but that we should surrender to our God.

Illustrating the Text

All is grace.

Quote: **François Mauriac.** Sometimes our Shepherd God, says the psalmist, fed his people with "the bread of tears" (80:5), one of the mysteries of Israel's relationship with God, and ours too. Why does God choose to feed us with the "bread of tears"? A helpful analogy may be that of parents whose knowledge of the laws of nutrition and love for their children combine in their insistence that their children eat those foods they don't like—and tears are often present (even in the eyes of determined parents). But the parents have a broader view than the children, and it is tempered by grace. In the foreword to Elie Wiesel's book *Night*, François Mauriac comments on the rise of the modern state of Israel with this observation, "We do not know the worth of one single drop of blood, one single tear. All is grace."[8] That is what we have to remember: all is grace.

God's hidden hand practices his healing art in our lives.

Church Fathers: The faith strategy that allows the psalmist to drink God's "bowlful of tears" (see 80:5) is his trust in the Lord who can "make [his] face shine on us, that we may be saved" (80:7 and 19). The fact that this form of the priestly benediction becomes the refrain, and thus the theme or subtheme of the psalm, points to the underlying trust in the Lord. As Augustine says it so well, God's "hidden hand of healing art" works contrary to the program of our own plans and will: "Inside me your good was working on me to make me restless until you should become clear and certain to my inward sight. Through the hidden hand of your healing art my swelling abated and from day to day the troubled and clouded sight of my mind grew better through the stinging ointment of a healthy sorrow."[9]

True faith

Literature: *The Vicar's Daughter*, **by George MacDonald.** In MacDonald's novel, Wynnie, the narrator of the story, recalls her father's wisdom: "My father says, . . . that a true faith is like the pool of Bethesda—it is when it is troubled that it shows its healing power."[10] This analogy, like the psalmist's "bowlful of tears," describes the crucible from which the psalmist prays, "Restore us, God Almighty; make your face shine on us, that we may be saved" (80:7).

"If My People Would Only Listen to Me"

Big Idea

In God's great mercy our bad decisions may lead not to the end of the road but to a cul-de-sac of grace where we can make a U-turn.

Key Themes

- God's call is both a plea and a command, "If they would just listen to me."
- The consequences of our bad decisions are not the final word but God's call to turn around.

Understanding the Text

Psalm 81 belongs to a trio of festival psalms (Pss. 50; 81; 95) and is traditionally associated with the festival of Rosh Hashanah (the New Year; see "Historical and Cultural Background"). It has a sermonic core in 81:6–16,[1] delivering a message of God's grace in Israel's history.

The Text in Context

This is one of the three Asaph psalms that incorporate a prophetic message as part of their design (Pss. 50; 75; 81; also Ps. 95, but it is not an Asaph psalm). Psalm 80 closes with the prayer that God will make his face shine on his people and save them (80:19), while Psalm 81 engages in the realism of Israel's history and their rebellious nature yet enunciates the divine promise that God will feed them with the finest wheat and honey from the rock (81:16), quite a departure from the diet of tears he had served them in their past history (80:5). Both psalms engage liberally in Israel's story of God's past actions on their behalf (80:8–13; 81:6–7, 10–12). In the context of Book 3 and its historical backdrop of the exile, Psalm 81 is a pronouncement that their tragedy fits the pattern of their history, yet God offers future hope.

Outline/Structure

1. Summons to the festival (81:1–5a)
   a. Call to praise (81:1–3)
   b. God's authorization of the feast (81:4–5a)
2. A review of Israel's history and obligations (81:5b–16)
   a. Transition to the prophetic word (81:5b)
   b. A review of Israel's history (81:6–7)
   c. Israel's obligations and disloyalty (81:8–16)
      i. God's commands (81:8–10)
      ii. Israel's disloyalty (81:11)
      iii. Yahweh's counterresponse (81:12)
      iv. The command to listen (81:13)
      v. Yahweh's counterresponse (81:14–16)
         (1) Subjection of Israel's enemies (81:14–15)
         (2) Promise fulfilled (81:16)

Historical and Cultural Background

Form-critical scholarship of the past century has promoted the idea that Psalm 81, especially with its reference to the "New Moon" (81:3), likely celebrated Israel's harvest festival that coincided, but was not identical, with the Feast of Tabernacles celebrated on the fifteenth day of the seventh month. However, the traditional Jewish association with the New Year (Feast of Trumpets; see the comments on 81:3) seems more likely. In the Jewish weekly reading of the Psalms, Psalm 81 is read on Thursdays.[2]

Interpretive Insights

Title gittith. *Gittith* also appears in the titles of Psalms 8 and 84 and may have been a musical instrument. See the comments on the title for Psalm 8.

81:2 *timbrel*. This instrument was used by women, especially while dancing (see Exod. 15:20; Pss. 149:3; 150:4). See the comments on 149:3.

harp and lyre. See the sidebar "Musical Instruments in Psalm 33" in the unit on Psalm 33.

81:3 *ram's horn.* After the mention of the musical instruments in verse 2, the command to "sound the ram's horn [*shopar*]" follows. The Mishnah says that it was the practice to play other instruments along with the shofar,[3] which was itself not a tuned instrument, and its inclusion with other instruments in Psalms 98:5–6 and 150:3–5 would imply that. This instrument was made of a ram's horn (Josh. 6:4–13) and mainly used to give signals and alert people to impending danger (Judg. 3:27; 6:34; 1 Sam. 13:3; etc.).

New Moon. The lunar months began with the new moon. Numbers 29:1 calls the festival of the first day of the seventh month (now the Jewish Rosh Hashanah, or New Year) the "day of the blowing of the shofar" (NIV: "a day for you to sound the trumpets").

our festival. Because the Feast of Tabernacles (Sukkot) was so prominent in ancient Israel (sometimes called "the feast"; see, e.g., 1 Kings 8:2, 65; 2 Chron. 7:8; Neh. 8:14 ESV), some believe this was the festival Psalm 81 celebrated. It began on the fifteenth day of the seventh month when the moon was full (Lev. 23:41–43). However, the general interpretation in Judaism is that the festival celebrated in this psalm is the "festival of trumpets" (Num. 29:1; see NLT), alluded to in verse 3 by mention of the ram's horn (shofar). See "Historical and Cultural Background."

81:4 *a decree for Israel, an ordinance.* The reference is evidently to the blowing of the trumpet at the New Moon.

81:5 *When God went out against Egypt.* "God" is not in the Hebrew text, and the subject could be either "God" or "he" (Israel). If it is God, then it probably alludes to God's punishing Egypt, probably with the plagues; if it is Israel, it would likely allude to the exodus. Based on the reference in Exodus 11:4 of the Lord's going out through the land of Egypt at midnight, I would prefer the former.

statute for Joseph. See 78:5, where the word "statute" (*'edut*) is a synonym for "law" (*torah*). The spelling of "Joseph" (*y^{e}hosep*) is not the normal orthographic form (*yosep*), but the suggestion that the two additional letters (*he* and *waw*) are a hint of the name Yahweh is not convincing. The fact that Joseph appears in the Asaph psalms (77:15; 80:2) has been taken as a pointer toward a northern provenance, and the phrase "the God of Jacob" (81:4) may support that idea, although we may be merely speaking of a northern adaptation of these psalms.

I heard an unknown voice say. The fact that an oracle follows this statement leads some, including the NIV, to insert the noun "voice," with verses 6–16 composing the content of the message. Translated literally, the statement is, "I heard a language I did not know,"[4] implying the Egyptian language (as some translations render it; see, e.g., ASV, KJV). While it is translated by the NIV as an introduction to the prophetic oracle that follows, there is no consistency in the Asaph psalms. In fact, the only unambiguous introduction to the prophetic oracles in the Asaph psalms is 50:16a. Psalm 95, which also contains a prophetic oracle but is not an Asaph psalm, introduces the oracle of verses 8–11 in verse 7b. Tate summarizes the interpretations that have accrued to this statement.[5]

81:6 *the burden.* The word translated "burden" is borrowed from the story of the exodus (see Exod. 1:11; 2:11; 5:4–5; 6:6–7 ESV).

the basket. In Egypt the basket was used to carry clay, bricks, or other materials. See Jeremiah 24:1–2.

81:7 *distress . . . thundercloud . . . waters of Meribah.* These three terms cover Israel's bondage in Egypt, the revelation of the law on Sinai (Exod. 20:18), and the wilderness era (Exod. 17), respectively.

I tested you. Generally in the Pentateuch and in other psalms (Exod. 17:7; Deut. 6:16; Pss. 78:41; 95:8–9), Israel tests God. Yet on occasion God tests Israel (Exod. 15:25; 16:4; 20:20). See the comments on 78:19 and the sidebar "Does God Deceive?" in the unit on Psalm 78.

81:8 *Hear me.* God speaks in the third-person plural ("their") in verse 6 and then switches to the second-person singular ("your") in verse 7, before he engages a direct address to the people in verse 8 and finally shifts back to the third person in verses 11–16. Such a grammatical change of person is not unusual in the Psalms.

I will warn you. The verb (also 50:7 [NIV: "testify"]) carries the sense of a warning to correct a relationship that has gone bad (cf. 1 Kings 21:10, 13; Mal. 2:14; Job 29:11).[6]

if you would only listen to me, Israel! Verse 13b is virtually a duplicate (lit., "if *my people* would only listen to / obey me"). This is very similar to 95:7b and is an implicit command.

81:9 *foreign god.* This is the substance of the first commandment (Exod. 20:3; Deut. 5:7; cf. "other god"). See also 44:20.

any god other than me. Literally, "You shall not worship a strange god," the substance of the second commandment (Exod. 20:5a; Deut. 5:9a).

81:10 *I am the* LORD *your God.* This is equivalent to Exodus 20:2; Deuteronomy 5:6, both as Yahweh's self-identity and his activity in the exodus.

Open wide your mouth and I will fill it. The question is "fill it" with what? This type of expression normally refers to filling one's mouth with words (e.g., Jer. 1:9). Yet verse 16 seems to suggest the content: "the finest of wheat" and "honey from the rock." Because this menu is so far from verse 10, however, some commentators would move it to the end of verse 15. Yet, the intervention of verses 11–15 is not necessarily so disruptive, which the following arrangement indicates:

"Open wide your mouth and I will fill it" (81:10)	Yahweh's first command and promise
"But my people would not listen" (81:11)	Israel's response
"So I gave them over to their stubborn hearts" (81:12)	Yahweh's counterresponse
"If my people would only listen to me" (81:13)	Yahweh's second command (implicit)
"In no time would I [NIV: "how quickly I would"] subdue their enemies" (81:14)	Yahweh's counterresponse (if Israel would be obedient)

"Those who hate the Lord would cringe" (81:15)	Yahweh's counterresponse continued (if Israel would be obedient)
"Then [resultative conjunction *waw*] he would feed him [Israel] with the finest of wheat" (81:16, author's translation)	Yahweh's promise of verse 10b fulfilled: "With honey from the rock I would satisfy you" (81:16)

81:12 *their stubborn hearts.* Both Deuteronomy and Jeremiah characterize Israel's reputation as "stubbornness" (e.g., Deut. 29:18; Jer. 7:24). See also 78:8.

81:15 *would cringe.* The metaphor is "cause to bow down" (under force), thus pay reluctant homage.

81:16 *But you would be fed.* The Hebrew is literally, "And he [the Lord] will feed him [Israel]," verse 15 already having engaged the third person "Lord" as the antecedent ("the Lord would cause him [their enemies] to cringe," author's translation). See Deuteronomy 32:13–14.

Theological Insights

Thankfully, in the Bible, grace is not so much in the *listener* as in the *speaker*, and that is where it is found in Psalm 81. We know what grace is because God has spoken in the Scriptures. That is not to suggest that listeners do not exhibit grace also—indeed they do—but the biblical doctrine of grace is revealed and explicated in God's words and replicated in human patterns of obedience. The Hebrew verb "hear/listen" occurs five times in this psalm, and except for the use of the verb in verse 5, all occurrences (81:8 [2x], 11, 13) have the nuance of "obey." So what God requires of Israel and of all believers is to listen obediently. That is the thrust of Psalm 81. Twice the Lord says, "If you / my people would only listen to me" (81:8, 13), thus calling us to obedient listening. It is only in that response that divine grace can be understood and replicated. To help us understand its reality, Isaiah describes the absence of obedient listening: "For when I called, no one answered, when I spoke, no one listened" (Isa. 66:4). But he also describes the reality of grace in the most beautiful words: "Before they call I will answer; while they are still speaking I will hear" (Isa. 65:24). Grace is always a step ahead of our human actions.

Teaching the Text

Psalm 81 provides the preacher/teacher with an opportunity to talk about bad decisions, a topic that we all find appropriate at some time in our lives. To allow the text to shape and direct our message, we may note two things in particular.

First, the Lord twice issues what is both a command and an entreaty: "If you would only listen to me" (81:8; cf. 81:13). The inference of these words amounts to a window into God's grace—if they would listen, God has good things in mind for them. In fact, his commandments were designed for Israel's good. This is a model of divine grace in Scripture, both Old and New Testaments: God is willing to forgive and forget our sordid past and the distasteful—even rebellious!—decisions we have made. But we must listen and obey. One of the most difficult tasks we humans engage in, and one of the most important, is *listening*. We often listen within the framework of our own desires and mentally shape the speaker's words accordingly—we hear what we want to hear. Or we listen out of politeness so that we do not offend the speakers, but in reality we hardly hear a word they say. Israel did both kinds of listening, and so do we. But there are genuine listeners— mark them when you find them!—and they listen to every word while they look you in the eye, and they take your words with utmost seriousness. In fact, they listen so well that they anticipate what you are going to say (see "Theological Insights").

Second, when God turns us over to the consequences of our bad decisions ("So I gave them over to their stubborn hearts," 81:12), that is still not the end of the road but a cul-de-sac of grace where we can make a U-turn in his direction. God's discipline is corrective rather than punitive.[7] And he posts the sign again, "If my people would only listen to me" (81:13). It is a second-chance grace, and that is the nature of divine grace. We may remind ourselves that God's abundant grace sets the model for us. We too must forgive seventy times seven (Matt. 18:22), for just as God's cul-de-sac of grace has given us the opportunity to turn around, we provide the same opportunity to those who have offended us. Thielicke describes it as taking the offender's guilt upon oneself (see "Illustrating the Text" in the unit on Ps. 144), which is precisely the transaction of grace effected by Christ on the cross: "'He himself bore our sins' in his body on the cross, so that we might die to sins and live for righteousness; 'by his wounds you have been healed'" (1 Pet. 2:24, quoting Isa. 53:4–5). Chesterton looks at the Christian faith and says the chief aim of the order of love is "to give room for good things to run wild" (see "Illustrating the Text"). While quite a different metaphor, that is probably close to what the psalmist means when he says the Lord would feed his people "with honey from the rock" (81:16).

Illustrating the Text

"If my people would only listen . . ."

Quote: Gerald Kennedy. Ruminating about how people often do not understand the preacher's message, and what can be done to fix that problem, Gerald Kennedy, an American preacher to preachers, creates an imaginary meeting with Amos and his "congregation" after some of Amos's honest, some would say caustic, sermons. The idea is that his message was subtle, and the people's understanding, ironically, was rather subtle too. In Kennedy's imagination, the Israelites wondered if they had heard the prophet right, and indeed they had.

Layman: Doctor, shouldn't the clergy be more careful in using the phrase: Thus saith the Lord?

Amos: By all means. That's why I remain a layman. And I'm not a doctor.

Layman: I think that when you suggest God says, "I hate, I despise your feasts," you are doing a disservice to the Church.

Amos: Really? How wonderful. That is what I was hoping for.

Layman: When you say such things as "Hear this word, you cows of Bashan," you are using language unbefitting a gentleman.

Amos: Right you are, brother. But who said I was a gentleman?

Layman: There is nothing more restful than a solemn worship service. Don't you believe in the liturgical revival?

Amos: Of course I believe in it. By the way, what is it?

Layman: The Church is to help people. When you say, "Woe to you who desire the day of the Lord. . . . It is darkness, and not light," you upset the people and take away their comfort.

Amos: Hurrah! That was the whole idea.

Layman: I do not come to church to hear the preacher talk about such things as injustice, the rich robbing the poor, and God's anger. I want a more positive message.

Amos: The Jewish Science Church meets down on the next corner.

Layman: The trouble with your sermons is that they have no solutions.

Amos: Wait a minute, brother. Remember my closing words this morning? "But let justice roll down like waters, and righteousness like an everflowing stream." Quite a solution, it seems to me.

Kennedy concludes his imaginary postsermon interview: "Perhaps the problem is not so much an inability to understand as an unwillingness to listen."[8]

Room for good things to run wild

Quote: G. K. Chesterton. Our psalmist says, "If my people would only listen to me, . . . you would be fed with the finest of wheat; with honey from the rock I would satisfy you" (81:13–16). Chesterton comments on the order of love that characterizes the Christian faith and observes, using a different metaphor from the psalmist, that the aim of this order is to "give room for good things to run wild": "Stated baldly, charity certainly means one of two things—pardoning unpardonable acts, or loving unlovable people. . . . The criminal we must forgive unto seventy times seven. The crime we must not forgive at all. . . . We must be much more angry with theft than before, and yet much kinder to thieves than before. . . . And the more I considered Christianity, the more I found that while it has established a rule and order, the chief aim of that order was to give room for good things to run wild."[9]

"Rise Up, O God, Judge the Earth"

Big Idea

Justice is so important to God that it becomes a yardstick to measure our faithfulness.

Key Themes

- God is the true Judge of the world.
- Justice in any society can be measured by the standards and delivery system of justice at the lowest level of the social hierarchy.

Understanding the Text

Psalm 82 does not fit easily into any of the psalm categories. If it fits into any type at all, it is closer to a community lament about Israel's failure to care for the social indigents of their community, and in this sense it is related to the preaching of the preexilic prophets. More precisely, the psalm is an oracle of sarcasm against other gods, similar to Isaiah 46:1–4 and Psalms 115:2–8; 135:15–18.

The Text in Context

In response to the allegation that he claimed divinity, Jesus quotes Psalm 82:6 in John 10:34. His interpretation is that the "gods" of Psalm 82 are humans. And he uses the argument from the minor to the major to say that since Scripture "called them 'gods,'" to whom the word of God came—even though they were humans—even more so should the one whom the Father set apart as his very own and sent into the world be called the "son of God!" (John 10:34–36).

Outline/Structure

This outline reflects the interpretation of "gods" as judges and rulers. The poem is framed by the psalmist's words in verses 1 and 8.

1. The voice of the psalmist: God's intervention in the council of the earthly judges and rulers ("gods") (82:1)
2. The voice of God through the prophet (82:2–7)
   a. God's first indictment of the judges (82:2)
   b. God's demand of the judges (82:3–4)
   c. God's second indictment of the judges (82:5)
   d. God's punitive actions against the judges (82:6–7)
3. The voice of the psalmist: Prayer that God will dispense justice in his world (82:8)

Historical and Cultural Background

Those who view the "gods" as the heavenly pantheon point to Marduk, who convenes the assembly of the gods in the Creation Epic, and the god El, who presides over the Canaanite pantheon,[1] but see "Additional Insights: The Meaning of 'Gods' in Psalm 82," following this unit.

Interpretive Insights

82:1 *God presides.* The verb "presides" means to "rise and remain standing." Isaiah 3:13–14 presents the Lord as standing to judge his people. The Asaph psalms emphasize God's judgment (50:4, 6; 74:10–11; 75:2–10; 76:8–10; 82:1–8). That this is a subtheme in this collection is underscored by the final psalm in the collection, which is concerned with Israel's justification and the nations' recognition that "you, whose name is the LORD—that you alone are the Most High over all the earth" (83:18).

the great assembly. "The great assembly" (*'adat-'el*, lit., "assembly of God") designates the people of Israel in Numbers 31:16 and Joshua 22:16–17 (*'adat YHWH*; see ESV). The word "God" (*'el*) is rendered by the NIV as the adjective "great."

gods. Whether or not the psalmists, or some of them at least, really believe other gods exist is debatable (see "Additional Insights: The Meaning of 'Gods' in Psalm 82," following this unit), but in any event, this psalmist takes the claim of their devotees seriously. In fact, to argue against one's opponents, one must sometimes assume their presuppositions are true in order to disqualify them. Quite clearly the writer of Psalm 82 believes the "gods" he refers to are no better than humans (82:7).

82:2 *How long will you defend the unjust.* This change of subject from God to the judges is signaled by the grammatical change of number ("will you defend" is plural), not apparent in modern English.

show partiality to the wicked? The expression is literally, "to lift up the face of the wicked" (in favor).

82:3 *Defend the weak and the fatherless.* In verse 2 the psalmist warns the judges of their unjust practices, and here he provides the details by commanding them to do what they have not been doing (see Isa. 1:23). The "weak" are the "marginalized," who are "the mass of small farmers, artisans, and day laborers in contrast to the ruling class and the great landowners."[2]

uphold. This verb means to "judge fairly." The Torah commanded Israel not to show partiality to the poor nor favoritism to the great (Lev. 19:15). The matter at stake is not merely the poor, but justice. The NIV's addition of "the cause" ensures that sense of the verb.

82:4 *Rescue the weak and the needy.* Since the verb has changed from the two judicial verbs of verse 3 ("defend" and "uphold"), this directive is probably spoken to the leaders who have the power to "rescue."

82:5 *The "gods" know nothing.* This clause has no specified subject (lit., "they know nothing"), so the NIV has supplied "gods," particularly since verses 1 and 6 refer to them, and the terms of this verse satisfy a caricature of the gods—they know nothing and understand nothing and, metaphorically speaking, walk in darkness because of their moral deficiency. The purpose of the scare quotes ("gods") is to allow for a different interpretation, in our case, the judges. Because justice fails, "the [moral] foundations of the earth are shaken."

82:6 *I said.* This verb can also mean "I thought." Evidently these words belong to the psalmist, or even the community, and they are emphatic ("I *myself* thought"), since the Hebrew text adds "I."[3] This is the only time in the psalm that we hear the psalmist speak in the first person.

You are "gods." See "Additional Insights: The Meaning of 'Gods' in Psalm 82," following this unit. While this may be an earlier opinion of the psalmist concerning the judges and rulers, it is more likely mere sarcasm. In view of the parallel term "sons of the Most High," "gods" should be understood here as "deities." That is, the judges ("assembly of the god[s]"; see the comments on 82:1) are acting as if they are gods. This statement is quoted by Jesus in John 10:34 (see "The Text in Context," above).

sons of the Most High. In the Psalter, seven out of eighteen occurrences of 'elyon ("Most High") occur in the twelve Asaph psalms,[4] suggesting that it is a preferential name for God in the Asaph collection, perhaps because the Elohistic Psalter prefers the more generic names for God, like 'elohim.

82:7 *you will die like mere mortals.* This is sarcasm in the sense that these judges and rulers make decisions *as if* they were divine, but despite their self-deification, they will die like all other mortals (lit., "like 'adam," which could be an allusion to Gen. 2–3).

82:8 *Rise up, O God, judge the earth.* The imperative is the same form as contained in the prayer of Moses (Num. 10:35), except that, rather than

Yahweh, God's name is *'elohim*, as would be expected in the Asaph psalms. It is a call for God to judge the nations, similar to the prayer of Moses that exhorts God to take action against his enemies. See the sidebar "The Divine Names in Psalm 50" in the unit on Psalm 50.

all the nations are your inheritance. Literally, "for you *yourself* [emphatic] will possess all the nations." That, of course, is the reason God can and should judge the world.

Theological Insights

Justice is one of God's communicable attributes that he imparts to his human subjects; he also makes his human subjects his agents to announce and enforce his standards of justice. The prophets and the Psalms are particularly focused on the depressed social classes as special objects of Yahweh's concern. And beyond that, God measures, in part at least, how well we human beings carry out our responsibility as his representatives in terms of how well we attend to the needs of the poor and oppressed. There is simply no way we can reflect the true character of God if we neglect to care for those who fall at the bottom of the social ladder, for God cares for them.

Teaching the Text

Preparing a sermon/lesson on this psalm will require that we first make a decision about how we should understand "gods" in the psalm (82:1, 5, 6). Once we have done that—and that will make the next step easier—then we must identify the speakers in the psalm, which I have suggested to be the psalmist (82:1 and 8), and a voice that speaks on God's behalf (82:2–4), which may also be the psalmist or a priest. While we must express a hefty degree of exegetical humility as we deal with these issues, Psalm 82 reveals some solid points for which no apology is needed.

First, the words of this psalm expose the deformed structures of human society. And sadly they seem most often unmasked at the level of the most vulnerable members of the social order, laid out in this psalm in verses 3–4—and that is a universal truth. Justice in any society can be measured by the standards and delivery system of justice at the lowest level of the social hierarchy. We might make the point presented in "Theological Insights," that justice is one of God's communicable attributes, which means that his Word gives us principles that must govern our behavior and attitude toward other human beings. The Ten Commandments form the classical set of those principles.

Second, those who work in the system of justice and make its decisions, both those who sit in the judge's seat and those who sit in the jury's box, plus all citizens who affect the dispensation of justice in various ways, should recognize that our responsibility is one that God has assigned us. We are really his representatives, and that means we should take our responsibility with utmost seriousness. Of course, it also puts us in a structure of the hierarchy of justice that can be easily abused. So we remind ourselves that we are not "gods" who lord it over the less fortunate, lest we forget this to our own peril (cf. Mark 10:42–45). So we should approach our task with humility, praying for God's wisdom to represent him truthfully and faithfully, remembering that God is the final Judge, and we too will stand before him to receive his verdict, which hopefully will be, "Well done, good and faithful servant" (Matt. 25:23).

Illustrating the Text

Interpret the psalm from the bottom up.

News Story: We have taken the position that the "gods" are false deities, whom the psalmist demotes to wicked human judges, and he sarcastically challenges them to "rescue the weak and the needy" (82:4), if they think they can (see "Additional Insights: The Meaning of 'Gods' in Psalm 82," following this unit). That is interpreting the psalm from the top down. But we can start with the "gods" in their demoted status, who "will die like mere mortals" and "fall like every other ruler" (82:7), and speak about those human rulers or leaders who act as if they are gods—and they are myriad in our world—decreeing the fate of the helpless and hopeless, shutting their ears to their cries for mercy, and then trying to cover their tracks when they have carried out their "godlike" judgments. While the following story involved some difficult judgments—we must try to put ourselves in the place of those who had to make them—it illustrates the kind of decisions and consequences that attach themselves to our complex world.

The *Chicago Tribune* relates the story of a young illegal alien who suffered a fall while working in America, and being uninsured and now a quadriplegic, he was cared for in a hospital of one of the country's leading hospital systems—they deserve commendation. But after his medical expenses had accumulated to more than half a million dollars, the "system" (should we say "gods," whether they were the subjects of such hubris or the victims?) transferred him against his will to a substandard health care facility in his home country, and thankfully, a few days later to a better-equipped hospital. He died approximately one year later.[5]

Squatter's rights?

True Story: Elder Kim was a wealthy and prominent businessman in Pyongyang, in what is now North Korea, before the First World War. He was a devout servant of Christ. Addressing the General Assembly of his church, he related the story about a young dentist friend who had asked him to find a property for him to establish an office in Pyongyang. After much searching, Elder Kim wrote to say he had found a place, but the building was in bad condition and located in a bad neighborhood, and moreover, the price was exorbitant. Despite those conditions, however, the friend telegraphed him to buy the property, which he did. The owner asked for a couple of days to vacate the building, a request Elder Kim graciously granted. But when the grace time expired, the former owner, now a six-month illegal occupant, would not vacate, and Korean Christians did not believe they should take people to court, even nonbelievers.

Elder Kim proceeded to ask his audience what he should do. Recognizing his legal rights, the audience voted unanimously that he could proceed legally to evict the squatter. Then the elder drew the address to a conclusion:

> "Thank you, Fathers and Brethren, for the way you have considered my problem. Before I sit down I wish to draw one conclusion. Nineteen hundred years ago the Lord Jesus Christ came down from Heaven to purchase for Himself a dwelling place." Then striking his hand upon his breast, he continued. "He bought this old shack rundown, in a bad neighborhood. He bought me because He wanted to take possession and dwell in my heart. He gave Himself for me, and He gave me the Holy Spirit as a down payment on my inheritance, bringing me innumerable blessings with His redemption. But I cling to my tenement and leave Him outside. Now if you say that I have the right to seek the help of the authorities to evict the man who is occupying my friend's house, what shall you and I say of ourselves when we deny the Lord Jesus the full possession of that for which He gave His own life?"[6]

This world belongs to God, as do we individually, and the psalmist declares that "all the nations are your inheritance" (82:8).

The Meaning of "Gods" in Psalm 82

Psalm 82 is one of a kind among the Psalms. Its interpretation really depends on how we interpret the term "gods" in verses 1 and 6. Traditionally, they were viewed as human "judges," who are called "gods" (*'elohim*) in Exodus 21:6; 22:8–9, 28; and so on. These judicial figures are corrupt and incapable of rendering impartial judgment (82:3–4). The voice of verse 1, then, is that of the psalmist, who sets the scene by announcing God's intervention in the earthly assembly of judges. A prophetic oracle follows (82:2–4), challenging the earthly judges ("gods"), and indicting them for their favoritism (82:2), demanding that they engage in corrective action (82:3–4). In a caustic accusation, this voice, speaking on God's behalf, arraigns them for their judicial ignorance and ethical insensitivity (82:5). Presumably this same voice continues in verses 6–7, and in a sarcastic tone registers a change in standing for the judges, reducing their self-deified status ("sons of the Most High") to that of all other mortals (82:6–7). Either they were looked upon as gods because of their power—"I said/thought, 'You are gods'" (popular opinion); or they exercised their power as if they were gods. Finally, the psalmist exhorts the real God to rise up and judge his world, a job the judges have failed miserably to do (82:7). The Geneva Bible of 1559 represents this view that has dominated Psalms interpretation until the modern era: "The Prophet declaring God to be present among the Judges and Magistrates, reproveth their partiality, and exhorteth them to do justice. But seeing none amendment, he desireth God to undertake the matter and execute justice himself."

A second view, and one that would probably not have shocked the psalmist's audience, is that "the great assembly" represents a pantheon of gods (the mythical view), since Israel lived in a pantheistic world. In fact, there is ample evidence that preexilic Israel at the level of their popular religion (the religion of the common people) was quite henotheistic.[1] That is, they believed in one God but did not deny that other gods existed. Indeed, it was during the exile that the popular religion became unapologetically monotheistic, although monotheism was certainly known and widely accepted by Israel's patriarchs, prophets, and priests. For the psalmist, however, to use such mythical language was a bold move, since we assume that he himself did not endorse or advocate polytheism Yet the notion of Israel's God standing in the assembly of the gods and indicting those deities for their defense of the unjust and their partiality toward the wicked is daring indeed (82:2). Thus, if we follow this view, the true God stands in the "assembly of the god[s]" and "judges" them, reducing them to their real status ("The 'gods' know nothing," 82:5); and they, if they exist at all, are mere mortals like all human beings (82:6b–7). Then the directive of verses 3–4 would be made with tongue in cheek: "Defend the weak and the fatherless," if you think you can (sarcasm). The psalm would thus be a sarcastic attack on the popular view of Israel's henotheistic religion, the religion that paved the way to Israel's tragic and humiliating demise at the hands of their enemies ("the nations," 82:8b).

A third view, appealing like the preceding view to the mythology of Israel's world, is that the "gods" are equal to "angels" or servants of the High God, who gather in assembly to deliberate the means and methods of carrying out the demands of the high god in earthly affairs, similar to the scenes in Job 1 and 2. These are supernatural beings, but not divine, and thus are themselves subject to death (82:7).[2]

In any case, the psalm closes with Moses's prayer (Num. 10:35): "Rise up, O God" ("May your enemies be scattered")—because this is your world ("your inheritance"). This final verse is the psalmist's claim that Israel's God is the High God (82:6) because the world (the nations) belongs to him (82:8). Creation is the title claim to deity, and even if the "gods" of Israel's world claim to be creator deities too, Israel's God is the heir of the nations and thus the Most High God.

"O God, Do Not Remain Silent; Do Not Turn a Deaf Ear, Do Not Stand Aloof, O God"

Big Idea

God and his people are indivisibly connected, so that what hurts God's people also hurts God.

Key Themes

- The Lord alone is the Most High God.
- The people of God are entrusted as the keepers of God's reputation.
- Shame is a constraint on sinful behavior.

Understanding the Text

This last of the Asaph psalms (Pss. 50; 73–83), and the final psalm of the Elohistic Psalter (Pss. 42–83), is a national lament that describes some of the historical enemies of Israel. Israel's enemies are essentially God's enemies too, and the psalmist prays that they may be put to shame and, by this humiliation, come to acknowledge that Yahweh alone is "the Most High over all the earth" (83:18).

The Text in Context

Elsewhere in the Psalter there are psalms that open, as does Psalm 83, with a plea that God not keep silent (28:1; 109:1). Psalm 50, the first Asaph psalm, declares that "our God comes and will not be silent" (50:3a), forming an arc to Psalm 83 and its petition that God not be silent. Some have also called attention to the theme of rebellion against Israel and their God, a theme that reverberates with Psalm 2:1–2. In connection with the preceding psalm, both poems utilize God's name "Most High" (*'elyon*, 82:6; 83:18).[1] The unjust judges of Psalm 82 are not gods at all ("sons of the Most High"), but Yahweh is the Most High God. Indeed, perhaps the capstone of the comparison is that with the nations' confession of Israel's God, the concluding petition of 82:8 is fulfilled.[2]

The allusions to the period of the judges mean that the psalmist may have reworked an older poem that spoke of ancient unsuccessful attempts to exterminate the nation of Israel; that message resounds again in their own world and against the background of Book 3, where the Babylonians have done the same, also without success.

Outline/Structure

1. Appeal to God to listen (83:1)
2. Reason why God should listen (83:2–8)
   a. The plotting of the enemies against Israel (83:2–4)
   b. The enemy alliance against Israel (83:5–8)
3. The petition for God to act (83:9–18)
   a. A model from Israel's history (83:9–12)
   b. A model from nature (83:13–15)
   c. A model from human experience (83:16–18)[3]

Historical and Cultural Background

Although some propose that the background for this psalm is 2 Chronicles 20, where the Ammonites and Moabites fight against Judah, there is no historical evidence of the coalition of nations listed in 83:6–8 arrayed against Israel. Rather, this is a list of Israel's historical enemies, with Assyria as the capstone foe. The fact that the Assyrian Empire rather than Babylonia rounds out the symbolic number of ten nations might suggest that the psalm stems from the Neo-Assyrian period (mid-eighth to late seventh century) and has been adapted for Book 3.

Table 1. History Cited from the Period of the Judges in Psalm 83

Historical Event in Psalm 83	Location in Judges
Midian (83:9)	Judg. 7
Jabin, king of Canaan, and his general Sisera at River Kishon (83:9)	Judg. 4–5
Oreb and Zeeb, Midianite chieftains (83:11)	Judg. 7:25
Zebah and Zalmunna, Midianite kings whom Gideon killed (83:11)	Judg. 8:5–21

Interpretive Insights

83:1 *O God, do not remain silent . . . O God.* Twice addressed to God to reinforce his entreaty (*'elohim* and *'el* [shortened form]), the three verbs request that God not remain silent, that he not act as though he is deaf, and that he not sit still and do nothing.

83:2 *your enemies . . . your foes.* Literally, "your enemies" and "those who hate you," two expressions that occur in the prayer of Moses (Num. 10:35). Note that the address is to God, and the enemies are not just Israel's but God's enemies too.

83:3 *those you cherish.* Literally, "your hidden ones," a term of endearment, in the sense that Yahweh protects them from harm.[4] Ezekiel 7:22 applies the same word to the temple that is about to be desecrated (NIV: "the place I treasure").

83:4 *let us destroy them.* As the second half of the verse clarifies, the enemies' intent is to wipe the nation of Israel off the map and thus destroy their historical witness (see also Jer. 31:36). This calls to mind the book of Esther, where Haman plans to bring an end to God's people.

as a nation. The word the enemies employ is not the theological word "people" (*'am*), normally applied to the covenant people Israel, but the political term "nation" (*goy*), probably intended as a derogatory term. While the destruction of Jerusalem is not referred to in the psalm, this is such a destructive event, both politically and historically, that some believe it alludes to that event.

83:5 *they form an alliance against you.* An alliance against Israel is an alliance against God. In rabbinic literature it is said that when the Roman general Titus was victorious over Israel and destroyed the temple in AD 70, he believed he had destroyed Israel's God.[5]

83:6 *tents of Edom . . . of Moab.* When the Israelites entered the Transjordan, Yahweh forbade them to take the territory of the Edomites and Moabites, because Yahweh had assigned them their land (Deut. 2:1–9).

the Ishmaelites. These are the descendants of Ishmael (Gen. 25:12–18).

the Hagrites. These are tribes associated with the descendants of Hagar, Sarah's maidservant.

83:7 *Byblos.* The Greek name of a city north of modern Beirut (Heb. name is Gebal). See Ezekiel 27:9.

Ammon and Amalek. Ammon and Amalek are both mentioned in Judges 3:13 as Israel's enemies. Amalek is a roving tribe of Edomite ancestry (Gen. 36:12, 16).

Tyre. Tyre is twenty-five miles south of Sidon and about thirty-five miles north of Carmel and is a formidable seacoast town (see Ezek. 26:1–28:19).

83:8 *Even Assyria has joined them.* While some suggest that this is the small tribe descended from Dedan mentioned in Genesis 25:3, it is most likely the Assyrians of the eighth century, who brought an end to the northern kingdom of Israel in 722 BC. Thus we have a list of enemies who fought against Israel at different times, and Assyria "joined them" to finish the job.

Lot's descendants. "Lot's descendants" are Moab and Ammon, descended from the incestuous relationship of Lot and his two daughters (Gen. 19:31–38).

83:9–12 See table 1.

83:9 *Midian.* Israel also fights with the Midianites in Numbers 31, but the details here apply to the battle described in Judges 6–8.

83:10 *dung on the ground.* This implies that they were not buried.

83:12 *pasturelands of God.* This is likely the land of Canaan.

83:13 *tumbleweed.* This word (*galgal*, from the verb meaning "to roll") designates the ball-shaped thistle that the wind uproots and rolls along the ground.[6]

chaff. See Psalm 1:4.

83:14–16 *pursue them with your tempest.* Verse 14 begins a new petition against the enemies, using the metaphor of the storm that God creates.

Cover their faces with shame, LORD. The impulse of shame motivates them to seek God's name.

83:17 *may they perish in disgrace.* The Song of Deborah, celebrating a decisive victory over the Canaanites, ends with a similar petition (Judg. 5:31). Since the prayer asks that they "perish in disgrace," the petition that "they will seek your name" (83:16) does not seem to imply saving faith, but rather implies that they will surrender to Yahweh's will and acknowledge that he is sovereign. Verse 18 suggests the same.

83:18 *Let them know.* This is similar to Ezekiel's hope that the nations may see God's work and recognize that he is sovereign ("They will know that I am the LORD," Ezek. 6:13), but it is not always a saving knowledge.

Most High. This divine name *'elyon* occurs also in 82:6 (see the comments on 82:6), and the sense is God's sovereign rule over "all the nations" (82:8). The judges of 82:6 who were mistakenly, or sarcastically, called "sons of the Most High" will, it is hoped, come to know that Yahweh is "the Most High over all the earth." If the word "gods" in Psalm 82 is intended to refer to deities, then the force of this recognition is just as powerful, or more so.

Theological Insights

The table of nations (83:6–8), while including Israel's military enemies, also includes the Phoenician city of Tyre, not a military enemy as such, but a spiritual one, "because it was through the various economic and political alliances with the Phoenicians that Israel learned ever anew the ways of infidelity to God"[7] (Amos 1:9; Ezek. 26–28). Not being a seafaring nation itself, Israel was connected to the sea and the larger world and its materialistic possibilities through the Phoenician cities of Tyre and Sidon. As Reardon says, "There is more than one way for the people of God to be destroyed. And the danger of destruction is the very theme and meat of this psalm."[8] Paul acknowledges that it is in fact our spiritual enemies that are the greatest threat to us: "For our struggle is not against flesh and blood, but against the rulers, against the authorities, against the powers of this dark world and against the spiritual forces of evil in the heavenly realms" (Eph. 6:12).

Teaching the Text

Psalm 83 provides a unique opportunity in the Psalms to develop the theme of the indivisibility of God's people and God himself. First, we can begin with the enemies' own words in 83:4, pointing out that the destruction of God's people is intended to obliterate Israel's name and thus the knowledge of God that their name represents. Zenger observes: "Israel here makes itself an advocate in God's own cause, out of conviction that Yahweh and Israel belong together like the two sides of a coin."[9] Our standing as God's people is so closely tied to God's that Paul can declare, "If God is for us, who can be against us?" (Rom. 8:31). And to demonstrate this truth, the apostle adds that Christ's death on the cross is the indisputable evidence of his love: "He who did not spare his own Son, but gave him up for us all—how will he not also, along with him, graciously give us all things?" (Rom. 8:32); and then Paul ends this symphonic movement of redemption with the declaration that nothing in all creation can separate us from "the love of God that is in Christ Jesus our Lord" (Rom. 8:38–39).

A second point is that the psalm in essence cries out to the Lord to do something for his own "survival."[10] On the one hand, we do not have to worry about God's survival—it is not threatened! Yet, on the other hand, God himself is concerned about his reputation, and we should be as well. Ezekiel records Yahweh's actions for the sake of his own name (Ezek. 20:14): "But for the sake of my name I did what would keep it from being profaned in the eyes of the nations in whose sight I had brought them out" (of Egypt). Although our psalm does not make this point, we might emphasize here that we ourselves also have a responsibility for assuring God's reputation. That we are God's representatives should be enough to keep us on course.

Illustrating the Text

Shame provides a constraint on our behavior.

Quote: **John Calvin.** Our psalmist asks God to cover his enemies' faces with shame (83:16), evidently for a constructive purpose. While shame can have negative as well as positive effects on individuals and societies, a total demise of shame is alarming. The demise of shame may be an indicator of the loss of our moral underpinnings. Calvin regarded shame as "a bridle to repress our wicked and extravagant passions." He wrote: "There is hardly one in a hundred, who is as steadfast as he ought to be when God alone is witness. But shame renders us courageous and constrains us to be constant, and thus, the vigor that is almost extinct in private is aroused in public."[11] (See Ps. 25:2, 3; see also "Illustrating the Text" in the unit on Ps. 25.)

If God is for us, who can be against us?

Story: The story is told of a plane full of passengers, years ago, that was just taking off when the copilot noticed a rattle in the rear door of the plane. He went back to check it out, and as he did, the door started to swing open; and the copilot clung to the handle with all his might. When the pilot realized that the copilot was hanging on for dear life, he slowed the plane and brought it to a stop. And when he did, they had to pry the copilot's hands loose from the door handle. On one side of the theological spectrum we might say we have to hold on to God just like that (for example, see the gospel song "Hold to God's Unchanging Hand"). But on the other side of the theological spectrum we would say that is just the way God holds on to us. In fact, he holds us so tightly that, unlike those who freed the copilot's hands, nothing—nothing among the conditions and circumstances of life, nothing among the cosmic powers of the universe—can pry us loose from the love of God that is in Christ Jesus our Lord (Rom. 8:35–39).

In Paul's Letter to the Romans, he follows a path that exposes the human condition over against the grace of Christ. In the book of Romans Paul metaphorically climbs a mountain, as it were, until in Romans 8 he faces the last challenge that leads to its crest. And there looming before him are the dreaded crevices and rock faces that mountain climbers encounter, and in Paul's message they take the names of trouble, hardship, persecution, famine, nakedness, danger, and sword—we could insert our own list. In this psalm, Israel's enemies imagine that they can destroy Israel's name (83:4) and thus destroy God's name (this seems to be the assumption). Yet, the psalmist prays that God will meet their malicious actions with a shame that leads to grace (83:16) and concludes with the thought that the enemies have still not destroyed God's name, for he is "the Most High over all the earth" (83:18). The message is not far from Paul's declaration: "If God is for us, who can be against us?" (Rom. 8:31).

"How Lovely Is Your Dwelling Place, Lord Almighty!"

Big Idea

The journey of faith is shaped by its destination.

Key Themes

- The temple is God's claim on creation.
- The temple represents God's re-creating power over his world.

Understanding the Text

Psalm 84 is one of the most beautiful and most beloved psalms in the entire Psalter. Spurgeon calls it "the pearl of Psalms." He comments: "If the twenty-third be the most popular, the one-hundred-and-third the most joyful, the one-hundred-and-nineteenth the most deeply experimental, the fifty-first the most plaintive, this is one of the most sweet of the Psalms of Peace."[1] It is a Zion psalm, and also related to the Songs of Ascents (Pss. 120–34). The prayer for the king in 84:9b ("your anointed one") suggests that the monarchy is still standing, so 586 BC would be the latest possible date for its composition.

The Text in Context

We have seen the affection for the Lord's house in the first Korah collection (Pss. 42–43). Indeed it is present in every book of the Psalter except Book 4. In Book 1 we saw it in such texts as 27:4, and in Book 2 in Psalms 42–43 and 63:1–2, all in Davidic collections. Finally in Book 5 we meet this theme again in 122:1.[2]

Outline/Structure

Here is one of those places where the enigmatic word *selah*, at the end of verses 4 and 8 (see the NIV footnote), marks out the three strophes of the

Book 3 was edited during the exile, when the community was contemplating the theological implications of the end of David's dynasty (Ps. 89). Within that context, there is, in fact, a minihistory of the temple contained in Book 3, extending from the Mosaic tabernacle to the destruction of the temple. To begin Book 3, Psalm 73 gives a refreshing and unique perspective on the temple: that the theological conundrum of the prosperity of the wicked came to a resolution for the psalmist when he entered the temple (73:17). Psalm 78 laps back in time to the tabernacle and its capture by the Philistines (78:60–61) and speaks of God's building "his sanctuary [temple] like the heights" (78:69). In fact, the kingship of God over Israel and the world is symbolized by his enthronement "between the cherubim" (80:1); and, in anticipation of Psalm 84, Psalm 76:2 informs us that "his dwelling place" ("tabernacles") is in Zion. Before the story is done, we are informed of the terrible devastation of the temple in 586 BC (74:3–7; 79:1), and then Psalm 84 begins a new Korah collection (Pss. 84–85; 87–88) by celebrating the temple and drawing a line back to the initial psalms of the first Korah collection (Pss. 42–43), with which Psalm 84 has so much in common. But it may be of significance that Book 3 concludes, not with the loss of the temple, but with the ostensible failure of the Davidic covenant, which underwrites and legitimates the temple. While Book 4 references the temple, its historical setting in the postexilic period, when the temple had lost much of its luster (Hag. 2), redirects attention from the temple as the Lord's dwelling place to the Lord as Israel's dwelling place: "Lord, you have been our dwelling place throughout all generations" (Ps. 90:1).

psalm. Note the pattern of the word "blessed." The term *concludes* the first and third strophes and *begins* the middle one.

Strophe 1	Blessing on those who dwell in God's house (84:1–4)	"Blessed" concludes this strophe.
Strophe 2	Blessing on those who journey to the Lord's house (84:5–8)	"Blessed" begins this strophe.
Strophe 3	Blessing on those who trust in the Lord (84:9–12)	"Blessed" concludes this strophe.

Historical and Cultural Background

The idea of sacred space was a concept that ancient Israel shared with their neighboring religions, and in fact with most major religions. In Scripture, the garden of Eden is designated by the assertion, "Now the Lord God had planted a garden in the east, in Eden" (Gen. 2:8), and the sacredness of that space is the object of the Lord's concern when he banishes Adam from the garden (Gen. 3:23). The garden is a place where God and humankind meet: "Then the man and his wife heard the sound of the Lord God as he was walking in

Names of God in Psalm 84

This is the first psalm after the close of the so-called Elohistic Psalter (Pss. 42–83), which has a preference for the divine name *'elohim* ("God"). Whether or not the editor of Book 3 intended to make his psalm an appropriate follow-up on these psalms, it nevertheless contains seven occurrences each of the tetragrammaton (*Yahweh*) and the generic name (*'elohim*), as if to equalize the usage, if not the significance, of the divine names. Perhaps our psalmist is trying to be quite inclusive of the divine names so as to mark the end of the Elohistic Psalter. Note that the following table includes the proper names for God as well as other appellations (such as "Sun").

Lord of Hosts (NIV: "Lord Almighty")	*YHWH tseba'ot*	84:1, 3c, 12a
Lord God of Hosts (NIV: "Lord God Almighty")	*YHWH 'elohim tseba'ot*	84:8a
Lord	*YHWH*	84:2a, 11a, 11b
God	*'elohim*	84:3c, 7b, 8b, 9a, 10b, 11a
Living God	*'el-hay*	84:2b
My King	*malki*	84:3c
Sun	*shemesh*	84:11a
Shield	*magen*	84:11a

Note: The verse numbering for Ps. 84 differs in the MT; the numbers are all one number higher than the English versification.

the garden in the cool of the day" (Gen. 3:8). We observe a similar phenomenon in the story of Babel, but in that instance the Genesis narrative gives it a mixed review. While human beings intend to build a tower "that reaches to the heavens," their purpose seems to be not so much to establish a sacred space where God and humans can have their mutual encounters but to build a place where humans can celebrate their own accomplishments ("so that we may make a name for ourselves," Gen. 11:4). In time the temple becomes the sacred space where God meets his people and they approach him with their earthly troubles and sinful ways and petition God to answer their prayers (1 Kings 8:22–53). Basically Israel is no different from their neighbors in this respect, for the Babylonian literature informs us that when the city of Babylon was built, one of the god Marduk's first acts was founding a temple where the gods and humans could meet.[3] (See also N. T. Wright's view of the temple as God's claim on creation in "Illustrating the Text" in the unit on Ps. 121.)

Interpretive Insights

Title gittith. *Gittith* is also contained in the titles of Psalms 8 and 81 (see the comments on the title for Ps. 81).

Sons of Korah. This is the second collection of Korah psalms (Pss. 84–85; 87–88). Psalms 42–49 compose the first collection. See "The Text in Context" in the unit on Psalms 42–43.

84:1 *lovely.* This word signifies love and devotion, as in Deuteronomy 33:12 (NIV: "beloved").

your dwelling place. The noun is plural, perhaps because the temple contains many compartments,[4] or it is a plural that emphasizes its importance. Psalm 43:3 uses a duplicate term.

LORD *Almighty.* Literally, "LORD of Hosts," which the NIV consistently renders "LORD Almighty" (see the sidebar "Names of God in Psalm 84"). This title is associated with the ark, the symbol of God's presence.

84:2 *yearns.* Genesis 31:30 uses this verb to describe Jacob's longing to return to his father's household.

courts of the LORD. These were the court of the priests and the court of Israel, where the congregation stood during worship. Herod's temple also had a court of women.

my heart and my flesh. That is, "my whole being."

the living God. See Psalm 42:2.

84:3 *Even the sparrow.* The open courts were an easy place for birds to make a nest, and the psalmist longingly reflects on their easy access to the temple.

84:4 *Blessed are those who dwell in your house.* Three exclamations (84:4, 5, 12 [84:5, 6, 13 MT]), beginning with "blessed" (*'ashre*), build on the idea of the temple (see "Outline/Structure"). The first strophe (84:1–4) stresses the privilege of being in the Lord's house; the second, the privilege of journeying to the Lord's house (84:5–8); and the third, the privilege of trusting in the Lord of the house (84:9–12).

84:5 *Blessed are those whose strength is in you, whose hearts are set on pilgrimage.* The temple is the "strength" of those "who dwell in your house" (84:4). Kidner makes the attractive suggestion that the word "blessed" is used three ways: first, *longingly* (84:4), second, *resolutely* (84:5), and third, *contentedly* (84:12).[5] Literally, the verse reads: "Blessed is the man whose strength is in you, (the) ways in their heart." The personal pronoun "you" may mean either the Lord or the temple. Since the pronoun in verse 4 is clearly the Lord, it logically follows that in verse 5a it also means the Lord ("whose strength is in you" [the Lord]); but in verse 5b, since this half line focuses on the journey ("paths," "roads"; cf. NET) the pronoun "their" at the end of the line (lit., "in *their* heart[s]") seems to be pilgrims: "[its] ways are in their heart[s]" (NIV: "whose hearts are set on pilgrimage"). See "Teaching the Text."

84:6 *Valley of Baka.* This could be a valley that pilgrims pass through on their way to the temple. Some propose the Valley of Rephaim, where mulberry trees grow (*b^eka'im* = mulberry trees).[6] The point is that these pilgrims, transformed by their love for the temple, in turn transform this valley into a spring.

84:7 *from strength to strength.* This is possibly an allusion to the walls of the city with their ramparts (see 48:13).

appears before God in Zion. This is the goal of the pilgrims and of the psalmist, and it contains virtually the same language as Exodus 23:17 where all males are instructed to "appear before the Sovereign LORD" three times a year.

84:9 *Look on our shield . . . your anointed one.* Modern translators generally consider "shield" as a term for the king, viewing "our shield" and "your anointed one" as parallel terms. The Septuagint understands "shield" as a word for God ("our defender"), and in verse 11 God is clearly referred to as "shield."

84:10 *Better is one day in your courts.* "A thousand elsewhere" is parallel to "tents of the wicked," and the message is that "one day in your courts" is better than a thousand in the ill-gotten opulence of the tents of the wicked.

doorkeeper. The Korahites were keepers of the temple gates (1 Chron. 9:17–27; Neh. 11:19). In David's plans for the construction of the temple, and after the Levites would be no longer needed for packing and moving the tabernacle, David assigned them to other roles, like doorkeepers, guards of the temple treasures, and singers (1 Chron. 24–25). Doorkeeping may have been among the more menial tasks, thus implying the lowest rung of the Levitical ladder.

84:11 *a sun and shield.* The Lord gives light to those who yearn for the courts of the Lord, and he protects them on their way to the house of God.

84:12 *blessed.* This is the third time the term occurs (84:4, 5), finally pronouncing blessing on "the one who trusts in you" (see "Outline/Structure").

Theological Insights

In the Psalter the life of faith is sometimes expressed under the metaphor of a journey to the temple, where one meets God and experiences his presence. It is not surprising that, given the temple associations of the Korah tradition, both of the Korah collections begin with a journey to the temple, at least in the psalmists' memories. The factors that often impede are distance, as here in Psalm 84, and political circumstances that hinder the psalmist from making the journey (Ps. 43:3). In the first Korah psalms (Pss. 42–43) the psalmist was isolated from the temple in a distant place, a condition that was evidently caused by political circumstances. The realities of place and presence are paired. The *place* where the worshiper met God was the sanctuary, and the sanctuary was characterized by God's *presence*.

As true as that is in the Psalter—and as wonderful!—Israel in their common life came to misunderstand the relationship between the two, so much so that they thought the place and presence could not be violated. If God's presence was there in the temple, then no harm could come to them (Jer. 7:8–15). Both Jeremiah and Ezekiel published their word of condemnation against this theological error, and Ezekiel even demonstrated, against the popular belief, how the "Glory of the LORD" moved from the holy of holies to the threshold of the temple (Ezek. 9:3) and then from the threshold to the east gate of the city (Ezek. 10:19) and finally to the Mount of Olives (Ezek. 11:23), before it later returned and filled the temple (Ezek. 43:4). God could not be confined to his dwelling place, as some people thought, and his presence could not be manipulated.

So as we grasp the truth that the Lord chose a place on earth to dwell (Deut. 12), we must at the same time recognize that just as the temple is the Lord's dwelling place, so is also the earth he made (Ps. 24:1–2). That truth is as applicable today as it was in Israel's time—God's places of worship are a claim on this world he made. Further, while the temple is the Lord's dwelling place (Ps. 84:1), when the temple was destroyed, the Lord himself was acknowledged as Israel's dwelling place (Ps. 90:1), which brings us a step closer to the New Testament doctrine of abiding in Christ. It is this abiding that produces joy (John 15:4–11).

Teaching the Text

Since a pilgrimage to the temple stands behind the psalm (see "Illustrating the Text"), we can look at the destination (temple) as the shaper of the journey. That is, while our journey represents an important destination, the destination has a way of shaping the journey, giving it a certain quality and nobility, as well as a determined focus.

One way to prepare our sermon/lesson on Psalm 84 is to follow the three occurrences of the word "blessed," each nuanced by its own strophe.[7] The first is nuanced by the psalmist's description of the joyous privilege of being present in the temple: "Blessed are those who dwell in your house; they are ever praising you" (84:4). To be in God's presence is to praise him, and as the psalmist ruminates on the experience, he is envious of the sparrow that flits back and forth so freely in the temple courts, preparing her nest and raising her young. We should emphasize both *joy* and *contentment* that create the psalmist's longing, and speak also about our own joy and contentment in the place and experience of worship. Since our spiritual longing for the Lord's house is in fact a longing for God, our yearning is not therefore so much for the house as for the presence of God that dwells in and among God's people who worship there. We may also stress that longing to be in God's presence to worship and being there are companion experiences (cf. 27:4–5). The anticipated joy of the destination gives a silhouette of joy to the journey.

The second "blessed" is nuanced, like the first, by its strophe (84:5–8) and focuses on the journey to the temple. The ardor of the journey comes into view as the psalmist sees the pilgrims' resolute spirit turning the landscape into a refreshing spring (84:6). Here we may reinforce the point made above that it is the spirit of the pilgrim, a spirit shaped by faith, that determines to a great extent the character of the journey. As pilgrims we find that the strength for the journey grows out of our anticipated arrival (see the first point), and we can say with the psalmist that we "go from strength to strength" (84:7). That is, rather than focusing on tired feet and worn sandals and the dangers of the road (there are, of course, other prayers in which these can be quite appropriate), our psalmist silhouettes the journey by its high points, "strength to strength," which puts the face of strength on the journey rather than weariness. In comparison to our first point, that the destination determines the joy of the journey, here the determinative factor is the character of the pilgrims themselves, "whose hearts are set on pilgrimage" (84:5b).

The third "blessed" is again nuanced by its strophe (84:9–12), emphasizing the blessing of trusting in the Lord, which is the companion experience of dwelling in God's presence. It finds the pilgrims at their destination, the house of God; and, finally having arrived in God's presence, or having become aware of God's presence in and among his people, the pilgrims acknowledge even the most inconsequential task in God's house to be a far greater privilege than to "dwell in the tents of the wicked" (84:10). This would also be an appropriate place to note N. T. Wright's observation that the temple established "a bridgehead for God's own presence within a world that has very determinedly gone its own way" (see "Illustrating the Text" in the unit on Ps. 121). His comment that God is determined to "re-create the world from within"[8] goes handily with the observation we have made on verse 5, that the "paths" to the temple have been internalized by the pilgrims (see the comments on 84:5). That is, we absorb God's ways, and through his power working in us he re-creates the world from within. Chesterton puts the matter in different words, but with essentially the same meaning, when he says of the believer, "Can he hate it [the world] enough to change it, and yet love it enough to think it worth changing?"[9] That is the thrust of "Blessed is the one who trusts in you" (84:12). Ultimately the arrival (not just the anticipated arrival) justifies the character of joy and strength with which its anticipation has silhouetted our journey.

To conclude this lesson on a New Testament note, the preacher/teacher might draw out Christ's teaching that he is the true temple (John 2:19) and that abiding in Christ is the true goal of the Christian life (John 15:4, 10; cf. 1 John 2:23–25), and note that the abiding power of Christ re-creates the world from within.

Illustrating the Text

A description of pilgrimage

Church History: Spurgeon compares the pilgrimage to the temple represented by this psalm to the English pilgrimages to the shrine of Thomas of Canterbury and Our Lady of Walsingham, religious pilgrimages that were so popular as to affect the entire country. Among their effects, they caused the formation of roads, the erection and maintenance of hostelries, and "the creation of a special literature. . . . Families journeyed together, making bands which grew at each halting place; they camped in sunny glades, sang in unison along the roads, toiled together over the hill and through the slough, and, as they went along, stored up happy memories which would never be forgotten. One who was debarred the holy company of the pilgrims, and the devout worship of the congregation, would find in this Psalm fit expression for his mournful spirit."[10]

The Psalms influenced religious orders.

Church History: Rowland Prothero gives a brief summary of the influence of the Psalms on the monastic life.[11] Through the Psalms men and women heard God's call to service, regulated their lives, ordered the canonical hours and activities, and were directed where to build their monasteries; to the chanting of the words of the Psalms they dedicated their abbeys and churches, baked their eucharistic bread, cast their bells, and buried their dead. Thomas Aquinas (1225–74), for example, the great Catholic theologian and author of the *Summa theologica*, heard the call of God to monastic life through Psalm 84:10 ("I would rather be a doorkeeper in the house of my God than dwell in the tents of the wicked"), and he became a Dominican monk. As a rule, the monastic orders required their members to memorize the entire Psalter.

A doorkeeper in the house of my God

True Story: British New Testament scholar N. T. Wright tells the story of his father, who returned from World War II in 1945, having spent five years as a prisoner of war. After his death in 2011, from his diaries and papers the family began to piece together some of his major life decisions. For example, the senior Mr. Wright was offered a position in the Territorial Army, a civilian organization that supported the regular army and encouraged the new generation. At the same time he had been approached with the offer to become a churchwarden in a local church, assuming responsibilities for many things in the life of the church, such as ringing the church bells, handing out books to congregants, and taking up the collection. He chose the job as churchwarden, and upon reflection, the family reckoned that his sentiments lay with Psalm 84: "I would rather be a doorkeeper in the house of my God" (84:10).[12]

"Righteousness and Peace Kiss Each Other"

Big Idea
God constructs his kingdom out of the building blocks of his own character.

Key Themes
- God's kingdom is a reflection of God's character.
- God walks the path righteousness has prepared.

Understanding the Text

Psalm 85 is a community lament, consisting of a review of God's past work in Israel (85:1–3), the lament proper that arises from divine displeasure with the people (85:4–7), and a glorious celebration of God's personal attributes personified (85:9–13). Amazingly, this portrait arises out of the ashes of the exile and presents us with a picture of the eternal kingdom of God.

The Text in Context

Some scholars have insisted, and rightly so, that this psalm needs to be viewed against the background of Isaiah 40–55, which celebrates the return of Israel from Babylonian exile. With respect to companion psalms, Psalms 85 and 44 have a similar structure and related contents, but some dissimilarities (see table 1 below). Psalm 126 is also similar in structure and content.

The first three Korah psalms in this collection conclude on the theme of God's goodness. In the historical context of the Babylonian exile, Book 3 develops a strong theme of faith in God's goodness (84:11; 85:12; 86:17) before it sounds the troubling theme of the ostensible failure of the Davidic covenant in Psalm 89.

Table 1. Comparison of Korah Psalms 44 and 85

Psalm 44	Psalm 85
Recalls what God has done for Israel, particularly in the times of Joshua and the Judges (44:1–8)	Recalls generally what God has done for Israel, with a view to forgiving their sins (85:1–3)
Acknowledges that God has rejected them and humiliated them before their enemies, although they have done nothing wrong (44:9–16)	Assuming Israel's guilt (on analogy of 85:1–3, that is, God's forgiving them in the past), prays that God will revive the nation again and show them his unfailing love (85:4–7)
(No priestly or prophetic word as in 85:9–13)	Transition through a priestly or prophetic word (note "I") (85:8)
Based on their faithfulness to the covenant, no rationale for their shame is evident except it is "for your sake"; prays that God will awake and not reject them forever, although the prayer is yet unanswered (44:17–26)	Priestly or prophetic word describes the state of God's favor when glory again fills the land (after the reversal of exile) and God's kingdom has come (85:9–13)

Outline/Structure

The psalm divides into three strophes. Note the suggested voices for each strophe, particularly since Psalm 85 was probably used in the sanctuary. The congregation recites the oracle received by the priest or prophet.

1. Congregation: God's past mercies on Israel (85:1–3)
2. Congregation: Appeal to God to repeat past mercies (85:4–7)
3. Transition—Leader: Listening for a positive response (85:8)
4. Congregation: The oracle (85:9–13)

Historical and Cultural Background

Appealing generally to the historical context of Book 3 (divided kingdom and early exile), the psalmist remembers God's past mercies (85:1–3) and alludes quite probably to the terrible devastation of the Babylonian destruction and the divine anger that it implied (85:4–7; "Will you be angry with us forever?" 85:5a). In fact, it sounds as though they were rather deep into the exile (by 586 BC they had already experienced three: 605, 597, and 586 BC) and had become weary with Yahweh's "displeasure" toward them (85:4b).

Interpretive Insights

85:1 *showed favor.* It is the opposite of God's wrath, illustrated by Isaiah 60:10: "Though in anger I struck you, in favor I will show you compassion."
Jacob. Jacob is a poetic name for Israel.
85:2 *You forgave the iniquity . . . and covered all their sins.* These two images of forgiveness also occur in 32:1. The idea behind "forgive" (*ns'*, "to

lift up, bear") is to bear one's burden of sin, and the Lord not only did that, but he also "covered" (*ksh*) their sin as to make them invisible.

85:3 *from your fierce anger.* This phrase occurs in the Song of Moses (Exod. 32:10) and suggests that Israel has, as in Moses's time, endured God's disfavor for some reason not specified in the psalm. Divine anger is also a way of describing the exile (e.g., Zech. 1:12).

85:4 *Restore us again.* This verb (*shub*, 85:5 MT) occurs three times in this strophe (also 85:6a [85:7a MT], translated adverbially as "again"; 85:8c [85:9c], "*turn* to folly"). While each usage carries a different nuance, this is one of the ways the psalmists keep an idea before their readers. They sometimes introduce a verb, in this case with its primary meaning first ("restore, return"), and then reuse the verb with its varying nuances, even though they may turn in a different semantic direction, thus keeping the idea before the readers. It is one of the beauties of Hebrew poetry.

85:5 *Will you be angry with us forever?* In verses 4 and 5, to emphasize God's anger behind the undefined tragedy, our psalmist uses three expressions: "your displeasure," "be angry," and "prolong your anger."

85:6 *revive us again.* This verb is used in Ezekiel 37 (e.g., 37:3; NIV: "live") to describe the resuscitation of the people who went into exile.

85:7 *unfailing love . . . your salvation.* These are covenant terms, the first denoting Yahweh's enduring commitment to Israel, and the second, deliverance from their troubled circumstances.

85:8 *I will listen.* This verse transitions to the oracle that follows in verses 9–13. In view of the Korah connection with the temple, we might conjecture that these are the words of a priest or prophet or most likely the Korahite psalmist himself who led the worship. Habakkuk 2:1 describes a similar waiting for a word from God.

let them not turn to folly. In view of God's promises of peace, the plea is to let the people not return to the "folly" (or "stupidity") that brought about their devastating tragedy in the first place. See Proverbs 26.

85:9 *that his glory may dwell in our land.* If we are assuming an early exilic date for the psalm (see "Historical and Cultural Background"), Habakkuk's reassurance that God's glory will again fill the earth gives some illumination to this verse (Hab. 2:14, 20). If the psalm speaks of the time between the exile of 597 and the destruction of the temple in 586 BC, the hope was not quickly fulfilled but must wait for Zerubbabel's temple or some eschatological day, or perhaps both.

85:10 *Love and faithfulness meet together; righteousness and peace kiss each other.* These divine attributes personified provide a description of the eschatological day of restoration. While the primary condition described by the inimitable language of this verse is most likely the restoration from exile, it is much more the perfect picture of the eschatological day of salvation depicted in Scripture (see "Illustrating the Text"). "Love" (*hesed*) and "faithfulness/truth" (*'emet*), certainly not strangers to each other (Exod. 34:6; Ps. 89:14b), are God's emissaries of salvation in this meet-and-greet moment of God's eternal kingdom (see also 57:3 and "Teaching the Text" in the unit on Ps. 57). The parallel kiss of "righteousness" and "peace" forms the capstone of what God has prepared for those who love him. "Righteousness" has primarily associations with social justice (Deut. 16:18–20), and when righteousness prevails, "peace" results.[1] This is the opposite of the allegory of Isaiah 59:14–15, where others of God's attributes are barred from the city of Jerusalem (see also Isa. 1:21). Kidner is right when he says: "The climax is one of the most satisfying descriptions of concord—spiritual, moral and material—to be found anywhere in Scripture."[2]

85:11 *Faithfulness springs forth from the earth, and righteousness looks down from heaven.* This is another perspective on the truth of verse 10, the meeting of earth and heaven, when the human faith and heavenly grace meet in mutuality, in a sense, the objective of the entire plan of salvation in Scripture: "Your kingdom come, your will be done, on earth as it is in heaven" (Matt. 6:10; see "Illustrating the Text").

85:12 *what is good.* God's gift of "the good" underwrites his entire kingdom. It is God's good nature stamped on his kingdom. The Lord's "good(ness)" describes the blessing of his kingdom (84:11c; 86:17).

our land will yield its harvest. That God's gift of his goodness will cause the land to yield "its harvest" suggests that the problem that lay behind the lament of verses 1–3 might have been a severe drought (see Hag. 1:10).

85:13 *Righteousness . . . prepares the way for his steps.* Now we see the path that God walks, prepared by "righteousness," and he walks the same path that Isaiah describes for the "redeemed" who are on their joyful return to Zion (Isa. 35:8–10). In other words, God walks the path he has prepared for his people.

Theological Insights

In terms of God's eternal kingdom depicted in 85:9–13, we have a description of the personal imprint of God's character attributes that give his kingdom its moral and theological face and content. In the Lord's Prayer it is expressed in terms of God's will done "on earth as it is in heaven" (Matt. 6:10). In other instances, the imagery of that "moment" in the world's eschatological future, when heaven and earth blend in perfect harmony, is less personal and more metaphorical, like the "wedding supper of the Lamb" (Rev. 19:9) and "the Holy City, the new Jerusalem, coming down out of heaven from God" (Rev. 21:2). In Scripture the kingdom of God has multiple faces: the social (e.g.,

Isa. 11:6–9), legal (Isa. 11:1–4; Ps. 89:14), and theological (here in Ps. 85:10). All of these images are significant because each reveals an essential aspect of God's kingdom, but here in Psalm 85 we see God's personality profile, so to speak, much as Moses saw when the Lord caused his "goodness" to pass by Moses (Exod. 33:19).

Teaching the Text

One approach to building a sermon/lesson on this psalm is to concentrate on 85:9–13 and use the divine attributes of "love and faithfulness [or, "truth"]" and "righteousness and peace" (85:10) as the building blocks. This type of sermon is perhaps more difficult to develop because it relies heavily on word studies. But some preachers/teachers appreciate the kind of detail this study will require,[3] and if this study is done well, their congregations will too. In that case, start with a study of these terms in the Psalms and look at 57:3 and 89:14 (see also "Teaching the Text" in the unit on Ps. 57), as well as other occurrences of the terms, especially when they occur in these pairs. It is significant that the word pair of "love and faithfulness" appears in Moses's prayer of Exodus 34:6, and using Moses's language to describe the coming blessing is to draw on a major authority of the Hebrew Scriptures that the psalmists and their hearers highly respected. Moreover, the psalmist's prayer in 85:7, "Show us your unfailing love, Lord, and grant us your salvation," is reminiscent of Moses's prayer in Exodus 33:18, "Now show me your glory." The object of the verb is different, but the point is virtually the same—Moses wanted to "see" or experience God's presence in an intimate way. And the Lord answered with, "I will cause all my goodness to pass in front of you, and I will proclaim my name, the Lord, in your presence" (Exod. 33:19), which is comparable to 85:12, "The Lord will indeed give what is good, and our land will yield its harvest." This is an opportunity to speak about how God's spiritual blessings are translated into material gifts. Here God's "unfailing love" (*hesed*) and "good(ness)" are translated into the "harvest." The spiritual and material are not synonymous, but they are related. Yet, we should not force God's promise of the harvest into the mold of the prosperity gospel. The problem with this "gospel" is that it links divine grace to material blessing and fabricates a gospel of works, binding grace to our human efforts. And that means that grace is no longer unmerited. When "righteousness and peace kiss each other" (85:10b), it is God's righteousness that "looks down from heaven" (85:11b) and plants a kiss of peace on the troubled earth. And it is God's faithfulness, demonstrated by the harvest (85:12), that reveals the new age of peace. In the psalmist's perspective, God's "faithfulness" seems more earth-bound (85:11a) and righteousness more heaven-bound (85:11b). Now they have united in perfect harmony. In Paul's broader theological perspective, this is the peace of God that transcends all understanding (Phil. 4:7), when heaven and earth are no longer at cross-purposes (see "Illustrating the Text").

At this juncture we may take up a second and reflective point that this psalm makes in verse 13, "Righteousness goes before him and prepares the way for his steps." God's righteousness prepares the way for his appearance in the world, both in Israel's history and in the world's. It represents the spiritual infrastructure of God's kingdom, and God not only builds his kingdom out of the spiritual fabric of righteousness, but he also builds the road on which he appears as the reigning and coming monarch of that kingdom. It is the "processional way" that Isaiah calls the "way of holiness" (Isa. 35:8–10).

It is of the utmost importance that we understand that God's kingdom—and that means the way we conduct our kingdom lives—reflects God's character of righteousness, faithfulness (truth), and love. These three compose the formula for peace, and these qualities working together provide peace for our world and our personal peace.

Illustrating the Text

Heaven and earth are no longer at cross-purposes.

Bible: "Faithfulness springs forth from the earth, and righteousness looks down from heaven" (85:11). No longer at cross-purposes, here earth and heaven meet. It is that eschatological moment when God's will is done "on earth as it is in heaven" (Matt. 6:10), that moment in God's salvation timing when John sees the "Holy City, the new Jerusalem, coming down out of heaven from God, prepared as a bride beautifully dressed for her husband" (Rev. 21:2). Another way to think of the harmony and reconciliation alluded to here is to recall Paul's description of Christ's reconciling work: "For God was pleased to have all his fullness dwell in him, and through him to reconcile to himself all things, whether things on earth or things in heaven, by making peace through his blood, shed on the cross" (Col. 1:19–20).

Righteousness is "not to see what I see, not to feel what I feel."

Quote: Martin Luther. Luther probably understood Paul's concept of righteousness as well as, if not better than, anyone else. In his pamphlet *The Freedom of a Christian*, Luther says of forgiveness: "This is wonderful news to believe that salvation lies outside ourselves. I am justified and acceptable to God, although there are in me sin, unrighteousness, and horror of death. Yet I must look elsewhere and see no sin. This is wonderful, not to see what I see, not to feel what I feel. Before my eyes I see a gulden, or a sword, or a fire, and I must say, 'There is no gulden, no sword, no fire.' The forgiveness of sins is like this."[4] That is, it is *as if* we had no sin, *as if* we had not sinned at all. God has removed our sin from us "as far as the east is from the west" (Ps. 103:12).

While "righteousness" involves a consciousness of our sin and a repentant spirit, it further means a new relationship to God. That is, when our righteous Judge pronounces us "forgiven" or "righteous," it does not mean merely that we are now in harmony with the God whose law we violated. In fact, in the Old Testament Prophets "righteousness" is a relational term (e.g., Isa. 1:21–31) whose meaning is ultimately that we have a right relationship with God. When "righteousness and peace kiss each other" (Ps. 85:10b), our relationship to God has been restored to wholeness.

"Give Me an Undivided Heart, That I May Fear Your Name"

Big Idea

We cannot truly acknowledge God as Master (Lord) until we come to see ourselves as servants.

Key Themes

- The LORD alone is God and demands united worship and devotion.
- Only a united heart can be in right relationship with God.

Understanding the Text

Psalm 86 can be classified as an individual lament, particularly based on parts 1 (86:1–7) and 3 (86:14–17). The crisis behind the lament is not evident (86:7a, 14), but presenting it in subjective terms is quite typical of the psalmic laments.

While the speaker is an individual speaking in David's voice, his personality profile has also changed from that of the king to the suffering servant who trusts in the God of Moses revealed in the Torah (86:15; cf. Exod. 34:6). Now in this new crisis era, David (rhetorically; see endnote 9 in the unit on Psalm 73) both identifies with his suffering people and affirms the covenant faith of ancient Israel.[1] In fact, in Books 3, 4, and 5 a virtual quotation of the formula of grace (Exod. 34:6) appears in three strategically placed David psalms (Pss. 86:15; 103:8; and 145:8), having the effect of David's endorsement of the Mosaic covenant. To hear Moses's words in David's voice is indeed powerful and effective to this community. While it is, in one respect, a reminder of the covenant issued in the voice of their greatest and most esteemed king, it also has a messianic effect—David has appeared again, David *redivivus*.

The Text in Context

Commentators generally emphasize the piecemeal nature of this psalm, but that in no way detracts from its beauty. As many as forty borrowed phrases or terms have been identified, although many of them are merely allusions (in table 1 I give the most easily identifiable ones). Two observations are in order. First, this psalm is an example of how the poets were steeped in the language of the Psalms, as well as other portions of Scripture. Most likely this poet is merely drawing on his memory as he brings forward the verses and phrases he would like to put into David's service as he composes this new "prayer of David." Second, the poet (who is perhaps the editor of Book 3) adds to the profile of David *the king* the profile of the servant who is *poor and needy* (see table 3, "The 'Poor and Needy' toward the End of Book 2," in the unit on Ps. 70). He picks that portrait up from the end of Book 1 (40:17) and reemploys it at the end of Book 2 (70:5a; 72:12, 13). Israel's ideal king then identifies with his people in their defeat and captivity (see "Additional Insights: David, the Prototype of the 'Poor and Needy,'" following this unit). There are no placebos in human suffering—everyone takes the bitter pill at some point—and the very idea that even the king suffers, whether *for* or *with* his people, is a comfort of great proportions.

Table 1. Intertextuality of Psalm 86

Psalm 86	Other Texts
"I am poor and needy" (86:1b)	"I am poor and needy" (40:17a)
"Guard my life . . . who trusts in you" (86:2)	"Guard my life . . . for I trust in you [NIV: "for I take refuge in you"]" (25:20)
"Teach me your way, Lᴏʀᴅ" (86:11a)	"Teach me your way, Lᴏʀᴅ" (27:11a)
"Arrogant foes are attacking me, O God; ruthless people are trying to kill me— they have no regard for you" (86:14)	"Arrogant foes are attacking me; ruthless people are trying to kill me—people without regard for God" (54:3)
"But you, Lord, are a compassion- ate and gracious God, slow to anger, abounding in love and faithfulness" (86:15)	"The Lᴏʀᴅ is compassionate and gracious, slow to anger, abounding in love" (103:8) "The Lᴏʀᴅ, the Lᴏʀᴅ, the compassionate and gra- cious God, slow to anger, abounding in love and faithfulness" (Exod. 34:6)
"Turn to me and have mercy on me" (86:16a)	"Turn to me and have mercy on me [NIV: "be gra- cious to me"]" (25:16a)

Note: I have made some adjustments in the NIV translation to make the comparisons more easily recognizable.

Outline/Structure

Some scholars have identified a chiastic structure and located the central theme of the psalm either in verse 9 (international homage to Yahweh)[2] or verse 10 ("You are great" and "You alone are God").[3]

1. The lament: A cry for the Lord's help (86:1–7)

   Note these features:

   "Answer" forms an *inclusio* (86:1a and 7b)

   Eight imperatives undergird the lament, which is largely a petition

2. Praise of the Sovereign Lord, who alone is God (86:8–13)

   Note these features:

   The "gods" are invoked and dismissed as incomparable to Yahweh (86:8)

   The nations make pilgrimage to worship God (86:9)

   God's "marvelous deeds" are invoked as evidence of his uniqueness (86:10)

   Suppliant prays that God will teach his way and give him an undivided heart (86:11)

   Vow to praise God with this new heart ("all my heart") for deliverance (86:12–13)

3. Lament and petition (86:14–17)

   Note these features:

   The suppliant's foes appear for the first time (86:14)

   The poet's faith is anchored in the Mosaic covenant (86:15)

   Prayer for a sign of God's goodness (86:17)

Historical and Cultural Background

While the psalms contained in Book 3 were not all written during the Babylonian exile but were adapted for the editorial purpose of Book 3, some were likely composed to deal with the uncertainties and demands of the time, such as Psalm 89. It is likely that Psalm 86 belongs in this category as well, to satisfy the absence of a Davidic psalm in Book 3, and to provide a profile of David as the suffering servant, "poor and needy" (86:1), who identifies with his suffering people.

Interpretive Insights

Title *A prayer of David.* This exact phrase also occurs in the title of Psalm 17 and links the psalm to the "prayers of David" mentioned in 72:20.

86:1 *Hear . . . answer.* Although the verb "hear" in verse 6 is a different verb, it is nevertheless a synonym, and this pair of verbs constitutes an *inclusio* for this strophe (86:1–7).

86:2 *I am faithful.* The word translated "faithful" (*hasid*) is related to *hesed* ("covenant love") and carries the sense of "godly."

your servant. The psalmist's humility is incorporated in this phrase (also 86:4a). He uses *'adonay* ("my Master," "Lord") seven times in the psalm, perhaps to emphasize his servanthood.

86:5 *abounding in love.* See Exodus 34:6b. See also verse 15, which has the longer phrase. This phrase and verse 15 identify the psalmist as a covenant believer.

86:8 *Among the gods.* Since our psalmist declares in verse 10b that "you alone are God," it seems unlikely that he is acknowledging that other gods exist. Kidner proposes that they are angels.[4] Another possibility is that he is merely accommodating the popular belief.

86:9 *All the nations you have made will come and worship.* Schaefer suggests that this is the middle (main) point of the psalm, international worship—thus, Yahweh's sovereignty.[5] See the sidebar "Yahweh and Other Gods in the Psalter" in the unit on Psalm 7.

86:10 *For you are great.* This is a standard exclamation of praise in biblical worship (e.g., Deut. 10:17; Jer. 10:6; Pss. 48:2; 95:3; 147:5).

you alone are God. This psalm likely originated in the late exilic or early postexilic period, when Israel had come to embrace a pure monotheism (see the comments on 86:8).

86:11 *an undivided heart.* The KJV's memorable "unite my heart to fear thy name" (see also ESV) puts the idea in a positive setting. The verb translated "unite" signifies "to designate exclusively, concentrate."

86:13 *from the realm of the dead.* The Hebrew word behind this phrase is *she'ol*. It could also be metaphorical, describing a life-threatening experience. See the sidebar "Sheol" in the unit on Psalm 6.

86:15 *a compassionate and gracious God.* This is a virtual quotation of Exodus 34:6b.

86:16 *show your strength in behalf of your servant; save me, because I serve you just as my mother did.* Literally, "Give your strength to your servant, and save the son of your handmaid." The sense is that David prays for God to turn his favor to his servant and save him, the son of another faithful servant (handmaid). The NIV translation puts the emphasis on "serve" and constructs a comparison with his mother. The Hebrew text recognizes David's mother's piety, but it does not compare David's piety to hers; thus the NIV gives an unintended reading.

86:17 *your goodness.* In light of the quotation from Exodus 34:6b in verse 15, this is likely an allusion to Exodus 33:19, where the Lord causes all his "goodness" to pass before Moses. This term is a connecting link among Psalms 84 (v. 11); 85 (v. 12); and 86 (vv. 5, 17).

Theological Insights

Scripture has a good deal to say about a heart or mind that is not united. Psalm 12:2 refers to those who say one thing but mean another and describes them as having a "double heart" (RSV). James speaks of doubt as the obstacle to a united heart and declares that "such a person is double-minded and unstable in all they do" (James 1:8). Augustine expresses a similar state of his own heart in his prayer "O Lord, grant me purity, but not yet."[6]

Paul speaks of the tug-of-war going on inside him and asserts that sin has taken advantage, for example, of the commandment against coveting and has made him even more covetous (Rom. 7:7–12). He seems to be addressing the same kind of divided heart that our psalmist recognizes to be devastating to his life of faith (86:11). With our psalm it is probably too early in the history of Old Testament thought to suggest that this concept represents the "good inclination" and the "evil inclination" that later would come to describe this condition in Jewish thought (see Rom. 7:21), but it would not be too early to recognize the initial stage of such an understanding of the human struggle.

Teaching the Text

Picking up on the "Key Themes," we may focus on the "undivided heart" (86:11). The preacher/teacher may want to use another translation besides the NIV to put it in positive terms, that is, to speak about a "united" rather than "undivided" heart: "Unite my heart to fear your name" (ESV). The meaning is obviously the same, but the Hebrew verb is "unite," and that immediately puts the sermon/lesson on a positive footing. While our psalmist prays for a united heart, as if he has not yet achieved this goal, the elements of his faith spelled out in the psalm certainly provide the spiritual ingredients for such a disposition of heart.

First is *trust*, and twice he affirms his trust in the Lord (86:2b, 4b). Second is his sense of *servanthood*. In fact, the two occurrences of "trust" are connected with his acknowledgment that he is a servant, so the master/servant model is very strong in the psalm. As indicated above (see the comments on v. 2) the sevenfold use of the substitute noun *'adonay* ("my Master") for Yahweh (the tetragrammaton) suggests that he wants to stress the idea that God is his Master. One of our problems with celebrating Christ's lordship is acknowledging that we are servants. Lordship and servanthood are a pair of ideas that cannot be severed from each other. Third, David's confidence is in *God alone* (86:10) and in God's gracious character (86:15). Even though verse 8 seems to accommodate the "gods," to confess "you alone are God" in verse 10 runs contradictory to that idea. This trio of ideas—trust, servanthood, and God alone—gives us a picture of the united heart.

Illustrating the Text

Mr. Facing-both-ways

Christian Literature: *Pilgrim's Progress*, **by John Bunyan.** In *Pilgrim's Progress*, the main character, Christian, after leaving the town of Vanity Fair, meets Crafty (called "By-ends" in Bunyan's original work), from the town of Fairspeech. When Christian questions Crafty about his wealthy kinfolk in his hometown, he lists them by name, all of whom are the opposite of the psalmist's "undivided heart" (86:11b). Here is Crafty's way of answering Christian's question "Who are your kindred there?": "Almost the whole town; and in particular, my Lord Turn-about, my Lord Time-server, my Lord Fair-speech, (from whose ancestors that town first took its name), also Mr. Smooth-man, Mr. Facing-both-ways, Mr. Any-thing; and the parson of our parish, Mr. Two-tongues, was my mother's own brother." Crafty's description of the nobility of his hometown continues: "And to tell you the truth, I am become a gentleman of good quality, yet my great-grandfather was but a waterman, looking one way and rowing another."[7] Obviously we earthlings have difficulty dealing with a person of split loyalty, and so does God.

Humility is knowing and acknowledging who we are.

History: Our psalmist acknowledges that he is the Lord's servant (86:2), and he uses the servant's name for God, *'adonay*, which further reinforces his humility. In January 1864, Ulysses S. Grant, in response to those who were urging him to run for president, said: "I aspire only to one political office. When this war is over, I mean to run for Mayor of Galena, and if elected, I intend to have the sidewalk fixed up between my house and the depot."[8] Grant had proved to be a great general and knew who he was.

David, the Prototype
of the "Poor and Needy"

In several ways, Psalms 70–72 correspond to the conclusion of the First Davidic Psalter (Pss. 3–41). First, Psalm 70 is, with minor variations, a duplicate of Psalm 40:13–17, forming a corresponding psalm of David that portrays him as the prototype of the *poor and needy*, not just their defender (see 34:6). Second, Psalms 40 and 41 portray David as the prototype of the *righteous person*, and then in Psalms 70–72 he has taken his paradigmatic place in the company of the poor and needy—a condescension, to be sure, but only in the sense that he has joined this company as the righteous individual who is now identified as the poor and needy. The editor of Book 2 again affirms that portrait by including the words of 40:13–17 in the conclusion to the Second Davidic Psalter (70:5a). Indeed, Psalm 41 begins with the pronouncement "Blessed are those who have regard for the weak" (41:1), and the portrait of the ideal king drawn in Psalm 72 includes this character trait in the royal profile: "He [the king] will take pity on the weak and the needy" (72:13).

The editorial ordering of the psalms to present this Davidic portrait may be explained as a product of the time in which the Second Davidic Psalter was shaped. We only have to recall that the obvious interest in the monarchy marks the end of Book 3, as it does the beginning and end of Book 1 (Pss. 2 and 41),[1] and the conclusion of Book 3, as Psalm 89 formulates its probing inquiry into the failure of the Davidic dynasty. So the "final" editing of Books 1–3 reflects the time of the Babylonian exile or early postexilic period (69:33; note also the prayer to "rebuild the cities of Judah," 69:35). But we should be aware that the time of editing and the historical period reflected in each of the five books are not necessarily the same. While Book 3, for example, reflects the historical period of the divided monarchy and its tragic end, it was edited later. Only with that long-range perspective could the editor(s) provide this profile of David as the "poor and needy." In that political context, David's identity with this humiliated and captive people as the "poor and needy" (70:5) would provide a dimension of great comfort—their ideal king identified with them and entered their condition of humiliation. When the editor or writer of Psalm 86 adds this "prayer of David" to the otherwise David-less collection of Book 3, it is, as Hossfeld and Zenger observe, a "recapitulation" of the two Davidic psalters (Pss. 3–41 and 51–72).[2]

"The LORD Will Write in the Register of the Peoples: 'This One Was Born in Zion'"

Big Idea
We are citizens of the city of God (God's kingdom) by grace.

Key Themes
- The historical realities of the Old Testament become the spiritual realities of the New.
- God bestows citizenship in his kingdom by grace.

Understanding the Text

This psalm belongs to the Zion songs (Pss. 46; 47; 48; 76; 84; 87; 122) and celebrates Jerusalem as the "center of the community of God on earth,"[1] indeed the mother of the world's salvation. As a Zion song it goes beyond the historical significance of Jerusalem and reflects the surpassing worth of the city of God as a metaphor for God's kingdom.

The Text in Context

The third psalm in this second series of Korah psalms, Psalm 87 connects immediately to the preceding psalm: "All the nations you have made will come and worship before you, Lord" (86:9a). There is a reverse parallel between the Zion songs in the first Korah collection and Psalm 87. That is, Psalm 46 celebrates the "city of God" where "the Most High dwells" (46:4), and by his power the nations are subdued. In this second Korah collection, Psalm 87 reverses this message and celebrates the salvation of the nations rather than their subjection.[2] (See table 1.) Psalms 47 and 87 have different expressions for the salvation of the nations. In Psalm 47:9 "the nobles of the nations assemble as the people of the God of Abraham," whereas in Psalm 87 the nations are recorded in God's registry as having been born in Jerusalem (see "The Text in Context" in the unit on Ps. 48).

Table 1. Comparison of Korah Psalms 46–48 and 87

Psalm 46	Psalm 47	Psalm 48	Psalm 87
		"His holy mountain" (48:1)	"The holy mountain" (87:1)
"Dwellings of the Most High" (NIV: "the holy place where the Most High dwells") (46:4)			"Dwellings of Jacob" (87:2)
"City of God" (46:4)		"City of the Lord Almighty [or "of Hosts"] . . . city of our God" (48:8)	"City of God" (87:3)
"Know that I am God" (46:10)			"Those who know [NIV: "acknowledge"] me" (87:4)
"Will establish her forever" (NIV: "makes her secure forever") (46:8)			"Will establish her" (87:5)
"The Most High" (46:4)	"The Most High" (NIV: "the Lord Most High") (47:2)		"The Most High" (87:5)
"Whose streams make glad" (46:4)			"All my fountains are in you" (87:7)

Note: I have made some adjustments to the NIV to make the comparisons more easily recognizable.

Outline/Structure

This psalm is one of those poems where the word *selah* (after 87:3 and 6; see NIV footnotes) seems to mark it off into two strophes with a celebratory conclusion.

1. A Zion song (87:1–3)
2. "Glorious things" spoken about the city of God (87:4–6)
   Celebratory conclusion: Response of the nations to their new city of birth (87:7)

Historical and Cultural Background

In Babylonia during the first millennium BC, people were known by their city of origin ("a son of city X"), which meant that they enjoyed the rights and privileges of citizenship in that city and were protected by its deities.[3]

That concept, which was much wider than Babylonia, seems to stand behind the thesis of this psalm.

Whether this psalm is preexilic, exilic, or postexilic—any one is possible—it represents the spirit, if not the historical fact, that in the Old Testament there was conversion from other religions to Israel's religion, a fact attested by the story of the healing of the Syrian general Naaman (2 Kings 5:17).

Interpretive Insights

Title *Of the Sons of Korah. A psalm. A song.* See the same title in Psalm 48, except the phrases are reversed.

87:1 *He has founded his city.* See Isaiah 14:32; 28:16; Psalms 78:69; 102:16.

on the holy mountain. These are the mountains that surround Jerusalem (Ps. 125:2).

87:2 *gates of Zion.* This is metonymy for the city of Jerusalem. The social, economic, and legal activities took place in the gates, so they were a microcosm of the city. Generally the two places in an ancient Israelite city where there was enough space for a crowd to gather were the gates and the temple court.

the other dwellings of Jacob. It is possible that this alludes to other places where the tabernacle had stood (Shiloh and Gibeon). Or it could also mean the nonauthorized sanctuaries that competed with Jerusalem (such as that uncovered at Arad).

87:3 *Glorious things are said of you.* These are the stories of God's glorious acts, the "marvelous deeds" of 86:10a. More specifically it may refer to the oracle that follows in verses 4–6 regarding the nations' citizenship in Zion. The pronouns "I" and "you" alert us to direct speech and prompt us to ask who is the speaker and who is the object. Four times we have direct speech (87:4, 5, 6, and 7). The speaker in the third instance is clear, the Lord. But in the first instance it could be either the psalmist or a personification of Zion. I would prefer the personification since the whole psalm is about Zion and the psalmist seems to be the reporter. The second is unnamed ("it will be said," 87:5), but perhaps is the congregation or the general populace, or even the nations themselves. The fourth instance is the content of the song.

87:4 *I will record.* This is the voice of Zion filling in the meaning of "glorious things" of verse 3.

Rahab. A poetic name for Egypt (Isa. 30:7; Ps. 89:10). The list of countries is not exclusive but represents major nations that figure into Israel's history and surround Israel geographically. Egypt, located to Israel's southwest, belonged to the great story of redemption (the exodus), and Babylon, located to the southeast, belonged to the second great story of redemption (the return from exile). Philistia, located on the coastal plain to the west, was a thorn in Israel's side for centuries, and Tyre (Phoenicia), located on the coast to the north, was generally on friendly terms with Israel but sociologically and economically led Israel toward a materialistic worldview. Cush, or Ethiopia, lay far south of Israel, completing the four directions of Israel's world, with Zion as the center.

This one was born in Zion. "Zion" is not in the Hebrew text but is inferred (the Hebrew is "This one was born there"). It is as if the poet is pointing his finger at the individual nations, saying, "This one [Egypt, Babylon, etc.] was born in Zion."[4]

87:5 *Indeed, of Zion it will be said, "This one and that one were born in her."* Now the psalmist declares that the real country of their birth, at least in a spiritual sense, was Zion.

the Most High. This is an appropriate name to use for God here since it has associations with Abraham and Melchizedek where Abraham identifies the Lord as "God *Most High*, Creator of heaven and earth" (Gen. 14:22). We may note that the same identification occurs here, with "Most High" in verse 5 and "Lord" in verse 6 as clarifying terms. See the comments on 82:6.

87:6 *This one was born in Zion.* As in verse 5, "Zion" is not in the Hebrew text, but "there" certainly means Zion.

87:7 *As they make music they will sing.* The participle translated as "they make music" also means "they dance"; thus, the sense of the phrase would be "and they sing as they dance."[5] It is the image of a feast of celebration over their newly declared citizenship in Zion.

All my fountains are in you. This may be the song they sing, celebrating the spiritual fountains of faith (Isa. 12:3; Ps. 46:4). There seems to be, at least textually, no reason why the expression "my fountains" (lit., "springs") should be here, especially after the psalm has spoken about countries and cities. The Septuagint translator, perhaps also stumped by this awkward statement, says "the *habitation* of all is in you," and "habitation," in the context, is a much better fit. However, the Hebrew "my springs" likely has a more subtle explanation. When people in the biblical world thought about places, the most important associate idea was whether those places had water. And the psalmist's readers would recognize that Jerusalem had only one spring (Gihon), so this would be contrary to fact; and rather than this being a descriptive sentence about the physical resources of the city, they would recognize this as a "spiritual" descriptor, just as these geographical entities mentioned in the psalm had their "spiritual" birthplace in Jerusalem. Verse 7 thus turns out to be a hermeneutical key to the psalm—the entire psalm should be interpreted in a spiritual sense.

Theological Insights

I recall being in a worship service once when guest singers rendered so beautifully John Newton's hymn "Glorious Things of Thee Are Spoken, Zion City of Our God," and for some reason, certain individuals in the congregation were perplexed by the choice of hymn, thinking it had political implications. Perhaps it was their lack of understanding that the Christian church has identified itself with ancient Zion, the city of God, which is not a Crusader idea. Rather, the historical realities of the Old Testament often become the spiritual realities of the New, and this is such an instance. Just as Jesus and his apostles sought to demonstrate the roots of their ministry and teaching in the Hebrew Scriptures, the church has followed suit and plotted its foundation and historical moorings in the Old Testament. In the Epistle to the Romans, Paul insists that the children of Abraham are those who come by faith rather than by human descent, and he argues this point along the chronological lines of the story itself (Rom. 4:9–12). That is, when Abraham believed the Lord, he became the father of the faith (Gen. 15:6), and when he subsequently received the covenant of circumcision, he became the father of the race (Gen. 17:9–14). The latter, asserts Paul, was a "seal of the righteousness that he had by faith while he was still uncircumcised" (Rom. 4:11). Thus the apostle declares that, chronologically speaking—and in this case theology follows chronology—faith is the primary basis for determining membership in the family of God. In Psalm 87 the criterion is election under the metaphor of birth.

Teaching the Text

An appropriate way to begin our sermon/lesson is to speak about citizenship and its privileges in the ancient as well as the modern world (see "Historical and Cultural Background"). A citizen of a particular country or city has certain rights and privileges, as well as responsibilities. Psalm 87 is more concerned with privileges than responsibilities. That is, it celebrates the connection to Zion by recognizing, "All my fountains are in you" (87:7). And for a city that had only one physical spring of water, that is quite a declaration of faith.

Newton received the inspiration for his hymn "Glorious Things of Thee Are Spoken" (see "Theological Insights") from this psalm, and he captured the theme of verses 5–6 in the final verse: "Of Zion's city I through grace a member am." To develop this theme we may make three points. First, this psalm opens up a vision of the world community with its spiritual center in Zion (Jerusalem). That too is symbolic. It is not so much the geographical city but what happened in that city that is so important for Judaism and Christianity. While the psalmist does not go so far as Paul's inclusive statement of Galatians 3:28, he nevertheless harmonizes with Paul's theme: "There is neither Jew nor Gentile."

Second, the method by which this transaction takes place is birth: "This one was born there" (87:4c ESV). Since the psalm recognizes the native lands where the visitors to Jerusalem were born, and then issues the decree that "this one was born in Zion" (87:6), the legitimation of their birth is adoption rather than natural birth. This keys into Paul's description of the gentiles as adoptees into Abraham's family (Rom. 8:15; Eph. 1:5). In fact, from the time of Abraham the nations were included in God's plan (Gen. 12:3), and here we see them enrolled on the international roster of grace by the Lord himself.

We may look at this truth from another angle, the new birth. While it is not the New Testament theme of Christ's "You must be born again" (John 3:7), there are, as we have recognized above, two births in view. The first is an acknowledgment of the nations' births in their native lands (natural birth, 87:4c), and the second is a divine transaction, a spiritual birth no less, as the Lord registers the peoples and welcomes them as spiritual citizens of Zion: "This one was born in Zion" (spiritual birth, 87:6b). It is the truth Augustine speaks of as "the city of God," whose "Founder has inspired us with a love which makes us covet its citizenship" (see "Illustrating the Text").

Third, there is a hint that not only nations but their individual members receive rights of citizenship in Jerusalem: "This one and that one" (87:5). The expression is literally "a man and a man" (= each person) and implies that these are the individuals who make up the nations that find their birthright in Zion.[6] The point is that God's grace, not mentioned specifically in the poem, underwrites the registry of nations and individuals. At this juncture we may use Newton's hymn and recite the final stanza:

> Savior, if of Zion's city
>   I through grace a member am,
> let the world deride or pity—
>   I will glory in thy name;
> fading are the worldlings' pleasures,
>   all their boasted pomp and show,
> solid joys and lasting treasures,
>   none but Zion's children know.

Illustrating the Text

The city of God

Church Fathers: Psalm 87:3 is a key text in Augustine's monumental work *The City of God*, where he uses this term to allude to the commonwealth of God, or the church: "From these and similar testimonies, all of which it were tedious to cite, we have learned that there is a city of God, and its Founder has inspired us with a love which makes us covet its citizenship."[7] In contrast to Psalm 83:13–18, where Israel's enemies are subdued by force, Psalm 87 illustrates conquest by grace, as God writes each nation and individual in his registry of love. Wilcock appropriately asserts: "If it is about anything, it is about the grace that brings in undeserving outsiders, and blesses them with the privileges of citizenship."[8]

The universal unifier

Bible: The presence of the nations is not the major constituting factor of the universality of the gospel. Rather it is place of birth. This picture in Psalm 87 is unique, for here we observe a theological principle that runs through Scripture in various strands, here in the principle that the Lord is the Founder (87:1) and the Namesake (87:3) of the universality of the gospel ("city of God"): "he has founded" (87:1), and "this one was born there" (87:6 ESV). He has also elected to proclaim "glorious things" of this city (87:3), which is essentially "glorious things" about its Founder and Namesake. When Nicodemus questions Jesus about the "new birth," Jesus emphasizes that this birth is spiritual, not physical (John 3:5, 8). When Paul makes his universal statement in Galatians 3:28, he too identifies the universal unifier, not as place or ethnicity, but as spiritual, centered in the person of Jesus Christ: "There is neither Jew nor Greek, neither slave nor free, nor is there male and female, for you are all one in Christ Jesus."

"Darkness Is
My Closest Friend"

Big Idea
In its deep desolation this psalm takes us all the way to the cross, where we confront a deeper desolation.

Key Themes
- When hope does not materialize, it still sustains.
- Sometimes we have to live with death on the edge of life.
- When we cry out to God, who saves, we are not hopeless.

Understanding the Text

This psalm has been called "the most desolate in the Psalter."[1] The psalmist has suffered from some unspecified but isolating illness from his youth (88:15), leprosy being one of the proposals (see 88:8, 18), and he has lived life on the edge of death. It was composed as an individual lament but may be used here in the Korah collection as a community lament (especially suggested by its closeness to Ps. 89), and as such it forms an appropriate prelude to the somber hues of Psalm 89.

The Text in Context

This psalm has affinities with the book of Job, but it is not driven by the wisdom question of God's righteousness.[2] Wilcock points to Lamentations 3 and identifies the basic elements in this psalm as belonging to that lament, and he proposes that this psalm be understood not as an individual lament but with reference to the nation mourning over the fall of Jerusalem to Babylonia.[3]

There is also some correlation in subject matter between certain psalms in the first Korah collection and those of the second Korah collection: Psalms 42–43 correlate with Psalm 84; Psalm 44 correlates with Psalm 85; Psalm 48 with Psalm 87; and Psalm 49 with Psalm 88.[4]

Outline/Structure

The psalm is marked by three different verbs for "cry," giving us an outline of the psalm.

1. Cry (*tsaʿaq*) to the Lord for help (88:1–9a)
   a. Anguished cry for help (88:1–2)
   b. Lament of the afflicted one (88:3–9a)
2. Cry (*qaraʾ*) to the Lord for help (88:9b–12)
   a. Loud cry for the Lord's help (88:9b–c)
   b. Rhetorical questions about death (88:10–12)
3. Cry (root, *shwʿ*) to the Lord for help (88:13–18)
   a. Cry for the Lord's help (88:13)
   b. Rhetorical question about the Lord's abandonment of him (88:14)
   c. Lament of the afflicted one (88:15–18)

Historical and Cultural Background

The Hebrew Scriptures give us a range of thoughts on life after death (see the sidebar "Sheol" in the unit on Ps. 6; see also "Additional Insights: The Afterlife and Immortality in the Old Testament," following the unit on Ps. 49), but in the Psalter, Psalm 88 stands by itself in having vacated all hope.

Interpretive Insights

Title *According to* mahalath leannoth. The word *mahalath* appears in the title of Psalm 53. In both locations it may be a tune name.

A maskil *of Heman the Ezrahite.* For *maskil,* see the comments on the title for Psalm 74. There are several references to a person named *Heman* in the historical books (1 Kings 4:31; 1 Chron. 2:6; 15:17; 25:1, 5). If the person referenced is that of 1 Chronicles 25:1 and 5, a temple musician in David's time, the poem could have been written by him and then reused in Book 3 as a community lament. The purpose would be to shape the mood of the collection for the approaching topic of Psalm 89, the end of the Davidic dynasty and its theological implications.

88:1 *the God who saves me.* This is virtually the only hopeful phrase in the psalm, and it does not seem to describe the realities of his situation but relates the change he hopes for.

day and night. This phrase implies the intensity of the psalmist's prayers.

88:2 *my cry.* This is a ringing cry of joy or sorrow.

88:5–7 *I am set apart from the dead.* The KJV has translated more literally, "Free among the dead, like the slain that lie in the grave," and this adjective ("free") has led some Christian interpreters to view this as a description of the fact that death could not hold Jesus.[5] While some commentators consider this a corrupt text, there are no textual variants to replace it, and the Septuagint translates the Hebrew text quite literally. The sense of the verse is hopelessness, as the NIV's rendering represents. It is as if the suppliant, because of his troubles, is already in the netherworld. The terms "lowest pit" and "darkest depths" (88:6) are descriptive of death (Job 10:21; Ps. 143:3). Moreover, the psalmist perceives that divine wrath is directed against him (88:7, 14, 16–17). In view of that, and quite surprisingly, he still does not accuse God of injustice.

88:8 *my closest friends.* These could include relatives too. Note that verse 18 suggests that his "closest friends" have been replaced by darkness.

I am confined and cannot escape. Sickness was a common reason for a person's isolation from the community (Lev. 13:45–46; Job 19:13–22; 30:9–23; Ps. 31:9–12).

88:9 *my eyes are dim with grief.* This expresses the pain of disappointment (Deut. 28:32). There are four questions in verses 10–12, and the implied answer to them is "no."

88:10 *their spirits.* This Hebrew term (RSV: "shades"; ESV: "the departed"; KJV: "the dead") elsewhere in the Hebrew Bible refers to a pre-Israelite people (e.g., "the Rephaites" in Deut. 2:20–22; Josh. 12:4). Contextually it clearly refers to "the inhabitants of Sheol, who are little more than shadows of their former selves."[6]

praise you. The dead are separated from Yahweh and thus unable to praise him. See "Theological Insights."

88:13 *But I.* The conjunction "but" signals a shift in emphasis, calling attention to the psalmist's plight and his third call for help. His situation includes unanswered prayer, spurning by God (88:14), almost a lifetime of affliction (88:15), God's frightful wrath (88:16–17), and shunning by others (88:18)—how much more hopeless could one be!

88:14 *Why, LORD, do you reject me and hide your face from me?* Nowhere in the psalm does the suppliant acknowledge sin; so, unlike Job, he does not argue his case on the basis of his righteousness, although his "why" implies that he does not know why the Lord has assumed this attitude toward him.

88:18 *darkness is my closest friend.* The curtain of hope has closed on the suppliant, and he is shut off, at least mentally, in the darkness of death. If this psalm is spoken by the community, or adapted as a community lament, as is often the case (also suggested by Rashi),[7] then it is an appropriate prelude to Psalm 89, which deals with the death of Israel as it has been known for centuries. Even the statement "From my youth I have suffered and been close to death" (88:15a) may be intended by the compiler of Book 3 to be a general lament about Israel's history, which for centuries has been lived on the edge of death. And now, on the verge of exile, they lament that they are without "friend and neighbor" and darkness is closing in.

Theological Insights

Death is a huge topic for Holy Scripture—in fact, it is addressed in one of the introductory stories of the Bible (Gen. 3). In varying degrees the Scriptures deal with the power of death and how human beings can cope with its sheer inevitability and horrifying prospects (e.g., Ps. 49). Psalm 88 is located near the bottom rung of the ladder with its preoccupation with death—indeed, a preoccupation with life lived on the brink of this frightening inevitability, a "living death," we might say.

Unfortunately we sometimes read "Sheol" as the New Testament concept of "Hades" or "hell." But while related, they are not the same (see the sidebar "Sheol" in the unit on Ps. 6). In the Hebrew Bible, Sheol involves separation from God, but in the sense that communication between the dead and Yahweh is no longer possible. Separation is not punitive as it is in the New Testament (see Luke 16:19–31), but the lament here is to the effect that death cuts off the possibility of praising God, so precious to human beings and so strategic to a proper relationship with God. Given the importance of praise in the Psalter, closing down its potential is a serious impairment of the spiritual life and a subtle reminder of the reality that death annuls the most vital spiritual aptitude available to humankind, the praise of God (see "Theological Insights" in the unit on Ps. 103).

Teaching the Text

Psalm 88 is one of those psalms that preachers and teachers may never choose as their text. But I certainly hope not. From one angle, it is a testimony to those who live with some life-threatening disease and are never free of the threat of death, and they can never let go of God. That is the circumstance of this person of faith. From another angle, it is a testimony to that person who lives such a life and blames God, even questions him courageously, but never accuses God of injustice. We infer from 88:14 that such a prospect is lurking beneath the surface—it just never has materialized. Psalm 88 has some things in common with Job, who also blames God but, unlike Psalm 88, accuses God of injustice. Yet, our psalmist does not have the advantage of God's words to him, as Job has (Job 38–41). The psalmist is utterly shut off in darkness. Of course, this is also a wonderful opportunity to deal with the New Testament promises of resurrection and eternal life (e.g., John 3:16; 1 Cor. 15; 2 Cor. 5:1–15).

The preacher/teacher who chooses to take one or both of the angles mentioned above may also integrate into that message the triple use of the suppliant's verb of petition (see "Outline/Structure"). The three verbs are synonyms. And while we must be careful that we do not overreach for their semantic extensions, here is a case where three synonyms carry a slightly different nuance of meaning—that's the reason the psalmist uses three different verbs, and from them we learn something about the character of prayer.

First, the psalmist says, "day and night I *cry out* [*tsa'aq*] to you," a verb that basically means "to cry out for help"—it is a plea to the "God who saves," the prayer of faith (88:1 [88:2 MT]). The fact that the suppliant cries out "day and night" implies the intensity of his prayers and also his trust in the "God who saves."

Second, the psalmist says, "I *call* [*qara'*] to you, LORD, every day" (88:9 [88:10 MT]), and the verb carries the basic meaning of "call out loudly." It is his prayer when he edges up against the reality of death (88:10–12). This is a cry of desperation. Like the first cry, this may also be a cry for help, but it is tinted by his frequent brush with death. Our prayers, depending on the immediate circumstances, take on different hues of passion and urgency. The writer to the Hebrews reminds us that our Lord himself prayed with this kind of passion "unto him that was able to save him from death" (Heb. 5:7 KJV).

Third, the psalmist says, "But I *cry* [*shiwwa'ti*] to you for help, LORD" (88:13 [88:14 MT]). This verb implies utter intensity, or as Koehler and Baumgartner describe it, citing Ernst Jenni, "to utter a successive series of screams."[8] The intensity has not subsided since his first cry, because it comes before the Lord in the morning. But a weariness has come to characterize his prayer, because now he feels rejected and is convinced that God is hiding his face from him (88:14). The closing of the psalm is virtually the opening of Psalm 22, "My God, my God, why have you forsaken me?" And it takes us as Christians all the way to the cross, where our Savior uttered those same words, and where we can be comforted that the utter cry of desolation should never be ours, because Christ exhausted its depths (see "Illustrating the Text" in the unit on Ps. 22). If the psalmist could only have heard and believed the strong words of the Song of Songs that "love is as strong as death" (Song 8:6), and taken a giant step beyond that to hear, "I am the resurrection and the life" (John 11:25), that would have lit up the landscape of his world. Yet he has cried out to the God who saves, and that means his faith is not in a holding pattern. We should not disparage the pattern of faith that, rather than advancing in wide strides, progresses in small increments.

Illustrating the Text

Attitudes toward death

Quote: **C. S. Lewis.** Writing to an American friend about longing for the life to come, Lewis says: "What a state we have got into when we can't say, 'I'll be happy when God calls me' without being afraid one will be thought 'morbid.' After all, St. Paul said just the same. If we really believe what we say we believe—if we really think that home is elsewhere and that this life is a 'wandering to find home,' why should we not look forward to the arrival[?] There are, aren't there, only three things we can do about death: to desire it, to fear it, or to ignore it. The third alternative, which is the one the modern world calls 'healthy' is surely the most uneasy and precarious of all."[9] Psalm 88 seems to illustrate the second attitude. But we can be thankful that Psalm 88 is not the last word about death. On another occasion, and in somewhat different circumstances, another writer declares that the darkness is not dark to God (Ps. 139:12). So why should we fear it?

God has planned eternal life.

Biography: **Malcolm Muggeridge.** In 2003 Wheaton College celebrated Malcolm Muggeridge's one hundredth birthday with *Firing Line* host William Buckley. As part of the celebration, Buckley showed some clips of *Firing Line* that he and Muggeridge did together. In one of them, Muggeridge talked about looking forward to death, because he knew eternal life was waiting for him. This was a man who had been an agnostic and had come to faith in Christ. The marvel is that God planned eternal life for us, planned it from eternity, and by faith in Jesus Christ we receive this plan as our own. This plan—so noble, so amazing, so truly wonderful—God has made known in stages throughout history, until finally he revealed it in all its fullness and glory in Jesus Christ. Even Psalm 88, which presents a dark picture of death, by that very picture configures the vacuum that exists in human hearts and waits to be filled with God's gift of eternal life.

"I Will Sing of the LORD's Great Love Forever"

Big Idea

How do we live with God when he ostensibly says no to his own promises or leaves them in suspension?

Key Themes

- We can—and should—lament God's unfulfilled promises.
- We humans are "yes" creatures, and living with the God who says no is a challenge of faith.
- God's unfulfilled promises are suspended, not only in time, but in God's own certain character, and that is where our hope lies.

Understanding the Text

Psalm 89 is, by verse count, the third-longest psalm in the Psalter, behind 119 and 78. It is composed of a general lament (89:38–51) that is at the same time both individual (89:47a) and community, a feature I have claimed for other psalms, most recently Psalm 88. Like an unresolved discordant chord (Kidner),[1] the psalm leaves in theological suspension the question of the failed Davidic covenant (2 Sam. 7:4–17). This psalm is also classified as a royal psalm and is distinguished by its final position in Book 3, reverberating with royal psalms that begin Book 1 (Ps. 2) and conclude Book 2 (Ps. 72), while anticipating the royal psalms to come (Pss. 110 and 132).[2]

The Text in Context

The contextual background of Psalm 89 is Nathan's prophecy to David regarding his dynasty and the building of the temple in 2 Samuel 7:4–17. Table 1 provides an overview of these two texts.

2 Samuel 7:4–17	Psalm 89
"[To] my servant David" (*'el-'abdi 'el-dawid*) (7:5) "[To] my servant David" (*l^e'abdi l^edawid*) (7:8) *In both texts David is called "my servant" (the LORD's)*	"To David my servant" (*l^edawid 'abdi*) (89:3) "David my servant" (*dawid 'abdi*) (89:20) "Your servant" (89:39, 50)
"Forever" (*'ad 'olam*) (7:13, 16 [2x])	"Forever" (*l^e'olam* or *'olam*) (89:1, 2, 4, 28, 36, 37, 52)
The technical term "covenant" is not used in 2 Sam. 7	"I have made a *covenant* with my chosen one" (89:3a; cf. 89:28b, 34a, 39a)
"My people Israel" (7:7, 10, 11) "My people" (7:8) "Israelites" (lit., "children of Israel") (7:6, 7)	"Your faithful people," "people" (89:19) *Israel as God's people is not the focus of Ps. 89*
"Throne of his kingdom," "your throne" (7:13, 16) *Both texts are concerned about David's throne because that is at the heart of 2 Sam. 7*	"And make your throne firm through all generations" (89:4b; cf. 89:14, 29 [2x], 36b, 37, 44) *Both texts celebrate the perpetual reign of David*
No reference to divine oath to seal the promises	"I have sworn" (89:3b, 35a; cf. 89:49b)
"Wicked people will not oppress them anymore, as they did at the beginning" (7:10)	"The wicked will not oppress him" (89:22b)
"I have cut off all your enemies from before you" (7:9a)	"I will crush his foes before him" (89:23a)
"His [David's] kingdom" (7:12, 13) "Your [LORD's] kingdom" (7:16) *Both David's royal line and its perpetual continuance are assured*	*In light of the end of the Davidic dynasty with the Babylonian conquest, David's kingdom is not even mentioned*
The promises of 2 Sam. 7 are not called a covenant	"A/the covenant," "my covenant" (89:3a, 28b, 34a, 39a)
David is not called anointed one	"Your anointed one" (David) (89:38b, 51b)
"*Built/build* me a house" (7:5, 7; cf. 7:13)	"Your love stands firm forever" (lit., "*will be built forever*") (89:2a) "Make your throne firm" (lit., "*I will build your throne through all generations*") (89:4b) *The temple is not even mentioned in Ps. 89, but this could be a veiled allusion to the building imagery of 2 Sam. 7*
"I will be his father, and he will be my son" (7:14)	"He will call out to me, 'You are my Father, my God, the Rock my Savior'" (89:26)
"I will raise up your offspring to succeed you" (7:12)	"His/your [David's] line" (89:4a, 29a, 36a)
Naturally, the end of the Davidic dynasty would have no place in this text	"You . . . have defiled his crown in the dust" (89:39b) "Cast his throne to the ground" (89:44b)

Outline/Structure

Traditionally this psalm is divided into three parts: the hymn (89:1–18), the oracle (God's words) (89:19–37), and the lament (89:38–51). Yet, the following outline follows the flow of the text.[3]

1. Introduction: God's everlasting "love" and "faithfulness" (89:1–4)
   a. Established in the heavens (89:1–2)
   b. Manifested on earth in his covenant with David (89:3–4)
2. A hymn of praise (89:5–18)
   a. Praise of the heavenly beings (89:5–8)
   b. God's rule over the world he created (89:9–13)
   c. Blessing on those who walk in the light of God's presence (89:14–18)
3. God's promises to David (89:19–37)
   a. David's everlasting kingship (89:19–29)
   b. David's perpetual dynasty (89:30–37)
4. God's unfulfilled promises to David (89:38–45)
   a. God's rejection of his "anointed one" (89:38–39)
   b. God's devastation of David's kingdom (89:40–41)
   c. God's elevation of David's enemies (89:42–45)
5. The lament (89:46–51)
   a. How long will God's anger last? (89:46)
   b. Man's life is short and his creation vain (89:47–48)
   c. Why has God not fulfilled his promises to David? (89:49)
   d. Enemies have mocked the psalmist (89:50), the Lord (89:51a), and David (89:51b)[4]
   Closing Doxology (89:52)

Historical and Cultural Background

While a few commentators give a preexilic date to this psalm, the greater likelihood is that it belongs to the exile, when the Babylonians had destroyed the temple and dethroned the Davidic king Zedekiah (2 Kings 25), thus bringing an end to David's dynasty. Psalm 89 was likely composed when the dew of this tragedy lay fresh on Israel's conscience, although some scholars would date it near the rebuilding of the temple under Zerubbabel (520–516 BC), when the hope of reviving the Davidic kingship was bursting into flower (e.g., Hossfeld and Zenger).[5] In historical reality, however, David's dynasty was never restored. The brief Hasmonean kingship established under the Maccabees (ca. 140–116 BC) was a priestly dynasty, not a Davidic one. See "Theological Insights."

Interpretive Insights

Title *maskil.* See the comments on the title for Psalm 74.

Ethan the Ezrahite. Book 3 of the Psalter mentions three men who, according to 1 Chronicles 15:17 and 19, were Levitical singers in the time of David: Heman, Asaph, and Ethan. To that mix is added Korah, a descendant of the Levitical family of Korah, who was punished for his rebellion against Moses (Num. 16); Korah's descendants were gatekeepers in David's time (1 Chron. 9), and some of them were obviously musicians in the sanctuary. All four of them are represented in Book 3: Asaph (Pss. 73–83); Korah (Pss. 84–85; 87–88); Heman (Ps. 88); and Ethan (Ps. 89).

In view of an exilic or early postexilic date for the composition of Book 3, these psalms may be, in a symbolic way, the celebration of the temple that David's aspirations and preparations helped make possible, and so we hear symbolically from the singers of his own musical staff. Even David himself, by virtue of the editor's ingenuity, adds his own voice in Psalm 86, and Ethan concludes the chorus: "I will sing of the LORD's great love forever . . . through all generations" (89:1). The symbolic song is not only in the content of these psalms but in their attributed authorship as Davidic representatives. There is a deafening silence in Psalm 89 regarding the temple (see table 1)—it's all about David and his covenant. Yet David's temple musicians, at least symbolically, sing the descant.

89:1–4 These verses form the first part of the psalm, the introduction.

89:1 *I will sing of the* LORD's *great love forever . . . your faithfulness.* Verse 1 forms a virtual vow to praise the Lord, generally a feature of the lament that occurs toward the end of the psalm, and the psalmist vows to sing this song "forever," that is, in perpetuity. And that hints at the major issue of the psalm: Why has the Lord's covenant with David not continued? Indeed, the content of the song celebrates God's "great love" (*hesed*) and "faithfulness" (*'emunah*), much like the overture of a symphony introduces the musical theme or themes that the composer develops in the major piece.[6] When we recall that 88:11 laments that God's "love" cannot be declared in the grave, then the very fact that this poet trumpets God's "love" stretched across the generations implies that Israel, at least in the suppliant's faith, is not yet a tomb, even though David's dynasty is defunct and the temple lies in ruins. It is a song of life.

89:2 *your love stands firm forever.* Literally, "[your] love will be built forever." Perhaps this verbal imagery is a veiled allusion to the "building" of the temple, which is a theme of 2 Samuel 7 but is mysteriously absent from Psalm 89. Both documents share the phrase "David my servant" (see table 1).

89:3 *You said, "I have made a covenant."* Verse 3 introduces God's words (he speaks twice: 89:3–4 and 19–37), while the psalmist's voice is heard in verses

1, 2, 47a, and 50. Even though Nathan's words to David in 2 Samuel 7:4–17 do not engage the term "covenant" (see table 1), it obviously was a covenant (also implied by "I have sworn" in 89:3) and is so called in Psalm 132:11–12. Verses 19–37 are a description of that covenant, and God's ostensible annulment of it is the topic of the lament (89:38–51).

89:5–18 The second part of the psalm is a hymn of praise in language intended to form the foundation on which to base God's promises that follow in part 3 (89:19–37). In verses 5–8 the psalmist lauds the Lord's majestic preeminence over the heavenly beings (89:5); then in verses 9–13 he extols God's ruling and creating powers over the universe, followed in verses 14–18 by the heart of this hymn that extols "righteousness" and "justice" (89:14) as the underpinnings of God's throne.

89:15–18 *Blessed are those who have learned to acclaim you.* Our psalmist pronounces blessing on "those who have learned to acclaim" the Lord as King. The Hebrew uses the term "shout(s) of joy," an expression that alludes in this case to the acclamation of a new king (see also 47:5).

Since the topic of the poem is so morose, it is important that the psalmist present the reader with a portrait of the majestic God and provide a background of praise and confidence for the final lament.

89:19–37 These verses describe the Davidic covenant, although its terms are taken only in part from 2 Samuel 7 (see table 1). The gist of the covenant is expressed in verses 28–29: (1) the Lord's everlasting love for David, (2) a covenant that will not fail, and (3) David's perpetual line of rulers.

89:29 *as long as the heavens endure.* The cosmic picture of the enduring heavens (89:28–29) becomes the model for the endurance of God's covenant with David. Reinforcing that further in verses 35–37, and coming to the main thrust of the psalm, the psalmist declares that the disappearance of David's dynasty was equivalent to breaking the covenant with the sun and moon of the created order (see also Jer. 33:20–21). There is an exception clause inserted in the narrative of Solomon's dedication of the temple (1 Kings 8:25), perhaps to satisfy the tension created by the question of God's faithfulness raised by the exile and the discontinuation of David's line: "You shall never fail to have a successor to sit before me on the throne of Israel, if only your descendants are careful in all they do to walk before me faithfully as you have done" (see also 89:49).

89:38–45 The fourth section begins with a different tone, "But you," and rehearses God's unfulfilled promises to David, which include God's rejection of his "anointed one," that is, David's dynasty (89:38–39), which amounted to his renunciation of the Davidic covenant, the devastation of David's kingdom (89:40–41), and the exaltation of David's enemies (89:42–45), a serious slate of offenses indeed.

89:40–41 *You have broken through all his walls.* While we do not have a clear description of the Babylonian conquest in this psalm, the terms of verses 40–41 may be allusions to the devastation, as are the almost exact words in 80:12 ("Why have you broken down its walls?"). See also Psalms 74 and 79. We are also reminded of the Edomite plunder of Jerusalem after the fall, which is the subject of the prophecy of Obadiah.

89:46–51 Two realities are impressed on the psalmist: the Lord has hidden himself, and his wrath just seems to continue (89:46). In the face of these dreadful facts, he reminds God of his (the psalmist's) own mortality and the futility of human life (89:46–47).

89:49–51 *Lord, where is your former great love, which in your faithfulness you swore to David?* Now the central question in the psalmist's subconscious mind, even when he is praising God, is posed in terms of God's character and reliability. He reminds God of how the enemies have mocked him (the psalmist, 89:50), the Lord (89:51a), and David's royal descendants (89:50 "your servant" = Heb. "your servants").

89:52 *Praise be to the LORD forever!* As is the case with all five books of the Psalter, the doxology closes the psalm as well as Book 3. See "Trends in Psalms Studies" in the introduction in volume 1.

Theological Insights

Psalm 89 is one of the best examples of an unfulfilled Old Testament prophecy and propels us toward the New Testament, "where we find that the fulfillment will altogether outstrip the expectation."[7] Our psalmist finds this propulsion in two sources. First, he appeals to the natural course of the created world, affirming that David's line will continue as surely as the sun and moon follow their assigned functions in the universe (89:36–37). Second, the psalmist appeals to the Mosaic covenant, where the Lord self-defines his character as one that abounds in "love and faithfulness" (89:14b; Exod. 34:6, *hesed* and *'emet/'emunah*). On these sure grounds, the psalmist then raises the question, "Where is your former great love, which in your faithfulness you swore to David?" (89:49). After the appeal to God on these two firm claims, the lament of verses 38–51 leaves this question in suspension—not in uncertainty, but in the certain character of God.

Yet the suspension does not continue forever. Matthew and Luke, in different ways, trace Jesus's lineage through David (Matt. 1:1–17; Luke 3:23–38), and Peter declares that Jesus fulfilled God's oath that he would place one of David's descendants on the throne (Acts 2:25–36). Of course, the New Testament writers are speaking of a spiritual kingdom—indeed, a new kind of kingdom in whose principles Jesus instructs us in the Beatitudes (Matt. 5:3–12), and he affirms before Pilate, "My kingdom is not of this world" (John 18:36).

Teaching the Text

Psalm 89 is an opportunity to consider one of the questions that trouble so many people: How do we live with a God who says no, particularly no to his own promises, as it would seem?

First, when we face adversities, we should ask what part our sins have had in bringing forth the adversities in our lives. While the psalmist does not give evidence that he has engaged in any kind of soul searching regarding the causes of the exile, Ezekiel and Zechariah reveal that such introspective thinking did take place (Ezek. 18:2, 25; 33:10, 17, 20; Zech. 1:2–6). Of course, we know that God's grace covers our sins, but our adversities also call us to spiritual introspection, and that too is a mark of divine grace.

Second, we may consider the state of faith reflected in the psalm: the God who set the sun and moon in their unchangeable positions and whose self-description is that of a God whose attributes are "love" and "faithfulness" would not leave his promise to his people in timeless suspension. God's promises are as sure as his character, his character is established in heaven (89:2), and the heavens belong to him (89:11). There is no wonder, then, that we can sing of the Lord's great love forever. In fact, our poet draws on the language of the Lord's self-identity in Exodus 34:5–7 as code language to establish the deity's character (e.g., 89:1, 2, 14) and then appeals to two witnesses, the sun and moon (89:35–37), to establish the reliability of God's oath. In other words, the worshiper assures us that this is who God always has been and always will be, and there is no other place to turn in order to ascertain his unchangeable character, except to his creation and redeeming love.

Now the psalmist has set the stage for the puzzling question of verse 49: "Lord, where is your former great love, which in your faithfulness you swore to David?" That's where the lament of verses 38–51 seems to form a sharp theological drop-off. Yet, in the frame of the psalm, creation and covenant promise are intended to provide an assurance on the other side of the ledger. The effect is to make the question of God's inattention to his covenant promises a suspension *in* the certainties of God, not apart from them—and the psalmist can leave it there because he is confident in God's unchangeable character. This is a formula for a resolution to our skepticism, especially when life's circumstances seem to contradict what God has promised to do. It is a summons to affirm that our faith is anchored in the character of God and a reminder that his promises both grow out of his character and are founded on that unchangeable truth.

Third, in this state of suspension, our psalmist does a beautiful thing that is instructive for all believers who face the question of God's "unfulfilled" promises. He sets the spiritual hierarchy in order by using the substitute term for Yahweh, the term "Lord" (*'adonay*, "my Master"); this is followed in the next verse by "your servant." Lord, servant—that is the proper structure of command and obedience in the universe. And now in that reality, the psalmist, and we too who have come to acclaim God King, can abandon ourselves to God's character. That is, we can abandon ourselves to the God who put the sun and moon in place as witnesses of his character and unchangeable nature. Moreover, to submit ourselves to God's character of "love" and "faithfulness" is to commit ourselves to his will. And to commit ourselves to his will is to submit ourselves as servants to our Master. That is the ultimate and the only place of security. Ultimately life's questions have to be posed and posited in terms of the person of God. They are safe there, and so are we, "because I know whom I have believed, and am convinced that he is able to guard what I have entrusted to him until that day" (2 Tim. 1:12).

Illustrating the Text

In Christ, God's promises have always been "Yes."

Bible: 2 Corinthians 1:15–20. We human beings are "yes" creatures in that we like to hear the affirmation of our plans and proposals. "No" is not a response we by nature and conditioning like to hear. In Psalm 89 our writer deals with the suspension of God's promises to David that his dynasty would continue, but with the Babylonian conquest in 586 BC the dynasty came to an end and never revived, at least not in a physical and historical sense (see "Additional Insights: The Priest-King Ruler Model," following the unit on Ps. 110). Yet it did revive in a spiritual sense in the person and kingship of Jesus Christ. Our psalmist's point is that, even though history may have brought the Davidic line to an end, God's promises are still anchored in God's character of love and faithfulness, which he has established in heaven (89:1–2). Paul makes a similar point in 2 Corinthians 1:15–20 when he builds off the uncertainty that the Corinthians had regarding his planned visit. Paul's plans, he assures them, were not "yes, yes" and "no, no" at the same time, but they were, like God's own promises, a definite "yes" in Jesus Christ: "For no matter how many promises God has made, they are 'Yes' in Christ. And so through him the 'Amen' is spoken by us to the glory of God" (2 Cor. 1:20). Our response of faith is to say the "Amen." So the promises of God to David are only suspended in God's character, and his character is impeccable: "For the Son of God, Jesus Christ, who was preached among you by us—by me and Silas and Timothy—was not 'Yes' and 'No,' but in him it has always been 'Yes'" (2 Cor. 1:19). God would, in his own time and way, carry through with his promises because his character is their eternal indemnity.

Authentic praise comes from submitting to God's will.

Bible: We cannot overemphasize the centrality of God's will in our lives and our submission to it. As difficult as the servant-master relationship may be, and as humbling, our Lord himself provides the perfect example. In the Lord's Prayer he teaches us to pray, "Your will be done, on earth as it is in heaven" (Matt. 6:10); and in the garden of Gethsemane the Savior prays, "My Father, if it is possible, may this cup be taken from me. Yet not as I will, but as you will" (Matt. 26:39). The clarification of the spiritual hierarchy with Master and servant in their proper places (see "Teaching the Text") is, at least in part, the reason that the psalmist can close the psalm on a note of praise, "Praise be to the LORD forever!" (89:52a). It is only those who truly submit to God's will who can render authentic praise.

"Lord, You Have Been Our Dwelling Place throughout All Generations"

Big Idea

Life's brevity silhouettes both our security in God and our need to redeem the time.

Key Themes

- Human mortality and sin remind us of the brevity of life and the need for grace.
- All of our unfulfilled desires, and especially God's unfulfilled promises, are suspended in the character of God.

Understanding the Text

Psalm 90, a community lament, introduces the voice of Moses to set the uncertainty of Psalm 89 and the future of David's monarchy in the light of God's eternal being. What greater and more reassuring voice could be heard than the voice of Moses, "the man of God," speaking in the assuring tones of Israel's "dwelling place" in God throughout their history! Whatever Israel's loss in the tragic exile—and it was gigantic—the recognition that the eternal God is "our dwelling place throughout all generations" (90:1) is a gigantic gain.

The Text in Context

This prayer of Moses, the only psalm attributed to him, has affinities with the Song of Moses in Deuteronomy 32, both setting Israel in the context of creation (Deut. 32:6; Ps. 90:1–2), and both providing historical perspective.

After the golden calf incident Moses pleads with Yahweh to turn and have compassion on Israel once again (Exod. 32:12), and with the positioning of Psalm 90 at the beginning of Book 4, following Psalm 89, again Moses enters this plea for his people.

While Deuteronomy is more a review of Israel's history (cf. Ps. 78), Psalm 90 puts Israel and human life generally in the perspective of God's eternal nature. In contrast to Psalm 89, this psalm incorporates a spirit of confession, evidently acknowledging that the failure of the Davidic covenant, though not mentioned in the psalm, was Israel's moral failure (90:8), not God's. Van-Gemeren makes the plausible proposal that Book 4 (Pss. 90–106) answers a series of questions raised by Psalm 89.[1]

Second Peter 3:8 quotes Psalm 90:4 to make the point that God looks at time differently than we do. Psalm 90 stops short of declaring that there is no human time with God but states that a thousand years are like a day to him, or like the even more diminished "watch in the night." See "Illustrating the Text."

Outline/Structure

1. The eternal God and the transience of human life (90:1–12)
   a. The eternal God (90:1–2)
   b. Humankind's transient life (90:3–6)
   c. God's wrath on humanity (90:7–10)
   d. The power of the wrath of God and the fear of God (90:11–12)
2. Seven petitions for grace (90:13–17)
   a. "Relent, LORD!" (90:13a)
   b. "Have compassion" (90:13b)
   c. "Satisfy us in the morning with your unfailing love" (90:14)
   d. Equalize the number of our glad days to our afflicted ones (90:15)
   e. Show your deeds to your servants and their children (90:16)
   f. May the Lord's favor rest on us (90:17a)
   g. "Establish the work of our hands" (90:17b)

Historical and Cultural Background

The wrath of God that is so prevalent in the thought of the psalm is a theme woven through the story of Israel's history, especially in Numbers and Deuteronomy. While some take the attribution to Moses as a later note, the subject matter certainly belongs to the literature about Moses, and the concept of God as "our dwelling place" is found in the Blessing of Moses (Deut. 33:27 ESV). Moses could very well have written the psalm, which the editor of Book 4 adapted for his purposes. See "The Text in Context."

Interpretive Insights

Title *A prayer of Moses the man of God.* Only once in the Pentateuch is Moses called "the man of God" (Deut. 33:1), implying his intimacy with God, and connecting this psalm to the Blessing of Moses.

90:1 *Lord.* Rather than the name Yahweh ("LORD," indicated by small caps), this is the substitute term *'adonay* ("Lord," indicated by lowercase letters). Since it means "lord" and "master," it may, like 89:49a, suggest that "the man of God" stands before the deity as a slave.[2]

dwelling place. In the Blessing of Moses he uses a similar expression, "The eternal God is your refuge" (same noun as "dwelling place," Deut. 33:27).

90:2 *Before the mountains were born.* The birth imagery to describe God's creating activity is found elsewhere in Scripture (e.g., Deut. 32:18; Prov. 8:22–25). The point of this verse is that God existed before the world, and the world is the evidence that he exists.

90:3 *You turn people back to dust.* "People" (*'enosh*) often implies frail humanity, here the generation that is dying, and the second term for humanity, "you mortals" (*bᵉne-'adam*), implies the generation that is replacing it. The term "dust" (*dakka'*) alludes to Genesis 3:19 (there dust is *'apar*) but adds to it the idea that human life often comes to an end with a violent crushing.[3] Verses 3–10 include metaphors that describe human brevity and insecurity: dust, a watch in the night, a flash flood that sweeps people away, new grass that springs up in the morning and is withered by evening, a moan, and a bird that flies quickly away. Similar descriptions of life's brevity are found in Psalms 102:3–11, 23–24; 103:15–17; and Isaiah 40:6–8.

90:4 *A thousand years . . . like a day . . . like a watch.* Generally there were three watches in the night. God views time differently than human beings do. Metaphorically speaking, long stretches are mere hours on his "clock."

90:5–6 *sleep of death.* "Sleep" implies death (the latter is not in the Hebrew text).

new grass. The story of human life, both its agony and ecstasy, is written in the cycle of nature.

90:7 *We are consumed by your anger.* The reference is to Israel, or the more immediate community in exile.

terrified. This verb is used elsewhere to describe terror generated by an impending doom (Judg. 20:41) or by divine judgment (Exod. 15:15; Pss. 6:3; 83:17; Isa. 13:8; etc.).[4]

90:8 *our secret sins in the light of your presence.* These are probably sins that Israel tried to hide from God and others, but God knows the secrets of all hearts (44:21), and no wrongs can be hidden from him (69:5). Following up on Psalm 89, this may be a confession that Israel's sins are behind the failure of the Davidic covenant and the exile, which would certainly be in line with 1 Kings 8:25.

90:9 *All our days pass away under your wrath; we finish our years with a moan.* The description of life as years that wane away like "a moan" employs a Hebrew word that refers to the sound of one's speech, as if history had a voice of its own, telling its own story. The KJV even renders this term as "a tale that is told." Israel's story, and ours, is chanted in the muffled tones of history's events and actors. Applied to the historical setting of Book 4, the pronoun "our" is the community voice.

90:10 *seventy years, or eighty.* Seventy is hardly the normal life span in the psalmist's time but is a desirable age for a good life, while eighty would be a special gift of longevity. See *Jubilees* 23.15.

the best of them. Following other translations, the NIV accepts the idea, perhaps based on the LXX, of "the best of them." KJV has "strength," but the Hebrew term (*rahab*) implies "width" and "length," thus ESV's "span." That is, humankind's years are lived under God's wrath, and "the length of them" can be described as "trouble and sorrow."[5] It is a pretty sad description of human existence, and not far from the reality of Israel's world, and the world as countless people have experienced it. It is a lament of the same nature as Ecclesiastes (e.g., Eccles. 4:1–3).

90:12 *Teach us to number our days.* An awareness of life's brevity will lead to "a heart of wisdom." This term probably defines the "fear that is your due" in the previous verse, for the "fear of the LORD is the beginning of wisdom" (Ps. 111:10; cf. Deut. 32:29). This is really the center of the psalm. At this point our poet thinks of death as the factor that helps the believer to realize "that God shows him the way to the true and ultimate meaning of life."[6]

90:13 *Relent, LORD! How long . . . ?* If the prayer was written by Moses, and it might well have been (90:13 is similar to Exod. 32:12), we do not know what circumstances prompted it. However, the editor(s) of Book 4 applies the psalm to the exile and the troubling loss of the Davidic dynasty, interpreting these events as the result of God's wrath that can be traced to Israel's sins (90:8). Verse 13 begins a section of seven petitions for a better future (see "Outline/Structure").

90:14 *Satisfy us in the morning with your unfailing love.* The "morning" means that God's covenant love (*hesed*) will come soon, or, in the sense of 46:5, that a new tomorrow will come with the breaking day.

90:15 *for as many years as we have seen trouble.* Judging from the plethora of troubles that filled Israel's history, this would be an age of joy and gladness (90:14), and in reverse proportions of God's wrath, a golden age indeed.

90:17 *the favor of the Lord.* This is a prayer for grace. Our work, without God's blessing, is futile.

the work of our hands. The composition of Book 4 may be dated in the early postexilic age, and this could very well allude to the reconstruction of the temple (520–516 BC) and the hopes of reestablishing David's dynasty (see 92:4).

Theological Insights

The roots of New Testament theology are found in the Old Testament, especially the Psalms, and there is at least one such theological truth in Psalm 90. To speak about God as our "dwelling place" points in the direction of the teaching of Jesus in John's Gospel. Speaking of the coming of the Holy Spirit, Jesus says: "On that day you will realize that I am in my Father, and you are in me, and I am in you" (John 14:20). This theological truth goes beyond the security and intimacy of Psalm 90 and involves the framing of one's will in accordance with God's will. This is the sense of Jesus's statement in the parable of the vine: "If you abide in me, and my words abide in you, ask whatever you wish, and it will be done for you" (John 15:7 ESV). That is, believers become so absorbed in Christ's words that their will has been refined by the will of God.

Teaching the Text

Psalm 90 gives the preacher or teacher an opportunity to deal with some of the most profound spiritual truths in the Hebrew Bible, truths that connect to New Testament theology. In the first place, we need to take into account the opening statement that sets the stage for the entire psalm (90:1–2). It is, in fact, a confession of faith, acknowledging the Lord as our "dwelling place." This concept, incorporated in the Blessing of Moses (Deut. 33:27), is not so much a mystical view of dwelling in God—yet that is not to be ruled out—but the practical and historical notion of security in God that Moses attests to ("Underneath are the everlasting arms"). This is so difficult for us to comprehend that C. S. Lewis compares us to a child who cannot be enticed away from his mud pies to a vacation by the sea, because he has no notion of the splendor of the sea (see "Illustrating the Text"). It is a hint of the intimacy that regulated Israel's relationship with God and reminds us of Jesus's own statement regarding the new age the Holy Spirit would inaugurate (see "Theological Insights"). In our discussion of Psalm 89, I suggested that the Davidic covenant was suspended not so much in time as in God's character of "love" and "faithfulness," and there Israel could leave the unfulfilled promises of God.

Second, this psalm's view of time and the eternal God can become a corrective for our own flawed view of time, often the *carpe diem* ("seize the day") philosophy of life, with its hedonistic approach to life. When we get a view of the brevity of human life, measured against the eternity of God, in whom we abide, it silhouettes both our security in God and the need to measure the short days we have in this life. Verse 12 petitions God for that purpose.

Third—and this is also related to the second point—we can stress the relationship between mortality and sin. Weiser suggests that the nature of sin is to numb us to the effect of our mortality on our love of sinning. Our own mortal nature, especially without a consciousness of God's eternal nature, dims our view of the battle between the divine will and the human will that is always raging, tilting us in the direction of our will rather than God's.[7]

A fourth point can be an appropriate capstone on this sermon or lesson: the grace that permeates the psalm. Moses believes in divine grace, and to reinforce this point we may observe that he does not pray for wealth, health, or possessions, but in verse 13 his entreaty is for divine compassion—not compassion earned, but compassion generated from the character of the one who is our "dwelling place." In the Sermon on the Mount, Jesus admonishes us that we ought not to make the necessities of life our primary aim, because our heavenly Father knows we need them and will abundantly supply them out of his grace; but seek first his kingdom and righteousness, for the necessities are a gift of God's grace (Matt. 6:25–34). Psalm 90 acknowledges this from another angle, not from our need of life's necessities, but from our need for God to make our work in this short life a success. That too is reliance on God's grace, without which our work cannot succeed: "Establish the work of our hands for us—yes, establish the work of our hands" (90:17).

Illustrating the Text

In our ignorance, we prefer making mud pies instead of taking a holiday at the sea.

Quote: C. S. Lewis. The idea of the Lord as our dwelling place is a bit difficult for us humans to comprehend. But the psalmist wants us to understand that ever since God brought the world into existence, he has been our dwelling place (see Deut. 33:27, "The eternal God is your refuge"). The psalmist breaks that down into the components that make up human existence, which include our fleeting sense of life and the sins that are ever before the Lord—these are primary—but apart from that, we must not exclude a mystical dimension of dwelling in God that is hinted at in this psalm, a sense of dwelling in the care and protection of a power beyond our imagination. Speaking of our inability to comprehend the eternal (and that is the ultimate dimension of dwelling in God), Lewis said we are like "an ignorant child who wants to go on making mud pies in a slum because he cannot imagine what is meant by the offer of a holiday at the sea."[8]

Only what is eternal is important.

Architecture: On the triple doorway of Milan's majestic cathedral are three inscriptions. Over one doorway is carved a beautiful wreath of roses, and underneath is the inscription "All that pleases is but for a moment." Over a second doorway is a cross, with these words beneath it: "All that troubles is but for a moment." Underneath the great central doorway is written, "That only is important which is eternal." In Psalm 90 Moses puts Israel's life and our human life in general in the context of God's eternal being, raising the importance of our human existence to immeasurable heights in this universe. The two flanking doors of the Milan cathedral are reminders that while both life's pleasantries and troubles are momentary, our relationship to God ("our dwelling place") is eternal. We are reminded of Paul's memorable assurance in Romans 8:18: "For I reckon that the sufferings of this present time are not worthy to be compared with the glory which shall be revealed in us" (KJV).

"I Will Say of the LORD, 'He Is My Refuge and My Fortress, My God, in Whom I Trust'"

Big Idea

God's grace turns us into witnesses, not victims.

Key Themes

- The story of faith is written in God's names.
- God's protective care is ultimately found in God, our "dwelling place" and "refuge."
- When God acknowledges our faith, it is not merely commendation but a word of grace.

Understanding the Text

Psalm 91 has been described as a psalm of trust in a class all its own.[1] It certainly contains the confession of trust and multiple descriptions of dangers that have taught the psalmist to trust (91:2). At the same time it has no vow of sacrifice or praise to fulfill. See the sidebar "Psalms of Trust" in the unit on Psalm 16.

The Text in Context

Psalm 91 has a hand-in-glove relationship to Psalm 90. In the previous psalm the poet laments that "we are consumed by your anger and terrified by your indignation" (90:7), and Psalm 91 gives the complementary picture of how God's protecting care operates in a world of danger. Moreover, Psalm 90 petitions God to "have compassion on your servants" (90:13b), while Psalm 91 spells out the saving compassion of the Lord, who protects his children under his wings like an eagle (91:4a–b) and commands his angels to bear them safely over the rugged paths (91:11–12). The obvious challenge of the suppliant to his audience is to make the Most High their "dwelling [place]" (91:9; same Hebrew word as 90:1), just as Moses in Psalm 90 confesses that this relationship truly has been the historical reality of Israel's relationship with God.

In the Gospels, when the devil quotes Psalm 91:11–12 to support his challenge for Jesus to cast himself down from the pinnacle of the temple, Jesus counters with a word from Deuteronomy 6:16 that suggests the words of our psalm to be a promise of grace, not a reason to test God and see if he would fulfill his promise (Matt. 4:6–7 // Luke 4:10–12).

Some have, quite defensibly, ventured that Psalms 46 and 91 are the two psalms that most clearly lay out the benefits of trust in the Lord.

Outline/Structure

After a general confession of trust (91:1–2), the psalm is divided into three major parts by the Hebrew conjunction *ki* ("because," "for," "surely"), each time introducing an affirmation:

"Surely (*ki*) he will save you from the fowler's snare." (91:3)

"Because (*ki*) you, LORD, are my refuge . . ." (91:9, author's translation)

"Because (*ki*) he loves me, says the LORD, . . ." (91:14)

We also hear two or three voices in the psalm: the psalmist (91:1–8, 9b–13), a second person (91:9a; "you" may be the person(s) to whom the psalm is addressed, "whoever dwells in the shelter of the Most High" [91:1]), and the Lord's voice (91:14–16). As early as the Targum,[2] multiple voices have been recognized in the psalm, the Targum hearing the voices of David, Solomon, and the Lord.

Franz Delitzsch surmises that there may be some literary significance in the fact that God's voice in the final verses is phrased in a seven-line strophe of the psalm (91:14–16 consists of seven lines in the Hebrew text), perhaps suggesting the pervasive and protective presence of Yahweh, a truth the psalm has highlighted. We have seen in other instances that literary features sometimes function as a code. See the sidebar "Names of God in Psalm 84" in the unit on Psalm 84; in that psalm the poet uses *YHWH* and '*elohim* (God) seven times each to conclude the Elohistic Psalter that has overwhelmingly preferred '*elohim* (God) rather than *YHWH*. See also the sidebar "Number Symbolism" in the unit on Psalm 150.

Introduction Psalmist's affirmation of the Lord as "my refuge" (91:1–2)

1. "Surely" (*ki*): Psalmist's first affirmation of trust in God (91:3–8)
   a. Surely "he will save you from the fowler's snare" and from the noisome pestilence (91:3)
   b. [Surely] "he will cover you with his feathers" (91:4)
   c. [Surely] "you will not fear the terror of night, nor the arrow . . ." (91:5)
   d. [Surely] you will not fear "the pestilence . . . nor the plague . . ." (91:6)
   e. [Surely] you will be saved in the heat of battle (91:7)
   f. [Surely] you will only *see* the danger but not experience it physically (91:8)
2. "Because" (*ki*): Psalmist's second affirmation of trust in God (91:9–13)
   a. [Because] *you, Lord, are my refuge*, [and because] "you made the Most High your dwelling" (91:9)
   b. [Because] *you, Lord, are my refuge*, "no harm will overtake you, no disaster will come near your tent" (91:10)
   c. [Because] *you, Lord, are my refuge*, "he will command his angels . . . to guard you in all your ways" (91:11–13)
3. "Because [*ki*] he loves me": God's affirmation of trust in the psalmist (91:14–16)
   a. "'Because he loves me,' says the LORD, 'I will rescue him'" (91:14a)
   b. [Because] he loves me, "I will protect him" (91:14b)
   c. [Because] he loves me, "I will answer him" (91:15a)
   d. [Because] he loves me, "I will be with him in trouble" (91:15b)
   e. Because he loves me, "I will deliver him and honor him" (91:15c)
   f. [Because] he loves me, "I will satisfy him [with long life] and show him my salvation" (91:16)

Historical and Cultural Background

In view of the tragic events that brought the Davidic dynasty to an end in 586 BC (see Ps. 89), Psalm 91 reviews the dangers of the times—of all times, for that matter—and reaffirms Yahweh as Israel's "dwelling [place]" (91:9), securing them from the dangers that lurk in their world. Those dangers are expressed with the metaphors of hunting, nature, disease, and war.

Interpretive Insights

91:1–2 *shelter of the Most High*. Some scholars consider verses 1–13 to be a wisdom psalm, since they encourage the pursuit of godliness and promise God's protection.[3] Yet, while those terms are found in Wisdom literature (especially Proverbs), they are also characteristic of the psalms of trust, so we need not look any further for its genre. "Shelter" has the sense of protection or covering. Both this phrase and "the shadow of the Almighty" allude to the temple, where one could take refuge. By using military terms of "refuge" and "fortress" the psalmist may allude to some military invasion,[4] most likely the fall of Jerusalem, or military activity in general. Or the psalm may have come from an earlier period and been reapplied in Book 4 to allude to the disastrous events surrounding the fall and the end of David's dynasty (Ps. 89).

will rest. The verb means "spend the night" and suggests the protection one would feel when taking refuge in the temple from some peril, or in the tent of one's own dwelling.

I will say of the LORD . . . *my God.* Four names are used for God in these verses. "Most High" (*'elyon*), a patriarchal name, implies that God is above all other gods (91:9; cf. 18:13; 47:2; 83:18; 97:9; see also Gen. 14:22). The "Almighty" (*shadday*), another patriarchal name for God (Exod. 6:3), appears elsewhere in the Psalter only in 68:14. These terms from ancient history call to mind Yahweh's presence with Abraham and Moses (Gen. 14; Exod. 6:2–3). "LORD" (*YHWH*) is God's personal name and implies his covenant relationship with Israel (Exod. 3:13–15). "My God" (*'elohim*) identifies Yahweh as the suppliant's God and is a virtual confession of faith.

91:3 *Surely he will save you . . . fowler's snare.* Verses 3, 9, and 14 are introduced by a Hebrew conjunction (*ki*) that is translated as "surely" or "because" (see "Outline/Structure"). With the first two occurrences the conjunction is followed by the psalmist's affirmation of trust in God, and in the third instance it is followed by God's affirmation of trust in the psalmist. The metaphor in the first half of verse 3 is a hunting metaphor (see "Historical and Cultural Background" in the unit on Ps. 57; also Ps. 124:7).

91:4 *his feathers.* The hunting imagery of verse 3—the fowler's snare—transitions to the protecting wings of the eagle (Deut. 32:11; Matt. 23:37), representing the pattern of the psalm that moves from danger to God's protection.

91:5–6 *the terror of night . . . arrow that flies by day.* Note the alternation between night and day, a "round-the-clock threat," as Schaefer calls it: terror by *night*, arrow that flies by *day*, pestilence that stalks in the *darkness*, plague that destroys at *midday.*[5]

the pestilence that stalks . . . the plague that destroys. "Plague" is coupled with the word "pestilence" in Deuteronomy 32:24, and some commentators associate the latter word with the deity of pestilence and war in the ancient Near East.[6] By association, then, they suggest that "plague" (Ps. 91:6) alludes to demonic forces.

91:8 *only observe with your eyes.* That is, you will be a spectator, not a victim.

91:9–10 *If you say, "The* LORD *is my refuge."* The Hebrew word *ki* in verse 9 begins a new section of the psalm (see "Outline/Structure"); the NIV translators did not translate the word, but it should be translated "because" (see ESV, NRSV). The NIV's "if you say" is not in the Hebrew text but is intended as a connective. The problem in verse 9 is that the subject of the first clause is *"you"* (the Lord): "Because *you*, LORD, are my refuge." Then in the second clause the subject changes to the person the psalmist is addressing, represented by the "you" of verses 3–8. So the NIV has essentially made "you" (the addressee of the psalmist) the subject of both halves of the verse. Thus verses 9 and 10 would read

> Because [you say,] You, LORD, are my refuge,
> [and because] you have made the Most High your dwelling place,
> no evil shall befall you, nor plague come near your tent. (author's translation)

This preserves the integrity of the text, making sure the strophe marker *ki* of the three strophes (vv. 3, 9, and 14) is not lost, and, further, it recognizes that the psalmist is engaged in reassuring his audience of Yahweh's protection.

91:11–12 *his angels . . . strike your foot against a stone.* The final clause alludes to the rocky terrain of Israel where travelers can easily trip and fall (Pss. 35:15; 37:31; 38:16; Prov. 3:23). "Angels" is used of both human and heavenly beings in the Old Testament (Gen. 24:7; Exod. 23:20; Ps. 34:7), and here it could mean either. In light of divine intervention posed by the poem, heavenly beings seem more appropriate to the context.

91:13 *great lion and the serpent.* These two species of animals represent the enemies of individuals and of Israel (e.g., Ps. 17:12; Jer. 51:34).

91:14–16 These verses are the divine oracle, most likely delivered by a priest or Levite or temple prophet.

91:14 *"Because he loves me," says the* LORD. "Because" is the Hebrew word *ki*, which begins a new section of the psalm (see "Outline/Structure"), and God is the speaker in this section. The verb "loves" connotes affection (cleaving, yearning, desiring) and is used of one's love for another person (Gen. 34:8; Deut. 21:11), of Yahweh's love for Israel (Deut. 7:7; 10:15), and of one's devotion to God (Ps. 91:14). The subject of the verb (NIV: "he") is the psalmist or Israel. But to whom is God speaking that he would reference the psalmist and Israel in the third person rather than speaking to them in the second person, "you"? Perhaps this would be the point in a temple service that the priest or Levite would respond to this psalm of trust with these words of God.

he acknowledges my name. The verb is "know" and implies an intimacy with God, not merely information about who he is. It is essentially synonymous with "loves" in the first half of the verse.

91:16 *long life.* In verses 14–16 the Lord promises not only protection but fullness of life, which constitutes, at least in part, the concept of "salvation," in this case, consisting of security, freedom from harm, and long life.

Theological Insights

Sometimes when something wonderful happens to us, out of a sense of unworthiness we ask why. Somewhere in God's eternal plan there is no doubt an answer, but from our limited perspective in time and space, there is only one answer to this question: it is God's miracle for us, or God's grace—there is no difference. Grace is the great miracle, unexplainable by the natural laws of the universe. Of course, there is a descriptive answer in the character of God: God is love; but that is not an explanation. Why does he love us? Why do we even need an explanation? Is not what we need the reality itself, and the explanation becomes a secondary issue? While the question why is not posed by the psalmist, it is nonetheless implicit in the psalm, and it is to that question that God is responding in verse 14: "Because he loves me." But that still does not tell us why. Rather it states the reality, and that is enough. Yet, while God does not explain his love, he shows it, and "he loves me" is broken down into the components of God's protective care in the oracle at the end of the psalm (91:14b–16).

Moreover, the psalmist's experience of God's protection is a wonderfully personal matter: "Only with your own eyes will you see it" (author's translation). When we are aware of the dangers but are beneficiaries of God's protection and security, it is certainly safe to say that we are carried by angels (91:11). This expression reminds us of the metaphor of 77:19, that God led the Israelites through the sea, "though [his] footprints were not seen." Like the reality of love without its explanation, we experience the reality of God's presence even though we may see only the product and not the process—we are safe! That is the special grace associated with trust in God, and it is with "our own eyes" that we see it—we are observers, not victims. And God's grace calls for no apologies.

Teaching the Text

An observation about the text of Psalm 91 might give the preacher/teacher a good starting point. The Hebrew conjunction *ki* is a key term in the structure of the psalm, introducing all three parts (see "Outline/Structure"). It is so important in the psalm that it should be understood as a prefix to every statement that follows. This "one little word," like Martin Luther's line in "A Mighty Fortress Is Our God" (see "Illustrating the Text"), functions in the psalm to assure us that God will always be with us and we can always trust him.

This one little word, "surely," dominates part 1 (91:3–8) in the first affirmation of trust, an assurance of God's deliverance from the extraordinary dangers of life, like war and pestilence: "Surely he will save you from the fowler's snare and from the deadly pestilence" (91:3). In fact, "surely" ought to prefix every clause of part 1, as the outline indicates. It functions as a signpost of God's wonderful love, reminding us that we can trust God, even in the most threatening circumstances. In essence our psalmist is affirming his words in verses 1 and 2.

We should note that our psalm *begins* with the assurance that we can trust God, and it does so by the use of God's names by which he was known to Abraham and Moses: "Most High" (*'elyon*), "the Almighty" (*shadday*), and "the LORD" (*YHWH*) (see the comments on 91:1–2). These names are code for the story of these two great ancient men of faith. God was known to Abraham as the Most High (Gen. 14), and God was known to all three patriarchs as God Almighty (Gen. 17:1; 28:3; 35:11; 43:14; 48:3; 49:25). "The LORD" (*YHWH*) was the name revealed to Moses (Exod. 3). We commonly confess our faith in the language of others, even the saints of our own world, as a generation of students has done in the pithy and memorable sayings of the revered president of Wheaton College Dr. V. Raymond Edman (see "Illustrating the Text").

This one little word (*ki*) occurs a second time to introduce part 2 of the psalm (91:9–13), and the suppliant's second affirmation of trust: "[Because] you say [in verse 2], 'The LORD is my refuge,' and [because] you make the Most High your dwelling, no harm will overtake you, no disaster will come near your tent" (91:9–10). In this part of the psalm we hear how we can trust the Lord in those circumstances of life that we call domestic, indicated by "your tent" and "your ways" (91:11). We also note that the assurance is in the remarkable detail that God commands his angels "concerning you"—that is very personal and specific! In the Old Testament, angels sometimes have the appearance of divine beings and sometimes of humans (cf. Heb. 13:2). The story of the lady in the gray dress and yellow sweater is a striking example of the human form (see "Illustrating the Text").

The third occurrence of this one little word (*ki*) introduces part 3 of our psalm (91:14–16), which is remarkably God's affirmation of trust in the psalmist, rather than the psalmist's affirmation of trust in God. This is the first time we hear God's voice in the psalm: "Because he loves me" (literally, "because he clings to me" [in love]). There are other notable moments in Scripture when God affirms us, tells us that we are doing something right, or reminds us that he is pleased with us (e.g., Matt. 25:21, 33–36; Heb. 11:16), and when we hear such affirmations, it is an extraordinary moment of grace, that God should deem us worthy of his acknowledgment. And like the other two instances of this one little word, "because" should be understood as a prefix to each statement of blessing (see "Outline/Structure"). That one little word highlights the reasons we can trust God and the reasons God can trust us, an extraordinary formula of grace.

Illustrating the Text

He will command his angels concerning you.

History: On May 15, 2014, the National September 11 Memorial & Museum was dedicated and opened to the public in New York City. Among the many artifacts from that horrible day in American history is the following letter of a survivor rescued by an unknown policeman. Her letter does not mention "angels," but sometimes angels choose to use human hands to pick us up lest we dash our foot against a stone (cf. 91:12 KJV):

> You literally picked me up off the sidewalk that day. I was on the east side of City Hall Park and after the second WTC collapse I was running from the wall of dust and flying debris when I fell. I was terrified—people were running over me and past me. You lifted me off the ground and said "run with me." After a few blocks when I said I didn't think I could run anymore, you said run just a little further and then if you can't run I'll carry you. You got me to a safe place and went back to help others. I didn't get your badge number or your name but I will never forget you. I pray that you are safe. You and your brother and sister officers are one of the great things about this city.
>
> With love and gratitude,
> Ann (the lady in the gray dress
> and yellow sweater)

We sometimes confess our faith in others' words.

Biography: V. Raymond Edman. As president of Wheaton College from 1940 to 1965, Dr. Edman was well known for his memorable and pithy sayings, which were an expression of his own faith and an inspiration to thousands of students through the years. Among his sayings were

"Not somehow, but triumphantly!"
"Never doubt in the dark what God told you in the light."
"Chin up, knees down!"
"It's always too soon to quit."

These faith expressions give one a sense of this man of God's persistent, trusting, and prayerful faith, and when Wheaton College students recalled these words, they often became a confession of their own faith in the words of Dr. Edman, just as our psalmist confesses his faith in the language of Abraham and Moses. In Dr. Edman's book *Not Somehow, but Triumphantly!* he includes a letter from a Wheaton alumnus who was a resident in neurosurgery at a New York hospital and was called on to assist in emergency surgery on another Wheaton alumnus. During the operation the patient had a cardiac arrest, and the surgical staff tried unsuccessfully for almost an hour to restart the patient's heart. Then as the unnamed alumnus began to take his turn, someone said, "We might as well quit." Immediately the young resident remembered Dr. Edman's saying "It's always too soon to quit," and he began to pray. Suddenly the EKG spontaneously reverted to a normal rhythm, pulse and blood pressure rebounded, and the patient survived and recovered.[8]

When we hear the name *Shadday*, we think of Abraham, and the name *Yahweh*, we think of Moses, and in a real sense key in to their lives of faith.[9] Of interest, and somewhat of an uncanny nature, Dr. Edman gave a chapel talk at Wheaton College on September 22, 1967, entitled "In the Presence of the King," which, one might say, became his "password" to glory, for during that sermon he suddenly passed into the eternal King's presence.

One little word

Hymn: "A Mighty Fortress Is Our God," by Martin Luther. While Luther in his reformation hymn did not necessarily have in mind the "one little word" that I have stressed in the psalm, he nevertheless used this phrase as an expression of how God, by his character of power and grace, can defeat his foes with "one little word":

> And though this world, with devils filled,
>   should threaten to undo us,
> We will not fear, for God hath willed
>   his truth to triumph through us.
> The Prince of Darkness grim,
>   we tremble not for him;
> His rage we can endure,
>   for lo, his doom is sure;
> One little word shall fell him.

"I Sing for Joy at What Your Hands Have Done"

Big Idea

God's power to reverse the forces of evil in our lives creates joy.

Key Themes

- The joy of the kingdom is derived from God's works and the triumph of righteousness.
- There is no age limitation on bearing the fruit of the gospel.

Understanding the Text

This is a psalm of thanksgiving (see the sidebar "Psalms of Thanksgiving" in the unit on Pss. 9–10).[1] Its status in Judaism as the Sabbath psalm is assured by its title, and it exhibits, whether coincidentally or intentionally, the joy that came to be associated with the Sabbath and the fact that Sabbath prayers include not petitions but only praise. In the late exilic or early postexilic background of Book 4, the title may not be coincidental but intentional, to draw attention to the Sabbath, a religious institution that came to be a dogma of Second Temple Judaism.

The Text in Context

This is the only psalm in the Hebrew Psalter that is assigned to a day of the week. The Mishnah (*Tamid* 7.4) lists the psalms for each day of the week (ca. AD 200), and the Septuagint too has added all the daily designations (day 1, Ps. 24; day 2, Ps. 48; day 3, Ps. 82; day 4, Ps. 94; day 5, Ps. 81; day 6, Ps. 93; day 7, Ps. 92).

Outline/Structure

1. The hymnic introduction: God's constant love "in the morning" and "faithfulness" at night (92:1–4)
   a. Making music to the name of the Most High (92:1–3)
   b. God's works, the general reason for the worshiper's joy (92:4)

The biblical world was a musical world, illustrated by this Sabbath song that was to be sung or recited to the music of three instruments: the ten-stringed instrument, the lyre, and the harp. The NIV reads the first two instruments as a single one, following the Septuagint and Syriac, and also the term for a single instrument in Psalms 33:2 and 144:9 ("ten-stringed lyre").

While opinions vary on the nature of these instruments (see the sidebar "Musical Instruments in Psalm 33" in the unit on Ps. 33), Hossfeld and Zenger insist that the traditional lute, harp, and cithara do not accurately represent them. Rather, they are three different types of lyres, requiring differing playing techniques and representing different tone ranges. Hossfeld and Zenger propose the following: the "ten-stringed" instrument was probably a lyre, as was also the second instrument (a tenor or bass instrument; not translated in the NIV), played without a pick, and the third, the "harp," was a hand lyre, small and higher pitched than either of the other two.[a]

[a] Hossfeld and Zenger, *Psalms 3*, 437.

2. The hymn: The first reason for the worshiper's joy—the defeat of God's enemies (92:5–11)
   a. The destruction of God's enemies (92:5–7)
   b. The center of the psalm (92:8)
   c. The destruction of God's enemies (92:9–11)
3. The hymn: The second reason for the worshiper's joy—the triumph of the righteous (92:12–15)

Historical and Cultural Background

One might wonder why Psalm 92 is the only psalm that bears the daily psalm designation in its title. The Mishnah interprets the psalm as a description of the eschatological Sabbath (*Tamid* 7.4), and, as "Teaching the Text" seeks to illustrate, the psalm exposes both aspects of God's kingdom: the destruction of evil and the triumph of right. Book 4, having been edited in the exilic or early postexilic age, would naturally sound the hopeful theme of God's kingdom. It is all the more appropriate when we recognize that this hope grew out of the smoldering ashes of Israel's greatest tragedy, that of the Babylonian exile.

Interpretive Insights

Title *A psalm. A song. For the Sabbath day.* The double designation of this psalm as "a psalm" and "a song" also occurs with Psalms 30; 48 (terms reversed); and 67, but the Masoretes separated "song" from "for the Sabbath day," suggesting that the last phrase could have been added as a later designation. The Levites sang the psalm of the day during the daily sacrifice that was held in the morning and afternoon (Exod. 29:38–42; Num. 28:1–8). In our psalm the speaker may be the king.

92:1 *It is good to praise the* Lord. See "Theological Insights." See also Psalm 147:1.

make music. This verb (root, *zmr*) means to sing or to play a musical instrument. In view of the instruments mentioned in verse 3, we may assume the latter.

92:3 *melody of the harp.* The Hebrew word for "melody" occurs also in Psalm 19:14 (NIV: "meditation"), and in Lamentations 3:62 with a nonmusical sense ("mutter"). Here it may suggest "strumming" of the instruments while the poem is recited.[2]

92:4 *make me glad.* Verses 4 and 9 begin with the word "because" (NIV: "for"), giving the reason for the psalmist's singing of God's love and faithfulness (cf. v. 2). The tone of the song is one of joy, which is quite in keeping with the "joy of the Sabbath" in Judaism.

92:5 *How great are your works.* Verses 5–15 seem to be the song itself.

92:6 *Senseless people . . . fools.* As in wisdom literature, the "fool" (synonym of "senseless people") is one who ignores God and his ethical requirements.

92:7 *that . . . they will be destroyed forever.* The NIV appropriately begins this verse with "that" (not in the Hebrew text) to indicate the object of the verbs "know" and "understand" of verse 6. See 103:15–16.

92:8 *But you,* Lord, *are forever exalted.* There is general agreement that this is the theological center of the psalm, not in the sense that it is the theme, but the verse provides a climax toward which the psalm builds. Even though the wicked will be destroyed, God will be eternally exalted.

92:9 *For surely.* Like verse 4, this verse begins with "because" (NIV: "for") to provide further reason for the psalmist's rejoicing—the Lord's enemies will perish.

92:10 *my horn.* The metaphor of the ox's horn implies strength.

fine oils have been poured on me. "Poured" is a different Hebrew verb from that of 23:5 and carries the sense of "to mix," perhaps suggesting a more generous use of oil than the usual "anointing" required.

92:11 *My eyes have seen.* The verb "have seen" implies "to gaze" with a spirit of triumph ("gloat").

92:12 *like a palm tree.* The palm tree blossoms every year, whereas the "evildoers" of verse 7 flourish like the grass and then fade. See the sidebar "The Palm and the Cedar."

92:13 *planted in the house of the* Lord. Since there were no trees in the "courts" of the temple, this is a metaphor describing a truth we have seen many times in the Psalms, that the Lord's house is a place where the righteous not only gather but flourish, as if they were plants growing there.

92:14 *bear fruit in old age.* Even as our physical powers decline with advancing age, the spiritual nature of the righteous produces fruit in old age. This is typically a wisdom motif (see 71:18).

92:15 *The Lord is upright.* God is "straight" (NIV: "upright") in his relations with his creatures (see Deut. 32:4).

Theological Insights

When understood fragmentarily, the biblical faith will sometimes, lamentably, produce a fragmented understanding of God. Yet there are key concepts that serve to obviate this tendency and promote wholeness in our understanding of God. In our psalm the unifying concept is *good* or *goodness*, which occurs often in the Psalter. This psalm begins with the assertion that "it is good to praise the Lord" (92:1a). The word "good" (*tob*) is inclusive of the aesthetic and the ethical. The Scriptures begin with the narrative of creation in Genesis 1, and that creation narrative is interspersed with the observation, "And God saw that it was good," and at the end of the narrative, the superlative pronouncement, "It was very good." The aesthetically "beautiful" and the ethically "good" are comprehended together in this observation.[3] From the beginning of the world, therefore, we are justified, indeed compelled, to think comprehensively about God's goodness.

When Moses prays that the Lord show him his glory, that request is denied, but the Lord volunteers an alternative: he will cause all his "goodness" to pass before Moses and will proclaim his name in Moses's presence (Exod. 33:19). God's glory is the ultimate glimpse of God, described as seeing his face, but the Lord permits Moses only to see his goodness, suggesting that it is short of his glory. Another psalmist, perhaps reflecting Moses's own experience, exclaims: "O, how abundant is your goodness" (Ps. 31:19 ESV).

In Psalm 69:16 the phrase "the goodness of your love" brings together two of God's communicable attributes, each defining the other. It is God's "loving goodness" and God's "good love," divinely revealed, and also portrayed in human life, that is the ultimate ethical dimension of God's character. And the aesthetic beauty of humanity and the created world is an expression of that.

Teaching the Text

Referring to the "Outline/Structure" rubric above, we may build our sermon or lesson around the theme of joy. In this case, we should make the emotional tone of the sermon or lesson one of joy. Verse 4 begins with the word "because" (NIV: "for"; see the comments on 92:4 above) and sets forth the first reason for the worshiper's joy: God's works. Specifically, the enemies of the kingdom of God will perish like grass that flourishes and then dies (92:7). We may define the "wicked" as those who oppose God and his gospel—that is the primary meaning. Yet there are many other enemies that sometimes make this world a miserable place for us: disease, broken relationships, death, and so forth. The thought of God's reversal of these threatening conditions is enough to create a new sense of joy (see also "Illustrating the Text" in the unit on Ps. 21).

The second reason for the worshiper's joy is the triumph of the righteous (92:12–15). It is the reverse of the evil that has plagued the psalmist, or the positive picture of the coming kingdom of God. We can take advantage of the metaphor of the palm and cedar planted in the house of the Lord and flourishing "in the courts of our God" (92:12–13). The lesson is that God's house is the place where believers mature and flourish. Admittedly, the temple and the church are not the same kind of institution, but they both serve, though not exclusively, as the place and the symbol of worship in Judaism and Christianity, respectively. The lesson we draw from our text, however, is that worship is a lifelong endeavor, for the righteous "bear fruit in old age" and stay "fresh and green." We also may point out how it is easy to succumb to the idea, culturally generated, that we grow too old to be of any benefit to the church and kingdom; the psalmist is unaware of any such limitations.

Moreover, the righteous do not or should not lose their verbal witness as they advance in age, barring, of course, mental and physical impairments. This all sums up these two reasons for the worshiper's joy: the Lord is in a right relationship with his people, and "there is no wickedness in him" (92:15). We might further observe that the Jewish understanding of the psalm was that of the future Sabbath of the kingdom of God.

Illustrating the Text

God's majesty is proclaimed in nature.

Biography: **Lilias Trotter.** In 1876, when only a teenager, Lilias Trotter (1853–1928), a member of a wealthy London family, was befriended by John Ruskin of Oxford University, perhaps the greatest art critic and social philosopher of the Victorian era. Their friendship would last until Ruskin's death in 1899. Ruskin recognized Trotter's phenomenal artistic ability, and at a critical stage in her life, he articulated the future in art that lay before her, predicting that if she would devote herself to her art, "she would be the greatest living painter and do things that would be Immortal."[4] But Trotter was torn between her art and God's call, and in 1879 she made the choice in favor of God's call, writing, "I see as clear as daylight now, I cannot give myself to painting in the way he [Ruskin] means and continue still to 'seek first the Kingdom of God and His Righteousness.'"[5] Subsequent to that decisive moment of surrender to God's will, she wrote about "the liberty of those who have nothing to lose, because they have nothing to keep."[6] Yet her sense of God's majesty portrayed in the beauty of nature (92:4) and the proclamation of God's love in the morning and his faithfulness in the evening continued to mark her life and witness: "Is it not so that the Lord looks down on the earth, it may be, alongside the radiant beauty of His Kingdom already set up in other worlds? He sees the slowly swelling buds of His dawning springtime here, and is glad."[7]

The righteous are "planted in the house of the Lord."

Quote: **Daniel Poling.** The description of the righteous "planted in the house of the Lord" and flourishing "in the courts of the Lord" is an apt description of the life of faith. It is a life that produces fruit, irrespective of advancing years—"They will still bear fruit in old age," and their ongoing witness is not to their own vitality but to the Lord's strength and purity (92:15). Daniel Poling tells the story of his friend E. Francis Hyde, a gifted musician, business entrepreneur, and patron of the arts. On one occasion Poling asked him what his secret was, and Hyde, somewhat hesitatingly, said, "I never reminisce." And then he proceeded to relate something of his life's story. Poling commented, "He had his memories, but he did not live in them. They traveled with him, but always his face was front and he was on the march."[8] We might say the same for Israel. They traveled with their memories but did not live *in* them; they lived *with* them. And this is the secret power of memories in life and faith. In fact, the life of the righteous is extended in the direction of proclaiming the character of God: "The LORD is upright; he is my Rock, and there is no wickedness in him" (92:15).

"The Lord Reigns, He Is Robed in Majesty"

Big Idea

God's sovereignty is one of the most pervasive and intimate doctrines in Scripture: God is in control of the world and of our lives.

Key Themes

- God's sovereign reign means that he holds claim to every square inch of our lives.
- God's throne and God's house are symbols of God's sovereignty, and his laws are the instruments by which he rules.

Understanding the Text

This psalm is generally classified as a hymn that celebrates Yahweh's kingship, thus a psalm of the heavenly King. It begins with the declaration, "The Lord reigns," which is also the opening declaration of Psalms 97 and 99. As a hymn, it is characterized by the praise of God for his wonderful works in history and for his character.[1]

The Text in Context

The major contextual issue with Psalm 93 is the cadre of psalms concentrated in Book 4 that declare Yahweh's kingship: "The Lord reigns" (see the sidebar). Psalm 47 contains the same acclamation ("God reigns," 47:8), though being found in the Elohistic Psalter, it exhibits a preference for the divine name "God" (*'elohim*).

There are also verbal links between Psalms 93 and 92 ("exalted" in 92:8, 10a and "on high" in 93:4c [same root]; "very" in 92:5b and 93:5a [ESV]; "house" in 92:13a and 93:5a), suggesting their close relationship. In fact, Psalm 93 complements Psalm 92 by exalting Yahweh as king. An extrabiblical reason for reading these two psalms together is that Psalm 93 was recited by the Levites in the second temple on the sixth day (Friday), and Psalm 92 on the seventh day (the Sabbath).

Of special interest is the kinship of the poem in 1 Chronicles 16:8–36, which celebrates David's bringing the ark to Jerusalem, an event of gigantic proportions in the history and theology of ancient Israel, virtually comparable to the crossing of the Red Sea.

This psalm shares language and ideas with Moses's Song of the Sea (Exod. 15), as represented by table 1. It is significant that the triumphant song of victory following the miracle at the Red Sea becomes an instrument to celebrate the hope that is still enshrined in Israel's soul, even though they have suffered the humiliation of the exile. With the awakening of new hope, however, the exiles' "Red Sea," like the Red Sea of the exodus, seems to be behind them as they celebrate Yahweh's sovereign reign.

Table 1. Shared Vocabulary between Psalm 93 and Exodus 15

Psalm 93	Exodus 15
"The Lord reigns" (93:1a)	"The Lord reigns for ever and ever" (15:18)
"He is robed in *majesty* [*ge'ut*]" (93:1b)	"For he is *highly exalted* [*ga'oh ga'ah*]" (same root; 15:21b)
"And armed with *strength*" (93:1c)	"The Lord is my *strength*. . . . In your *strength* you have guided [NIV: "you will guide"] them to your holy dwelling" (15:13b)
"Your throne was *established*" (93:2a)	"The place, Lord, you made for your dwelling, the sanctuary, Lord, your hands *established*" (15:17c)
"The *great waters, mightier*" (*mayim rabbim 'addirim*) (93:4a–b)	"In the *mighty waters* [*bᵉmayim 'addirim*]" (15:10b)
"Breakers of the *sea*" (93:4b)	"He has hurled into the *sea*" (15:1b)
"*Holiness* adorns your house" (93:5b)	"To your *holy* dwelling" (15:13b)

Note: Based on Hakham's list of parallels (*Psalms*, 2:382).

Outline/Structure

1. Acclamation: "The Lord reigns" (93:1a)
2. Declaration: (Because the Lord reigns) the world is firm and secure (93:1b–2)
3. Declaration: (Because the Lord reigns) he was Victor over the chaotic waters (93:3–4)
4. Declaration: (Because the Lord reigns) his laws, like the world, are firm, and holiness adorns his house (93:5)

Historical and Cultural Background

This psalm's composition has been dated as early as the tenth century BC and as late as the postexilic era.[2] Howard argues for a date of the tenth century BC, perhaps even earlier.[3]

"The Lord Reigns": Psalms of the Heavenly King

The declaration "the Lord reigns" occurs in 93:1; 96:10; 97:1; 99:1; and in 47:8 ("God reigns"). Mowinckel, with virtually no supporting evidence in the Hebrew Bible, has proposed that Israel celebrated an annual "enthronement festival," patterned after an annual Babylonian festival that acclaimed Marduk as king. He thus translates this clause as "Yahweh has become king."[a] The proponents of this hypothesis surmise that the ritual of this "enthronement festival" involved removal of the ark from the holy of holies and its return with this acclamation. The discussion, of course, has advanced well beyond the initial proposal, for example, with Petersen's *Royal God*, which provides a negative critique of the hypothesis, and Geller's article "Myth and Syntax in Psalm 93," in which he proposes a divine combat motif over an enthronement motif.[b]

Quite contrary to an annual royal coronation, Psalm 93 traces Yahweh's kingship back to creation, and I would prefer to call these psalms "the psalms of the heavenly King," or the "kingship of Yahweh psalms," in that they acclaim Yahweh king and confirm his reign over Israel and the world. We can further restrict these psalms to those that (1) include the acclamation (see above), and/or (2) call Yahweh king (95:3; 98:6; 99:4). This gives us Psalms 47; 93; and 95–99.[c]

The function of the psalms of the heavenly King in Book 4 is to divert attention from the ostensible failure of the Davidic kingship (Ps. 89) and to reaffirm Yahweh's kingship, upon which Israel's kingship is built. Book 4 does that in two ways, by (1) sounding this clear theme that Yahweh is still king over Israel and the universe, regardless of the state of the Davidic kingship, and (2) shifting the dramatic focus from the Davidic covenant to the Mosaic and Abrahamic covenants (103:7; 105:6, 26; 106:16, 23).[d] Since Book 4 probably received its present form sometime in the late exilic or early postexilic period, we need to view these psalms, with their optimistic perspective on the future, against such hopeful developments as the Decree of Cyrus (538 BC) and the rebuilding of the temple (520–516 BC). See Ezra 1:1–3; Haggai 1; see also Isaiah 52:7.

[a] Mowinckel, *Psalms in Israel's Worship*, 1:115.
[b] Petersen, *Royal God*; Geller, "Myth and Syntax in Psalm 93."
[c] See Howard, *Structure of Psalms 93–100*, 119–31, for an expansion of this group of psalms to 47 and 93–100. Watts ("Yahweh Malak Psalms," 343) finds four features of the psalms of the heavenly King: (1) a universal concern for all peoples and the whole earth, (2) references to other gods, (3) characteristic acts of Yahweh (making, establishing, sitting, judging, etc.), and (4) expressions of the attitude of praise before the heavenly King. This has led him to define this group as Psalms 47; 93; and 95–99.
[d] See Bullock, *Encountering*, 188–94.

The metaphors that describe God's majestic reign are images of royalty. First is the king's stately apparel, "robed in majesty" (93:1), with the fuller picture left to the reader's imagination. Second, Yahweh is "girded with strength" (NIV: "armed with strength"), a word picture of an athlete's clothing worn around his waist to assure him of more physical power.

Interpretive Insights

Title Psalm 93 has no title, but the Septuagint provides one, "A Psalm for the Eve of the Sabbath."

93:1 *The Lord reigns.* The verb is a Hebrew perfect, which can mean "the Lord has become king" and his reign continues (e.g., 2 Sam. 15:10; 16:8; 1 Kings 1:11, 13, 18). In the Hebrew of this verse, the subject precedes the verb, drawing attention to the fact that it is Yahweh who reigns.[4] See the sidebar.[5]

robed in majesty and armed with strength. Spurgeon observes that the Lord is clothed, "not with emblems of majesty, but with majesty itself."[6]

the world is established. This clause connects the images of "king" and "creator," implying that Yahweh has been king from the time of creation.

93:2 *Your throne . . . ; you are from all eternity.* God's throne is a metaphor for his sovereignty and justice (9:4; 89:14; 122:5). While "from all eternity" can mean "from of old," the fact that God reigns from the beginning of the world takes the reader back to "eternity," a concept that is probably more implied than explicit in the Psalms, but nevertheless, in the broad biblical perspective, it is an acceptable translation. After God's work of creation, he takes his place on the throne, an idea alluded to in Genesis 2:2–3 ("On the seventh day he rested from all his work"). See also Psalms 95:11; 132:14; Exodus 31:16–17. David's rest from all his enemies models the rest of God after creation (2 Sam. 7:1).[7]

93:3 *The seas.* Most likely influenced by the reference to creation (as well as "sea" in 93:4b), the NIV translates the Hebrew word "rivers/floods" as "seas." Isaiah 17:12–13 uses the metaphor of the roaring of many waters to speak of the tumult of the nations. Delitzsch endorses this view, understanding "rivers" as an allusion to the rivers of the powerful empires of the world (the Nile of Egypt, the Euphrates and Tigris of Assyria and Babylonia).[8] Others view it as an allusion to creation, suggesting the threat of the primordial waters of Genesis 1, where God speaks to the waters and, like any loyal subject, they obey (Gen. 1:9–10). The powers of chaos are symbolized by "the seas" in other places (Job 38:8–11; Pss. 74:12–17; 104:7–9). Either position is possible, but with the allusions to creation in verse 1, the connection to Genesis 1 and 2 seems preferable.

93:4 *mightier than the breakers of the sea.* God is the reference, and the obedient waters of Genesis 1:9–10 are the evidence of his overwhelming power.

93:5 *Your statutes, Lord, stand firm.* Connecting the truth of God's statutes to the Lord of creation is an effective way to validate the law, whose truth stands as long as creation stands. The fact that God's house stands apart from all other institutions of creation ("holiness adorns your house") can be attributed to God's laws (Torah), which make it holy. This fact is not disassociated from God's rule over the world, for just as God has created the world (93:1c) and summoned it to obedience (symbolized by the throne of 93:2), so he has established the operating standards ("your statutes") for the good of humankind. The fact that we have this clear reference to God's "statutes" here in Book 4 is likely in celebration of the Torah, already acclaimed by Psalms 1 and 19 and in anticipation of the Torah emphasis that we find in Book 5 (see "Additional Insights: The Egyptian Hallel [Psalms 113–18]," following the unit on Ps. 113).

holiness adorns your house. Both "your statutes" and "your house" connect the Creator of the world to the real life of Israel. The Creator calls Israel to a life of obedience to his "statutes" and manifests his presence in the "holiness" of his house.

Theological Insights

God's sovereignty means that he must have power over every aspect of the created order. The psalms of the heavenly King spell that out in multiple dimensions. For God to be sovereign, he must have power over all other gods—if, indeed, they exist (96:4–6; 97:7, 9)—and have control over creation (93:1b–3; 96:1–5, 10–13; 97:9; 98:7–9). And his power does not stop there—he must have sovereign sway over the nations (96:1, 3, 9; 97:1, 5–7; 98:7–9), be sovereign in justice (96:10–13; 97:2, 6; 99:4) and judgment (96:13; 97:8; 98:9), and be sovereign over the future (97:2–7; 98:9).[9] Obviously, this is a big order, and the question that arises is whether or not Yahweh indeed reigns in all these dimensions of his world. For those who wonder, the messianic interpretation is a necessary hermeneutic to complete this picture. Both Calvin and Delitzsch, for example, consider these psalms to be a description of the messianic kingdom.[10] They declare that the present reality of God's kingdom on earth gives us a picture of the coming kingdom (96:1–13; 98:7–9), a picture that will be complete only when heaven's voices announce: "The kingdom of the world has become the kingdom of our Lord and of his Messiah, and he will reign for ever and ever" (Rev. 11:15).

Teaching the Text

The theme of Psalm 93 is God's sovereignty, a theme we hear often in the Psalter, and never more clearly than here. When we speak of divine sovereignty, it sometimes sounds so distant and theoretical. But God's sovereignty is one of the most intimate messages of Scripture. It means, quite simply, that God is in control of the world and of our lives. This psalm spans history from the time "the world is established" (93:1c) to the era of God's revelation of his "statutes" (93:5a) to his people's response of worship in God's "house" (93:5b). To drive this point home, we can focus on the three associated ideas that support the theme of divine sovereignty: God's throne, God's statutes, and God's holiness.

First is God's throne, which represents no newly sprung kingdom, for it was "established long ago" (93:2a), suggesting all the accoutrements of kingship, which we may choose to spell out briefly. Homiletically, one of the principles of good preaching and teaching is to know the larger context of our text. This is an opportunity to bring into focus the dimensions of the Lord's sovereignty as spelled out in "Theological Insights," especially to stress the practical nature of divine sovereignty. What if we did not have the assurance that God is sovereign and that the world's affairs—and ours too—do not happen helter-skelter? It would be appropriate to bring in Romans 8:28 to assure our listeners that God is in control of every aspect of our lives (also 2 Cor. 4:15)—and that is intimate!

The second associated idea is God's "statutes" (93:5a). Every absolute monarch issues decrees that his or her subjects are to obey. God's decrees are as "firm" as the world God has established (93:1c). We should explain to our listeners that the divine "statutes" are reasonable and capable of being obeyed. God's commandments are his enablements, as the saying goes. If we want to reduce these to a manageable number, we can remind our audience that they may be summed up in the commandments to love God and to love our neighbor (Mark 12:28–31).

The third associated idea is God's "holiness" (93:5b). "Holiness" implies that God is separated from this sinful world, and he calls Israel and all adherents of the biblical faith to exhibit his character in a holy life (Lev. 19:2; 1 Pet. 1:16). In Leviticus 19:2, which commands us, "Be holy because I, the LORD your God, am holy," that command is followed by a series of practical prescriptions for living, climaxing in "Love your neighbor as yourself" (Lev. 19:18).[11] In keeping God's "statutes" we are made holy, and by our worship in his "house" we celebrate his holiness. This psalm binds these three associated ideas together to celebrate God's sovereign reign in the world and in our personal lives. They are a single piece.

Illustrating the Text

The one truth is God.

History: In the beginning of 1939 the *British Weekly* invited two prominent pastors, Dr. J. D. Jones and Dr. D. G. Campbell Morgan, to write a New Year's special greeting. Working independently, they both wrote on the sovereignty of God, an appropriate topic for that tumultuous time. Referring back to the First World War, Dr. Jones said, "That was my own sheet-anchor during the dark and testing years of the Great War. The ultimate issues were not in the hands of the Kaiser and his soldiers. The destinies of nations were not settled by machine-guns and Big Berthas. . . . The future of the world was not at the mercy of the big battalions—it was God's world, and it was His will that would get done. I preach that same great truth in these days of crisis and terror." Dr. Morgan wrote similarly, "What is the message that was in the past, and is still, the one all-inclusive word that I am attempting to utter? It is that, to quote the old-fashioned phrase, of the Sovereignty of God. I am firmly convinced that what I once heard you say is an abiding and inescapable truth, namely, 'The one fact is God, all other things are circumstances.'"[12]

Christ cries "Mine!" over every square inch of the domain of our human life.

Quote: **Abraham Kuyper.** When we hear the commanding words that begin this psalm, "The LORD reigns" (93:1a), we are hearing the Old Testament term—note that it is *verbal*—that Christians describe as the "sovereignty of God." Every person who falls on his or her knees in prayer to the God of Scripture in effect acknowledges that God is sovereign. Otherwise the prayers would be meaningless, because people would be praying to a God who may or may not be able to do anything for them. And if God is surrounded by that kind of uncertainty, he is not sovereign. Abraham Kuyper (1837–1920), Dutch theologian and a prime minister of the Netherlands, gave the inaugural address at the founding of the Free University of Amsterdam on October 20, 1880, in which he said that "there is not a square inch in the whole domain of our human life of which Christ, who is our Sovereign of *all*, does not cry 'Mine!'"[13] In our psalm the seas "lifted up their voice" to declare God's sovereign reign (93:3–4), much like the heavens in Psalm 19, with the immediate manifestation visible in the Lord's "statutes" (93:5a).

"The LORD Knows All Human Plans; He Knows That They Are Futile"

Big Idea

God's blessing is his primary mode of relating to humanity, and lest we misunderstand God's judgment, when we are disobedient, his judgment is the secondary mode, not the preferred.

Key Themes

- When God gives us his best, our response should be to return his favor in kind.
- God's sovereignty is not unchallenged as long as there is injustice in the world.

Understanding the Text

In view of the destruction of Jerusalem by the Babylonians, the historical backdrop of Book 4, Psalm 94 is appropriately a community and individual lament (see "Outline/Structure"), sounding the urgency for God to shine forth as the God who will not let injustice rule the day.

The Text in Context

Howard insists that there is significant cohesiveness between Psalms 93 and 94, with Psalm 93 affirming Yahweh's "sovereignty over rebellious nature, and Psalm 94 affirming his sovereignty over rebellious humanity."[1] So long as human injustice is an issue in the world, it poses an obstacle for the doctrine of divine sovereignty ("The LORD reigns," 93:1). Psalm 94 unmasks the problem to a degree and offers a solution (94:23), even if delayed. The wicked's oppressive behavior (94:5–6, 20–21) is the bottom line of injustice, as evidenced by the fact that it spans the full spectrum of prophetic preaching from Amos to Malachi and is among the reasons the Judean kingdom fell to the Babylonians in 586 BC (Ezek. 16:49; 22:7–8).

In 1 Corinthians 3:20 Paul quotes Psalm 94:11 from the Septuagint to make the point that the Corinthians who think they are "wise" should be aware that "the Lord knows that the thoughts of the wise are futile." These leaders value their thoughts over God's wisdom.

Outline/Structure

The psalm falls into two parts: a national lament (94:1–15) and an individual lament (94:16–23):

1. National lament (94:1–15)
   a. Address to God (94:1–7)
   b. Address to the wicked (94:8–11)
   c. Address to God (94:12–13)
   d. Corrective plan of justice (94:14–15)
2. Individual lament (94:16–23)
   a. Psalmist's complaint (94:16–17)
   b. Address to God (94:18–20)
   c. Psalmist's assurance (94:21–23)

Historical and Cultural Background

According to the Mishnah, this psalm was recited by the Levites in the second temple on Wednesdays (*Tamid* 7.4). The Septuagint also includes this notation in its title, as well as an attribution of the psalm to David.

Interpretive Insights

94:1 *a God who avenges. O God who avenges.* The repeated clause is similar to the repetitive style of 92:9 and 93:3, obviously for emphasis (see 94:23). The beginning of the psalm may allude to the Song of Moses (Deut. 32:35–43).

94:2 *Rise up, Judge of the earth.* The universal tone suggests the universal nature of the problem of injustice (see Gen. 18:25).

the proud. These are individuals who have lifted themselves up against God, who refuse to recognize God as God, a disposition that also distorts one's relationship to one's fellow human beings (e.g., Job 40:11, 12; Ps. 123:4; Isa. 2:12).[2]

94:3 *the wicked.* These could be either individuals within the community or foreigners. The internal social oppression mentioned in verses 5–6 resembles that described by the prophets (e.g., Isa. 1:17, 23; Jer. 7:5–7; Mic. 3:5), so it is likely internal, not foreign, for in Book 5 the wicked are more internal than external. The psalmist's response to the arguments posed by the wicked in verses 9–10 is similar to Isaiah's words in Isaiah 29:16. The wicked thought God took no notice of their oppressive behavior (94:7), but the Babylonian exile, the backdrop event of Book 4, is evidence that he did and that he punishes wickedness. Further, the exile was divine punishment for Israel's internal sins (Zech. 1:2–6).

94:5 *your inheritance.* This can mean both the people of Israel and the land of Israel. Given the historical situation, both meanings are probably intended.

94:6 *the widow . . . the foreigner . . . the fatherless.* These terms represent three defenseless classes of people, whom the Torah often issues warnings about (e.g., Deut. 24:17; 27:19).

94:7 *The LORD does not see.* Even though the Lord made our sense of sight, the wicked claim he does not see their wickedness.

94:8 *you senseless ones.* The term parallels the word "fools" in the second half of the verse, as in 92:6. Now they are addressed directly (cf. 94:7).

94:9 *ear not hear . . . eye not see.* The human senses are a copy of the Creator's senses, and certainly he uses his own senses to discern what is going on in the world. The wicked have grossly underestimated God's ability to perceive what is going on in his world (see Prov. 20:12).

94:10 *Does he who disciplines nations not punish?* The Babylonians may be in view here as the object of God's punishment for their destructive behavior. The Lord disciplines both nations and individuals (94:12).

teaches mankind. While the source of God's teaching is not specified with regard to the nations, it is stipulated as "your law" in regard to Israel (94:12).

94:11 *The LORD knows all human plans . . . that they are futile.* This verse answers the questions of 94:9–10. In God's eternal master plan only his plans succeed, regardless of how we insist on putting our own plans into place (see Prov. 16:3).

94:12 *Blessed is the one you discipline, LORD.* This beatitude is reminiscent of those in 1:1; 32:1, 2; and 41:1. It is characteristic of wisdom thought, as are other features of this psalm (94:9–10, Creator; 94:8, "fools"; 94:10b, God as Teacher).

from your law. This implies that the "law" (*torah*) contains a wide spectrum of instruction, rather than a restricted body of instruction.[3] The *torah* is a sourcebook of instruction for life.

94:13 *you grant them relief.* The righteous, whom God instructs from the "law" (94:12b), do not cry out in their affliction but wait until the wicked are punished, which is the goal of God's instruction (94:13).

94:14 *For the LORD will not reject his people.* This psalm is a reassurance that the circumstances do not portend the Lord's abandonment of Israel, and this verse contains the first promise that grows out of the beatitude of verse 12 (see 94:5). If this psalm, as the other psalms of the heavenly King, comes from the exilic or early postexilic period, affirming God's election of Israel, it would arise naturally out of the messianic atmosphere that had developed around the Decree of Cyrus (538 BC) and the rebuilding of the temple (520–516 BC).

94:15 *Judgment will again be founded on righteousness.* A second promise, that the perverted justice of the time will again be turned to righteous judgment, accords with Isaiah's view of Jerusalem's renewed future (Isa. 1:26; 59:9–21).

and all the upright in heart will follow it. This is probably not a corrective for the righteous ("upright in heart") but a prediction that they will no longer suffer their earlier oppression.[4]

94:16 *Who will rise up for me against the wicked?* This verse begins the individual lament. Twice the psalmist speaks in the first-person singular (94:16–19 and 22–23; note the plural "our" in 94:23b). In the first instance he speaks about his fate under the dispensation of the wicked (94:16–17), and in the second instance, about God's help in his time of trouble (94:22–23). The "wicked" may be those who, by their immoral and idolatrous practices, have brought down the Judean kingdom.

94:17 *Unless the* Lord *had given me help.* This is the answer to the question of verse 16: the one who will arise against the wicked is the Lord; and had the Lord not intervened into Israel's precarious situation, the psalmist individually and the people corporately might have been destroyed.

94:20 *a corrupt throne.* Literally, "a throne of destructions." It may refer to the king or to the judges, or perhaps both.

94:23 *He will repay them for their sins and destroy them.* The object is the "wicked" who "band together against the righteous" (94:21a), and they are slated for divine judgment.

Theological Insights

One of the arguments of our psalmist to counter the claim of the wicked, that God does not see their evil works, is that God, the Creator of our senses, certainly uses his cognitive abilities to perceive the work of evildoers. It is an interesting way to phrase the argument; in fact, it is a reflection of our creation in the image of God: we hear, see, and reason as God does. God is the macrocosm of our human existence. That ought to alert us to the Lord's cognizance of all our human plans, which he knows are "futile" (94:11). This is the basis of the question and answer put forth in verses 16–17. This answer is confirmed in God's "unfailing love" of verse 18. Thus the poem asserts that God, by his nature reflected in our own (94:9–11), is certainly cognizant of evil and will avenge it, and by his nature, characterized by "unfailing love," will give the righteous relief while they wait for God's vengeance.

Teaching the Text

It is really difficult to preach a sermon or teach a lesson on divine judgment, unless, of course, divine love is laid alongside it—no, placed above it! How does God, in fact, govern the universe? Admittedly the observations made by the psalmist, and our personal observations, can be confusing. Thus, we might begin this message by stressing Paul's point in Romans 2:4–5, that God's primary mode of governance is to bless his people: "God's kindness is intended to lead you to repentance." God's judgment is his alternate mode of operation, and certainly not his preferred: "Because of your stubbornness and your unrepentant heart, you are storing up wrath against yourself for the day of God's wrath" (Rom. 2:5).

Psalm 94 reflects both aspects of God's mode of operation in the world. As our first point we can focus on verse 11 of part 1. There are two views in this section: the wicked claim that "The LORD does not see" (94:7); the counterclaim is that the God who gave us the capacity of perception, a capacity that mirrors God's own cognitive capabilities, knows that our human plans are futile. That is, the wicked cannot get by with their schemes.

We may make two subpoints here. One is to remark that, interestingly, the problem of injustice occurs in the midst of those psalms that declare the Lord's sovereign reign. We would expect God's sovereignty, by its very nature, to be exclusive of the problem of injustice. But the point of the juxtaposition of these two ideas is that, until we have offered some satisfactory solution to the problem of injustice, the doctrine of divine sovereignty is held in suspension.[5] The psalmist offers such a solution in verse 23, even though it may be delayed. Vengeance belongs to God. It is not our prerogative (Deut. 32:35; Isa. 63:4; Rom. 12:19; Heb. 10:30). As a second subpoint we can stress the sense of verse 13 that the righteous, who sometimes become weary of waiting for God to make all things right, can still expect some respite in the interim period while we are awaiting the day of judgment. So the pain of the delay is assuaged by the hope that the righteous are given some respite from trouble, "till a pit is dug for the wicked" (94:13). Justice delayed is not justice denied. The suppliant of Psalm 73 provides a connection to this weary waiting, for faced with the same arrogance of the wicked (73:11), he was deeply troubled until he entered the "sanctuary of God" (73:16–17). We may express this as God's grace in waiting.

The second point of our message may then focus on verse 18 of part 2. Like the psalmist of Psalm 73, our suppliant's faith was becoming uncertain ("My foot is slipping"), and then he discovered that God's "unfailing love" was his stabilizing support. We might also refer to the covenant description of the Lord in Exodus 34:6–7, where his "love" is extended "to thousands, . . . forgiving wickedness, rebellion and sin. Yet he does not leave the guilty unpunished." This is a summary of the theology of Psalm 94, and it is not coincidental that this description puts God's love first and leaves his judgment as the secondary mode of dealing with humanity. Rather than conclude the message on the note of judgment (although that is what the psalmist does, 94:23), we may stress the necessity of living a life that honors and responds favorably to the Lord's kindness (94:12, 17).

Illustrating the Text

We should give God our best.

Architecture: I have climbed the belfry towers of many of the great cathedrals in Europe and looked out over the embellishments that grace the steeples. And I have always been impressed that those details that one can't see from the ground level were crafted with the finest workmanship and from the finest materials. The craftsmen could have used the cheap stuff way up there—nobody would notice, one might think. Or they could have let the novice craft those parts of the cathedral—novices had to learn sometime, one might explain. But God saw them, and that's what really mattered. The principle of God's governance out of his goodness demands that our response be to give God the very best, even when nobody else will know: "Or do you show contempt for the riches of his kindness, forbearance and patience, not realizing that God's kindness is intended to lead you to repentance?" (Rom. 2:4). Because God gives us his best, should we not, out of the sincerest gratitude, return his favor in kind?

But for the grace of God, there go I.

Applying the Text: Psalm 94:12 pronounces a benediction on those whom the Lord disciplines, and the verbs "discipline" and "teach" are parallel. Spiritual instruction without spiritual discipline is deficient. Sadly, much of the Christian community in the Western world has lost the sense of Christian discipline and thus the sense of being instructed by God's law. In fact, many Christians believe no one has the right to "discipline" them for moral infractions. Their sense of accountability is so meager that if discipline seems to be on the horizon, they move from one faith community to another to avoid such an action, or drop out of the community altogether. But our accountability to God's church is, or ought to be, synonymous with our accountability to God. And our love for our brothers and sisters must reflect God's unconditional love. Individual believers and the community of faith must also understand that there are two things necessary for moral accountability: a strong sense of community and an unimpeachable climate of Christian love. In that climate of community and love, our manner of discipline should be, "But for the grace of God, there go I."

"Come, Let Us Sing for Joy to the LORD"

Big Idea
We can truly worship God only when we embrace God as Creator.

Key Themes
- We worship God because he is Creator and Redeemer.
- The doctrine of creation is inseparable from the doctrine of grace.

Understanding the Text

Psalm 95 begins with a hymn that sets the tone for a festive occasion, and then in the midst of the joy the psalm ends with a prophetic admonition. But the admonition grows out of the security of the covenant relationship spelled out in verse 7. It is quite likely that, given the warning in verse 11 issued to the wilderness generation ("They shall never enter my rest"), the psalm was written on the verge of the return from Babylonian exile. This new generation, much like the disobedient wilderness generation, needed to learn from the past that disobedience would prevent them from entering the promised land ("my rest") like it had prevented their ancestors, and this admonition summons them to "hear his voice," which is equivalent to "obey me." The two generations constitute an appropriate parallel, and now the psalmist, in a prophetic voice, issues this warning. The festive call to worship in verses 1–2 would then be in anticipation of the restoration of temple worship and the reconstruction of the sanctuary. Verse 7, in this context, is a confession in the words of the covenant formula, "He is our God and we are the people of his pasture."

While the psalm does not contain the declaration "the LORD reigns," it does qualify for the psalms of the heavenly King by its royal language (95:3b, "great King"; 95:7, royal shepherd imagery; see the sidebar "'The LORD Reigns': Psalms of the Heavenly King" in the unit on Ps. 93).

The Text in Context

Some scholars have compared this psalm to Psalms 50 and 81, two other festive psalms. Psalm 96, its neighboring psalm, already has temple worship in view (96:8–9) and, in light of God's glorious deeds, the psalmist summons the whole earth to sing a new song in this new era when "the LORD reigns" (96:10) and comes to judge the earth (96:13).

Psalm 95:7–11 is quoted in Hebrews 3:7–11, where the writer applies "today" to the time and circumstances of the recipients of that letter. Their "today" becomes the day of decision regarding the salvation won by Christ through his suffering, which, in the writer's application, is the spiritual "rest" promised so long ago to the wilderness generation. Sadly, the wilderness generation did not enter the promised rest, because of their disobedience; but now, as in the time of the psalmist, God's people have a renewed opportunity to enter that rest, which today is not the promised land, as it was to the wilderness and exilic generations, but salvation through Christ's redemptive sacrifice. And more than that, it is no less the Sabbath rest that God himself entered after creation (Gen. 2:2–3).

Outline/Structure

1. The hymn (95:1–7b)
   a. Praise of the Creator (95:1–5)
   b. Praise of the covenant God (95:6–7b)
2. Prophetic admonition (95:7c–11)
   a. Call to hear God's voice (95:7c)
   b. A warning from the wilderness (95:8–11)

Historical and Cultural Background

Earlier we observed that one of the ways Book 4 offsets the lament of Psalm 89 regarding the ostensible failure of the Davidic dynasty is to emphasize the kingship of Yahweh. Psalm 95, probably written in the late exilic or early postexilic age, represents a strong piece of that effort. The Lord is hailed as "the great King above all gods" (95:3). This double theme of divine kingship and the inferiority of other gods is advanced in Psalm 96, where the suppliant declares that "all the gods of the nations are idols, but the LORD made the heavens" (96:4b–5). As the exiles were attempting to throw off the yoke of idolatry, it was important that they understood the impotence of their idols and that Yahweh, whom they had scorned by their idolatrous history, "made the heavens" (the idols did not!) and therefore had a right to their worship and loyalty.

Interpretive Insights

95:1 *Come, let us sing for joy.* The first verb ("come") is a second-person plural imperative that exhorts others to worship, and the second verb ("let us sing for joy") a first-person plural cohortative ("let us") that includes the speaker.

let us shout. This should be interpreted as a festal shout. It has parallels in 47:1 and 81:1.

Rock of our salvation. This is a military term suggesting a place of refuge from danger (see also 89:26).

95:2 *thanksgiving.* While the first part of this psalm is categorized as a hymn, it is a hymn of thanksgiving.

95:3 *great King above all gods.* The sphere of God's reign begins with the heavenly ("above all gods"), extends to the earth and sea (95:4–5), then to the sanctuary (95:6), and ultimately to Israel itself ("his pasture, the flock under his care," 95:7), the universal scope of God's reign (see the sidebar "Yahweh and Other Gods in the Psalter" in the unit on Ps. 7; see also 96:4–5).

95:4 *In his hand are the depths of the earth, and the mountain peaks belong to him.* The "depths of the earth" and the "mountain peaks" are two extremities of the world, implying that the whole world belongs to God, for the reason given in verse 5: "for he made it."

95:5 *his hands formed the dry land.* In Genesis 1:9–10 God commands and the dry land appears, but our writer gives it a personal touch here, similar to Genesis 2:7 ("Then the LORD God formed a man from the dust of the ground and breathed into his nostrils the breath of life").

95:6 *Come, let us bow down in worship, let us kneel.* Three cohortative verbs ("let us") describe the bodily movements of worship. The NIV has conflated the first two ("let us *bow down* in *worship*"), but the reader can see them clearly in the RSV: "Let us worship [prostrate oneself] and bow down [sitting in an upright position], let us kneel [bend the knee]."[1] Israel's worship was more than speech and involved the whole person.

before the LORD our Maker. Physically, they worshiped in the court and faced the sanctuary and holy of holies. Theologically, this call to worship is in response to the Creator of the world (95:4–5), "the LORD our Maker."

95:7 *for he is our God.* The conjunction "for" introduces the reason for the call to worship given in verse 6. The confession affirms the first two parts of the covenant formula (see "Teaching the Text").

the people of his pasture, the flock under his care. In the biblical world it was common for the king to be depicted as the shepherd of his people, the implied image here (see Pss. 23; 77:20; 78:52; 80:1; 100:3; Isa. 53:6; Ezek. 34:11–16; John 10:14). The clause "we are the people of his pasture, the flock under his care" is virtually duplicated in Psalms 79:13 and 100:3.

Today. This echoes Deuteronomy 4:40; 5:3; 6:6; 7:11; 9:3; and 11:2. Here begins the prophetic admonition, which I propose was directed to the exiles awaiting the return to their homeland (the second exodus) and the reconstruction of the temple. The psalmist did not want them to miss the promise of this occasion by indulging in the same disobedience as the wilderness generation.

if only you would hear his voice. This conditional clause expresses the idea of a wish that they would listen (see Deut. 11:13, where the same construction occurs).

95:8 *Meribah . . . Massah.* In the wilderness the Israelites complained of thirst, and Moses struck the rock at Rephidim to give them a miraculous spring of water (Exod. 17:1–7), naming the place Massah ("testing") and Meribah ("contention"). A parallel story occurs in Numbers 20:1–13, when the Lord instructs Moses to speak to the rock at Kadesh, but he strikes it instead. As a consequence, the Lord bars Moses from the promised land.

95:9 *tested me.* See the comments on 78:18.

95:10 *forty years I was angry.* Not only did the water-out-of-the-rock incident contribute to Yahweh's anger during the forty-year wilderness period, but other incidents were also factors (see Deut. 1:37). The verb "be angry" (*qut*) appears only here in the Old Testament with Yahweh as the subject. Generally the wilderness era is referenced in negative terms. Jeremiah 2:2–3 is an exception.

95:11 *on oath.* In the Old Testament, God sometimes swears an oath, but he does not make vows (see the sidebar "Vows" in the unit on Ps. 76 and the sidebar "Oaths" in the unit on Ps. 7).

my rest. This is a reference to the promised land (Deut. 12:9–10; Josh. 1:13). The first exodus generation rebelled against Yahweh, and their penalty was that they were prohibited from entering Canaan ("my rest"). The speaker warns them not to repeat the mistake. Waltner makes the observation that this story contributes to the Mosaic character of Book 4.[2] See "The Structure and Composition of the Psalter" in the introduction in volume 1.

Theological Insights

Psalm 95 contains two exhortations to worship and the reasons for it. The first exhortation is "Come, let us sing for joy to the Lord" (95:1); the reasons: because "the Lord is the great God, the great King above all gods" (95:3), and he is "our Maker" (95:6). And we note that the English Reformers used this exhortation as a call to worship in the Book of Common Prayer (see "Illustrating the Text"). The second exhortation is "Come, let us bow down in worship" (95:6), with the stated reason that "he is our God and we are the people of his pasture" (95:7). While the first exhortation draws our attention to creation (95:6), the second calls attention to the redeeming relationship between Yahweh and Israel, alluding to the first two items of the covenant formula ("I will be your God" and "you will be my people"), which amounts to a faith confession. This brings to mind a feature of the theology of the Psalms: our worship should reflect our basic confession of faith. This can take at least two avenues, Holy Scripture and the historic creeds of the Christian church. We should be conscious that it is through these confessions that we tap the roots of our faith, and worship should reflect these confessional roots. When the church gathers to worship, we reflect on who God is and who we are in relationship to him. Here the psalmist confesses that the Lord "is our God and we are the people of his pasture, the flock under his care" (95:7; cf. 100:3), and that is the heart of worship.

Teaching the Text

As we begin constructing our sermon or lesson, we may point to the fact that Psalm 95 is a confession of faith. We too can confess our faith by using this psalm with its two confessional statements. First, "The LORD is the great God, the great King above all gods" (95:3). This confession arises out of the deep conviction that the earth belongs to God because he made it (95:4–5) and we should worship God because he made us (95:6). God as Creator is a fundamental presupposition of the biblical faith, and we can worship God in spirit and in truth (see John 4:24) only when we embrace God as Creator. That means we are totally dependent on him for our existence as well as our care. It would be quite appropriate to talk about the implications of this understanding for the doctrine of grace. Creation and grace are inseparable. God created the world and pronounced it very good, and he created humankind in his own image. That in itself was an act of grace. And all of God's acts of grace flow out of that gracious act, because he is always concerned with his own image—how could he not be, for that is who he is!—and ultimately restores humanity to the image of Christ, who is the image of God (Col. 1:15–16). Indeed, Paul calls us to put on "the new self, which is being renewed in knowledge in the image of its Creator" (Col. 3:10). That image has been grossly deformed by our rebellion against God (Gen. 3) (see "Illustrating the Text").

The second statement is "He is our God and we are the people of his pasture, the flock under his care" (95:7). In the Old Testament the covenant formula is a three-part program of redemption (see the sidebar "The Covenant Formula" in the unit on Ps. 79; see also "Theological Insights"). The goal of redemption is that God would become our God, that we would become his people, and that he would dwell in our midst. It is a wonder of the biblical faith that God wants to be with us, wants to dwell among us, and ultimately wants to dwell in us and wants us to dwell in him. For the Creator of the world to relate to us as "the people of his pasture, the flock under his care" is for us to experience the wonder of redemption, "God with us" (see Matt. 1:23).

Illustrating the Text

Life is the portrait studio where we are to be painted in the image of Christ.

Human Metaphor: In one of his sermons Dr. Elam Davies, late pastor of Fourth Presbyterian Church in Chicago, related the story of a hospital visit with a lady in his church who had been badly burned. As he talked with her, she asked him to look in the chest by her bed. In the drawer he found a photo of a beautiful woman with perfect skin and a beautiful countenance. She said to him, "This is the way I want you to see me." The Heidelberg Catechism asks the question, "Why, then, does God have the ten commandments preached so strictly since no one can keep them in this life?" And the answer is given: "First, that all our life long we may become increasingly aware of our sinfulness, and therefore more eagerly seek forgiveness of sins and pray to God for the grace of the Holy Spirit, so that more and more we may be renewed in the image of God, until we attain the goal of perfection after this life" (Q & A 115). We need to think of our renewal in the image of God as God painting a portrait of us, and as he does, he paints the features of the image of his own Son into our portrait (Rom. 8:29), for his Son is so beautiful that God wants every one of us to look like him. This world is the portrait studio, and we are here for a live sitting.

The corporate voice

Church History: The English Reformers used the first verse of this psalm in morning prayer as a corporate call to worship: "O come, let us sing unto the LORD; let us heartily rejoice in the strength of our salvation."[3] Note that the psalmist joins his voice to the congregation in worship ("let us sing," "let us bow down"). I have made the point that in Book 5 the "I" of these psalms is often, and likely most often, the corporate "I"—the whole nation is praying. There is power in corporate prayer, not because God regards the prayers of the community of faith more than he does the prayers of the individual, but because there is unity in corporate prayer, a unity of purpose and petition, and God honors that unity (Ps. 133:1). Several times in Solomon's prayer of dedication of the temple he refers to Israel's prayers with the clause "when they pray toward this place" (1 Kings 8:30, 35; cf. 8:44, 48). These were their individual prayers combined into a petitionary chorus before God. When we pray as a church on behalf of our common concerns, that contributes to the unity of the body of Christ and is one of the strengths of corporate prayer. The Chronicler affirms the power of corporate prayer in his account of the dedication of the temple by inserting the Lord's promise: "If my people, who are called by my name, will humble themselves and pray and seek my face and turn from their wicked ways, then I will hear from heaven, and I will forgive their sin and heal their land" (2 Chron. 7:14). A nation cannot repent vicariously through the repentance of one or two individuals (Ezek. 14:13–14). It requires all of God's people to pray with a united voice and singular purpose. When the church in Jerusalem prays for Peter in prison, the Lord miraculously looses his shackles, and Peter appears a free man before the praying church ("The church was earnestly praying to God for him," Acts 12:5).

Thus corporate prayer has at least two functions. First, it unites God's people in a singular purpose and petition, and God is always attentive to the united prayers of his people. Second, coming together with a singular purpose formulated in a single petition contributes to the unity of the people of God, and the unity of God's people, corresponding to the unity of the Father and the Son, is the ultimate goal of the Spirit of God (John 17:11, 20–26).

"Sing to the LORD a New Song"

Big Idea

The joy of redemption elicits a new song from the redeemed.

Key Themes

- God's "comings" are multiple.
- The kingdom of God is welcomed with rejoicing.

Understanding the Text

While Psalm 95 is addressed to the worshiping congregation of Israel, Psalm 96 is addressed to the gentiles and the natural order (the heavens, the earth, and the sea; 96:11). It is not enough to announce to Israel that the Lord reigns; the whole world must hear the proclamation, and this hymn fulfills that function. Moreover, it is the fulfillment of the call of 95:1, "Come, let us sing for joy to the LORD." Indeed it is a "new song" (96:1), celebrating the second exodus (return from exile). Other texts provide glimpses of this new-world vision (47:1–3; 66:1–3, 7–9; 87; see also 9:8, where the words of 96:10c appear: "He will judge the peoples with equity"). But, as Wilcock observes, "a psalm whose entire background is the grand panorama that we have here is a new thing in the Psalter."[1]

The Text in Context

As with Psalm 86, the text of Psalm 96 is shared by several other psalms. It includes verses from Psalm 29 (see "The Text in Context" in the unit on Ps. 29). Portions of Psalm 96 also appear in 1 Chronicles 16: the Chronicler celebrates David's transfer of the ark of the covenant to Jerusalem by using a portion of this psalm (1 Chron. 16:23–33); he also draws on Psalms 105 (1 Chron. 16:8–22) and 106 (1 Chron. 16:34–36) for the occasion.

The psalm is not exactly quoted in the New Testament, although there are some allusions, for example, the "new song" in Revelation 5:9 and 14:3 (see also Rev. 9:20 and Ps. 96:5; Rev. 12:12 and Ps. 96:11; Rev. 19:11 and Acts 17:31).

In the context of Book 4, Psalm 96 most likely summons the earth to sing a "new song" in view of the history-transforming events of the return from captivity and the restoration of the temple.

Outline/Structure

This psalm is written in two parts. The first is indicated by the *inclusio* "all the earth" (96:1 and 9), and the second also by an *inclusio* formed by "judge the peoples" (96:10 and 13).

1. Summons to the earth and nations to praise the Lord (96:1–9)
   a. Summons to the earth to praise the Lord (96:1–3)
   b. Reasons for praise (96:4–6)
   c. Summons to the families of nations to praise the Lord (96:7–9)
2. Announcement that the Lord reigns (96:10–13)
   a. Announcement that the Lord reigns (96:10)
   b. Call to the heavens and earth to rejoice before the Lord (96:11–13)

Historical and Cultural Background

The Septuagint titles this psalm "When the house was built after the captivity." The backdrop of Book 4 is the Babylonian exile and the time of the return and the rebuilding of the temple. It was a time of renewed messianic enthusiasm, with new hope for the advancing kingdom of God.

Interpretive Insights

96:1 *Sing to the LORD a new song.* The trifold verb "sing" (96:1–2), addressed to "all the earth," is matched by the trifold "ascribe" in verses 7 and 8, addressed to the "families of nations." "A new song" occurs several times in the Psalms (33:3; 40:3; 96:1; 98:1; 149:1; see also Rev. 5:9; 14:3). In all of these references the "new song" is connected to God's wondrous works, and here, in the context of Book 4, it may very well be the miraculous work of God that shapes the return of the exiles to their homeland, the second exodus (see Isa. 42:10).

96:2 *proclaim his salvation day after day.* As the exile was ending, the Decree of Cyrus and the initial return under Zerubbabel, with the reinstitution of sacrifice, represented a new era of "salvation" (see Isa. 52:7).

96:3 *his marvelous deeds.* These are God's saving deeds in history, like the exodus from Egypt and the return from exile (the second exodus), through which he manifests his "glory" (see Num. 14:22).

96:4 *For great is the* LORD . . . *he is to be feared above all gods.* The Hebrew verse begins with "that," which represents the content of the declaration anticipated by verse 3, "Declare his glory . . . , his marvelous deeds among all peoples, that great is the LORD and most worthy of praise" (v. 4, author's translation). Yahweh's superiority over the gods is lauded here, as it is in 95:3.

96:5 *idols.* The Hebrew word *'elilim* means "worthless" or "nothing" (see Job 13:4; Jer. 14:14). In Isaiah 2:20 it bears the meaning "idols," as here. The word is considered to be a parody of "God" (*'elohim*).

but the LORD *made the heavens.* This is the reason he is worthy to be called God. See the same idea in Jeremiah 10:11.

96:6 *Splendor and majesty . . . strength and glory.* Strength and majesty are the accoutrements of kingship that awaken reverence and adoration (Pss. 21:5; 45:3), anticipating the declaration of Yahweh's royal reign in verse 10.[2]

his sanctuary. There is some evidence in Book 4 that the temple was standing when some of these psalms were written. This may suggest the preexilic period before 586 BC or the postexilic period, when the second temple had become a reality (e.g., 92:13; 100:4).

96:7 *ascribe to the* LORD *glory and strength.* This section of the psalm is a virtual duplicate of a portion of Psalm 29 (29:1b = 96:7b; 29:2 = 96:8a and 9a). See "The Text in Context" in the unit on Psalm 29.

96:8 *bring an offering and come into his courts.* Psalms 68:29 and 72:10 speak of an offering in honor of the king. In view of the new temple, this may also mean that the nations will bring an offering and worship in the temple. "His courts" is plural because the temple had several.

96:9 *splendor of his holiness.* The KJV renders this as "beauty of holiness," which was interpreted spiritually as holy deeds and behavior. It is hardly the beauty of the second temple, as Calvin would prefer to think,[3] particularly in light of the disappointment that the generation that returned from exile faced when the second temple took shape (Hag. 2:1–9).

tremble before him, all the earth. As in 96:1b, "all the earth" is addressed because "his marvelous deeds" (96:3) are such as to create awe in the whole earth. The fear of God that causes the earth to tremble is not a saving fear but a fear of God's judgment (96:10c). This verse admonishes believers, says Calvin, to approach worship with reverence "instead of rushing without consideration into God's presence."[4]

96:10 *The* LORD *reigns.* This is one of the characteristic features of the psalms of the heavenly King, and here it is for the benefit of "the nations," for his reign means that "he will judge the peoples with equity," the same standard by which he judges his own people and far more than the nations, who had done so much harm to Yahweh's people, could have hoped for.

96:11–13 *Let the heavens rejoice, let the earth be glad; let the sea resound.* This hymnic conclusion gathers together the components of the created order (96:13a): "heavens," "earth," and "sea" (96:11). Four verbs carry the sense of joy at God's judgment of the earth ("rejoice," "be glad," "be jubilant," "sing for joy"; 96:11–12). The judgment of the nations is a prominent theme in the postexilic age, especially the books of Haggai and Zechariah. But we should note that it is not the nations that are rejoicing. Even though Israel declares Yahweh's glory "among the nations" (96:3), the nations are the object of his judgment (96:13). The clause "for he comes" (96:13a) speaks of a theophany (Hab. 3:3). Yahweh, having already established his reign, now comes in the events of the early postexilic age, especially in the return from exile and the reconstruction of the temple, repeating his wondrous works of the first exodus.

Let all creation rejoice. These words are not in the Hebrew text, nor are they in the Septuagint. The duplicate text in 1 Chronicles 16:33 connects the second half of verse 12 and verse 13: "Then let the trees of the forest sing for joy before the LORD, for he comes to judge the earth" (author's translation). Quite probably we should read our psalm the same way: "Then let all the trees of the forest sing for joy before the LORD, for he comes, for he comes to judge the earth" (96:12b–13a).

Theological Insights

Paul speaks of the "frustration" of creation and declares that creation is waiting to "be liberated from its bondage to decay and brought into the freedom and glory of the children of God" (Rom. 8:19–23). Psalm 96 (vv. 11–13), while it does not address creation's "frustration," certainly suggests the joy of creation's liberation from its "bondage to decay." The ultimate New Testament declaration comes when the voice from the throne announces, "I am making everything new!" (Rev. 21:5).

The goal of this renewal as well as its avenue is the kingdom of God. The announcement "The LORD reigns!" is, in fact, the declaration that the kingdom has come and is coming. It is the already–not yet dilemma in which every believer lives, reflected in the prayer that Jesus taught us to pray, "Thy kingdom come, thy will be done, on earth as it is in heaven." It has come so near, yet still its fulfillment eludes us, evidenced by the disparity between God's will done on earth as it is executed in heaven. The tension is real, and the moment it loses its hold on us is the moment we lose sight of the kingdom. It is in the vision glorious that we find our peace, but it is due to the peace of Jesus Christ, not the world's, that we can live and thrive in that tension (John 14:27). And this is a major stanza of our "new song."

Teaching the Text

This psalm should send a surge of joy through our hearts as we realize that God cared enough about the world, and the new world order, which we call the kingdom of God, to announce to the gentiles that "the LORD reigns!" That is, he included them/us in this earth-shattering proclamation, and he even publicized that he would judge the rest of the world by the same standard by which he judged Israel (96:10c).

With that in mind, we may form our sermon or lesson on the universal premise of this psalm. First, we may observe that the addressees of the psalm are both rational and nonrational. The rational are composed of "all the earth" (96:1b) and "families of nations" (96:7a; cf. 96:10a), and the nonrational is the natural world, composed of the major objects of the creation story: "heavens," "earth," and "sea" (96:11). God made them all, and they are all objects of his redeeming love. As stated above, God wants the whole world, both Israel and the nations, both rational and nonrational, to know that he reigns. The very fact that God would make such a proclamation to the gentile world is evidence, in a side-view way, that he cares for the whole world, and through Israel he would bless the world (Gen. 12:3). Alongside this great verity is the revelation that God will judge the whole world by the same standard of "righteousness" and "truth" (Ps. 96:13; the NIV has "faithfulness," but "truth" is a better term for a standard of judgment).

Second, in this same vein of thought, we may comment on the clause, occurring twice, "he comes" (96:13). It is quite appropriate that this should be the concluding thought, for the reigning Lord is now coming "to judge the earth." "He comes" is a clause that describes the Lord's appearance, or theophany, and we may observe that there are many "comings" in Scripture. They occur, as a rule, at the junctures of history when God is doing a marvelous work among his people. In this case, it is probably the return from exile when the valleys are lifted up and the mountains made low to make "a highway for our God" (Isa. 40:3). And it is not only a victory parade for the King of glory, but he is the vanguard and rearguard for his people as they make their way home (Isa. 52:12). "He comes" is the proclamation of the voice on a high mountain, "Here is your God" (Isa. 40:9).

"He comes" from Nazareth in Galilee to announce the good news that "the kingdom of God is at hand; repent, and believe in the gospel" (Mark 1:15 RSV). And we have beheld his glory! Miracles, mercies, and God's love in human form light up the world in the glowing face of Christ.

And finally "he comes" in the urgency of history that has run amok in the evils of a rebellious world, with the announcement "Look, I am coming soon!" (Rev. 22:12). And his church calls out in answer, "Come, Lord Jesus" (Rev. 22:20).

Illustrating the Text

Dramatic joy fills the earth when "The Lord reigns" is proclaimed.

History: On January 1, 1863, the document was spread out on a table in the president's office, and Abraham Lincoln dipped his pen in an inkstand, held it in the air over the document, hesitated, looked around the room, and said: "I never, in my life, felt more certain that I was doing right than I do in signing this paper. But I have been receiving calls and shaking hands since nine o'clock this morning, till my arm is still and numb. Now this signature is one that will be closely examined, and if they find my hand trembled they will say, 'he had some compunctions.' But anyway, it is going to be done." And with that he slowly and carefully wrote the name "Abraham Lincoln" at the bottom of the Emancipation Proclamation.[5] Carl Sandburg's description of the electric atmosphere that pervaded President Lincoln's office that day is a reminder, on a smaller scale, of the dramatic joy that fills the earth when the proclamation "The Lord reigns" is published among the nations (96:10–13) and they experience God's reign that brings liberty and salvation.

The church has hope that "he comes," again and again.

Church History: The following description of the spiritually desolate state of England and the English church in the first half of the eighteenth century is a reminder, even a parallel, of our own age of spiritual darkness, waiting for the light to dawn. It is a reminder, even a parallel, that it is because "the Lord reigns" that he comes, and comes again, to bring salvation and renew his people, as this psalm announces. And further, because he reigns and because he comes again and again, Christ's church has reason to rejoice in hope. The editors of a collection of John Newton's letters summed up the conditions of the time:

> In the first half of the 18th century England was in a state of religious and moral decay. For many years the land had been sinking into darkness and paganism. Intemperance and immorality, crime and cruelty were increasingly becoming the characteristics of the age. The National Church was in such a dead condition that instead of being the salt, preserving the nation from corruption, she was only adding to the immorality by weakening the restraints which Christianity imposed on the lusts of men. The teaching from the pulpit consisted of natural theology and cold morality which were utterly impotent to awaken the Church or to stem the flood of iniquity. If the nation was to be saved the Church would first have to be revived. And that is what took place.[6]

It was in that seemingly hopeless situation that God raised up George White-field, John Wesley, John Newton, and others to proclaim the power of Christ to revive his church and renew a morally despairing nation, thus creating a major wave of the First Great Awakening. As long as "the LORD reigns," he will continue to come and come again to renew his people who call on God in repentance and faith (2 Chron. 7:14).

"The LORD Reigns, Let the Earth Be Glad"

Big Idea

Joy is more than an emotion; it is a state of mind, a disposition of the heart, and it reaches its highest decibels in the proclamation that God reigns.

Key Themes

- God's sovereign reign is universal.
- When the "gods" worship the Lord, that is the ultimate symbol that "the LORD reigns!"
- "The LORD reigns" means the Lord is King of kings and Lord of lords.

Understanding the Text

Psalm 97 provides both an oral and a visual presentation of the Lord's coming announced in 96:13. In Israel's tragic circumstances of the exile, with the loss of king and reputation, hope is revived in the announcement that "the LORD reigns," and it is further bolstered by the word picture of the Lord's coming (97:2–6).

The Text in Context

Above we noted the coming of God announced in 96:13, and Psalm 97 provides a literary complement, giving us a graphic word picture of his coming.

The only New Testament quotation of Psalm 97 is found in Hebrews 1:6, where the author is giving reasons why Jesus is superior to the angels. The author of Hebrews uses the Septuagint, which renders "gods" (*'elohim*) as "angels": "And again, when God brings his firstborn into the world, he says, 'Let all God's angels worship him.'" Some commentators (e.g., Calvin) prefer this translation over that of "gods" (see Ps. 8:5). It certainly is possible, but Yahweh's superiority over the "gods" is the ultimate claim of sovereignty and is preferable here.

Outline/Structure

The psalm falls into three parts, each distinguished by an *inclusio*.

1. Call to rejoice in the Lord's reign (97:1–6)
   Inclusio: Verse 1, "earth" / verse 6, "heaven" (combined terms = all creation)
   a. Declaration that "the LORD reigns" (97:1)
   b. The Lord's appearance (97:2–6)
2. Effects of the Lord's appearance (97:7–9)
   Inclusio: Verse 7, "gods" / verse 9, "all gods"
3. Exhortation to those who love the Lord (97:10–12)
   Inclusio: Verses 1 and 12, "rejoice" (*smh*)

Historical and Cultural Background

As with Psalm 96, the Septuagint positions this psalm in the late exilic or early postexilic age (see the comments on the title for Ps. 97). The cultural setting is that of an ancient king who leaves his own province to visit other provinces of his kingdom, and his processional way is accompanied by the accoutrements of royalty, in our case, divine royalty that exceeds the affects of earthly monarchs (97:3–5).

Interpretive Insights

Title While the Hebrew psalm has no title, the Septuagint gives it the superscription "For David, when his land is established/restored."

97:1 *The LORD reigns.* See the sidebar "'The LORD Reigns': Psalms of the Heavenly King" in the unit on Psalm 93.

let the earth be glad. The reason is that the Lord reigns.

let the distant shores rejoice. "Distant shores" is a poetic term for distant foreign lands (see Ezek. 27:3, 15).

97:2 *Clouds and thick darkness surround him.* Here begins the description of the theophany, patterned after earlier appearances (e.g., Exod. 13:21–22). God's majesty is obscured by the "clouds and thick darkness."

righteousness and justice. Psalm 96:13 says Yahweh judges "the world in righteousness," and this clause adds "justice" (or "law"). See also 89:14.

the foundation of his throne. God's "throne" is a metaphor for the fundamental principles of God's reign, and these principles are also set forth in 89:14.

97:3 *Fire goes before him.* Sometimes fire accompanies Yahweh's appearances in the Old Testament and consumes or refines (e.g., Exod. 3:2; 19:18; Ps. 50:3).

97:4 *lights up . . . sees and trembles.* The verbs are Hebrew perfects, and if we take this to be the Lord's future appearance, they may be understood as perfects of certitude: "His lightnings enlightened the world: the earth saw, and trembled" (KJV). That is, the psalmist is so sure it is going to happen that he speaks as if it already has, using the past or present tense (compare Isa. 9:2). In addition to the fire that goes before him, the lightning also illuminates the world and radiates Yahweh's processional way, so the earth trembles at his approach, and "the mountains melt like wax" (97:5), depicting an awesome theophany. See Exodus 19:18 and also Micah 3:1–4 for a similar picture.

97:5 *before the Lord of all the earth.* The explanation for the effect the Lord's appearance has on creation is that "the LORD reigns!"

97:6 *The heavens proclaim his righteousness.* Verses 6–8 describe the result of Yahweh's appearance. In a metaphorical way, or perhaps even a mystical way, creation announces the king's righteousness, by which he judges the world (96:13). See also 19:1.

and all peoples see his glory. Now we hear that the lights that illumine the world for Yahweh's procession also light up the world so that "all peoples see his glory." God's "glory" and "righteousness" are parallel, as they are in Isaiah 62:2, and in Isaiah 51:5 God's "righteousness" is equivalent to his "salvation." This fits well into the time frame of the return from Babylonian captivity (see Isa. 35:1–2, 8–10; Ps. 98:3).

97:7 *All who worship images are put to shame.* In view of the luminating assistance the creation provides the world of humans for seeing God, the worshipers of idols are put to shame, because their gods do not come to their aid (cf. Isa. 46:1–2).

idols. See the comments on 96:5.

worship him, all you gods! The psalmist calls on the "gods" (*'elohim*) to worship Yahweh, who is above all the gods (96:4). The Septuagint has "angels" instead of "gods." For the "gods" to worship the Lord is the final acknowledgment of God's sovereignty.

97:8 *Zion hears and rejoices.* The sense is that the world has not yet begun to rejoice in the knowledge that "the LORD reigns," but Zion has. This would imply that the long period of soul-searching during the exile has come to an end, and now as the political and spiritual horizons reconfigure, Zion (Jerusalem), as well as the "villages of Judah" (lit., "daughters of Judah"), is happy about this good news.

97:9 *the Most High over all the earth.* Verse 9 concludes part 1 of the psalm by continuing the direct address to Yahweh in verse 8, lauding his sovereign reign over all the gods, essentially a confirmation of "the LORD reigns" in verse 1. "Most High," an ancient epithet for God (*'elyon*), draws Abraham's witness into the story (Gen. 14:22), for he identified Yahweh with Melchizedek's

"God Most High." See "The Text in Context" in the unit on Psalm 83, and the comments on 83:18.

97:10 *Let those who love the LORD hate evil.* Now the suppliant addresses the congregation and admonishes them to "hate evil," which is a call for a radical change in their personal behavior (cf. Prov. 8:13). Since Zion and Judah's villages recognize God's "judgments" (or "laws"), they should hate evil as those laws require. Tate insists, and quite credibly, that the universal aspect of the psalms of the heavenly King "is secondary to their purpose of encouraging and empowering the people of Yahweh."[1] In the absence of a Davidic king, this community needed to be reassured that a greater King was on the throne.

for he guards the lives of his faithful ones. These are synonymous with "those who love the LORD," at whose disposal God puts his protective resources and "delivers them from the hand of the wicked" (see 2 Tim. 2:19). The verb "delivers" is a Hebrew imperfect verb and implies that God has done this many times.[2]

97:11 *Light shines on the righteous.* The NIV opts for an alternate and plausible reading ("shines," *zarah*) of the verb "sown" (*zarua‘*) (see the NIV footnote). The difference is the final Hebrew letter *heth* rather than *ayin*, which is attested by a few versions. If one insists on the Masoretic reading, the Hebrew verb "sown" mixes metaphors and suggests that light, like a seed, is sown in the earth and will sprout in its proper season.[3] The combination of "light" and "joy" as the accompaniments of the "righteous" suggests both an intellectual ("light") and an emotional ("joy") disposition for the righteous (see 30:5).

97:12 *Rejoice in the LORD, you who are righteous.* A second time the congregation is addressed and admonished to "rejoice in the LORD," based on Yahweh's profile provided by the psalm: "The LORD reigns"; the foundations of his throne are "righteousness and justice"; Yahweh is the Most High over all the earth; and he is exalted above all gods. "Righteous," says Calvin, "comprehends integrity of heart, more being required to constitute us righteous in God's sight than that we simply keep our tongue, hands, or feet, from wickedness."[4]

his holy name. Literally, "the memory of his holiness." Here the Hebrew word for "memory" has the sense of "name," as it does in Exodus 3:15, and the expression "his holiness" functions as an adjective, thus "his holy name."

Theological Insights

In our discussion of Psalm 96 we made the observation that God's "comings" are multiple (see "Teaching the Text" in the unit on Ps. 96). Even by the time of our psalmist, there was a general understanding that history repeats itself. Indeed, Jeremiah assures Israel that God's deliverance from Babylonian exile will be so glorious that it will displace the axiomatic memory of deliverance from Egyptian bondage (Jer. 16:14–15; see "Additional Insights: The Model of Historical Double-Tracking," following the unit on Ps. 138). In this regard, Weiser remarks that the Christian cannot read this psalm without the reminder of "the similar tones and word-pictures with which the Christmas Gospels in Luke and John report the fulfillment of that promise" (see Luke 1–2; John 1:1–18).[5] Israel saw God's glory in prophetic word pictures, but his coming in human flesh has revealed "the glory of the one and only Son, who came from the Father, full of grace and truth" (John 1:14). Even the joy of the earth and Zion, ordered by this psalm, is the tone of Mary's Song (Luke 1:47). It is no wonder that the church has assigned Psalms 96; 97; and 98 as lectionary readings for Christmas Day, celebrating God's involvement in the world through his incarnate Son.

Teaching the Text

There are many occasions in the Psalter that present the preacher and teacher an opportunity to speak about joy. Our first point can be that joy is not merely an emotion but a state of mind, a disposition of the heart, that exudes from the exultant believer. Joy, which Chesterton has called "the small publicity of the pagan" but the "gigantic secret of the Christian"[6] (see "Illustrating the Text" in the unit on Ps. 21), is the major tone of God's comings (see "Theological Insights"). Having found this joy in Christ, Paul directs the Philippian church, "Rejoice in the Lord always. I will say it again: Rejoice!" (Phil. 4:4). Calvin makes the perceptive comment that the psalmist's invitation for people to rejoice "is a proof that the reign of God is inseparably connected with the salvation and best happiness of mankind."[7] Joy is the emotional state of being that God commands for all believers. And it is not always an easy state of being to achieve, but it is a duty too. Lewis quotes William Wordsworth, who said we know nothing more beautiful than the "smile" on Duty's face—her approval of duty done.[8] It is the sad and morose who loiter around the edges of the kingdom.

Once we have registered this truth in our listeners' minds, the second point we must be sure to make is that the reason we rejoice is that "the LORD reigns," not merely over Israel but over the entire world. This means that the Lord is King of kings ("the Lord of all the earth," 97:5) and Lord of lords ("Worship him, all you gods!"; 97:7), and his authoritative reign is unopposed by other powers. Further, it means that the world ought to be filled with joy, which Calvin understands to be evidence that the kingdom extends to the entire world.[9] Obviously the world, like Israel, needs something to rejoice about, and there can be nothing better and more assuring than God's sovereign reign. This was the point of Hugh Latimer's soliloquy in the pulpit of Westminster Abbey in the presence of King Henry VIII (see "Illustrating the Text"). The bold summons to the "gods" to worship Yahweh is the ultimate evidence of God's reign. God's reign relegates the idols and false deities of this world, and all the egomaniacal monarchs and presidents who represent them, to nothingness. Whether they are "gods" our minds have conceived or our material world has manufactured for us, they must necessarily fall down before "the Lord of all the earth" in acknowledgment of his lordship.

A third point is that this new reality of God's reign has moral implications. Thus the psalmist admonishes "those who love the LORD [to] hate evil" (97:10). It is a duty incumbent on us all, and we can be assured that we are not alone in our struggle with evil (see "Illustrating the Text"). No, indeed, for the Lord "guards the lives of his faithful ones and delivers them from the hand of the wicked" (97:10). That state of faith is characterized by the shining light of understanding and the substantive joy of being right with God (97:11). Textually, that completes the circle, for we conclude our discourse on the same note and the same verb as we began, "rejoice." It is joy that has its source not in ourselves but in God's sovereign reign. "The LORD reigns" means "He is Lord of lords and King of kings" (Rev. 17:14).

Illustrating the Text

The King of kings is here.

Classic Sermon: Hugh Latimer, one of the great preachers and leaders of the English Reformation in the sixteenth century, was once preaching in Westminster Abbey when King Henry VIII was in the congregation. As he stood in the pulpit, he soliloquized: "Latimer! Latimer! Latimer! Be careful what you say. The king of England is here!" Then his soliloquy continued: "Latimer! Latimer! Latimer! Be careful what you say. The King of kings is here."[10]

The path of duty is plodding.

Literature: *Paul Faber, Surgeon,* by George MacDonald. While Psalm 97 exudes joy, one gets the impression that it is not a joy that is entirely spontaneous. Rather it comes, at least in certain times and circumstances, with a bit of effort. One gets this impression from verse 10 when the psalmist commands those "who love the LORD" to hate evil, implying that they probably don't, or that they don't hate it as much as they should; otherwise the call to animosity toward evil would probably be unnecessary. Our ethical duty includes a call to hate evil. The path of duty is a plodding path, and a necessary one. In his novel *Paul Faber, Surgeon*, MacDonald describes Dr. Paul Faber as being on the dutiful path to faith:

> The thing that God loves is the only lovely thing, and he who does it, does well, and is upon the way to discover that he does it very badly. When he comes to do it as the will of the perfect Good, then is he on the road to do it perfectly. . . . The doing of things from duty is but a stage on the road to the kingdom of truth and love. Not the less must the stage be journeyed; every path diverging from it is "the flowery way that leads to the broad gate and the great fire."[11]

"Sing to the LORD a New Song, for He Has Done Marvelous Things"

Big Idea

What God has done for Israel is key to understanding his relationship to the world.

Key Themes

- God's salvation of Israel is the dress rehearsal for universal salvation.
- In the biblical economy of faith, salvation and judgment belong together.

Understanding the Text

The world and Israel are intertwined in this psalm, for the Lord, with his "right hand" and "holy arm," has "worked salvation" for Israel and also "revealed his righteousness to the nations," all in a single package (98:1–2). This psalm is most likely set in the late exilic or early postexilic period; Israel and the nations have witnessed the "marvelous things" God has done (98:1), which is likely an allusion to the return and the rebuilding of the temple.

The Text in Context

Isaiah 40–55 shares language and imagery with Psalm 98, especially in view of the return from Babylonian exile, which they both celebrate. Moreover, Psalm 98's kinship to Psalm 97 is also striking in both vocabulary and theme. Both psalms mention "the world" (97:4; 98:9), "nations" or "peoples" (97:6; 98:2, 9), and "the earth" (97:1, 4, 5, 9; 98:3, 4, 9); and both speak of "righteousness" and "judgment" (97:2, 6, 8; 98:2, 9). While the Lord's "coming" is spelled out in cosmic terms in 97:5, this psalm (in 98:9) returns to the unembellished language of "he comes" that we find in 96:13.

While the language of Psalms 96 and 98 is strikingly similar, Psalm 96 directs "all the earth" to "sing to the LORD a new song," based on his character

(96:1), and Psalm 98 begins with the same injunction based on the Lord's deeds (98:1b). The language shared by the two psalms is so impressive that some scholars have suggested they were written by the same author (see table 1).

Table 1. Shared Vocabulary between Psalms 96 and 98

Psalm 96	Psalm 98
"Sing to the Lord a new song" (96:1a) "Sing to the Lord, all the earth" (96:1b) "Sing to the Lord" (96:2a)	"Sing to the Lord a new song" (98:1)
"The Lord" (96:1 [2x], 2, 4, 5, 7 [2x], 8, 9, 10, 13)	"The Lord" (98:1, 2, 4, 5, 6, 9)
"All the earth" (96:1, 9) "The earth" (96:11, 13)	"All the earth" (98:4) "The earth" (98:3, 9)
"His salvation" (96:2)	"His salvation" (98:2) "The salvation of our God" (98:3)
"Peoples" (*'ammim*) (96:5 [NIV: "nations"], 10) "All peoples" (*kol-ha'ammim*) (96:3) "You families of peoples ['*ammim*; NIV: "nations"]" (96:7)	"Peoples" (*'ammim*) (98:9)
"The nations" (*goyim*) (96:3, 10)	"The nations" (*goyim*) (98:2)
"Marvelous deeds" (96:3)	"Marvelous things" (98:1)
"The world" (*tebel*) (96:10, 13)	"The world" (*tebel*) (98:7, 9)
"The Lord reigns" (96:10)	"The Lord, the King" (98:6)
"Let the sea resound, and all that is in it" (96:11)	"Let the sea resound, and everything in it" (98:7)
"He comes" (96:13 [2x])	"He comes" (98:9)
"To judge the earth" (96:13b) "He will judge the world in righteousness and the peoples in his faithfulness" (96:13c–d; cf. 96:10c: "he will judge [*yadin*] the peoples with equity")	"To judge the earth" (98:9b) "He will judge the world in righteousness and the peoples with equity" (98:9c–d)

Outline/Structure

Although the addressees are most likely Israel in part 1, the nations are definitely the object of the address in part 2. The parallel injunctions in verses 1 and 4 each have a reason attached, beginning with "for" (Heb. *ki*), the first immediately following the injunction (98:1b–3), and the second occurring at the end of the stanza (98:9b–c).

1. The new song of Israel (98:1–3)
   a. Command to sing a new song (98:1a)
   b Reason for singing a new song ("for," *ki*) (98:1b–3)
2. The new song of creation (the earth and sea) (98:4–9)
   a. Command to praise the Lord (98:4–9a)
   b. Reason for praising the Lord ("for," *ki*) (98:9b–c)

Historical and Cultural Background

We interpret Book 4 against the historical backdrop of the return from Babylonian exile (ca. 536 BC), prompted by the Decree of Cyrus in 538 BC, and followed by the reconstruction of the temple in 520–516 BC. The fact that the verb "revealed" (98:2) occurs only here in the Psalter is significant, for the content of this revelation to the nations is "his righteousness," or his vindication. The Decree of Cyrus as recorded in Ezra 1:2–4 and 2 Chronicles 36:22–23 implies a revelatory occasion ("The LORD, the God of heaven, . . . *has appointed me* to build a temple for him at Jerusalem," Ezra 1:2). Isaiah announces this era in 41:10, using a synonymous term (NIV: "righteous right hand"; RSV: "victorious right hand").

Interpretive Insights

98:1 *Sing to the LORD.* The plural verb is addressed to Israel, suggested by the pronoun "our" in verse 3b. The message, as appropriate to the nations as to Israel, is that the Lord has "revealed his righteousness to the nations" (98:2b) and "remembered his love and his faithfulness to Israel" (98:3a).

a new song. The marvelous deeds on behalf of Yahweh's people prompt the "new song." It is "new" in the sense that it celebrates God's "new" works on Israel's behalf (see Jer. 16:14–15).

marvelous things. This expression refers to God's saving acts in Israel's history, like the exodus (Exod. 34:10; see also Pss. 72:18; 86:10; 106:7).

his right hand and his holy arm. These are metaphors of God's power (Exod. 15:6), and "his holy arm" implies that the standard by which the Lord has won victory is his holiness. Isaiah 52:10a is a virtual duplicate.

98:2 *revealed his righteousness to the nations.* This likely alludes to the Decree of Cyrus and the return from exile, both of which are symbols to the nations that Yahweh is sovereign Lord and King (98:6b), or more generally alludes to the complex of events reflected in Isaiah 40–55.

98:3 *He has remembered his love and his faithfulness to Israel.* The two nouns "love" and "faithfulness" are shorthand for the Mosaic covenant (Ps. 89:33; Exod. 34:6).

the salvation of our God. Based on the timing of Book 4, this is likely the deliverance of Israel from Babylonian captivity (see the comments on 98:2). It certainly numbers among the "marvelous things" God has done (98:2; cf. Jer. 16:14–15).

98:4 *Shout for joy to the LORD, all the earth.* This shout of victory is prompted by the Lord's "love" and "faithfulness" (Pss. 66:1; 95:1–2; 100:1).

98:5 *the harp.* See the sidebar "Musical Instruments in Psalm 33" in the unit on Ps. 33.

98:6 *the trumpets . . . ram's horn.* The "trumpet" was made of silver or bronze (Num. 10:2), and the "ram's horn" (*shopar*) made, obviously, of the ram's horn. See the comments on 81:3.

shout for joy before the LORD, *the King.* This is the language of acclamation when a new king is elevated to the throne (1 Kings 1:39; 2 Kings 9:13; 11:12–14). The use of the word "King" suggests that this psalm belongs to the psalms of the heavenly King (see the sidebar "'The LORD Reigns': Psalms of the Heavenly King" in the unit on Ps. 93).

98:7–9 *Let the sea resound . . . the world.* Now the psalmist commands creation (98:7, "the sea" and "the world," although "world" [*tebel*] is a synonym of the word "earth" ['*erets*], which is the term in the creation narrative of Gen. 1), with the rivers and mountains (98:8), to resound with praise (see, e.g., Isa. 44:23). They are enjoined to "sing before the LORD, for he comes to judge the earth" (98:9), and in verse 9c we learn why the created order can sing for joy although the Lord comes "to judge the earth." It is because he "will judge the world in righteousness and the peoples with equity." The language of verse 9 is virtually identical with that of 96:10c, 13b–d (see table 1). The rivers "clap their hands" (98:8), celebrating God's reign (2 Kings 11:12).

Theological Insights

As noted above, Israel and the nations are interwoven in the content of this psalm. In fact, except for the pronoun "our" in 98:3, one can hardly determine whether the addressees of part 1 are Israel or the nations. Their destinies are tied together, and it is noteworthy that the Lord "has made his salvation known and revealed his righteousness to the nations" (98:3). One would not be surprised to hear this declaration with Israel as its object, but having "the nations" as object is more of a surprise. Of course, if we understand "righteousness" as vindication, then the announcement is less startling, for this revelation is more a hint of Isaiah's proclamation to Israel in exile "that her hard service has been completed, that her sin has been paid for" (Isa. 40:2). While the sense of vindication is probably intended (see "Historical and Cultural Background"), the meaning of the psalm goes beyond that and enjoins the nations to "shout for joy before the LORD, the King" (Ps. 98:6b). The reason for this rejoicing is found in 98:9, "for he comes to judge the earth . . . in righteousness and the peoples with equity." Judging from God's standard of justice, "in righteousness" and "with equity," the nations can expect divine judgment to be based on that standard, rather than an arbitrary one. And it should be noted that it is the same standard of judgment the Lord uses for Israel. Indeed, as Reardon says, God saves humankind by the "forceful intrusion of His holiness" into human history.[1]

In biblical terms, Israel's history is the world's history, and that makes a lot of sense since Israel's God is the world's God—"salvation is from the Jews" (John 4:22). "The church," says Goldingay, "can never grow out of or escape its indebtedness to the Jewish people. Yahweh's relationship with Israel remains the model for Yahweh's relationship with the church."[2] Isaiah 52:7–10 constitutes the prophetic counterpart of Psalm 98. It is the belief that God has shaped Israel's history in order to demonstrate and establish his rule over all history.[3]

Teaching the Text

The real performance of salvation history on Israel's stage becomes the dress rehearsal for universal salvation. That is not, however, to suggest that it is not real for Israel. Rather, it is a microcosm of salvation history, first offered to Israel. Israel's salvation, first spoken of in this psalm in verse 1, is revealed to the nations in verse 2. One of the interesting features of this text is that "the ends of the earth have seen the salvation of our God" because the Lord "remembered his love and his faithfulness to Israel" (98:3). This psalm resounds with the promise to Abraham that "all peoples on earth will be blessed through you" (Gen. 12:3), and it shouts aloud of God's "love" and "faithfulness" revealed to Moses (Exod. 34:6).

We may then make our first point to be God's work in Israel's history that becomes the reason for all the earth to "shout for joy to the LORD" (98:4) and "shout for joy before the LORD, the King" (98:6). This injunction immediately calls the world to loyalty and obedience. It is of great importance that "all the earth" (98:4) praise the Lord, the King. In the broad scope of Scripture, it is quite clear that universal salvation was still not fully embraced by exilic Israel, even though they were moving in that direction. The rehearsal had begun, and God was demonstrating that when he "remembered his love" for Israel (98:3), that remembering had implications for the world: "For God so loved the world . . ." (John 3:16). We might make this more personal by saying that God always had the universe, and its individual inhabitants, in his salvation scope, even from the beginning of history. That ought to make us joyful in the Lord.

The second point, which we unfortunately embrace with less enthusiasm, is the dress rehearsal for another universal event, divine judgment. Here is one of God's "comings." In the biblical story salvation and judgment belong together, as they do in the parable of the sheep and the goats (Matt. 25:31–46). Our psalm reminds us that God "comes to judge the earth," but he judges "in righteousness" and "with equity" (see the comments on 98:9). So we have no reason to fear a king who is equitable. Today we talk a lot about accountability—and so we should—but, sadly, in our lexical warehouse it has little to do with judgment. Yet, the idea is similar: we are accountable by a set of standards. That is, we are answerable to someone for our actions, as we are morally answerable to God.

The Revelation of John is about salvation and judgment, and here, as in other places in the Psalter and the Hebrew Bible, we have a dress rehearsal for that final phase of salvation history when the whole world will rejoice in God's salvation and his judgment on evil (Rev. 20:11–15).

Illustrating the Text

We are to "fear not" but to have the fear and awe of God.

Television: *A Charlie Brown Christmas.* While the "fear of God" is a standard feature of Old Testament theology, the phrase refers to a saving fear, or awe of God's saving power and reigning majesty. When the Scriptures enjoin us to fear God, it is precisely that kind of mood we are directed to have. The fear that repels us from rather than draws us to God is the type we are commanded not to have, the kind of fear the angel at Christ's birth instructed the shepherds not to have: "Fear not; for, behold, I bring you good tidings of great joy" (Luke 2:10 KJV). Christmas 2015 marked the fiftieth anniversary of the television special *A Charlie Brown Christmas* by Charles M. Schulz. At the Christmas pageant in this classic cartoon, Linus, a figure of a culture of insecurity, recites the angel's announcement of Christ's birth to the shepherds (Luke 2:8–20), and when he pronounces the words "Fear not," he drops his security blanket as a symbol of the new security Christ had brought to the world; one of the later scenes shows his security blanket as the skirt lying under the Christmas tree.

"No one ever—ever loved us like this."

Biography: **Lilias Trotter.** In 1888, after turning away from a potentially promising career in art to obey Christ's call to missionary service in the Muslim world, Lilias Trotter arrived in Algiers with two companions, Blanche Haworth and Lucy Lewis. They were so overjoyed to see their place of service looming before them that while still aboard the ship, they joyfully sang together, "Crown Him Lord of All." Thus began Trotter's forty-year ministry among the Muslims of Algeria. Our psalmist recognizes the Lord's love and faithfulness to Israel and summons the earth to "shout for joy to the LORD" (98:4), bringing together God's covenant with Israel and the salvation of the nation (98:3). Trotter's passion to reach Muslim women and children with the love of Christ was sweetly recapped in the words of an Arab woman whose sick child had received Lilias's loving care: "No one ever—ever loved us like this."[4]

"The LORD Our God Is Holy"

Big Idea

God's holiness not only distinguishes God from us humans but summons us to be like him.

Key Themes

- God's call to a new life is based on an old principle.
- God's reign is sovereign.

Understanding the Text

This hymn of praise incorporates a trifold declaration that God is holy and describes his holiness in terms of his sovereign reign, his justice, and his forgiving and avenging character.

The Text in Context

With some justification, Psalm 99 is sometimes said to be a hymn composed on the "Holy, holy, holy" of Isaiah 6:3, the trifold refrain mirroring the Isaiah text (Ps. 99:3, 5, 9). Delitzsch calls this "an earthly echo of the trisagion of the seraphim."[1]

Quite certainly Psalm 99 is a recollection of Psalm 93 (see table 1), summing up the theology of the psalms of the heavenly King and transitioning to Psalm 100, which is the crowning psalm of the collection.

Table 1. Comparison of Themes in Psalms 93 and 99

Theme	Psalm 93	Psalm 99
Yahweh's reign	"The LORD *reigns*" (93:1)	"The LORD *reigns*" (99:1)
Yahweh's power	"Armed with *strength* ['oz]" (93:1)	"The King is *mighty* ['oz]" (99:4)
Yahweh's throne	"Your *throne*" (93:2)	"*Enthroned* [or "dwelling"] between the cherubim" (99:1)

Theme	Psalm 93	Psalm 99
Yahweh's exaltation	"The Lᴏʀᴅ *on high* [root, *rum*] is mighty" (93:4)	"He is *exalted* [root, *rum*] over all the nations" (99:2) "*Exalt* [root, *rum*] the Lᴏʀᴅ our God" (99:5, 9)
Yahweh's laws	"Your *statutes* ['*edoteyka*], Lᴏʀᴅ, stand firm" (93:5)	"They kept *his statutes* ['*edotayw*] and the decrees he gave them" (99:7)
Yahweh's holiness	"*Holiness* adorns your house" (93:5)	"He is *holy*" (99:3, 5) "The Lᴏʀᴅ our God is *holy*" (99:9)

Note: See Hossfeld and Zenger, *Psalms 2*, 491n18.

Outline/Structure

The psalm consists of three parts, each ending in a refrain:

1. "The Lᴏʀᴅ reigns" (99:1–3)
   a. "The Lᴏʀᴅ reigns" (99:1–2)
   b. Address to the Lord (99:3a)
   c. Refrain: "He is holy" (99:3b)
2. The King acts equitably toward Jacob (Israel) (99:4–5)
   a. The mighty King loves justice (99:4a)
   b. Address to the Lord (99:4b–c)
   c. Address to the congregation (99:5a–b)
   d. Refrain: "He is holy" (99:5c)
3. The Lord answers those who call on him (99:6–9)
   a. Moses, Aaron, and Samuel as intercessors and God's answer (99:6–7)
   b. Address to the Lord (99:8)
   c. Address to the congregation (99:9a–b)
   d. Refrain: "The Lᴏʀᴅ our God is holy" (99:9c)

Historical and Cultural Background

Our thesis for Psalms 93–99 is that these psalms were written, or were adapted, for the late exilic or early postexilic age when Israel realized they had been forgiven by their gracious covenant God (see Exod. 34:5–6), after having been punished by the exile for their sins. As they emerge from this experience that might be compared to the prodigal's coming "to himself" (Luke 15:17 KJV), Psalm 99 proclaims God's holiness as a principle of renewal on the basis of an old commandment (Lev. 19:2).

Interpretive Insights

99:1 *The LORD reigns.* This declaration of Yahweh's reign is joined by the acknowledgment in 99:4 that "the King is mighty." Against those who claim that this psalm belongs to a fall festival that annually elevated Yahweh as King, Kraus insists, and I agree, that this is "a call for homage" (Yahweh is King), not a cry of coronation.[2]

let the nations tremble. See 18:7 for this same verb (NIV: "shook"). This and the final clause of the verse, "let the earth shake," describe the effect the Lord's reign should have on the nations.

he sits enthroned between the cherubim. The empty space between the cherubim, which were attached to the ark in Moses's tabernacle (Exod. 25:10–22) but were also separate-standing figures flanking the ark in Solomon's temple (2 Chron. 3:10–14), was perceived to be the place where Yahweh's presence dwelt (Exod. 25:22; 1 Sam. 4:4).

99:2 *Great is the LORD in Zion.* This is a localization of the declaration in 99:1a. The Lord's greatness is particularly recognized in Zion because that is where his dwelling is.

99:3 *Let them praise your great and awesome name.* The subject of this verb is not stated, but since the nations have been the topic of verses 1 and 2, the subject is likely the nations ("Let them").

he is holy. This refrain (99:3, 5, 9) may be a congregational response. Holiness implies that God is distinct from human beings. And it is certainly not without significance that this psalm suggests that the holy God loves justice (99:4) and forgives sins (99:8). In fact, the call to be holy in Leviticus 19:2 stands in the context of a description of the holy life, intended to be a description of what "Be holy" means in Israel's world and ours, the necessary changes for historical context being made. See "Theological Insights."

99:4 *The King is mighty, he loves justice.* This is a problematic text, but the NIV captures the sense of it.[3] It is most likely a statement about Yahweh's kingship and not about a human king. Because Yahweh the King is "mighty" and "loves justice," he has established righteous rules for his kingdom, and moreover, he himself has "done what is just and right." Psalmic prayer is not always a direct address to God. Rather it is often, as here, a combination of third-person ("The King is mighty") and second-person singular verbs and pronouns ("you have done"). In the prayers of the church and our personal prayers, the pattern is to use the second-person address almost exclusively.

you have established . . . ; you have done. The pronoun "you" is emphatic with the sense, "*you*, and not humans." The allusion may be to the Torah, especially since "footstool" in 99:5 implies the ark of the covenant (cf. Ezek.

43:7; see also Ps. 132:7), in which Moses was instructed to deposit a copy of the Torah ("the testimony," Exod. 25:16 KJV; see the comments on 99:7).

just and right. These two terms describe one principle of action, "righteousness judgment" (see also 2 Sam. 8:15).

99:5 *worship at his footstool.* In ancient Near Eastern iconography, monarchs are sometimes depicted sitting on their throne with their feet resting on a footstool (see the description of Solomon's throne in 2 Chron. 9:18). Some take this as a reference to the temple (e.g., Isa. 60:13), but since Yahweh is described as "enthroned between the cherubim" in 99:1, we probably should understand this as the ark of the covenant. Although the ark had been captured by the Babylonians in 586 BC and consequently never stood in the second temple (Zerubbabel's), the Israelites evidently still thought of the ark as being there.

99:6 *Moses and Aaron . . . , Samuel.* These three heroes of the faith are cited as men who "called on the LORD" and who "kept his statutes and the decrees he gave them." All three in their biblical contexts are attested as having prayed for Israel (Moses, Exod. 32:31–32, etc.; Aaron, Lev. 9:23; Samuel, 1 Sam. 7:9). Only one of the three, Aaron, was an official priest, but both Moses and Samuel were Levites and functioned as priests on certain occasions (e.g., Moses, Exod. 32; Samuel, 1 Sam. 7:9). One of the functions of a priest, of course, was to pray for the people. This example taken from among Israel's great leaders is similar to Ezekiel's statement that "even if these three men—Noah, Daniel and Job" were in the country, "they would save only themselves by their righteousness" (Ezek. 14:14, 20).

Mention of Moses, Aaron, and Samuel invokes images of the exodus and Davidic kingship. The era of the return—a new exodus—was upon the Israelites, and the prophet who anointed David king had interceded for Israel, and God forgave their sins, even though he punished them for their transgressions—both realities were realized in the exile and return. This new era reverberated with the prayers of this trinity of heroes, as well as their warnings.

99:7 *from the pillar of cloud.* Scripture speaks of God speaking to Moses and Aaron from the pillar of cloud (Exod. 33:9; Num. 12:5) but not to Samuel. Some commentators understand the allusion to be to the night voice that Samuel heard when God first called him, suggesting that the call came from above the ark (1 Sam. 3:3–4).

his statutes. This expression is used in Exodus 25:16 (NIV: "covenant law") to refer to the law that Moses deposited in the ark of the covenant, and here it likely designates the Mosaic law in general.

99:8 *you answered them.* In a direct address to Yahweh, the psalmist echoes the explanation of the divine name (see 99:6b) given in Exodus 34:6–7: the Lord is a forgiving God, but because of his love and truth, he also punishes sin.

99:9 *the* LORD *our God is holy.* This last refrain reissues the theme of this psalm and transitions to Psalm 100, and it applies the qualities of "the LORD our God" (used twice) to the nations.[4]

Theological Insights

In Israel's exilic/postexilic climate, our psalmist takes this community back to one of the constituting principles of Israel's nationhood: "Be holy because I, the LORD your God, am holy" (Lev. 19:2). If Israel should be restored to a new life after the exile, it must be on this old principle that Yahweh established in the patriarchal phase of the covenant relationship.[5] Further, Leviticus 19 provides a description of what this holy mandate means and builds toward the commandment, indeed the climax, of "Love your neighbor as yourself. I am the LORD" (Lev. 19:18).[6] We often use the word "holy" (*qadosh*) routinely in our theological conversation, assuming that everyone knows its meaning. Basically the word implies that God is absolutely distinct from us humans. Yet it is more than that. At once it raises the issue of grace, that God, who is the "other," would allow himself to be accessed by us earthlings, who are the opposite of holy, and that he would put us into an intimate relationship with himself.[7] The human reaction to God's holiness is described by the prophet Habakkuk as silence: "But the LORD is in his *holy* temple; let all the earth be silent before him" (Hab. 2:20). Yet Psalm 99 summons the community of faith to vocal praise of God. Perhaps we should not distinguish too sharply between *awesome silence* and *vocal praise*, because the latter is the former in words. God's holiness, however, is not an absolute separator but involves a reciprocal relationship, and that is the sense of Leviticus 19:2. God holds up his character to Israel and commands them to be like him. In the context of God's holiness, supplied by this psalm, we can understand God's actions in Psalm 99:4 to be, at least in part, a description of his *holy grace*: he loves justice, establishes an equitable standard of relationship, and conducts himself by that standard as well. And we, by keeping his word, are to become like him, not demigods but reflections of his person.

Teaching the Text

Psalm 99 is one of those psalms whose refrain provides us with a natural outline for a sermon or lesson. The themes of the three stanzas—Yahweh's exaltation (99:2), justice (99:4), and forgiveness (99:8)—all lead to the same refrain, the declaration that "he/God is holy" (99:3, 5, 9), and thus define what is meant by holiness. The first stanza (99:1–3) begins with the declaration "the LORD reigns" and concludes with the refrain "he is holy." The two terms mutually inform each other. The Lord, "enthroned between the cherubim," reigns, and that is the fundamental premise of this stanza. This premise means that ancient Israel, who lived under subjection to a foreign power and hoped for deliverance, could nevertheless rejoice in the holy God, who reigns. This truth reapplied to our lives, especially when enemies are rampant—disease, personal foes, economic disasters, and so forth—gives us confidence that all is well because God is sovereignly in control.

The second stanza (99:4–5) moves into a description of God the King as one who is "mighty," "loves justice," and has "established equity." Like each of the stanzas, this one engages in a summons to praise/exalt the Lord, followed by the declaration that Yahweh is "holy" (99:3, 5, 9). The definition reinforces the idea of God's sovereign reign by proclaiming that he is "holy." When a deity of this character is in control, we can "worship at his footstool." And it is of consequence that he lives by his own rules: "In Jacob you have done what is just and right."

The third stanza (99:6–9) puts to rest any doubt that Yahweh takes our misdeeds lightly, for he is a forgiving God (99:8), echoing the character description of Yahweh in his revelation to Moses (Exod. 34:5–6). When the psalmist declares that "the LORD our God is holy," he does so with this image of the forgiving and avenging God to provide the context. We might want to continue this idea into the New Testament, and the following texts will support the theme of this psalm: Luke 4:18–19; Romans 12:1; Hebrews 10:19–25; 1 Peter 1:15–16; 2:5, 9; Revelation 15:3–4.

Illustrating the Text

A different choice of terms cannot change the nature of the deed.

Church Fathers: Augustine, in *The City of God*, tells the story about a pirate whom Alexander the Great had taken captive. The emperor asked his captive pirate how he dared to violate the safety of the sea, and this frank and insolent answer was his response: "And how do you venture to make the whole earth unsafe? When I do this with a small boat, they call me a robber, but when you do it with a large fleet, they call you an emperor."[8] Unlike Alexander the Great, God does not operate by a double standard, doing one thing while demanding another, but he commands his followers to be like him. It is not a copycat effort but the spiritual discipline of imitation. Our English adage "Imitation is the highest form of flattery" is our earthly way of speaking about the social discipline of imitation, but the spiritual discipline operates in the realm of glorifying God, where flattery becomes praise. Flattery is self-focused, but praise turns us away from ourselves toward God, whose worthiness is beyond all telling—the only discipline that can turn our selfish adulation into selfless praise of God, who is holy.

Be holy!

History: Thomas Jefferson inscribed the "pursuit of happiness" into the Declaration of Independence and into our American culture, and we duly accept that as one of the basic tenets of our way of life. However, Jews and Christians put a spin on the phrase that does not completely overlap with the popular interpretation. Wolpe incisively observes that "happiness is a by-product, not an aim. You cannot be made happy, paradoxically, by pursuing happiness alone. Perhaps you can be comfortable, even satisfied; but happiness, deep contentment of soul, can arise only from the pursuit of something greater, a sense of life well lived. Happiness itself is elusive, and, moreover, contentment is hardly the highest human accomplishment."[9] For Jews and Christians, the directive is not "Be happy" but "Be holy" (Lev. 20:7).

"Shout for Joy to the LORD, All the Earth"

Big Idea

With this psalm we celebrate the gospel given to the whole world.

Key Themes

- The gospel of God's love and faithfulness is extended to all the earth.
- The gospel is the one and only saving gospel, because it is the gospel of the one and only God.

Understanding the Text

One of the most discussed collections of psalms is represented by the psalms of the heavenly King (Pss. 93–99), and Psalm 100 is their capstone. This psalm celebrates the universal gospel of grace that is proclaimed with joy in this psalm.

The Text in Context

In a literary sense, Psalm 100 borrows language from the cadre of psalms it concludes, especially Psalms 95; 96; 97; and 98 (see table 1), to celebrate the theme of Yahweh's kingship. Even though our psalm does not contain the declaration "The LORD reigns" or the word "king," it nevertheless celebrates God's kingship in its calls to "serve [NIV: "worship"] the LORD with gladness" (100:2)—the language of subservience—and to "enter . . . his courts with praise" (100:4), both reflecting the language of monarch and servant, although they also have another meaning (see "Interpretive Insights"). If Psalm 100 did not conclude an earlier macrocollection of the Psalter, it was likely the logical conclusion to the cadre of the psalms of the heavenly King.[1]

Psalm 100 picks up threads from other psalms in the psalms of the heavenly King (Pss. 93–99), emphasizing God's love and the joy of this new era of restoration.

Table 1. Dependence of Psalm 100 on the Language of Psalms 95–98

Psalm 100	Psalm 95	Psalm 96	Psalm 97	Psalm 98
"*Shout for joy to the* Lord, *all the earth*" (100:1)		"*All the earth*" (96:1, 9)	"*All the earth*" (97:5, 9)	"*Shout for joy to the* Lord, *all the earth*" (98:4)
"Worship the Lord *with gladness*" (100:2)		"*Let* the heavens *rejoice, let* the earth *be glad*" (96:11)	"*Let* the earth *be glad*" (97:1) "Zion hears and *rejoices*" (97:8) "Light shines on the righteous and *joy* on the upright in heart" (97:11) "*Rejoice* in the Lord" (97:12)	
"*His love . . . his faithfulness*" (100:5)		"*His faithfulness*" (96:13)		"*His love . . . his faithfulness*" (98:3)
"*Enter* his gates *with thanksgiving* and *his courts* with praise" (100:4)	"*Let us come before him with thanksgiving*" (95:2)	"*Come into his courts*" (96:8)		
"*Praise his name*" (100:4, human beings as subject)		"*Praise his name*" (96:2, human beings as subject)		
"*Shout for joy*" (100:1)	"*Let us shout aloud*" (same verb, 95:1) "*Let us . . . extol* him" (95:2)			
"We are his; *we are his people,* the *sheep of his pasture*" (100:3)	"*He is our God* and we are the people *of his pasture,* the *flock* under his care" (95:7)			

Outline/Structure

1. Four imperatives to worship and reason for worship (100:1–3)
   a. Four imperatives (100:1–3a)
      i. "*Shout for joy* to the Lord" (100:1)
      ii. "*Worship* the Lord with gladness" (100:2a)

iii. "*Come* before him with joyful songs" (100:2b)

iv. "*Know* that the LORD is God" (100:3a)

  b. Reason: "It is he who made us, and we are his; we are his people, the sheep of his pasture" (100:3b–c)

2. Three imperatives to worship and reason for worship (100:4–5)

  a. Three imperatives (100:4)

    i. "*Enter* his gates with thanksgiving" (100:4a)

    ii. "*Give thanks* to him" (100:4b)

    iii. "*Praise* his name" (100:4c)

  b. Reason: The Lord is good, and his love and faithfulness continue to all generations (100:5)

Historical and Cultural Background

The idea of universal salvation—that is, salvation offered to the whole world—while not exclusive to the postexilic period, gained traction in that time of Israel's history. Psalm 100 is a virtual conversion ritual, the nations confessing themselves to be believers in Yahweh's revelation to Moses (Exod. 34:5–6). It is a distinctive component of Book 4, and one that needed to be included in a theology that proclaims, "Yahweh reigns!" This proclamation implies that Yahweh's reign is universal, for he made the world (95:6; 96:5), and all must bow in humble submission to his lordship—in fact, to his saving lordship.

Interpretive Insights

Title *For giving grateful praise.* The Hebrew title is "A Psalm for the Thanksgiving" (or "the Thank Offering [*todah*]") (see 107:22; 116:17). In a liturgical sense this psalm was used when the thank offering was made. The thank offering celebrates God's special benefits to the individual and community (Ps. 107).

100:1 *Shout for joy to the LORD, all the earth.* This is a festal shout, celebrating an important event or festival, evidently the fact that the earth has come to acknowledge that the Lord is God. This call to worship would have been spoken by the worship leader, probably a priest or Levite.

100:2 *Worship the LORD with gladness.* The verb "worship" is literally "serve," which often carries the nuance of worship.

100:3 *Know that the LORD is God.* Knowing God is accepting his lordship (1 Chron. 28:9). This verse may have been recited outside the gates of the temple while the worshipers were waiting for entry (cf. Ps. 24). If we consider the psalm a miniature treatise on universal salvation, then this is a call to the nations to recognize that Yahweh is the true God.

It is he who made us, and we are his. The first-person plural object and subject ("us" and "we") put this statement on the lips of the earth's inhabitants or kings. Significantly, this is the abbreviated covenant formula on the lips of the inhabitants of the earth, acknowledging the Lord as God and confessing themselves to belong to him. We hear the covenant formula on Israel's lips in 79:13 and 95:7, and elsewhere, but here on the lips of the inhabitants of the earth or their kings it is both shocking and hopeful. The nations have come to confess Yahweh as God!

The clause "we are his" is written in Hebrew as "*and not [lo']* we ourselves" (see the NIV footnote; this reading is supported also by the LXX and the Targum). But the Jewish scribes of the Middle Ages (Masoretes) provided a correction in the margin (*lo*; lit., "to him"), giving the meaning, "and we belong to him" (i.e., "we are his"). The parallel text of Psalm 95:6–7 supports the corrected reading ("we are his"), but either meaning is theologically within bounds.

100:4 *Enter his gates with thanksgiving.* The imagery is that of the "gates" and "courts" of the temple. These words may have been spoken by the gate-keeper, giving the worshipers permission to enter. If this psalm was recited in the temple in a service of thanksgiving, the psalm implies either a preexilic date, when the temple was still standing, or, most likely, a postexilic date, when the temple had been reconstructed. Further, the idea that the salvation of the nations is celebrated in the temple courts is a proclamation of a new theological boldness, arising out of the developing theology of the postexilic community. While it is difficult to imagine that the occasion issues an invitation to gentiles to enter the temple, it is likely an expression of the new theology's openness to the universal perspective, but it is still quite wonderfully shocking.

100:5 *For the* LORD *is good and his love . . . his faithfulness.* The psalmist now gives the reason why worshipers are commanded to enter the temple gates with thanksgiving: the Lord is good. This verse reflects the formula of God's self-revelation when he made his "goodness" to pass in front of Moses (Exod. 33:19) and proclaimed his name, "the LORD" (Yahweh) (Exod. 34:6). "All the earth" (Ps. 100:1) joins in Israel's confession of God's covenant goodness, represented by his name and displayed in his "love" and "faithfulness." While not yet a historical reality, the future of God's universal grace is envisioned here and is eventually revealed in the New Testament gospel (Matt. 28:19–20).

Theological Insights

The psalm begins with a call to "all the earth" to worship the Lord, yet 100:3b sounds like Israel's confession rather than the nations', and the idea of inviting all the earth to enter the courts of the temple (100:4) is not spatially plausible. But it is symbolic of the universal entrance of all peoples into God's presence and kingdom. Psalm 100 may be considered a theological treatise in miniature that sets forth the salvation of the nations. While we may legitimately try to distinguish the terms that apply to the nations and those that apply to Israel, the call to the nations to worship Yahweh is laid down on the grid of temple worship, and the acknowledgment that "he made us" (100:3) may very well be a significant point of theological conflation. That is, the nations are summoned to worship Israel's Lord, to come into his courts, and ultimately into his presence. Israel's faith and that of the nations are rolled into a single, universal faith. In this moment of truth, Israel has shared the noblest and most intimate aspects of their faith with all the world, for they have invited all the nations to worship the Lord, not in their pagan sanctuaries, but in the courts of the Lord, and they have summoned the nations into the Lord's presence. Nothing could be more intimate than that. Here we come as close to the mystery of universal salvation, laid out more clearly in the New Testament (e.g., Eph. 1:3–10), as we do in any of the psalms.

Teaching the Text

Psalm 100 is the basis for a sermon or lesson celebrating the gospel given to the whole world, not just to Israel. We might begin with a brief summation of the psalms of the heavenly King, explaining that this psalm is the capstone of that collection (Pss. 93–99). While we should not give our listeners more than they can digest, it would be helpful, for the preacher's or teacher's benefit, at least, to review table 1 in order to grasp the dependence of Psalm 100 on the language of that collection; then mention it briefly without elaborating. In the setting of the classroom, however, it will be appropriate to review table 1, since the students are likely to have it before them and will be interested in discussing the implications.

We may begin our first point by mentioning that this is a psalm of thanksgiving. Such psalms are intended to give praise to God for some personal or corporate benefit the worshiper(s) has received. Since this psalm is a community psalm of thanksgiving, it is most likely a celebration of Israel's release from Babylonian exile and their return to Judea. That complex of events was the occasion to give God thanks for their miraculous delivery. The rebuilt temple was the intended venue for the celebration, and the psalm may have been written for some occasion in the new temple. The whole world is invited.

We sometimes fail to recognize that the tone of joy in the psalms, and in our prayers, is an index to God's joy that he made us and we are his. The words of verse 3 are not merely words about our joy of being in the family of God but are also reflective, and thankfully so, of God's joy that we are in the family, for "he made us, . . . we are his people, the sheep of his pasture." Shouldn't the shepherd be proud of his sheep? And when God's people "shout for joy to the LORD," our God takes pleasure in that joy. As many parents will affirm,

"No parent is happier than his or her least happy child" (see "Illustrating the Text"). That may not be absolutely applicable to God because he is God, but our joys and sorrows affect him, as do our sins.

The Message renders verse 4 with a paraphrase from our technological age: "Enter with the password: 'Thank you!' Make yourselves at home, talking praise." We may speak about the necessity to come into God's presence in the proper attitude, even with the proper language (see "Illustrating the Text"). The German theologian Rudolf Otto believed that England was the most religious country in the world, and he attributed that in part to the Book of Common Prayer, whose history goes back to the sixteenth-century Reformation (see "Illustrating the Text"). God is so eager to hear us utter any words of praise and thanksgiving, and also petition, which are sometimes babbling, sometimes flawless. The Lord said, "Before they call I will answer; while they are still speaking I will hear" (Isa. 65:23). Prayer is a conversation with God, and thanksgiving is an opportunity to "talk praise." God is listening to the utterances of our hearts as well as to those of our lips. Sometimes they are in perfect coordination, and sometimes they are not. But we need to remember that love always connects to some heavenly chord (see the MacDonald quote in "Illustrating the Text" in the unit on Ps. 130).

Second, this psalm assumes that the world is the object of the gospel message ("all the earth," 100:1). Israel's horizons were not always so wide, but even when they were more restrictive, the universal note had already been built into God's plan of grace, for through Abraham's descendants God would bless the world (Gen. 12:3). Psalm 100 is a witness to the joy of that discovery and the rapture of that announcement. The psalm is permeated with joy, the joy of the gospel to the world. Here we should mention the Great Commission (Matt. 28:18–20).

Third, there is one saving gospel because there is one saving God. Psalm 100 celebrates the gospel given to the world. In the Old Testament that gospel is represented by God's covenant with Israel, and although 100:3b–c is Israel's confession, the call to the nations to worship (100:1) implies that the nations too are invited to recite the confession (see "Theological Insights"). Jesus reminds his audience, "Your father Abraham rejoiced at the thought of seeing my day; he saw it and was glad" (John 8:56). Even God's revelation of himself in Jesus of Nazareth is the Old Testament gospel of God's "love" and "faithfulness" incarnate (Ps. 100:5). The nuances change, and the covenant assumes various forms, but the substance is the same: the character of the one self-revealing God. Christ's words in John 14:6 are to the effect that Christ is the all-comprehensive God: "I am the way and the truth and the life"—there is no reality outside that three-dimensional reality. Thus Christ puts the statement that follows in this light as he declares the exclusive nature of the saving gospel: "No one comes to the Father except through me." That is, there is only one saving gospel, because there is only one saving God, who has revealed himself in Jesus Christ. The covenant formula, in fact, points in the direction of Yahweh's comprehensive relationship to Israel: Yahweh is Israel's God, and Israel is Yahweh's people, and Yahweh will dwell in their midst. When we apply that to the world, then there is no room for other gods. We may also continue the emphasis on God's abiding presence with Israel and with us by applying the teaching of John's Gospel that the Holy Spirit undertook that role of God's/Christ's dwelling among us when Christ bodily ascended into heaven (John 16:12–15).

Illustrating the Text

The Old One Hundredth and more

Church History: While Psalm 100 is not a liturgical piece in the sense that other psalms, such as Psalm 136, are, it has taken its place in Reformation hymnology as a standard praise hymn. The popular paraphrase appears in the Genevan and Scottish Psalters, with the common tune, "The Old One Hundredth," composed by William Kethe, an English cleric who fled for refuge from anti-Protestant persecution to Geneva, where he wrote this tune and assisted in the composition of the Genevan Psalter. The English Reformation, though lacking a single central figure like John Calvin in Geneva, Martin Luther in Germany, or John Knox in Scotland, was nevertheless a powerful and transformative Reformation, with leadership shared by many commanding figures. One of the great products of that movement was the Book of Common Prayer, first published in 1549, and reedited by Thomas Cranmer, archbishop of Canterbury, in 1552 (with many more editions to follow).[2] Even in the modern era, the German theologian Rudolf Otto, in his *Idea of the Holy*,[3] expresses the view that England was the most religious country in the world, and he attributes that, in large part, to the influence of the Book of Common Prayer. Thomas Cranmer, and many other leaders and followers of the English Reformation, gave their lives for the Reformation cause. Cranmer, for example, was burned at the stake by Mary, queen of Scots in 1556.

A parent's happiness is equal to that of the least happy child.

Quote: Chuck Swindoll. Ben Patterson in his insightful book of meditations on the Psalms attributes this quote to Chuck Swindoll: "No parent is happier than his or her least happy child."[4] Every loving parent can identify with that sentiment. While it is wrong to read our human emotions and sentiments back into God, this one, I believe, is reflected in the biblical revelation of God's relationship to us human beings. He is our Father, and when our life is not joyful (happy), it affects our heavenly Father, just as our sins do (Ps. 51:4). We have failed to recognize this as we ought. The joy the earth is summoned to express in God's presence is an index to the joy that God has in us, for when he had created the world, he saw that it was "very good" (Gen. 1:31). And that is more than an ethical pronouncement; it is demonstrative of God's joy in his creation. This is not to suggest, however, that our joy determines our Father's, but it is to recognize that he identifies with us, with our joy and sorrow, just as earthly parents do, and as our heavenly Father he sorrows when we do and is joyful when we are. This truth belongs to the doctrine of the incarnation, as the writer to the Hebrews says: "Since the children have flesh and blood, he too shared in their humanity so that by his death he might break the power of him who holds the power of death. . . . For this reason he had to be made like them, fully human in every way, in order that he might become a merciful and faithful high priest in service to God, and that he might make atonement for the sins of the people" (Heb. 2:14, 17).

Why the Universal Perspective in the Wake of the Exile?

As this collection of the psalms of the heavenly King draws together the implications of Yahweh's kingship, the lines of grace fall wide and encompass the universe. If Yahweh is King, then he must be King over the whole world, not just over Israel. The thought that the kings of the earth will serve the Lord is expressed by 2:11 and 102:22. While we hear the voice of Israel confessing their faith through the covenant formula in 79:13 and 95:7, we hear also the voice of the nations making that same confession in 100:3, and it is a monotheistic confession (see 46:10 and 83:18).[1] Further, God's goodness that Moses and Israel had experienced, displayed in his covenant "love" and "faithfulness," was the dress rehearsal for the salvation of the world (100:5; see also Ps. 96).

One of the perplexing questions regarding this truth is, why should Israel widen its horizons universally at the close of the humiliating era of the exile? Why do the psalmists, especially in Book 4, become more universally extroverted, rather than withdrawing into themselves? This is a difficult question, of course, but we may consider these thoughts. First, the loss of kingship and the hope of its revival were overshadowed by the reassertion of Yahweh's kingship—that was intentional. The latter was not a substitute for the Davidic dynasty but was a reassurance that Yahweh's kingship was primary and all other monarchies, even Israel's, were mere shadows. After the Davidic dynasty came to its humiliating end at the hands of the Babylonians, it was time for Israel's real King to reassert himself as Lord of the universe. This self-assertion did not occur under the aegis of a new theological program, however, but was exercised within the framework of Yahweh's covenant with Israel, thus showing himself to be the one God over the world he had created, and governing the world by his one covenant (see the comments on 100:5).

Second, Isaiah calls the Persian king Cyrus "my shepherd" and says that he will "accomplish all that I please"; part of Yahweh's pleasure is the rebuilding of Jerusalem and the temple (Isa. 44:28). The fact that Cyrus issued his decree, allowing the exiles to go home and rebuild their temple, was evidence that he was acting under Yahweh's influence. Yet Psalm 100 takes the story beyond that and summons "all the earth" to join Israel in the temple to worship Yahweh (100:1, 4). Perhaps this story, more than any other, inspired the composition and editing of the psalms of the heavenly King.

Building off the developments that led to Israel's return from exile and restoration to the land, Book 5 definitely incorporates a universal note. This takes the form of a declaration that Yahweh is in heaven and does what he pleases and that the idols of the nations are the product of human hands and have no capacity for doing or saying anything (115:2–8; 135:15–18); Yahweh is God over all gods (135:5); and finally, everything that has breath is summoned to praise the Lord (150:6). While "those who fear the LORD" is sometimes viewed as a reference to non-Israelite devotees of Yahweh, the use of the phrase in Book 5 seems to refer rather to Israelites, associating them with the commandments (112:1; 119:79; 128:1). This is a phrase for the new community that is known for its devotion to the Torah. Psalm 119:79 seems to suggest some kind of "conversion" decision: "May those who fear you turn to me, those who understand your statutes." While it might be argued that this "universalism" that we see in Books 4 and 5 does not involve a saving confession, it is on the verge of that great moment of grace when the covenant of grace widens its scope to include all humanity.

"I Will Conduct the Affairs of My House with a Blameless Heart"

Big Idea

A true leader must be careful to lead a blameless life before he or she requires this standard of others.

Key Themes

- Our public life should be a reflection of our private life.
- A leader can only demand that followers live up to the level of his or her own moral standards.
- Our ultimate commitments shape our personal life and world.

Understanding the Text

This royal manifesto sets out the principles of the king's rule. Luther calls it "David's mirror of a monarch."[1] It defines the statement about the king's governing principle of "justice" mentioned in 99:4. Some view it as a vow that the Davidic king makes when he ascends the throne. However, the absence of a Davidic king after the exile leaves this vow suspended without fulfillment. If it was not messianic in its original intent, it became messianic when no Davidic king arose. In that case, it can be viewed as the vow the messianic King will take when he assumes his royal throne.

The Text in Context

Psalm 101 is the first Davidic psalm in Book 4, joined only by Psalm 103. We also observed earlier that Psalm 86 is the only Davidic psalm in Book 3. Since the Psalter is largely Davidic, the editors seemed to assume that David must be represented in all five books. Further, whereas Psalms 99 and 100 conclude with scenes of the temple, this psalm ends in "the city of the LORD," purged of evildoers (101:8). We can see this as an Old Testament version of the new Jerusalem where the temple and the new Jerusalem have merged into a single reality (Rev. 21:22).

Outline/Structure

1. The king's personal vow to walk in integrity (101:1–3a)
2. The king's public standard of ethics (101:3b–7)
3. The king's vow to maintain justice (101:8)

Historical and Cultural Background

"The one whose walk is blameless" (101:6) was most likely an official in the king's court (see 2 Sam. 8:2–18; 20:23–26; 1 Kings 4:1–6), and his faithfulness in carrying out the king's program was critical to the king's success.[2] This psalm could have been written for the accession of a preexilic Israelite king to the throne and later applied to the messianic King after the exile when there was no Davidic king forthcoming. Or we may view it eschatologically as a royal psalm (see Ps. 45) in which the ascending king, or the messianic King, vows to restore justice and right behavior to Jerusalem.

Interpretive Insights

Title *Of David*. This is the first Davidic psalm in Book 4. In fact, the only two persons to whom psalms are attributed in Book 4 are Moses (Ps. 90) and David (Pss. 101 and 103).

101:1 *love and justice*. These are characterizing qualities of the kingdom of God, both present and future (Pss. 89:15; 119:149; Hosea 12:7; Mic. 6:8; Jer. 9:23). The first noun refers to the Lord's conduct that issues from his loving character. The second refers to conduct according to the principles of justice.[3]

I will sing. Singing was a typical way of presenting a royal psalm (see Ps. 45, title).

101:2 *my house*. This is most likely the house of the king, or more widely, the kingdom itself. However, in light of the idea that the king is the guardian of the Lord's house, by extension it might also be the temple.[4] In that case, the ethical standard that will govern the king's house, as well as the temple, reminds us of Psalms 15 and 24, with their entry rituals. Also it is a fitting picture of the statement of Psalm 93:5, "Holiness adorns your house."

with a blameless heart. The intent of the psalm is to define how the king will conduct his affairs "with a blameless heart." The opposite of a "blameless heart" is a "perverse" heart, which the king explicitly rejects in verse 4. Seven ethical stipulations describe his administrative policy:

"I will not look with approval on anything that is vile." (101:3)

"I hate what faithless people do; I will have no part in it." (101:3)

"The perverse of heart shall be far from me." (101:4)

"Whoever slanders their neighbor in secret, I will put to silence." (101:5)

"Whoever has haughty eyes and a proud heart, I will not tolerate." (101:5)

"No one who practices deceit will dwell in my house." (101:7)

"No one who speaks falsely will stand in my presence." (101:7)

Proverbs 6:16–19 lists seven things the Lord hates, and the list is similar to this one, but not a duplicate.

101:3 *anything that is vile.* The Hebrew word is made up of two elements: *beli* ("without") and *ya'al* ("worth"), basically "without worth."

I will have no part in it. Literally, "It will not cleave to me." This is a descriptive disavowal of evil's clinging power (see Heb. 12:1, "sin which clings so closely" [RSV]).

101:4 *The perverse of heart.* The NIV translates the phrase as people rather than a condition, but the psalmist is basically describing the condition of the human heart that he rejects as his personal and administrative ethical policy. One cannot maintain the latter without the former. The adjective "perverse" means "crooked" or "twisted" and is the opposite of "straight" or "upright." The condition is the opposite of a "blameless heart" in verse 2 (see Prov. 11:20; 17:20).

101:5 *Whoever slanders their neighbor in secret, I will put to silence.* The Hebrew verb rendered "put to silence" means "to cut off." The Syriac has "I will silence," which is the effect of being cut off, and which the NIV prefers.

haughty eyes. See Proverbs 6:16–17.

proud heart. Literally, "a wide heart," wide enough to allow evil to dwell there. This term is found also in the Wisdom literature (e.g., Prov. 21:4; cf. 28:25 [NIV: "greedy"]).

101:6 *the faithful in the land.* These are most likely the officials in the king's court and a parallel with "the one whose walk is blameless." The king's officials must emulate the king's own character (101:2). Verses 5–8 outline the psalmist's public life, while verses 2–4 prescribe his public policy. Here the king outlines his vetting process that will lead to selecting those individuals who comply with his ethical program as officials in his court. The phrase is a superlative, meaning "the most faithful in the land."[5]

101:7 *No one who practices deceit.* Six times the psalmist uses the negative ("not," "no," etc.) to exclude certain behaviors from his royal program of operations.

101:8 *Every morning.* Justice was generally dispensed in the morning when the elders of the city met at the city gate to deal with any problems the people of the city brought them (2 Sam. 15:2; Jer. 21:12; Ruth 4). Here the king expunges the city of evil every morning so that it can be truly "the city of the LORD." Compare Ezekiel's name for the city, "THE LORD IS THERE" (Ezek. 48:35).

Theological Insights

In Psalm 101, verses 2–4 set forth the personal ethic of this ruler, and verses 5–8 lay out his public policy, which gives us a "format for the examination of conscience."[6] Perhaps the greatest disqualification of a leader is to be found in personal violation of the standard of conduct that he or she requires of his or her own subordinates. "It is the character of the governor and the character of those in his government," says Mays, "that really determine what the effect of their governing is on the governed. In this the psalm is radical but history is replete with examples that prove it is right."[7] A true leader must "be careful to lead a blameless" life before he or she requires this standard of others. The pattern has its origin in God himself, who says to Israel: "Be holy because I, the LORD your God, am holy" (Lev. 19:2). The biblical faith is one of the *imitation of God*. The metaphor of walking in the Lord's ways is another evidence of imitating God, walking in his steps as he leads the way (Deut. 10:12–19; Mic. 6:8).[8]

Teaching the Text

The divine name occurs only twice in this psalm (vv. 1 and 8) and forms an *inclusio*, which implies that the ethical standard of the psalm is based on the Lord's covenant with Israel and is also confirmed by the term "love" (101:1), a central concept of the Mosaic covenant. In this vein, Mays comments: "The psalm also teaches that conduct depends on character and character is shaped by ultimate commitments. It would insist that 'you cannot be good without God,' a lesson for more than rulers."[9] This psalmist's "ultimate commitments" to God and his covenant are undeniable.

Just a few years ago before the Christmas season, the atheists in a major American city posted a billboard that read: "Why believe in a god? Just be good for goodness' sake." But is it possible to be good just for the sake of being good? The problem is this: Can goodness exist without God? Can a society endure without anchoring its morality in God? Or to put it in terms of our American system, when moral goodness is shifted from the religious sphere to the political, and moral goodness becomes a ward of the state rather than the church, can it endure?

The covenantal orientation of this psalm is evidenced in the *inclusio* of the divine name Yahweh and in the covenant terms "love" and "justice"

(101:1). Those two observations point to the "ultimate commitments" of the psalmist that Mays alludes to, that is, the Mosaic covenant and the God who stands behind it. Most Western societies have taken their standard of morality from the Bible. In the present social and political climate, however, we are emerging from that ethic and are cutting ourselves loose from our moral moorings. This advertisement is evidence of that: "Just be good for goodness' sake." The question then becomes even more urgent: Can we be good without God?

Christianity has constructed a bulwark against this kind of thinking. It has done so with the ethic of love: "God is love" (1 John 4:8). John wrote, "For God so loved the world that he gave his one and only Son" (John 3:16), and this kind of self-giving love has become the model of love and the basis of moral goodness. The New Testament even uses a special term to describe this love, the Greek term *agapē*. It is a completely selfless love, the kind that gives and expects nothing in return, and it is a divine gift that works against our sinful inclinations. This is the vertical dimension of Christian morality: God is love. But it is also the horizontal dimension. God's love is one of his communicable attributes, and we are commanded to communicate this love on a horizontal plane: "A new command I give you: Love one another. As I have loved you, so you must love one another" (John 13:34). It is from this foundation of *agapē* love that the dignity and worth of the individual arises. *Agapē* love gives birth to the idea that every individual is of equal worth in God's sight, whether rich or poor, intelligent or simpleminded. All of the distinctions that develop in the course of human culture are erased in the light of God's love (Gal. 3:28). The alternative is human reason, which produces the idea that our self-worth is determined by our contribution to society. However one might interpret Genesis 1 in the light of modern science, the important message is, as Sir John Eccles puts it, that a human is not merely "an insignificant animal" (see "Illustrating the Text"). The result of ignoring this message is euthanasia and abortion on demand, to mention only two consequences. But the Christian faith, on the other hand, elevates the individual through *agapē* love, and that is God's love, God's ultimate commitment to his creation, and the goal of all human commitments.

Illustrating the Text

The misjudgment of science

Science: In the February 1985 issue of *US News and World Report*, in an article titled "Science Can't Explain," Sir John Eccles, an Australian neurophysiologist and Nobel Prize winner, writes: "Science has gone too far in breaking down man's belief in his spiritual greatness and has given him the belief that he is merely an insignificant animal who has arisen by chance and necessity on an insignificant planet lost in the great cosmic immensity."[10]

The death of the sacred

Story: There was a time in our social development when it was considered particularly heinous to steal from the church. But as our ethical moorings have cut us free from all things sacred, every institution is fair game for those with evil intent. From the late nineteenth and early twentieth centuries, when the church was still considered sacred, there is a story about a legendary Presbyterian pastor in Birmingham, Alabama, affectionately known as Brother Bryan. He was frequently out on the streets befriending homeless people, and the story goes that one night as he walked the streets of Birmingham, a would-be robber came up behind him, stuck his gun in Brother Bryan's back, and demanded his money. When the pastor turned around, the thief cried, "Oh, it's Brother Bryan!" and scurried away without any loot.[11] But the church today is fair game in a society where one's own needs and desires are the only criteria for determining one's actions.

The vertical world has been replaced by the horizontal.

Culture: A few years ago the Jewish novelist Chaim Potok spoke at Wheaton College, and he made the point that two hundred years ago the world was a vertical world, but it has now become a horizontal world. By that he meant that two hundred years ago people believed there was a God who stood above the world and governed it, and they knew they were in relationship to him, whether they liked it or not. But now in our horizontal world, God no longer is viewed as a force with whom we have to reckon, and we are concerned only about ourselves and the world around us. We relate only to the horizontal dimensions of life. There is no God above us, it is assumed, governing our world, pursuing us with love, calling us to a responsible and holy life.

The prince's psalm

History: Ernest the Pious, Duke of Saxe-Gotha (1601–75), once sent an erring minister a copy of Psalm 101 as a corrective, and it became a proverb in the country that when an official had done wrong, he would soon receive the prince's psalm to read.[12]

"The Heavens . . . Will Perish, but You Remain"

Big Idea

Our world may change, but God remains the same.

Key Themes

- Hope need not be tangible, but it must be substantive.
- The peoples of the world have become God's people.

Understanding the Text

This individual lament expresses distress about three things: God's anger directed against Israel, the insults the psalmist has received from his enemies, and the thought of humanity's swiftly passing life.[1]

The Text in Context

This fifth of the seven penitential psalms of the ancient church (Pss. 6; 32; 38; 51; 102; 130; 147) contains, like Psalm 6, no open expression of penitence. Yet the confession of sin in verse 17 may be the reason it was included among the penitential psalms.

Lamentations 1; 2; 4; and 5 are, for the most part, personifications of Jerusalem, and Lamentations 3, the center lament of Lamentations, is the nation lamenting her fate. Similarly, Psalm 102 depicts the speaker as "the destitute" (102:17), "the prisoner" (sg.), and "those condemned to death" (102:20), plausible figures for a personification. The title itself leaves that possibility open, identifying the speaker as "an afflicted person who has grown weak." Thus we may view 102:1–11 as a personification of Jerusalem, using the imagery of destruction and a life languishing in exile. This literary form is sustained through verse 11, at which point the speaker ruminates (note the first person, "I," "me," and "my") about the destruction and restoration of

Zion (102:12–22), and then the personified city resumes the first-person lament in verses 23–24, praying, "Do not take me away, my God, in the midst of my days."

Metaphorically, the speaker's days "vanish like smoke," and his bones "burn like glowing embers" (102:3). He is emaciated by his stark conditions (102:5) and living "like an owl among the ruins" (see Ezra 9:9). Further, the metaphor of a "bird alone on a roof" suggests one deserted by his mate, perhaps an allusion to widowhood (see Lam. 1:1). Even the violence that brought an end to the city is alluded to in 102:10: "you have taken me up and thrown me aside." The time of the lament seems to be toward the end of the exile, "for it is time to show favor to her; the appointed time has come" (102:13b).

Outline/Structure

Note the correspondences in the following outline, implying the cohesive nature of the poem: (1) parts 1 and 2 close with a lament over Zion's abbreviated history (102:11, 23–24); (2) part 2 opens with praise of Yahweh as heavenly King and Redeemer of Zion (102:12–13), and part 3 opens with praise of Yahweh as Creator of the earth and heavens (102:25).

1. Petition and lament (102:1–11)
   a. Petition (102:1–3)
   b. Psalmist laments his affliction (102:4–10)
   c. Psalmist laments his waning days (102:11)
2. Praise and hope (102:12–24)
   a. Praise of Yahweh as heavenly King and redeemer (102:12)
   b. Hope of Yahweh's favor on Zion (102:13–14)
   c. Hope of the nations and kings to become God-fearers (102:15–17)
   d. Yahweh's compassion on Zion (102:18–22)
   e. Zion's lament of her short history and prayer for extended days (102:23–24)
3. Praise and hope (102:25–28)
   a. Praise of Yahweh as Creator of the earth and heavens (102:25)
   b. Praise of Yahweh as the unchangeable constant (102:26–27)
   c. Zion's children and posterity in Yahweh's presence (102:28)

Historical and Cultural Background

The rich similes of this psalm give us pictures of Israel's world, describing the physical decline of the psalmist or most likely, the devastation and desecration of Zion. The birds are probably unclean.

"Days vanish like smoke." (102:3a)

"Bones burn like glowing embers." (102:3b)

"My heart is blighted and withered like grass." (102:4a)

"I am like a desert owl." (102:6a)

"[I am] like an owl among the ruins." (102:6b)

"I have become like a bird alone on a roof." (102:7)

"My days are like the evening shadow." (102:11a)

Interpretive Insights

Title *A prayer.* The title is written in parallel clauses, something that Hakham says does not occur in any other heading[2] and may be original to the psalm:

> A prayer of an afflicted person
> who has grown weak
> and before the LORD
> pours out a lament. (Hebrew order of the phrases; author's
>   translation)

102:1 *Hear my prayer, LORD.* The verb is emphatic: "LORD, *please* hear my prayer."

102:3 *my days vanish like smoke.* This refers to the days of his suffering when his life seemed to vanish away and he called on the Lord for help.

my bones burn like glowing embers. This may be an allusion to fever and suggests a physical illness. Or it may be simply the description of an emotion. Most likely, the psalmist is suffering from emotional and physical ailments, with the emotional being primary.

102:4 *My heart is blighted and withered like grass.* The metaphors that build on the body parts, plus the last statement, "I forget to eat my food," support the emotional interpretation as the primary cause of the suppliant's suffering. We must keep in mind too that this is personification.

102:5 *I . . . am reduced to skin and bones.* Literally, "My bone(s) cleave to my flesh [or "skin"]." While it sounds like a physical disease, he is overwhelmed with grief, which can also cause emaciation.

102:6 *desert owl.* The species of animal is not certain. Hakham renders it a "small owl."[3] The word "owl" (*kos*) may designate owls generally.[4] The fact that the psalmist identifies with a ritually unclean bird may imply that he himself is ritually unclean or is isolated and lonely like an unclean fowl, maybe even crying out in pain with screeching sounds like an owl. Of course, as a personification of Jerusalem, now in ruins, a ritually unclean bird is an appropriate metaphor.

the ruins. This may have a double meaning, the ruins where the "owl" dwells and the ruins of the temple (Ezra 9:9). Jerusalem personified laments the lonely ruins of the city.

102:8 *All day long my enemies taunt me.* The psalmist is the subject of the previous seven verses (102:1–7), and now he turns his attention to the enemies who react to his troubles in a taunting way (102:8–9). If the suppliant speaks for the suffering community, the enemies are likely the nations (see 102:15).

102:11 *the evening shadow.* Literally, "stretched out / lengthening shadow" that announces approaching death. Now the subject is Yahweh, who, in the suppliant's view, has treated him violently ("taken me up and thrown me aside," 102:10). Job perceives that God has also treated him the same way (Job 30:22), so a personal interpretation is in order, but a corporate interpretation, describing Yahweh's violent treatment of Jerusalem, is also quite possible.

102:12–13 *But you, Lord, sit enthroned forever.* "But *you*, Lord" of 102:12 stands over against "*I wither*" (102:11). Yahweh's kingship is the reason he can intervene in Zion's history. While Yahweh is not called king in the psalm, the verb "to sit" is the language of kingship. The confession of verse 12 parallels Lamentations 5:19.

Yahweh is "enthroned" (102:12; cf. 92:8; 93:2;); he rules over the kings of the earth (102:15); he is eternal (102:26; cf. 90:1; 92:8; 93:2); and he is enthroned on high (102:19; cf. 93:4). Note that the language of Yahweh's kingship in Book 4 is part of the editorial strategy of shifting the emphasis from David's failed dynasty to Yahweh's kingship, which is the primal kingship and all that ultimately matters. References to Zion in Book 4 are 97:8; 99:2; 102:13, 21.

102:15 *The nations will fear the name of the Lord.* Now the subject changes to the nations (102:15–17) who "fear the name of the Lord" because of Yahweh's restoration of Zion (102:16).[5] See also Isaiah 59:19.

102:18 *Let this be written for a future generation.* Writing down the glorious deeds that Yahweh has done (102:19–22) is a way to remember and ensure that his renown should last.

102:19 *The Lord looked down from his sanctuary on high.* This statement implies, by Yahweh's attentive survey, that the psalmist's prayer has been answered.

102:20–22 *release those condemned to death.* "This" in verse 18 evidently refers to the three events mentioned in these verses: the release of the exiles (102:20), the restoration of Jerusalem (102:21), and the restoration of the temple (102:21).

102:23–24 *In the course of my life he broke my strength.* Literally, "He afflicted (me) in the way of my strength." The city is speaking, and she says that the Lord has cut her life short in her prime. The petition that follows compares the psalmist's years (cf. ESV), which are short, to Yahweh's years, which endure throughout the generations.

102:25–27 *In the beginning.* Literally, "before," thus "before" the generations of humankind "you laid the foundations of the earth." Yahweh created the heavens and the earth, but they are not eternal as God is. Not only did Yahweh create them, but he controls them, changing them "like a garment."

102:28 *The children of your servants will live in your presence.* Reading this in the light of 102:18, we observe that the God who created the heavens has also looked down from "his sanctuary on high" and had pity on the "prisoners" and "those condemned to death." He is eternal and omnipotent, but he still has pity on his human creatures. The phrase "in your presence" in the second half of the verse may be an allusion to the new temple. The sense of the text, however, is about the security of future generations: "The children of your servants will dwell securely; their descendants will be established before you" (author's translation).

Theological Insights

Hope must be based on some reason, or else it is false hope. It does not have to be tangible, but it has to be substantive. This psalm leans on the substance of hope in God's changeless character. Even the heavens may perish and wear out like a garment, but God remains (102:26), and his years, unlike humanity's, have no end. Hebrews 13:8 is a restatement of this truth, applied to Christ, as that writer also applies the truth of verses 25–27 to Christ in Hebrews 1:10–12. The fact that God does not change provides stability in our changing world and undergirds our hope for the future.

Teaching the Text

Psalm 102 presents us with the challenge of preaching the whole psalm or developing one or two of its ideas, not an unusual dilemma in preaching the Psalter. If we decide to preach a single idea, it should be one that is very prominent, if not the main theme of the psalm. In this instance, the brevity of human life and the eternity of God are central. Preaching the whole psalm, however, is a better strategy because it does not risk the problem of an imbalance of ideas.

First, the brevity of human life compared to God's eternity is central to the psalm. The human condition includes much suffering, as this psalm attests (102:3–11), and God's eternal existence puts it in perspective. God will arise and have compassion on Zion (102:13). James also stresses the ephemeral nature of humanity and insists that we are totally dependent on God's will as we face the future (James 4:14–17).

Second, it is the responsibility of this generation to record God's mighty deeds in history for the instruction of coming generations (102:18). The Christian faith, like Judaism, is a historical faith, anchored in history and lived out in historical lives and events. Each generation lives not only for itself but for the next generation. This is a lesson of history that is difficult to learn and even harder to implement, but it is mandatory for the good of humankind and of God's eternal purposes. The human life cycle also illustrates this truth. Parents live for their children, and as they become grandparents, they begin to sense they are living for the next generation. In 1 Corinthians 10, Paul reviews some of Israel's history and reminds this church that these things were written to warn future generations (1 Cor. 10:11).

Third, this psalm speaks of the great transaction that makes the peoples into God's people (102:15). When the nations see the Lord's restoration of Zion, they "will fear the name of the LORD." This puts Israel's faith in the wider perspective of the salvation of the world. God's grace is universal (see "Theological Insights" in the unit on Ps. 100). The apostle Peter writes to the gentiles, dispersed throughout Asia Minor, and applies the sense of Hosea 2:23, originally written to Israel, to the gentiles: "Once you were not a people, but now you are the people of God" (1 Pet. 2:10). We should emphasize divine mercy as the reason we gentiles, as well as Jews, enjoy the grace of God. Out of the freedom of his electing grace, God called Abraham, so he has the same freedom to call the gentiles to join this awesome company.

Fourth, 102:26 speaks of the hope that, in the eschatological day, the heavens will perish. Second Peter 3:7 and 10 describe that day when the first heaven and the first earth will have passed away (Rev. 21:1), as God makes all things new (Rev. 21:5). This message of renewal would carry a high level of comfort for the exiles as they anticipate the renewal of Zion. And as God conducts his program of restoration, they are reminded of God's constancy (102:26–27). So the God who has revealed himself to Israel in past generations is the one unchangeable force and stable presence in their lives. It is in that past revelation that Israel has received something substantive on which to hope for the future. That truth, of course, retains the same high level of comfort for believers in all ages!

Illustrating the Text

The seeds in the crevices

Quote: **Mark Twain.** The psalmist's description of his emaciated body in 102:3–11 is a bit reminiscent of the decrepit estate in Ecclesiastes 12:1–8. While the psalmist does not openly confess his sins, the early church included this psalm among the penitential psalms for a reason; likely they saw this lament as a description of the deteriorating state of sin in the psalmist's life. Our sins, though they may seem small and insignificant, have a way of growing in boldness and audacity and, with time, disrupting and even destroying our lives. On one of his world tours Mark Twain and his fellow travelers visited the Crusader-era fortress of Nimrod near the city of Banias in what is today the Golan Heights. He wondered how the mighty structure could have been toppled, even by the massive forces of an earthquake, though the facts spoke clearly that such a disruption had occurred there:

> We wondered how such a solid mass of masonry could be affected even by an earthquake, and could not understand what agency had made Baniyas a ruin; but we found the destroyer after a while, and then our wonder was increased tenfold. Seeds had fallen in crevices in the vast walls; the seeds had sprouted; the tender, insignificant sprouts had hardened; they grew larger and larger, and by a steady, imperceptible pressure forced the great stones apart, and now are bringing such destruction upon a giant work that has even mocked the earthquakes to scorn! Gnarled and twisted trees spring from the old walls everywhere, and beautify and overshadow the gray battlements with a wild luxuriance of foliage.[6]

"No stranger did that to us."

Quote: **H. M. Kuitert.** The suppliant reviews his suffering (102:3–11) and prays, "Do not hide your face from me when I am in distress" (102:2a), inferring that he does not see God's face in his suffering. Theologian H. M. Kuitert speaks of the catastrophes the farmers of the province of Zeeland (Netherlands) often suffered, and when their pastors sought to comfort them, they were prone to say, "Minister, no stranger did that to us." Kuitert comments that "the 'face' [that they saw in tragedy] is not the real face; behind it is hidden the friendly face of God."[7] That is what our psalmist is looking for.

"The LORD Is Compassionate and Gracious, Slow to Anger, Abounding in Love"

Big Idea

The praise of heaven is the tuning fork for our earthly praise.

Key Themes

- The brevity of human life is painted in relief against God's eternity.
- God's love is the reason for his works.

Understanding the Text

Weiser has called this psalm "one of the finest blossoms on the tree of biblical faith."[1] It is a psalm of praise par excellence. As the editor(s) completes the configuration of Book 4, he chooses four psalms of praise (Pss. 103–6; Pss. 105 and 106 are also thanksgiving psalms) to conclude the book, and the editor of Book 5 begins that collection with another thanksgiving psalm (Ps. 107).

The Text in Context

Psalm 102:13 says, "You will arise and have compassion on Zion," and Psalm 103 is a complement to that hope, as it projects the image of Yahweh's love to a community whose sins have all but destroyed it. Kidner calls Psalms 103 and 104, both psalms of praise, "twin stars of the first magnitude,"[2] although they are more fraternal twins than identical. Their major resemblance is that both poems begin and end with the self-call to praise. Looking retrospectively,

Waltner proposes that the editor(s) of Book 4 placed Psalm 103 after Psalm 102 because he saw that divine forgiveness was the answer to the horrors Israel had suffered in the Babylonian exile (102:13–14).[3]

Some commentators mention the thematic similarities between Psalms 103 and 90: forgiveness of sin (103:3, 10, 12; 90:7–8), the Lord's love and mercy (103:4, 8, 11, 17–18; 90:14), humanity's brief life (103:15–16; 90:5–6), and the Lord's rule over all (103:19; 90:1–2).[4]

Outline/Structure

The psalm opens and closes with the same line, forming an *inclusio*, which defines the whole psalm as a psalm of praise.

1. Praise of the Lord for his benefits (103:1–5)
   a. Self-call to praise (103:1–2)
   b. God's benefits (103:3–5)
2. The Lord's nature as experienced by "those who keep his covenant" (103:6–18)
3. A call to universal praise (103:19–22)

Historical and Cultural Background

The clause "so that your youth is renewed like the eagle's" (103:5b) has spawned speculation about several eagle legends that we need not rehearse here. What stands behind this simile is most likely the eagle's natural loss of its plumage and its subsequent renewal, giving it a beautiful and youthful appearance.[5] Isaiah too seems to know this aspect of the eagle's nature when he says, "youths shall faint and be weary," but "they who wait for the Lord shall renew their strength; they shall mount up with wings like eagles; they shall run and not be weary; they shall walk and not faint" (Isa. 40:30–31 ESV).

Interpretive Insights

Title *Of David.* Only this psalm and Psalm 101 are attributed to David in Book 4. Other occurrences of the phrase "of/to David" as the sole title of the psalm are found in Psalms 25–28; 35; and 37.

103:1 *Praise the Lord, my soul.* The psalmist addresses his own person with this self-exhortation. The "soul" is not the Greek concept of "soul" but is the person, often used in poetry in place of the pronoun "I." Here it is synonymous with "my inmost being," which includes the suppliant's mind and heart.[6] The divine name ("Lord") occurs eleven times in the psalm and, along with the term "covenant" (103:18) and the language of Exodus 34:6, positions this psalm in the center of the Mosaic covenant. It is a virtual reaffirmation of the covenant.

my inmost being. These are the internal organs, representing the whole person. Perowne encapsulates the idea as "expressing the desire to enlist every thought, faculty, power, the heart with all its affections, the will, the conscience, the reason, in a word the whole spiritual being, all in man that is best and highest, in the same heavenly service."[7] See also 42:5 and 11 for the use of this self-address.

103:2 *his benefits.* This term, speaking in an earthly sphere, is used of deeds that require recompense.[8] Since these are Yahweh's deeds, by that definition they require the human response of praise.

103:3 *all your sins . . . all your diseases.* The psalmist begins to list the benefits: forgiveness, healing, redemption from death, love, compassion, good things, and renewal of life (103:3–5). The Hebrew word for "diseases" (*tahalu'im*) occurs in Deuteronomy 29:22 (see "Theological Insights" in the unit on Ps. 32).

103:4 *the pit.* This term (*shahat*) designates the netherworld (Sheol) or death itself. To "redeem" one's life from the "pit" is to rescue one from death (e.g., 6:5). The metaphor of redemption is based on the practice of a kinsman who rescues a relative from slavery or captivity by paying a price. While this text may not relate to life after death, Psalm 16:9–11, where this term also occurs, certainly points in that direction (see Acts 2:25–28; 13:35–37; see the comments on 16:10).

crowns you with love and compassion. These two attributes of Yahweh echo Exodus 34:6, one of the defining portraits of God in the Hebrew Bible. Delitzsch calls "love" (*hesed*) "the primal condition and the foundation" of all the other attributes of Yahweh and refers to it as "sin-pardoning mercy."[9] The crown is woven out of "love and compassion,"[10] a crown jewel beyond all comparison. See Psalm 8:5.

103:5 *satisfies your desires with good things.* This includes all that love can embrace. The translation "your desires" is influenced by the Septuagint, but the same Hebrew word in Ezekiel 16:7 denotes a well-proportioned body (see "Historical and Cultural Background" for the simile "like the eagle's").[11]

103:6 *The Lord works righteousness . . . for all the oppressed.* The term "righteousness" is a Hebrew plural, and in Judges 5:11 (NIV: "victories"); 1 Samuel 12:7; and Micah 6:5, it means God's saving ("righteous") deeds.

103:7 *his ways.* This indicates "his attributes." Moses asks God to show him his "way" (Exod. 33:13), and the Lord says, "I will cause all my goodness to pass in front of you" (33:19) and then informs him of the thirteen attributes of mercy (34:6–7; see the sidebar "The Thirteen Attributes of God" in the unit on Ps. 111).

his deeds. "Deeds" are wondrous deeds, synonymous with miraculous deeds, which include the exodus from Egypt. This term is used synonymously with "wonders" in Psalm 78:11.

103:8 *compassionate and gracious.* This is a description of Yahweh's ways. These words are drawn from Exodus 34:6, where Yahweh gives his self-portrait.[12] The omission of the last word of Exodus 34:6 ("abounding in love and *faithfulness* [or "truth"]") may imply that the psalmist wants to emphasize Yahweh's "love" (*hesed*), a point that the context bears out. See also Psalms 86:15; 145:8; Joel 2:13; and Nehemiah 9:17 for the use of Exodus 34:6.

103:10 *he does not treat us as our sins deserve.* He does not pay us in kind for our sins. Rather, Yahweh forgives out of love.

103:11–13 *as high as the heavens are above the earth, so great is his love.* The psalmist uses three metaphors of comparison to convey the greatness of God's care for his human creatures: the height of the heavens above the earth, to measure God's love (*hesed*); the distance between the east and the west, to measure God's forgiveness; and the father's pity for his children, to measure God's compassion. Neither of the first two measurements can be quantified, and, of course, that is the point—they exceed our capability to measure them. The concept of God as father (103:13) is common in the Old Testament (e.g., Exod. 4:22; Deut. 14:1; Isa. 1:2), as it is in ancient Near Eastern literature.

103:14–16 *he knows how we are formed.* "Our frame" in 103:14 (RSV; Heb. *yetser*; NIV: "how we are formed") occurs in Genesis 8:21 in the sense of "desire" or "inclination." Here it carries both the nuance of "desire" and "frame" ("he remembers that we are dust"). Our heavenly Father "knows how we are formed" and "remembers that we are dust," obviously because he made us (Ps. 100:3). The "he" is emphatic: "*he* knows."

he remembers that we are dust. The life of mortals is like grass. The suppliant employs two expressions to state how frail is human life: (1) the Lord "remembers that we are dust" (103:14), evidently alluding to Genesis 2:7; and

(2) humanity's life is "like grass" that withers when the hot wind blows over it (Ps. 90:5; cf. 102:4a, 11b; Isa. 40:6–8; 51:12).

To emphasize the idea of our humanity, the Hebrew of verse 15 begins with a *casus pendens* ("pending case"): literally, "*As for mankind*, his days are like grass."[13] God's love (103:17) puts humanity's short life in relief by comparing it to God's eternity. The covenant, the functional heart of the Torah, was not merely God's gift to Israel, but it demanded obedience.

103:19 *his throne . . . his kingdom rules over all.* God's "throne" and "kingdom" are parallel terms referring to God's rule over the world. The word "all" is prefixed by the definite article, giving the phrase definiteness, "his kingdom rules over *everything* [lit., "the all"]," that is, the universe.[14] See 1 Chronicles 29:12 for the same usage of the definite article with "all" (*kol*).

103:20–22 *Praise the LORD.* The first "Praise the LORD" bids "his angels," adding the descriptive "you mighty ones who do his bidding" (cf. Joel 3:11)[15] and "who obey his word," to praise the Lord. The second "Praise the LORD" summons "all his heavenly hosts," adding the descriptive "you his servants who do his will," to praise the Lord. The third "Praise the LORD" calls "all his works," with the descriptive "everywhere in his dominion," to praise the Lord. And the fourth "Praise the LORD" bids the psalmist's own person to praise the Lord, "that his voice may not be wanting in the mighty anthem,"[16] thus combining a heavenly and earthly choir of praise (also Ps. 148).

Theological Insights

The praise of God in Psalm 103 begins and ends on an inclusive note that involves both God ("Praise the LORD") and humanity ("my soul"). And this praise command is inclusive of the entire hymn of praise, symbolized by the *inclusio* ("Praise the LORD, my soul," 103:1a and 22c), and we might say, of life itself, for the life of the believer should be a life of praise. Waltner reminds us that our "forgetting and turning away from God begins when we no longer praise" him.[17]

The psalmist tunes into God's praise, first by specifying seven "benefits" for which we ought to praise God (see the comments on 103:3). Then in strophe 2 (103:6–18) these benefits are further described, all stemming from God's "love." As the psalmist tunes his voice to the universal praise of God (103:20–22b), he begins to hear the perfect melody sung by the angels and servants of God ("mighty ones") "who do his bidding." Then another voice, God's creation, with perfect pitch, joins the heavenly chorus, and finally, listening in on heaven's performance, the psalmist adds his voice again. Heaven and creation become the tuning fork for our own praise. The great hallelujah of Revelation 19 exhibits the same incremental praise of God. The praise of God is more than a mode of worship; it is the language of perfection for talking to God. Yet, on the way to perfection, as we would expect, it has its degrees and intensities, and we humans join in at our particular level and intensity as we move, by God's grace, to the level and intensity of the perfect pitch of the heavenly hosts. And so our psalmist moves us on that scale to the ultimate level and intensity of the "heavenly hosts, you his servants who do his will" (103:21). Von Rad sums up this truth: "Praise is man's most characteristic mode of existence."[18]

Significantly, this unique level and intensity of praise in its ultimate utterance includes us human beings ("all his works"), as our earthly praise merges into this heavenly language of praise ("Praise the LORD, my soul"). Heaven and earth are joined in perfect harmony.

Teaching the Text

This psalm is a minor treatise on God's love (*hesed*) and shares a kinship with 1 Corinthians 13. As suggested in the "Interpretive Insights" (see the comments on 103:8), our psalmist ends the quotation of Exodus 34:6 with "love," omitting the last word ("faithfulness/truth") of the formula of grace, most likely in order to put stress on the "love" of Yahweh, a point that the context of 103:8 bears out. The psalm, in fact, downplays God's anger ("nor will he harbor his anger forever," 103:9b) and accentuates God's love (130:8) and forgiveness (103:10–12).

As our first point, we may recognize, indeed emphasize, that the psalm does not deal with God's love in a vacuum, because the language of the psalm recognizes that Israel has sinned, and it is precisely against that backdrop that the love of God is so powerfully forceful (103:13), summing up Israel's human frailties—and ours—in the words "we are dust" and "the life of mortals is like grass" (103:14, 15). In a similar setting, Paul writes his "love chapter" (1 Cor. 13) to a church that has been fragmented into special interest groups with presumptuous attitudes of superiority. It is the real world, the world we all know, where people hurt, and worry disquiets, and conflict pushes its way into our lives, and unchecked resentment grows into the cancer of hatred.

As our second point, we may emphasize that our psalm, and Paul's rhapsody of love, is the eye of the storm in a world where the "wind blows over" the flower of life and it is gone (103:15–16), and we are never free of that dreadful threat. This peaceful sanctuary is composed of the Lord's love, which is from everlasting to everlasting to "those who fear him" (103:17), on whom he has compassion like a father for his children (103:13).

A third point (see "Theological Insights" for further illumination) is that this perspective on God's gracious love and forgiveness draws out our praise, which blends with the praise of the heavenly hosts and culminates in the perfect harmony between heaven and earth: "Praise the LORD, my soul!"

Illustrating the Text

"Praise, my soul, the King of heaven."

Hymn: "Praise, My Soul, the King of Heaven," by Henry Francis Lyte. Lyte, an English minister, composed a hymn based on Psalm 103, published in his collection of paraphrased psalms, *The Spirit of the Psalms*, in 1834. This hymn draws together the doctrines of the exalted Lord of the universe and his gracious benefits provided to his people. Queen Elizabeth II chose this hymn to be sung at her wedding in Westminster Abbey on November 20, 1947.[19]

> Praise, my soul, the King of heaven,
> > To His feet thy tribute bring;
> Ransomed, healed, restored, forgiven,
> > Evermore His praises sing:
> Alleluia! Praise the Everlasting King!
> Alleluia! Praise the Everlasting King!
>
> Angels in the height, adore Him,
> > Ye behold Him face to face;
> Sun and moon, bow down before Him,
> > Dwellers all in time and space:
> Alleluia! Praise with us the God of grace!
> Alleluia! Praise with us the God of grace!

The eye of the storm

Personal Testimony: I was on a teaching mission in Kingston, Jamaica, in late 1988, just after Hurricane Gilbert had devastated that island in September of that year. Our host drove my wife and daughter and me around the island, and, of course, the horrible damage was everywhere. Friends reported that one of the interesting memories about the hurricane was that when the eye of the storm passed over the island, they had clear, blue skies and bright sunshine before the storm resumed its trail of destruction. Psalm 103, as mentioned in "Teaching the Text," is aware of the storm of sin's devastation, but that lies underneath the story line of God's love and forgiveness, drawn from the formula of grace in Exodus 34:6. In the troubled climate of the Corinthian church, Paul's symphony of love in 1 Corinthians 13 functions as another "eye of the storm" created by love.

"I Will Sing Praise to My God as Long as I Live"

Big Idea

God's intimate and ongoing work of creation is directed toward the goal of the new creation.

Key Themes

- The creation is a present reality, not just a historical memory.
- We experience God in the fabric of our world.

Understanding the Text

This psalm of creation is a meditation on the creation record of Genesis 1. As a meditation, it need not follow the order of creation in Genesis 1, nor articulate the wonders of the created order in the precise same language. In fact, it is written with a postfall perspective (104:29), closing with the prayer that "sinners vanish from the earth and the wicked be no more" (104:35). The poem is an individual hymn of praise (see "The Anatomy of Praise" in the introduction in vol. 1) and as such may very well have been used in the temple as an instrument of praise to the Creator of the world.

The Text in Context

Using its own poetic language, this psalm reflects on the days of creation and their works as laid out in Genesis 1.

Outline/Structure

A division of this psalm into seven sections has virtually become standard practice among commentators.

1. Praise of the Lord, clothed with splendor and majesty (104:1–4)
2. The created earth, exposed by the separation of the waters (104:5–9)

Table 1. Days of Creation in Psalm 104

Day	Creation	Genesis 1	Psalm 104
Preface	(Gen. 1:1–2)	"In the beginning God created the heavens and the earth. . . . And the Spirit [or "wind"] of God was hovering over the waters" (1:1–2)	"When you send your Spirit, they are created" (104:30a) "And rides on the wings of the winds" (104:3c)
		"In the beginning God created the heavens and the earth" (1:1)	"He set the earth on its foundations" (104:5a)
		"Darkness was over the surface of the deep [t^ehom], and the Spirit [or "wind"] of God was hovering over the waters" (1:2b)	"You covered it [earth] with the watery depths [t^ehom] as with a garment; the waters stood above the mountains" (104:6)
Day 1	Light (Gen. 1:3–5)	"And God said, 'Let there be light,' and there was light" (1:3)	"The Lᴏʀᴅ wraps himself in light as with a garment" (104:2a)
Day 2	Firmament (NIV: "vault") (Gen. 1:6–8)	"And God said, 'Let there be a vault between the waters to separate water from water. . . . God called the vault 'sky'" (1:6, 8a)	"He stretches out the heavens like a tent and lays the beams of his upper chambers on their waters" (104:2b–3)
Day 3	Waters (Gen. 1:9, 10)	"And God said, 'Let the water under the sky be gathered to one place, and let dry ground appear'" (1:9)	"The waters stood above the mountains. But at your rebuke the waters fled, at the sound of your thunder they took to flight; they flowed over the mountains, they went down into the valleys, to the place you assigned for them. You set a boundary they cannot cross; never again will they cover the earth" (104:6b–9)
	Vegetation and trees (Gen. 1:11–13)	"Then God said, 'Let the land produce vegetation: seed-bearing plants and trees on the land that bear fruit with seed in it, according to their various kinds. And it was so" (1:11–13)	"He makes grass grow for the cattle, and plants for people to cultivate. . . . The trees of the Lᴏʀᴅ are well watered" (104:14–18)
Day 4	Planets as timekeepers (Gen. 1:14–19)	"And God said, 'Let there be lights in the vault of the sky to separate the day from the night, and let them serve as signs to mark sacred times, and days and years, and let them be lights in the vault of the sky to give light on the earth.' And it was so" (1:14–19)	"He made the moon to mark the seasons, and the sun knows when to go down" (104:19–23)

Day	Creation	Genesis 1	Psalm 104
Day 5	Sea life and birds (Gen. 1:20–23)	"And God said, 'Let the water teem with living creatures, and let birds fly above the earth across the vault of the sky . . .'" (1:20–23)	"There is the sea, vast and spacious, teeming with creatures beyond number—living things both large and small. There the ships go to and fro, and Leviathan, which you formed to frolic there" (104:25–26) "The birds of the sky nest by the waters; they sing among the branches" (104:12) "The trees of the Lord are well watered. . . . There the birds make their nests . . ." (104:16–17)
Day 6	Animals (Gen. 1:24–28)	"And God said, 'Let the land produce living creatures according to their kinds: the livestock, the creatures that move along the ground, and the wild animals, each according to its kind.' And it was so . . ." (1:24–25)	"They give water to all the beasts of the field; the wild donkeys quench their thirst" (104:11) "The high mountains belong to the wild goats; the crags are a refuge for the hyrax" (104:18) "All the beasts of the forest" (104:20) "The lions roar for their prey" (104:21)
	Humankind (anticipated, Gen. 1:26–28)	"Then God said, 'Let us make mankind in our image, in our likeness, so that they may rule over the fish of the sea and the birds in the sky, over the livestock and all the wild animals'" (1:26–28)	"Wine that gladdens human hearts, oil to make their faces shine, and bread that sustains their hearts" (104:15) "Then people go out to their work, to their labor until evening" (104:23) (This reflects Gen. 2:15 more than Gen. 1.)
	Food for humankind and animals (Gen. 1:29–30)	"Then God said, 'I give you every seed-bearing plant on the face of the whole earth and every tree that has fruit with seed in it. . . . And to all the beasts of the earth and all the birds in the sky and all the creatures that move along the ground—everything that has the breath of life in it—I give every green plant for food.' And it was so" (1:29–30)	"All creatures look to you to give them their food at the proper time. When you give it to them, they gather it up; when you open your hand they are satisfied with good things" (104:27–28) "The lions . . . seek their food from God" (104:21)
Conclusion	(Gen. 1:31)	"God saw all that he had made, and it was very good" (1:31)	"May the Lord rejoice in his works" (104:31b)

Note: The table is built on Kidner's brief outline of these correspondences, *Psalms 73–150, 368.*

3. Provision of water for life (104:10–18)
   a. By springs and rivers (104:10–12)
   b. By rain (104:13–18)
4. Creation of the moon and sun and their functions for life in the world (104:19–23)
   a. Regulation of animal life by the moon (104:19–21)
   b. Regulation of human life by the sun (104:22–23)
5. The two main divisions of the cosmos: Earth and sea (104:24–26)
   a. The earth (104:24)
   b. The sea (104:25–26)
6. The Lord's providential care of the creation (104:27–30)
7. The Lord's joy in his creation and the psalmist's joy in the Lord, with a vow to lifelong praise (104:31–35c)
   Hallelujah (104:35d)

Historical and Cultural Background

Some scholars have drawn attention to similarities between Psalm 104 and a hymn to the Egyptian sun god, Aten, which comes from the time of Akhenaten, king of Egypt (ca. 1350 BC). While there are definitely correspondences of imagery between these two hymns, dependence of Psalm 104 on the Egyptian hymn is hardly plausible, even though both pieces of literature share sensibilities regarding the created world. One big difference, however, is that the Creator in Psalm 104 definitely stands above the world and apart from it and is decidedly not synonymous with the sun.[1]

Interpretive Insights

104:1 *Praise the LORD, my soul.* This call to praise closes the psalm also, thus forming an *inclusio* (see the comments on 103:1). The beautiful metaphor of the third part of the verse describes God as "clothed with splendor and majesty," denoting brightness and beauty (21:5; 45:3).[2] Note that this anthem of praise alternates between the second person, "you" (God), and the third person ("he," "they," etc.). While the psalm is based on Genesis 1, it is not about a static past but a living present, evidenced by the participles (twelve) and imperfect verbs (forty-six) that give it a present-tense flavor, and the "you" of the verbs (the stand-alone personal pronoun "you" never occurs). The psalmist is meditating on God's presence ("you") in his creation, so that the Creator himself is present and not merely a historical memory.

104:2 *The LORD wraps himself in light.* The psalmist has captured the relationship of the Creator to light, poetically describing him as putting it on like a garment. This recalls other psalms that associate the Lord's being with light, for example, Psalm 27:1.

he stretches out the heavens like a tent. This poetic expression corresponds to the creation of the firmament (NIV: "vault") in Genesis 1:6–8. See table 1.

104:3 *and lays the beams of his upper chambers on their waters.* This poetic expression corresponds to the separation of the waters in Genesis 1:6–8. See table 1. Also see Isaiah 40:22.

He makes the clouds his chariot and rides on the wings of the wind. The word "chariot" (*rᵉkub*) has the same sounds as the word for "cherub" (*kᵉrub*), except interchanged, and the parallel phrase, "wings of the wind," suggests that the poet intended for "chariot" to summon the thought of the cherubim that are attached to the ark and of the winged creatures that occupy the chariot throne in Ezekiel's vision (Ezek. 1).

104:4 *He makes winds his messengers, flames of fire his servants.* The poetic language suggests that God, more than controlling the universe, uses the "winds" and "flames of fire" (lightning) to do his will. The word "messengers" (*mal'akim*) is sometimes translated "angels" (see the NIV footnote). The Septuagint has turned the clause around, taking the first noun in each clause as the object of the participle "makes" ("He makes his angels spirits ["winds"], and his servants flames of fire"; see Heb. 1:7). It is quite possible to read the Hebrew as the Septuagint has done, but there may be another motivation behind the Greek translation: the translator may have been bothered by the strong anthropomorphisms of the Hebrew text, which he has tried to soften.

104:6 *the waters stood above the mountains.* This is a picture that is only assumed in the Genesis narrative. The mountains were submerged beneath the waters, and when the waters were separated, the mountains appeared.

104:7–9 *at your rebuke.* Our psalmist is interpreting the Lord's creative command in Genesis 1:9 (see table l) as a "rebuke," which, at first glance, is a surprising nuance. Yet, we remember that Yahweh was bringing order to the world, part of which involved exposing the land mass, already created but covered by the waters. Thus the psalmist might easily have read God's word of command as "rebuke." The Lord's voice is interpreted as "the sound of your thunder" (104:7b).

they flowed over the mountains. Verse 8 gives the fuller picture depicting the waters as they first advance to the top of the mountains (a reflex to God's "rebuke"), and then "they went down into the valleys, to the place you assigned for them" (very likely the sea). The tops of the mountains were not the place God had intended (*ysd*, "establish," "assign") for the waters to go, but it was the seas, further justifying the psalmist's interpretation of the Lord's command as "rebuke."

You set a boundary. Although not mentioned specifically, the "boundary" is the sand or seashore (Jer. 5:22; Prov. 8:29; Job 38:8–11), and it serves as a boundary "they cannot cross," that "never again will they cover the earth" (Ps. 104:9a). Again the reader sees the order of God's creation taking effect, further justifying the nuance of "rebuke" that lies behind the psalmist's interpretation.

104:10–13 *He makes springs pour water.* The poem continues with a description of the normalization of the waters and their purpose (104:10a and 11a).

104:14–18 *He makes grass grow . . . and plants.* The purpose of plants is to provide food for animals and humans. Of some interest is the observation that plants are the food for human beings as well as animals, not taking into account the permission to eat meat given in the Noah story (Gen. 9:3–4). It is hard to believe that the psalmist intentionally ignored this fact, a fact that anyone familiar with the sacrificial system would know very well, but he evidently has chosen to limit his correspondences to the initial creation story of Genesis 1, although there may be hints of Genesis 2 in the poem (compare 104:10a and Gen. 2:6, although they employ different words for "springs"; 104:14b, 23 and Gen. 2:5 and 15; also 104:29b and Gen. 2:7). Bread, wine, and oil are the three main life-sustaining products of the earth (Ps. 104:14).

The trees of the LORD . . . the cedars of Lebanon. These phrases are parallel, so that the majestic reputation of the "cedars of Lebanon" corresponds to the superlative "trees of the LORD" (for "cedars of Lebanon," see the sidebar "The Palm and the Cedar" in the unit on Ps. 92). The topic shifts from the well-watered "trees of the LORD" to the animals that make their nests in them to the mammals that make their home in the mountains, returning to the description of verses 10–11, which mixes the images of the waters and the mountains. The "high mountains" are the home of the "wild goats" and the rock hyrax, the latter a herbivorous mammal and included among the unclean animals (Lev. 11:5; Deut. 14:7).

104:19–23 *He made the moon . . . and the sun.* The topic of these verses extends beyond that of moon and sun to deal briefly with the way the habits of animals and human beings are regulated by them. The moon and the sun coordinate their functions so that the animals can find food at night and human beings can earn their food by day.[3] Such is the order of God's world.

104:24–26 *How many are your works, LORD! In wisdom you made them all.* With a burst of praise our hymnist lauds the Lord's works as a product of wisdom (Prov. 3:19), pointing to the earth and the sea.

Leviathan. Since "Leviathan" is listed among other created beings, it is more likely also a created being rather than a mythological creature. For more on Leviathan, see the comments on 74:13–14.

104:27–30 *All creatures look to you to give them their food.* The topic of this section is the food that God gives to his creatures. In a series of clauses that begin in Hebrew with second-person singular verbs ("you" = Yahweh), the psalmist describes God's power over the gift of food and life in alternating positive (104:27–28) and negative (104:29) clauses, concluding with the positive announcement that God's Spirit is the creating and renewing force of the cosmos (104:30).

104:31–32 *may the* LORD *rejoice in his works.* With a second burst of praise, the psalmist exalts the Lord (104:31), reminding us of Genesis 1:31, which is a close equivalent to God rejoicing in his works: "God saw all that he had made, and it was very good. And there was evening, and there was morning—the sixth day."

104:33–35 *I will sing to the* LORD *all my life; I will sing praise to my God as long as I live.* Except for the first verb ("I will sing"), verse 33 occurs also in 146:2. Delitzsch may be right in recognizing a reflection of the Sabbath in this verse, and the hope of the eschatological Sabbath in verse 35 when "sinners" and "the wicked" "vanish from the earth."[4]

as I rejoice in the LORD. While joy is not the explicit topic of the creation narrative, an underlying stream of joy nevertheless runs through the narrative. For example, the pronouncement that the creation is good, interspersed through the narrative, exudes the spirit of joy. Moreover, the reader should sense the joy of the first human offspring when Eve declares, "With the help of the LORD I have brought forth a man" (Gen. 4:1).

Praise the LORD, *my soul. Praise the* LORD. "Praise the LORD, my soul" forms the *inclusio* with verse 1. The final "hallelujah" (*hal*ᵉ*lu-yah*; NIV: "Praise the LORD") occurs here in the Hebrew text, but the Septuagint has it as the opening words of Psalm 105 (see the NIV footnote; see also table 2). "Hallelujah" occurs here for the first time in the Psalter and does not occur outside the Psalter (in fact, it is exclusive to Books 4 and 5 of the Psalter), except in Revelation 19.

Table 2. Pattern of the Hallelujahs in Psalms 104–50

Psalm	Occurs at Beginning	Occurs at End	Comments
104		104:35	"Praise the LORD" (*hal*ᵉ*lu-yah*).
105		105:45	105:1: "Give thanks [*hodu*] to the LORD" (NIV: "Give praise to the LORD").
106	106:1a	106:48	106:1b: "Give thanks [*hodu*] to the LORD, for he is good; his love endures forever."
107–10			This is the first group of psalms in Book 5 that do not contain "hallelujah" at all. Note 107:1: "Give thanks [*hodu*] to the Lord, for he is good; his love endures forever."
111	111:1		
112	112:1		
113	113:1	113:9	The first and the second to last of the Egyptian Hallel psalms (113, 117) begin and end with "hallelujah."

Psalm	Occurs at Beginning	Occurs at End	Comments
114			
115		115:18	
116		116:19	
117	(117:1)	117:2	
118–34			This is the second group of psalms in Book 5 that do not contain "hallelujah" at all. Note 118:1, 29: "Give thanks [*hodu*] to the Lord, for he is good; his love endures forever."
135	135:1	135:21	"Hallelujah" also occurs in 135:3. This is the only internal occurrence of "hallelujah" in a psalm, and we should note that here it concludes the opening stanza of the psalm.
136–45			This is the third group of psalms in Book 5 that do not contain "hallelujah" at all. Note 136:1: "Give thanks [*hodu*] to the Lord, for he is good. *His love endures forever*" (with variations in verses 2, 3, and 26). Then the *hodu* is dropped in all the intervening verses, but "*His love endures forever*" concludes each verse.
146	146:1	146:10	This group of psalms (146–50) has "hallelujah" at the beginning and end of the psalm.
147	147:1	147:20	
148	148:1	148:14	
149	149:1	149:9	
150	150:1	150:6 (2x)	"*Hallelujah*" occurs as the final word of the psalm, and is preceded by a slightly different form of the verb, "Let every living being *praise the Lord*" (*tᵉhallel yah*).

Note: With one exception (135:3), "hallelujah" does not occur internally in the psalms, but only at the beginning and ending of the psalms.

Theological Insights

As Calvin points out, this psalm is a reminder that we need not think we will find God only in the lofty clouds, but "he meets us in the fabric of the world."[5] In view of the animated world depicted by this psalm, Perowne speaks of Genesis 1 as "a picture of still life" and the world depicted in the psalm as "crowded with figures full of stir and movement."[6] Perowne's beautiful prose gives a sense of the sights and sounds of this picture of creation:

> The wild ass roaming the sands of the wilderness, stooping to slake his thirst at the stream which God has provided; the birds building their nests, and breaking forth into song in the trees which fringe the margin of the torrent-beds; the wild goats bounding from rock to rock, and finding their home in the inaccessible crags; the young lions filling the forest by night with their roar, and "seeking from God their prey"; and the sea with the same plentitude of life, its depths peopled with huge monsters and swarming myriads of lesser fish,

and its surface studded with sails, the image of the enterprise, the traffic, the commerce of the world; and lastly, in fine contrast with this merely animal activity of creatures led by their appetites, the even tenor, the calm unobtrusive dignity of man's daily life of labour: take all these together, and we have a picture which for truth and depth of colouring, for animation, tenderness, beauty, has never been surpassed.[7]

We can be grateful for both scenes, but especially grateful for the world of crowded figures and animated movement, the world we know and live in, the fabric of the world where God meets us.

Teaching the Text

Our psalmist vows, "I will sing praise to my God as long as I live" (104:33). Indeed this is a noble calling, and incumbent on every believer. A sermon/lesson on this topic can open up a number of faith vistas and give us a new perspective on life.

First, a life of praise will inevitably transform our attitude toward God and ourselves. We will begin to see God for what he has done, which is always an expression of who he is. That is the thrust of this psalm. As Calvin reminds us, it is "in the fabric of the world" that we meet God (see "Theological Insights"). And we will see ourselves as God's special creation, created for his glory.

Second, Psalm 104 describes God's sovereign care of the world in the orderly function of nature. The moon reigns over the elusive movements of the animals who seek their food in its quiet light (104:20–21), and humankind takes their work directive from the rising and setting sun (104:23). These planetary timepieces are part of the Lord's design to provide food for all of his creatures.

Third, a life of praise is pleasing to God (104:34). It affects our relationship with God, which is the goal of faith. And the ultimate outcome of God's continuing creative work in the world is the moral purge of the world's evil (104:35). The praise of God, especially a lifelong engagement, will raise our consciousness of evil and its detrimental effect on creation and will cause us to rejoice at the thought of its elimination. In this psalm the intimate and ongoing sense of creation is no accident. Rather, it is the work of redemption that is—amazing grace!—built into the order of creation and dramatized in the history of the biblical faith. Even when Moses went up on Sinai to receive divine revelation, the cloud covered the mountain for six days, and on the seventh "the Lord called to Moses from within the cloud" (Exod. 24:16). The sixth-day/seventh-day pattern is a flashback to creation, and God's word to Moses on the seventh day is no less than a reassertion of its significance, in this case redemptive significance, as was the seventh day of creation. In a real sense, the biblical story is a story of creation and redemption, and the two cannot be separated. When the final chapter of redeeming grace is told, it is the story of "a new heaven and a new earth" (Rev. 21:1)—that is, the story of redemption enunciated in the language of creation: "Behold I make all things new" (Rev. 21:5). The language of praise, indeed, is a diverse language, and the rich vocabulary of praise is endowed with different nuances, intended to do justice, so far as humanly possible, to the God who is worthy of all praise. Indeed, one praise term may overlap in meaning with another but will incorporate a different degree of meaning (e.g., "bless" and "give thanks"). In a sense, our lifelong endeavor of praising God is intended to have an advancing level of effectiveness until we join the redeemed church and its myriad of voices in the ultimate song of redemption (Rev. 19; see "Theological Insights" in the unit on Ps. 103 and "Illustrating the Text" in the unit on Ps. 150).

Illustrating the Text

"Improve the world, begin with Geneva."

Church History: Calvin acutely states that we meet God "in the fabric of the world." This is the world the Lord created and set in order, and by his power and grace he brings an end to the evil of this world (104:35) and gives us a song to sing throughout our life (104:33). I suspect it is the song of redemption, for that is what the psalm celebrates: "When you send your Spirit, they are created, and you renew the face of the ground" (104:30; perhaps an allusion to the curse of the ground in Gen. 3:17). We are the objects and instruments of that grace. Calvin's motto for the progress of the Christian gospel and the holy life was "Improve the world, begin with Geneva." The gospel must begin locally, both in our personal lives and in the churches where we worship, and we cannot hope to bring saving grace to the world unless that spiritual reality begins in us.[8]

"The price of power is weakness."

Biography: Lilias Trotter. This psalm exudes the power of the Creator, who brought the world into existence and, in the marvelous pictures of the psalm, continues to sustain it. The psalmist is an observer of the Almighty's power and word-paints the vignettes of the Lord's providential care of the universe he made. But the other picture of the writer is that he is helpless and totally reliant on God's mercy (104:28–30). Lilias Trotter had served the Lord faithfully in Algiers for more than three and a half decades; in the last four years of her life her failing health continued its downward movement, during which she continued to write, paint, and minister in various ways, largely out of her weakness while confined to her bedroom, yet with powerful results. In her diary she records the following lines from George Fox:

> Two glad Services are ours
> Both the Master loves to bless
> First we serve with all our powers
> Then with all our helplessness.

And she wrote that these words "link on with the wonderful words 'weak with Him'—for the world's salvation was not wrought out by the three years in which He went about doing good, but in the three hours of darkness in which He hung stripped & nailed, in utter exhaustion of spirit, soul & body, till His heart broke. So little wonder for us, if the price of power is weakness."[9] We are reminded of the Lord's assurance to Paul: "My grace is sufficient for you, for my strength is made perfect in weakness" (2 Cor. 12:9 NKJV; see also 1 Cor. 1:25).

God speaks through the crowd and through the quiet.

Hymn: "Where Cross the Crowded Ways of Life," by Frank Mason North. North (1850–1935) wrote this beautiful hymn and affirmed that it is in the crossroads of our world that we hear the voice of the Son of Man:

> Where cross the crowded ways of life,
>> Where sound the cries of race and clan,
> Above the noise of selfish strife,
>> We hear Thy voice, O Son of Man!

Yet, we must be careful that we do not intimate that God can only speak to us in the humming noise of life, because he has all kinds of venues where he can address us, even a "still small voice" (1 Kings 19:12 KJV).

The Hallelujahs of Books 4 and 5

The word "hallelujah" (*hal*ᵉ*lu-yah*; NIV: "Praise the LORD!") is composed of two elements: the masculine plural imperative *hal*ᵉ*lu* ("praise!") and the shortened form of the divine name, *yah* ("LORD").[1] Its Greek form in the Septuagint is *allēlouia*. Zenger proposes that it likely originated in the temple as a festival "cheer" in the liturgy, or as a congregational response to a hymn or prayer,[2] somewhat like "The LORD is great" (40:16; 135:5). "Hallelujah" occurs for the first time in the Psalms at 104:35 and is the last word in the Psalter (150:6), there occurring twice (see table 2, "Pattern of the Hallelujahs in Psalms 104–50" in the unit on Ps. 104). It occurs nowhere else in the Hebrew Scriptures. That would strongly suggest that this praise-command/response was connected with temple worship, with the view that the Psalms were shaped by temple worship and in turn had a strong hand in shaping the same. Further, the exclusive use of this term at the end of Book 4 and at well-selected points in Book 5 gives the impression that it belonged to the final edition of the Psalter. Its use here sets it off as a unique feature of the Psalms, so unique that it belongs only to the final approach to the temple and God's presence represented by Book 5 (compare also the finality of the hallelujah chorus in Rev. 19) and should not be replicated in other places in the literature. The fact that it occurs after the doxology of 106:48, which closes Book 4, implies that it is a later addition to Psalm 106; that is supported by the superscriptive and subscriptive use in the Hallelujah Psalter (Pss. 146–50). Only once does "hallelujah" occur internally in a psalm (135:3). The idea of a "hallelujah redaction" is generally recognized by Psalms scholars, even if there is no consensus on when it was made. Dates range anywhere from the time of Ezra and Nehemiah (ca. 450 BC) to the second or first century BC.

This praise imperative begins to form a pattern in Psalms 104–18, with three triads of psalms (104–6, 111–13, 115–17), separated by breaks (caesuras) in the use of "hallelujah" (107–10, 114, and 118).[3] The function of the three triads is to prepare for the announcement of the return and rebuilding of the temple in the Songs of Ascents (Pss. 120–34). As table 2 in the unit on Psalm 104 shows, the first triad of hallelujah psalms, which concludes Book 4 (Pss. 104–6), "hallelujah" occurs at the close of the first two psalms and at the beginning and close of the third psalm (Ps. 106). The purpose of the first "hallelujah" triad is to alert the reader to the announcement of the end of the exile (106:44–46; see "The Text in Context" in the unit on Ps. 107), thus forming a transition from Book 4 to Book 5.

The break in the pattern, represented by Psalms 107–10, is certainly no break in the message, for after Psalm 107 has announced the end of the exile (107:10–16), Psalm 108 announces a new day of history, so momentous that it is an awakening of the dawn (108:2), and assures Israel that the Lord is still the owner of the land and will parcel it out according to his own pleasure (108:7–9). Psalm 109 is David's summative curse against his enemies of Books 1 and 2 and the summative word of justice delivered against the enemies of the kingdom of God. Psalm 110 concludes the caesura by a second Davidic psalm that echoes the blessing of Melchizedek, priest of Salem, on Abraham. This psalm thus anticipates the leadership role that is about to be assumed by the high priest in the new community (see "Additional Insights: The Priest-King Ruler Model," following the unit on Ps. 110), a role that has messianic proportions.

The second triad of hallelujah psalms (Pss. 111–13) exhibits a departure from the pattern of the first "hallelujah" triad in that "hallelujah" occurs at the beginning of the first two psalms (Pss. 111 and 112), and in the final psalm (Ps. 113) at the beginning and ending (see table 2 in the unit on Psalm 104). The pattern change is perplexing, but it may simply be an alternative way to sound the alert that an important message is about to follow (exodus from Egypt), with the third "hallelujah" triad completing the symmetry by returning to the first triadic pattern. In any event, the break represented by Psalm 114 announces the subject of the exodus from Egypt (114:1), which is the focus of the Egyptian Hallel and which becomes the template on which Israel would celebrate its new exodus from Babylonian exile. Illustrating the multidimensional nature of the "hallelujah redaction," Robertson compares the final hallelujah collection (Pss. 146–50) and the seven psalms of 111–17 and points out that the latter collection forms a pyramid configuration, with Psalm 114, the "Egyptian" psalm, at the apex.[4]

The third triad of hallelujah psalms (Pss. 115–17) completes the symmetry of the hallelujahs by returning to the original pattern of Psalms 104–6. Its function in the Egyptian Hallel and Book 5 is to lay out the covenant basis of the first exodus—that is, Yahweh's "love and faithfulness" (Exod. 34:6)—which is also the basis of the second exodus, the return from exile. It further answers the question that has been thrown in Israel's face time after time, and most blatantly by their latest enemies, "Where is their God?" (Ps. 115:2b). The answer asserts that their God is in heaven (115:3a), and he is not a product of human engineering but the God who made heaven and earth (115:15). Psalm 116 repositions Israel theologically by the affirmation "I love" (116:1; see Deut. 6:5) and turns their eyes to the temple (116:19), anticipating the journey from Babylonia to Jerusalem, celebrated by the Songs of Ascents. Psalm 117 is the praise colophon to the Egyptian Hallel, announcing the covenant basis of God's great deliverance from Egypt—"love" (*hesed*)—which is, as noted, also the basis of the second exodus (the return). In climactic terms, Psalm 118, the final break in the collection, celebrates God's "love" and encloses their celebration in a declaration of God's goodness and love: "Give thanks to the LORD, for he is good; his love endures forever" (118:1, 29). And most appropriately, Israel confesses Yahweh as their God (118:28), in compliance with the covenant formula that overarches Israel's history from Abraham forward.

The break (caesura) between the Egyptian Hallel and the climactic pair of psalms that capstones the Pilgrim Psalter (Pss. 135–36) is brought to an end with Psalm 135, which begins and ends with "hallelujah," again an announcement that Yahweh's "love" (*hesed*) has finally accomplished its purpose in history (Ps. 136). The position of Psalm 137 in Book 5, while at first seeming to stick out with its offensive message like Psalm 109, nevertheless serves an important function in the book. It presents a graphic picture of Israel's greatest suffering since Egypt, before Psalm 138 declares that Yahweh has looked "kindly on the lowly" (138:6) and triumphed over the gods and that the kings of the earth will praise Yahweh for carrying out his decrees. Like Psalm 109, which exults in Yahweh's justice against Israel's (David's) enemies, Psalm 138 exults in Yahweh's power to fulfill his purpose for his people: "You stretch out your hand against the anger of my foes; with your right hand you save me" (138:7b–c).

The voice of David merges into the Hallelujah Psalter of Psalms 146–50 after he, confessedly a servant, has proclaimed Yahweh the real King (145:1), and these psalms gather the voices of creation, Israel, and all humankind into a gigantic chorus of praise to God the King.

"He Remembered His Holy Promise Given to His Servant Abraham"

Big Idea

God's promises, not our plans, are the energizing force of saving history.

Key Themes

- God first gives before he makes demands.
- Suffering is inherent to God's plan for history and for our salvation.
- The process and the product of God's redeeming work are to restore us to his likeness.

Understanding the Text

In the broadest category, this psalm belongs to the hymns, or psalms of praise,[1] in which historical content is common. It can also be classified as a psalm of thanksgiving whose purpose was to lead the postexilic community in celebration of Yahweh's providential guidance from the time of the patriarchs through the Egyptian bondage and exodus into the land of Canaan. As a subgenre, however, it is one of the historical psalms, which include Psalms 78; 105; 106; 135; and 136.[2]

The Text in Context

The most obvious intertextual observation regarding this psalm is its use in 1 Chronicles 16. The Chronicler has put together a composite psalm to celebrate David's transfer of the ark to Jerusalem. He pieced together Psalms 105:1–15 (1 Chron. 16:8–22); 96:1–13 (1 Chron. 16:23–33); and 106:1, 47–48 (1 Chron. 16:34–36), evidently to provide a liturgical instrument for the second temple (built in 520–516 BC). On a theological note, Robertson makes a convincing case for the use of the poem in 1 Chronicles 16 in Book 4 as a way of highlighting the "YHWH reigns" / "YHWH is king" theme. Drawing on

David's transfer of the ark to Jerusalem, Psalm 96:1–13 articulates the central theme in the psalms of the heavenly King (Pss. 93–99), "YHWH reigns" (Ps. 96:10; 1 Chron. 16:31). It further asserts that as the creator of all things, he alone reigns: "For all gods of the nations are idols; but the LORD made the heavens" (Ps. 96:5; 1 Chron. 16:26). Psalms 105 and 106 have a particular link in the theme of the patriarchal covenant (105:8–11 and 106:45–46), which is a theme that also links them to Deuteronomy. It was this covenant that governed the course of history during the exile and "caused all who held them captive to show them mercy"[3] (see the comments on 106:44–48). Moreover, the perspective on the covenant in Psalm 105, as Hossfeld has pointed out, is not the law as such but God's promise of the land to the patriarchs.[4] At this juncture of history, this emphasis supports the view that the historical backdrop of Book 4 is the return from exile. The intertextual dependence of Psalms 105 and 106 on the Pentateuch further highlights the underlying patriarchal covenant and emphasis that concludes Book 4. This, of course, is preparation for the repatriation of the exiles to the land in Book 5.

Outline/Structure

1. A call to Abraham's descendants to give thanks (105:1–6)
2. A review of Yahweh's covenant works from the patriarchs to the land of Canaan (105:7–45)
   a. Yahweh's covenant with Abraham (105:7–11)
   b. The patriarchs in Canaan (105:12–15)
   c. Joseph in Egypt (105:16–22)
   d. The Israelites in Egypt (105:23–25)
   e. The plagues on Egypt (105:26–36)
   f. The exodus from Egypt (105:37–38)
   g. The wilderness wanderings (105:39–41)
   h. The Abrahamic covenant fulfilled in the promised land (105:42–45)[5]

Historical and Cultural Background

The span of history in this psalm stretches from the patriarchs, through the sojourn in Egypt and the exodus, to the wilderness wanderings and the entrance to Canaan.

Interpretive Insights

105:1–6 The introduction is a call to "give thanks" (NIV: "give praise"), "proclaim," "make known," "sing," "sing praise," "meditate" (NIV: "tell"), "glory," "rejoice," "seek" (NIV: "look to"), and "remember." This aggregate of instructions is addressed to the descendants of Abraham (105:6), who entered the promised land because the LORD "remembered his holy promise given to his servant Abraham" (105:42).

105:1 *proclaim his name.* Literally, "Call on [his] name." This is not prayer to God as such but a proclamation of his name and reputation ("Call out [his] name"). In 116:13 and 17, the psalmist is "proclaiming" the Lord's name by making a sacrifice of thanksgiving, probably in the presence of the congregation.

105:4 *Look to the LORD and his strength.* The possessive noun "his strength" is an epithet for God (96:6), whereas in 78:61 "his strength" (NIV: "the ark of his might") is obviously a reference to the ark of the covenant.

105:5 *Remember the wonders he has done.* "Remember" is both a mental and a historical experience (105:8). Wilcock points out that "remembering is a matter of action, not just of memory."[6] The descendants of Abraham are enjoined to "remember the wonders" God has done, while the Lord "remembers . . . the covenant he made with Abraham" (105:8–9). Verses 12–41 rehearse those wonders.

105:6 *you his servants, the descendants of Abraham.* The Hebrew of this verse begins with an implied plural ("seed"; NIV: "descendants"), and thus the translators make the nouns plural in the second half of the verse, "his chosen ones, the children of Jacob." In Hebrew, verses 42 and 43 repeat "Abraham his servant" (sg.) and "his chosen one" (sg. = Jacob).

105:7–11 *the LORD our God.* Verse 7 begins the second part of the psalm, a review of Yahweh's covenant works (105:7–45). Verses 7–11 address God's covenant with Abraham. Only in verse 7 does the suppliant implicitly include himself ("our") among the people of God, but, of course, that is understood elsewhere without making a point of it.

105:12–15 *for their sake he rebuked kings.* Here begins the story of the patriarchs in Canaan, and to show how Yahweh was directing their history, in verse 14 the psalmist recalls that the Lord "rebuked kings," very likely referring to several encounters with rulers in Canaan.

105:16–22 *He called down famine on the land.* The story of Joseph in Egypt is a large part of the historical review, which implies its significance in Israel's history, quite in keeping with the prominence given the story in Genesis. The "famine on the land" (105:16) obviously refers to the famine in Canaan that prompted Jacob to send his sons to Egypt to buy grain (Gen. 42:1–2), although it may double for the famine in Egypt too. God is the cause of the famine, as he is the mover of history, and its universal extent is indicated with the words "and destroyed all their supplies of food." Literally, it reads, "he broke every staff of bread" (cf. Lev. 26:26), which is likely the imagery of the "staff" on which the round loaves of bread were hung to transport them and protect them from mice.[7]

sold as a slave . . . till the word of the LORD *proved him true.* Verses 17–19 allude to the brothers' selling Joseph and his subsequent imprisonment. In that context the clause "till the word of the LORD proved him true" (lit., "the word of the LORD tested/refined him") is a reference to Joseph's dreams in Canaan (Gen. 37:5–11). The verb "proved" is used in other contexts for the refining of metal (e.g., Ps. 12:6 [NIV: "purified"]; Jer. 6:28–30; Mal. 3:3), suggesting here that Joseph's hardships "refined" his character.

105:23–25 *The* LORD *made his people very fruitful . . . too numerous for their foes.* Israel's four hundred years in Egypt are covered concisely because it is Joseph's suffering, not Israel's, that the psalmist wants to stress. In fact, "his people" in verse 24 may hint at Egypt as the place where Israel really became the people of God, and moreover, "the LORD made his people very fruitful . . . and too numerous for their foes."

105:26–36 Verses 26–36 cover the plagues on Egypt.

105:27 *They performed his signs.* Although the psalmist makes Moses and Aaron the subject of the verb "performed," it is quite obvious that the subject of the psalm—beginning, in fact, at the start of the historical review in verse 5, and with only a few exceptions—is Yahweh ("he").

105:28 *for had they not rebelled against his words?* These words present a textual problem. The negative word (*lo'*, "not") is the crux of the problem, and literally the text would read, "and they did not rebel against his word." The Septuagint and Syriac delete the negative word to make the statement positive ("for they had rebelled against his words"; the RSV, NRSV, and NASB follow that lead). Then the statement would refer to the Egyptians. Other translations, in order to preserve the integrity of the text, turn the declarative sentence into a question, as the NIV does. Another alternative is to leave the negative word "not" in place and understand it to refer to Moses and Aaron's obedience to the Lord's commands.[8] This preserves the integrity of the text.

105:36 *Then he struck down all the firstborn.* As to the order of the plagues, the place of the tenth is sacrosanct, and it occupies its proper place in the list. As for the other nine, the psalm begins the review with the ninth plague (darkness), the third and fourth plagues are inverted, and the fifth and sixth plagues are omitted. Based on the psalmist's familiarity with the Genesis narrative and the Exodus account of the plagues, however, it is likely that he is simply using his poetic license when he departs from the Torah narrative.[9]

Table 1. Order of the Plagues in Psalm 105

Plague	Biblical References	Psalm 105
Ninth plague: darkness	Exod. 10:21–23	105:28
First plague: Nile to blood	Exod. 7:20–21; Ps. 78:44	105:29
Second plague: frogs	Exod. 8:6	105:30

Plague	Biblical References	Psalm 105
Fourth and third plagues: flies and gnats	Exod. 8:16–18, 21–24	105:31
Seventh plague: hail	Exod. 9:22–25	105:32–33
Eighth plague: locusts	Exod. 10:12–15; Ps. 78:46	105:34–35
Tenth plague: death of the firstborn	Exod. 11:4–8; 12:29–30; Ps. 78:51	105:36

Note: The fifth (death of the livestock) and sixth (boils) plagues are not included.

105:37–38 *He brought out Israel.* Like Israel's time in Egypt, the exodus is given short shrift because the psalmist intends for the patriarchs in Canaan and the Joseph story to take center place. Part of the beauty of this review is the way the writer joins the patriarchal story and Joseph's suffering and triumph in Egypt, the result of which is the fulfillment of God's promise to Abraham (105:42–43). The thread that runs through verses 8–45 is God's overpowering control of history. This message is especially useful in their historical circumstances that are marked by the "wonders" and "miracles" of the return and restoration from exile.

105:39–41 *He spread out a cloud as a covering, and a fire to give light.* Again we notice that the period of the wilderness wanderings warrants short notice, not because it was unimportant but because it did not serve the purpose of the psalmist's message of God's power to fulfill his promises. In the wilderness narrative, the cloud (105:39) is normally a guide during the daytime, as is the fire at night, rather than a covering as here.

105:42–45 *he remembered his holy promise given to his servant Abraham.* The final section returns to the ideas of verses 6 and 8, the Lord's covenant with Abraham. In verses 43–45 we have the picture of Israel in the promised land, concluding with allusions to Sinai ("his precepts" and "his laws," 105:45). In view of Canaan as God's gift (105:44), followed by the mention of God's laws (105:45), Weiser comments that "God is first the Giver before he makes demands."[10] See Deuteronomy 6:10–11.

Praise the LORD. Verse 45 ends with "hallelujah" (see the NIV footnote). If the "hallelujah" of 104:35 (NIV: "Praise the LORD") is shifted to 105:1, as the Septuagint does, thus matching the pattern of Psalm 106, then "hallelujah" in verses 1 and 45 forms an *inclusio.* But we are working with the pattern of the Masoretic Text rather than the Septuagint.

Theological Insights

Psalm 105 is a strong lesson in divine providence. By its historical review, it opens up the first part of the covenant formula, "I will be your God," providing a poetic account of how the Lord has carried out that promise, first by making a covenant with Abraham, and then by working through his human servants Moses and Aaron. The Westminster Shorter Catechism has a succinct definition of God's providence: "God's works of providence are, his most holy, wise, and powerful preserving and governing all his creatures, and all their actions."[11] The subject of this psalm is Yahweh, whose work in history is so awesome that he should be made known to all nations (105:1). This reminds us of the Great Commission, to "go and make disciples of all nations . . . teaching them to obey everything I have commanded you" (Matt. 28:19–20). The substance of the psalm's message is God's gracious care of Israel, and the subject, of course, is Yahweh, who "sent Moses his servant, and Aaron." But even though the psalmist attributes signs and wonders to them, the works are in effect Yahweh's ("his") signs and wonders (Ps. 105:27). Then when the psalmist has interjected this brief notation about Moses and Aaron's ministry, he again shifts the subject to the Lord: "he sent," "he turned," "he spoke," "he struck," "he brought out," and so on. God's providential work is written in the story line of Israel's history, and as Waltner says, "The purpose of knowing history is that people may know God. Israel's historiography was all theology."[12]

Teaching the Text

There are two methods that we may use to build our sermon/lesson. One is to draw out of the psalm the spiritual lessons from Israel's story. That means we take Israel's history at face value and understand the theological values that the psalmist perceives to be written in the story line.

First, God keeps his promises, and they become the principle by which we interpret God's work in our world and in our lives. On the macrolevel, it is God's plan to redeem the world, which has its beginning in God's eternal decrees, articulated in his promises to give Abraham the land of Canaan. The program of divine providence is shaped by that promise. We can remind ourselves that it is God's promises, not our plans, that shape saving history. Historical circumstances and events, however, are not extraneous to the divine purposes, but they are God's instruments by which he fulfills his purposes (see "Theological Insights"; see also "God's work is perceptible only to those who believe" in "Illustrating the Text" in the unit on Ps. 53).

Second, we human beings are instruments of God's providential care for his people, as were Moses and Aaron. While we should be reluctant to equate our work with God's, in effect, that is precisely the way God does his work in the world and in our personal lives. So we must do our work in such a way that we perform it as if God were our personal employer and we were expecting to undergo a performance evaluation: "So whether you eat or drink or whatever you do, do it all for the glory of God" (1 Cor. 10:31). Jesus also expresses this truth in a memorable way in one of his kingdom parables: "Whatever you did for one of the least of these brothers and sisters of mine, you did for me" (Matt. 25:40).

The second method we may employ is to interpret Israel's history as a parable that illustrates how God works in his people's lives. The two methods are not mutually exclusive, and the same truths may be drawn from the text. Yet this second method views Israel as a type of the church or the individual believer, and the truths drawn from the text are instructive of how divine providence works in history. For example, the Joseph story, as a type, instructs us that suffering is part of God's plan to bring his promises to pass. "Joseph's experience was that of Israel in miniature. The path to glory lay through suffering."[13] Weiser's comment that suffering is "capital invested with God" is quite apropos here. Moreover, we might mention Paul's statement in Romans 8:28, that God has so constructed his plan for us that everything has a place, even those things that don't seem to fit into the picture—Joseph's imprisonment seemed alien to the larger plan. While God is the Actor in the psalm, he is not unresponsive to our pleas: "They asked, and he brought them quail; he fed them well with the bread of heaven" (Ps. 105:40). We know that God gave both quail and manna at Israel's request. All of his gifts were for the purpose "that they might keep his precepts and observe his laws" (105:45). Augustine mentions God speaking to him with the words "I am the food of grown men. Grow and you shall feed upon me. And you will not, as with the food of the body, change me into yourself, but you will be changed into me."[14] Both the process and the product of God's redeeming work are to restore us to his likeness (1 John 3:2), and that is rooted in Old Testament theology: "Be holy because I, the LORD your God, am holy" (Lev. 19:2; see Gen. 1:27). Paul speaks of both the process and the product in terms of "the new self, which is being renewed in knowledge in the image of its Creator" (Col. 3:10).

Another example is to look at the way the Lord sent Moses and Aaron, and through them brought his providential care of his people to reality. This means that God has so established the church as his instrument to bring in the kingdom of God that not even the "gates of Hades" can prevail against it (Matt. 16:18). There is no way, with Yahweh as the power in and behind history, that God's larger plan for his people could ever fail.

Illustrating the Text

God has a purpose for our lives.

Church History: The broad purpose of history, of the church's history generally, and of our history personally, is to bring in the kingdom of God, or for

God's will to be done on earth as it is in heaven. God's purpose for individuals, much narrower in scope than his purpose for the church, fits into that broader purpose, as it did for Joseph. Edward Kimball was the Sunday school teacher who one day walked into the shoe store where Dwight L. Moody was employed in Boston, put his hand on this young man's shoulder, and invited him to consider Jesus as the Lord of his life. Neither Kimball nor Moody could later recall the exact words Kimball said to the young shoe salesman, but it was the turning point in Moody's life.[15] One of my colleagues, Dr. Walter Elwell, in a class lecture in his popular course "The Life and Teachings of Jesus," queried whether God's purpose for Kimball's life might have been no more than putting his hand on Moody's shoulder and inviting him to come to Christ.

This comment raises an intriguing question for us: How does God assign and distribute his purposes for individuals? If God's purpose for our lives is that particular—we can't be sure—we still don't have to worry, because we won't fail to fulfill it if we live our lives by Paul's principle, "Whether you eat or drink or whatever you do, do it all for the glory of God" (1 Cor. 10:31). In fact, Jesus's parable of the kingdom in Matthew 25 may suggest that God does not evaluate our actions so much quantitatively as he does qualitatively. And his eternal decree of grace is: "Well done, good and faithful servant; you were faithful over *a few things*, I will make you ruler over many things. Enter into the joy of your lord" (Matt. 25:21 NKJV).

Suffering is capital invested with God.

Bible: **Genesis 50:20.** Weiser says: "Suffering, as it were, is capital invested with God, booked by him (cf. Mal. 3:16; Job 19:23) and collected by him."[16] The story of Joseph is a good illustration of this principle. He said to his brothers: "You intended to harm me, but God intended it for good to accomplish what is now being done, the saving of many lives" (Gen. 50:20). According to the story line, Joseph's brothers initiated this deed with evil intentions, but God wove it into the fabric of history to accomplish his will, and in such a way that we are hard put to say that it was not part of God's design. He is the Master Weaver. Whether it was "booked by him"—that is the difficult question—it was certainly "collected by him."

"We Have Sinned,
Even as Our Ancestors Did"

Big Idea

Our personal sins and those of past generations are often inextricable.

Key Themes

- Historical solidarity with our ancestors' guilt has its place in our confession of sin.
- Prayer can change God's mind in certain circumstances, but not his eternal purposes.

Understanding the Text

Psalm 106 is a multiple-genred psalm. It begins like a psalm of praise (106:1–3), but then it moves into a psalm of lament, which is the driving force of the poem. The reasons for lament are multiple also, focusing on Israel's disobedience. Further, Yahweh's deliverance as a reality is distributed throughout the psalm (106:8–11, 23, 43, 45–46). Yet it also carries the marks of a psalm of thanksgiving (106:1b and 47b). Like Psalm 105, which celebrates God's covenant with Abraham and spans Israel's history from the time of the patriarchs to the entrance into Canaan, Psalm 106 reviews Israel's history from the time of the exodus from Egypt to the second exodus—that is, the return from exile—cataloging the seven sins of the wilderness generation[1] and the three sins of the promised-land generation (see the comments on 106:34–39).

The Text in Context

In 1 Chronicles 16, the Chronicler has put together a medley of psalms (with minor differences) to celebrate David's moving the ark to the new tent he had erected for it in Jerusalem: he pieced together Psalms 105:1–15 (1 Chron. 16:8–22); 96:1–13 (1 Chron. 16:23–33); and 106:1, 47–48 (1 Chron. 16:34–36).[2]

Outline/Structure

Four historical paradigms form the heart of the poem; they are designed to present the double theme of "Israel sinned" and "the Lord saved."

Hallelujah (106:1a)
1. Introduction (106:1b–5)
    a. Call to give thanks (106:1b)
    b. Psalmist's opening challenge to praise (106:2)
    c. Beatitude on those "who always do what is right" (106:3)
    d. Psalmist's prayer to be included in the upcoming restoration of God's people (106:4–5)
2. Historical paradigm 1: Israel sinned in Egypt and at the Red Sea (106:6–12)
    a. Israel sinned: "We have sinned . . . [with] our ancestors" (106:6–7)
        i. In Egypt: "They gave no thought to your miracles" (106:6–7a)
        ii. At the Red Sea: "They rebelled by the sea, the Red Sea" (106:7b)
    b. The Lord saved: "Yet he saved them for his name's sake" (106:8–12)
3. Historical paradigm 2: Israel sinned in the wilderness by demanding manna and quail, in the rebellion of Korah, and at Horeb by making the golden calf (106:13–23)
    a. Israel sinned (106:13–22)
        i. By demanding manna and quail: "But they soon forgot what he had done" (106:13–15)
        ii. By the rebellion of Korah: "In the camp they grew envious of Moses and of Aaron" (106:16–18)
        iii. By making the golden calf: "They exchanged their glorious God for an image of a bull" (106:19–22)
    b. The Lord saved: "Moses, his chosen one, stood in the breach before him" (106:23)
4. Historical paradigm 3: Israel sinned by sending the spies into Canaan, worshiping Baal of Peor, and rebelling at the waters of Meribah (106:24–33)
    a. Israel sinned (106:24–29, 32–33)
        i. By sending the spies into Canaan: "They did not believe his promise" (106:24–27)
        ii. By worshiping Baal of Peor: "They yoked themselves to the Baal of Peor" (106:28–29)

iii. By the waters of Meribah: "By the waters of Meribah they angered the Lord" (106:32–33)

b. The Lord saved: "But Phinehas stood up and intervened, and the plague was checked" (106:30–31; see the note below)

5. Historical paradigm 4: Israel sinned by not destroying the Canaanites (106:34–45)

a. Israel sinned: "They did not destroy the peoples as the Lord had commanded them" (106:34–42)

b. The Lord saved: "Many times he delivered them"; "Yet he took note of their distress when he heard their cry" (106:43–45)

6. Conclusion (106:46–48)

a. Concluding observation from the historical paradigms: "He caused all who held them captive to show them mercy" (106:46)

b. Concluding prayer for mercy (106:47)

c. Concluding doxology (106:48a–c)

Hallelujah (106:48d)

Note that in the third historical paradigm our writer has taken the liberty of introducing the saving event (Phinehas's intervention) before he gives the final sin in this paradigm, sin at the waters of Meribah (106:32–33). In verse 34 he moves to a different paradigm.

Historical and Cultural Background

This closing psalm of Book 4 edges up on Book 5 with a somber survey of the historical sins of Israel and the Lord's gracious acts of forgiveness. The psalmist confesses his and Israel's sins ("We have sinned with our fathers," 106:6 KJV) in the tones of the prophets and declares the gracious act of liberation from the exile that is taking place before their eyes ("He caused all who held them captive to show them mercy," 106:46), God's latest and most decisive act of grace yet.

In this psalm also we have a window into one of the technical arts of the ancient biblical world, the manufacture of idols. The NIV's phrase "an idol cast from metal" (106:19b) is a rendering of the Hebrew word *massekah*, which derives from the root "to pour" (*msk*). This is one of those words that preserves the technical process in its makeup. To make their idols, they poured metal into a cast and overlaid it with gold or silver (see Isa. 40:19).

Interpretive Insights

106:1 *Praise the Lord.* Literally "Hallelujah." See table 2, "Pattern of the Hallelujahs in Psalms 104–50," in the unit on Psalm 104.

Give thanks to the LORD, *for he is good; his love endures forever.* This leads the reader to think this psalm may be a psalm of thanksgiving (see the comments at the beginning of "Understanding the Text"), and as was the practice of this category of psalms, the congregation celebrated together the reasons for giving thanks. The plural imperative address (*hal^elu*; NIV: "praise") suggests just such an occasion, especially since "his love endures forever" is, elsewhere in the Psalter, a congregational response (e.g., Ps. 136). This observation is reinforced by the fact that the psalm also ends with a congregational response, "Let all the people say, 'Amen!'" (106:48). The two key words "good" and "love" come from Yahweh's own self-description in Exodus 33:19 ("goodness") and 34:6–7 ("love," *hesed*), setting this poem in the context of Yahweh's covenant.

106:2–3 *Who can proclaim . . . or fully declare his praise?* The question-and-answer style may expose a wisdom influence, but it does not mean that it is a wisdom psalm. Verses 3 and 48 (NIV: "Praise be to the LORD") frame this main section of the psalm with the two words for "blessed" (*'ashre* and *baruk*). In fact, it is not coincidental that these two terms occur in the concluding psalm of Book 1 (Ps. 41:1, 13), and in the same order as in this concluding psalm of Book 4 (106:3, 48). (See "The Text in Context" in the unit on Ps. 41.)

106:4–5 *that I may share in the joy of your nation.* Some commentators insist that the terms of verses 4–5 sound like the writer is a proselyte,[3] since he ostensibly stands outside the people of God and hopes to be included among Yahweh's saved people (but see the comments on 106:6–7).

106:6–7 *We have sinned, even as our ancestors did.* Here the psalm shifts to a prayer of penitence, and contrary to the notion that he is a proselyte, the psalmist includes himself in the subject of the prayer ("*We* have sinned"). While different authorship of verses 1–5 may explain this shift, I suggest that it is the suppliant's strong sense of sin that causes him to speak like an outsider in verses 4–5—he seeks the reinstatement of forgiveness. Definitely the writer of verses 6–7, if the same, is a member of the covenant people ("*our* ancestors"). If he is not the same writer, then why did he allow the obvious inconsistency to stand?

Only here in the Hebrew Bible do we have the verb "to sin" (*ht'*) in combination with the preposition "with" (*'im*), literally, "We have sinned *with* our fathers," or "together with our fathers"[4] (the NIV's "*even as* our ancestors" interprets the preposition as "like"). The psalmist's self-confession of solidarity with his ancestors, even in their sins, gives a profound and powerful sense of guilt (see "Illustrating the Text").

When our ancestors were in Egypt . . . they rebelled by the sea. The historical era in the psalmist's mind becomes identifiable here for the first time—his mind falls back to Egypt and the Red Sea (106:7b–12).[5]

106:13–15 *he gave them what they asked for, but sent a wasting disease.* The events in the wilderness alluded to here, manna and quail, are recorded in Numbers 11 (also Ps. 78:21–31). The "wasting disease" is the plague that the Lord sent among the Israelites as they were eating the meat they had craved (Num. 11:33–34).

106:16–18 *In the camp they grew envious . . . The earth opened up.* The Levitical rebellion led by Korah, and joined by the Reubenites, Dathan, and Abiram (Deut. 11:6), is recorded in Numbers 16. The psalmist tells us that the earth swallowed Dathan and Abiram, but he does not mention Korah, who seems to have survived. The fact that the Korah psalms (Pss. 42–49; 84–85; 88–89) are a prominent part of the Psalter may have influenced the omission of Korah's name. See "The Text in Context" in the unit on Psalms 42–43.

106:19–22 *they made a calf and worshiped an idol.* Not surprisingly, the choice of subjects from the Horeb/Sinai event is the golden calf (Exod. 32), especially since the psalm is focused on Israel's disobedience. The effect was that the Israelites "exchanged their glorious God [lit., "their glory"] for an image of a bull, which eats grass" (Ps. 106:20), offending in at least two ways. First, they violated the second commandment (Exod. 20:4), and second, they embraced the "bull" as their god, a symbol of Baal (note the apostasy at Baal of Peor in Ps. 106:28).

106:23 *had not Moses . . . stood in the breach before him.* The story of Moses's intercession for his offending people is summed up in Exodus 32:32, where he identifies with them so radically that he declares to Yahweh that he will accept their punishment too: "But now, please forgive their sin—but if not, then blot me out of the book you have written" (Exod. 32:32).

106:24–27 *they did not believe his promise.* The story of the spies in Canaan is found in Numbers 13–14. The focus is on the scornful attitude of the people toward the minority report by Joshua and Caleb, recommending that Israel should go directly into Canaan and take it (Num. 13:30; 14:5–9). The punishment for the Israelites' rejection of their plan was that the first generation to come out of Egypt would die in the wilderness and their descendants would be taken into exile (Ps. 106:27), a prediction not included in the Numbers account.

106:28–29 *They yoked themselves to the Baal of Peor.* As if the golden calf incident were not enough, Israel again committed apostasy after they had left the wilderness and crossed over into the Transjordan (Num. 25:1–13; Deut. 4:3).

106:30–31 *But Phinehas stood up.* The zealous intervention of Phinehas, Aaron's grandson, into the situation, merits for him the distinction accorded to Abraham: "This was credited to him as righteousness for endless generations to come" (see Gen. 15:6). This attribution gives Phinehas a religious status equal to Abraham's. Of course, this equal standing is not developed further in the Hebrew Scriptures; however, it may suggest that the priesthood of the postexilic period, based on their ancestor's zealous act, should be accorded a noble standing. This would be of great importance in the absence of the monarchy and the restoration of temple worship.

106:32–33 *By the waters of Meribah they angered the LORD.* This brief report of the incident at Meribah is based on the accounts in Exodus 17:1–7; Numbers 20:1–13; and Deuteronomy 32:48–52. Our writer seems to be dependent on Deuteronomy 9:7–8, 22 for his description that "they angered the LORD." Two "rock" incidents are recorded, one at Rephidim (Exod. 17:1–7), renamed "Massah" and "Meribah," where Moses struck the rock, and another at Kadesh, when the Lord instructed him to speak to the rock but he struck it instead (Num. 20:8–13). It was the latter incident of disobedience that barred Moses from the promised land. In Deuteronomy, Moses blames his action in the latter incident on Israel (Deut. 1:37; 3:26; 4:21). See Psalms 81:7 and 95:8.

106:34–45 The behavior of the Israelites in Canaan, like their actions in the wilderness, was characterized, tragically, by the adoption of Canaanite "customs" (106:35) and idols (106:36). It was a failure to distinguish themselves as God's people, as spelled out in Deuteronomy. Among their failures were the following: (1) they did not destroy the Canaanites as directed (106:34); (2) they adopted the practices and worship of the gods of Canaan (106:35–36); and (3) they sacrificed their children to demons (*shedim*, "demons/spirits" [NIV: "false gods"]; this name for pagan gods occurs elsewhere only in Deut. 32:17).[6]

106:40–43 *he delivered them, but they were bent on rebellion and they wasted away in their sin.* We note the pattern of the Lord's deliverance of his people to the power of the nations (106:40–42), followed by their liberation (106:43a), but then their rebellious nature dominated their life ("They wasted away in their sin," 106:43c). It is a modified model of the Deuteronomic pattern that characterizes the book of Judges: apostasy, oppression, distress, repentance, deliverance.

106:44–45 *he heard their cry; for their sake he remembered . . . out of his great love.* Israel's "cry" was the incentive for the Lord's remembering his covenant "for their sake" (106:45a).

106:46–48 *He cause all who held them captive to show them mercy.* The outcome was the release from captivity, Yahweh's "great love" being the basis for his relenting (Exod. 34:6).

Save us, LORD our God. The suppliant's prayer is that God will do to his generation what he has done for former disobedient generations: "Yet he saved them for his name's sake" (106:8a). (See "Teaching the Text" in the unit on Pss. 9–10.) The prayer is to the effect that Yahweh will return the people from exile that "we may give thanks to your holy name and glory in your praise" (106:47c–d). Duplicated in 1 Chronicles 16:35–36, which celebrates David's transfer of the ark to Jerusalem, this moment in history was comparable to that decisive event when Yahweh's covenant with the patriarchs was reaffirmed (1 Chron. 16:15–22) and Yahweh was again acclaimed king (1 Chron. 16:31).

Praise be to the LORD, *the God of Israel . . . Let all the people say, "Amen!"* The psalmist or editor already anticipates the historical setting of Book 5, the return and restoration, and quite likely, the fivefold ending of the Psalter (Pss. 146–50) that fulfills this desire to "give thanks to your holy name and glory in your praise" (106:47). The psalm closes with a doxology (106:48) that also closes Book 4. It is a virtual duplicate of the doxology that closes Book 1 (41:13) and is the only one of the five closing doxologies that includes a congregational response. A further observation is that the first three closing doxologies have "Amen and Amen," while this one, the fourth, has a single responsive "Amen." Already observed is the additional fact that Psalm 106, like Psalm 41 that closes Book 1, employs the two words for "blessed" (see the comments on 106:2–3). The fact that these two doxologies are duplicates may suggest that the compiler of Book 4 considered his task to include an appropriate conclusion to the penultimate version of our present Psalter, and he consciously intended to replicate the doxology that closed Book 1, providing an *inclusio* for the book.

Theological Insights

Moses's practice of prayer gives us an angle, among others, that is both perplexing and instructive. Moses had a way of challenging God, of calling God's decisions into question. In Exodus 32 and 33, and in Numbers 14, he seems to step into the situation to protect God against himself, to keep God from damaging his reputation (that's the sense of Num. 14). The psalmist recalls such an occasion when he writes: "So he said he would destroy them—had not Moses, his chosen one, stood in the breach before him, to turn away his wrath from destroying them" (Ps. 106:23). This statement raises the question, can we change God's mind through prayer? God's mind is essentially his character, or his nature, or we might say his purposes. It is that which defines him as God— his infinite, eternal, and unchangeable being, wisdom, power, holiness, justice, goodness, and truth. The Westminster Shorter Catechism (Q & A 7) asks:

> Question: What are the decrees [i.e., purposes] of God?
>
> Answer: The decrees of God are his eternal purpose, according to the counsel of his will, whereby, for his own glory, he hath foreordained whatsoever comes to pass.

The catechism suggests that the decrees of God can be reduced to God's "eternal purpose" (note the singular): "They are not successively formed as the emergency arises, but are all parts of one all-comprehending plan."[7]

God's purpose is one great master plan that we might summarize as the plan to save humanity "for his name's sake" (106:8), as expressed in our psalm, and ultimately through the sacrifice of Christ on the cross, according to the gospel. God will not change that plan. Perhaps in the minor details of the master plan, it makes little difference whether we dot an *i* or cross a *t*, but the fundamental purpose will not, cannot, change. We say the shortest distance between two points is a straight line. If we apply this to God's purpose, it seems that while God wants to work according to the most efficient method—the straight-line method—in reality, the straight line turns out to have some curves and digressions here and there. And in these cases, such as the Joseph story (Gen. 37–50), the accommodation is so seamless that we cannot tell where it begins and where it ends, but the purpose is clear: to save the people of Israel (Gen. 50:20). And whether or not God endorsed the brothers' devious plan, his purpose was accomplished. Moses's purpose of standing in the breach was the same, to save Israel, and God honored his action. Changing God's mind in prayer is not equivalent to changing his eternal purpose, to bring salvation to the world. Prayer may change the itinerary, but it will not change the destination. The mystery is why God would even contemplate destroying Israel. Yet the important thing is that God's purpose was preserved.

Teaching the Text

The preacher/teacher might move in several directions to explicate this multigenred and multithemed psalm. One approach is to focus on the topic of national and personal sins and their relationship. Are they in a mutual, parallel, or exclusive relationship to each other? Is it possible, or appropriate, for the believer to ignore the national sins and only deal with his or her personal sins? To what extent should public worship incorporate confession of our national sins? This topic, however, must be thought through carefully so that we neither depreciate personal repentance in favor of corporate or acclaim personal repentance to the disregard of the corporate. The story of the pastor who sought the patriarch's forgiveness for a nation's past sins (see "Illustrating the Text") is an example of one who felt so attached to the nation's past sins that he could not proclaim forgiveness, since he felt he had not confessed his nation's sins and received forgiveness.

A second approach is to highlight God's grace as a response to our sinning, pointing out that even though Israel rebelled against the Lord at the Red Sea, he still saved them "for his name's sake" (106:8). The psalm, in fact, follows a pattern of "they sinned" and "the Lord saved them" (see "Outline/Structure"). The psalm is a log not only of Israel's sin but of God's forgiveness—sadly, a paradigm of human history, but happily, a paradigm also of God's grace. The cycle of sin and forgiveness is the abbreviated cycle of apostasy, oppression, distress, repentance, and deliverance in the book of Judges. In light of this pattern, and our own pattern of asking forgiveness for sins that we will, sadly, repeat, we may ask if such prayers are authentic prayer (see "Illustrating the Text"). In answer to our question, we may point out that these prayers remind us that we are called to live a repentant life, and that includes false starts and more restarts, and those are evidences of God's grace. This may also be a proper place to insert Paul's statement that "where sin increased, grace increased all the more" (Rom. 5:20).

We may further observe another divine response to our sinning, that when Israel "exchanged their glorious God for an image of a bull, which eats grass" (106:20), the Lord spared them when Moses stood in the breach on their behalf (106:23). While Moses's status as God's servant was unique, God's servants are still called to stand in the breach on behalf of God's people, at least in prayer, and sometimes they are summoned to perform particular actions as they represent the people of God before the God of grace.

Illustrating the Text

Forgiving the sins of the fathers and mothers

True Story: A number of years ago I was able to reconnect with a former student of mine who had become a prominent leader in a Middle Eastern church. A man of deep faith, he told me this story. A few years earlier, a Turkish Christian pastor had come to him and asked him to forgive him. "Forgive you for what?" he asked. "You haven't done anything to me." (He didn't even know the man.) This Turkish pastor then told him his story. He said that every time he got up to preach, the blood of the Armenian holocaust of 1915, in which one million Armenian Christians were killed by the Turks, rose up to haunt him, and as a result, he could not preach forgiveness. Then the leader understood, and said, "I forgive you." They cried together and prayed together. This pastor, in the same spirit as our psalmist (106:6), sensed his solidarity with the past generations of his people. We might wonder how a greater sense of historical solidarity with the sins of past generations might affect us. Would we, for example, be less likely to repeat them? I suspect the answer is in the affirmative.

Repentance is both prayer and practice.

Church History: Repentance is a reversal of course, a change of attitude, and an alteration of acting and thinking. Starck's *Prayer Book* is a wonderful book of devotions written by a Lutheran pietist in seventeenth-century Germany.[8]

It contains prayers that represent the true nature of repentance, asking God to forgive us and start us on a totally different course. They even petition God not to let us commit the sin anymore. The question this raises in regard to our prayers of repentance and confession is this: Is it authentic for us to ask God to forgive us and help us not to commit the sin again, when our experience tells us that we will probably repeat the old offense again? Now, we must acknowledge that some people can, and some people do, by the wonderful grace of Christ, make the 180-degree turn immediately, and never go back to the sin of which they have repented. That is what every earnest sinner desires. But most of us make our turn toward the good life in incremental degrees, not 180-degree turns.[9]

In answer to our question, that's the reason it is important for us to keep praying our prayers of repentance, asking God to change us totally, even though we are not surprised—but hopefully disappointed—when we repeat the same sin again. Yet, those prayers remind us that a change of mind has indeed taken hold of us, and even if incrementally, we want to move toward a total transformation. In fact, it is authentic prayer when we come to God and ask forgiveness for sins that we suspect are going to keep holding on to us for a while. But our desire to be changed is ground zero. So we have to *pray* and *practice* repentance, developing a *repentant life*, so that as we are changed from one degree to another, the old sin begins to lose its glamour, and we begin to exercise a resistance we could not put forth in our unrepentant state of heart.

In our prayers we, by the grace of God, write a quitclaim deed to the old life and start a new one (2 Cor. 5:17). That may take some negotiations with ourselves, with our circumstances, with others who can help us—the practice of a repentant life—but no negotiations with God, for there is no compromise regarding our offenses against him, only repentance. A total transformation is the only acceptable object: "'Come now, let us settle the matter,' says the LORD. 'Though your sins are like scarlet, they shall be as white as snow; though they are red as crimson, they shall be like wool" (Isa. 1:18).

What many of us want, unfortunately, is *repentance lite*, just enough confessing to make us feel better, though we have every intention of committing the sin again. That's inauthentic prayer. But even that degree of insincerity can be exposed in the prayer room and can be turned into both true repentance and practice as we turn incrementally to a changed life.

"Let the Redeemed of the LORD Tell Their Story"

Big Idea

Our personal faith stories are vignettes of grace in the larger story of God's kingdom.

Key Themes

- Prayers of individuals become the prayers of the community of faith, and the reverse.
- Our faith story is a line or paragraph, some even a chapter, in the story of God's kingdom, but none is a footnote.
- The story of redemption is the sum of its parts.

Understanding the Text

Book 5 of the Psalter begins with this beautiful community psalm of thanksgiving, celebrating the return from exile. The worship leader summons those "redeemed from the hand of the foe" (Isa. 62:12) to give thanks to the Lord. The psalmist breaks these worshipers into four categories, and he reviews their troubles and celebrates God's deliverance (see "Outline/Structure," below; see also the sidebar "Psalms of Thanksgiving" in the unit on Pss. 9–10).

The Text in Context

Psalms 106 and 107 share complementary features. First, 106:47 prays that the Lord will save Israel and "gather" them from the nations so that they "may give thanks" to his holy name. Psalm 107 begins as a response to that prayer (107:1). Second, 106:27 declares Yahweh's oath to scatter the descendants of the wilderness generation "throughout the lands," and now Psalm 107 is situated on the verge of the new exodus, this time from Babylonian exile, with an eye on the return to the land. Third, 106:34–46 reviews the cycle of apostasy, foreign oppression, and deliverance, which is virtually matched by the structure of the four strophes of our poem, especially as celebrated in the double refrain (see "Outline/Structure"). Fourth, 106:45 asserts that God's merciful response to Israel's rebellion was based on his covenant, and "out of his great love" (using the plural of *hesed*, lit., "out of the abundance of his great love" [see Exod. 34:6]) he saved them. Not surprisingly, 107:43 summons the wise to "ponder the loving deeds of the LORD" (also, like 106:45, the plural of *hesed*), where the plural could be translated as a plural of magnitude ("ponder the LORD's *great love*"). Zenger suggests "proofs of the love of YHWH," and refers to 107:1, 8, 15, 21, and 31, as the evidences.[1] Schaefer suggests that these links between Psalms 106 and 107 indicate that the two psalms were already linked together before the Psalter was divided into five books.[2] However, the compiler of Book 5 may merely have intended to provide an organic link between Books 4 and 5, as is the case with those psalms that link Books 1 and 2 and Books 3 and 4 (see "The Text in Context" in the units on Pss. 42–43 and on Ps. 90).

Although these psalms are not quoted in the New Testament, God's provisions for these celebrants have parallels in Jesus Christ. Jesus gives bread in the wilderness (Matt. 14:13–21), releases prisoners (Luke 4:18), heals and forgives (Mark 2:10–12), and calms the sea (Mark 4:39).[3]

Outline/Structure

This psalm is a beautiful piece of literary artistry, the exemplary psalm of thanksgiving in the Psalter. The heart of the poem is composed of four parallel scenes that depict Israel's troubles, their cry for help, and the Lord's subsequent deliverance, followed by the review of God's acts of unfailing love. In a literary sense, the last section of strophe "d," which gives a longer list of God's acts of unfailing love, forms an *inclusio* with 107:1, which introduces the fundamental reason for thanksgiving: "for he is good, *his* love [*hesed*] endures forever." In a more restricted sense, reflected by the outline below, the final verse forms a perfect *inclusio* with 107:1 since it calls for pondering "the loving deeds of the LORD" (the plural form of *hesed*). Further, as we would expect of a psalm of thanksgiving, the celebrants are gathered in the temple for worship, where they rehearse the acts of the Lord's unfailing love.

1. Call for the redeemed to give thanks to the Lord (107:1–3)
2. Four categories of a thankful people (107:4–42)
   a. Some who were redeemed from their wanderings (107:4–9)
      i. Their trouble (107:4–5)
      ii. Refrain: Their cry for help (107:6)
      iii. The Lord's deliverance (107:7)

iv. Refrain: Call to give thanks (107:8)

v. God's acts of unfailing love (107:9)

b. Some who have been freed from prison (107:10–16)

i. Their trouble (107:10–12)

ii. Refrain: Their cry for help (107:13)

iii. The Lord's deliverance (107:14)

iv. Refrain: Call to give thanks (107:15)

v. God's acts of unfailing love (107:16)

c. Some who were healed of their afflictions (107:17–22)

i. Their trouble (107:17–18)

ii. Refrain: Their cry for help (107:19)

iii. The Lord's deliverance (107:20)

iv. Refrain: Call to give thanks (107:21)

v. God's acts of unfailing love (107:22)

d. Some who were saved from the perils of the sea (107:23–42)

i. Their trouble (107:23–27)

ii. Refrain: Their cry for help (107:28)

iii. The Lord's deliverance (107:29–30)

iv. Refrain: Dual call to give thanks and praise (107:31–32)

v. God's acts of unfailing love (107:33–42)

3. A concluding word to the wise (107:43)

Historical and Cultural Background

Israel was not a seafaring people until the time of Solomon (1 Kings 9:26–28) and did not likely have a competitive sea-trading industry for a long time (1 Kings 22:48–49). The reason was largely geographical, for the country's coastline ran shallow up to Tyre and Sidon in the north, where a natural deep harbor could accommodate ships and thus allow sea trade to become a profitable industry. That is the reason Tyre was known for its sea trade. The engineered harbor at Caesarea was built much later by Herod the Great, thus increasing the potential for seafaring activities.

Interpretive Insights

107:1–3 *Give thanks to the* LORD *. . . his love endures forever.* The psalm begins with a call to the congregation to give thanks, to which they make a liturgical response ("His love endures forever"), which also occurs in 106:1b, the Egyptian Hallel (118:2–4), and the Great Hallel (136:1–26). In fact, Jeremiah predicts that the return from exile will be celebrated with this liturgical response (Jer. 33:11), and Ezra records this response by the congregation when the second temple foundations are laid (Ezra 3:11). Perhaps this is the psalmist's affirmation that Jeremiah's prophecy has been fulfilled as he summons the people to give thanks to the Lord.

Let the redeemed of the LORD *tell their story.* The story of the "redeemed" is the account of release from captivity, and the following four strophes, with their distinct stories of redemption, are the parts that make up the whole. A thanksgiving offering also marked the occasion (see 107:22).

107:4–9 The first strophe can be viewed on two levels. First, the imagery is that of the wilderness era: a people wandering in desert places, facing all the dangers of that situation—hunger, thirst, loss of orientation, and inability to find a habitable place to dwell.[4] Second, metaphorically and literally, that was the situation Israel faced during the Babylonian exile, from which they have now been delivered. This is an excellent example of how the Psalms use the colors from the palette of past historical eras to paint the picture of another era.

107:4–5 *Some wandered in desert wastelands.* The major English translations have distinguished among the four categories of thankful people with the word "some" (107:4, 10, 17, and 23). This first group of the "redeemed of the LORD" (107:2) are those who "wandered in desert wastelands, finding no way to a city where they could settle" (107:4). Two words (*midbar* and the poetic term for "wilderness," *yᵉshimon*) are behind the phrase "desert wastelands," which seems to allude to the wilderness period (107:5), perhaps even alluding to the patriarchs who also looked for a permanent dwelling.

107:6–7 *Then they cried out to the* LORD *in their trouble, and he delivered them.* The refrain is composed of two parts, the first in verse 6, coming after the description of trouble (107:4–5; also occurs in 107:13, 19, and 28). The historical cycle described in the book of Judges (e.g., Judg. 2:11–16) is reflected in the first part. Note that Yahweh, the Director of history, is the subject of the statement after each occurrence of this refrain (Ps. 107:7, 14, 20, and 29). The second part of the refrain is a jussive (imperative force, "let them") call to give thanks to the Lord for his unfailing love (107:8, 15, 21, and 31).

to a city where they could settle. The need for food and water characterizes the wilderness generation (107:5; see the comments on 106:13–15 and 106:32–33), as does Yahweh's response to their distressful cry: "He led them by a straight way to a city where they could settle" (107:7), probably with Jerusalem in mind as the ultimate destination (see also Heb. 11:10). The fact that verse 4 asserts that they could not find that city may hint at both the wilderness generation's refusal to go directly into Canaan (Num. 13) and the alternative route they had to take through the Transjordan rather than passing along the King's Highway (Num. 21:21–30; Deut. 2:26–37). Significantly, the psalmist begins Book 5 with the theme of looking for a city, and Jerusalem was obviously the unnamed city of their aspirations (see Deut. 12, where the place is also unnamed), as it was the goal of those returning from exile.

107:8–9 *Let them give thanks to the* LORD. Verse 8 ends this section with the last half of the double refrain (also 107:15, 21, and 31), calling the congregation to give thanks for God's "unfailing love" (*hesed*) and "wonderful deeds."

he satisfies the thirsty and fills the hungry with good things. The first two strophes (107:4–9, 10–16) are followed by a brief enumeration of God's "wonderful deeds" (107:9 and 16), the third strophe (107:17–22) by a call to sacrifice thank offerings (107:22), and the fourth strophe (107:23–42) closes with an extended enumeration of God's "wonderful deeds" (107:33–42). The ultimate reaction to God's "wonderful deeds" is astonishment in the upright and a stunning silence in the wicked (107:42). The final word is a call to the wise to "ponder the loving deeds of the LORD" (107:43).

107:10–16 *Some sat in darkness, in utter darkness, prisoners suffering in iron chains.* The second group of the "redeemed" (107:2) is composed of "prisoners suffering in iron chains" (107:10), like their ancestor Joseph (105:18). Yet, since Book 5 is set against the background of the return, we may assume the phrase "in darkness, in utter darkness" is a metaphor for various periods of Israel's suffering because of disobedience, most recently the exile. "Utter darkness" (see also 23:4 where NIV has "darkest" for the term *tsalmawet*, also used in 107:10) intensifies the noun "darkness." The word pair "darkness and the shadow of death" (NIV: "in darkness, in utter darkness") occurs elsewhere only in Job (e.g., Job 10:21, which alludes to the world of the dead).[5] Verse 11 explains why they were prisoners: "They rebelled against God's commands."

Then they cried to the LORD . . . *Let them give thanks to the* LORD. The twin refrain occurs for the second time (107:13 and 15), with three minor variations in the first part (107:13). First, instead of the Hebrew verb *tsʿq* ("to cry out") used in the first and fourth refrains (107:6, 28), our author here uses a synonym *zʿq* ("to cry out"—different first letter; 107:13, 19). Second, he makes another synonymous substitution, using the verb *yoshiʿem* ("he saved them") in the two middle refrains (107:13, 19) for the verb *yatsilem* ("he delivered them") in verse 6, but he employs a different verb in verse 28 (*yotsiʿem*), all for literary effect:

"Then they cried out [*yitsʿaqu*] . . . and he delivered them [*yatsilem*]." (107:6)
"Then they cried out [*yizʿaqu*] . . . and he saved them [*yoshiʿem*]." (107:13)
"Then they cried out [*yizʿaqu*] . . . and he saved them [*yoshiʿem*]." (107:19)
"Then they cried out [*yitsʿaqu*] . . . and he brought them out [*yotsiʿem*]." (107:28)

he breaks down gates of bronze and cuts through bars of iron. Yahweh's deliverance (107:16) is expressed in the terms that Isaiah uses to describe

Cyrus's conquest of Babylon that resulted in Israel's release from Babylonian exile (Isa. 45:2).[6]

107:17–22 *suffered affliction . . . He sent out his word and healed them.* The third group of "the redeemed" (107:2) is composed of those whose transgressions have caused their illness (107:17). But when they cried to the Lord (see the comments on 107:10–16), "he sent out his word and healed them" (107:20). The language is the same as that used by Isaiah to describe Yahweh's sending forth his word, like an emissary to do his bidding, and it does not return unfulfilled (Isa. 55:11; also 40:8; 45:23).

Let them give thanks to the LORD . . . Let them sacrifice thank offerings. The second half of the twin refrain (107:21–22) is consistently framed in the third-plural jussive verb, obviously addressed to the subjects of the four categories of the psalm. The scene takes place in the sanctuary, as the leader turns to the congregation and instructs them now to make thank offerings (Lev. 7:11–15). It may be that while they are accomplishing this task, the others are rehearsing the "wonderful deeds" that have prompted the occasion of their thanksgiving offering.[7]

107:23–32 *Some went out on the sea in ships . . . they were at their wits' end.* The fourth group of the "redeemed" (107:2) are the sailors (see "Historical and Cultural Background"). The focus is on the storms they have encountered on the high seas, to the point that they were "at their wits' end" (107:27), which is the sense of the same verb in Isaiah 28:7 (NIV: "befuddled"). The word visuals are vivid, as we see the ship tossed by the winds and waves "to the heavens" and "to the depths" (Ps. 107:26). Just as in the book of Jonah, Yahweh was in control of the storm, both as its cause and as its calm (107:25, 29).

As with the other descriptions of trouble, the rescue from the sea speaks on multiple levels of meaning. The sea in biblical theology is the metaphor of God's fiercest foe (e.g., 65:7; 74:12–14), and the Red Sea is a paradigm of God's great victory over his enemies (e.g., 77:16–19; 78:13; 106:6–12). In the context of the exile, the sea with its perils, in addition to its literal meaning, is also very likely a metaphor for the dangers of that era, from which Yahweh eventually "guided them to their desired haven" (107:30).

107:33–42 *He turned rivers into a desert . . . He turned the desert into pools of water.* Just as each call to give thanks is followed by a brief summary of Yahweh's acts of unfailing love (see "Outline/Structure"), here the pattern continues with an extended description that both expands and reinforces the reasons to "give thanks to the LORD" (107:31). Falling outside the liturgical pattern, this extended strophe seems appropriate for the thanksgiving of the entire congregation.

the parched ground into flowing springs. This fourth strophe picks up themes from the first strophe (107:4–9): a city where they could settle (107:4, 7, 36), the hungry (107:5, 9, 36), and no way found (107:4, 40; NIV: "trackless waste"). The words "parched ground" and "flowing streams" (107:35) are the exact language Isaiah uses to describe the return from Babylonian captivity (Isa. 41:18), which is the historical setting of this psalm.

107:43 *Let the one who is wise heed these things.* This final verse offers a concluding word to the wise, much like Hosea 14:9, and may have been appended to the psalm by a later editor, although the writer himself, functioning in a time when wisdom language and thought were current, could have formulated his conclusion in wisdom language.

Theological Insights

The psalm is framed by the *inclusio* of God's "unfailing love" (107:1 and 43). The first occurrence (107:1) is rendered by the NIV as simply "love" (*hesed*), while the final occurrence (107:43) is the plural noun and probably should be understood as "the LORD's great love" (NIV: "loving deeds"; see "The Text in Context"). This term centers the poem theologically by its fourfold occurrence in the first half of the double refrain (107:8, 15, 21, 31). As we have observed in other instances, an *inclusio* may provide a hint of a central theme in a psalm. That is, Israel, both corporately and individually, is enclosed in God's love. That includes the four categories of individuals who give thanks to God for his delivering mercy, and it especially explains their deliverance as a gracious reflex of God's love. Indeed, the psalm illustrates the principle that redemption is the effect of God's love and is both a corporate and a personal transaction. Neither operation stands alone—they are mutually dependent. In Psalm 107 the "redeemed of the LORD" are composed of the congregation, while the four categories of individuals in trouble break that corporate entity down into its component parts: the homeless who have found a city, prisoners freed from chains, sinners forgiven, and sailors rescued from the perils of the sea. The prayers of the community of faith become the prayers of the individuals that compose that community, and the statement could be reversed: the prayers of the individuals become the prayers of the community of faith.[8] The psalm is an Old Testament version of Paul's lesson on the unity of the body of Christ in 1 Corinthians 12, and just as the encompassing love of God characterizes this psalm, it further illustrates the "more excellent way" of love that the apostle expounds in 1 Corinthians 13.

Teaching the Text

This psalm has so much potential for a message about the nature of the community of faith, or the church. We have already observed in "Theological Insights" how the people of God spiritually lean into and on the prayers of its members, and its members lean into and on the prayers of the people of

God. This is not merely a liturgical phenomenon but a spiritual dynamic. At some point in our sermon/lesson we could beneficially advance this concept by opening up Paul's discussion of the body of Christ in 1 Corinthians 12. There is a spiritual dynamic that operates in the body of Christ, binding the parts into the whole, and making the whole responsive to the parts. There is no member of the community of faith, however seemingly insignificant, who is dispensable. The story of all believers, however insignificant, is written into the story of the kingdom, some only a sentence, others a paragraph, some a full chapter, but none a footnote. Our understanding of this spiritual dynamic is critical to the functioning of the church in an orderly and effective way.

We can demonstrate this from Psalm 107 in at least three ways. First, we can emphasize the interdependence of the prayers of the body of Christ and the individual (see "Theological Insights"). The balance between the community and the individual, so beautifully illustrated in Book 5, is critical to our understanding of Old Testament faith and its New Testament counterparts (see 1 Cor. 12; see also "Historical and Cultural Background" in the unit on Ps. 116 and the comments at the beginning of "Understanding the Text" in the unit on Ps. 139). This relational principle involves the members of the body of Christ in mutual prayer (Rom. 15:30) and reciprocal service to one another (Rom. 15:27). Second, our individual troubles are those of the body of Christ, and the troubles of Christ's body, the church, are those of its individual members: "If one part suffers, every part suffers with it; if one part is honored, every part rejoices with it" (1 Cor. 12:26). In this same vein, Zenger observes that the four categories of the redeemed "deal with the rescue of individuals in different situations, and, on the other hand, they are about the restoration of Israel. Both aspects are interwoven."[9] Third, we can focus on telling our story as a personal faith narrative, much like the four categories of the redeemed. While we sometimes feel that our story is not important, especially compared to those that have a flourish ours does not have, the individual stories of the redeemed are vignettes of grace in the larger story of the people of God (see the illustration from Luther in "Illustrating the Text"). In light of the storytelling nature of this psalm, the NIV renders the verb "say" in verse 2 as "tell their story," and that is precisely what the redeemed do. Our personal narrative, even if it is only a line or two, is integral to the larger narrative of God's kingdom, and it is not to be disparaged, however inconsequential our story may seem to be.

Illustrating the Text

Safe harbor at last

Biography: John Newton. Psalm 107:23–30 describes occasions of peril on the seas when God intervenes and brings those who cry out to him into safe harbor. John Newton, known for his hymn "Amazing Grace," was himself a seafaring man, and he tells his own story in his autobiography. In February 1747, after having spent several years in Africa in various jobs and circumstances, Newton boarded a ship whose captain Newton's father (also a sea captain) had asked to bring Newton home to England. But the captain considered Newton, having sunk into moral decadence, to be another "Jonah" on board and at times told him the only way they would arrive safely at their destination was to throw him overboard. In the final stages of their journey, they encountered a powerful storm that threatened to fill the ship with water and sink it. For several weeks it caused no shortage of consternation among the crew, even bringing them to despair that they would ever reach their destination. During those days of a threatening death at sea, several strands of the gospel came together for Newton: Scriptures he had learned early in life, a New Testament on board, Stanhope's book on Thomas à Kempis, and a volume of sermons. As the crisis drew to an end, Newton realized that a spiritual transaction had taken place in his heart. In his own words, he recognized: "I stood in need of an Almighty Saviour, and such a one I found described in the New Testament. Thus far the Lord had wrought a marvelous thing; I was no longer an infidel."[10] Like the typical sea travelers of 107:23–30, his voyage brought him to the safe harbor of Northern Ireland and into the safe harbor of faith in Christ.

The story of the carter of manure

Church History: As historian Roland Bainton explains, Luther believed the work of the common laborer was just as important as the work of the apostles, and that is the gist of the following statement, even though it might sound like he is putting the labor of the carter of manure over the singing of the Carthusians[11] (and, in good Luther style, it may in fact be a subtle taunt of the Carthusians): "As God, Christ, the Virgin, the prince of the apostles, and the shepherds labored, even so much we labor in our callings. God has no hands and feet of his own. He must continue his labors through human instruments. The lowlier the task the better. The milkmaid and the carter of manure are doing a work more pleasing to God than the psalm singing of a Carthusian."[12]

"I Will Awaken the Dawn"

Big Idea

When a new era of life begins to dawn, we should praise God that he has both promised this new era and brought it to reality.

Key Themes

- Circumstances may change, but God does not.
- Our exaltation of God is enabled by God's self-humiliation.
- Human effort, necessary as it is, does not save us, but God does.

Understanding the Text

This psalm is a liturgical piece to announce and celebrate a new era, in this case, a time when Israel was emerging from the long, dark night of exile into the dawning day of return and restoration ("I will awaken the dawn," 108:2). Further, the psalm is a good example of how the writers of the Psalter sometimes use other psalms to reapply them for a different purpose in different circumstances. In this case the compiler has taken a psalm of praise from 57:7–11 and prefixed it to a lament, borrowed from 60:5–12, reapplying these old texts to the challenges faced by the returnees from Babylonian exile. With the verses from Psalm 57 our poet announces the dawn of a new day, the return from exile, and with the verses from Psalm 60 he reaffirms the Lord's promise of the land of Canaan, thus reassuring the returning exiles that their homeland is waiting for them.

The Text in Context

While the two lending psalms (Pss. 57 and 60) are contained in the Elohistic Psalter (Pss. 42–83), which favors the use of the generic *'elohim* ("God"), the one occurrence of *YHWH* (108:3, a change from *'adonay* in 57:9) is quite in concurrence with the nature of the Elohistic Psalter. The tetragrammaton (*YHWH*, "Lord"), in fact, does occur in strategic places in the Elohistic Psalter (e.g., 54:6; 55:22; 56:10; also see the sidebar "The Divine Names and the Elohistic Psalter" in the unit on Pss. 42–43).

Psalm 108 is composed of two Davidic psalms from Book 2, Psalm 57 being an individual lament and Psalm 60 a community lament. By this combination of an individual and a community lament the compiler alerts the reader to the fact that in Book 5 the community is most often the speaker, even when the psalmist is using the first-person singular "I."[1]

Outline/Structure

Evidently for liturgical purposes, the compiler of Psalm 108 has joined together pieces of two earlier psalms in order to praise God for the "dawn" of a new day and to pray for God's help in a situation where human efforts have proved "worthless."

1. A psalm of thanksgiving reapplied (108:1–5 // 57:7–11)
2. A psalm of lament reapplied (108:6–13 // 60:5–12)

Historical and Cultural Background

Most likely the geographical references, having been lifted from another historical setting, have become metaphors with new meaning for the postexilic community. Theoretically, the new kingdom those who repatriate the promised land inherit was the core of David's kingdom, but its enemies (Moab, Edom, and Philistia) have changed (see the comments on 108:7, 8, and 9), and these names are now applied metaphorically (see Ezra 4–5).

Interpretive Insights

108:1 *My heart, O God, is steadfast.* "My heart is steadfast" is repeated in the second line of 57:7, but here the second instance is left out, perhaps due to a copyist's error,[2] or it may be omitted for poetical reasons. "Steadfast" implies confidence in the surpassing worth of God's "love" (*hesed*) and "truth" (*'emet*; NIV: "faithfulness," 108:4). The latter terms are a pair that occurs in God's revelation to Moses, describing God's character (Exod. 34:6). Circumstances have changed, but God has not.

I will sing and make music with all my soul. The word rendered "soul" is literally "my glory" (*kᵉbodi*). One proposal is to give the word different vowels to make it "my liver" (*kᵉbedi*), which was the seat of the emotions (Lam. 2:11). Kirkpatrick notes that it is grammatically in apposition to "I," the noblest part of our being, which seems to be the sense of the NIV's "my soul."[3]

108:2 *Awake, harp and lyre!* The writer of Psalm 137 remembers, perhaps metaphorically, that the exiles had hung their harps (*kinnor*) on the willow trees of Babylonia (137:2), which may have become an adage to describe the exiles' dejection. Here our psalmist issues a call for the repatriates to emerge from their state of dejection and praise the Lord. The harp and the lyre, symbolically speaking, will "awaken the dawn" of the new era of restoration.

I will awaken the dawn. With the declaration "I will sing and make music" (108:1), the summons to harp and lyre to awake, and the statement here "I will awaken the dawn," we have reason to think this service of worship was a musical event of great melodic proportions.

108:3 *among the peoples.* The repatriation of the exiles to their homeland was unmatched in Hebrew history (98:2–3), so this event is one that will demonstrate God's power and love, and one the nations should hear about (96:3; 105:1). The covenant name *YHWH* ("LORD") is overwhelmingly used for God in Book 5, so there was no reason to use the alternate name *'adonay* (57:9) here (see "The Text in Context").

108:4 *your love . . . your faithfulness.* See the comments on 108:1 above; see also Exodus 34:6.

108:5 *Be exalted.* In 57:5 and 11 this invocation forms a refrain. The imperative verb could be translated "exalt yourself" (21:13; "I will be exalted" [or "exalt myself"] occurs in 46:10: "I am exalted" [RSV], or "I will be exalted" [ESV]; see "Theological Insights"). This verse forms an appropriate transition to the following strophe of hope and confidence for the future, lifted from 60:5–12.

108:6 *help us.* The Hebrew vowels give the reading "help me" (lit., "answer me"), which the Masoretes confirm in the margin of the text, and the first-person singular of the verbs in 108:1–5 is supportive of this reading. Other versions, however, have the first-person plural, "help us," which agrees with the plural ("us/our") of 108:11–13. A decision on the textual variants could go either way, and either makes sense. Yet our decision ought to be based on the literary nature of the second strophe. Note that the beginning and final verse (108:6 and 13) speak of the victory this community seeks, and that is the key: the second strophe is basically a community lament, thus the plural seems appropriate in 108:6, and the "I" of 108:1–5 is the corporate "I."

those you love. These are the Israelites (Deut. 33:12; Jer. 11:15), and this petition, which opens the second strophe, suggests a bit of desperation in the community as the restoration is taking place.

108:7 *God has spoken from his sanctuary.* Literally, "God has spoken by his holiness." In Psalm 89:35 and Amos 4:2 God's "holiness" is used with the verb "to swear," and here the verb "spoken" seems to carry that nuance. The content of the divine oracle, delivered by a prophet or priest, is given in verses 7b–9.

Shechem . . . Sukkoth. Shechem is on the western side of the Jordan and symbolizes the major portion of Canaan, while Sukkoth lies on the eastern side of the Jordan and symbolizes the Transjordan portion of the promised land. Together they are inclusive of the whole land. Jacob had stopped at Sukkoth and Shechem in his return after his self-exile in the Transjordan, and he built an altar at Shechem, symbolizing his claim on the land (Gen. 33:17–20).[4] These terms are intended to bring this patriarch and his land claim, based on God's promises, to the reader's mind.

108:8 *Gilead . . . Manasseh.* Similar to the terms of 108:7, Gilead and Manasseh (the half tribe of Manasseh settled on the eastern side) were located in the northern part of the Transjordan, while Ephraim and Judah were on the western side of the Jordan, further symbolizing the eastern and western lands promised to the Israelites. They are code language for the whole of Canaan. God is again swearing that he will give Israel the land of Canaan, and that message is most appropriate in this context of the return from exile.

108:9 *Moab . . . Edom . . . Philistia.* These three countries were Israel's mortal enemies who occupied territory within Israel's tribal claims. Nevertheless, their territories too belonged to God, and he could parcel them out to whomever he wished.

108:10–13 *Who will bring me to the fortified city?* The nation is now speaking, and the "fortified city" is probably Edom's capital city, Petra, which was carved out of a stone fortress. While Edom was a political problem when Jerusalem fell to the Babylonians in 586 BC (see Obadiah), we do not know of any problems with Moab and Philistia in the early postexilic period. We should assume, therefore, that the historical context of Psalm 60 ("Is it not you, God, you who have now rejected us and no longer go out with our armies?"; 60:10; see 108:11) has now been transformed into a metaphor, suggesting the difficult challenge that lay ahead for the exiles. Verse 11 answers the question of verse 10: only God can restore them to their land. In verse 13 the present historical circumstances emerge more clearly as the psalmist asserts that God has "rejected us" (108:11). This note in Psalm 60 refers to some unknown military defeat, but here in the new context it is an allusion to the exile.

Give us aid against the enemy, for human help is worthless. At this point, the suppliant moves into a petition (108:12). Historically, early postexilic Israel faced much opposition from the nations around them (see Ezra 4–6). One wonders if the clause "for human help is worthless" is not a hint of Cyrus's unfulfilled promise to assist in the rebuilding of the temple (see Ezra 6). This affirmation is another way to declare that it is "you, God" (108:11a), who will lead them. Divine assistance is their only hope. The last word of confident faith (108:13) would fortify the returning exiles for their challenging task. See "The biblical protocol of blessing" in "Illustrating the Text" in the unit on Psalm 134.

Theological Insights

In the strict sense of the verb of 108:5 "be exalted" ("to raise, be high"), we human beings cannot raise God any higher than he already is. And when we pray "Be exalted, O God," we are only acknowledging his preeminence in the universe, not elevating him with our praise above his already exalted status. We have the capacity for increasing only the estimation of God's worth but not his worth itself. We tend to merge the two functions, but they are not the same. And even the function of elevating God in our own eyes and the eyes of others is possible only if God condescends and allows us humans to praise him, to "lift him up," "to exalt him," as in 34:3. David's words in 22:3 (God is "enthroned on the praises of Israel," NRSV) is a clue of God's condescension (see the comments on 22:3; see also "Teaching the Text" in the units on Pss. 22 and 78). If God is truly exalted by us human beings, it must be because he humbled himself to receive our words of exaltation. Only he can truly recognize his own worth and majesty, and only he has the capacity to express it, but God condescends to allow us human beings to employ our deficient capabilities to exalt him. It might not be too bold to say that God incarnates our human praises (see 22:3). And here "Be exalted, O God" is another hint of his condescension.

Teaching the Text

In order to explain how the old material is being reused (see "Interpretive Insights") we will need to give some historical details, but caution must be exercised that our sermon not become a lecture in history (though this may be acceptable for a teaching occasion), as important as that may be. Rather, we want to stress the spiritual lesson that the historical events highlight. To do that, we may utilize Psalm 126 to help us fill in the picture, since this psalm is drenched with the emotions of joy and hope that filled the souls of those who made their way back to Judea from their exilic home in Babylonia.

The main thrust of our sermon/lesson may take the shape of an announcement that the old has passed away and the new has come: from exile to a new home, which parallels the spiritual motif of moving from the depressed life of our sins to a life of freedom and joy in God's forgiving love (108:4). Other dimensions may be that we have faced a time of discouragement or crisis in our congregational life, and now we are beginning to emerge into a new time of joy and freedom. This psalm gives us an opportunity to celebrate the passage, especially emphasizing the idea that our human efforts, as necessary as they were, did not accomplish our goal, but it was ultimately God who gave us the victory.

We may also want to stress another idea that can complement the featured announcement of a new day: we have arrived at the occassion because "human help is worthless," and "with God" we have gained the victory (108:12–13).

This part of the lesson is our opportunity to explain not so much where we are but how we got there. We ought not speak of human effort as absolutely worthless—that's not what the psalmist is saying. Rather, we want to recognize the need for human effort and at the same time acknowledge that, in the beautiful metaphor of another psalm, "Unless the LORD builds the house, the builders labor in vain" (127:1). Then we may bring these two themes together by stressing that this new phase of our personal life, or the life of our congregation, has been brought to reality because of God's promises (as he promised to bring the Israelites home) and God's power to save us and defeat the evil forces in our lives (108:13).

Illustrating the Text

Divinity at your feet

Church Fathers: Augustine ruminated on the mysterious doctrine of the incarnation and confessed that God's self-humiliation is built into the order of his redemptive plan. God's eternal truth raises up those who are humbled and, more than that, builds for itself a humble dwelling of clay, so as to identify with them. Then we, seeing his condescension in human flesh, should cast ourselves on God in his "coat of skin" and find that it is there, it is *from there*, and it is *only from there*, that he lifts us up out of our sinful humiliation.

> I was not humble enough to possess Jesus in His humility as my God, nor did I know what lesson was taught by His weakness. For your Word, the eternal truth, high above the highest parts of your creation, raises up to itself those who are subdued, but in this lower world He built for Himself a humble dwelling out of our clay, by means of which He might detach from themselves those who were to be subdued and bring them over to Himself, healing the swelling of their pride and fostering their love, so that instead of going further in their own self-confidence they should put on weakness, seeing at their feet divinity in the weakness that it had put on by wearing our "coat of skin"; and then, weary, they should cast themselves down upon that divinity which, rising, would bear them up aloft.[5]

While there can certainly be occasions in life when persons and circumstances lift us out of our social and material depression, the incarnation of God in Christ is uniquely different in that he lifts us up in saving grace, provides us with a new identity as children of God, and "from his fullness we have all received, grace upon grace" (John 1:16 ESV).

Humility, humility, humility

Quote: John Calvin. Paul describes God's condescension, or self-humiliation, in these memorable words: Christ "humbled himself by becoming obedient to death—even death on a cross!" (Phil. 2:8). Christ's taking upon himself our humanity and bearing our sins on the cross models a humility for his followers to imitate. Calvin makes a commanding statement in this regard:

> A saying of Chrysostom's has always pleased me very much, that the foundation of our philosophy is humility. But that of Augustine pleases me even more: "When a certain rhetorician was asked what was the chief rule in eloquence, he replied, 'Delivery'; what was the second rule, 'Delivery'; what was the third rule, 'Delivery'; so if you ask me concerning precepts of the Christian religion, first, second, third, and always I would answer, 'Humility.'"[6]

"He Stands at the Right Hand of the Needy, to Save Their Lives"

Big Idea

God in his mercy replaces our accusers and becomes our advocate.

Key Themes

- We can deceive others through our prayers, but we cannot deceive God.
- Believers are called to be like God.
- The Lord, as counsel for the defense, takes the place of our accusers.

Understanding the Text

Psalm 109 is the classical imprecatory psalm (see "Additional Insights: Imprecatory Psalms," following the unit on Ps. 34), which pronounces a series of curses against the psalmist's accusers. Some consider this psalm an individual lament (109:2–5),[1] while there is also language of a psalm of thanksgiving (109:30). Zenger identifies the psalm as a petition and draws attention to the cry for help that extends throughout the psalm—verse 1 → verse 21 → verse 26 → verses 30–31 (culminating in the vow to praise).[2] Most significantly, he proposes that this is not a psalm of cursing but a psalm of justice.

Waltner suggests that Psalm 109, the most vitriolic of the imprecatory psalms, deserves a new reading.[3] I think he is right (see "Teaching the Text"). Some have provided this new reading in the form of the "quotation" theory, understanding verses 6–19 to be the imprecations of the psalmist's enemy against the psalmist himself, not vice versa.[4] I have followed the traditional interpretation, that the curses are pronounced by the psalmist (the voice of David) against his enemies, phrased in the singular but aimed at Israel's corporate enemies. It is both a final word of judgment on David's enemies of Books 1 and 2 and judgment on Israel's enemies in the postexilic era that constitute the background of Book 5. Psalm 109 points to one of the missing pieces in the program of restoration, which is justice on Israel's enemies (see "Additional Insights: A Hypothesis on Psalm 109," following this unit).

The Text in Context

As Book 5 opens with the summons to "give thanks to the LORD, for he is good," Psalms 108 and 109 continue the theme of thanksgiving. Psalm 107 sets Book 5 in the context of the return from exile (107:2–3), while Psalm 108 rejoices in the dawn of a new day when the Lord renews his promise to give the land of Canaan to Israel. Psalm 109, not surprisingly, deals with David's enemies, who are also God's adversaries, and prays that their punishment will take the form of a reversal of their own wicked deeds (compare 137:9). While the curses the suppliant prays down on his adversary are in the singular (109:6–19), the picture broadens to the plural number, to include the enemies of God's people at large (109:20, 25, 27–29). Even though this psalm may have been written to apply to personal enemies, in the postexilic context the pluralization may constitute a corporate curse against Israel's enemies.

In Acts 1:20 Peter quotes Psalm 109:8b, "May another take his place of leadership," in the selection of an apostle to replace Judas, suggesting that the psalm was speaking of the psalmist's enemy (the offender or object of the curses) and the psalmist is praying that someone else will replace him (in Acts 1:20 Judas is the enemy/offender).

Outline/Structure

The psalm consists of four parts: a lament, imprecation, prayer, and vow to praise.

1. Prayer of lamentation (109:1–5)
   a. Petition for deliverance (109:1)
   b. Lament (109:2–5)
2. Imprecation: An extended curse (109:6–20)
   a. The juridical setting (109:6–7)
   b. The hoped-for sentence (109:8–15)
   c. Reasons for the curse (109:16–19)
   d. The reward: The curse turned upon the accusers (109:20)
3. Prayer of trust and petition (109:21–29)
   a. Grounds for appeal to the Lord (109:21–25)
   b. Imprecation that the accusers be punished (109:26–29)
4. Vow to give thanks and praise (109:30–31)[5]

Historical and Cultural Background

In the historical setting of Book 5, the exile or after the exile, Psalm 109 uses the singular number to curse the psalmist's enemy in verses 6–19, and the plural number to curse his enemies in verses 27–29 (see "Additional Insights: A Hypothesis on Psalm 109," following this unit). Also the setting of the curses is not specifically identified, but based on the description of the court ("let an accuser stand at his right hand," 109:6; see the comments on 109:6–20), with the accuser standing on the "right hand" of the accused, it seems to be the city gate, where courts normally convened (see Ruth 4).

Interpretive Insights

Title *Of David.* The book of Psalms is stamped with David's personality and character. Except for Book 3, which has only one Davidic psalm (Ps. 86), and Book 4, which has only two (Pss. 101 and 103), the other books have a generous presence of Davidic psalms (see "The Structure and Composition of the Psalter" in the introduction in vol. 1). The purpose of that is to be sure there is no absence of David's strong reputation. The compilers of Books 1 and 2, particularly, have intentionally built David's profile into the collection so that he is the prototype of the "poor and needy" (see the sidebar "The Editing of Book 2" in the unit on Ps. 70), and this profile is not lost on the compiler(s) of Book 5.[6] In fact, Psalm 108 concludes with the confidence that God "will trample down our enemies" (108:13), and Psalm 109 showers them with curses, as it declares that the Lord "stands at the right hand of the needy, to save their lives from those who would condemn them" (109:31), thus preparing the way for the picture of the vanquished enemies in Psalm 110. There we see the Lord, as the counsel for the defense, having displaced the accusers on his "right hand" (110:5). This small cadre of Davidic psalms (Pss. 108–10), both by their titles "of David" and by the declaration of the final psalm in the cadre (110:1), appropriately presents David as the beneficiary of the Lord's sovereign rule over the universe. In reaction to his enemies who said he would never rise again (41:8), David prays at the end of Book 1, "Raise me up, that I may repay them" (41:10), and in the opening section of Book 5, the compiler depicts the Lord at David's right hand as his ultimate defense counsel, having defeated David's enemies and given him a drink from the "brook along the way" (110:4–7).

109:1–3 *My God . . . do not remain silent.* First the psalmist petitions God not to be silent (109:1; also 83:1), and then he explains why: "People who are wicked and deceitful have opened their mouths against me; they have spoken against me with lying tongues. With words of hatred they surround me; they attack me without cause" (109:2–3). The opposition that the psalmist faced was largely belligerent language. It appears that he was ill (109:24–25), and perhaps his opponents' opposition was a malicious interpretation of the cause of his illness.

109:4–5 *but I am a man of prayer.* In contrast, David says, "I am a man of prayer" (109:4). Literally, this reads, "I am/was prayer," which means "and I prayed"[7] (compare 120:7). The psalmist's impeccable character silhouettes his opponents' bad behavior in two sets of opposites. They paid him "evil for good" and "hatred for love [NIV: "friendship"]" (109:5). See Proverbs 17:13; 1 Samuel 25:21.

109:6–20 The NRSV prefixes "They say" (lacking in the Hebrew) before verse 6 and puts quotation marks around verses 6–19, suggesting that these are the curses the accusers pronounced against the psalmist, rather than the psalmist against the accusers. Kraus is among those scholars who insist that the curses (109:6–19) are the psalmist's report of the imprecations his accusers had brought against him—the psalmist is merely reporting them.[8] Yet, Peter's quotation of 109:8b in Acts 1:20 implies that these words are the psalmist's against his enemies (see "The Text in Context").

109:6 *let an accuser stand at his right hand.* A court trial seems to be the setting for these verses, which are formulated in the singular. The clause "let an accuser stand at his right hand" suggests that in the court of law, the accuser was on the right and the accused on the left (see Zech. 3:1). And quite interestingly, in 109:31 the Lord takes the accuser's place at the right hand of the needy and becomes their defender.

109:7 *may his prayers condemn him.* The literal translation of this clause is "may his prayer become a sin," suggesting that the accuser's prayers, in view of his duplicitous character (109:2) and insincerity, should accomplish the opposite of forgiveness (see Prov. 28:9).

109:8–10 *may another take his place of leadership.* The prayer continues regarding the accuser's "place" (from root *pqd*, "to appoint"; 109:8). The NIV's "place of leadership" implies the accuser held an official position. The Septuagint renders this term as *episkopē*, probably a reference to a role of leadership within the community.[9] The opponent was obviously a person of influence, or he could not have brought such havoc to the psalmist's life. "May his days be few" (109:8) is obviously a death wish, but the most dreadful fate was social—"May his children be fatherless and his wife a widow" (109:9)—for no one would help the man's family if he were executed as a criminal.[10]

109:11–15 *May a creditor seize all he has . . . may the sin of his mother never be blotted out.* The picture is expanded further by the ruthless "creditor" (109:11), an example of whom is seen in 2 Kings 4:1. Moreover, to have the sin of his mother never be blotted out would be a violation of one of the most tender and affectionate relationships of the human family, a punishment second only to the impoverishment and disgrace of his wife and children. In fact, the imprecations of 109:9–15 all affect the accused's family, his most precious and vulnerable asset.

109:16 *he never thought of doing a kindness.* Verse 16 puts his violation of human relations in slightly different language from verses 4 and 5 but nevertheless reveals how heartless he was. He finished killing those who were already on their way to death, "the poor and the needy and the brokenhearted" (the Polel conjugation means "to finish someone's death"; see 2 Sam. 1:9).

109:17–20 *He loved to pronounce a curse . . . He found no pleasure in blessing.* The operative in this series of curses is a reversal of acts and attitudes: he cursed, and may his curses return upon him (109:17a); he did not bless, so may he not be blessed (109:17b); he wore cursing like a garment, so may he wear it always like a belt tied around his waist (109:18–19). The suppliant's prayer in verse 20 is not for vengeance but that the Lord may repay the accuser in like kind (an eye for an eye). Essentially this verse summarizes verses 6–19.

109:21 *help me for your name's sake; out of the goodness of your love.* For the first time in the psalm the basis for Yahweh's sovereign action, his "love" (also 109:26, "unfailing love") becomes evident. Their lack of "kindness" (*hesed*, 109:16) toward others should be met with the absence of "kindness" toward them (109:12). In verse 21 the phrase "your name's sake" is parallel to God's "love," suggesting that when God acts for "his name's sake," he is acting out of his love, and these two ideas are analogous transactions (see "Theological Insights"; see also "Teaching the Text" in the unit on Ps. 74, and the sidebar "For His Name's Sake" in the unit on Ps. 23).

109:22–25 *I am poor and needy, and my heart is wounded within me.* In verse 16 the adversary pursues to death "the poor and the needy and the brokenhearted," and in verse 22 the psalmist identifies himself as that person, even though here his broken heart is described with a different word ("to perforate, break"). Then the suppliant describes his physical condition with two metaphors (109:23): first, he is so gaunt that he fades away like a shadow (i.e., he looks like a shadow when he walks); and second, he is so emaciated that, like the locust, the wind could blow him away.[11] Verse 24 describes his weakness from fasting, probably fasting as he prays for God's mercy (see also 69:10).

109:26–29 *save me according to your unfailing love.* Having described his condition and the scorn of his accusers, he now invokes God's help according to his "unfailing love" (109:26), praying that the Lord will "let them know that it is your hand, that you, LORD, have done it" (109:27)—that is, that the Lord has accomplished his deliverance. He prays not for himself but for God's glory. The prayer takes the form that God will act in reverse order of the accusers' cursing, and rather than wearing cursing as his garment (109:18), the suppliant's "accusers" may be "wrapped in shame as in a cloak" (109:29).

109:30–31 *I will greatly extol the* LORD; *in the great throng of worshipers I will praise him.* Now the psalmist vows to praise God in the presence of a great crowd of worshipers (109:30), most likely in the temple, acknowledging that the Lord is the defender of the "poor and needy" as the suppliant has prayed he would be (109:21). The vow to give thanks (109:30; NIV: "I will greatly extol the LORD") in the presence of other worshipers puts this psalm in the thanksgiving category (see the sidebar "Psalms of Thanksgiving" in the unit on Pss. 9–10). Psalm 108 opens with the vow to give God thanks, and after the suppliant of Psalm 109 curses his enemies, he closes with the same vow of thanksgiving (see "The Text in Context").

Theological Insights

We are quick to identify, and ought to be quick to praise, those whose actions flow out of their good character. Psalm 109:21 puts in parallel lines the two phrases "for your name's sake" and "the goodness of your love," suggesting an analogous relationship. This may be as close to an equivalent of John's "God is love" as we have in the Old Testament (1 John 4:8; see "Teaching the Text" in the unit on Ps. 101). God's actions originate in his character, which is "the goodness of [his] love." Verse 26 is essentially a repetition of the petition in verse 21, using synonymous verbs of petition for effect ("help me" // "deliver me"; "help me" // "save me"). Despite the varied portraits of God that are contained in the Hebrew Bible, it is remarkable, especially in a world like Israel's, with its constant conflict and devaluation of human life, that the Hebrew faith rises to this height of religious preeminence. The New Testament, in one sense, is not as "new" as the title would suggest, though it is that. But so often its grandest figures and beliefs represent a refocusing, sometimes a reframing, sometimes even a reconfiguring, and sometimes even a revamping, of Old Testament concepts (see Jesus's Sermon on the Mount in Matt. 5). The love of God is one of those concepts that might qualify for all of those terms, with the exception of revamping, because the God of the Old Testament is a God of love, whatever other portrait we may have to reconcile with this one.

Teaching the Text

In spite of the challenges presented by this psalm, I hope every serious reader will give Psalm 109 a new hearing. As we prepare to convert the theological overtones of this poem into a sermon or lesson, we may focus on one of its striking metaphors.

First, we may observe that the court generally met inside the city gate in the morning as the people were leaving the city to work their fields and tend their sheep. Second, as the "curse" section (109:6–19) opens, the psalmist gives us a partial description of the court in verse 6; and evidently here, but not always, it was composed of three persons: the "evil" person (*rasha'*), who has already been mentioned in verse 2 but is evidently a different person, yet "evil" like him in character, perhaps an unscrupulous judge; "an accuser" (*satan*), who stands physically on the right side of the accused (109:6; cf. Zech. 3:1); and the accused, against whom the psalmist is about to deliver his invectives. Verse 7 explains the purpose of the evil judge: "Let him [the accused] be found guilty."

Third, in order to better understand the offensive nature of the enemy in 109:6–19, we may call attention to verse 16: "For he never thought of doing a kindness [*hesed*], but hounded to death the poor and the needy and the brokenhearted." He was a violator of the moral instruction of Micah 6:8—he did not love mercy (*hesed*). His behavior was the opposite of that. The phrasing of verse 16 gives us an opportunity to speak of our human responsibility to imitate God. Just as God has shown love and mercy to us, we are to act in like manner toward others. The assumption of this statement is that we are to be like God: "Be holy because I, the LORD your God, am holy" (Lev. 19:2). Jesus gives us a commandment to that effect: "A new command I give you: Love one another. As I have loved you, so you must love one another" (John 13:34; also 15:12). It would not be inaccurate to say that the most serious sin of the psalmist's adversary was that he failed to reflect God's character. And compounded with that, he directed his failed conduct at the most vulnerable and most-to-be-pitied members of society, "the poor and needy and brokenhearted" (Ps. 109:16).

Fourth, in verse 31 we hear that the Lord "stands at the right hand of the needy," having replaced the accuser as the suppliant's advocate. Paul puts the matter into the Christian context when he attests that Christ Jesus is at the right hand of God interceding for us (Rom. 8:33–34; cf. Heb. 10:12). That is, rather than our accuser standing at our right hand to condemn us, our Advocate Savior is standing there instead to defend and forgive us.

Illustrating the Text

Two issues

Quote: **David Wolpe.** Despite all the uneasiness the imprecatory psalms raise, at least two issues lie imbedded in the lines of Psalm 109. One is divine justice, which underlies the curses of 109:6–20. They are counterbalanced against the psalmist's innocence, which was met by his opponents' hatred (109:2–3); the psalmist's friendship and prayers, met by their accusations (109:4); and the psalmist's good actions, met by their animosity (109:5).

In any person's good judgment, does not this kind of abhorrent behavior deserve justice? And if justice is not forthcoming, then what kind of God do we think we serve?

The second issue is what it means to be human, certainly human in the biblical sense. Does our psalmist's behavior toward his enemies not define precisely what it means to be human: friendship, love, prayer, goodness? The psalmist has discovered the meaning and exercised his knowledge toward his human companions, even toward his enemies. Whether the psalmist had asked the questions about our humanity, he certainly found some answers. Wolpe comments, "Part of being fully human is asking the most important questions that confront us, asking them again and again, not letting them go until we figure out what it means to be a human being, why we were put here, whether we were put here for any reason at all."[12]

Designs to delay death

Culture: Psalm 109 is not about death per se, but the pall of death hovers over the psalm, particularly in the curses that, once effected, would make the psalmist's enemies' lives worse than death (e.g., his children fatherless and wandering beggars; 109:9a, 10a). Of course, the psalmist is even more direct when he wishes the enemy's wife a widow (109:9b). And further, the enemies themselves enforced a philosophy of death, for they mercilessly "hounded to death the poor and the needy and the brokenhearted" (109:16). So, operating on the *lex talionis* (eye for an eye) principle, the suppliant prays that they may be victims of the doom they have enacted on others (109:17–19). Even the proprietors of death in our culture fear it and do everything they can to escape it. Wolpe describes how our culture tries to delay death in ways that are positive and normal but nevertheless motivated by the threat of death: "How much human activity is designed to delay death! A hospital is the spangled, solid monument to the overt struggle, taking hostilities to the front. But there is also exercise, diet, the vast ingenuity devoted to accident prevention of all sorts, coiffures and cosmetics: our unceasing struggle to look young is but another frantic and even angry way of insisting how far we are from the end."[13]

A Hypothesis on Psalm 109

Psalm 107 sets Book 5 in its historical context and provides a spiritual history of Israel's looking for a city to dwell in while wandering in desert places, sitting in darkness created by their own rebellion against God's commandments, suffering affliction because of their own iniquities, and ultimately being threatened with shipwreck on the high seas of their moral decay. Then out of the Lord's unfailing love, they found the city they were looking for, and God rescued them from the tempest at sea and "stilled the storm to a whisper" (107:29). In this miraculous climate, Psalm 108, in David's name and in a spirit of victory, awakens the dawn of a new day that crowns the hope of Psalm 107 (107:42–43). There the psalmist rejoices in God's love and his authoritative oath sworn "by his holiness [NIV: "sanctuary"]" (108:7), returning the land to this disenfranchised people. This program of celebration is not complete, however, without a sure word of justice on Israel's enemies, an event that belongs to all of her ages, and especially to the age of the return, whose magnitude outstrips the exodus from Egypt (Jer. 16:14–15). Psalm 109 provides that missing piece in this opening unit of psalms in the book that will conclude the Psalter. This book of praises, like the God it extols, surpasses all other efforts to exalt "the God of my praise" (109:1; NIV: "My God, whom I praise").

But how does this poet accomplish that? First of all, he dedicates the psalm "to David" (NIV: "of David"), which is essentially the same as hearing David's melodious voice to the accompaniment of his own instrument (108:1), and in that voice he accomplishes his objectives: to express his passion against his enemies and his passion for his people, the two sides of David's public profile. David's passion against his enemies, as in Psalms 35 and 69, takes the form of a series of curses (109:6–19). The plurality of David's enemies is replicated in verses 2–5 and 21–29, and the singular number in verses 6–19 particularizes those enemies in a single person, perhaps the appointed representative of the accusers in the court of law.[1] To highlight the court setting, they are not called by the usual term "enemies," but the poet uses the verb that means "accuse" (*stn*, 109:4, 20, 29; the same verb that gives us the "accuser," *satan*, in Job 1 and 2; see also Ps. 109:6). The belligerent language often used in reference to foreign enemies, while absent from the curses (109:6–19), is not absent from the invocation, where the psalmist says that "they surround me" and "they attack me" (109:3), both military terms. Yet their battle ranks are composed of big mouths and lying tongues (109:2). Even the imprecations take a form that is more appropriate to their "wicked and deceitful" character and assume the form of imprecation that we have in Psalm 137 against Babylon and Edom. The absence of the names here (but not in Ps. 137) may indicate that the psalm belongs to a time when such mention of these political foes would have jeopardized the security of the community. In fact, the mode of apocalyptic writings (not to suggest that this is apocalyptic) in those politically charged settings was to use generic and symbolic language so as not to perturb the enemies. Our psalmist substitutes metaphors for symbols ("cursing as his garment; it entered into his body like water, into his bones like oil," 109:18). But he hits his enemy hard with caustic curses that bring the doom of ethnic extinction, phrased in domestic terminology (109:9–15).

The second aspect of his passion is David's concern for his people, humbled by exile. And they could have no greater comfort than to know that their revered King David identified with them. Our writer is evidently aware of the effort the psalmists and compilers of the book have expended to present David as the prototype of his suffering people, under the image of the "poor and needy."[2] That point of identity comes in 109:16 and 21 ("needy" also in 109:31). David is the "suffering servant" (note 109:28), and in that role he joins his suffering people. And climactically, in that role he also assures them that the "accusers" at court, standing at the plaintiff's right hand, have now been supplanted by the Lord, who "stands at the right hand of the needy, to save their lives from those who would condemn them" (109:31). The return and restoration make that message a historical reality.

"The LORD Says to My Lord: 'Sit at My Right Hand Until I Make Your Enemies a Footstool'"

Big Idea

Our Messiah is the King whose decrees we follow, and he is the Priest who prays for us that we may fulfill them.

Key Themes

- The Messiah is both King and Priest.
- The accuser of God's people is replaced by their Advocate.

Understanding the Text

Psalm 110, a royal psalm,[1] reflects the three main offices of ancient Israel: prophet, priest, and king. It begins with a prophetic word that invests David with his kingly office and makes him the vice-regent of Yahweh himself (see the comments on 110:1). What Psalm 8 does for humanity, declaring them a little lower than God (8:5), Psalm 110 does for the king, declaring him next in power to God (110:1). The king's investiture with royal power is augmented by his investiture with the priestly office in the line of Melchizedek, thus giving us the office of priest-king modeled in the Jebusite monarch Melchizedek (Gen. 14; the name means "king of righteousness").

The Text in Context

Following Psalm 107, which positions Book 5 in the postexilic era, Book 5 introduces a small Davidic collection (Pss. 108–10), evidently to focus Book 5 more closely on the hopes of the restoration. Psalm 108 summons the new dawn of history when God renews the promise of the land of Canaan to his people, now on the verge of returning to the homeland. Psalm 109 follows with curses on Israel's enemies, concluding with a picture of Yahweh, standing at the right hand of the needy as their Advocate. With Psalm 110 we hear the victor's strategy in relation to Israel's enemies of Psalm 109: Yahweh will make the enemies Israel's footstool. Further, Psalm 110 opens onto the new Davidic dynasty, configured according to the ancient model of Melchizedek, king of Salem (Jerusalem) and priest of God Most High (Gen. 14:18). While David never lived up to that prototype—nor was he expected to—it nevertheless was likely an ideal for his dynasty; and in the wake of the return, Zechariah reiterates this ancient priest-king model as he hopes for the revival of the monarchy (Zech. 6:9–15). It is significant that this psalm, perhaps ancient on its own merits, reaches back into patriarchal history and configures the renewed hopes of the monarchy's revival along the lines of the ancient priest-king of Salem who blessed Abraham. And what better credentials could this new era of history afford!

Along with Psalms 22 and 69, Psalm 110 shares the honor of being among the most frequently quoted psalms in the New Testament. The uses of the psalm fall basically into two categories, both based on the two oracles of the psalm. The first is that of the investiture of the king with power second only to God: "Sit at my right hand" (110:1). When Jesus's opponents test him with questions about taxes, the resurrection, and the greatest commandment, he uses this language to assert his divine sonship and turns the question on his accusers, "What do you think about the Messiah? Whose son is he?" When the respondents answer, "The son of David," Jesus then chidingly rejoins, "If then David calls him 'Lord,' how can he be his son?" (Matt. 22:41–46; cf. Mark 12:35–37 // Luke 20:41–44). On the day of Pentecost, Peter draws on that exegetical tradition and quotes this same verse to prove that Jesus the Messiah (not David) has been exalted to God's right hand by his resurrection from the dead (Acts 2:34–36). In a similar train of thought, the writer to the Hebrews quotes this verse to make the case that Jesus the Son is superior to the angels (Heb. 1:13). The theme of Christ's power and authority is further echoed in Mark 16:19; Romans 8:34; 1 Corinthians 15:25; Ephesians 1:19–22; Colossians 3:1; and Hebrews 10:13.

The second oracle (110:4–7) is used in the New Testament to establish Jesus's priestly office. The writer to the Hebrews makes verse 4 the hinge verse for Christ's high-priestly ministry according to the order of Melchizedek, distinguishing his priesthood from the Aaronic. In Hebrews 5:6 the writer quotes Psalm 110:4 (and 2:7) in order to make the point that Christ received his high-priestly office not by genealogical descent but by divine appointment. Then in Hebrews 7, drawing on the details of Genesis 14, the writer continues to develop this theme, ultimately citing Psalm 110:4 again to make the point that Christ was the only priest whose office was established by an oath, setting him apart from the Aaronic (Levitical) priests (Heb. 7:14–21). The themes of Christ's priestly work/intercession and kingly power are combined in Romans 8:34; Hebrews 8:1–2; 10:12–14; and 12:2.

Outline/Structure

Psalm 110 is composed of three parts, following the three oracles or divine words (110:1, 2–3, 4–7). Each divine word is introduced by a formula signaling the oracle to follow: "The LORD says" (110:1), "The LORD will extend your mighty scepter from Zion, saying" (110:2), and "The LORD has sworn" (110:4).

1. First oracle: Appointment of king as vice-regent (110:1)
   a. Introductory formula (110:1a)
   b. Oracle of appointment: "Sit at my right hand until I make your enemies a footstool for your feet" (110:1b)
2. Second oracle: Empowerment of vice-regent to rule over his enemies (110:2–3)
   a. Introductory formula (110:2a)
   b. Oracle of empowerment: "Rule in the midst of your enemies!" (110:2b)
   c. The king's troops: willing, spiritually endowed, and youthful (110:3)
3. Third oracle: Appointment of vice-regent as priest (110:4–7)
   a. Introductory formula (110:4a)
   b. Oracle of priestly investiture: "You are a priest forever, in the order of Melchizedek" (110:4b)
   c. The Lord's advocacy and revenge on the priest-king's behalf (110:5–6)
   d. The king's refreshment and victory (110:7)

Historical and Cultural Background

This psalm is often considered to be very early, perhaps from David's own time, and in Book 5 it is just reapplied to the new historical circumstances of the postexilic period. Despite renewed hopes that the Davidic monarchy might revive after the demise of the Babylonian Empire (539 BC), especially with Cyrus's appointment of Sheshbazzar, a descendant of David, to the governorship of Judah (Ezra 5:13–15), it did not happen. In fact, the Davidic monarchy never revived, except, as Christians insist, in the messianic rule of Jesus of Nazareth. However, when the Maccabeans, four centuries later, seized the opportunity to reestablish the monarchy, at least in titular form, it was a priestly monarchy.

The reference to "footstool" in verse 1, an image well represented in ancient iconography, alludes to the place where the monarch rested his feet, and here it is a symbol of subordination.

Interpretive Insights

110:1 *The Lord says to my lord.* Literally, "Oracle of the Lord to my master." The word "oracle" (*ne'um*) designates words of prophecy (Num. 24:3–4, 15–16; 2 Sam. 23:1). "My lord," on the historical level, refers to the king, whereas Jesus interprets the speaker of the psalm to be David, and "my lord" to designate the Messiah (Matt. 22:43–45). The occurrence of the tetragrammaton (*YHWH*, "Lord") and the word for "lord" (*'adoni*) indicates a vast difference between these two terms, one divine and the other human. The latter term is used in respect, much as we use "sir" (Gen. 23:6; 1 Sam. 22:12).

Sit at my right hand. This is the first of three oracles that God speaks to the king (110:1b, 2b, and 4b). Here God invites the king to take the position of second-in-command ("Sit at my right hand"). It is the typical protocol of biblical kingship, for the king is God's representative. The imagery, of course, is that of the conquering king who seats conquered kings at his right hand to signify his favor toward them and their loyalty toward him.[2] However, in the context of Psalm 109:6 and 31, we see another level of meaning, that of the Advocate who has replaced the accuser.

footstool. This is the place where the king rested his feet and is a symbol of subordination.

110:2 *The Lord will extend your mighty scepter from Zion.* The "scepter" symbolizes royalty and power. Its source is Yahweh, and its place of dispatch is Jerusalem.

Rule in the midst of your enemies! This is the second time we hear God's voice, or the second oracle in the psalm. This verse is Yahweh's investiture of the king with royal authority and power to rule over his enemies.

110:3 *Your troops will be willing on your day of battle.* "Your troops" is literally "your people," but in light of Judges 5:2, where the same verbal root describes the willingness of the soldiers to join the battle, it probably alludes to the troops' loyalty to David (1 Sam. 18:7).[3]

Arrayed in holy splendor. "Holy splendor" is an equivalent of a similar phrase in 29:2, "splendor of his holiness." Rather than the colorful uniforms that some of the neighboring armies wore, Israel's troops were arrayed in the "splendor" of Yahweh's holiness. The noun "splendor" is plural (*hadre*), whereas the noun in 29:2 and 96:9 is singular (*hadrat*). Hakham explains that the masculine plural is sometimes used to express an abstract idea, just as does the feminine singular, reinforcing the abstract (spiritual) "splendor" of Yahweh's holiness over against the literal brilliance of the enemy army, which is only imagined here.

from the morning's womb. This is a difficult phrase. Literally, it is "from the womb of the dawn [*mishhar*]." The NIV's translation is dependent on the Greek (LXX), which has "from the morning," a metaphor for youth. The sense of verse 4 seems to be that the young men will join themselves in loyalty to the king in his fight against his enemies, and they will be arrayed in "holy splendor" rather than the colorful uniforms of the enemy armies.[4] So the king's army is described in three ways: willing, spiritually endowed ("holy splendor"), and youthful.

110:4 *The Lord has sworn.* Only in 132:11 does the Lord take an oath to establish David's throne. Here the oath is for the purpose of establishing his priesthood. Both David and Solomon exercised some priestly functions, or directed those functions to be exercised by the priests (2 Sam. 6:18; 1 Kings 8:62–63), but neither can hardly be called a priest-king (see "The Text in Context"). This verse may allude to Israel's priestly function incorporated in the Mosaic covenant (Exod. 19:6), but beyond that, it is a reference to the messianic priest-king whom Zechariah predicted would appear (Zech. 6).

You are a priest forever, in the order of Melchizedek. This is the third oracle that the Lord speaks, assigning the king a priestly role after the non-Aaronic priest Melchizedek of Genesis 14.

110:5–7 *he will crush kings on the day of his wrath.* In verses 5–7 the scene shifts to the battlefield, for which the king's loyal subjects willingly volunteered (110:3). While in 109:6 the accuser stands at the right hand of the accused, the oracle of 110:1 invests David with ruling power by commanding him to sit at the deity's right hand. In verse 5 the position has changed ("The Lord is at your right hand"), and the Lord ('*adonay*, substitute name for *YHWH*) has now taken the place of the accuser in 109:6. While "Lord" in verse 5 is the same terms as "Lord" in 110:1 ('*adonay*), referring to the king, in 110:5 many Hebrew manuscripts substitute the tetragrammaton (*YHWH*, "Lord") for this term, indicating that the Lord has now taken his place at the right hand of the king as his defender, in the same sense as 109:31, where the Lord stands at the right hand of the needy as the counsel of the defense.

He will drink from a brook along the way, and so he will lift his head high. The subject changes abruptly in verse 7 from Yahweh to the king, to describe the physical and spiritual refreshment that Yahweh provides.

Theological Insights

As we have explained under "The Text in Context," the messianic portrait in Psalm 110 consists of two parts, the messianic king and the messianic priest, although they are the same figure. As Reardon observes, the initial oracle of the psalm, "Sit at my right hand," became "the foundation of some of the most important christological and soteriological statements of the New Testament."[5] And he proposes that in this one line of the psalm we have a summary of the eternal identity of Jesus Christ, his triumph over sin and death, and his glorification at God's right hand.[6]

The third oracle, "You are a priest forever, in the order of Melchizedek," is just as significant in church doctrine, since Christ's sacrificial death on the cross became the once-for-all-time oblation for the sins of the world, and his eternal intercession at God's right hand the extension of his priestly work (Rom. 8:34). In one sense we can say that the kingly role of Christ is to represent God to the world, and at the same time, he is our intercessor at God's right hand, thus completing a two-way relationship, God to humankind and humankind to God, and each way is fulfilled by God's Son, Jesus Christ. That is to suggest that what God requires of us is communicated by the messianic King, and what we need from God is also communicated by the messianic Priest, not two persons but two functions, thus constituting a perfect system of intercommunication. Our Messiah is the King whose decrees we follow, and he is the Priest who prays for us that we may fulfill them.

Teaching the Text

The temptation to preach or teach this psalm eschatologically is strong, and there is some justification for that (see "Additional Insights: The Priest-King Ruler Model," following this unit). If the preacher/teacher chooses that option, I suggest that he or she highlight the theme I have laid out in "Theological Insights," that the psalm presents the absolute model of divine/human communication, whereby God speaks his word to us through Christ our King and speaks our word (prayers) to God through Christ our Priest. We can make the point that this is the system by which God communicates his grace in terms of his will and intercedes with God that we may fulfill it (Rom. 8:27).

If we choose to follow the historical/eschatological interpretation, which I have opted for, we need to explain how the priest-king can be both historical and eschatological. The compiler of Book 5 has evidently placed this psalm here to present, at least in a rhetorical sense, David as both king and priest. The postexilic community desperately needed the voice of king and priest in their hopes of restoration, that is, the voice of authority and the voice of intercession, in order for the tenuous circumstances they faced to turn in their favor. In this regard, we may stress that we also need the divine voice of authority, speaking God's will, as well as the divine voice of intercession, praying that God's will might be done on earth as it is in heaven. With that combination of voices God's kingdom cannot fail, and we cannot fail to live in accord with its principles.

Illustrating the Text

Prayer is God talking to himself through us.

Quote: C. S. Lewis. However articulate and fluent our prayers may be, we have our inarticulate moments when either our language is impeded or our thoughts are incoherent, and the Spirit intercedes for us with "wordless groans" according to the will of God (Rom. 8:26–27). This is another way to say that God prays his prayers through us ("in accordance with the will of God"), even calling our speech impediment and incoherence into his service. The priest-king Messiah both issues his decrees and through his intercession enables us to obey them. "God's commandments are his enablements," as the saying goes. When our prayers are shaped and reshaped into petitions that express God's will for us and our world, then these are equivalents of God's prayers. C. S. Lewis, writing to an American friend, asserts that God moves us to pray for the things he wants us to have, fulfilling, we might add, Paul's declaration that "the Spirit intercedes for God's people in accordance with the will of God" (Rom. 8:27): "Not (lest I should indulge in folly) that your relief had not in fact occurred *before* my prayer, but as if, in tenderness for my puny faith God moved me to pray with especial earnestness just before He was going to give me the thing. How true that our prayers are really His prayers; He speaks to Himself through us."[7]

Additional Insights

The Priest-King Ruler Model

After the Davidic dynasty ended with the Babylonian exile, the dynasty, despite hopeful expectation, never revived, except in the spiritual kingdom of Christ. In fact, the only time Israel had a king again was during the Hasmonean era (157–37 BC), and this was a priestly dynasty. The book of 1 Maccabees informs us that when Simon, one of the Maccabean sons, won Jewish independence from the Syrians (Seleucids), the people "made him ruler and high priest" (1 Macc. 14:35, 38, 41), thus assuming a priest-king model. This psalm, especially with its Melchizedek connection, provides a bridge for the institution of the priest-king ruler. This office, canonically speaking, has its origins in the story of Melchizedek, who blesses Abraham when he returns from victory over the coalition of Canaanite kings (Gen. 14).

Psalm 110, then, assumes three functions in Book 5. First, taking our cue from the psalm itself, David's conquest of the Jebusite city of Jerusalem (2 Sam. 5:6–10; 1 Chron. 11:4–9), by the very nature of the connection with Melchizedek and Abraham, conveys the priest-king office of Melchizedek on David. Of course, no evidence suggests that David lived out this hybrid leadership role in real life, but we might say that he did in a rhetorical sense, particularly in view of his portrait in the Psalms as intercessor between God and Israel (see "Theological Insights" in the unit on Ps. 34).

The second function of Psalm 110 in Book 5 is that it anticipates the reconstruction of the temple and reestablishment of a functioning priesthood, which, especially in connection with the newly developing centrality of Torah, opened the way for a new prominence for the high priest, particularly in the absence of a king. We see this in the prominence of Joshua the high priest (Hag. 1:1; Ezra 3:1–6) and Ezra the priest (note Ezra's leadership of a group of returnees in Ezra 8:1). While no monarch of preexilic Israel functioned in such an obvious priestly role, Zechariah records the transition to the priest-king model in the appointment of Joshua the high priest as king (Zech. 6:11–15). This prophetic instruction should probably be viewed in connection with Psalm 110, producing a nexus among Genesis 14; Psalm 110; and Zechariah 6:11–15. Since this model was not fulfilled in history, the New Testament—followed by the Christian church—has interpreted Christ's person and role in terms of this psalm. In fact, Jesus seems to bypass the idea that the psalm may have a double meaning, interpreting the psalm to speak of both David and the Messiah (Matt. 22:41–46 // Mark 12:35–37). The intent of his words in the Gospels (see "The Text in Context" in the unit on Ps. 110) is to distinguish "LORD" and "lord," obviously understanding Yahweh as the speaker of the oracle in Psalm 110:1, and "lord" as referring to Christ, God's Son seated in power at God's right hand. If we press this point, then the oracles of Psalm 110 are exclusively eschatological and not historical. I would, however, prefer to understand Jesus's interpretation of Psalm 110:1 in the double sense, David fulfilling, at least in a spiritual sense, the priest-king model of the psalm, especially in his role as intercessor in the Psalms, where he is both king and intercessor, and Christ fulfilling it in the eschatological sense. Generally speaking, Old Testament future prophecies are tied to historical events and persons. Isaiah's Immanuel prophecy (Isa. 7:14) may serve as an illustration. While we might view Immanuel as exclusively an eschatological figure, fulfilled in the person of Christ (Matt. 1:22–23), he may also be both a historical and eschatological figure—that is, Isaiah's son (Isa. 8:8) and the Savior of the world.

Third, Psalm 110 contributes a piece to the portrait of the new postexilic community in that it indicates a priestly role for the new community, suggested also by 132:9. Just as Psalms 111–12 contribute a feature of this new profile, that of the centrality of Torah (see "The Text in Context" in the unit on Ps. 111), so Psalm 110 alludes to the retrieval of the priestly role assigned to Israel by the Mosaic covenant (Exod. 19:6). Of course, this is assuming that the singular pronoun "you" refers to the postexilic community of faith, as is often the case in Book 5, as well as to a historical figure of priest-king, most likely a messianic person.

"Glorious and Majestic Are His Deeds, and His Righteousness Endures Forever"

Big Idea

Since God's character is the support system that upholds his works, his precepts are trustworthy, as is he.

Key Themes

- God's character is reflected in his works.
- God's commandments are not burdensome.

Understanding the Text

Psalms 111 and 112 are alphabetic acrostics (except for the initial "hallelujah"; NIV: "Praise the LORD"),[1] using all twenty-two consonants of the Hebrew alphabet, each new line beginning with a new letter of the alphabet. They have been called "twin psalms" because of their mutual acrostic structure, matching terminology (see table 1 in the unit on Ps. 112), and mirror imaging. Psalm 111 extols the Lord by lauding his works, which are a reflection of his character (111:4), and Psalm 112 personalizes the character of God, especially with the duplicate clause of 111:3b and 112:3b, "and his righteousness endures forever" (NIV pluralizes the singular ["he" to "they"] of Ps. 112), describing the wise individual. Psalm 111:10 builds the first half of the bridge between the two psalms, and Psalm 112:1 builds the other half: "The fear of the LORD is the beginning of wisdom; all who follow his precepts have good understanding" / "Blessed are those who fear the LORD, who find great delight in his commands." In view of the opening verse of Psalm 111 ("I will give thanks"; NIV: "I will extol"), and God's works as an accomplished fact of creation and history, we may call this an individual psalm of thanksgiving. See the sidebar "Psalms of Thanksgiving" in the unit on Psalms 9–10.

The Text in Context

While the word *torah* does not appear at all in Psalms 111 and 112, they nevertheless represent a turn toward Torah wisdom, much as we see in Psalms 1, 19, and 119. In addition to the keeping of the commandments (see 111:7, "precepts"), Zenger describes this genre of wisdom as a shift from "the earlier emphasis on nature and social interaction to the saving works of Yahweh."[2] Psalm 112, in fact, contains a reflection back to 1:1–2 and 41:1 and a forward glance to 119:1–2. The connecting word is "blessed" (*'ashre*), which lauds the one who "fears the LORD, who delights greatly in his commandments" (112:1, author's translation; see also 1:1 and 111:2), who in 41:1 is modeled as David the righteous man "who considers the poor" (ESV; see "The Text in Context" in the unit on Ps. 41). In Book 5 the writer of Psalm 112 now uses Torah-wisdom language to describe that individual as one "who fears the LORD" (see Prov. 1:7; 9:10).[3] And in view of the Babylonian captivity and restoration, which is the backdrop of Book 5, Psalm 112 looks forward in hope, like Psalm 41 (vv. 1, 2c–d, 11): "Their hearts are secure, they will have no fear; in the end they will look in triumph on their foes" (112:8). The need to hear this word of triumph—the same note of triumph over their enemies that was so appropriate at the end of Book 1, where war and personal conflict were pervasive—was as fresh at this stage of history as in David's time. Although David is clearly the voice of Psalms 108–10, Psalms 111 and 112 begin a long silence for David (we do not hear his voice again until Psalm 124), but his voice still echoes in the triumphant words of Psalm 41 translated into the words of Psalm 112:8 (see 41:11–18). Just as Psalm 41:12 celebrates David's victory over his enemies and the fulfillment of his lifelong desire to be in the presence of the Lord, thus concluding Book 1 on a triumphant note, so Psalm 112:8–9 gathers up the threads of David's character as a righteous man who is not afraid and looks forward to triumph over his enemies as the historical David did.

Outline/Structure

> Hallelujah (111:1a)
> 1. Vow to praise the Lord (111:1b–c) ("works of the LORD" constitutes an *inclusio*; see 111:10b, "all who follow his precepts")
> 2. Extolling God's works (111:2–9)
>   a. Delighting in God's works (111:2–3a)
>   b. Theme: "His [Yahweh's] righteousness endures forever" (111:3b)

c. The Lord's works reflect his character (111:4)
d. Provision of food (111:5)
e. Gift of the land (111:6)
f. Trustworthy precepts (111:7–8)
g. Redemption of God's people (111:9)
3. The fear of the Lord (bridge to Ps. 112) (111:10)
a. The fear of the Lord (111:10a)
b. Following the Lord's precepts (111:10b)[4]

Historical and Cultural Background

Psalms 106:46–47 and 107 have already set the Babylonian captivity and the early years of the restoration as the historical backdrop for Book 5, and Psalms 111 and 112 fall within that frame. Similar to the way Psalm 41 establishes David as the "righteous" individual, these twin psalms aim to establish the identity of the wise person (see "The Text in Context"). After a period of seventy years without the temple, the Torah or commandments had begun to take center place in developing Judaism, and that development surfaces here in the declaration that the one who fears the Lord and keeps his commandments is truly the wise person (111:10; 112:1).

Interpretive Insights

111:1 *Praise the* Lord. Literally, "Hallelujah." This word of praise, which stands outside the acrostic pattern, belongs to the edition of the Psalter that is sometimes called the "hallelujah redaction." "Hallelujah" begins both Psalms 111 and 112 and so ties them to Psalm 113, which begins and ends with "hallelujah." Thus these twin psalms provide a bridge between the opening psalms of Book 5 and the Egyptian Hallel of Psalms 113–18.

I will extol the Lord. Literally, "I will give thanks to the Lord"; see also 9:1. This is the language of the psalms of thanksgiving, and the location of this service of thanksgiving is the temple, "in the company of the upright, in the congregation" (ESV; see 33:1–2).[5]

111:2–3 *Great are the works of the* Lord. Here the psalmist begins what he pledged to do in verse 1 and lauds the "works of the Lord" as his reason for giving thanks. The Lord's works, which include both his saving deeds and marvels of his creation, are a testimony to his greatness (see Deut. 11:7). "Glorious and majestic" implies that the Lord's deeds are the exercise of his kingship, as attested by other psalms (21:5; 45:3; 96:6; 104:1; 145:5; see 1:2 for the idea of delighting in God's law).

111:4–6 Verses 4–6 give a concise review of Israel's covenantal history. These historical allusions go hand in hand with the two references to Yahweh's "covenant forever" (111:5b, 9b). Verses 4–5 have been used in the Christian church as a prayer of thanksgiving at the table.[6]

111:4 *He has caused his wonders to be remembered.* Yahweh's "wonders" (111:4) echo his mighty deeds, which may refer specifically here to the plagues (Exod. 3:20).

The Thirteen Attributes of God

The thirteen attributes of God (Exod. 34:6–7) are understood as ethical terms that define who God is. Some variation exists in their enumeration, but the following is typical:

1. "The LORD, the LORD" (*YHWH*): God's personal name connotes his attribute of mercy.
2. "God" (*'el*): The generic name for God (in this case the shortened form) connotes God's almighty power by which he rules over nature and humankind.
3. "Merciful" (*rahum*; NIV: "compassionate"): This term is taken to refer to God's compassion for human misery and suffering.
4. "Gracious" (*hannun*): With humanity the qualities of grace and mercy are quite inconsistent, but with God they are permanent, and this particular attribute suggests that God is active and constant in his application of mercy and grace.
5. "Long-suffering" (*'erek 'appayim*; NIV: "slow to anger"): God is not hasty to punish but gives offenders opportunity to change their evil ways.
6. "Abundant in goodness" (*rab-hesed*, lit., "plenteous in mercy"; NIV: "abounding in love"): God gives his human creatures more than they deserve.
7. "Truth" (*'emet*; NIV: "faithfulness"): God is true to his own nature and faithful to fulfill his plans of redemption.
8. "Keeping mercy to the thousandth generation" (NIV: "maintaining love to thousands"): God remembers the good deeds of the ancestors and rewards them by fulfilling his promises to future generations.
9. "Forgiving iniquity" (*nose' 'awon*; NIV: "forgiving wickedness"): God forgives those sins that are committed from our evil disposition.
10. "Transgression" (*pesha'*; NIV: "rebellion"): God forgives those evil deeds that humans do out of malice and rebellion against God.
11. "Sin" (*hatta'ah*): God forgives those sins that arise out of human weakness.
12. "Will by no means clear the guilty" (NIV: "He does not leave the guilty unpunished"): God will not ignore the sins of humankind, even though he forgives but appropriately punishes them. He can never obliterate the difference between good and evil.
13. "Visiting the iniquity of the fathers upon the children" (NIV: "He punishes the children and their children for the sin of the parents"): God appropriately metes out consequences for the sins of humans, even though he has forgiven them. Forgiveness removes the sinfulness but not the penalty, and this extends to the third and fourth generation, but to those who love him God shows mercy.[a]

[a] See Hertz, *Pentateuch and Haftorahs*, 364–65, notes on Exodus 34.

gracious and compassionate. These words the Lord uses to describe his own character to Moses (Exod. 34:6); these are among the thirteen attributes of God as recognized in Judaism (see the sidebar).

111:5 *He provides food.* The provision of manna and quail is likely the "wonder" referred to by the rather peculiar use of the Hebrew word for "food" (111:5), which usually refers to animals of prey, but in Malachi 3:10 it means "food"; the use of the word here may be dictated by the fact that the poet needs a word beginning with the letter *teth*, which the Hebrew word *terep* supplies.

he remembers his covenant forever. The reference to "his covenant forever" is a summary of what the poet is doing here, referencing the Mosaic covenant and its provisions (see Exod. 31:16).

111:6 *the lands of other nations.* This is an allusion to the conquest (see Ps. 105:8–11; Deut. 7:1).[7]

111:7–9 *all his precepts are trustworthy.* "Precepts" (111:7) are God's commandments, a term that occurs only in the Psalms (19:8; 103:18; 119 [21x]). The DNA of this noun, coming from the verb that occurs in 8:4, suggests that it may evoke God's care and concern: "What is man that you are mindful of him, and the son of man that you *care for* him?" (ESV). (See "Theological Insights.") The language of verse 8 suggests that God's commandments, as Zenger says, "are continually 'supported' by YHWH."[8] The terms "redemption" and "covenant" in verse 9 are parallel terms, implying that the covenant was an instrument of redemption. Now in the early postexilic era, without the temple, the law was becoming, as Psalm 1 asserts (1:2) and the Lord's works acclaim (111:2), the delight of Israel (112:1). The psalmic road ahead, paved by the Egyptian Hallel, which celebrates Israel's redemption from Egypt (Pss. 113–18), is leading the way to the meditation on the law represented by Psalm 119.

111:10 *The fear of the* LORD . . . *To him belongs eternal praise.* See "The Text in Context." Since God's Torah is everlasting, his "righteousness" is also everlasting (111:3), and now, says the psalmist, this calls for "eternal praise." The Hebrew word "praise" (*tᵉhillah*) is a derivative from the verb "hallelujah" (root *hll*), which introduces the psalm.

Theological Insights

As Israel emerged from the exile and set out on the uncharted road to restoration, the long absence of the temple and the sacrificial system had already given rise to much soul-searching. In the absence of the temple, the Torah had begun to occupy a new and commanding place in Israel's communal life. More personally, the stipulations of Deuteronomy 6:4–9 were beginning to take effect in the life of faith, and Psalms 111 and 112 are indicators of that shift. Psalm 111:7–9 puts the "works" of God's hands and his "precepts" in parallel relationship, assuring that God enacted the works of creation out of his covenant character—he is "faithful and just" (111:7)—just as he has his precepts. In a similar mode, 19:7–9 characterizes the Torah in ethical terms, disclosing the positive nature of the Torah, and by implication the corresponding nature of the Giver of the Torah. Our text, in comparison, discloses the positive character of the Giver and thus the virtuous nature of the Torah (111:4, 7–8). In 111:8 the passive participle ("supported"; NIV: "established") describes the Lord's continuous "upholding" of his "precepts." One is reminded of John's assertion that God's "commandments are not burdensome" (1 John 5:3).

Teaching the Text

Building off the "Theological Insights," we can construct our sermon/lesson on the idea that God's works are a reflection of his character, and his character is "gracious and compassionate" (111:4), which means that "the works of his hands are faithful and just; all his precepts are trustworthy" (111:7). God's "precepts" come with good character credentials.

Biblical ethics describes individual character as a single piece, proceeding from the innermost being, often referred to as "the heart." In this ethical system, character is not fundamentally the result of external forces and circumstances, although they certainly affect and shape who we are, but the real determinant is what happens between us and God in our innermost being. Our words and behavior are the indices of the shape of our hearts. Jesus teaches that it is not what one ingests that defiles but what comes from one's heart: "For out of the heart come evil thoughts—murder, adultery, sexual immorality, theft, false testimony, slander. These are what defile a person" (Matt. 15:19–20a; see also Luke 6:45). Hypocrisy is the epitome of inauthenticity, and a condition of the heart that God cannot endure. Jesus speaks strongly against outward actions that betray the evil condition of the heart: "On the outside you appear to people as righteous but on the inside you are full of hypocrisy and wickedness" (Matt. 23:28; cf. Luke 12:1; see also 1 Pet. 2:1).

This character model is laid out in Psalm 111, exhibiting the fact that the character and actions of Yahweh are a single piece (see "Theological Insights"; see also 111:4, 7–8). We can trust God's words. The Jerusalem Bible expresses the sense of verses 7 and 8 quite vividly: "All that he does is done in faithfulness and justice, in all ways his precepts are dependable, ordained to last for ever and ever, framed in faithfulness and integrity." This psalm's confession also reveals the underlying principle of prayer, which is a petition that God enact his character in human history and in our personal lives (see "Illustrating the Text").

Illustrating the Text

Prayer is a petition that God enact his character.

Bible: Genesis 18:25. Psalm 111 is a declaration and an affirmation that God's character and his works are a single piece—there is no inconsistency. His works are "gracious and compassionate" (111:4b) and "his precepts are trustworthy" (111:7b), the offspring of his character as described in the formula of grace in Exodus 34:6. While Psalm 111 is a confession and not a prayer, this psalm is nevertheless instructive in how to shape our prayers, the principle being, "Thy will be done," which is a prayer that God enact his character of love and grace in the world. As an example, when Abraham haggled with God over Sodom and Gomorrah, he based his negotiations on the principle that God would not "kill the righteous with the wicked, treating the righteous and the wicked alike" (Gen. 18:25). Abraham was merely asking God to act according to his character. We can be sure that when we pray, God is not going to answer our prayers if they don't shape up with who he is—that is, if they don't agree with his character.

There is a God in the world.

Story: Our psalmist's keen consciousness of justice and righteousness provides the aura for this psalm, and this aura is secured by God's commitment to his people through his everlasting covenant (111:1–5). It is God's justice and righteousness that bind him and the world he made to a sense of morality (111:4; also Exod. 34:6–7). There is a story that Rabbi Levi Yitzhak (eighteenth century) once announced a meeting in the town square to hear an important announcement. The townspeople, preoccupied with their various occupations and duties, were a bit annoyed that they had to drop what they were doing and gather for the meeting. But respect for their rabbi took precedence over their chores. And when they came to the meeting, Rabbi Levi Yitzhak said: "I wish to announce that there is a God in the world." A brief announcement, but the people understood that it was a reminder in the midst of their busy lives that there was a God in the world where they were engaged so feverishly. To restrict him to the religious rituals and forget his place in their daily lives was immoral. In fact, without God there is no moral compass for our routine lives.[9]

"Blessed Are Those Who Fear the LORD, Who Find Great Delight in His Commands"

Big Idea

The imitation of God, to which all believers are called, involves not merely words but actions.

Key Themes

- The blessing of those who fear the Lord continues to their children.
- The imitation of God is built into the prayers and praises of the Psalms and calls all believers to an imitation of God's character and actions.

Understanding the Text

Psalm 112 is a representative of the wisdom psalms in that it commends the fear of the Lord and keeping the commandments and contrasts the way of the righteous and the wicked. The acrostic structure, while sometimes providing the frame for a wisdom psalm (e.g., Pss. 34 and 37), is not necessarily a wisdom framework (see the sidebar "Wisdom Psalms" in the unit on Ps. 37).

The Text in Context

While Psalms 111 and 112 are sometimes called "twin psalms," Goldingay downplays their similarities and calls them a "niece or nephew (rather than twins)."[1] As table 1 shows, however, there is a considerable amount of shared language, making the "twin" kinship justifiable. Wilcock calls Psalms 111 and 112 a diptych, the left-hand panel (Ps. 111) being a portrait of the Lord, and the right-hand panel (Ps. 112) a portrait of the believer.[2]

Table 1. Shared Vocabulary between Psalms 111 and 112

Psalm 111	Psalm 112
"Hallelujah" (111:1a)	*"Hallelujah"* (112:1a)
"And his righteousness endures forever [la'ad]" (111:3b)	*"And his righteousness endures forever"* (112:3b) *"His righteousness endures forever [la'ad]"* (112:9b)
"They are established *forever and ever [la'ad lᵉ'olam]"* (111:8a) "He remembers his covenant *forever [lᵉ'olam]"* (111:5b) "He commanded his covenant *forever [lᵉ'olam]"* (111:9b)	"Surely he will not *forever [lᵉ'olam]* [or "never"] be shaken" (112:6a)
"Gracious and merciful" (111:4b)	*"Gracious and merciful* and righteous" (112:4b)
"They are *established* forever" (sᵉ*mukim la'ad*) (111:8a)	"His heart is *established"* (*samuk libbo*) (112:8a)
"In the council of the *upright* and congrega-tion" (111:1c)	"The generation of the *upright"* (112:2b)
"He has made his wonders a *remembrance"* (111:4a)	"The righteous will be an everlasting *re-membrance"* (112:6b)
"The works of his hands are truth and *justice [mishpat]"* (111:7a)	"He conducts his affairs with *justice [mish-pat]"* (112:5b)
"The fear of the Lᴏʀᴅ is the beginning of wis-dom" (111:10a) "He gives food to *those who fear him"* (111:5a)	"Blessed is the one *who fears the Lᴏʀᴅ"* (112:1b)

Note: All translations are the author's.

Regarding the relationship between Psalms 112 and 113, there are also several links that show how Psalm 112 marks the path to the Egyptian Hallel (Pss. 113–18). Structurally it exhibits the mark of the "hallelujah redaction" that was imposed on the text at a later time (111:1; 112:1; 113:1, 9). On the compositional level, Zenger mentions four links. First is the blessing of the generation of the upright (112:2b), which is matched in 113:2 by bless-ing Yahweh ("Let the name of the Lᴏʀᴅ *be praised"*; same verb). Second is the enduring influence of the righteous (112:3b, 6a, "never"; lit., "will not forever"; and 112:6b, 9, "forever"), linked to the enduring praise of Yahweh in 113:2 ("forevermore"). Third is the exaltation of the righteous (*"lifted high* in honor," 112:9c), linked to the exaltation of Yahweh's glory in 113:4 (*"exalted* over all the nations," same verb: *rum*). Fourth, the theme of the poor links the two psalms together. In 112:9c they are the recipients of the generosity of the righteous, while in 113:7–8 they are the objects of Yahweh's direct elevation of them from the "dust" and "ash heap" to seat them with princes.[3]

Outline/Structure

Hallelujah (112:1a)
1. A beatitude for those who fear the Lord (112:1b–c)
2. Benefits and responsibilities of those who fear the Lord (112:2–9)
   a. Wealth and riches (benefit) (112:2–3)
   b. Light dispelling darkness (benefit) (112:4)
   c. Actions growing out of their good character (responsibility) (112:5)
   d. Stability of the righteous (benefit) (112:6)
   e. No fear of bad news (benefit) (112:7)
   f. Triumph over enemies (benefit) (112:8)
   g. Generosity to the poor (responsibility) (112:9a–b)
   h. Honor (benefit) (112:9c)
3. Fate of the wicked (112:10)

Historical and Cultural Background

Psalms 111 and 112 are an expression of the expanding importance of the law (Torah) in emergent Judaism in the late sixth century BC. The absence of temple and sacrifice during the exile (which were so central to the preexilic faith) had helped to create a rising prominence of the Torah. Psalms 1; 19; and 119 are attestations to this fact, and the twin psalms (111:7, 10; 112:1) lend further evidence. After Psalms 107–10 introduce the reader to the postexilic age and the challenges that the exile and restoration represent, Psalms 111 and 112 serve a purpose in Book 5 similar to the purpose that Psalm 1 serves in the book as a whole. They orient the community to the new standard of reference, the Torah, whose precepts are trustworthy. Even when the temple had been rebuilt and worship restored, the Torah continued to share center stage with the temple. See "Historical and Cultural Background" in the unit on Psalm 111.

Interpretive Insights

112:1 *Praise the* LORD. Like Psalm 111, this psalm also begins with "hallelujah" (NIV: "Praise the LORD!"; see the comments on 111:1).

Blessed are those. The phrase here is the same as that in 1:1, with the exception of the definite article before "man" in 1:1 ("Blessed is *the* man," 1:1 ESV; the NIV has pluralized the terms in 112:1 to make the translation more gender inclusive). In fact, the first and last words of Psalms 1 and 112 are identical (*'ashre,* "blessed," and *to'bed,* "perish"; see the comments on 112:10).

112:3 *Wealth and riches.* These are legitimately acquired possessions (Prov. 8:18). "Their righteousness," parallel to "wealth and riches," implies the righteous person's walk of life.[4]

112:4 *Even in darkness light dawns for the upright.* The allusion may be to the plague in Egypt when light shined on the Israelites while the Egyptians were in darkness (Exod. 10:23), and in the same way God's light shines on the "upright" of every generation (Ps. 97:11), particularly the present one, as the exile comes to an end and return to the land becomes a reality. The terms "gracious and compassionate and righteous" combine to describe the good person, and the first two terms (in reverse order) occur in Exodus 34:6 to describe God. These divine attributes are permanent with God, while they are inconstant with us humans.

112:5 *Good will come to those who are generous and lend freely.* This is a character description of the good individual rather than an assertion about the reward of being good, as the NIV renders it. It is the same construction as "Blessed is [the] man" in verse 1 (see the comments on 112:1), another character description, and the character description of the righteous in Psalm 1. The second clause of the sentence ("who conduct their [lit., "his"] affairs with justice") is a general description of the specific conduct described in this lead clause.

112:6 *Surely the righteous will never be shaken.* Even though "the righteous" is not in the Hebrew text, the statement seems to be about them nevertheless, reflecting back on the "righteous" of verse 4b and forward to verse 6b.

112:7 *They will have no fear of bad news.* This is a description of the wise man, Job being our most sterling example, whose faith, according to the prologue, sustained him in the face of his loss of everything in one day— "Their hearts are steadfast, trusting in the LORD" (112:7b; cf. Job 1:20–22).

112:8 *Their hearts are secure, they will have no fear.* This continues the description of the wise individual who is "trusting in the LORD" (112:7b) and includes their enemies, as we would expect Psalm 112 to do, especially with the upcoming theme of deliverance from Egypt, and the enemies the postexilic community also faced.

112:9 *They have freely scattered their gifts to the poor.* The ethical conduct described in verse 5 is continued here and applied specifically to the poor.[5] The metaphor in the second clause, "their horn will be lifted high in honor," suggests the strength of the bull, and thus victory, which is the sense of "their [lit., "his"] righteousness" in verse 9b. Quite plausibly, the community or nation is now the referent, and thus the NIV's plural should be viewed in that way. The ethical life is both an individual and a corporate concern, and the individual person of verse 1 has become the corporate person (community) of the psalm.

112:10 *The wicked . . . the longings of the wicked will come to nothing.*
The poem is mostly about the righteous, but this final verse engages in a
comparison of the two ways, as is typical of Wisdom literature. Just as Psalm
1 declares that "the way of the wicked *will perish*" (ESV) so Psalm 112 ends
with the same verb (*to'bed*, "come to nothing"), commending the way of the
righteous life and warning that the life of the wicked will come to nothing.

Theological Insights

There is some justification for looking at Psalms 111 and 112 as a diptych
(see "The Text in Context"), with the portrait of Yahweh in the forefront of
Psalm 111 and the portrait of the believer in the forefront of Psalm 112. The
fear of the Lord (111:10; 112:1) is complemented by his gracious and compassionate character (111:4; 112:4), which is reflected in "those who fear the
Lord," who are indeed a mirror image of their Lord. It is another example
of the Old Testament imitation of God (*imitatio Dei*). One gets the impression from 112:4 that the darkness of Israel's humiliating defeat and exile has
begun to dispel, and this renewed community of faith can expect good from
a life that reflects God's character ("gracious and compassionate"). Nor is
the blessing limited to themselves and the present generation, but it extends
to their posterity. Such is the nature and life of those who fear the Lord.

Teaching the Text

We may build off "Teaching the Text" in the unit on Psalm 111, where we
stressed the truth that God's character and his works/words are a single piece.
To speak anthropologically about God, his character is the infrastructure that
supports his works and words, and his own character description, found in
Exodus 34:6, is that he is "gracious and compassionate" (111:4). His actions
and precepts necessarily fall within that frame of reference.

Our lesson on Psalm 112 can build off the idea that Psalm 111 gives us a
portrait of God, and Psalm 112 gives a portrait of the believer who is a reflection of God's portrait. It is the mirror image. The Psalms, in fact, teach
us the lesson that the righteous, by virtue of their relationship to the Lord,
reflect his righteousness, and his laws are designed to convey his character to
those who keep them (119:137–38). He is "upright" and expects his people
to be the same (94:15). The Lord is "holy," and he commands his people to
be holy, a spiritual principle established in Leviticus 19:2. And, as I have emphasized from time to time, the Lord's love (*hesed*; see "Theological Insights"
in the unit on Ps. 109) is the central concept of the covenant, and as God's
love sets the standard for his actions, so God's people are to exhibit his love,

which will also set the standard for their actions (the imitation of God). In Psalm 109:16 the wicked are indicted because they "never thought of doing a kindness [*hesed*, which is essentially imitating God's *hesed*], but hounded to death the poor and the needy and the brokenhearted." Wenham concludes incisively: "So in a sense the obligation to imitate God is built into the grammar of prayer and praise."[6]

In John's Gospel Jesus gives this commandment: "Love each other as I have loved you" (John 15:12). We follow the principle of imitation, and Jesus is our model: "As the Father has loved me, so have I loved you" (John 15:9). John's first letter traces this truth back to the character of God: "Dear friends, let us love one another, for love comes from God. Everyone who loves has been born of God and knows God. Whoever does not love does not know God, because God is love" (1 John 4:7–8). John further describes love in these words: "This is how we know what love is: Jesus Christ laid down his life for us. And we ought to lay down our lives for our brothers and sisters. If anyone has material possessions and sees a brother or sister in need but has no pity on them, how can the love of God be in that person? Dear children, let us not love with words or speech but with actions and in truth" (1 John 3:16–18). The imitation of God, to which all believers are called, involves not merely words but actions.

Illustrating the Text

"It is more blessed to give than to receive."

Literature: *What's Mine's Mine*, by George MacDonald. One of the treasured characteristics of the righteous, according to 112:4, 9, is their generosity. In Acts, the apostle Paul quotes a memorable saying of Jesus not recorded in the Gospels but quite in keeping with his kingdom teachings, "It is more blessed to give than to receive" (Acts 20:35). In MacDonald's novel *What's Mine's Mine*, the main characters are two Highlander brothers, Ian and Alister. At one point Ian says to Alister, "We must be constantly giving ourselves away, we must dwell in houses of infinite dependence, or sit alone in the waste of a godless universe."[7] That's the essence of our Lord's saying. But in our upside-down world, that beatitude runs against the grain of human greed. This sinful world screams in our ears, "Get what you can while you can," and we are tempted to live by this philosophy. Yet, those who practice the gift of generosity often find that being on the receiving end is not so easy. Joy Davidman, commenting on her dependency on others (receiving), remarked how difficult it was for her, and she suggested that the difficulty provided the givers with the opportunity to practice their gift: "It *is* difficult having to accept all the time! But unless we did, how could the others have the pleasure, and the spiritual growth, of giving? And—I don't know about you, but I was very proud; I liked the superior feeling of helping others, and for me it is much harder to receive than to give but, I think, much more blessed."[8] Charles Williams resolves the tension: "The giver's part may be harder than the taker's; that is why, here, it may be more blessed to give than to receive, though in the equity of the kingdom there is little difference."[9]

When the self obscures even the crescent of the moon

Quote: Flannery O'Connor. Psalm 112 does not mention God's love (*hesed*), but its description of the righteous person instills an aura of love in the psalm. This spiritual disposition is characterized by the fear of the Lord (112:1) rather than a fear of the bad things that could happen. That is to say, the focus is on the Lord, not on one's self. O'Connor confesses that it is her own self that keeps her from seeing God: "Dear God, I cannot love Thee the way I want to. You are the slim crescent of a moon that I see and myself is the earth's shadow that keeps me from seeing all the moon. The crescent is very beautiful and perhaps that is all one like I am should or could see; but what I am afraid of, dear God, is that my self shadow will grow so large that it blocks the whole moon, and that I will judge myself by the shadow that is nothing."[10]

"Who Is like the LORD Our God, the One Who Sits Enthroned on High?"

Big Idea

When God manifests his sovereignty by stooping to involve himself in human affairs, he in no way relinquishes his absolute sovereignty over the world.

Key Themes

- The Lord is sovereign in heaven and on earth.
- Divine sovereignty involves the dual aspects of exaltation and condescension.
- The kingdom of the world requires a right-side-up correction to make it the kingdom of God.

Understanding the Text

This is the first psalm of the Egyptian Hallel (sometimes called the Passover Hallel), so named from 114:1 ("When Israel came out of Egypt"). Psalms 113 and 114 are sung before the meal during the Passover seder in Jewish homes, and Psalms 115–18 are sung after the meal, when the fourth cup has been filled. We assume the latter collection was the "hymn" Jesus and his disciples sang at the end of the Passover seder before his arrest (Mark 14:26). In the Christian liturgy, Psalms 113; 114; and 118 are the proper psalms for Evensong on Easter Day.[1] The literary form is that of a hymn.

The Text in Context

The psalmist could hardly have chosen a more appropriate metaphor for his text to represent the postexilic community, "barren" (NIV: "childless," 113:9), having been deprived of its political, social, and, to some extent, physical fertility by the Babylonian exile. So he quotes the Prayer of Hannah (1 Sam. 2:8a–c) and uses other vocabulary from the prayer (see the sidebar) to describe this new era, now on the hopeful verge of becoming "a happy mother of children" (Ps. 113:9b). Like Hannah's prayer, it is a dedication of this child of hope, the new era of promise, to the Lord (see 1 Sam. 1:21–28).

Outline/Structure

This poem can be subdivided into two parts, with the entire poem framed by the "hallelujah" trademark. Part 1 (113:1b–4) is a summons to praise the Lord, introduced by the programmatic "hallelujah" (NIV: "Praise the Lord"). Part 2 (113:5–9a) is introduced by the question of God's incomparable sovereignty ("Who is like the Lord our God?"), understood in terms of God's sovereignty in heaven ("on high") and God's sovereignty on earth, two parts of the whole.

Hallelujah ("Praise the Lord") (113:1a)
1. Summons to praise Yahweh's name (113:1b–4)
   a. Summons to Yahweh's servants to praise Yahweh's name (113:1b–c)
   b. Praise of Yahweh's name in universal time (113:2)
   c. Praise of Yahweh's name in universal space (113:3)
   d. Praise of Yahweh, exalted over the nations (113:4)
2. Yahweh's incomparable sovereignty "on high" and in condescension (113:5–9a)
   a. The question of Yahweh's incomparable sovereignty posed (113:5a)
   b. The question answered: Yahweh's incomparable sovereignty: who sits enthroned "on high" (113:5b)
   c. The question answered: Yahweh's incomparable sovereignty: who "stoops down" in condescension (113:6)
   d. Yahweh's condescension demonstrated (113:7–9a)
      i. Yahweh's elevation of the poor (113:7–8)
      ii. Yahweh's elevation of the barren woman (113:9a)
Hallelujah ("Praise the Lord") (113:9b)

Historical and Cultural Background

See "Additional Insights: The Egyptian Hallel (Psalms 113–18)," following this unit.

Interpretive Insights

113:1 *Praise the* L<small>ORD</small>. This phrase translates the Hebrew "hallelujah." At some point, very likely one of the final editorial operations that fixed the present form of the Psalter, the "hallelujah redaction" of Books 4 and 5 (see "Additional Insights: The Hallelujahs of Books 4 and 5," following the unit on Ps. 104) gave the macrocollection the quality of praise. The exclusive use of "hallelujah" in this portion of the Psalter (and nowhere else in the Hebrew Bible) is a distinguishing mark of significant value. Along with the emphasis on the Torah, signaled by Psalm 1 and reemphasized by the Torah psalms Psalms 19 and 119 (see "Additional Insights: The Egyptian Hallel [Psalms 113–18]," following this unit), this editorial touch puts praise and Torah alongside one another as the key tonal qualities of the Psalter. That is, the Psalter is a meditation on the Torah and is no less a book of praises to the Lord (the Hebrew title of the book, *Tehillim*, means "praises").

you his servants. The address is to Yahweh's "servants" (113:1b), who are the same as the "poor" and "needy" whom he stoops to help (113:7 and 8).

113:2–3 *both now and forevermore.* The praise of God is universal in both time (113:2) and space (113:3). The expression "forevermore" as an eternal note of praise sets off a sympathetic vibration of praise in all of the doxologies that close the five books, thus detonating this "big bang" of worship that does and always will characterize the world God made and redeemed.[2]

113:4 *exalted over all the nations, his glory above the heavens.* Verse 4 functions as a concluding affirmation of praise.

113:5 *Who is like the* L<small>ORD</small> *our God . . . ?* Some scholars divide the psalm between verses 3 and 4, but this momentous question begins a new train of thought. This question, perhaps rhetorical, is posed in the Song of the Sea in light of the Lord's mighty deliverance of Israel at the Red Sea (Exod. 15:11). Moses reintroduces the question in his review of the challenge of the conquest awaiting Joshua in Deuteronomy 3:24. It also occurs two other times in the Psalter (Pss. 35:10; 71:19). Here the implied answer is that no gods are higher than the heavens and supreme over the nations like our God (113:4), and God's sovereignty is not compromised by his stooping down to see what is going on in the earth (condescension), where he corrects the upside-down social (spiritual!) order by revoking the humiliation of the poor and needy and seating them beside princes (113:7–8; compare Joseph). Nor does he stop there. He revokes the most degrading state of childless women, thus restoring them to the honorable estate of creation, to replenish the earth (113:9). These last two works are part of the answer to the question of verse 5a (see "Outline/Structure").

113:6 *who stoops down to look on the heavens and the earth?* While the Lord is above the heavens (113:4), he bends low to see the earth. The Lord does not merely observe the earth but involves himself in human affairs; he

The Song of Hannah and Psalm 113

Psalm 113 contains a direct quotation (113:8 quotes 1 Sam. 2:8a–c), as well as several echoes, from the Song of Hannah (1 Sam. 2). This shared vocabulary makes it very clear that the Samuel text is in the mind of the psalmist, and he is building a picture of Israel as a barren woman (exile) whom the Lord is now blessing with children and transforming from a "poor and needy" people into a respected community (to "sit with princes").

1 Samuel 2	Psalm 113
"There is no one *like the* Lord . . . ; for there is no one besides you; there is no rock *like our God*" (2:2)	"Who is *like the* Lord *our God* . . . ?" (113:5)[a]
"A *barren woman* ['*aqarah*] bears seven" (2:5)	"He settles the *barren woman* ['*aqeret*] in her home as a happy mother of children" (113:9)
"The Lord causes [one] to inherit and makes rich; he *humbles* [*mashpil*] and raises them up" (2:7)	"He *stoops down* [*hammashpili*, same Hiphil participle] to look on the heavens and the earth" (113:6)
"*He raises the weak/poor from the dust; he elevates the needy from the refuse dump, to make [them] sit with princes*" (2:8a–c)	"*He raises the weak/poor from the dust; he elevates the needy from the refuse dump, to make [them] sit with princes*" (113:7–8a)

Note: All translations in this table are the author's.
[a] The declaration in 1 Samuel 2:2 has been turned into a question in Psalm 113:5, and the two phrases have been joined.

"raises the poor from the dust and lifts the needy from the ash heap; he seats them with princes" (113:7–8). "To sit in the dust" is a metaphor for extreme degradation (Isa. 47:1)[3] and may symbolize the humiliation of the exile. The author exhibits clever literary shrewdness by the inversion of the order of verse 4 (113:4, earth and heaven; 113:6, heaven and earth).

113:8 *he seats them with princes.* This is a figure of speech for elevation to the highest rank of human society (Job 36:7). Verse 8 is a quotation from the Song of Hannah in 1 Samuel 2:8a–c (see the sidebar).

113:9 *the childless woman . . . as a happy mother of children.* "The reference in verses 6 and 7 to the Prayer of Hannah suggests this further reference to the experience of Hannah, as an instance of the way in which Jehovah has compassion on those who are despised"[4] (see Isa. 54:1; 66:8). The Greek (LXX) transfers the final "hallelujah" (NIV: "Praise the Lord") to the beginning of Psalm 114.

Theological Insights

The sovereignty of God is presented in Scripture, and particularly in this psalm, in multidimensional perspective: God is sovereign in heaven and on the earth. That simply means that God reigns and rules over all aspects of his creation. In the historical context of Book 5, Israel was emerging from the humiliation of the Babylonian exile, and it was not enough merely to proclaim the Lord's sovereign rule, but this suffering community would be comforted to know that the Lord's sovereignty encompasses human affairs, especially the suffering of God's people. So our author takes the most extreme cases of humiliation, the poor and needy and the childless woman. The poor were the objects of abuse, and the woman without children was the object of humiliation and scorn (1 Sam. 1:6–8). The "on high" sovereignty of God is less visible to us human beings, but when God's sovereign reign expresses itself at the lowest echelons of our world, that is a validation of his sovereignty "on high." Yet, to hear that God "stoops down" to see what is going on in the earth in no way depreciates his sovereignty "on high." Rather, his condescension is an expression of his sovereignty in heaven, thus the two-dimensional perspective.

Teaching the Text

We may open up the spiritual dimensions of this psalm to our congregation and students first by calling attention to the Lord's servants and the summons to praise the Lord. As the community of faith is shaped by their historical circumstances, the Lord shapes himself, historically speaking, to the needs of that community (divine condescension). In that frame of thought, the terms "servant" / "your servants" / "servants of the LORD" become a more frequent occurrence in Books 4 and 5 of the Psalms.[5] These terms are an index to the spiritual reformation that has been occurring in the suffering community of faith. The psalmist has called on them to be shaped by the Torah. And they make up the new community who is faithful to God, and their praise of the Lord has become not merely a ritual but a way of life. We can then stress the need to have our lives so shaped by the Word of God that we are worthy to be called "servants."

Second, following the order of the psalm, we may now turn our attention to the psalmist's description of the Lord, in both his heavenly exaltation and his earthly condescension. I have explained in "Theological Insights" that God's sovereignty in Scripture carries a dual meaning. By God's own eternal decrees, it is not enough for him merely to show himself as sovereign in heaven (that is, God rules the universe), but he shows himself sovereign on the earth (that is, God rules in and over earthly affairs). We sometimes refer to the latter aspect of divine sovereignty as "providence." And we must remember that God often demonstrates his providence in suffering, both human and divine (that's both the mystery and the wonder of grace) and in the relief of suffering (that's the expression of divine mercy) (113:7). In our psalm he "stoops down" and "raises the poor from the dust" (113:6, 7), but he in no way relinquishes his sovereignty over the world. Paul's statement in Philippians 2:5–11 is the classic expression of divine condescension to redeem humanity, and the apostle introduces this mystery with the directive: "In your relationships with one another, have the same mindset as Jesus Christ" (Phil. 2:5). This is also the perfect place to complete the circle and speak of the "servants of the LORD" who reflect God's condescension in service, to which Paul calls the Philippian church and us all. While we are not called to imitate God's sovereignty—human sovereignty is an oxymoron—we are certainly called to imitate his humility. And in that imitation, we relieve the suffering of our fellow servants. However, at this point we should be aware that we are applying the text in the Christian context, not drawing this from the psalm itself. We might employ another of Paul's statements to conclude this point, and perhaps conclude the sermon/lesson: "God chose the foolish things of the world to shame the wise; God chose the weak things of the world to shame the strong" (1 Cor. 1:27).

Illustrating the Text

God's sovereignty encompasses suffering.

Quote: Dorothy Sayers. As we see in Psalm 113, God's sovereign reign in our lives and our world encompasses suffering (see "Teaching the Text"). Sayers says that we do not choose suffering but must expect it.

> The creative will presses on to its end, regardless of what it may suffer by the way. It does not choose suffering, but it will not avoid it, and must expect it. We say that it is love, and sacrifices itself for what it loves; and this is true, provided we understand what we mean by sacrifice. Sacrifice is what it looks like to other people, but to that-which-loves I think it does not appear so. When one really cares, the self is forgotten, and the sacrifice becomes only a part of the activity. . . . The time when you deliberately say, "I must sacrifice this, that, or the other" is when you do not supremely desire the end in view. At such times you are doing your duty, and that is admirable, but it is not love. But as soon as your duty becomes your love the self-sacrifice is taken for granted, and, whatever the world calls it, you call it so no longer.[6]

When I read this statement a few years ago, I penciled in the margin of the book names of a dear couple in a church where I was interim pastor. In infancy their daughter was mistakenly administered a drug that made her an invalid for life, and she had to be cared for like a baby. I had once mentioned to them the "sacrifice" they were making, and her mother responded, "It's no sacrifice at all." The care of their daughter was neither duty nor sacrifice, but it was love.

Imitating Christ

Church History: Dietrich Bonhoeffer's book *The Cost of Discipleship* is one of his best-known and most-loved works. At its core it is an exegesis of the Sermon on the Mount, which shows us how deeply Bonhoeffer had wrestled with that text. Sifton and Stern comment on and quote from a letter that Dietrich Bonhoeffer wrote to his older brother, Karl-Friedrich: "His [Dietrich's] exasperation with the tedious, hair-splitting maneuvers among German clergy over how, when, and whether to disobey Nazi strictures is clear in his letter to Karl-Friedrich: 'I believe I know that inwardly I shall be really clear and honest only when I have begun to take the Sermon on the Mount seriously. That is the only source of strength that can blow all this stuff and nonsense sky-high, with only a few charred pieces of the fireworks remaining. The restoration of the church will [only] come from . . . a life of uncompromising adherence to the Sermon on the Mount in imitation of Christ.'"[7] We can assume that Bonhoeffer was thinking about the radical change in human behavior and conceptualization of the world that Jesus requires in the Sermon on the Mount (see "Teaching the Text" in the unit on Ps. 146).

The Egyptian Hallel (Psalms 113–18)

This collection of psalms, in a literary sense, has a view to the reconstruction of the temple and the reconstitution of the community in Jerusalem as the people emerge from the Babylonian captivity.[1] Psalm 114:1 provides the collection with the ambiance of the exodus from Egypt ("When Israel came out of Egypt"). Indeed, so momentous was this "new exodus" from Babylonia that it set the new standard of redemption (Jer. 16:14–15; Mic. 7:15–17) and would become the reference point of God's wonders of redeeming love. This principle of reapplying God's great works in Israel's history to another time and to another event underlies Moses's statement in Deuteronomy 5:3: "It was not [only] with our ancestors that the LORD made this covenant, but with us, with all of us who are alive here today" (see "Additional Insights: The Model of Historical Double-Tracking," following the unit on Ps. 138). The Egyptian Hallel is, as it were, a pamphlet that describes the community and its developing qualities, configuring the return and restoration in the images of the elevation of the poor to princedom and of Hannah's barrenness turned to motherhood. In view of its singular purpose, it is quite possible that all of the psalms in this collection come from the same author.

The qualities and events of the new community featured in these psalms are, first, a picture of the community itself, described with images and a direct quotation from 1 Samuel 2 (see the sidebar "The Song of Hannah and Psalm 113" in the unit on Ps. 113). With the hues from the palette of Hannah's prayer, which our astute writer uses to paint the picture of the community, particularly a barren woman emerging with joy from her childlessness, Psalm 113 describes the community as one of barrenness (the exile) now emerging to a new day "as a happy mother of children" (113:9b). It was a time of joy (see Ps. 126).

Second, the Egyptian Hallel sets forth certain identifying qualities and developments of this era by focusing on Yahweh's care of the poor and needy in 113:7–8. While the cause of the poor was championed by the preexilic prophets, by this time the poor had become virtually synonymous with the righteous, and emerging from the depressed conditions of political domination, the social and economic condition of this majority population was symbolic of the spiritual state of Israel. The imagery of the Lord's lifting the poor and needy from their ash heap suggests that they have now become a favored class, princes no less. We are reminded of the Sermon on the Mount, which virtually turns the world as we know it upside down to give us the true picture of the kingdom of God:

"Blessed are the poor in spirit, for theirs is the kingdom of heaven" (Matt. 5:3). Only a radical correction could set the depraved kingdom right-side up and establish the new community that Isaiah 40–55 and the psalmists envision.

Third, the emerging community had undergone a period of soul-searching and spiritual transformation and had at last abandoned idolatry, alluded to in Psalm 115:4–8, and embraced a monotheistic faith. In fact, we should take this denunciation of idolatry as the community's statement on the matter. It was part of their new identity as the community of faith (115:8, 9; also 135:15–18).

Fourth, with the new temple now likely coming to completion (compare Hag. 2:1–5), the natural development would be the reaffirmation of the priesthood, similar to Haggai 2:10–19. Moreover, the house of Aaron, along with Israel, rather than blessing Israel, receives Yahweh's blessing (115:12) and responds with its affirmation: "His love endures forever" (118:3). It is the same affirmation that the congregation made when the foundation of the new temple was laid (Ezra 3:11).

Fifth, in view of Yahweh's deliverance of Israel from the "sorrow and distress" of political oppression, the natural response from the worshiper, and now from the community of faith, was to sacrifice a thank offering, which Psalm 116 vows to do (vv. 14, 17–19), and that in the new temple ("the courts of the house of the LORD," 116:19a; see also 118:19–20). To conclude the cadre of songs that have their eyes set on this new era, Psalm 117 serves as a benediction after the Egyptian Hallel, its vocabulary reflecting the formula of grace (*hesed* and *'emeth*; Exod. 34:6). Psalm 118 then constitutes the liturgy of thanksgiving that fulfills the vows of Psalm 116 (see 118:1), thus completing the Egyptian Hallel.

Sixth, a final observation outside the Egyptian Hallel but connected to it, and a feature that crowns the collection, is the new emphasis on the Torah, introduced by the Torah theme of Psalms 111 and 112 (111:7–8, 10; 112:1) and given its zenith treatment by Psalm 119. The procurement of the Torah's central importance is represented by the length, the acrostic style, and the content of Psalm 119. As we have already observed, in the absence of the temple and sacrifice, the Torah was becoming the central focus of developing Judaism, and Psalm 119 might be viewed as a representation of the new Torah community that was taking shape and would hopefully result in this new era of Yahweh's love and faithfulness. Whether or not Psalm 119 represents a conclusion to an intermediate stage in the developing collection that became Book 5 is, at least, a suggestion that merits consideration. Mays proposes that the editor(s) intentionally locates Psalm 119 at a place in Book 5 to suggest that Torah piety positions the new community for the coming of the kingdom of God.[2]

Zenger has made a convincing case for a double arc that joins Psalms 113–15 and 116–18, giving the first arc a theocentric or monotheistic accent, and the second arc a universalistic accent.[3]

"Tremble, Earth, at the Presence of the Lord"

Big Idea

Israel's story of redemption from Egypt is the story of God taking up residence among his people and thus is a microcosm of our story, Christ dwelling with us and ultimately in us.

Key Themes

- Creation functions in service to our journey of redeeming grace.
- The goal of redemption is to be in the presence of God.

Understanding the Text

This lovely hymn illustrates how a literary artist, in terse and crisp verse, can weave a tapestry of grace out of the threads of history and theological understanding. Its compact story of redemption, witnessed by an observant creation (sea and river, mountains and hills), is completed in the call to the "earth" to tremble before the epiphany of the "God of Jacob." In comparison to Psalm 113, which celebrates redemption cosmically (from the rising of the sun to its setting), Psalm 114 celebrates redemption historically (from Egypt to Canaan).

The Text in Context

The second psalm of the Egyptian Hallel, Psalm 114 gives this collection (Pss. 113–18) its name (114:1). Psalms 114 and 115 are considered a single psalm in the Greek (LXX) and Latin (Vulgate) versions. However, Psalm 114's perspective on Israel's miraculous journey from the Red Sea to the Jordan River, along with its distinct literary beauty, sets it off from both Psalms 113 and 115.

Outline/Structure

The poem consists of four brief strophes, each two verses long.

1. The miraculous journey of redemption from Egypt to Canaan (114:1–2)
2. Nature's exuberant response to the miracles at the Red Sea and the Jordan River (114:3–4)
3. The poet's reaction to nature's response (114:5–6)
4. The summons to the earth for a comparable response (114:7–8)

Historical and Cultural Background

See "Additional Insights: The Egyptian Hallel (Psalms 113–18)," preceding this unit.

Interpretive Insights

114:1 *When Israel came out of Egypt.* This verse sets the tone for the psalm in that the following verses are a poetic account of Israel's journey of redemption from Egypt to the promised land. "A people of foreign tongue" faces in two directions: Egypt, which they left centuries ago, and Babylonia, from which they have only recently departed. Deuteronomy 28:49–50 speaks of a "nation whose language you will not understand" to predict that Israel's disobedience will lead to conquest by a foreign power.

114:2 *Judah became God's sanctuary, Israel his dominion.* The words "sanctuary" and "dominion" (lit., "dominions") are parallel, and we should understand them to mean that Judah, the name by which the land was known, became the place of God's sanctuary and the place where God rules (God is not directly mentioned until v. 7, although the NIV has inserted "God" as the subject of the verb in v. 2a).

114:3 *The sea looked and fled, the Jordan turned back.* Poetically speaking, these two miracles at the Red Sea and the Jordan River are the beginning and the end of the journey of redemption that leads to the sanctuary in Judah. The two events are compared in Joshua 4:14 (see also Ps. 66:6). We are not told what the sea "sees" (*ra'ah*; NIV: "looked"), which is enough to generate the questions of verses 5–6. We assume, however, that the poet's answer fills in the blank—the sea sees the appearance "of the God of Jacob" (114:7).

114:4 *the mountains leaped like rams.* The allusion may be to Sinai and the giving of the law when Sinai "trembled violently" (Exod. 19:18). Here the verb "leaped" has the sense of "danced" and may imply a joyful celebration.[1]

114:5–6 *Why was it, sea, that you fled?* This brief stanza is a follow-up on the poetic description of the miracles at the Red Sea and the Jordan River and the metaphors that describe the awesome reaction of nature to those miracles (114:3–4). Weiser comments that nature "becomes a visible witness to and interpreter of the divine epiphany."[2] The questions are rhetorical (cf. 29:6; Exod. 19:18), but the psalmist's sense of history as present reality is a mark of his piety.[3] Nature is still amazed at God's redeeming work!

114:7 *Tremble, earth, at the presence of the Lord, at the presence of the God of Jacob.* These verses may give the answer to the questions of verses 5–6. We know from verse 2 that God has already reached his sanctuary (*qodsho,* "his holiness"), and now in verse 7 the poet introduces the real goal of Israel's journey, which is, indeed, the spiritual objective of much of the Psalter, to enter "the presence of the Lord."

In the broader interpretation of the psalm, the "earth" can mean the world and be viewed as inclusive of the items of creation already mentioned: the sea, the Jordan, mountains, and hills. Or in view of the universal note of 113:4, we might see "earth" in the sense of the "land" of Israel; since the psalm is concerned with the new community that is forming after the exile, that would be my preference. But we certainly can be more definite about the observation that the deity's name appears for the first time in the poem in verse 7, and that is part of the poet's literary plan. The first word for the thus-far-unnamed deity is "Master" (*'adon,* "Lord"), which is not the normal substitute for the tetragrammaton (that substitute is *'adonay*); this term carries the sense of "Master," Master of creation and Master of his people too. The second name is the singular term for *'elohim* (*'eloah*), which does not occur frequently in the Psalter (see, e.g., 50:22; 139:19).[4] This accomplished writer leaves the deity unnamed in verses 1–6, even interrogating the Red Sea, the Jordan River, and the mountains and hills on the way to Judah, but they, perhaps stunned by the wonders of the journey, remain speechless (114:5–6). Yet the awestruck psalmist reveals the secret himself and answers for the created elements: it was the Lord's appearance that put the creation in awe.

In view of the postexilic setting of the Egyptian Hallel, "the presence of the God of Jacob" in verse 7 may very well be an allusion to Zerubbabel's temple. And, further, perhaps the singular form of the divine name *'eloah* is intentional so as not to leave any ambiguity regarding Israel's monotheistic faith.

114:8 *the rock into a pool, the hard rock into springs of water.* The allusion is likely to the rock that Moses struck and from which water came out to slake the Israelites' thirst (Deut. 8:15; 32:13; Exod. 17:6; Num. 20:10–11). Isaiah employs this metaphor to describe the superlative effect of the return from Babylonian exile (Isa. 41:18). So the parable concludes by assuring Israel that a supply of water—and what could be more precious!—will be abundant. The return will be nothing short of a miracle.

Theological Insights

The sheer literary and theological beauty of this psalm is enough to put every reader in awe of God's majestic work in history—and that is the writer's purpose. Our psalmist introduces the mystery of God's dwelling in the midst of his people, an old idea in a new literary context ("I will walk among you," Lev. 26:12). Here is the emerging expression of God's dwelling among his people (see the sidebar "The Covenant Formula" in the unit on Ps. 79), which in John's Gospel becomes even more intimate as God's dwelling *in* his people (e.g., John 15). Thus Israel's story of redemption from Egypt has the mysterious effect of God taking up residence among his people ("Judah became God's sanctuary") and becomes a microcosm of our story of redemption, that Christ dwells in us (John 15:4–5).

Teaching the Text

We should understand this psalm as a description of the journey of deliverance. It is the microcosm of biblical redemption, whose story begins with the deliverance from Egypt and climaxes in God's mysterious redeeming grace through the cross of Christ. The story of our psalm begins in Egypt and concludes in the "presence of the Lord" (in the temple). The psalmist virtually skips the wilderness period, except for an allusion to the miracle of water from the rock. It is quite a valid point to observe that this psalm's design, and often our own story too, is to hit the highlights of God's acts of grace in our lives—and that is only natural and a valid reflex of thanksgiving to God. That too can be the first point of our message. In the text itself, the only negative aspect of the people's past is the implication borne by the detail that they had lived among "a people of foreign tongue," but that was more for identity purposes than for alarm. Often we bring in the sordid details of our own "Egypt" to establish identity with those who are suffering and who need to hear the story of our deliverance—and that is important. Yet some of us do not have such a story to tell. But even then, the story of God's love expended to fallen humanity is enough. Not even the most dramatic story of deliverance can top that one! The psalmist rejoices when he says, "You have given me the heritage of those who fear your name" (Ps. 61:5). The rest of our story, though important and effective, is mere commentary. God's wonderful works of grace are the chapter headings: the exodus, the Jordan, the return, the birth, the cross, the resurrection.

A second point is to observe that the world, or our own personal world, often looks at our lives of grace with great astonishment, maybe even incredulity that a redeemed life is even possible. Admittedly, the miraculous events in Israel's past were spectacular enough to deserve both negative and positive reactions by those who observed them, in this case nature personified (114:5–6), and in our case, by those witnesses who are skeptical and those who are "almost . . . persuaded" (Acts 26:28 KJV). While the verbs "fled" and "turned back," as they are applied to the sea and river (Ps. 114:3), suggest that the waters were repulsed by fear, the verb "leap" (114:4, 6) edges on the nuance of joy (lit., "to skip about gaily"; cf. Eccles. 3:4). We may draw out of this idea that the mountains and hills, at least in anticipation, already expect (and joyfully!) the presence of the Lord. One may wonder if Paul did not have this psalm in mind, or some similar Old Testament text, when he wrote that "the creation waits in eager expectation for the children of God to be revealed" (Rom. 8:19). The joyful end is incorporated in the events that compose the journey. This is a world in anticipation of God's coming (Gal. 4:4). The fear will fade into joy.

A third point to stress is that the goal of redemption is "the presence of the Lord" (114:7). Ultimately, the goal is to be in relationship with God, the most intimate relationship—that's the sense of "the presence of the Lord." As we have already observed, Book 1 of the Psalter is replete with references to that goal (e.g., 16:11; 17:15; 23:6; 27:4). Book 1 even closes with the assurance, "Because of my integrity you uphold me and set me in your presence forever" (41:12). That sounds very much like a relationship that reflects God's character. Just as God's integrity brings him to enact his character toward his people in the story of redemption (e.g., "love" and "faithfulness"), we are also called to enact our integrity in our journey into God's presence. We may note also that "the presence of the Lord" is not only the goal, but it is the experience along the journey (21:6), which is imbued with joy.

Fourth, we want to make the point that creation (sea, river, mountains, and hills) is observant of the story of redemption. While God's created world is beautiful and remarkable, it is the drama of redeeming grace to which even creation pays attention. Indeed, creation deserves its own special tribute, but God's unique relationship with humanity is the magisterial dogma of Holy Scripture (8:3–9). One of John's many beautiful portraits of redemption in Revelation is the 144,000 redeemed from the earth. When they sing their new song before God's throne, "No one could learn the song except the 144,000 who had been redeemed from the earth" (Rev. 14:3). We can explain, without demeaning the created order, that the truly authentic story is the gospel of grace that only the redeemed can sing, a mystery that even angels long to look into (1 Pet. 1:12).

Illustrating the Text

We should have seamless integrity from where we preach to where we live.

True Story: John Stott was one of the pioneers of the modern evangelical movement in England and around the world, and his friend Richard Bewes notes that he was also known for his tidiness and order, not only in his preaching and ministry but also in his housekeeping. Once, Bewes recalls, when he was speaking at the Keswick Convention in the United Kingdom, and the convention guests were staying in the Castlerigg Manor Hotel, Bewes was talking to the hotel staff woman who came to clean his room. The conversation revealed that she was also attending the convention. When Bewes inquired how she was finding the meetings, she replied, "Well, I hear a good deal of how people have liked hearing one speaker and then another. But I judge these men not by their speeches, but by their bedrooms!" This further prompted Bewes to ask, "And on that basis, who in your opinion is the outstanding speaker at Keswick this year?" She lost no time to answer, "Oh, there's absolutely no doubt about it—it's John Stott."[5] In psalmic theology there is much to be said in favor of a seamless integrity—from pulpit to bedroom—of those who trust in the Lord.

Singing the song of redemption

Poetry: *The Divine Comedy*, by Dante Alighieri. In Dante's *Divine Comedy*, Dante stands with Virgil, his guide through hell, on the edge of purgatory as they see a ship filled with souls swept up to the shore of purgatory by the momentum of an angel who accompanies the ship, and all of the souls, seeking divine forgiveness for their sins, sing Psalm 114 in its entirety: "When Israel came out of Egypt, . . . Judah became God's sanctuary, Israel his dominion." For Dante this was the song of redemption, first sung, of course, by Israel to celebrate their deliverance from Egyptian bondage. But their deep search was for God's ultimate forgiveness that would come through the messianic exodus from Egypt (Hosea 11:1; Matt. 2:13–15). On the one hand, this is an illustration of how Psalm 114 has been used in literature, and on the other hand, it demonstrates how the Psalms have been seen to have multiple layers of meaning, an interpretive principle demonstrated within the Psalter itself.

"Those Who Make [Idols] Will Be like Them"

Big Idea

The makers of idols themselves become like the gods they make.

Key Themes

- God is not the prisoner of circumstances but their master.
- This psalm witnesses to the faith in which God's will has become the psalmist's will.
- We become like the God (or gods) we worship.

Understanding the Text

This psalm is considered by many to have been used liturgically in the temple, and its structure and the three groups addressed (Israel, house of Aaron, those who fear the Lord) seem to point in that direction, but it is difficult to determine precisely how the liturgy looked and whose voices we hear. In form this psalm has traits of both a psalm of trust (115:9–11) and a psalm of praise (115:1, 16–18), with even an element of lament (complaint, 115:2). Obviously it is one of those psalms that does not fit comfortably into any of the form-critical categories.

The Text in Context

Psalm 115 begins the third triad of hallelujah psalms (Pss. 115–17) and completes the symmetry of the hallelujahs by repeating the original pattern of Psalms 104–6. It lays out the basis of the first exodus, Yahweh's "love" and "faithfulness" (115:1), which is also the basis of the second exodus, and alludes to the golden calf incident by discrediting idolatry (115:4–8; see also Exod. 34:6). We should recall that the return from exile marked a new beginning in Israel's life of faith, in that they gave up their idolatry and embraced Yahweh as the only God (see also 135:15–18).

Outline/Structure

1. Giving God the glory alone (115:1)
2. The crisis and satirical reply (115:2–8)
   a. The crisis created by the nations: "Where is their God?" (115:2)
   b. The theological answer: The God who acts (115:3)
   c. The satirical answer: The idols who cannot act (115:4–7)
   d. The effect of idols on their worshipers (115:8)
3. Call to the new community to trust in the Lord (115:9–11)
4. The Creator's blessing on the new community and delegation of authority (115:12–15)
   a. The blessing on the new community's three constituent groups (115:12–13)
   b. The Creator's blessing of posterity (115:14–15)
5. Yahweh credentials as compared to idols (115:16–18)
   a. Creator of the world and benefactor of humanity (115:16)
   b. The idols ("the dead") do not praise the Lord, but Israel does (115:17–18a)
   c. Israel's concluding "hallelujah" (115:18b)

Historical and Cultural Background

The historical setting for this psalm, like the Egyptian Hallel in general, can be discerned only by implication. In verses 9–13 of our psalm and 118:2–4 we have the three constituent groups of the new community (see the comments on 115:9–13). The "house of Aaron" represents the newly prominent priesthood, now necessary to the proper function of Zerubbabel's new temple, and "those who fear the LORD" represent the spiritual awakening that has resulted from the dark night of exile. The crisis that generated the psalm, symbolized by the defiant question of verse 2, is likely the exile itself, which was a challenge to Yahweh's power and even brought his existence into a questionable light so far as the nations were concerned.

Interpretive Insights

115:1 *Not to us,* LORD, *not to us but to your name be the glory.* Here our poet sets up a series of contrasts, intended to show that Yahweh is the true God and the gods represented by the idols are nonexistent:

- Not to us but to God be the glory (115:1).
- God does whatever he pleases, but the idols have no capabilities to do anything (115:3–7).

- The lifeless gods cannot praise the Lord, but we who trust the Lord—the opposite of dead idols—can (115:8, 17–18).
- The heavens belong to the Lord, but the earth has been given to humankind (115:16).

because of your love and faithfulness. The preposition translated "because" (*'al*) may also mean "for the sake of" (ESV), and this is preferable here since "your name" is parallel to "your love" (*'emet*) and "faithfulness" (*hesed*), which are virtual synonyms for Yahweh (see Exod. 34:6).

115:2–3 *Why do the nations say, "Where is their God?"* This taunting question, raised by the idolatrous nations, suggests a time of crisis, most likely the exile in general. The question is essentially a denial of God's existence, and the impudent claim of the fool of Psalms 14 and 53 who says there is no God amounts to the same unbelief. In fact, the internal denial of the latter two psalms is probably more blasphemous, because it rises from a community where unbelief was the counter position within the covenant community.

Our God is in heaven; he does whatever pleases him. The answer to the question of verse 2 is verse 3. The first of the Hallel psalms establishes God's transcendent position "above the heavens" (113:4). The declaration that God "does whatever pleases him" is not so much a statement about God's freedom—though that is not to be denied—but an assertion about his activity in contrast to the inactivity of the idols who "cannot speak" or "see" or "hear" or "smell" or "touch" or "walk" or "utter a sound." In contrast, "our God" acts—in fact, does whatever one would expect a god to do (see Isa. 46 for a similar idea).

115:4–8 Psalm 135:15–18, with some differences, is a duplication of verses 4–8 (see table 1 in the unit on Ps. 135). This is a mockery of the idols and their worshipers.

115:8 *Those who make them will be like them.* The grammar of this verse lends itself to several possibilities. It is (1) a prayer ("May those who make them be like them," author's translation); (2) a prediction (NJPS: "Those who fashion them, all who trust in them, shall become like them"); (3) an assessment (NIV: "Those who make them will be like them"); (4) an imprecation ("May it be that those who make them will become like them," author's translation); or (5) equivalency (KJV: "They that make them are like unto them"). The implication is that the makers, who have a human body with its senses and capacities, make their idols in their own image, which is a projection of themselves. The order of the terms seems to favor numbers 3 and 5.[1] In the context of the psalm, however, the writer, by his description of the lifeless idols in verses 4–7, has assigned them to "silence" (115:17b), another term for Sheol (see 94:17). That is, the makers of these lifeless idols will become like them, lifeless, and "It is not the dead who praise the LORD" (115:17a).

115:9–13 *trust in the* LORD—*he is their help and shield.* The three addressees are "all you Israelites," "house of Aaron" (priests), and "you who fear him," with each word of instruction followed by the refrain "He is their help and shield." The refrain opens up the meaning of "trust in the LORD": the Lord himself is the alternative—and more—to trusting in the weaponry of war (see 20:7). The major comparison, however, is not Yahweh versus military might but Yahweh versus idols (see 115:4–8). While the first and third groups could be identical, the third category seems to add a defining word to Israel, in regard to not only their spiritual commitment ("you who fear him," 115:11a) but their social status ("small and great alike," 115:13b). They are the new Israel that now, due to the refining effect of the exile, can be described as "you who fear" the Lord, whose spiritual renovation has had a socially leveling effect (see 113:7–8). The same three groups are mentioned a second time in 115:12–13, and here they are not the subjects of "trust" but the objects of blessing. Thus two things are highlighted: some kind of religious transformation has occurred in the community of Israel that now merits the phrase "those who fear the LORD" (it is not a call to trust but a recognition of their trust); and the priests merit a separate recognition from "Israel" and "those who fear the LORD," suggesting their new responsibilities in the new temple. The same three groups are addressed in 118:2–4, hinting that these three designations have become standard categories of the new community.

115:14–16 *May the* LORD *cause you to flourish, both you and your children.* Literally, "May the LORD add to you, to you and to your children," which is another way to pray for posterity (cf. 113:9), and this is the essence of "be blessed" in 115:15, bringing to mind the blessing of Genesis 1:28: "God blessed them and said to them, 'Be fruitful and increase in number.'" The allusion to the Genesis text is strengthened by two things: first, the appellation "Maker of heaven and earth" in 115:15b, and second, the acclamation that the "heavens belong to the LORD, but the earth he has given to mankind" (115:16). This custodial care of the earth is the essence of the last half of Genesis 1:28.

115:17–18 *It is not the dead who praise the* LORD. See the comments on 115:8. Here we have a contrast between the idols, who are essentially "dead" since they have no physical capacities to do anything, and those who make them, who are "dead" too (115:8), and they cannot praise the Lord (see 6:5).

Theological Insights

I have suggested that the makers of the lifeless gods, who can do nothing, will become like them (115:8), in the sense that the makers will also be lifeless (dead), and the dead cannot praise God (115:17). Based on the nature of idolatry, however, and worship of the true God, for that matter, the striking lesson of this satire is, as the NIV renders it, that we become like our gods. If our god is small, we become small; if our God is big, we grow in likeness; if our god is vindictive, we become vindictive too; if our god is loving, we learn to love as well.[2] Hakham aptly observes: "And he who attaches himself to something without substance will ultimately lose any substance he himself may possess."[3]

Teaching the Text

This psalm is loaded with possibilities for preaching and teaching. I suggest, first, that we begin with an idea that Kidner interjects regarding idolatry: it is tied to what we see and not what we do not see.[4] In this regard, we should make the point that the covenant faith prohibits making images of Yahweh (Exod. 20:4; Deut. 5:8), and while the reason for this commandment is not explained, the reason can more generally be perceived from the Hebrew Scriptures: we human beings tend to become attached to the things we can see, and the idols become our gods, and they are helpless to assist us (Isa. 46:1–2). The inevitable consequence of this religious conviction is that the "maker," who crafts the idol in his or her own image, becomes the god.

That observation can bring us to the second point that we may draw, from verse 8: we become like our God (gods), or inevitably we project ourselves in the visible objects, and they are lifeless, so we have to act and speak for them, and effectively we ourselves become the deity. We can recall that God created humanity in his own image (Gen. 1:26–27), and that was the defining character of humankind. This is precisely how the maker of idols is operating: the idols are a projection of the maker. Thus idolatry is not only a projection of ourselves in lifeless images but a projection of ourselves into God's own place and role as the Creator. It is simply another version of the serpent's strategy: "For God knows that when you eat from it your eyes will be opened, and you will be like God" (Gen. 3:5).

As preachers/teachers of the gospel, this is where we may bring forward Paul's theology of the conforming work of Christ, who is the image of God (he is not made "in" God's image but "is" the image of God; see Col. 1:15; 3:10) and who conforms us again to the image of God (Rom. 8:29). We might take our point even further and suggest that our fallen nature is prone to repeat the human couple's strategy in Eden: to project ourselves into God's place. There's no problem, of course, with creating our offspring in our own image, as Adam did—that's our mandate! But the problem is putting ourselves in God's place, and that's the inevitable outcome of making idols, whatever form they take.

One way we can conclude our sermon/lesson is to use John's statement to the effect that our efforts to "be like them" (idols) can be turned in the direction to "be like him" (Christ), and join this to Paul's theology mentioned above. This is God's re-creative work in Christ: "But we know that when Christ appears, we shall be like him, for we shall see him as he is" (1 John 3:2).

Illustrating the Text

Becoming our real selves means being restored to the image of God.

Quote: *Mere Christianity*, by C. S. Lewis. The idea of this psalm is absolutely correct: we become like the God we worship, and that is the way it should be (Lev. 11:44). The gross error of the idolaters is that they become like their god too, but their god is lifeless. Made in the image of God, we are conformed into his image, making us the real persons God intended us to be—as Paul phrases it: "For those God foreknew he also predestined to be conformed to the image of his Son, that he might be the firstborn among many brothers and sisters" (Rom. 8:29). The firstborn is Christ ("the firstborn over all creation," Col. 1:15), and that is the image to which God seeks to conform us (Col. 3:10), remaking us in the image of our Creator. Thus the object of saving grace is our reimaging. It is only in that redemptive process that we become our real selves, restored in the image of our Creator. C. S. Lewis makes the point that it is only when we are looking for God that we become our real selves:

> Your real, new self (which is Christ's and also yours, and yours just because it is His) will not come as long as you are looking for it. It will come when you are looking for Him. Does that sound strange? The same principle holds, you know, for more everyday matters. Even in social life, you will never make a good impression on other people until you stop thinking about what sort of impression you are making. Even in literature and art, no man who bothers about originality will ever be original whereas if you simply try to tell the truth (without caring two pence how often it has been told before) you will, nine times out of ten, become original without ever having noticed it. The principle runs through all life from top to bottom. Give up yourself, and you will find your real self. Lose your life and you will save it. Submit to death, death of your ambitions and favourite wishes every day and death of your whole body in the end: submit with every fibre of your being, and you will find eternal life. Keep back nothing. Nothing that you have not given away will be really yours. Nothing in you that has not died will ever be raised from the dead. Look for yourself, and you will find in the long run only hatred, loneliness, despair, rage, ruin, and decay. But look for Christ and you will find Him, and with Him everything else thrown in.[5]

By no other name

Story: After the nations challenge Israel with their taunting, "Where is their God?" (115:2), in the following psalm our psalmist calls on the name of the Lord (*YHWH*; see 116:2, 4, 13, 17), using the divine name eighteen times. Israel does not serve just any god; he has a name, Yahweh (see Exod. 3:13–15). No lifeless and generic god like the gods of the nations will do (115:4–8). James Mulholland tells the story of his five-year-old brother getting separated from his mother in a grocery store. When he realized that he was lost, he called out in a quivering voice, "Helen, Helen!" His mother found him quickly and wiped away his tears. And then she said, "Why did you call me Helen?" He answered, "I knew there were lots of mommies here, but I thought there would only be one Helen." There are lots of gods in the world, but there is only one Lord.[6]

"Return to Your Rest, My Soul, for the LORD Has Been Good to You"

Big Idea

To love and to believe absolutely arise out of the crucible of suffering.

Key Themes

- The psalmist (and the community of believers) was the suffering servant.
- The spiritual journey from death to life in God's presence is the travelogue of our journey of faith.

Understanding the Text

This psalm of thanksgiving was likely sung over the thank offering. It is framed in the first person, "I," but most probably was spoken on behalf of the entire community, now emerging from the exile to a new life of freedom.

The Text in Context

Zenger speaks of the "anthology style" of this psalm—that is, it draws on other psalms.[1] Psalm 86 is another example of this style, and, like Psalm 116, it is virtually pieced together from terms, phrases, and longer borrowings from other psalms to express the suppliant's own thoughts (see table 1 in the unit on Ps. 86).

Table 1. Intertextuality of Psalm 116

Psalm 116	Other Psalms
"The cords of death encompassed me" (116:3a)	"The cords of death encompassed me" (18:5a)

Psalm 116	Other Psalms
"*Gracious* is the Lord *and righteous*" (116:5a)	"[The Lord is] *gracious* and merciful *and righteous*" (111:4b) "*Gracious* and merciful is the Lord" (see Exod. 34:6) (114:4b)
"*For you have delivered my life from death,* . . . *my feet from stumbling. I will walk before* the Lord *in the land(s) of the living*" (116:8–9)	"*For you have delivered my life from death,* indeed *my feet from stumbling,* to *walk before* God *in the* light *of the living*" (56:13–14)
"Please, Lord, for I am *your servant,* I am your servant, *the son of your handmaiden;* you have loosed my bonds" (116:16)	"Give strength to *your servant,* and save *the son of your handmaiden*" (86:16)

Note: All translations are the author's.

In 2 Corinthians 4:13 Paul quotes 116:10a from the Greek (LXX), suggesting that it was in a crisis like the psalmist's that he discovered his belief.[2]

Outline/Structure

1. An absolute love (116:1–9)
   a. Arising out of God's grace (116:1–2)
   b. Breaking the "cords of death" (116:3)
   c. Answering the psalmist's call for help (116:4)
   d. Confessing the Lord's help (116:5–6)
   e. Reviewing the rescue (116:7–9)
2. An absolute faith (116:10–19a)
   a. Believing amid the crisis (116:10–11)
   b. Giving thanks for the Lord's goodness (116:12–19a)
      i. Remembering the Lord's goodness (116:12)
      ii. Lifting up the "cup of salvation" (116:13)
      iii. Fulfilling his vows to the Lord (116:14)
      iv. Remembering the faithful (116:15)
      v. Celebrating release from exile (116:16)
      vi. Making the thank offering (116:17–19a)
   Hallelujah ("Praise the Lord") (116:19b)

Historical and Cultural Background

Psalm 116 recalls the anguish of exile in the words "cords of death" (116:3), "when I was brought low" (116:6), and "I am greatly afflicted" (116:10b, which has the sense of exile in Ps. 119:67, 71). The personal "I" is the voice of the corporate community about to observe the service of thanksgiving to celebrate their deliverance from exile. It is quite possible that this service was celebrated in Zerubbabel's new temple (dedicated in

516 BC). See also "Historical and Cultural Background" in the unit on Psalm 115.

Interpretive Insights

116:1–2 *I love.* The verb "love" does not have an object (absolute use of the verb), which is an unusual construction (compare 26:8; 31:23).[3] Most English translations move the tetragrammaton (*YHWH*) to this position and make "the LORD" the object (but see also the absolute "I believe" [NIV: "I trusted"] in 116:10).

116:3–6 *cords of death entangled me, the anguish of the grave.* These verses describe how repeatedly the psalmist, or, following our interpretation, the new community, has been "entangled" by the "cords of death," or the "anguish of the grave [*sheʾol*]." That is, they were on the verge of death, and when he/they called on the Lord ("LORD, save me!"; 116:4a), "he saved me" (us) (116:6b). Here we have two features of the psalm of thanksgiving, a report of the crisis (116:3) and the assurance of deliverance (116:6b; see the sidebar "Psalms of Thanksgiving" in the unit on Pss. 9–10).

when I was brought low. This verb bears the sense of being materially poor, but in 79:8 it carries a spiritual meaning, which may be the sense here,[4] or more likely it may be an allusion to Israel's Egyptian bondage and the Babylonian exile, as 116:7–9 implies.

116:7–9 *Return to your rest, my soul.* This is an account of the psalmist's personal experience, or Israel's experience in the exile, or both. Now the celebrant gives an abridged account of what God has done and calls the congregation, which stands for the whole of Israel, to return to resting in God, "for the LORD has been good to you" (116:7). The new era of "rest," like the new era David entered when "the LORD had given him rest from all his enemies" (2 Sam. 7:1), opened upon a new opportunity to "walk before the LORD in the land of the living" (Ps. 116:9), a metaphor of the restoration and an expression of the new life of the restored community ("before the LORD").

116:10–11 *I trusted in the LORD when I said.* For the absolute use of the verb "I believe" (NIV: "I trusted"), see the comments on 116:1–2, above. The Greek (LXX) has: "I believed, therefore I spoke." The Hebrew construction, however, can have a temporal sense, "when." So the psalmist may be recalling those times of suffering during the exile (116:10b), and in verse 11 remarks about his cynical feelings during that time ("Everyone is a liar"—i.e., you cannot trust anybody). Yet he still "believed" despite the suffering and cynicism. Thus verses 10 and 11 would read: "I believed [even] when I would say: 'I am greatly afflicted.' I was the one who said: 'Everyone is a liar'" (author's translation).

116:12 *What shall I return to the* L'ORD *for all his goodness to me?* This question is answered by the following verses, which describe the psalmist's worship (116:13–19), culminating in a service of thanksgiving in the temple (118:19–27). The problem he had faced was most likely the exile itself (116:3), and he describes his deliverance with a prison metaphor, "You have freed me from my chains" (116:16).

116:13 *I will lift up the cup of salvation.* While we do not have any references to a libation accompanying the thank offering, this may be symbolic language celebrating the Lord's salvation of Israel from the exile.

116:14 *I will fulfill my vows to the* L'ORD *in the presence of all his people.* The suppliant is stationed in the temple to carry out his promise to make a thank offering. "All his people" refers to the congregation present, not all of Israel, in the sense that those gathered in the temple represented the entire nation (see the sidebar "Vows" in the unit on Ps. 76).

116:15 *Precious in the sight of the* L'ORD *is the death of his faithful servants.* In verse 8 the psalmist acknowledges that God has delivered him from death, probably the exile, in which so many died. This is an epitaph for those precious believers who lost their lives in this tragic era.

116:16 *Truly I am your servant,* L'ORD. See "Theological Insights."

just as my mother did. Literally, "the son of your handmaid."[5] In 113:9 the Lord's compassionate nature, celebrated also here in this psalm, is the reason he "settles the childless woman in her home as a happy mother of children." And in 115:14 the suppliant prays that this time will be one of many children. Now the worshiper acknowledges that he, and the congregation too ("the son of your handmaid"), is the fulfillment of those hopes and prayers.

freed me from my chains. In 2:3 the word "chains" (or "bonds") is a metaphor to describe foreign domination, and this is most likely the sense of the term here (see 107:14).

116:17 *I will sacrifice a thank offering.* The Hebrew imperfect verb (future) carries the present sense—he is now about to carry out this vow.

116:18–19 *I will fulfill my vows . . . in the presence of all his people.* This conclusion reiterates the worshiper's intention (116:14) to pay his vows for what the Lord has done for him (them). It will occur "in the presence of all his people" (116:14b and 18b). Wilcock reminds us that "the Old Testament knows of no private faith which is not also in some way public. And the psalm itself shows the same two faces"[6] (note 116:19, "in the courts of the house of the L'ORD").

Theological Insights

Psalm 116 introduces the postexilic community's developing portrait in a significant way. Emerging from the exile, this people sees itself as the "servant of the LORD,"[7] indeed, a suffering servant (116:16; compare the Servant Songs of Isaiah). In fact, verse 10 rehearses the servant's reflection on his suffering during the exile: "I believed [even] when I would say: 'I am greatly afflicted'" (author's translation; see the comments on 116:10–11, above). The verb "afflicted," in fact, is used of the exile in 119:67, and the virtual transformation from wayward sinner to obedient servant is the subject of that strophe of Psalm 119: "Do good to your servant, O LORD, according to your word. . . . Before I *was humbled* [went into exile], I was straying; but now I am obedient to your word" (119:65–67, author's translation). The writer of Psalm 119 even acknowledges that the exile has taught him (or, the community) the Lord's decrees (119:71). There is no hint of vicarious suffering, however, as there is in Isaiah's fourth Servant Song (Isa. 53:4–6). Yet, they have been delivered from death that they "may walk before the LORD *in the land of the living*" (that is, Judah; Ps. 116:9), a virtual resurrection of the servant who was "cut off from *the land of the living*" (exile; Isa. 53:8). Israel's self-understanding has already taken the shape of the suffering servant.

Teaching the Text

Psalm 116 logs for us what has been called a "religious topography."[8] If we choose to use this term, we should explain it by mentioning the stages from the brink of death (116:3, 8), through the psalmist's recognition of God's mercy as God rescued the worshiper from the state of despair (116:4–6), giving us a glimpse of his restored life ("your rest," 116:7; and "the land of the living," 116:9). It is a parable of the exile and return. The "courts of the house of the LORD" (116:19) signify that the worshiper's final destination is worship, or his relationship with God—the two overlap significantly (cf., e.g., 23:6; see also "The Text in Context" in the unit on Ps. 69). This can be our first point.

Second, we may want to enlarge on this journey, particularly because it provides a spiritual travelogue for so many life experiences, from death to life ("that I may walk before the LORD in the land of the living," 116:9). In fact, it might be helpful to point our listeners to the structure of verses 7–9 that form part of our travelogue. Deliverance from death (116:8) is surrounded by the two descriptive phrases about the new life, one being "rest" (116:7) and the other "the land of the living" (116:9). We might even find it helpful to compare the Samuel story of David's new era of rest that comes after his conquests are done (see the comments on 116:7–9).

Third, we may stress the idea that the whole of our spiritual posture can be described with the two absolute verbs of the psalm: "I love" (116:1) and "I believe" (116:10). They are not successive stages of faith but parallel, even though they put faith in two different frameworks. Since "I love" has no object, the worshiper is expressing his spiritual status, much as John does when he says (again with no verbal object): "*We love* because he first loved us" (1 John 4:19). While Deuteronomy 6:5 has the Lord as the object ("Love the LORD your God with all your heart and with all your soul and with all your strength"), at the same time it describes a posture of faith that is all-encompassing. These commandments are first of all to be "on your hearts" (internal); and then they must constitute our heritage ("Impress them on your children"); and further, they must be the substance of our daily living ("Talk about them when you sit at home"); and that means they will be the earmarks of our very existence ("Tie them as symbols on your hands"); and finally they are to lay claim to our private and public life ("Write them on the doorframes of your houses [private] and on your gates [public]") (Deut. 6:6–9).

Fourth—and this could easily be a message by itself—we may take advantage of Jesus's Last Supper with his disciples. We know that by the first century AD the Egyptian Hallel was sung during the Passover seder, and two of the Gospels mention the detail that "they had sung a hymn" (Matt. 26:30; Mark 14:26), most likely a reference to the Egyptian Hallel, or the concluding portion, and Psalm 126, which was also part of the Passover liturgy. Psalm 116 particularly presents the framework for this messianic moment and the terms that easily connect to the setting of the Last Supper, extending even to Gethsemane. As we have observed above, the psalmist has suffered the "cords of death" and the "anguish of the grave," and was overcome with "distress and sorrow" (116:3). Moreover, he was the suffering servant (116:10, 16).

Illustrating the Text

Both sides of the equation

Quote: **John Newton.** Our psalmist is intent on describing both sides of the spiritual equation. On the one side, the exile was a time of death and sorrow (116:3), and on the other side of the equation was God's salvation (116:6). This death/life cycle (116:3–4, 6–9) is the point of the psalm: when death entangled him (them), he cried, "LORD, save me!" (116:4) and then testified to that reality (116:8–9). In one of his letters, Newton (1725–1807) describes this equation, filling in the factors on either side.

> [God's] patience likewise is wonderful. Multitudes, yea nearly our whole species, spend the life and strength which he affords them, and abuse all the bounties he heaps upon them, in the ways of sin. His commands are disregarded, his name blasphemed, his mercy disdained, his power defied, yet still he spares. . . . He preserveth man and beast, sustains the young lion in the forest, feeds the birds of the air, which have neither storehouse nor barn, and adorns the insects and

the flowers of the field with a beauty and elegance beyond all that can be found in the courts of kings.[9]

"O Jesus, look at father!"

True Story: The psalmist's opening statement is, "I love the LORD, for he heard my voice; he heard my cry for mercy. Because he turned his ear to me, I will call on him as long as I live" (116:1–2). Lilias Trotter, missionary to the Muslims of Algiers, records a tender moment among her beloved villagers. A two-year old girl with a sensitive heart and a precocious mind was attracted by a picture on the wall of Jesus calling a child to him, and she wanted her almost blind father to see Jesus. In Trotter's own words, the little girl "went right up to her nearly blind father & pointed to one of the pictures on the wall—one of the Lord calling a little child to Him—& said 'Look at Jesus.' 'I have no eyes O my daughter—I cannot see,' was the answer. The baby thing lifted head & eyes to the picture & said, 'O Jesus, look at father!' . . . Was not that a bit of heavenly wisdom! (28 July 1909)."[10]

Our psalm does not employ the language of God looking on us humans, but it does say that "he turned his ear to me" (116:2b), which has the same effect. This precious child in Trotter's story was, in her childlike way, expressing her love for Jesus by her attraction to the picture and desire that her father see him. Then when she realized that this was not possible, she turned in the same trusting faith to Jesus, that he might look at her father. Sometimes we cannot, for whatever reason—our sins, our spiritual blindness—look at Jesus, but he can look at us. And that is the prayer of a childlike faith, "O Jesus, look at father!" And heavenly wisdom!

That's beatiful!

"Great Is His Love toward Us"

Big Idea

Praising the God of "love" and "faithfulness" is more than admiration.

Key Themes

- The universal praise of God is based in God's character of love and faithfulness.
- Only when Israel and all nations join together in the praise of Yahweh will God's praise be complete.

Understanding the Text

This psalm, the briefest in the Psalter, is an interlude before the powerful conclusion to the Egyptian Hallel, Psalm 118. It may function like a liturgical benediction. It is also an affirmation of the formula of grace in Exodus 34:6.

The Text in Context

While some scholars have proposed that Psalm 117 is the conclusion to Psalm 116, and others have suggested it is the beginning of Psalm 118, both of these psalms have their appropriate ending and beginning, respectively. The general opinion is that this brief hymn of praise is independent in its own right. While the Greek Septuagint moves the "hallelujah" (Greek *allēlouia*) that follows Psalm 116 to the beginning of Psalm 117, it is quite obvious that the Greek translator was trying to establish a consistent pattern of hallelujahs in Psalms 112–19 by placing *allēlouia* at the beginning of each of these psalms, even before Psalm 119 (see table 2 in the unit on Ps. 104). The irregular pattern of the Hebrew text (MT) is more difficult to explain, so we are inclined to assume its originality, and the fact that the Septuagint translator gave it another order may suggest that he did not understand it either.

Paul quotes verse 1 in Romans 15:11 to support the point that the inclusion of the gentiles in the plan of salvation was not an afterthought on God's part.

Outline/Structure

1. Summons to all nations to praise the Lord (117:1)
2. The Lord's "love" and "faithfulness" warrant praise (117:2a)
   Hallelujah ("Praise the LORD") (117:2b)

Historical and Cultural Background

See "Additional Insights: The Egyptian Hallel (Psalms 113–18)," following the unit on Psalm 113.

Interpretive Insights

117:1 *Praise the* LORD, *all you nations; extol him, all you peoples.* The full tetragrammaton (*YHWH*) is used here rather than the shortened form that occurs in the praise imperative "hallelujah" (lit., "praise Yah"). The verb translated "extol" occurs only three times in the Psalter in this form (63:3 [NIV: "glorify"]; 145:4 [NIV: "commends"]; 147:12), and twice in Ecclesiastes (4:2 [NIV: "declared"]; 8:15 [NIV: "commend"]). The same root in a different verbal form occurs in Psalm 106:47 (= 1 Chron. 16:35 [NIV: "glory"]). The Hebrew phrase "all nations" also occurs in 118:10 in reference to the threat of the nations.

117:2 *For great is his love toward us, and the faithfulness of the* LORD *endures forever.* The verb that the NIV and most English translations render "is great" suggests strength that prevails. Here the subject is Yahweh's "love" (*hesed*), and that is a potent image (see 103:11): Yahweh conquers by his love. But "faithfulness" (Heb. *'emet* also means "truth") in the second half of the verse completes the picture of Yahweh's character revealed to Moses (Exod. 34:6) and assures Israel and the nations that his love will never fail. Some understand the phrase "toward us" to apply only to Israel, but it is not outside the theological frame of this period of time to expect that Israel was much more inclusive (see "Historical and Cultural Background" in the unit on Ps. 87).

Theological Insights

While the salvation of the nations (gentiles) is not explicit here, the call to the nations to praise the Lord is clearly connected to God's covenant with Israel, for the formula of grace in Exodus 34:6, the Lord's "love" (*hesed*) and "faithfulness" (*'emet*) is a favorite covenant code in the Psalms. The perplexing feature of the psalm is that the suppliant affirms Yahweh's love "toward us" (117:2a) and does not explicity include the nations, even though he had summoned them to praise the Lord in 117:1. Why then should the nations praise the Lord for God's covenant with Israel, unless, of course, the nations are being implicitly invited into the covenant, or are already viewed as sharing its benefits? That seems to be the case in Psalm 100 (see "Teaching the Text" in the unit on Ps. 100), which shares the covenant terms "love" and "faithfulness" with Psalm 117 (100:5 has an alternate form for the second term). It is likely that by the time of this psalm's composition, the salvation of the nations had become a plank in Israel's theological platform, and without apology or explanation the nations are summoned to praise God with Israel for his covenant love and faithfulness, in which they share.

Teaching the Text

By the time of the postexilic era Israel had become more religiously inclusive. We could begin with a brief explanation, and unapologetically. Kidner remarks: "It may also be that the 'us' of verse 2 has already found room for the 'you' implied in verse 1, by seeing Israelites and Gentiles as one people under God."[1] This can be our first point of emphasis. We might even suggest that the hallelujah redactor has combined both the nations and Israel in his redaction as he summons them to "Praise the LORD!" There is a hint of that in Psalm 148, where the hallelujah redactor has founded the praise of Yahweh in Yahweh's creative activities and on that foundational premise has summoned all creation, including "kings of the earth and all nations" (148:11), to praise the Lord.

The creation story begins with a view to all humankind (Gen. 1–3), and the Abrahamic covenant involves blessing to the entire world (Gen. 12:1–3; cf. Gal. 3:8–9). Now Psalm 117 reflects the more inclusive point of view. While it does not depict the salvation of the nations, that is implied, because we can hardly expect the nations to praise the Lord without some acknowledgment that his "love" and "faithfulness" have implications for their own existence. There are those occasions, of course, when humanity is summoned to acknowledge God's sovereignty (e.g., Isa. 45:23; Rom. 14:11; Phil. 2:10)—unconditional surrender!—but there is no hint of that here.

The New Testament writers celebrate the inclusion of the gentiles in the plan of salvation through Jesus Christ, a doctrine we Christians do not celebrate as often as we should. Delitzsch beautifully remarks, "Mercy [love] and truth are the two divine powers which shall one day be perfectly developed and displayed in Israel, and going forth from Israel, shall conquer the world."[2] Paul bases the salvation of the gentiles in the faith in God's promises to Abraham (see "Theological Insights" in the unit on Ps. 87), and that is something to celebrate. He even quotes 117:1 in Romans 15:11 to further affirm this point. The consummate praise of the Scriptures is found in the Revelation of John, where "every nation, tribe, people and language" join together in extolling

God's salvation through Jesus Christ (the Lamb; Rev. 7:9–10); and "a great multitude" sings the fourfold "hallelujah" to celebrate God's victory over evil (Rev. 19:1–8). Then, and only then, will the praise of God be complete.[3] See "Illustrating the Text" in the unit on Psalm 150.

Illustrating the Text

Picking up the threads

Literature: *The Maiden's Bequest*, **by George MacDonald.** This psalm, brief in words, is monumental in content, for it is an announcement that the Lord's love and faithfulness are great; and all nations, whether they are participants or observers, are summoned to praise the Lord. Psalm 117 picks up the threads of the covenantal theme of God's love and faithfulness revealed to Moses in Exodus 34:6. This formula of grace appears as a golden thread at various points in the Psalter. It is the preamble to Psalm 118 that celebrates God's love (*hesed*; 118:1–4). The last piece of the Egyptian Hallel, Psalm 118 begins with the same words that open the final psalm of Book 4 (106:1) and the initial psalm of Book 5, "Give thanks to the LORD, for he is good; his love [*hesed*] endures forever." God's "love" is the essence of his being, and his faithfulness is a function of his love. Or we might suggest that they are near equivalents ("faithfulness" can also be translated "trust" or "truth"). MacDonald, in his novel *The Maiden's Bequest*, says of the boldness of one of his characters, Tibbie, blind of sight but keen of love, "Possibly the darkness about her made her bolder; but I think it was her truth, which is another word for *love*, however unlike love the outcome may look, that made her able to speak in this fashion."[4] However the equivalency of these two terms is judged, the fact that the nations acknowledge Israel as the beneficiary of God's love and faithfulness means that the nations are on the verge of the greatest moment in their history, a theme that Book 5 sounds out in various ways.

"Give Thanks to the LORD, for He Is Good; His Love Endures Forever"

Big Idea

It is in our weakness, not our strength, that we learn how strong God is to save.

Key Themes

- God sometimes takes the things we disparage and makes them the cornerstone of faith.
- Human resources cannot match God's love.

Understanding the Text

A psalm of thanksgiving, Psalm 118 closes the Egyptian Hallel with a festive celebration of God's love (*hesed*), which has had an encompassing effect in Israel's history, illustrated by the encompassing feature of the refrain (*inclusio*), "His love endures forever." Through many hardships the people of Israel have come to celebrate God's saving grace (118:14, 21) and have come to confess him as their God (118:28).

The Text in Context

As the final psalm in the Egyptian Hallel, Psalm 118 celebrates Yahweh's love (*hesed*) and repeats this affirmation of faith that began the Hallel in 113:1: God's love was experienced, perhaps best experienced, in the crucible of suffering (118:5–7, 18), and it just goes on and on ("His love endures forever," 118:1b, 2b, 3b, 4b, and 29b).

Wilcock compares this psalm to some of the cathedrals of England that required generations to build. When one visits such a monumental worship structure, one can see clear evidences of successive architectural styles: Norman, early English, decorated, perpendicular. Analogously, he calls attention to the "architectural" styles of the psalm, drawn from other psalms and biblical texts.[1]

Table 1. Intertextuality of Psalm 118

Theme/Text	Psalm 118	Other Texts
David's distress turned to a spacious place (*merhab*)	118:5	Ps. 31:8 (31:9 MT)
David struck down his enemies	118:10–12	2 Sam. 8
Moses's Song	118:14: "The LORD is my strength and my song; he has become my salvation" (ESV)	Exod. 15:2: "The LORD is my strength and my song, and he has become my salvation" (ESV)
The LORD's right hand	118:15b, 16	Exod. 15:6
Aaron's blessing	118:27	Num. 6:25

Jesus himself quotes verses 22 and 23 of this psalm to put his generation's rejection of him in the broader light of redemption history (Mark 12:10–11). The writer to the Hebrews takes another theological perspective from this psalm, quoting verse 6 to make the point that the Lord's help takes away the fear of mortals (Heb. 13:6). Since Psalm 118 is a psalm that celebrates God's love stretched across the troubled years of Israel's history, it is the knowledge of God's unchanging love that underwrites the affirmation of the author of Hebrews that "Jesus Christ is the same yesterday and today and forever" (Heb. 13:8).

Outline/Structure

Table 2 is an attempt to represent the four voices we hear in Psalm 118: the framer's/celebrant's voice, the congregation's voice (includes both "Israel" and "those who fear the LORD"), the voice of the priests ("house of Aaron"), and the voice of the gatekeepers.

Historical and Cultural Background

Our working hypothesis is that this psalm, although it uses the first-person singular (I/me/my) in verses 1 and 5–22, is spoken on behalf of Israel, broken down into "[all] Israel," the priests ("house of Aaron"), and the temple worshipers gathered for this service of thanksgiving. The occasion is not clear, but based on the allusions to the temple in verse 26, and possibly also verses 19–20, it could have been used, perhaps even composed, for the occasion of the laying of the foundation of the temple, its dedication (516 BC), or the Passover of that year, which followed the dedication (Ezra 6:16–22). Some would prefer the time of Ezra and Nehemiah in the middle of the fifth century BC.

Table 2. Four Voices in Psalm 118

Framer's/ Celebrant's voice	Congregation's voice ["Israel" and "those who fear the Lord"] (see 115:9)	Priests' voice ("house of Aaron")	Gatekeepers' voice
Opening call to thanksgiving (118:1; cf. 118:29)			
Call to Israel to give thanks (118:2a)			
	Congregation's (Israel's) response (118:2b)		
Call to the priests ("house of Aaron") to give thanks (118:3a)			
		Priests' response (118:3b)	
Call to "those who fear the Lord" (118:4a)			
	Congregation's ("those who fear the Lord") response to give thanks (118:4b–18)		
	Congregation's call to the gatekeepers (118:19)		
			Gatekeepers' invitation to enter the temple gates (118:20)
	Congregation's continued response to give Yahweh thanks (118:21–25)		
	Congregation's affirmation of the temple building (118:22–25)		
		Priests' blessing of the congregation and faith affirmation ["The Lord is God"] (118:26–27)	
	Congregation's response to priestly blessing and their affirmation of faith ["You are my God"] (118:28)		
Concluding call to thanksgiving (118:29; cf. 118:1)			

Interpretive Insights

118:1 *Give thanks to the* LORD, *for he is good; his love endures forever.* The opening and closing verses are precisely the same as the opening verse of Psalms 106 and 107, as well as the lead line of Psalm 136. In Psalm 106 it signals a transition to Book 5, while its occurrence in Psalm 107 begins a prolonged thanksgiving unit, composed of Psalms 107–36. Its double occurrence in Psalm 118 forms a proper conclusion to the Egyptian Hallel, anticipating the Great Hallel of Psalm 136.

118:2–4 *Let Israel say: "His love endures forever."* We hear the voice of the celebrant addressing the same three groups addressed in 115:9–11: all Israel, the priests ("house of Aaron"), and "those who fear the LORD," who are probably the congregation of the faithful gathered with the celebrant for the thank offering. Liturgically, the response ("His love endures forever") may be made by all three groups in their proper order, and then there follows an extended review of Israel's history in generic terms, likely spoken by the congregation (the "I" is a corporate "I").

118:5–6 *I cried to the* LORD. The divine name is the short form of *YHWH* (*Yah*), and the sign of the indirect object ("to") is missing. It may be that *Yah* ("LORD") is his one-word prayer: "I cried: 'LORD' [*Yah*]." The declaration that the psalmist was "hard pressed" (exile, 118:5a) and that the Lord "brought [him] into a spacious place" (return, 118:5b; see also 4:1b) may be a shorthand account of the exile and restoration. It was in that experience that Israel learned the weakness of human power (118:6) and the "mighty things" the Lord can do (118:15–17).

118:7 *The* LORD *is with me; he is my helper.* See 54:4–5 for similar language. The image of the Lord as helper is used many times in the Psalter. For the Christian reader, 46:1 is the classic text.[2] This psalm celebrates some great deliverance from the psalmist's enemies (118:7b), which may be the monumental return from exile and restoration.

118:8–9 *It is better.* Still employing military language, twice the poet uses the comparative degree ("It is better") to elevate trust in the Lord as the superior alternative (see 20:7). It was either the Lord or humans, and on another level, the Lord or human leaders.

118:10–12 *All the nations surrounded me, but in the name of the* LORD *I cut them down.* A rabbinic interpretation of "all the nations" is that it refers to the numerous nations throughout Israel's history that had assaulted them,[3] most recently the Babylonians. "I cut them down" is also a general reflection on Israel's victories. The poem is phrased in the first-person singular (I/me/my, 118:5–22) and then interjects a first-person plural section (we/our/us, 118:23–27), returning to "I" in verse 28, concluding with the refrain that also opens the psalm: "Give thanks to the LORD, for he is good; his love endures forever" (118:1 and 29). The "I" is evidently the corporate "I" that includes the whole congregation of Israel. It shows signs of being a liturgy (see "Outline/Structure").

They swarmed around me like bees, but they were consumed as quickly as burning thorns. The description of attack is reinforced with the simile "like bees" (see Deut. 1:44)—and that needs no explanation—and the doom of the attackers with the simile "as burning thorns" (see 2 Sam. 23:6–7). In fact, a thorn fire flares up quickly and then goes out quickly, suggesting a fierce battle followed by a sudden lull. This is a general description of Yahweh's intervention into Israel's threatening circumstances throughout history, not a description of any one instance.

118:13 *I was pushed back and about to fall.* The Hebrew text literally reads, "You harshly pushed me back so that I would fall," but the NIV follows the Greek (LXX) and Syriac, making it the first-person singular: "I was thrust, and sorely shaken, that I might fall: but the Lord helped me" (LXX). Quite obviously, if the Lord is the subject of the verb ("You [LORD] harshly pushed me back"), the Greek and Syriac have deflected the blame from Yahweh so as not to attribute evil intent to him. But this is unnecessary because Yahweh is often credited with causing weal *and* woe (see "Theological Insights" in the unit on Ps. 71).

118:19–20 *the gates of the righteous.* These are either the gates of the city or the gates of the temple, and now the worshiper, along with those who are accompanying him, has arrived and seeks to enter (see Ps. 24). Verse 19 is the words of those who seek to enter, and verse 20 is probably the words of the gatekeeper (see table 2).

118:22 *The stone the builders rejected has become the cornerstone.* The cornerstone is placed on the ground floor where two walls meet, strengthening the structure. The stone the builders rejected was deemed unworthy of the structure (see Neh. 4:1–3, where Sanballat and Tobiah mock the stones of the walls of Jerusalem), but now—for whatever reason, we are not informed—they have used it nevertheless. With the focus on the temple in verses 3 and 26–27, the "cornerstone" is likely that of the new temple.

118:27 *With boughs in hand, join in the festal procession up to the horns of the altar.* Literally, "Tie the sacrifice with ropes to the horns of the altar" (see ESV). According to the Mishnah (*Tamid* 4.1) the sacrificial animal was tied until it was slaughtered, and then it was offered at the northwestern corner of the temple court.

118:28 *You are my God.* Israel now offers a confession that amounts to the first and second parts of the covenant formula (see "Theological Insights"). This is a paraphrase of the first two parts of the covenant formula, (1) I will be your God, and (2) you will be my people. What makes the confession all the more powerful is that, in Leviticus 26:11–12, it is made in the context of the exodus from Egypt, and what could be more impressive than to hear God's people confess the reality of this relationship that has at last come true as the new exodus and occupation of the land of Canaan is occurring (exodus from Babylonia and return to Judah)? The psalmist may, on the ground level of meaning, refer to a real stone that was rejected as the cornerstone of the new temple, but it symbolized Israel, and it is the reversal of the builders' decision to reject the stone. It is a parable of God's election of Israel, as related in Deuteronomy 7.

118:29 *Give thanks to the* LORD, *for he is good; his love endures forever.* In addition to forming an *inclusio* with verse 1, the ending of this psalm is the same as the beginning of Book 5 (107:1) and the beginning of the final psalm (136:1) in this major thanksgiving unit (107–36) and constitutes the capstone not only to the Egyptian Hallel but also of this major thanksgiving unit of Book 5. Now we are ready for the massive treatment of the Torah that Psalm 119 provides. The Lord's goodness, in fact, is represented by his gift of the Torah.

Theological Insights

The Egyptian Hallel closes with a celebratory psalm that reflects Israel's renewed faith. We have already observed the character of this new community (see "Additional Insights: The Egyptian Hallel [Psalms 113–18]" following the unit on Ps. 113). In our discussion of the present psalm we have proposed that it is a corporate psalm of thanksgiving to celebrate some special event ("The LORD has done it this very day," 118:24), perhaps the laying of the temple foundation (see "Historical and Cultural Background"). As Israel emerges from the exile and enters the new era of salvation history, their confession is a monotheistic one, a theological conviction that developed more concretely during the exile: "The LORD is God" (118:27a). We may stress the shaping power of historical events, and whatever the event, it had changed Israel's perspective: "The LORD has done this, and it is marvelous in our eyes" (118:23). There is a conflict that lies behind 118:22, for the builders, for some unnamed reason, rejected the stone that others, assumedly, favored. This is likely an in-community controversy, for the "builders" of the temple would have been a vital part of the community, perhaps even priests and Levites. This presents us with the opportunity to speak about the internal controversies of the community of faith, and to stress the fact that God builds his temple, and also his church, out of "stones" that do not necessarily merit the overall acclaim of the faith community. While we do not know the particulars of the outcome, the decision to include this stone had a positive effect on the community.

Moreover, the language of the psalm reflects the three components of the covenant formula. First, the confession that the Lord, already acknowledged in verse 27, is their God: "You are my God, and I will praise you [or, "give thanks to you"]; you are my God, and I will exalt you" (118:28). It appropriately comes after the universal praise of Psalm 117 and the acknowledgment of God's love and faithfulness. And as they confess that Yahweh is their God, they are implicitly confessing that they are Yahweh's people (the first two parts of the covenant formula: "I will be your God, and you will be my people"). But the third element of the formula, the presence of God in their midst, though not mentioned here per se, is represented by the temple (118:26). So as the era of warfare and trust in human resources fades into the past (118:7, 8–9), their renewed faith, made in terms of the ancient covenant formula, marks the new era: "The LORD has done this, and it is marvelous in our eyes" (118:23). Jeremiah declares that the monumental event of the return and restoration will become the new theological watchword of Israel (Jer. 16:14–15). See the sidebar "The Covenant Formula" in the unit on Psalm 79.

Teaching the Text

Utilizing the "Key Themes" above, we can draw two lessons from the many potential ones that could be taken from this psalm. First, we may put forth the idea that the psalm depicts Israel on the verge of disaster (118:5–7, 10–12, 13), and sometimes seemingly doomed to ruin (118:18) and abandonment (118:22a), but the Lord has rescued them (118:14, 18b, 21, 22b). Indeed, it was in the midst of these seemingly hopeless situations that Israel learned that their weakness was the Lord's strength, and the lesson resounded strong and clear: "It is better to take refuge in the LORD than to trust in humans" (118:8–9). It is in our weakness, not our strength, that we learn how strong God is to save (note Paul's affirmation in Rom. 8:26: "The Spirit helps us in our weakness"). Paul learned this lesson from his experience with the proverbial but very real "thorn in the flesh," when the Lord reassured him: "My grace is sufficient for you, for my power is made perfect in weakness" (2 Cor. 12:9). In 1 Corinthians 1:25 the apostle wrenches this truth from his experience of proclaiming the gospel: "For the foolishness of God is wiser than human wisdom, and the weakness of God is stronger than human strength." Our psalmist also observes this verity as he surveys Israel's history, and he exclaims: "The LORD's right hand has done mighty things!" (Ps. 118:15, 16). Quite importantly, Israel was, as the metaphor implies, almost passed by because of their insignificance, but the Lord elevated them to a position of importance (118:22), and given the five occurrences of the Lord's "love" in the psalm, we can safely attribute that to his love. This is the lesson of Deuteronomy 7:7–11, which informs Israel that, if the Lord had considered their numbers ("You were the fewest of all peoples"), he would have bypassed this nation on that score alone: "But it was because the LORD loved ['hb] you and kept the oath he swore to your ancestors that he brought you out with a mighty hand and redeemed you from the land of slavery. . . . Know therefore that the LORD your God is God." The confession Israel makes in the psalm (118:27–28) is virtually the same that Moses calls them to. The "stone the builders rejected" (118:22a) is equivalent to the potential devaluation of this people ("You were the fewest of all peoples") mentioned by the Deuteronomy text.

Since Jesus was so clear in his choice of verses 22 and 23 when he explained his rejection by his generation, this would be an appropriate place in the sermon/lesson to cite that incident (Mark 12:10–11) and observe that Jesus is putting himself in the place of Israel, which "the builders rejected,"[4] and declaring that God, whom we may call the Master Architect, bypassed the poor judgment of the "builders" and imposed his design on history, both literally and messianically, and accomplished one of the marvels of all salvation history ("It is marvelous in our eyes").

The second point is certainly a companion of the first, especially in the sense that the Lord's choice of the weak and insignificant to accomplish his will is a sign of the power of his love. His love, in fact, is the real power that works his saving will, and human resources cannot match trusting his love. The centrality of God's love (*hesed*) is the key to understanding the covenant, and it is the key attribute of his nature (Exod. 34:6). Its centrality in this psalm represents the centrality of God's love as it occurs in his covenant commitment (also Deut. 7:9, "keeping his covenant of love [*hesed*] to a thousand generations of those who love him and keep his commandments"). John's Gospel recognizes the supremacy of God's love (John 3:16). Depending on the nature and biblical understanding of our audience, we might even stress the covenant formula that is embedded in this psalm to demonstrate God's faithful commitment to carrying through with his love (see "Theological Insights"). At this important juncture of history this community confesses that "the LORD is God," a virtual acknowledgment of the Lord's exclusive existence, that they are God's people, and that God is with them.

Illustrating the Text

Praying out of our weakness

Church Fathers: Even in our prayers we find that we need to take refuge in the Lord, for we sometimes mark out the Lord's route for accomplishing our desires and expect him to stamp them with his approval. But our prayers often arise out of our weakness, and that includes our inability to know God's will and trust him, so especially in our prayers we take refuge in God rather than trust our human strategies (118:8–9). Paul speaks of how the "Spirit helps us in our weakness" and prays the prayer that our faith is too weak to pray or our insight is too defective to perceive (Rom. 8:26–27). Before Augustine was converted to Christ, he headed for Rome to teach, and his mother went with him to the port of departure, weeping and pleading with him not to go. In his *Confessions*, Augustine wrote:

> What was it, my God, that she sought from you with so many great commissions, except that you would not let me sail away. But in your deepest counsels you heard the crux of her desire: you had no care for what she then sought, so that you might do for me what she forever sought. . . . She did not know how great a joy you would fashion for her out of my absence. She knew nothing of this, and therefore she wept and lamented. By such torments the remnant of Eve within her was made manifest, and with groans she sought what she had brought forth with groans."[5]

H. C. G. Moule summed up the work of the Spirit in that situation: "Did He not so intercede for Monnica, and in her, when she sought with prayers and tears to keep her rebellious Augustine by her, and the Lord let him fly from her side—to Italy, to Ambrose, and so to conversion?"[6]

Allow life, not death, to reign.

Quote: David Wolpe. The plain meaning of 118:17 ("I will not die but live") is that the psalmist, even though threatened by death, will nevertheless live. One Hasidic rabbi, however, saw a different nuance in the statement and interpreted it as, "I will not die while I am alive."[7] The idea is that, as long as we exist in this world, we should allow life to reign and not death. Wolpe comments, "To the Jewish way of thinking, the shame of a life ill-lived is not only in having wasted time wanting that which one could not have, but in *not having pursued that which one could have had, should have had*." He also quotes Rabbi Menachem Mendle of Kotzk (eighteenth century), who was asked what had been most important to his teacher who had recently died; he thought for a moment and replied, "Whatever he was doing at the moment."

"I Have Hidden Your Word in My Heart That I Might Not Sin against You"

Big Idea

Knowing and doing the will of God, and living by it, are the joy and substance of life.

Key Themes

- God is the Master Teacher, and the Torah (God's will) is the life-saving curriculum.
- Knowing and doing the Torah is the joy of life.
- God's law is the revelation of his love.
- God's law is the liberating force for his servants.
- God's promises are the sustaining power of life.

Understanding the Text

This psalm is an alphabetic acrostic,[1] containing all twenty-two letters of the Hebrew alphabet (thus twenty-two strophes), and each strophe has eight verses, all of which begin with the letter of the alphabet appropriate to that stanza. The main topic, of course, is the Torah, named by ten different terms (see the sidebar "Ten Words for 'Law' in Psalm 119") and examined from multiple angles of faith and life. The psalm's literary type can also be viewed from several angles, since there are elements of the hymn that praise the Torah and laments grieving over the opposition to the power and merits of the Torah, as well as elements of wisdom piety. Of course, the safest literary category is a Torah psalm.[2]

The Text in Context

The Egyptian Hallel is bookended by two acrostic poems, Psalms 112 and 119, both celebrating the Torah: Psalm 112 blesses those "who fear the LORD, who find great delight in his commands [*mitswot*]" (112:1), and Psalm 119 celebrates the Torah in all 176 verses except verse 122, which has no word for Torah or law[3] (see the comments on 119:122).

Other Torah psalms are Psalms 1 and 19, strategically placed in the collection to highlight the importance of God's word (see the sidebar "Torah Psalms" in the unit on Ps. 19 and "The Text in Context" in the unit on Ps. 20).

Like Lamentations 3, where the poet speaks for the nation, Psalm 119 also has a corporate dimension, and the "I" of the poem is the covenant community praying for the success of the restoration community, especially the young potential leaders of the community (119:9).

Outline/Structure

Rather than duplicating the outline provided by the acrostic pattern, I have followed that outline in "Interpretive Insights" and not repeated it here.

Historical and Cultural Background

Historians sometimes characterize the fall of Judah to the Babylonians in 586 BC as the end of the history of the nation Israel and the beginning of Judaism. As Kaufmann says: "It was not only the people that went into exile, but their religion as well."[4] The people's survival in a foreign land, without their central sanctuary and sacrifice, was dependent on the reformation of their religion. The leading reformation principle was that they gave up their idolatry and adopted monotheism.[5] Alongside that revolutionary development, the centrality of the sanctuary was replaced by the invisible presence of God, who became their sanctuary (Ezek. 11:16; Hag. 2:4), and principles that regulated their new life were incorporated in God's word that came to be hidden in their hearts (Ps. 119:11). Zenger calls this developing emphasis on the Torah as represented by Psalm 119 "proto-rabbinic."[6]

Interpretive Insights

119:1–8 *Aleph*. **Strophe 1.** This strophe begins with a pronouncement of blessing (119:1–3) and continues with a prayer that petitions the Lord for help in obeying his decrees (119:4–8). The prayer begun here continues to the end of the psalm (119:4–176). The opening verses are reminiscent of the beginning of the Psalter (119:1–2; cf. 1:1). The fact that Psalms 112 and 119 form an *inclusio* to the Egyptian Hallel (see "The Text in Context") is further evidenced by the use of "blessed" (*'ashre*) in 112:1 and 119:1 and 2. The tone, however, is almost totally positive (except for 119:3a), and the two ways of Psalm 1 have been replaced with "his [the Lord's] ways" (119:3b). This positive tone is intentional in order to stress the way of Torah that now governs, or must govern, this new community's way of life. The spiritual reformation that had occurred during the exile put Israel on the way of Torah, which Psalm 119 celebrates.

119:9–16 *Beth.* Strophe 2.

119:9 *How can a young person stay on the path of purity?* This question, posed of youth ("young person"), is answered in the second half of the verse: "By living according to your word."

119:10–11 *I seek you with all my heart . . . I have hidden your word in my heart.* Seeking God with all one's heart is a Deuteronomic idea (Deut. 4:29) and forms Jeremiah's message to the exiles (Jer. 29:13). Note also that hiding Yahweh's word in the psalmist's heart is a guard against sinning against God.[7] This is a prescription for the control of youthful passions.[8] (See Prov. 8:10–11; 16:16.) Further, the new community had little hope of renewal without the participation of the young men, potential leaders of the community. In fact, the early introduction of this audience of young men may suggest that this group of the community is so critical to the success of the restoration that the poem is basically directed to them, the students of that generation.

119:17–24 *Gimel.* Strophe 3.

119:17 *Be good to your servant.* Now our poet identifies himself as "your servant" (119:17, 23; see also 119:38, 49, 65, 76, 84, 122, 124, 125, 135, 140, 176), in contrast to "the princes" (NIV: "rulers," 119:23).[9] When the psalmist refers to himself as "your servant," he may very well be identifying with David, whose devotion to the Torah was also of great acclaim (Ps. 19; note that David refers to himself as "your servant" in 19:11 and 13; also 69:17).[10]

119:18 *that I may see wonderful things in your law.* We have a window here into the "classroom" of the postexilic community, for the "wonderful things" in verse 18 are likely the matters that Deuteronomy speaks of as being "too difficult" (Deut. 17:8 uses *yippale'* as "difficult matters," same root *pl'* as "wonderful things") for the local judges, and for which they must appeal to the priests, Levites, and judges. For these, says our psalmist, one must appeal to God for understanding, although that does not rule out human arbitrators (see also the comments on 131:1).

119:23 *rulers sit together and slander me . . . Your statutes . . . are my counselors.* Quite interestingly, we see another aspect of the learning experience, represented by the "rulers" (lit., "princes"), who scorn the psalmist, but he still finds the Lord's "statutes" to be his delight and even his "counselors."

119:25–32 *Daleth.* Strophe 4.

119:25–26 *I am laid low in the dust . . . I gave an account of my ways and you answered me.* The suppliant, perhaps because of his sins or the sins of Israel ("I" may be the corporate "I"), was depressed ("My soul cleaves to the dust," 119:25 RSV).[11] So he confessed them, and Yahweh answered (119:26). Perhaps as a result, the psalmist chose "the way of truth" (NIV: "way of faithfulness," 119:30) rather than the "way of falsehood" (NIV: "deceitful ways," 119:29).

teach me your decrees. Yahweh as Teacher figures prominently in Psalm 119. The critical role of teaching in ancient Israel is a Deuteronomic idea (e.g., Moses teaches Israel [Deut. 4:1], and they are to teach their children [Deut. 6:7]) (e.g., Ps. 119:12, 26, 64, 66, 68, 108, 124, 135, 171). Once in Psalm 119 other "teachers" are referenced (119:99). However, the teaching function is mostly assigned to Yahweh himself, who is obviously the Master Teacher (e.g., 119:12, 26, 64, 66, 68, 108, 124, 135, 171), and the suppliant is the pupil "learning" God's laws (e.g., 119:7, 71, 73).

119:33–40 *He.* **Strophe 5.** The urgency of the psalmist's petitions is seen in the fact that the first seven verses of this strophe begin with imperatives.

119:35 *Direct me in the path of your commands.* After having affirmed in strophe 4 that he had rejected the "way of falsehood" (NIV: "deceitful ways," 119:29) and chosen the "way of truth" (NIV: "way of faithfulness," 119:30), he now prays that Yahweh will guide him and teach him the way of the commandments.

119:41–48 *Waw.* **Strophe 6.** This strophe begins each line with the Hebrew letter *waw*, which also means "and." The poet did not have many other options open to him since very few Hebrew words begin with this letter. In fact, Koehler and Baumgartner's lexicon of biblical Hebrew contains only thirteen entries for it.[12] Hakham observes that prefixing the first verb in each of the eight verses with the letter *waw* ("and") in effect expresses a sense of longing: for example, "And may your unfailing love come to me, LORD, your salvation according to your word" (119:41, author's translation).[13] Thus while strophe 5 ends with the psalmist's longing for Yahweh's precepts (119:40a), strophe 6 is essentially an elongated expression of that longing.

119:42, 46 *anyone who taunts me.* The suppliant's engagement with the Torah is not devoid of opposition (119:42), even though it is worthy to be rehearsed before kings (119:46).

119:49–56 *Zayin.* **Strophe 7.**

119:49 *Remember your word.* The choice of words that begin with the seventh letter of the alphabet, *zayin*, is not as limited as the words that begin with *waw*, but our poet nevertheless begins three verses with the same verb "remember" (*zkr*, 119:49, 52, 55). Obviously we remember what has already happened, or what we have already learned, while we only contemplate the future. The past is our source of knowledge that supplies the portrait of who God is and what he has done.

119:51 *The arrogant mock me unmercifully.* Again, the conflict that students faced in the community is suggested by verse 51. The mockers try to reduce the Torah keepers to powerlessness, but do not succeed.[14]

119:57–64 *Heth.* Strophe 8.

119:57–58 *You are my portion,* Lord . . . *I have sought your face with all my heart.* The psalmist declares that the Lord is his "portion" (see also 16:5; 73:26; 142:5)—that is his privilege as well as responsibility, as it is the Levites'. If the writer is not a Levite (see the comments on 16:5), who has no landed portion but whose "portion" is the Lord (Num. 18:20; Deut. 10:9; 18:1), he is using this term metaphorically to express his total devotion to God (see also Ps. 119:55 and 62).[15] That is evident in his declaration that he has "sought your [Yahweh's] face [or, "prayed"] with all my heart." The prayer that he offered may be summed up in the brief petition in the second half of the verse: "be gracious to me according to your promise."

119:59 *I have considered my ways and have turned my steps to your statutes.* Verse 59 represents a turning point in the psalmist's life. He has considered his "ways," and that has resulted in turning his devotion—total devotion—to the law, even despite the opposition, though the wicked "bind me with ropes" (119:61a).[16]

119:64 *The earth is filled with your love,* Lord; *teach me your decrees.* The strophe closes with a declaration that "the earth is filled with your love [*hesed*]," the magnificent truth in which the psalmist lives and the splendid reality in which he prays, "Teach me your decrees" (119:64). Who would not like to know the "decrees" of a God like this!

119:65–72 *Teth.* Strophe 9.

119:67 *Before I was afflicted I went astray, but now I obey your word.* The interesting perspective in verse 67 on the difference the commandments have made in the psalmist's life is illuminating. The English translations generally render the first verb as "I was afflicted" (and so the LXX), but Hakham connects it to the same root in Ecclesiastes 3:10, where it has the sense of "be engaged/ busy with," and he translates it "studied." Either translation, "afflicted" or "engaged/studied," fits the context, but since he has just spoken in verse 66 about the difference the commandments have made in his behavior and here (Ps. 119:67) refers specifically to his former sinful conduct (unintentional),[17] "engaged/studied" is an attractive alternative, especially in the context of the classroom setting of the psalm. "But now" is the line of separation between the suppliant's former life and the life that has been changed by his engagement with the Torah. He speaks of the same turning point described in verse 59.

119:73–80 *Yodh.* Strophe 10.

119:73 *Your hands made me and formed me.* This strophe begins with an echo from the Song of Moses (Deut. 32:6–7), assuring Israel that God is their Father and Creator.

119:75–76 *in faithfulness you have afflicted me. May your unfailing love be my comfort.* Verse 75 picks up another Deuteronomic idea, sounded in the previous strophe (119:67, 71), that the Lord has "afflicted" the psalmist (see the comments on 119:67). The idea occurs also in Deuteronomy 8:3, to say that God afflicted the Israelites in the wilderness, "causing you to hunger and then feeding you with manna, . . . to teach you that man does not live on bread alone but on every word that comes from the mouth of the LORD." The stress on the verb "afflicted" matches perfectly, as Moses assures us that affliction has a purpose, and its product is to teach us that the true essential is God's word. Behind that principle is God's "unfailing love" (*hesed*; Ps. 119:76), which is parallel to Yahweh's "faithfulness" in the previous verse (see also 100:5 for these two attributes together). Yet, God's love is of little value to us human creatures unless God is faithful to distribute it; and already we have been reminded that the earth is filled with God's love (119:64).

119:78 *May the arrogant be put to shame for wronging me without cause.* A parallel track in the psalmist's life is the opposition posed by the "wicked" (NIV: "arrogant"), who, in the previous strophe (119:69), have "plastered" (NIV: "smeared") him with lies.[18] Now the psalmist says they have "dealt perversely" with him (NIV: "wronging me"), perhaps causing the faithful to distance themselves from him.

119:79 *May those who fear you turn to me.* The psalmist prays that "those who fear" the Lord will be restored to fellowship.

119:81–88 *Kaph.* **Strophe 11.** Zenger's comment is well taken when he refers to strophes 11 and 12 as the "compositional center,"[19] for they emphasize certain ideas that justify this label. The poet recounts personal and communal suffering as he waits for Yahweh's comfort, which is founded in his unfailing love (*hesed*; 119:88). Yet another word of assurance caps the ideas of these two strophes as strophe 12 declares the eternal nature of God's word (119:89 and 93; in the Hebrew, "eternal" comes first in these two sentences), rooted in creation (119:90), and always at Yahweh's service (119:91).

119:81–82 *My soul faints with longing . . . "When will you comfort me?"* The affliction of the suppliant surfaces again (see 119:75) and reveals the lapse of time between the suppliant's desire and God's fulfillment of his word (119:82).[20] The poet partly does this by using a Hebrew verb that begins with the letter *kaph* three times in the strophe (*klh*, "to fade away/pine"; "to be finished"): "My soul *faints*" (119:81); "My eyes *fail*" (119:82); "They almost *wiped* me *from* . . ." (119:87). The emphasis falls on his affliction and waiting for Yahweh's help. In fact, he is the "suffering servant," no less, although he does not claim to be suffering for Israel's sake (cf. Isa. 53:4–5), even though that may be written between the lines.

119:83 *like a wineskin in the smoke.* This simile is difficult, especially since the wineskin would dry up in heat. Kirkpatrick mentions the practice of improving the quality of wine by putting it in a leather bottle and smoking it. However, as he observes, regardless of the purpose of the practice, the image here is negative, since the suppliant affirms that despite the treatment, he does not forget God's decrees.[21]

119:89–96 *Lamedh*. **Strophe 12.**

119:89–90 *Your word . . . stands firm in the heavens . . . you established the earth*. After affirming the eternal status of God's word in the heavens, our poet reaffirms God's creative work, as he did in verse 73 (see also Prov. 3:19; 8:22–29). The order and enduring nature of creation form a link that, most of all, reveals the nature of the Creator.

119:91–93 *for all things serve you*. The creation and the Creator are not synonymous, but creation serves the Creator, "for all things serve you" (Ps. 119:91b); and that is most obvious in the "delight" and the preservation of life that the Torah has brought to the psalmist (119:92–93).

119:96 *To all perfection I see a limit, but your commands are boundless.* Verse 96 sounds very much like Ecclesiastes, "where every earthly enterprise," says Kidner, "has its day and comes to nothing, and where only in God and His commandments do we get beyond these frustrating limits."[22] It is close in meaning to the Preacher's final word: "Now all has been heard; here is the conclusion of the matter: Fear God and keep his commandments, for this is the duty of all mankind" (Eccles. 12:13).

119:97–104 *Mem*. **Strophe 13.** Our poet does an interesting thing in this strophe. Rather than finding nouns or verbs that begin with *mem*, he uses the interrogative word *mah* ("how," "what"; e.g., 119:97: "How I love your law!") to begin the sentence. Or he prefixes the preposition *min* ("from") to the first word of the sentence to express the comparative degree (e.g., 119:100: NIV: "I have more undersanding than the elders, for I obey your precepts"; but see my objection below), or to express the prepositional idea "from" (e.g., 119:101: lit., "From every evil path I have kept my feet").

119:99–100 *more insight than all my teachers . . . more understanding than the elders*. The NIV's translation of verses 99 and 100 elevates the student over the teacher, which is hardly intended here. It is better to translate the preposition *min* as "from" rather than reading it as the comparative degree ("more than"): "I have gained insight from all my teachers; indeed [*ki*][23] I meditate on your statutes. I have gained understanding from the elders; indeed [*ki*] I have kept your precepts" (author's translation). Our psalmist is expressing his gratitude for his instructors and is certainly not so arrogant as to boast that he is smarter than they are.

119:103 *How sweet are your words to my taste*. The translation of this phrase depends on a verb (*niml[e]tsu*) that occurs only here in the Hebrew Bible. Some interpreters relate it to the Hebrew noun *m[e]litsah* ("pleasant speech").

However, the last half of the sentence clearly refers to "honey," implying the idea of "sweet."

119:105–12 *Nun.* Strophe 14.

119:105 *a lamp for my feet, a light on my path.* Although Psalm 119 is not given to articulating specific laws, the presentation of the Torah under the ten different synonyms (see the sidebar "Ten Words for 'Law' in Psalm 119"), as well as the benefits of the Torah life under various metaphors, gives the reader a picture of the world set right under the reign of the sovereign God. Here the metaphor of light and lamp[24] suggests a life radiated with light, God's initial creation (Gen. 1:3–5), and distinguished from the uncreated darkness that could never overcome the light (cf. John 1:5).

119:106 *I have taken an oath . . . that I will follow your righteous laws.* While the psalmist has exceeded the requirements for keeping the commandments by taking an oath, the rabbis say this suggests that one fulfills the commandments more zealously when one takes an oath.[25]

119:111 *Your statutes are my heritage . . . the joy of my heart.* The end result of the Torah life is indicated by another significant metaphor, "my heritage" (see 119:57 for a similar metaphor, "portion"; see also the comments on 74:2), which alludes to the land of Canaan (see Exod. 15:17). In that inherited land of the Torah life, joy is the tone of existence.

119:113–20 *Samekh.* Strophe 15.

119:113, 115 *I hate double-minded people . . . Away from me, you evildoers.* This strophe contains the only instance in the psalm of a direct address to someone ("evildoers") other than God. The evildoers' merit of this direct word of rebuke points to the trouble and opposition they have caused the psalmist individually and the community at large. The term "double-minded" may suggest the nature of their opposition—at times sympathetic and at other times blatantly opposed to the Torah. The use of the verb "stray" and the noun "deceitfulness" (NIV: "delusions," 119:118) supports this view. Indeed, the transition of the psalmist and the community to the centrality of the Torah is not accomplished easily, but along the way of this psalm we see the progress that has been made.

119:121–28 *Ayin.* Strophe 16.

119:122 *Ensure your servant's well-being; do not let the arrogant oppress me.* Three times in this strophe the suppliant refers to himself as "your [the Lord's] servant" (119:122, 124, 125). This conviction may very well justify his prayer that God will "be surety for your servant for good" (119:122a; NIV: "Ensure your servant's well-being"), which means that God should stand in as a guarantee for his well-being—quite a bold request, in the spirit of the audacious Job (Job 17:3). Yet, the ground of his confidence is ultimately in Yahweh's "love" (*hesed*), which Yahweh has spoken in his decrees. In fact, the parallelism of verse 124 suggests the virtual synonymity of the words "according to your love [*hesed*]" and the imperative "teach me your decrees." Moreover, the psalmist's love for God's "commands" is a response to God's love, not the reason for it (119:127–28).

Verse 122 is the only verse in Psalm 119 that does not have a word for the law (see "The Text in Context").[26] The reason for this is a mystery, since there seems to be no literary explanation for it.[27] I suggest that it may be that the suppliant, having affirmed his own obedience to the will of God ("what is righteous and just"; lit., "I have done judgment and righteousness" [author's translation], 119:121) and having assessed the critical situation ("your law is being broken," 119:126b), challenges God, without any mediating agent (Torah) and without delay, to act (119:126). The absence of the Torah word in verse 122 then is intended to call our attention to this challenge. One is reminded of Moses's challenge to Yahweh, when Yahweh informs him that Yahweh will not go up to Canaan with them but will send his angel. Moses counters with his own challenge that rules out any intermediary agent: "If your Presence does not go with us, do not send us up from here" (Exod. 33:15). Also verse 123 sounds as if the suppliant is almost apologetic about the absence of the Torah word in verse 122 when he laments, "My eyes fail, looking for your salvation, looking for your righteous promise." Essentially, that verse becomes a symbol of the absence of God's promise.

119:126 *It is time for you to act,* LORD; *your law is being broken.* The psalmist boldly says this to God, in view of the delay that he and the community have experienced as they wait on the fulfillment of God's promises and observe the brash violation of God's laws (119:126).

119:129–36 *Pe.* Strophe 17.

119:135 *Make your face shine on your servant.* Verse 135a is an echo of the priestly benediction (Num. 6:25) and a virtual equivalent of verse 124, where the suppliant prays that God may deal with him "according to your love [*hesed*]," which sets the context for his petition in the second half of the verse, "Teach me your decrees" (119:135b). Here God's shining face, the equivalent of his love, is the interpretive context of God's instruction. That is, the Torah is God's revelation of himself, of his love and of his favor.

119:137–44 *Tsadhe.* Strophe 18.

119:137–38 *You are righteous,* LORD, *and your laws are right.* Verse 137 continues the description of the character of God (119:124, 135), with whom the Torah originates. The adjective "righteous" (*tsadiq*) in the first half of verse 137 is parallel to the adjective "upright" (NIV: "right"), which describes God's laws in the second half of the verse. Verses 137 and 138 reflect the words of Moses's prayer in Deuteronomy 32:4 ("The Rock, his work is perfect, for all his ways are *justice*. A God of *faithfulness* and without iniquity, *just* and *upright* is he," ESV), using the Hebrew words for "justice," "faithfulness," "just," and "upright." There could be no stronger encouragement than to have God reveal himself to the current situation in Mosaic tenderness and strength.

119:141, 143 *Though I am lowly . . . Trouble and distress have come upon me.* The Hebrew word behind "lowly" in verse 141 also means "young," which reminds us of the description of the speaker as a "young person" in verse 9. And as we have observed, the mature level of the suppliant's understanding and the long and strong opposition he has faced are an overlay of the poet's experience with those, regardless of age, who have committed themselves to the Torah. Their lives have not been easy, for "trouble and distress," in hot pursuit of the psalmist, have again "found" him (NIV: "have come upon me," 119:143).

119:145–52 *Qoph.* Strophe 19.

119:149 *in accordance with your love . . . according to your laws.* Just as the Torah defines God's character (119:124, 135, 137), it also assures the psalmist that God lives by the laws that define him (119:149; also 119:132).[28]

119:150–51 *Those who devise wicked schemes are near . . . Yet you are near,* Lord. Our suppliant is still conscious of his opponents who actively scheme against the Torah and his devotion to it, and he is confident of the Lord's nearness that is far more effective and powerful than his enemies' nearness.

119:153–60 *Resh.* Strophe 20. This strophe echoes the language of the exodus, employing the verbs "see/look" (119:153, 158, 159; see Exod. 6:6, etc.) and "redeem" (119:154; see Exod. 6:6, etc.), and the noun "affliction" (NIV: "suffering," 119:153; see Exod. 3:7). As we have seen in other instances (see "Theological Insights" in the unit on Ps. 23), the exodus becomes the literary artist's palette from which he chooses his "colors" to describe events in his own and Israel's life.

119:161–68 *Sin and Shin.* Strophe 21.

119:161–62 *Rulers persecute me without cause . . . I rejoice . . . like one who finds great spoil.* Verse 161a sounds like the familiar battle assessment that we find in the imprecatory psalms, and the strong implication is that, while the rulers, perhaps, would think the psalmist ought to fear them, the opposite is the case: "My heart trembles at your [Yahweh's] word" (119:161b). The battle imagery continues in verse 162, implying that when the battle is over ("peace," 119:165),[29] the joy of the battle won and the dividing of the spoil is like the joy of the Torah (*'imrah*, 119:162a, = "word").[30]

119:163–64 *I hate and detest falsehood . . . Seven times a day I praise you.* As Wilcock says: "To develop a real love for it [law] is to develop a corresponding distaste for the illusions and the perversions of truth in which the world deals."[31] Indeed, the study of God's word must become an encompassing endeavor, signified by the psalmist praying "seven times a day" (119:164; see also 1 Thess. 5:17).[32] Yet it is not the number but the constancy of prayer that the suppliant has in mind; and whatever that number may be, it is totally sufficient (seven taken as the perfect number).

119:166 *I wait for your salvation,* LORD. The echoes from Jacob's final blessing of his sons reflected in this verse ("I wait for your salvation, O LORD" [Gen. 49:18 ESV]) are most appropriate, especially on the precipice of the transition from exile to a new age, much like Jacob's sons were facing. This blessing *before* the Egyptian bondage and now *after* the Babylonian bondage, is a type of *inclusio*, and it would not likely be lost on the psalmist's hearers.

119:169–76 *Taw.* **Strophe 22.** We might have thought that the last strophe would be a word of total confidence in God's word and triumph over its enemies, but it is less, in that it is a summary of the psalmist's state of heart, still crying out to God (119:169), still trusting God's promise (119:170), still singing a grateful song in celebration of the Lord's decrees (119:171–72). He is still conscious of his need for the Lord's help (119:173), longing for his salvation (119:174), praying for life (119:175), and confessing that he has strayed like a lost sheep (119:176). It is the quality of the believer's life that can never allow him or her to put sin out of consciousness and forget that where sin abounds, grace much more abounds (Rom. 5:20). See "Teaching the Text" below.

Theological Insights

We know that during the exile some monumental changes took place in the developing Jewish community, changes that came to maturity in the Second Temple period. In the absence of sacrifice, prayers (also reading of sacrificial texts) came to be a substitute for sacrifice, and in the absence of the central institution of the temple, the Torah (the law) came more and more to prominence. Already in this section of Book 5, we see signs of that development. Psalms 112 and 119, for example, both psalms celebrating the Torah and both acrostic psalms, bookend the Egyptian Hallel. They are a signature of the growing centrality of the Torah in Jewish life. It is hard to measure the devastating effect the destruction of the temple had on this community, but its ability to regenerate itself, by God's grace, is a remarkable sign of a vitality that could not be suffocated, even by immeasurable losses. As Israel pondered their inestimable losses, Jeremiah, himself a prophet of the exile, assured them that the return and restoration from exile would be no less a covenant event than had been the exodus from Egypt and that this new covenant would involve writing the Torah on their hearts (Jer. 31:31–34). While the temple was vulnerable to the vengeful passions of Israel's enemies, the Torah written on their hearts could not be the object of human warfare, and its beauty and treasure could never be sent into exile—this was part of the worth of the Torah. It was internal and so could not be destroyed by enemies of God. Moreover, this ultimate transaction of grace would be the final operation to establish the relationship between Yahweh and Israel that God had intended from the beginning: "I will be their God, and they will be my people" (Jer. 31:33). Again, that was something the Babylonians, or any other enemy, could not destroy. Psalm 112 is the proclamation that that day is coming, and Psalm 119 is a celebration that it has arrived, at least in its incipient form: "I have hidden your word in my heart that I might not sin against you" (119:11). See also Psalm 40:8; Proverbs 7:3; 22:18.

Teaching the Text

The preacher/teacher can turn in many directions to take advantage of the multivalent nature of Psalm 119. Obviously I can suggest only a few of these. I propose that the focus fall on one or two strophes, not more, or that the preacher/teacher choose a main topic found in the psalm, such as God's will (law) hidden in our hearts as the force of life (119:11), or unceasing prayer as a way of life (119:165), or the grace/love (*hesed*) that undergirds the whole universe. Not many of us can afford, either in time or energy, to preach 190 sermons on this psalm as did the seventeenth-century English divine Thomas Manton, preaching three sermons a week.[33] Yet, its riches are unfathomable and ought not be limited to one or two sermons.

We may follow Wilcock's example, using strophe 19 (119:145–52), or other strophes, as the basis of our sermon/lesson. He gives three things believers can rely on. First is God's love and laws (119:149). Obviously there is so much in this psalm about God's love (*hesed*), including the idea that it fills the earth (119:64) and is expressed in God's decrees (119:124, 135), and John reminds us that God's "commands are not burdensome" (1 John 5:3). Indeed, they are the psalmist's delight (119:24, 92–93, etc.), revealing God's true character. The emphasis on God's love underwrites well the powerful words of John Newton about grace from his new-covenant perspective: "Two things I know: I am a great sinner, and Christ is a great Savior."[34]

The second thing believers can rely on is God's nearness (119:150–51). By means of the Torah our suppliant has learned that wherever he is, in whatever circumstances, God is there.

The third thing is God's constancy (119:152). While this theme is sounded in several places of the psalm, the middle strophes (strophes 11 and 12, especially 12 [119:89–96]) present this idea, particularly in the "eternal" aspect of God's Torah that is emphasized in verses 89 and 93 (NIV: "never") by putting the term "eternal" first in these two sentences (see the comments on 119:89–96). We should remember that the world's evils, many of which the psalmist has encountered, are no match for God's love.

Illustrating the Text

Freedom in servitude

Hymns: "God's Help Sure," by Thomas Toke Lynch. One of the truly revolutionary principles that served the exilic community with liberating power was the idea that when the law became personal and internal, it lost its restrictive character and became the liberating force of God's people (Deut. 6:6; Ps. 37:31; Prov. 3:3; 7:3; Isa. 51:7; Jer. 31:33). The reason is that it binds us to God, who is the true Liberator; guards us from sinful ways that would distance us from him (Ps. 119:11); and assures us of God's love that fills the world (119:64). It is the shepherd who finds us in our wanderings and leads us home (119:176). Far from being a burden, when God reveals his will through his word, we discover that we are surrounded with God's liberating forces:

> Say not, my soul, "From whence
> Can God relieve my care?"
> Remember that Omnipotence
> Has servants everywhere.

This liberating word summarized here in Lynch's hymn was a welcome theme to a people who had spent seventy years as captives in a foreign land.

The Torah is a handrail.

Quote: Konrad Schaefer. We sometimes mistakenly identify the laws of the Hebrew Bible as regulations and restrictive rules—and those are included—but the Torah is much wider and richer than that. Schaefer offers a very helpful description of Torah in the Bible:

> Law, according to the use of the word Torah and its synonyms in Psalm 119, means wisdom or God's will. This poem represents an understanding of law akin to the *regula* of the ancient monastic tradition, a balanced ordering of human life. Law is a handrail which steadies and guides a person to walk rightly, and it represents divine revelation. Like the Torah, the first five scrolls of the Bible, which recounts God's marvelous acts and regulates human conduct to effect salvation, the law embraces all the movements of human life with God. God's law, an expression of his will, expresses perfection, and the poet gives shape to this sense in the composition of Psalm 119.[35]

Affliction and the loss of dignity can be dehumanizing.

Biography: Our psalmist is acutely aware of the "affliction/suffering" his opponents have served on him (119:50, 71, 75, 92, 153), and often affliction's companion is humiliation or the loss of dignity. In Laura Hillenbrand's book *Unbroken: A World War II Story of Survival, Resilience, and Redemption*, she describes the abuse and dehumanization that Louie Zamperini (bombardier) and Allen Phillips (pilot) endured after their crash into the sea:

> The crash of *Green Hornet* had left Louie and Phil in the most desperate physical extremity, without food, water, or shelter. But on Kwajalein, the guards sought to deprive them of something that had sustained them even as all else had been lost: dignity. This self-respect and sense of self-worth, the innermost armament of the soul, lies at the heart of humanness; to be deprived of it is to be dehumanized, to be cleaved from, and cast below, mankind. Men subjected to dehumanizing treatment experience profound wretchedness and loneliness and find that hope is almost impossible to retain. Without dignity, identity is erased. In its absence, men are defined not by themselves, but by their captors and the circumstances in which they are forced to live. One American airman, shot down and relentlessly debased by his Japanese captors, described the state of mind that his captivity created: "I was literally becoming a lesser human being."[36]

God both creates the hunger and provides the manna.

Biography: Miltos Anghelatos. Psalm 119 picks up the Deuteronomic idea that in the wilderness the Lord caused Israel to be hungry and then he fed them with manna (Deut. 8:3; Ps. 119:67, 71, 75). Miltos Anghelatos, late president of the Hellenic Scripture Union in Athens, Greece, experienced a quest for God as a young man that drove him to literature. One day, as he read a novel by Leo Tolstoy, his eyes fell on a quotation on the title page from a literary work he had never seen or heard of, the Bible. It was John 1:1. After searching his little town on the island of Corfu, he found one secondhand copy of the Bible and bought it for the price of eight pounds of potatoes that his dear mother had scraped together from the scarcities of World War II. As he read this book, he devoured it, and it devoured him, and he heard the call of God through the Scriptures to follow Jesus. His parents rejected him because they interpreted his love for the Bible and the evangelical faith as a rejection of their own church. But he had heard Jesus's call, and he went to Athens, where he was befriended by an evangelical pastor and his wife. It was the road less traveled by, but having heard the Savior's call, he followed and became an outstanding New Testament scholar and founder of the Hellenic Scripture Union of Athens, Greece.[37] When God creates the hunger, he also provides the "manna." And Jesus taught us, "Blessed are those who hunger and thirst for righteousness, for they will be filled" (Matt. 5:6).

"I Am for Peace; but . . . They Are for War"

Big Idea

The rules of the road for our journey of faith are grace and justice.

Key Themes

- Peace is a condition of the soul, as is also war.
- We are called to be pilgrims, not tourists, in our life of faith.

Understanding the Text

Psalms 120–34 are called Songs of Ascents, or less frequently, "gradual" (or "step") psalms, because they represent stages on the journey to Jerusalem or the fifteen steps of the temple. In the wider scope of their historical setting, and based on their rhetorical place in Book 5, they are the celebration of the returnees' long journey from Babylonia to Jerusalem;[1] and in the recurring cycle of history, they were sung by the Israelites on their journeys to the pilgrimage festivals in Jerusalem to which all Israelites were called three times each year (Deut. 16:16–17). The genre of Psalm 120 is that of an individual lament, although some consider it an individual psalm of thanksgiving.[2]

The Text in Context

Based on the recurring superscription of Psalms 120–34 ("A song of ascents"), this collection may have been a separate hymnal before it was installed in Book 5 of the Psalter.[3] The collection reveals an awakening consciousness of the new community and the new life the return from Babylonian exile was creating.

Outline/Structure

1. From distress to prayer (120:1–2)
2. Question about the deceitful and the answer (120:3–4)
3. The journey of peace in a world of war (120:5–7)

Historical and Cultural Background

One theory is that these psalms were written as an extended blessing on the postexilic community. The fact that they were sung by the Levites on the fifteen steps of the temple that led from the Court of the Women to the Court of Israel (*m. Middot* 2.5) suggests a later usage in the Second Temple period. While the Mishnah does not explicitly say the songs were sung on successive steps of the temple, the Tosefta is more explicit in this suggestion.[4]

Interpretive Insights

120:1 *I call on the* LORD *in my distress.* Psalm 120 speaks out of the country of exile (represented by Meshek and Kedar of verse 5). Thus, as Kidner remarks, "We join the pilgrims as they set out on a journey which, in broad outline, will bring us to Jerusalem in Psalm 122, and, in the last psalms of the group, to the ark, the priests, and the Temple servants who minister, by turns, day and night at the House of the Lord."[5] The phrase "on the LORD" comes first in the verse, emphasizing the psalmist's reliance on Yahweh rather than human resources. The nature of the distress is suggested by the "lying lips" and "deceitful tongues" of verse 2.

120:2 *Save me,* LORD, *from lying lips and from deceitful tongues.* Twice in the first two verses the divine name "LORD" (Yahweh) occurs, positioning this psalm in a strong mode of monotheistic faith. The later double use of "peace" (*shalom*) in verses 6 and 7 also has a positioning effect for peace over war, particularly since Yahweh is known as the giver of peace (Num. 6:26).

120:3 *What will he do to you . . . you deceitful tongue?* The suppliant is the speaker, and the subject seems to be Yahweh, but the verbs could be used impersonally ("What will be done to you?").[6] The problem, raised in verse 2, is the "deceitful tongue."

120:4 *with a warrior's sharp arrows, with burning coals of the broom bush.* Burning coals were often fastened to arrows in order to set their targets on fire. This is the answer to the question of verse 3: burning arrows are sharpened and ready for shooting at those who have "lying lips" and "deceitful tongues" (120:2). The root of the word for "deceitful" means "to throw" or "shoot,"[7] implying that a "deceitful" tongue, symbolically at least, shoots arrows.

120:5 *Meshek . . . Kedar.* Meshek was one of the sons of Japheth (Gen. 10:2), and his descendants lived in Asia Minor by the Black Sea (see Ezek. 38:2). Kedar was among the sons of Ishmael (Gen. 25:13) who lived in the Arabian Desert. They are called those "who draw the bow" (ESV) in Isaiah 66:19, since their ancestral father, Ishmael, was "an archer" (Gen. 21:20), reflected here in the "warrior's sharp arrows" of verse 4. These two places were in distantly opposite directions, Meshek to the north and Kedar to the south

The white broom bush (see 120:4) grows in the Negev on sandy hills and in other soils and reaches a height of six and a half feet, sometimes growing even to tree height. Its top is wide and its trunk narrow, giving shade in that hot climate, as it did for Elijah on his escape from Jezebel (1 Kings 19:3–8). The branches and roots are sometimes used to make a fire, and their embers can burn for a long time after the fire has died down, sometimes for days, and some traditions claim months (*y. Peah* 1.1; *b. Bava Batra* 74b). In February to March it blossoms with profuse white flowers.[a]

[a] See Hareuveni, *Tree and Shrub*, 27–33.

and southeast of Israel, in the Arabian peninsula.[8] It would hardly appear that the psalmist's wanderings were through such a large territory, and if we take them figuratively, the distance issue falls away—they represent the heathen place of exile (Babylonia), which was opposed to peace and dedicated to war.

120:7 *I am for peace; but when I speak, they are for war.* I have suggested that the Songs of Ascents were a celebration of the return from exile (Ezra 1–2), most likely written after the return, and later used as songs to celebrate the religious pilgrimages to Jerusalem. In view of that, it seems appropriate that the first psalm of the series should locate the celebrant in a foreign land, here metaphorically called Meshek and Kedar (120:5). Thus this description of the psalmist's position for "peace" compared to his captors' position for "war" is appropriate, reinforcing the symbolic meaning of Meshek and Kedar (representing Babylonia) as warring peoples. The literal rendering of the first line is "I [am] peace" (cf. a similar verbless clause in 109:4, "I [am] prayer"; NIV: "I am a man of prayer"), emphasizing the real substance of the psalmist's thought and life.

Theological Insights

Psalm 120 begins our "ascent" to the sanctuary in Jerusalem or, we could say, begins our journey into God's presence. It helps us realize that we sometimes live on the margins of this world (Meshek and Kedar), distant from God, and our real hope is to turn to the God who hears and saves. And those margins are often places of conflict, as they are symbolically here in Psalm 120 (see the comments on 120:5). But our psalmist realizes that he has been too long in the realm of conflict, for he is of a different character, a man of peace (see 120:7). His perspective as a man of peace living in the war-loving lands of Meshek and Kedar underlines the view that Israel's world was hostile, and they had to see themselves as a people of peace in an alien world.

As we prepare our sermon/lesson, we should keep in mind that Psalm 120, and all the Songs of Ascents, are songs for a journey, or rules for the road. They stretch from Israel's exile in Babylonia to their home in Jerusalem. We might focus on our life of faith as pilgrims rather than tourists, to use Peterson's metaphors.[9] We too often buy the spiritual trinkets and souvenirs of the world's hawkers, knowing full well that in a few years they will end up in our spiritual attics. Or, to put it another way, we are apt to be what Dallas Willard has called "consumers of religious goods and services."[10]

To help our listeners understand the nature of this collection (Psalms 120–34), Peterson calls them "an old dog-eared songbook,"[11] because they became songs the pilgrims sang on their way to Jerusalem for festival celebrations. We can use the analogy of a photo album, full of snapshots the first pilgrims took along the way, and each new set of pilgrims thumbed nostalgically through the photo album as they made their own journey to Jerusalem and sang these songs.

The first rule of the road is formulated out of the suppliant's backward glimpse of the journey past (the verbs are past tense ["I called"] and imply repetitive action, thus the NIV's "I call"): the poet had cried out to the Lord in his distress, and the Lord had heard him (120:1). So the first rule of the road is *grace*. That's where the Christian life begins. It's our reference point. When life's waves start tossing our ship of faith, we sometimes lose our orientation and need a still point to regain our bearings. A friend spoke to me a few years ago about his experience with deep-sea fishing. When the waves got high and people started getting seasick, the captain would say, "Look at the horizon." The horizon was the one point that didn't move and so had a settling effect. That's what grace is. It's the horizon of our spiritual world, the still point when the world is turning.

The second rule of the road the psalmist lays out before us is *justice* (120:2–4). The poet of the journey is confident that God will bring "the lying lips" to justice (120:4). One of the hardest things we do as Christians is to let God right the wrongs others have done to us. It's hard to leave these things in God's hands, but that is what the singer of Israel is doing. He is leaving the matter in God's hands, knowing that God will dispense justice (120:4).

Our psalmist was troubled by the "deceitful tongues" of his personal world (120:2), and that is not lost on us, because our world is full of them too. They are the advertisers who claim to know what we need and try to make us believe it; they are entertainers who offer us a quick fix of laughter but leave us with no joy; they are politicians who instruct us in morality and carry on their own private affairs; they are the pastors who, in Jeremiah's words, "heal the wound of this people lightly" (see Jer. 6:14; 8:11 ESV); they are the psychologists who explain our sinful behavior and leave our spiritual person unforgiven; they are the political correctors who level out all behaviors and all religious systems and leave us with a false sense of well-being, and no God who can save us. For healthy Christian discipleship we need to have a keen confidence in the God of justice. It's our sense of spiritual equilibrium.

The third rule of the road is God's call to a new *sense of destiny*. The poet realizes he has been a tourist too long, and now he needs to become a pilgrim. He uses the metaphor of Meshek and Kedar, symbols of a foreign land and alien life. He was not physically there, but he felt as if he were, living on a visa rather than a passport (120:5–6). Somewhere in the spiritual acoustics of his life the psalmist had heard God call him to become a pilgrim, to abandon the warring spirit of the world and embrace the spirit of peace (120:5–7). Paul says, "For the kingdom of God is not a matter of eating and drinking, but of righteousness, peace and joy in the Holy Spirit" (Rom. 14:17). See "Illustrating the Text."

And so may we exchange our tourist credentials for those of a pilgrim, to embark on a journey as we renew our sense of destiny. Thus we might emphasize that in Psalm 120 the Christian way of discipleship is marked by these three spiritual traits: a sense of God's grace, a sense of God's justice, and a sense of our destiny. Grace will orient us on the journey. God's justice will sustain our spiritual equilibrium. The sense of destiny will keep us looking to Jesus, the pioneer and perfecter of our faith (Heb. 12:1–3), who took the journey before us and "steadfastly set his face to go to Jerusalem" (Luke 9:51 KJV).

Illustrating the Text

Don't become a tourist instead of a pilgrim.

Christian Literature: *Pilgrim's Progress*, by John Bunyan. In *Pilgrim's Progress*, the character Christian carries a heavy burden on his back, looking for a way to escape his sinful conscience. And then he meets Evangelist, who points him to the Wicket-Gate, where he can enter and find rest for his soul. But on the way Christian meets Mr. Worldly Wiseman, who diverts him from his beeline path to the Wicket-Gate, and Christian dilly-dallies around, looking for the house on yonder hill where Mr. Legality lives. He becomes a tourist rather than a pilgrim.

Living into the kingdom

Bible: **Matthew 5.** Book 5 of the Psalter often deals with the theme of the kingdom of God, much like so many of the psalms, but there is an immediacy attached to this book, especially since it is shaped against the background of the return from exile and the rebuilding of the temple. The virtual miracle of the return, triggered politically by Cyrus's decree of 538 BC and powered spiritually by divine grace, led this community to believe that what was happening was more than a simulated portrait of God's kingdom but was in effect a reality. In fact, the biblical doctrine of the kingdom of God does not relegate its reality to the eschatological age but makes it an ongoing reality that calls for an ongoing *living into* the kingdom. Jesus's Beatitudes are set in the Sermon on the Mount, and in that context he makes the Beatitudes the principles by which the kingdom of God is lived and realized. E. Stanley Jones, in a series of meditations on the abundant life, explains that the kingdom is essentially living into the kingdom.[12] It is not merely a sphere of life but a way of life.

Songs of Ascents, the Pilgrim Psalter
(Psalms 120–34)

These fifteen psalms are connected by the title "A song of ascents," and four of them have "of David" in their titles (Pss. 122; 124; 131; 133), and one "of Solomon" (Ps. 127). Traditionally they are connected with the pilgrimage to Jerusalem (thus they are sometimes called "pilgrimage psalms" or, as a collection, the "Pilgrim Psalter"), the model pilgrimage being the return to the land of Israel from Babylonian exile, but the songs were used by pilgrims through the centuries, particularly for the journey to the temple for the agricultural festivals (Deut. 16:16–17). The Mishnah (*Sukkah* 5.4) associates these songs with the Feast of Water-Drawing, celebrated at the morning service on the seven days of Tabernacles. The Levites sang them to instrumental accompaniment on each of the fifteen steps that led from the Court of Women to the Court of Israel. Several explanations of the noun "ascents" have been put forward through the centuries.[1]

1. Songs sung to a high melody (Saadyah Gaon, ninth century AD). While the Hebrew root of the noun "ascents" means "to go up" (*'lh*), the travel terms evidenced in these psalms, with an absence of allusions to the use of the human voice, disqualify this explanation.

2. Songs sung when sacrificing burnt offerings (*'olah*, "burnt offering," is derived from the verb "to go up"). The evidence for this interpretation is not strong.

3. Songs sung by those who "ascended" to the land of Israel (the return from exile [Ezra 7:9] and the annual journey to Jerusalem at the agricultural festivals). This represents the traditional interpretation of "ascents." Some of the poems were probably composed specifically for the return from exile (see Ps. 121), while others speak of the return in retrospect (e.g., Ps. 126).

4. Liebreich offers a hypothesis that is an explanation more for the composition of these "songs" than for the term "ascents," but it has significance for the genre. He proposes that the "songs" (twelve directly, and three indirectly—Pss. 124; 126; 131) are built on four words of the priestly benediction (Num. 6:24–26): (1) "[The LORD] bless you" (*yᵉbarekᵉka*); (2) "and keep you" (*wᵉyishmᵉreka*); (3) "[the LORD] be gracious to you" (*wihunneka*); (4) "[and give you] peace" (*shalom*). To draw another link to the benediction, he suggests that the fifteen "songs" are intended to match the fifteen words of

the benediction.[2] When the collection was put together, it was a kind of homily on the priestly benediction, the precursor of the midrashic interpretations of the priestly benediction in *Sifre on Numbers*.[3] However, the fact that the composer does not complete the fifteen-song cycle, tying all fifteen "songs" to the benediction, brings this hypothesis into some doubt.

I think it is more likely that the composer uses the priestly benediction as his template in order to put a watermark of blessing on the "songs," especially since the return from exile represents such an epic development in Israel's history. The "watermark" then is composed of the four words from the benediction, and the community would certainly recognize the extension of that historic blessing on them in the word links to the priestly benediction. We may compare it to the Blessing of Moses in Deuteronomy 33, as he blesses Israel before his death and, most important, before Israel enters the great new era of Canaan. On the verge of this new era of their second entrance into the land, a priestly blessing is most appropriate, and Psalms 120–34 may be viewed as that extended blessing.

5. A poetic form identifiable in these poems that repeats certain words or expressions (anadiplosis) gives an advancing (traveling) or "going up" effect (Goldingay calls it "terracing"[4]; it is also called "step parallelism"). Most likely the advancing poetic form, which is consistent in these psalms, was inspired by the nature of the journey itself, and the stylistic movement of repeated words and phrases (illustrated below in Ps. 123) was intended to give the impression of the advancing journey (steps):

> "my eyes" (123:1a) →
>> "the eyes of slaves" (123:2a) →
>> "the eyes of a female slave" (123:2b) →
>> "our eyes look to the LORD our God" (123:2c)
> "the hand of their master" (123:2a) →
>> "the hand of her mistress" (123:2b) →
>> "[the hand of] the LORD our God" (123:2c)
> "till he shows us mercy" (123:2d) →
>> "have mercy on us, LORD" (123:3a) →
>> "have mercy on us" (123:3b)
> "we have endured no end of contempt" (123:3b) →
>> "we have endured no end of ridicule from the arrogant, of contempt from the proud" (123:4)[5]

The repeated use of this literary pattern gives support to the idea that Psalms 120–34 were written by a single author, or at least stylized by the same writer.

The two plausible time frames for the composition of the Songs of Ascents are the early postexilic era, in which the first exiles returned from Babylonia (ca. 536 BC) and the temple was rebuilt (520–516 BC), and the time of Ezra-Nehemiah in the middle of the fifth century. The freshness and general enthusiasm for the journey to Jerusalem and worship in the temple suggest, in my view, the early postexilic era, but the period of Ezra-Nehemiah is not implausible.

"My Help Comes from the LORD, the Maker of Heaven and Earth"

Big Idea

God's watchful care of his children includes all of their activities, as they "go out" and "come in."

Key Themes

- God our Helper is the Maker of heaven and earth, so what more effective help should we need!
- As our Protector, God keeps us from harm.

Understanding the Text

These are words of someone who is on a journey, and to assure the success of the journey he asks where his help comes from.[1] In form the psalm is a blessing, reminiscent of the priestly blessing (Num. 6:24–26). The vocabulary of the priestly benediction is present in verse 7 (*"may the LORD keep you from all harm,"* author's translation; see Num. 6:24).[2] The controlling motif is the Lord's watchful care of the traveler (121:2), the same care the people of Israel knew during their historic journey from Egypt (121:4). That motif is developed by the sixfold use of the verb "watch over / keep," with the name of the Keeper (*YHWH*) occurring five times in the psalm.

Liebreich analyzes the Songs of Ascents and concludes that they are an elucidation of four words in the priestly benediction (see "Additional Insights: Songs of Ascents, the Pilgrim Psalter [Psalms 120–34]," preceding this unit). While the connection to the priestly benediction is undeniable, it seems to me that rather than a formal series of homilies on the priestly benediction, the author intends to bless Israel, and he uses the language of the priestly benediction to do that. The congregation would readily hear the connection. Perhaps the author was a priest.

The Text in Context

In Psalm 120 the traveler, representing the entire community returning from exile, has already lamented his/their deplorable state of exile and set his/their eyes on the homeward journey to Jerusalem.

There are striking comparisons between Psalm 121 and Psalm 91. The difference is that the setting for Psalm 91 is battle, in which the Lord protects the supplicant, while that of Psalm 121 is a journey. Note the word similarities in table 1.

Table 1. Comparison of Psalms 121 and 91

Terms	Psalm 121	Psalm 91
The Lord is your "shade"	121:5	91:1
Psalmist's "right hand"	121:5	91:7
Psalmist's "eyes"	121:1	91:8
Psalmist's "foot"	121:3	91:12
Danger by "day" and "night"	121:6	91:5–6
God will keep the psalmist from "evil" (NIV: "harm")	121:7	91:10

Outline/Structure

1. The traveler's confession of trust (121:1–2)
2. Blessing on the traveler (121:3–8)

Historical and Cultural Background

Certain terms in this psalm enlighten us on the difficulties of travel in ancient Israel. One is the mountains decorating the terrain of Israel's world (121:1), which could be a challenge for travelers, particularly because of the need to traverse them and the dangers that might lurk from robbers and wild animals. A second, but related, feature is the rough and rocky terrain. One slip of the foot (121:3) could sprain an ankle or send the traveler over a precipice that could cause injury or even death. Third is the need for a constant watch on the journey (121:3–4), watching for perils along the way. Fourth is the bright, hot sun. If one is traveling north, the morning sun on one's right hand would not be too unpleasant—an advantage, in fact—but when one is traveling southward (such as from Galilee to Jerusalem; see "Teaching the Text"), the afternoon sun is on one's right side and can be scorching (121:6). To have a big, tall person walking on one's right-hand side (in this case, the Lord) can provide pleasant "shade" from the sun (121:5). A fifth, perhaps surprising, feature is the moon (121:6), whose light one would expect travelers to welcome. But since a negative effect of the moon is implied ("nor the moon [harm you] by night"), there seems to be a hint of some ill omen represented by the light of the moon, which may hint at the belief that the moonlight might bring trouble or illness.[3]

I am inclined to date this psalm in the early postexilic era, written before or after the exiles' journey home to Judah. Others would date it later, as late as 445 BC, celebrating Ezra's return to Jerusalem.[4]

Interpretive Insights

121:1 *I lift up my eyes to the mountains—where does my help come from?* The question is answered in verse 2. The "mountains" may be those that the returnees would encounter on the way back to Judah. Our suppliant recognizes that his help does not come from those mountains, so to clarify its source, he poses the question, "Where does my help come from?" There is also the possibility that the "mountains" are those that surround Jerusalem (125:2). The Masoretes divided the verse into two halves, the first ending with "mountains," and then follows the interrogative word "from where?" (*me'ayin*), which the King James translators rendered as a relative phrase: "I will lift up mine eyes unto the hills, *from whence* cometh my help." It appears to be intended as an interrogative, however, as the NIV and most modern English translations render it. In that case, the second half of the verse asks a question rather than gives an answer.

The two great journeys of Israel's history were the one from Egypt to Canaan and ultimately to Jerusalem, depicted so beautifully in 68:7–35, and the journey from Babylonia to Judah and, again, ultimately to Jerusalem. Psalm 121 is concerned, of course, with the second journey, and the challenge is the formidable terrain of the country with all of the attendant dangers. The description of this journey is still different from the Egypt-to-Jerusalem journey of Psalm 68, when Mount Bashan, as Israel passed by, was passionately jealous of Mount Zion (68:15–16).

121:2 *My help comes from the* LORD, *the Maker of heaven and earth*. This is the answer to the question of verse 1: the suppliant's help is not from the mountains but from the Lord who made them. The two must never be confused.

121:3 *He will not let your foot slip*. The general opinion is that we hear two voices in the psalm: the voice of the psalmist (121:1–2), and the voice of a priest or other religious official (121:3–8). The "I/my" may be the governor, perhaps Zerubbabel himself (see Ezra 2:2). If the psalm was written for the occasion of the journey from Babylonian exile to Judea, or in celebration of the occasion, the speaker of the blessing in verses 3–8 could be Joshua the high priest. There is, of course, the possibility that the psalm was composed earlier and the redactor adapted it for this purpose, but there is a freshness in these psalms that seems to suggest an emotional proximity to the historical events they celebrate.

121:4 *indeed, he who watches over Israel.* While these words may be those of a well-wisher,[5] or a third voice, the consistency of the blessing sounds as though it comes from a single speaker. The persistent theme is God's watchful care of the traveler(s).

121:5–6 *the* Lord *is your shade at your right hand.* The sun could, either by its brightness or its heat, hamper one's ability to protect oneself on a journey or defend oneself in battle (see 91:1). See "Historical and Cultural Background."

121:7–8 *The* Lord *will keep you from all harm . . . will watch over your coming and going.* Specifically, God will protect the traveler(s) from the harm that attended travels through the ancient world, and generally speaking, God "will watch over" their daily activities. "Your coming and going" is a word picture of daily life in the ancient world. Cities were very compact, with very little open space, and much of life, especially work, took place outside the city. In the morning the citizens, especially the men, would go out (Heb. "your going out") to the fields and pastures for the day's work, and in the evening they would come back into the city (Heb. "your coming in") to their homes and families. In light of 122:1 ("Let us go to the house of the Lord"), this expression may also reflect the journey to the temple. Viewed generally, however, the gist of the statement is that God will always and in all circumstances watch over his people—his care is comprehensive. This is essentially a summary statement that covers the specifics of his watchful care given in the psalm.

Theological Insights

The collection of psalms known as the Songs of Ascents, generally speaking, stretches across the return from Babylonian exile to the renewed temple of the Lord and provides a travelogue of Israel's return to Judea. While Psalm 123, for example, is concerned with the journey and the destination, Psalm 121 is focused on the journey itself. Recognizably, the constituent psalms give hints of their destination from time to time (e.g., 122:2), yet the collection itself is arranged to celebrate the destination at the end of the collection in Psalm 134. In the larger picture of Old Testament Israel the people were quite adept at celebrating both the journey and the destination, but in this era of their history, the destination was the ultimate symbol of God's watchful care of his people, and that needed to be positioned appropriately. Thus this travelogue of psalms moves us intentionally and sensitively toward the destination, which is the sanctuary, and there, to no surprise, we join the "servants of the Lord" in the presence of the "Maker of heaven and earth." In the meantime, the Lord makes sure that the journey is safe and secure.

Teaching the Text

Sometimes a familiar text is harder to preach/teach than an unfamiliar one, and the familiarity of Psalm 121, like Psalm 23, may prove to be more a challenge than an aid. So we want to take the simplest and most straightforward approach to the psalm, which is probably to give attention to the two voices of the psalm. Peterson calls it a "Travelers' Advisory,"[6] and that is a good metaphor to use as we construct our sermon/lesson.

The first voice is that of the traveler (the psalmist). We hear his voice (and, collectively, the community's) in the pronoun "I." He starts by making reference to the mountains, which could be the most formidable aspect of the journey from Babylonia to Jerusalem. First, and negatively, they may be the mountains where the pagan sanctuaries were built and from which their illicit worship proceeded (Jer. 3:23; 50:6; Ezek. 18:6, 15). Or, second, they could be the formidable mountains that posed such dangers to travelers, including topographical challenges, marauders, and wild animals. A third possibility, looking toward the journey's destination, is the mountains that surrounded Jerusalem and provided a defensive system for the city (Ps. 125:1). Since the entire blessing is focused on Yahweh's protection of the traveler, the second option is preferable. Yet, the question "Where does my help come from?" seems also to incline the reader toward the first option, for the psalmist does not stop with the mountains themselves—that is, creation—but his answer is that the Creator ("the Maker of heaven and earth") is the source of help, not the creation. This name for God, "the Maker of heaven and earth," appears three times in the Songs of Ascents (121:2; 124:8; 134:3), and once in 146:6. To have the Creator of the world as Guide and Protector on one's journey means that it will inevitably be a successful one. He knows every peculiar formation and dangerous precipice in those hills.

While the speaker is not identified, the nature of these verses suggests that the speaker is blessing the traveler(s) before the journey begins (see the comments at the beginning of "Understanding the Text"). Thus we may surmise that it is a priestly voice. His blessing includes the assurance that an unexpected accident won't occur on the way: "He will not let your foot slip" (121:3). One amazing thing about our Helper—this God who travels with us and who is nothing short of the "Maker of heaven and earth"—is that he never sleeps. If we fall asleep at the wheel or on the treacherous terrain of the journey—and we hope we never will—it would be great to know that someone who never sleeps is our traveling companion. The gods of this world take naps from time to time (see Elijah's taunt of the Baal prophets in 1 Kings 18:27–29). The powerful economic god we bow down to nods off periodically, and we never know when he might rouse himself again. The god of fame takes a snooze at the time of his own choosing and makes the popularity charts spiral downward. The stars of today will be the forgotten celebrities of tomorrow. But our God, Maker of heaven and earth, never slumbers. And as the Heidelberg Catechism reminds us, the Creator of the world is "my God and Father because of Christ the Son" (see "Illustrating the Text").

Now, if one is traveling from Galilee in the north to Jerusalem in the south (the route the exiles would have taken to Judea), for example, the morning sun is going to be on one's left-hand side, and it won't be too oppressive. But when the sun has passed its zenith and begun its movement toward the west, it gets very hot, and there are not many tree-studded roads to walk on. So a big and tall person walking on one's right-hand side will provide a great deal of relief from the sun. That also means, of course, that the companion is getting the brunt of it so the traveler won't. And the Companion is God, who shades us from the hot sun. That is the way God operates. He takes the brunt of the journey's hardships to protect us from the worst of them.

Illustrating the Text

See also "God's care of the world and of each person at the same time" in "Illustrating the Text" in the unit on Psalm 66.

God's faithful care

Church History: The Heidelberg Catechism (1563), in answer to a question about the first statement of the Apostles' Creed ("I believe in God, the Father almighty, Maker of heaven and earth"), captures, in the context of Christ's atoning work, the sense of Psalm 121:

> That the eternal Father of our Lord Jesus Christ, who out of nothing created heaven and earth and everything in them, who still upholds and rules them by his eternal counsel and providence, is my God and Father because of Christ the Son. I trust God so much that I do not doubt he will provide whatever I need for body and soul, and will turn to my good whatever adversity he sends upon me in this sad world. God is able to do this because he is almighty God and desires to do this because he is a faithful Father.
>
> We can be patient when things go against us, thankful when things go well, and for the future we can have good confidence in our faithful God and Father that nothing in creation will separate us from his love. For all creatures are so completely in God's hand that without his will they can neither move nor be moved. (Q & A 26, 28)

The temple is Yahweh's claim on creation.

Quote: N. T. Wright. Wright makes a point that connects to the Zion psalms (Pss. 15; 24; 42–43; 84):

The Temple turns out to be an advance foretaste of Yahweh's claim on the whole of creation. We are to see the Temple as establishing, so to speak, a bridgehead for God's own presence within a world that has very determinedly gone its own way. It is, institutionally speaking, God's purpose to recreate the world through his church, and that means the people in whom he lives. Though the pilgrims to the temple longed to be there and even contemplated being there permanently, it was not a state of static existence, but the state of exuberant life when God's power is ultimately manifested and his glory finally recognized. It is only in that incredible state of divine empowerment that God can do his highest work of re-creation, just as he did his work of creation in the beginning. John recognized that it was Christ who brought the world into existence, and that he is the exclusive Creator, "without him nothing was made that has been made" (Jn. 1:2). Thus Christ continues to be the dispensing Source of the two distinctive features of the initial creation, life and light (Jn. 1:4), and now they are life redeemed and light. So the creating work of God continues to renew and re-create the world from within the Word made flesh, to set up a place within his creation where his glory will be revealed and his powerful judgments unveiled.[7]

(Note also the connection between the creation of the world and entrance into the temple in Ps. 24:1–2.)

"I Rejoiced with Those Who Said to Me, 'Let Us Go to the House of the LORD'"

Big Idea

Worship is not an elective in the curriculum of faith but a required course.

Key Themes

- The passion of the spiritual journey is joy.
- The worship of God is the goal of faith.
- Peace is the quintessential outcome of our life in God.

Understanding the Text

The third of the Songs of Ascents depicts the suppliant, representative of the community, either in some stage of the journey on the way to Jerusalem for worship or in the early stage of arrival in the city. It is a Zion song (see also Pss. 46; 47; 48; 84; 87; 125; 126; and 132) and, like Psalm 84, reveals the personal passion of the psalmist and his company (addressed in 122:6) for Jerusalem and the temple.

The Text in Context

As a veneration of Zion, this psalm resembles Psalms 48 and 87. Its travel language corresponds to the terms of Psalm 121. For example, Psalm 121 ends with "your going out and coming in" (NIV: "your coming and going"), and Psalm 122 begins with "Let us go to the house of the LORD" (122:1b). The protection language of 121:3a, "He will not let your foot slip," has its correspondent in the victory language of 122:2, "Our feet are standing in your gates, Jerusalem"—the journey has been (or will be) a success!

Outline/Structure

A triple occurrence of several terms should be noted. While they are not distributed in such a way that they provide the formal structure, they nevertheless provide the substantive theology of the psalm. "Jerusalem" is a key to the content of the poem, occurring in all three strophes (122:2, 3, 6); "Lord" is also shared by the three strophes (122:1, 4, 9), as is also "house" (122:1, 5, 9); and "peace" (122:6, 7, 8) provides a capstone for the psalm, occurring only in the last strophe. The phrase "house of the Lord" forms an *inclusio* (122:1, 9).

1. The joy of the journey to Yahweh's house (122:1–2)
2. Praise of the Holy City (122:3–5)
3. Prayer for the peace of the Holy City (122:6–9)

Historical and Cultural Background

Based on the superscription "of David" and the phrase "thrones of the house of David" (122:5), some interpreters believe the psalm was composed during the monarchical period and installed in this collection to celebrate the return. On the other hand, the "thrones of the house of David," references to courts of justice, could apply to Israelite Jerusalem at any time, and it is only natural that any poem celebrating the "house of the Lord" be connected to David. It is also possible that the phrase alludes to the hopes of the restoration of the Davidic dynasty.

In the Second Temple period the psalm was most likely recited at the Feast of Tabernacles (Sukkot), which was called the "season of our rejoicing," and eventually became part of the water-drawing festival associated with Tabernacles.[1]

Interpretive Insights

Title *Of David*. Four of the Songs of Ascents have "of David" in the title: Psalms 122; 124; 131; and 133.[2] While this could be the result of a later redaction of this group of psalms, it could very well be original to the title, like "A song of ascents," since the entire collection has its eyes set on Jerusalem and the temple, and the author(s) of these poems would be intent on making a connection to David, who made preparations for the temple construction, and Solomon, who constructed it (Ps. 127). See "Additional Insights: Songs of Ascents, the Pilgrim Psalter (Psalms 120–34)," following the unit on Psalm 120.

122:1 *Let us go to the house of the* Lord. This psalm follows the blessing of the pilgrim(s) in Psalm 121 (see the comments at the beginning of "Understanding the Text" in the unit on Ps. 121), and the pilgrim ("me") has now become the pilgrims (plural: "let *us*" [122:1], "*our* feet" [122:2], "*our* God" [122:9]) who are on their journey to Jerusalem and who imagine themselves (or perhaps already are) "standing in your gates, Jerusalem" (122:2).[3]

122:2 *Our feet are standing in your gates, Jerusalem.* Psalm 121 is a blessing on the travelers, and Psalm 122 celebrates the journey itself. While the participle "standing" may be interpreted as a past tense, as the poet remembers how pleasant it was when "our feet *were standing*" within Jerusalem's gates,[4] the change of the language from the third person of verse 1 ("the house of the LORD") to the direct address of verse 2, "your gates, Jerusalem," and the second person of verses 6–9 have a present sound. In that case, the literary distance of the journey is very short and is either a mental picture or an actual report of arrival.

The direct address to a distant city or country, here Jerusalem, is not unusual in the prophetic books and should not surprise us here. Of course, it is possible that the journey, undocumented by the psalmist, occurs between verses 1 and 2 and the rest of the psalm is the pilgrim's description of the city (122:3–5) and blessings on it (122:6–9). The adverb "there" in verses 4 and 5 (NIV: "that is where," 122:4) and the fact that the city is not addressed in verses 3–5 make the places sound distant. In any case, we cannot insist on a stage-by-stage geographical movement in the Songs of Ascents, since Psalm 126 is obviously a reflection on the return already accomplished, and in 134:1 and 135:2 the pilgrims have already arrived in Jerusalem.

122:3–4 *a city that is closely compacted together.* The general view is that the expression "compacted together" (122:3) means one of two things: (1) the city is held together compactly due to its design (city plan), or (2) the people of Israel are joined together in unity when the tribes visit the city (122:4). The presence of the passive participle "built," describing Jerusalem, would seem to favor the first explanation.

to praise the name of the LORD *according to the statute.* The purpose of pilgrimage is to "praise the name of the LORD" (122:4), and the infinitive "to praise" is the verb "to give thanks," which suggests they will make a thanksgiving offering once they have arrived in Jerusalem. Psalm 107:4–9 describes the journey to "a city where they could settle," where they would "give thanks to the LORD for his unfailing love." The "statute" directing the tribes to go up to Jerusalem is quite possibly the Deuteronomic directive that three times a year all men "must appear before the LORD your God at the place he will choose" (Deut. 16:16).

122:5 *thrones for judgment, the thrones of the house of David.* Since David conquered Jerusalem and established his capital there, it had become known for justice (Jer. 21:12; Isa. 1:21; 9:6; 16:5). The office of king as judge is well attested.[5]

122:6–7 *Pray for the peace of Jerusalem.* These words may be spoken to the pilgrims who are beginning their journey to Jerusalem. Verses 6b–7b are a continuation of the blessing.

peace within your walls and security within your citadels. "Walls" and "citadels" also appear in parallel in 48:13. If we take the "walls" as real rather than visionary, then the time of Nehemiah (mid-fifth century BC), the re-builder of Jerusalem's walls, could also apply, although it is quite likely that "walls," "gates," and "citadels" are metonymy for the whole city. "Citadels" are towers built into the wall.[6]

122:8 *For the sake of my family and friends.* This interesting phrase opens a window to the sociological dimensions of Jerusalem. In the interest of the speaker's "family [lit., "my brothers"] and friends," he hopes that Jerusalem will truly become a "city of peace" (see "Theological Insights").

122:9 *For the sake of the house of the* LORD *our God, I will seek your prosperity.* Verses 8 and 9 revert to the first person, "I" (see 122:1), and the poet has the temple in view. The phrase "for the sake of the house of the LORD" implies that the city exists for the temple.

Theological Insights

The name Jerusalem, usually written *yᵉrushalaim*, was most likely written in an earlier form as *yᵉrushalem*. This name sounds a bit like the Hebrew phrase *'ir shalom*, "city of peace,"[7] although some modern interpreters understand the final part of the name (*-shalem*) as the name of a Canaanite god. In Genesis 14 it is the name of Jerusalem (sometimes rendered "Salem"; also Ps. 76:2). Our psalmist introduces "Jerusalem" in verse 2 (occurs also in 122:3a and 6a) and thereafter (122:6–8) uses "peace" (*shalom*) three times, evidently intended as a wordplay on the name Jerusalem. The directive "Pray for the peace of Jerusalem" (122:6a) stems both verbally and emotionally from the name of the city. When Jesus gets a glimpse of the city on his final journey there, he too addresses the city, as does our psalmist, and says, "If you, even you, had only known on this day what would bring you peace—but now it is hidden from your eyes" (Luke 19:42). Essentially he is saying that the city of peace should have known the Prince of Peace.

Teaching the Text

The spiritual effect of Psalm 122 is to project the reader into the worship of the Lord in the house of God in Jerusalem. Worship, therefore, can be the major theme of our sermon/lesson.[8] Worship is the common ground of Christian practice, the required curriculum of Christian discipleship—it is not an elective (note "statute" in 122:4). Peterson reminds us that worship "does not satisfy our hunger for God—it whets our appetite. Our need for God is not taken care of by engaging in worship—it deepens."[9]

In our psalm, the pilgrims are either on their journey or have already arrived in Jerusalem (122:2). The journey in any case is filled with joy (122:1). Another observant psalmist is so passionate with love for God and his sanctuary that he is envious of the bird that flits freely back and forth in the temple courts, making its home and raising its young (84:3).

To expand this theme we may observe, first, that this writer elevates not the geography or the beauty of the city or its temple but rather its design (122:3, the city was "closely compacted together"), suggesting perhaps that the architectural plan was a model of spiritual order.[10] It is like church architecture that reflects basic theological principles of our faith, such as the centered altar (or communion table) that represents the centrality of Christ's sacrifice, or the centered pulpit the centrality of the preached word. Our assumption, I think correctly, is that the plan of the city, in some respects at least, represented the orderly design of God's kingdom, and in that sense led the worshiper into the presence of God in the temple. Our spiritual application can be that worship is the place where we recognize how the pieces of God's plan for our lives fit together (compare Coverdale's translation of v. 3b, "that is at unity in itself").

Second, the design of the city and the place of worship in the people's lives suggest the orderly design of justice (122:5), a matter that is deep in the heart of God and deep in the hearts of all worshipers. Worship, we must remind ourselves, is worship of the God of justice, and the reputation of Jerusalem as the place of "the thrones for judgment" meant that justice was, and must be, written in and between the lines of the liturgy and articulated appropriately in its idioms (see Isa. 1:21).

Third, the orderly design of the city points to the quintessential outcome of our life in God, and that is peace. This must be the object of our prayers (lit., "Ask for the peace of Jerusalem," 122:6a). And the ubiquitous conflict of the psalmist's world—and our world too—demands that all true believers make peace an object of life and worship (see the comments on 120:7). MacDonald says of one of his characters that he read his philosophy by the light of wrong and suffering, and that was like reading it by the light of a burning house (see "Illustrating the Text"). Our psalmist wants us to read Jerusalem's biography by the light of the morning, and that is peace. The peace of Jerusalem, like the peace of any city or nation or individual, should permeate the whole, both political and personal. In our psalm it includes the city physically ("within your walls"), its defensive installments ("your citadels"), its inhabitants ("my family and friends"), and the sanctuary ("the house of the LORD") (122:7–9). Paul writes to the Philippian church about the "peace of God, which transcends all understanding" (Phil. 4:7) and assures them that this peace "will guard your hearts and your minds in Christ Jesus."

Fourth, and a side effect of our previous point, this peace will and should permeate our human relationships ("For the sake of my family and friends," 122:8). While peace and security within the environs of our world do not necessarily assure that our social relationships will be in accord, this condition will contribute ("for the sake of") to the well-being of our social and family life, which is not far from a wholesome spiritual existence. The object of our life in God is to *live into* the kingdom, a lesson we learn from the Beatitudes in their larger context of the Sermon on the Mount (see "Illustrating the Text").

Fifth, all of these will reverberate together for the good (NIV: "your prosperity," 122:9) of the whole. In our Christian context, "your" could be the church or our life of faith (one cannot be detached from the other), whereas in the psalmic context it is most likely Jerusalem. Yet, the city, like the church and our life of faith, is not the final object of devotion, but it is God, symbolized in our psalm by the "house of the LORD our God."

Illustrating the Text

The kingdom of God is righteousness, peace, and joy.

Bible: **The Sermon on the Mount.** Addressing the disagreement that some early Christians were having over what kinds of food to eat, Paul defines the kingdom of God as consisting of the spiritual triplets of "righteousness, peace and joy in the Holy Spirit" (Rom. 14:17). This peace, as for the psalmist also, is far more than an absence of military conflict. It is a peace that pervades every aspect of society and every fiber of our personal being. We know what it is to have a troubled mind, to spend a sleepless night because something has gone wrong between us and someone else. We know how it feels to be troubled by the past, insecure about the present, and anxious about the future. In fact, one might wonder if Paul is speaking against the backdrop of the Sermon on the Mount, in which Christ lays out a new constitution for the people of God, a constitution that forms the basis of the kingdom. And one of the things he advocates has to do with this peace that Paul is talking about: "Therefore I tell you, do not worry about your life, what you will eat or drink; or about your body, what you will wear. Is not life more than food, and the body more than clothes?" (Matt. 6:25). And one of the Beatitudes blesses "the peacemakers," who are the true "children of God" (Matt. 5:9). In a sense Paul is teaching the same lesson, for the kingdom is not what we ingest but the spiritual qualities of righteousness, joy, and peace that pervade our being.

Biography: **Corrie ten Boom.** The psalmist wants us to look at Jerusalem under the topic of "peace" (Ps. 122:6–8). In fact, the name of the city itself incorporates the Hebrew word "peace" (*shalom,* represented by the last part of Jeru-*shalem*). Peace should penetrate the whole of Jerusalem: "peace within your walls and security within your citadels." In Pam Rosewell Moore's book on Corrie ten Boom (*Life Lessons from the Hiding Place*), she writes about how Corrie loved to tell stories:

> *The Hiding Place* is powerful because of story itself—the telling of the past course of a person's life for a positive and sometimes life-changing end—is powerful. It cannot be said often or strongly enough that each of us who loves the Lord Jesus has his or her own story without which every other Christian is the poorer. If you and I can learn to tell our stories—not necessarily in writing but in talking about them, in daily living and in worship—we will affect our world in ways that only eternity will tell.[11]

Jerusalem's story certainly had its bright and dark hues, but the story had to be told with the controlling theme of peace; and ours, analogically, must be told with the controlling theme of the Prince of Peace. It should be like a Rembrandt painting with its strong beam of light as the center of attention. George MacDonald says of one of his characters that "he read his philosophy by the troubled light of wrong and suffering, and that is not the light of the morning, but of a burning house."[12] Our psalmist wants us to read Jerusalem's story, which was certainly marked in history by "wrong and suffering," by the "light of the morning." And the light by which we read our story makes all the difference.

"Have Mercy on Us, LORD, Have Mercy on Us"

Big Idea

In covenantal relationship with us, the God of power manifests himself as the God of mercy.

Key Themes

- God is enthroned in heaven as King.
- The Lord is the compassionate Master.
- God's people must wait "till he shows us his mercy."

Understanding the Text

Psalm 123 has traits of a community psalm of lament (123:3–4) but also of an individual psalm of trust (123:1–2). Delitzsch calls this poem that arises out of suffering "an upward glance of waiting faith to Jahve [Yahweh] under tyrannical oppression."[1]

The Text in Context

After the journey described by Psalm 122, this psalm opens the window onto the faith of Israel that has waited long enough (see the comments on 123:3) through a time of contempt and ridicule until Yahweh "shows us his mercy." On the other side of this psalm, Psalm 124 is the community's acclamation of the Lord's answer to this prayer ("We have escaped like a bird from the fowler's snare," 124:7). Psalm 121 begins with "I will lift my eyes to the mountains" (of Jerusalem), and the journey begins; in Psalm 122 the pilgrims receive a blessing for their journey and advance even to the city of Jerusalem; and in Psalm 123 they lift their eyes again (see 121:1) and see the one who sits "enthroned in heaven" (123:1), the vision glorious.

Outline/Structure

1. Trusting in the God of power and grace (123:1–2)
2. Entreating the God of grace and power (123:3–4)

Historical and Cultural Background

The slave-master relationship assumed by this psalm is one that troubles freedom-loving people, and so it ought. Even if the knowledge that slavery as practiced in the ancient Near East was often the product of economic impoverishment and relentless war does not ease our discomfort, in all fairness we should note that Israel had laws that regulated the slave-master relationship and turned it, or so it was intended, into a tolerable, or at least a more tolerable, relationship. For example, if the master maltreated the slave and caused bodily harm, the master had to free the slave (Exod. 21:26–27). Non-Hebrew slaves even had religious privileges within their master's household (e.g., Exod. 12:44; 20:10), and Hebrew slaves were to be released after six years of servitude (Exod. 21:1–6).[2]

Interpretive Insights

123:1 *I lift up my eyes to you.* The metaphor implies looking trustingly to Yahweh for help (see 121:1).

to you who sit enthroned in heaven. This picture of Yahweh, not named until verse 2, portrays God as sovereign King of the world (see also 93:4; 102:12); and because he sits enthroned in heaven[3] and is "our God" (123:2c), the suppliant can look to him to "have mercy" on Israel (123:3). "Enthroned in heaven" points to God's power, and "our God" (123:2c) sums up the special relationship Israel has to God and God to them (see the sidebar "The Covenant Formula" in the unit on Ps. 79).

123:2 *to the hand of their master.* The "hand of their master" turns in a giving gesture to fulfill their needs.

so our eyes look to the Lord our God, till he shows us his mercy. "Hand" is understood; that is, "so our eyes look to *the hand of* the Lord our God." The phrase "till he shows us his mercy" seems to locate the psalmist still under "contempt" (123:3) and "ridicule from the arrogant" (123:4), of which he/ they have had enough (NIV: "endured"; see 120:6). However, in the collective sequence of the Songs of Ascents, this is possibly a reflection on the exile as Israel slowly emerges—emotionally, physically, and geographically—from its powerful humiliation and suffering.

123:3 *Have mercy on us, Lord, have mercy on us.* Note that the repeated petitions are balanced on either side of "Lord." The psalm begins with the "I" of the suppliant and moves in verses 2–4 to the "we" of the suffering community, further evidence that the Songs of Ascents were written from the psalmist's personal perspective but have a community overlay. This is beautifully illustrated by the fact that Psalm 124 is the community's acclamation of the Lord's action in power and grace, and triumphantly they celebrate their escape from the threatening dangers of the exile: "*We have escaped* like a bird from the fowler's snare; the snare has been broken, and *we have escaped*" (124:7).

Theological Insights

We are often tempted to cut short our trust in God and look to our own resources to fix whatever problems have been thrown in our path. Verse 2c of this psalm unveils this community's heart and reveals a persistence, even a determination, to trust God "till he shows us his mercy," confident that he will do that because he is "our God." Verses 3 and 4 open another window into that long period of waiting—it has been one of contempt and ridicule (see Ps. 137), but now they have emerged with a faith refined by the mockery.

Teaching the Text

The homiletical standard of this commentary is to base our sermons/lessons on the text of the Psalms. Psalm 123 lends itself to this standard quite readily in that there is an unmistakable center, composed of the prayer "Have mercy on us, Lord, have mercy on us" (123:3).[4] And this prayer arises out of the faith that underwrites the psalm.

First, the psalmist knows the difference between his own powerlessness—which leads to his mercy cry—and the greatness of the heavenly King, who sits enthroned in heaven.[5] An ancient rabbi once said, "When you pray, know before whom you are standing."[6] Sadly, our age has lost a sense of the holy God before whom we stand. This manifests itself in the songs we sing, the prayers we pray, and the way we talk about God. Our psalmist, on the other hand, is aware that he is speaking to the one who sits "enthroned in heaven" (123:1).

Second, the suppliant reinforces this view of the exalted, reigning King by the example of slaves who look to their masters to turn their gracious hand in the slaves' favor. While it is quite humiliating for us human beings to assume this "slave" disposition, it is the proper one for believers, and the only proper one, when standing before the one "enthroned in heaven." And out of that disposition the people affirm, "Our eyes look to the Lord our God, till he shows us his mercy" (see the comments on 123:2). It is not the old kind of servitude but a new servitude that acknowledges that the one "enthroned in heaven" is "our God," not a tyrant but "our God," who has a special covenant with us ("I will . . . be your God, and you will be my people," Lev. 26:12). It is paradoxical thinking, of course, to perceive of ourselves as servants and privileged citizens at the same time, but that's precisely what our perception should be. We must hold in balance the perspective of distance (servants) and that of kinship with the God who sits "enthroned in heaven," just as the

Roman emperor's son was confident that his kinship to the emperor meant that he need not be afraid of the one sitting on the throne (see "Illustrating the Text").

Illustrating the Text

Keeping our royal distance from God

True Story: A few years ago Queen Elizabeth II came to the United States, and when one ordinary American lady was introduced to her, she hugged the queen.[7] It was a genuine response of joy and gratitude, but royal protocol does not permit hugging the queen—curtsy, yes; handshake, if she offers her hand. This dear American lady was just acting as we Americans do. She wanted the queen to know she was glad to meet her. But how could she have said that by her gestures and kept that royal distance too? This question can be applied to our relationship to God, in which we have to see ourselves as "slaves" (or "servants") but yet know by faith that we are children of the one "enthroned in heaven."

Freedom in slavery

Hymn: "Make Me a Captive, Lord," by George Matheson. Matheson put the paradox of slavery and freedom, expressed by this psalm and in the Christian gospel, in this hymn:

> Make me a captive, Lord,
>   And then I shall be free;
> Force me to render up my sword,
>   And I shall conqueror be.
> . . . .
> My heart is weak and poor
>   Until it master find;
> It has no spring of action sure—
>   It varies with the wind.
>   It cannot freely move
>   Till thou hast wrought its chain;
> Enslave it with thy matchless love,
>   And deathless it shall reign.

Your emperor, but my father

Story: In the psalmist's mind he saw, like Isaiah, the one who sits "enthroned in heaven" (123:1), and further, he knew that the relationship was not that of a tyrant and his miserable servant but that of the all-powerful ruler who shows his subjects mercy (123:2c–3a), the father-child relationship, no less.

William Barclay tells the story of a Roman emperor riding through Rome with his legions on his triumphal parade after a great victory. When the retinue approached the platform where the empress and the emperor's family sat, the emperor's youngest son, wild with excitement, jumped off the platform and pushed his way through the crowd to meet his father's chariot. But a guard caught the boy up in his arms and said, "You can't do that, boy. Don't you know who that is in the chariot? That's the emperor." The boy laughed and replied, "He may be your emperor, but he's my father."[8]

"We Have Escaped like a Bird from the Fowler's Snare"

Big Idea

The Creator of the world is our Helper, and he has not only the knowledge but also the experience.

Key Themes

- If God is for us, who can be against us?
- Our help comes from the Lord, who is both knowledgeable and faithful.

Understanding the Text

Psalm 124 is a combination of community thanksgiving and trust. It entertains, for a moment at least, the horrible thought, What if God had not intervened at so many points in Israel's history? The psalmist even spells out some of the consequences of such a divine withdrawal, had that been the case.

The Text in Context

Psalm 122 celebrates the successful pilgrimage to Jerusalem, and Psalm 123 closes with a prayer for mercy in view of the reality that Israel had "endured no end of ridicule" and "contempt" (123:4). Now Psalm 124 entertains the thought of what might have happened to God's people if Yahweh had not "been on our side" when they faced those seemingly formidable dangers. It has affinities with Psalm 129 in that the liturgical nature of both psalms is obvious ("let Israel say") and both deal with the threats and hostilities Israel has faced throughout history. It carries the same theme introduced in 118:6, articulated in a slightly different mode: "The LORD is with me; I will not be afraid. What can mere mortals do to me?" Another psalm of David declares the truth of the trustworthiness of the name of Yahweh in the declaration: "Some trust in chariots and some in horses, but we trust in the name of the LORD our God"

(20:7). The theme of Psalm 124 matches Paul's declaration in Romans 8:31: "If God is for us, who can be against us?" (The conditional clause in Ps. 124:1 is literally: "If the LORD had not been *for us*"; it is rendered by most English translations, going all the way back to Coverdale, as "on our side.")

Outline/Structure

1. The unreality of God's absence (124:1–5)
2. The reality of God's presence (124:6–8)

Historical and Cultural Background

While this psalm was probably composed in the postexilic era, verses 1 and 2 may be understood as a general reflection on Israel's many conflicts and Yahweh's many deliverances, including the great deliverance from the Babylonian exile. Goulder uses the grid of the book of Nehemiah, almost a century later (ca. 445 BC), to explain the origin and background of these poems, and this one he positions on the grid of Nehemiah 4:1–17, the opposition of Sanballat and Tobiah to Nehemiah's rebuilding efforts. The only psalm Goulder does not treat this way is Psalm 134, which he considers to be a conclusion to the collection.[1] While Goulder presents a rather convincing case, it is difficult to corroborate the general language of these psalms with the specific events of Nehemiah's work, and I prefer to understand them to be compositionally closer to the return from Babylonia, which is the primary event they commemorate.[2]

Interpretive Insights

Title *Of David.* Four psalms in the Songs of Ascents (also called the Pilgrim Psalter) have this phrase in their titles (Pss. 122; 124; 131; 133). See the comments on the title for Psalm 122.

124:1–2 *If the* LORD *had not been on our side—let Israel say . . . when people attacked us.* This is a conditional sentence introduced by a special Hebrew expression that could be rendered as "were it not for the fact that." This psalm exhibits well the repetition that characterizes the Songs of Ascents, and also the related step technique. See "Additional Insights: Songs of Ascents, the Pilgrim Psalter (Psalms 120–34)," following the unit on Psalm 120.

The singular person "I" of Psalm 123:1 transitioned to the plural "we/us" in 123:3–4, and the plural continues throughout Psalm 124. The writer sets up a set of unreal conditions ("if the LORD had not been on our side"), defining the real situation in verse 2b, "when people attacked us." "People" is the Hebrew word *'adam* ("humankind, humanity"), used as a collective.

The theme of Yahweh's favor to Israel against the opposition of mortals is frequent in the Psalms (118:6; 9:19–10; 56:4, 11; see also Isa. 31:3; 51:12–13).

124:3–5 *they would have swallowed us alive . . . the flood would have engulfed us.* Verses 1–2 form the protasis (the "if"/conditional clause), and verses 3–5 the apodosis (the potential outcome). The metaphors of the psalm were very familiar to the Israelites. They knew how destructive war could be (124:2b), how ruthlessly Sheol could swallow up its victims (124:3), and how the "earth opened its mouth and swallowed" Korah and his associates (Num. 16:31–32); and no one could ignore the devastating effects floods could have on a helpless population, especially the flash floods that burst Israel's wadis to overflowing.

124:6 *Praise be to the* LORD. Now the poet has dropped the metaphor of "raging waters" (124:5) and employs instead a metaphor about vicious animals, returning to the metaphor of verse 3. The Hebrew "blessed" (*baruk*; NIV: "praise be") often begins a new section of a psalm (e.g., 28:6; 68:19), as it does here. The psalmist breaks out in praise that the potential outcome was not realized, precisely because of the unreality of the "if" clause. To the contrary, the Lord *was* "on our side" (lit., "for us").

124:7 *We have escaped like a bird from the fowler's snare.* The hunting metaphor recalls how hunters lay a snare for birds (see the comments on 9:16 and 18:4–5; see also the painting from the tomb of Nebamun in the unit on Psalm 31). The broken snare was no ordinary event, because a good hunter would use the strongest material available.

124:8 *Our help is in the name of the* LORD, *the Maker of heaven and earth.* While the clause "the snare has been broken" in verse 7 does not specify who has broken it, the poet intends for us to understand this to be God, and here we understand that God could perform this task because he is "Maker of heaven and earth." This is really a theological summary of the entire psalm: the saving God and the creating God are the two sides of the coin of divine sovereignty (see "Teaching the Text" in the unit on Ps. 104). The statement "Maker of heaven and earth" appears also in 121:2 and 134:3.

Theological Insights

The conclusion of this psalm points to God, the "Maker of heaven and earth,"[3] not to the things he made. While the created world is good because God made it (Gen. 1:31), the Scriptures emphasize the Creator/Maker over the things he made. It is a serious aberration of biblical theology when we focus on things more than on their Maker. The pair in Eden shifted their focus from the Creator to the creation, which led them into disobedience: "When the woman saw that the fruit of the tree was good for food and pleasing to the eye, and also desirable for gaining wisdom, she took some and ate it. She also gave some to her husband, who was with her, and he ate it" (Gen. 3:6–7). But after entertaining the what-ifs of Israel's history, the psalm refocuses our attention on the one who is "our help," "the Maker of heaven and earth" (124:8). So we shouldn't be surprised that the enemies, described as "the flood," "the torrent," and "the raging waters," did not sweep us away. Indeed the Creator commanded them too, and they did his bidding at creation, so why would the waters be recalcitrant in other threatening circumstances!

Teaching the Text

One of my students called Psalm 124 the "what if" psalm. The psalmist ruminates about those circumstances that *could have materialized* into destructive forces "if the LORD had not been" on their side.

First, when the psalmist heard the stories of Israel's past, and when he looked at his own personal journal, he saw so many could-have-beens. Some would say we can't talk about the what-ifs of history, and, in a way, that is true. We don't know what would have happened, because it didn't happen. Yet sometimes talking about the what-ifs can make us appreciate more the "what dids"—the great things that God did!

The imagery in verses 4 and 5 reminds us of the cavernous wadis in Israel that dry up in the summertime, but in the wintertime, during the rainy season, they become potential torrents of destruction. When one drives along the shore of the Dead Sea and looks toward Jerusalem, one can see how those wadis stand there glaring at passersby with their mouths wide open. And during the rainy season, water can come rushing out of the Judean hills so forcefully that it can actually sweep a bus off the road.

We may mention to our listeners that this psalm reminds us of the fact that there are some hazards on the road of our Christian journey. Danger is lurking somewhere along the highway. To use another metaphor, the Psalms are a "journal of the soul" where the psalmists recorded their life experiences, the things that made them sad, the events that called for celebration, the people who energized them and those who bored them. Some of the psalms are virtually an accident report on the highway of faith, sometimes expressed in the most generic terms but in other instances containing the details of the tragedy and even the casualties that littered the road of life.

Second, we should make the point that the focus of Psalm 124 is not actually on the what-ifs of our lives—it treats those generically—but on the Lord's help. Calvin's services in Geneva began with this affirmation: "Our help is in the name of the LORD, who made heaven and earth" (see "Illustrating the Text"). So the psalmist breaks forth into praise in celebration of God's help

(124:6–7). In this case too, the terms are generic—no attempt to explain how, just the facts: "We have escaped like a bird." The worst scenario did not happen. We can remind ourselves and our listeners that verse 8 is the mammoth solution to our problems: "Our help is in the name of the LORD, the Maker of heaven and earth." And if God is for us, who can be against us? If we take our problems and *put God under them*, they look insurmountable. But if we take our problems and *put them under God*, they look so much smaller. We like to have the experts, the specialists, alongside us when we need help. If we are ill, we want a doctor who specializes in our particular malady. If we are building a house, we want an architect who knows the profession and builders who are skilled and do excellent work. But even as hard as we try, it is not always possible to get the best help available. But in our Christian life, we always have the best help possible—the Creator of the world! He not only has the knowledge but also is faithful. That's the truth that John sets forth in the frontispiece of his Gospel: that the Creator of the world has come to save the world (John 1:10–11) and help us in our personal crises. This is the God who put up a "No Trespassing" sign to the disease that stalked the alleyways of our anatomies, who said, "Do Not Proceed beyond This Point" to the spiritual viruses of our souls—"if it had not been the LORD who was on our side"!

Illustrating the Text

A Reformer's song of triumph

Church History: John Durie was one of the Scottish Reformers of the sixteenth century. He spent some time in Holland in exile from his homeland during the threatening years of Queen Mary's reign, and in 1582 he returned to Edinburgh to become the Protestant pastor of St. Giles Church, the church where John Knox had roared out his powerful sermons. As Durie and the Scottish believers made their way in procession up High Street to St. Giles Church for the service of restoration, they sang the metrical version of Psalm 124 in the Gaelic language, in four parts:

> Had not the Lord been on our side,
>   may Israel now say;
> Had not the Lord been on our side,
>   when men rose up to slay;
> They had us swallow'd quick, when as
>   their wrath 'gainst us did flame:
> Waters had cover'd us, our soul
>   had sunk beneath the stream.[4]

John Calvin's liturgy

Church History: In the liturgy that John Calvin wrote in Strassburg and Geneva, the service began with the sentence, "Our help is in the name of the LORD, who made heaven and earth." Calvin knew that this sentence expressed the powerful truth that every congregation needs to hear at the outset of worship. It is both a word of praise and a word of faith confession, and when our lives are directed by this truth, there is no gushing flood of trouble or stealthy trap of evil plans that can overpower us, because our Helper is the Maker of heaven and earth.

"Those Who Trust in the LORD Are like Mount Zion, Which Cannot Be Shaken"

Big Idea

God's presence gives security and peace.

Key Themes

- By God's grace, the power of the wicked will not replicate itself in the life of the righteous.
- Peace is the anteroom of God's presence.

Understanding the Text

Psalm 125 turns the reader's attention to the Lord's protective presence (much like Ps. 121), like Zion's encircling mountains, and focuses more closely on the moral life of the righteous that determines Israel's continuing occupation of the land (Deut. 28). The genre of the psalm is that of a Zion song (see also Pss. 46; 47; 48; 84; 87; 125; and 132), and it represents a view of the topography of Jerusalem, compared to 122:3, which gives us an internal view. It may also be viewed as a psalm of trust (125:1).

The Text in Context

What better picture of God's people could the poet provide after having announced their escape "like a bird from the fowler's snare" (124:7)? For here he describes the reason why the escape became a reality. Already the Pilgrim Psalter has directed the community of faith to "pray for the peace of Jerusalem" (122:6a) and assured them that the one who watches over this city would not let their feet slip (121:3, same verb as 125:1b, NIV: "be shaken").

Outline/Structure

1. The blessing: Mountains as symbol of God's encircling protection (125:1–2)
2. The curse canceled: The wicked's power will not replicate itself in the righteous (125:3)
3. Prayer, judgment, and blessing (125:4–5)

Historical and Cultural Background

The topographical information about Mount Zion (Jerusalem) in verse 2 of our psalm gives us a general sense of the city's natural defenses. Although Mount Zion is a hill, the mountains around the city are higher. East of the city lies the Mount of Olives, on the north lies Mount Scopus, and on the west and south are other hills, all of which are higher than Mount Zion. So the surrounding mountains provide a sense of security.

Interpretive Insights

125:2 *As the mountains surround Jerusalem, so the* Lord *surrounds his people.* Similarly, 34:7 says, "The angel of the Lord encamps around those who fear him, and he delivers them."

both now and forevermore. The NIV has accurately rendered the Hebrew phrase, which does not imply a new situation but indicates one that already exists and will continue and applies to the generation of the exile and those to follow.[1]

125:3 *The scepter of the wicked will not remain over the land allotted to the righteous.* The NIV has unfortunately not translated the Hebrew element that begins the verse, which here means "indeed" and lends an emphatic sense to the sentence. The assertion is that the authority of the wicked will not be permitted to dominate the righteous ("rod" [NIV: "scepter"] is the symbol

---

The Names Israel and Judah

Prior to the exile of the northern kingdom to Assyria in 722 BC, the southern kingdom was known as Judah, to distinguish it from the northern kingdom, Israel. After this momentous event, however, the southern kingdom of Judah tended to assume the name Israel, and by the postexilic period that name had been fully appropriated for the Judean kingdom. There is no specific information in the Old Testament about the return of the Israelite exiles (northern kingdom) to the land, although Jeremiah and Ezekiel, contemporaries of the exiles to Babylonia, allude to their whereabouts in their day.

of power). The allusion is to the Babylonian domination of the land, and this declaration anticipates Psalm 126, which, by celebrating the return, celebrates the relief from the "rod," or from Babylonian control. It may allude to Babylonian power that was broken by Cyrus the Great in the conquest of Babylon in 539 BC, thus breaking their control "over the land allotted to the righteous."

Psalm 132:12 issues a similar statement, clearly conditional in that instance, promising that if David's sons keep the covenant, they will occupy the throne forever. The expression "allotted to the righteous" is literally "the lot of the righteous," and English translations generally understand the phrase to allude to the land of Canaan, since Joshua used lots to apportion the land to the tribes. In light of the return to the land, this could also be an allusion to the Canaanites, who were the native inhabitants who led preexilic Israel away from the Lord and caused them to sin by worshiping other gods. In that case it would mean that the inhabitants of the land will not again be able to exercise influence over the Israelites and lead them into apostasy, as happened in the preexilic era ("For then the righteous might use their hands to do evil"), and thus bring about another forfeiture of the land.

125:4 Lord, *do good to those who are good, to those who are upright in heart.* As we observed on Psalm 123, the Songs of Ascents contain very few prayers, perhaps because the entire Pilgrim Psalter is a kind of "priestly blessing" on Israel (see "Teaching the Text" in the unit on Ps. 123 and the first endnote there). The petition recognizes that God blesses those "who are good" and are "upright in heart," which is likely a commendation of those who keep the Lord's commandments. The category of believers described here is synonymous with "those who trust in the Lord" in verse 1. Psalm 18:25–26 formulates a similar principle of reward ("To the faithful you show yourself faithful," etc.; see "Theological Insights" in the unit on Ps. 18).

125:5 *the* Lord *will banish with the evildoers.* The Hebrew behind the word "banish" means "lead away" ("to cause to walk"), and it may express the idea that the "evildoers" will be "led away" much as the exiles had been.

Peace be on Israel. This is a benediction, and it suggests that when the Lord banishes the evildoers, Israel will have peace (see the sidebar). Leviticus 26:5–6 links obeying the Lord's commands to peace in the land. The fact that the Pilgrim Psalter contains elements of blessing may suggest that it was written by a priest. See also "Theological Insights."

Theological Insights

We must not overlook the place of "peace" (*shalom*) in the Songs of Ascents. Psalm 119, the capstone psalm that follows the Egyptian Hallel, pronounces "great peace" on those who love God's law (119:165), and the writer (or writers) of the Songs of Ascents is quick to distinguish himself as a person of peace: "I am for peace; but when I speak, they are for war" (120:6–7); and that theme, though not an unbroken thread, is a prominent theme in the collection.[2] At the end of Psalm 122 the word "peace" is used three times within three verses, as the suppliant asks the community to "pray for the peace of Jerusalem" (122:6); and for the sake of family and friends, he pronounces a blessing of peace on Jerusalem (122:7–8), which he extends to the whole country in 125:5: "Peace be on Israel." The same blessing extends to the people in 128:6, "Peace be on Israel." Peace involves, obviously, a cessation of hostility and an end to conflict, and thus would be most apropos to this collection of psalms celebrating the end of a long period of war and captivity. But it also includes the welfare ("good") of the person and community (122:9b), and here in our psalm the blessing of God's presence (125:2; see also 128:6), which is the highest degree of *shalom*. Paul echoes this blessing in his own benediction on the Galatians, "Peace . . . to the Israel of God" (Gal. 6:16). It is of significance that the benedictory word the priests were to pronounce on Israel was "the LORD turn his face toward you and give you peace" (Num. 6:26). See Liebreich's hypothesis regarding the Pilgrim Psalter's dependence on the priestly benediction in "Additional Insights: Songs of Ascents, the Pilgrim Psalter (Psalms 120–34)," following the unit on Psalm 120.

Teaching the Text

First, we may observe that in our world much is said about security—financial security, health security, homeland security, even spiritual security—and these concerns meet us everywhere. That is the opening theme of Psalm 125: "As the mountains surround Jerusalem, so the LORD surrounds his people." Thus the psalmist, rather than beginning with his insecure world and working his way toward the theme of security, begins with a faith affirmation.

We may also make the point that Jerusalem does not occupy the highest mountain in the land, and not even the highest mountain in its region. The surrounding mountains, in fact, are not a circular wall, but, says Charles Spurgeon, "are, nevertheless, set like sentinels to guard her gates."[3] It is like a pyramid bowl turned upside down with smaller bowls having higher peaks situated around it, and those mountains symbolize the protecting presence of God. When standing on the Mount of Olives, for example, one looks down at the Temple Mount (City of David). While symbols can become a diversion, they can, used properly, remind us of spiritual realities (a picture of Jerusalem and the surrounding hills can be a good visual aid). The difference between believers and nonbelievers is not that believers in God don't have problems, but it is that they don't have to build their own security system, for God is their security. We can remind ourselves that we need, as Peterson says, to put our insecurities in their proper place, in the securing presence of God (see "Illustrating the Text"). Psalm 46 puts it in these words: "God is our refuge and strength, an ever-present help in trouble" (46:1).

Second, security in God carries a moral responsibility, and the psalmist penetrates beneath the simile of mountains to make this spiritual lesson. But we need to remind our listeners that Israel had lost their land and been taken into exile because of their moral infractions against God's law (see Deut. 28). The return from exile to their own land was evidence that they had made progress in turning their moral situation around, putting away their idols and the abominations that went along with the Canaanite worship (see Ezek. 8). It was when they came to God with empty hands, emptied of all their false supports and human resources and desperate to receive the gift of grace and peace that God so lovingly wanted to give them, that God could fill them (see "Illustrating the Text").

Verse 3 is a promise that God's commanding presence will not permit the wicked to replicate their evil in the land of Israel as they had done prior to the exile, thus leading Israel astray and into a long period of humiliation. This gives us an opportunity to speak about the powerful influence of evildoers over the righteous, a force that Christians must resist lest they lose their own spiritual standing. In Israel's recent history, apostasy had cost them their land, and no one would want to see that happen again. Paul speaks of Hymenaeus and Alexander, who "suffered shipwreck with regard to the faith" (1 Tim. 1:19–20). And as we make our point, we may also observe that our changed lives will inevitably bring God's favor, and that is the essence of the supplicant's prayer in verse 4.

The concluding benediction, "Peace be on Israel," is in essence the word of the Lord through his servant priest and a reiteration—in other words, of course—of the believers' affirmation of faith in verses 1–2: when God surrounds his people, they have peace. The word peace (*shalom*), which occurs twenty-three times in the Psalter, of which eight are in the Pilgrim Psalter, is evidently reflective of the priestly benediction, and twice it is benedictory (125:5 and 128:6). In Israel's life, as in ours, peace is the peak of blessing, the anteroom to the presence of God. In Augustine's *Confessions* he says, "God gives where he finds empty hands."[4] Sometimes our hands are so full of our earthly cares that we can't receive God's peace. Ultimately Christ is the peace toward which all human aspirations have striven (Eph. 2:14).

Illustrating the Text

Putting our fears in their place

Quote: **John Calvin.** Calvin said: "The best way, therefore, to maintain a peaceful life is when each one is intent on the duties of his own calling, carries out the commands that the Lord has given, and devotes himself to these tasks."[5]

Quote: Eugene Peterson. This psalm is not whistling in the dark, hoping that we can forget our sense of insecurity, hoping that our fears will subside, but it is facing the real darkness of life and putting our insecurities in their proper place—in the context of the securing power of God: "Those who trust in the LORD are like Mount Zion, which cannot be shaken but endures forever. As the mountains surround Jerusalem, so the LORD surrounds his people both now and forevermore"[6] (125:1–2).

Only empty hands can receive God's gift.

Quote: C. S. Lewis. Lewis tells this story of his wife, Joy:

> Joy tells me that once, years ago, she was haunted one morning by a feeling that God wanted something of her, a persistent pressure like the nag of a neglected duty. And till mid-morning she kept on wondering what it was. But the moment she stopped worrying, the answer came through as plain as a spoken voice. It was "I don't want you to *do* anything. I want to *give* you something"; and immediately her heart was full of peace and delight. St. Augustine says "God gives where He finds empty hands." A man whose hands are full of parcels can't receive a gift. Perhaps these parcels are not always sins or earthly cares, but sometimes our own fussy attempts to worship Him in *our* way.[7]

"The LORD Has Done Great Things for Us, and We Are Filled with Joy"

Big Idea

Tears may be a shaping force of life, but the main character trait of God's people is joy.

Key Themes

- Joy is a character trait of the people of God.
- The tears of the joy of arrival may be mixed with the tears of departure.

Understanding the Text

Since this psalm is a reflection on the return from exile, it was probably composed after the event, perhaps when the community realized that their crop failures were a consequence of their neglect of rebuilding the temple (Hag. 1:2–11; see Ps. 126:5–6). While it is a Zion song and shares a perspective with Psalm 85, it also has a lamentive tone (126:5–6). But the joy that pervades the poem (126:2, 3, 5–6) resists the lament label. If it is a lament, it is a lament clad in joy.

The Text in Context

Psalm 126 connects to Psalm 125 by the name "Zion" (125:1; 126:1), and the opening statement of 127:1 references the building of the temple ("Unless the LORD builds the house"), assuming a connection with Zion. Of course, Psalm 126 shares the same "ascents" style with the other Songs of Ascents in the Pilgrim Psalter with its repeated terms and phrases (e.g., "When the LORD restored the fortunes of Zion" [126:1] → "Restore our fortunes, LORD"

[126:4]; "The Lord has done great things for them" [126:2] → "The Lord has done great things for us" [126:3]; etc.).[1]

Zenger makes a case for Psalms 125 and 129 as the "outer psalms" of a collection of five psalms in the Pilgrim Psalter: "These two 'framing psalms' give the group of five *as a whole* a strongly political dimension. The trio of Psalms 126–128, standing between the two, sketch the daily world blessed by the God of Zion for those people who make the God of Zion the center of their lives."[2]

Psalm 126:2b–3a ("'The Lord has done great things for them.' The Lord has done great things for us") shares a few words with Joel 2:20–21, although they are not exact duplicates, and depending on how one dates the book of Joel, some take this to indicate a mutual dependence. Psalm 85 shares the perspective of restoration (85:1–3) and the abundant harvest (85:12).

Psalm 126 may be classified as a Zion song, along with Psalms 46; 47; 48; 84; 87; 125; and 132.

Outline/Structure

Two approaches to the psalm have characterized its interpretation, hinging on the Hebrew infinitive in verse 1 (*shub*, "to restore/return"). An infinitive has no tense and can be past, present, or future. One approach is to view verses 1–3 as future, understanding the infinitive of verse 1 as "*when* the Lord restores the fortunes of Zion" (NJPS, which is one of the few English version examples). The other view, more commonly accepted, is to interpret the infinitive as past tense, "*when* the Lord restored," as does the NIV. In light of the past tense (Hebrew perfect) "we were" (like dreamers) at the end of verse 1,[3] it would seem to tip the tense of the psalm toward the past, which means that the return from Babylonia has already happened.

1. Israel's reflection on the joy of return from exile (126:1–2a)
2. The nations' reflection on Israel's awesome redemption (126:2b)
3. Israel's confession that the Lord's awesome redemption was the source of their joy (126:3)
4. Israel's prayer for redemption (126:4)
5. Israel's/psalmist's reflection on the seed of tears that produce a harvest of joy (126:5–6)

Historical and Cultural Background

Glueck opens up the simile of verse 4 ("like streams in the Negev") by his description of how the rainfalls transform the arid landscape of the Negev into a virtual garden:

The grass and flowers fairly spring up after the first shower or storm, and the grim desert becomes a colorful garden overnight. It is as if a magic wand had been passed over the face of the earth. Flocks of birds suddenly make their appearance then, to sing and to swoop about in happy flight, and bands of gazelles and ibexes grace and cavort through the lush green.[4]

The fullness of joy attendant upon the restoration from captivity is compared to the *Afiqim ba-Negev* (Psalm 126:4), that is, the wadis in the Negev, whose soil has been saturated with life-sustaining waters of short-lived winter and spring freshets.[5]

The background of the psalm is most likely the Decree of Cyrus (538 BC) and the exiles' return to Judah described in Ezra 1.

Interpretive Insights

126:1–2a *When the* LORD *restored the fortunes of Zion, we were like those who dreamed.* One of two meanings is possible. First, this could refer to the restoration of the city of Jerusalem and the temple (Zion) to its former glory; second, it could refer to the return of the exiles. The Greek (LXX) opts for the second explanation, understanding the Hebrew phrase "the fortunes" (126:1, *shibat*; 126:4, *sheʿbit*) to be from the verb "to be in prison" (root *shbh*), and translates it "captivity" (*aichmalōsia*; "When the Lord turned the captivity of Sion"). Further, the Septuagint renders "like dreamers" as "like comforted ones."[6] While the second option seems preferable, it is possible that we should consider a much broader interpretation, including both options mentioned above.[7]

126:2b–3 *for them . . . for us.* These two prepositional phrases represent two different confessions. The first is spoken by the nations that see the incredible act of grace taking place in the return from exile. It is counter to their erstwhile and confrontational tactic that questions God's presence with Israel (42:3, 10; 79:10; 115:2; cf. Joel 2:17; Mic. 7:10). The second is Israel's own confession to the same effect. The nations and Israel together symbolize a worldwide phenomenon, and they are both confessing God's mighty acts ("great things"; lit., "The LORD has done greatly"; cf. Ps. 40:16b). One wonders if the clause "Our mouths were filled with laughter" may allude to Sarah's laughter of incredulity when she heard that she was to have a child in her old age (Gen. 21:6), and the following statement that "everyone who hears about this will laugh with me" is quite in keeping with the nations' affirmative response to this miracle in verse 2d, "The LORD has done great things for them." The nations speak first ("The LORD has done great things for them," 126:2d), before Israel makes the same statement, suggesting that the nations' pronouncement is filled with astonishment, and Israel's response is essentially, "That's right, the LORD *has done* great things for us" (126:3a).

126:4 *Restore our fortunes, Lord, like streams in the Negev.* The term "fortunes" alludes to the former life of the exiles in their own land. For "streams in the Negev," see "Historical and Cultural Background."

126:5–6 *Those who sow with tears will reap with songs of joy.* While this may be the answer to the request for restoration made in verse 4, spoken by a priest or prophet, it is also possible that it is a reflection on the crop failures that Haggai 1:2–11 speaks about, making the promise of verse 5, "Those who sow in tears will reap with songs of joy," essentially equivalent to that prophet's hopeful instruction in Haggai 1:8. In that case, it would refer to the real sowing of seed. A broader view would be to include the restorative work on the temple, which is my preference, and at that point it becomes a metaphor. For example, the laying of the foundation for the new temple was accomplished with tears but also with joy (Ezra 3:12).

Theological Insights

"Some things are too good to be true," says the adage. The Psalmist expresses this reality as "We were like those who dreamed" (126:1). In fact, neither the adage nor the psalmist's metaphor is a disclaimer of reality, but an acclamation that sometimes reality leaves us in virtual disbelief. This is the kind of joy of "dreams come true" that the exiles experienced when they realized that they were in fact, indeed, in reality, going home. It was a "pinch yourself" moment when goodness and truth came together in perfect harmony. "The past and the present meet in the presence of God," says Weiser,[8] and this community was experiencing that divinely appointed conclave, when human reality and divine grace touch each other, or perhaps we should say, when our human "dreams" become the gift of divine grace. That was what happened to Israel. And the antiphon of God's people is joy. In fact, the psalm begins with the Lord as subject, calls forth the witness of the nations, summons the confession of faith's community, and presents the final "video" of reapers loaded with sheaves and singing songs of the harvest's joy. It is a gathering of universal proportions in witness to God's phenomenal grace.

Teaching the Text

Today Psalm 126 is sung during the Passover Seder as a witness to what God has done for his people. This psalm itself comes out of the crucible of suffering. Like a stalagmite in a cave, it is shaped by the slow dripping of human tears. But while tears are a shaping power in this community's life, they are not the major attribute (Isa. 25:8). Rather, the emotional response to God's work is joy. And we can make this the main point of the sermon/lesson (there is nothing wrong with a one-point sermon/lesson). Chesterton has called joy the "gigantic secret of the Christian."[9] The psalmist's reflection on the past was all about the joy the return from exile brought these people: "Our mouths were filled with laughter, our tongues with songs of joy" (Ps. 126:2). It was simply unheard of in that world for political exiles to be repatriated. Isaiah had predicted it, but when it happened, it still seemed like a dream.

Joy, this "gigantic secret of the Christian," this fruit of the Spirit, as Paul calls it (Gal. 5:22), is not a transitory burst of emotion—though that's sometimes the external evidence—but it is one of the dispositional anchors of the Christian life. Jesus reminds his disciples that they should keep his commandments so "that my joy may be in you and that your joy may be complete" (John 15:11). George Bernanos was bold enough to say that the mission of the church was to rediscover the source of our lost joy (see "Illustrating the Text"). Joy is one of the earmarks of the Christian life. And Christ modeled this life for us, for it was joy that drew him to the cross ("For the joy set before him he endured the cross," Heb. 12:2), and this should even put a different perspective on the cross. When we gather around the communion table, for example, we are usually somber—and so we should be, but with a somberness clad in joy. What if we gathered around the Lord's table and burst into a gale of laughter? Would it be disrespectful? I don't think so, as long as it is the laughter of heaven, laughter that symbolizes the joy that Jesus knew in doing his Father's will, the joy that our sins are forgiven and that nothing can separate us from the love of Christ, the joy that he is coming again. At the Lord's table the tears ought to flow because of *what we have done to Christ*. But joy ought to bubble up in our souls because of *what Christ has done for us*. It's that latter reason that provokes the laughter of heaven. If we could hear the music of the spheres, it would be not a sinister laughter, not a get-even laughter, not an I-gotcha-at-last laughter, but the laughter of love, the laughter the exiles had as they made their way back home, the laughter that comes from the knowledge of sins forgiven, of the world made right with God, of a universe that declares the glory of God, of light that shines in the darkness and that darkness cannot overcome.

Genuine Christian joy is based on *what God has done*. That's the message of the psalm. Even the nations recognize God's wonderful works and proclaim, "The LORD has done great things for them" (126:2). It is after the nations make their proclamation that Israel then affirms that declarative truth. If we could recapture the joy of the Christian life, it would do a lot for us in the eyes of the world. This would be a great evangelistic witness, a spiritual outreach that would get the attention of our neighbors. It could transform us from weaklings into powerhouses of strength. That's what Nehemiah says to his congregation after they have heard the reading of the law of God.

When the people weep as they hear the Scriptures read, Nehemiah follows that with the proclamation, "Go and enjoy choice food and sweet drinks, and send some to those who have nothing prepared. This day is holy to our Lord. Do not grieve, for the joy of the Lord is your strength" (Neh. 8:10). He was sending them forth to their routine lives, to their workaday world, to live by the strength of the joy of the Lord. Let us labor and pray for the day when the Lord restores to his church that ability to become joyful about the great redeeming events of history, the great works of salvation that God has done and promised yet to do: the exodus, the return from captivity, the birth of Jesus, the cross, the resurrection, and Christ's promise to come again. When the church recaptures the power of Israel's witness to God's great works of saving grace, it will be a "pinch yourself" moment of recognition for the church and the world, to whom the church bears witness: "The Lord has done great things for us, and we are filled with joy" (Ps. 126:3). Our great God does great things.

Illustrating the Text

The tears of the joy on arrival may be mixed with the tears of departure.

Quote: *The Diary of a Country Priest*, by George Bernanos. The young priest in *The Diary of a Country Priest* says, "The mission of the Church is to rediscover the source of lost joy."[10] While that is only one aspect of the church's mission, it certainly is an important one. While the exiles of Psalm 126 find joy in their return home, we know that the ultimate source of their joy is the Lord. Their years of exile have been a sowing with tears (126:5), and we may assume that, after seventy years, those tears of joy upon returning home are mixed with tears of sorrow over leaving a place that has become home (only 50,000 of them will return, and that includes servants).

Quote: *Confessions*, by Augustine. Augustine speaks of his conversion in terms of joy displacing fear: "What I feared to be parted from, was now a joy to be parted with. For Thou didst cast them forth from me. . . . Thou castedst them forth, and for them enteredst in Thyself, sweeter than all pleasure."[11] The point is that often the fear of departure from a place or an experience or a life disposition is displaced, perhaps to our surprise, by the joy of arrival at a new experience in God. Our hearts have to be reequipped for the new phase of blessing, and sometimes that involves a bit of grief and pain. Indeed, "those who sow with tears," tears of the uncertainty of the harvest, maybe even tears of the grief of past harvest failures, will, in God's good plan and promise, "reap with songs of joy" (Ps. 126:5). This reminds us of David's transition from sadness to joy: "Weeping may tarry for the night, but joy comes with the morning" (Ps. 30:5 ESV).

"Big-godders" and "little-godders"

True Story: Donald Grey Barnhouse, former pastor of Tenth Presbyterian Church in Philadelphia, tells the story of his revered professor at Princeton Theological Seminary, Robert Dick Wilson, a renowned scholar of astounding linguistic ability. About twelve years after Barnhouse had graduated from the seminary, he was invited back to speak in chapel. Professor Wilson was present for the service, and afterward he approached the speaker with these words: "If you come back again, I will not come to hear you preach. I only come once. I am glad that you are a big-godder. When my boys come back, I come to see if they are big-godders or little-godders, and then I know what their ministry will be." When Barnhouse asked for an explanation, Wilson replied: "Well, some men have a little god and they are always in trouble with him. He can't do any miracles. He can't take care of the inspiration and transmission of the Scripture to us. He doesn't intervene on behalf of His people. They have a little god and I call them little-godders. Then there are those who have a great God. He speaks and it is done. He commands and it stands fast. He knows how to show Himself strong on behalf of them that fear Him. You have a great God, and He will bless your ministry."[12]

"Unless the Lord Builds the House, the Builders Labor in Vain"

Big Idea

God is both the Master Architect and the Master Builder, and we are merely his hired hands.

Key Themes

- God is the Master Architect and Builder.
- Children are our special inheritance from the Lord.

Understanding the Text

Zenger calls this psalm a proverbial poem or a psalm of wisdom instruction (see also Prov. 24:3–4).[1] The occurrence of "Solomon" in the title taps certain spiritual reserves, recalling his construction of the temple and his proverbial counsel to families in Proverbs.

The Text in Context

Zenger divides the Songs of Ascents into three groups of five: Psalms 120–24; 125–29; and 130–34, with each group having a center psalm. Table 1 presents that theory, and I have explained their interrelationships.

Table 1. The Centering Effect in the Pilgrim Psalter

1. Psalms 120–24	
Psalm 120	This set of psalms presents a general view of the return from exile, with the community's intent to escape the symbolic land of "Meshek" (120:5) in search of a country of peace (120:7).
Psalm 121	"Begins" the journey as the travelers "lift" their eyes toward the "mountains" of Jerusalem.

Centering Psalm:	"A song of ascents. Of David."
Psalm 122	Psalm 122 positions the perspective of this group at the "house of the Lord" in Jerusalem (122:1–2), celebrating their arrival in Zion, either in reality or in anticipation.
Psalm 123	Provides a picture of the people's ultimate vision, as they lift their eyes, not to Jerusalem as such, but to "you who sit enthroned in heaven" (123:1), acknowledging that they are slaves and the Lord is Master.
Psalm 124	Concludes this cadre of "travel" psalms with the answer to the prayer of 123:3, as they celebrate their escape from exile and their safe arrival through the power of "the Maker of heaven and earth" (124:7–8).
2. Psalms 125–29	
Psalm 125	Psalm 122 having given the centering perspective of Jerusalem and the temple, Psalm 125 begins this new group of psalms with a celebration of Zion and the Lord's protection of the city (125:1–2).
Psalm 126	Provides a reflection on the community's joy of their restoration to their beloved Zion.
Centering Psalm:	"A song of ascents. Of Solomon."
Psalm 127	Quite appropriately, the title of Psalm 127 refers to Solomon, intimating his role in building the "house" (temple) (127:1), and his proverbial counsel for family life (127:3–5; cf. Prov. 17:6; 20:7).
Psalm 128	Follows Psalm 127 with a blessing on Zion's inhabitants in terms of fruitful labor and offspring (128:1–4).
Psalm 129	Concludes on the triumphant note that Zion's enemies have not gained the victory (129:2).
3. Psalms 130–34	
Psalm 130	This group begins with a cry to the Lord, who does not keep a record of sins, thus explaining Israel's restoration by their forgiving God (130:3–4).
Psalm 131	Follows as a response to the call of 130:7 to hope in the Lord, and in effect also renews the call (131:3).
Centering Psalm:	"A song of ascents."
Psalm 132	While not attributed to David, the psalms on either side are, and judging from the content, it need not be attributed to David for it to be about the Davidic covenant, and that is the centering theme. It is a prayer that God will remember his covenant with David, thus positioning the Pilgrim Psalter in the Davidic covenant, and thus counterbalancing any issues left unresolved by Psalm 89; the congregation prays for the restoration of the Davidic dynasty (132:10) and the restoration of Israel as a priestly people (132:9).
Psalm 133	A blessing on the people of God as the renewed royal priesthood.
Psalm 134	Positions the Pilgrim Psalter in the temple with the people of God at worship and issues the final pronouncement of blessing on the people of God (134:3).

Note: The table is an adaptation of Zenger's "centering" theory on the Pilgrim Psalter (Hossfeld and Zenger, *Psalms 3*, 394). The summaries of the centering ideas are largely mine.

Outline/Structure

1. The Lord, the Master Builder of the temple (127:1–2)
2. The Lord, the Master Builder of the family (127:3–5)

Historical and Cultural Background

The attribution of this psalm to Solomon suggests not so much authorship but a Solomonic perspective, especially in relation to the "house," which, in connection with the title, carries a double meaning: the temple, which Solomon built, and the family, to which he offered so much advice in the book of Proverbs.

Interpretive Insights

Title *Of Solomon.* Since four Songs of Ascents have "to/of/for David" in their title, it certainly seemed appropriate to an editor (possibly even the psalmist, who was likely a contemporary of Zerubbabel's temple) to prefix Solomon's name to the idea of building a house, since he was the builder of the temple. Moreover, in 2 Samuel 12:25 the Lord sends the prophet Nathan to name Solomon *y^edidyah* (Jedidiah), meaning "beloved [*yadid*] of the Lord"; the same term is used in verse 2, "He gives sleep to his beloved [*yadid*]" (author's translation; NIV: "He grants sleep to those he loves"). Both the building of the house and "his beloved" bring Solomon to mind. While the attribution to Solomon could be later, it is also possible, with these word associations, that it is original to the psalm. In any case, it most likely means "about Solomon" (see also Ps. 72) rather than "by Solomon."

127:1 *Unless the* LORD *builds the house, the builders labor in vain.* Two verbs carry the sense of "build," the first ("to build") applied to the Lord, and the second ("to exert oneself") applied to the builders. The use of the verb "labor" ("exert themselves") emphasizes the effort put forth by these builders and thus makes the adverb "in vain" even stronger, "to no avail / useless" ("They exert themselves for nothing"; Coverdale: "Their labour is but lost").

Unless the LORD *watches over the city.* The second case is the city, and unless the Lord watches over it, the "guards stand watch in vain." While neither the house nor the city is named, the temple and city of Jerusalem are in view, especially since the title has prefixed "Of Solomon" to the psalm.[2]

127:2 *In vain you rise early and stay up late.* The NIV appropriately translates the term "in vain" as the first item of the sentence. The ascent pattern is obvious here in the use of the word *shaw'* ("in vain"). The poet puts that term first in the second half of each line of verse 1 (lit., "*In vain* the builders exert themselves"; "*In vain* the guards stand watch"), and here in verse 2 he puts it at the front of the sentence. The repetition of the term continues the "traveling" effect of the author's poetic style.[3] The terms "rise early" and "stay up late" are allusions to a long and intense workday, and likely with the assumption of wisdom thought that such toil is useless (e.g., Eccles. 4:4–8).

toiling for food to eat. Literally, "eating the bread of toil." This may be an echo of the Lord's curse against Adam in Genesis 3:17, which was a curse on the ground.

he grants sleep to those he loves. The Lord provides adequate sleep for those he loves and does not require them to "rise up early and stay up late" just to earn a living.

127:3–5 *Children are a heritage from the* LORD. The poet continues to enumerate God's gifts to "those he loves," children being the most significant. The term "heritage" is the same word used of the "heritage" of Israel as God's people (Deut. 4:20; 9:26, 29) and the land of Canaan as the heritage the Lord has given them (Josh. 13:6, 7; 23:4). So there is an implicit parable in these statements about children, who become "arrows" in the warrior's "quiver" (see Isa. 49:2). They are like God's claim on the world through his people Israel, and like the father and mother's claim on life, as the land was Israel's claim on the world, and the children are their weapons of conquest and agents of arbitration. The latter is implied by "They will not be put to shame when they contend with their opponents in court" (Ps. 127:5). See also Proverbs 5:18; 17:6; 20:7.

Theological Insights

This psalm speaks of those things that God gives to humanity to make them joyful: a house to live in, a city for safety, bread to eat, children, and protection of one's heritage. These are God's gifts—and that is the point—which he provides to "those he loves." And we must remember that they are God's *gifts*, and this does not imply that their absence is God's curse. The intent of the psalm is not to give passivity a stamp of approval but to provide an underlying understanding of the Lord's relationship to his people: the Lord is their provider and protector, and the fact that he chooses to use human beings to fulfill his will in no way puts them in control.

Teaching the Text

In Psalm 127 there is a delicate balance between human effort and God's enabling. While our human inclination is to get the job done, sometimes we unfortunately run ahead of God and forget Jesus's assurance: "My Father is always at his work to this very day, and I too am working" (John 5:17). Jesus knows that it is not merely his own hands that touch the blinded eyes; it is also the Father's hands that touch them through him.

We may make the point that there are two extremes that, unfortunately, often characterize believers, neither of which is valid. The first extreme is to do nothing because, in reality, only God can do things—so let him. But that produces passivity or slothfulness, and those who operate under this assumption fulfill the proverb "A little sleep, a little slumber, a little folding of the hands to rest—and poverty will come on you like a thief, and scarcity like an armed man" (Prov. 6:10–11; 24:33–34).

The second extreme is a spiritual workaholic posture that arises from the assumption that God is depending on us to do the job, so we have to expend every ounce of energy to accomplish the task. Hilary of Tours said we have to guard against a blasphemous anxiety to do God's work for him,[4] for this attitude will produce an unwholesome reliance on our human effort and resources and result both in frustration with ourselves because we could not accomplish our aims and in disappointment with God because the task turns out poorly.

The subject of this psalm, however, is neither of these positions but that of Proverbs 19:21: "Many are the plans in a person's heart, but it is the LORD's purpose that prevails." The assumption of this verse is that there is a larger plan of God ("the purpose of the LORD") and our plan or task fits somewhere within that purpose, and even when we have fulfilled ours, and fulfilled it well, it may still look inadequate or incomplete because we have not viewed it in the larger scope of God's kingdom. This is the time to remind ourselves that the larger plan has a Master Architect, and we are the Architect's workers, carrying out his plan. So the plan and the outcome are under the Master Architect's sovereign control. Luther, a man of inestimable stature and courage, realized that the Reformation could succeed only if the Lord was the Architect (see "Illustrating the Text"). Some of us need to post this motto on the lintel of our souls: "Unless the Lord builds the house . . ." (127:1). Maybe we ought even, and quite literally, to display it over the front door of our house. We are not the real Builder. We're just God's hired hands.

The verdict for forgetting this truth is clear in the psalm. Three times the psalmist uses the term "in vain," which means "for nothing" (127:1 and 2). The psalm teaches us that God is the key to everything we do and that we should do it all to the glory of God, as Paul instructs us in 1 Corinthians 10:31. That means we must recognize that the Lord is the Master Architect. Or to phrase it another way, we are the gloves into which God fits his loving and powerful hands. We need to acknowledge that the Lord is the Architect and the Builder; recommit ourselves, our work, and our plans to God's master plan and his masterful performance; and let God build his kingdom through us.

Illustrating the Text

We are the hired builders, not the architect.

Church History: Martin Luther was a doer if there ever was one. But he knew that all of his work in the reformation of the church was in vain if the Lord was not the real architect. When writing to friends or public bodies, Luther had a practice of sending one of his brief expositions of a psalm along with his letter. In November 1523, the Council of Riga sent him a letter of gratitude, and with his answer, he sent back his brief exposition of Psalm 127: "Except the LORD build the house, they labor in vain that build it." Luther's message was that the Reformation could not succeed if the Lord was not working through the efforts and toil of the churches.[5] He further expresses this truth in his hymn "A Mighty Fortress Is Our God," which draws on Psalm 46 (see "Illustrating the Text" in the unit on Ps. 46):

> Did we in our own strength confide,
>> our striving would be losing,
> were not the right man on our side,
>> the man of God's own choosing.
> Dost ask who that may be?
>> Christ Jesus, it is he;
> Lord Sabaoth his name,
>> from age to age the same,
> And he must win the battle.[6]

"Children are a heritage from the LORD."

Personal Testimony: One morning as I was reading my five psalms a day, Psalm 61:5 just jumped off the page at me: "You have given me the heritage of those who fear your name." The word "heritage" (root *yrsh*) is different from 127:3 (root *nhl*), but the two are virtually synonymous, often referring to Israel's landed heritage (Canaan). But they also include the spiritual heritage that is transmitted from one generation to the next. In a society that values real estate more than venerates it, I thought immediately about the spiritual heritage that my parents and my wife's parents passed on to us. We grew up in the church—it was our life—and don't have a testimony of a radical conversion (I rejoice to hear them from others, however), but our spiritual heritage is of the greatest value. In Psalm 127 the meaning of verse 3, "Children are a heritage from the LORD," involves at least two facts of significance: (1) that children are our "patrimonial claim" in the world, as was real property; that is, they give us a sense of permanence and belonging, and a hope for the future; (2) that they also represent the spiritual legacy that has been transmitted to us.

On a very personal level, in my early days of college teaching and my theological journey, I recall a major transition in my theological tradition that I knew I had to make if I was to maintain my theological integrity. Not knowing the full implications of this momentous decision, I recall kneeling in my study and praying one of those Hezekian prayers, tears and all, pouring out my concerns to the Lord, asking for not extended years but extended heritage, asking that my son, only two years old at the time, might come to know Christ—as I had come to know him, my most precious heritage, through my devout parents. God answered my prayer, and my son knows the Christian gospel even better than I did at his age.

"Blessed Are All Who Fear the LORD, Who Walk in Obedience to Him"

Big Idea

The fear of the Lord has three dimensions: theological, ethical, and practical.

Key Themes

- The fear of the Lord involves "walking in his ways" (commandments).
- To fear the Lord is to be "blessed."
- Family life is connected to the larger social circles of city and country.

Understanding the Text

Perhaps the best genre for this poem is that of a psalm of blessing or beatitude, with the priest in the temple likely pronouncing this blessing, in part or in whole, on the congregation. Zenger proposes that we might think of it as a "wedding blessing" (128:1–4), expanded by verses 5–6 into a blessing on "all who fear the LORD" (128:1).[1]

The Text in Context

Psalm 127 introduces two topics that are carried over into Psalm 128: a life that is filled with work and no sleep (127:2) and children as the Lord's blessing (127:3). Psalm 128 turns the first idea, a negative one, into a positive, that of the productive and prosperous life (128:2), and it extends the second idea, of children as a blessing, to many children as God's blessing (128:3). While Psalm 128 closes with a blessing (128:5–6), Psalm 129:1–4 is Israel's affirmation of the blessing prayed for them in 128:5–6. In effect, if Psalm 129:5–8, a curse, comes to pass, the positive blessing of 128:5–6 will become a reality. The final word of blessing, "Peace be on Israel" (128:6b), is a duplicate of the final blessing of 125:5c, which reaches further back into the Pilgrim Psalter to continue the theme of Psalm 122:6–8. When we consider the themes of work, posterity, and peace in the context of the postexilic age, they are perfect matches for those concerns that would have exercised a new community like the returning exiles.

Outline/Structure

The poem is composed of two parts, the first being a beatitude that is pronounced on "all who fear the LORD," which includes abundant offspring, and that is bounded at each end by the phrase "fear the LORD" (128:1a and 4b). The second is a blessing on the same group of believers and includes both prosperity and posterity.

1. Beatitude on all who fear the Lord (128:1–4)
2. Blessing on all who fear the Lord (128:5–6)

Historical and Cultural Background

While we cannot be certain when this psalm was composed, its background seems to be a time of peace and prosperity, at least a time of tenuous peace and prosperity. It may very well have been composed once the Jews had returned to Jerusalem and established a semblance of peace and normality, even in the early postexilic period. However, there is also the possibility that it was written during Nehemiah's time as an instrument of blessing used by the people when they "blessed all the men who willingly offered to live in Jerusalem" (Neh. 11:2 ESV).[2] Our working hypothesis is that the Pilgrim Psalter is a general blessing on the early postexilic community, newly returned from Babylonia and busily engaged in the work of restoration.

Interpretive Insights

128:1 *Blessed are all who fear the* LORD. This beatitude pronounces blessing on the God-fearers, as does 112:1 (other beatitudes are 1:1; 32:1, 2; 41:1; 94:12; 112:1). This term "blessed" (*'ashre*) sets those people who "fear the LORD" in a category of people who bring special pleasure to God and who enjoy an exceptional life in God. In other contexts, it also connotes those who receive God's special favor (e.g., forgiveness of sins, 32:1) but who also give to those in need ("Blessed are those who have regard for the weak," 41:1). See also the comments on 1:1 and 32:1, and "The Text in Context" in the unit on Psalm 41.

who walk in obedience to him. Literally, "who walk in his ways." Obedience is certainly the idea here, and it is obedience to Yahweh's "ways," or his Torah. See 119:1–3, where "ways" is a synonym for Torah.

128:2–3 *You will eat the fruit of your labor; blessings and prosperity will be yours.* Verse 1 formulates a general beatitude in the third person, with the bounding third-person idea occurring also in verse 4 ("Yes, this will be the blessing for the man who fears the LORD"), while verses 2 and 3 shift attention to the more specific "you" singular, applying the beatitude. One of the curses of the biblical world was that a family would grow their crops and not be able to eat their fruit because of enemy invasion or unjust seizure. Verse 2 expresses the opposite and is a metaphor for peace and prosperity.

fruitful vine . . . your children will be like olive shoots around your table. In the biblical world there was no greater blessing than children (Gen. 1:28; Ps. 127:3–5), and the more children, the greater the blessing. The metaphors "fruitful vine" and "olive shoots" represent the abundance of children. Infant mortality and disease took their toll on families in the ancient world, so many children would hopefully result in sufficient laborers in the family business and farm and also assure future offspring. "Olive shoots around your table" is a picture of the abundant shoots of new growth around the base of olive trees (see the sidebar "Olive Trees" in the unit on Ps. 52).

128:5–6 *May the LORD bless you from Zion.* Like verses 2–4, these final two verses are phrased with the second-person singular ("you"), but we should understand it to have a wider application to the community as a whole, as we have seen in other Songs of Ascents (see "The Text in Context" in the unit on Ps. 121, and the comment on 123:3). While the Songs of Ascents do not seem to have been placed in a chronological order, ever since Psalm 122, when the pilgrims declared, "Our feet are standing in your gates, Jerusalem" (122:2), the perspective of these psalms is almost exclusively Zion, the religious name of the city, and this term is used exclusively in the remainder of the collection,[3] with the exception of "Jerusalem" in 128:5b. "May you live to see your children's children" is an extension of the blessing of children in 127:3–4 and 128:3–4 to the grandchildren (see Prov. 17:6). Also of note is the literary style (anadiplosis) that repeats words and phrases in a steplike pattern; see "Additional Insights: Songs of Ascents, the Pilgrim Psalter (Psalms 120–34)," following the unit on Psalm 120. The peace of the individual and community (128:2) is inseverable from the peace of Jerusalem and the peace of Israel (128:5, 6).

Theological Insights

While the fear of God has various facets, its general meaning is that the person described as having the fear of God is religiously devout. We may think of the fear of the Lord as having three definitive dimensions: (1) the general, (2) the ethical, and (3) the practical. The general is here represented by "Blessed are all who fear the LORD" (128:1a; compare Prov. 9:10, "The fear of the LORD is the beginning of wisdom")—they are religiously devout (Job 1:1). The ethical is represented by "who walk in obedience to him" (lit., "who walk in his ways"; in Job 1:1 it is represented by those who "shunned evil")—they keep God's ethical demands. The practical is described in terms of the blessing of that state of religious devotion (Ps. 128:2–4)—they have a special relationship with God. The ritual dimensions of the "fear of the Lord," that is, devotion to worship and sacrifice, would be included most likely under "ethical" or "practical." It is difficult to make a sharp distinction between those two categories.

Teaching the Text

First, we may point out that Psalm 128 builds on the rhythm of Psalm 127, extending the idea of our children as "a heritage from the LORD" beyond their defensive usefulness ("arrows in the hands of a warrior," 127:4a) to productive fruit of the labor that parents and children alike enjoy around the table (128:2–3) and in an atmosphere of peace and prosperity (see the comments on 128:2–3).

Second, we can observe, in Zenger's words, that Psalm 128 "gives us another 'miniature of daily life.'"[4] The psalmist draws attention in verses 2 and 3 to those things that we human beings are inclined to take for granted.[5] They are the everyday blessings that we have been given—eating the fruit of our labor, the blessing of posterity (128:3), and peace (128:3b). It is also contextually appropriate to observe that the assumption of verse 2 is that the peace and prosperity in which the family lives and thrives is in part a product of the labor of the many children in the family. It is no less a family working together and eating together. While our society may be reluctant to take this picture to be instructional, it is at the same time given as a portrayal of happy family life, and it is hard to deny its merits.

Third, we ought to draw attention to the interrelationship between the blessing of children and the good things of the world, both of which are bounded by blessing and the fear of the Lord (128:1a and 4). And it is important to note that the clause "who walk in obedience to him" (see the comments on 128:1) is a parallel clause to "all who fear the LORD," offering a descriptive note (see "Theological Insights"), fulfilling the ethical dimension of "the fear of the LORD." That is, we cannot and will not keep God's commandments if we do not fear him, and the two go together to compose the meaning of "blessed" (*'ashre*). Sometimes the word "blessed" is translated "happy," but too often happiness in our world is self-indulgence, which has its place to some extent but must not become the dominant theme of our lives, and "happy" is an inappropriate translation of this religious term in the Psalter. In addition to the first great commandment ("Love the Lord with all your heart"), the second carries a similar if not equal weight, "Love your neighbor as yourself" (Matt. 22:34–40; cf. Deut. 6:5; Lev. 19:18).

Fourth, this portrait of blessedness is issued in verses 5 and 6 as a blessing on Jerusalem and on the country of Israel. Again, we need to be careful that we don't read a directive from this text that is not there, but we also should not ignore the connection between the present blessing of the family, living in peace and prosperity, and the transfer of the picture in the blessing pronounced over Jerusalem and Israel. Here we have three major social components of the world of the psalmist—the family, the city, and the country—and in this social order the family is foundational. Indeed, textually the psalmist establishes a link in verses 5–6 between the "prosperity" of Jerusalem (lit., "goodness"; the same word occurs in verse 2b with a variant spelling) and the person who fears the Lord, since verses 5–6 are an extended description of that person (community). We may make the point, and quite reasonably, that person and place are linked in biblical theology. As Zenger says, "The well-being of individuals and the well-being of Jerusalem are closely related: the happiness of the individual culminates in his or her rejoicing in the well-being of Jerusalem, and Jerusalem's prosperity is complete only when the individuals who love Jerusalem as their focal center are happy."[6] The Lord commanded Jeremiah to write to the exiles in Babylonia and direct them to "seek the peace and prosperity of the city to which I have carried you into exile. Pray to the LORD for it, because if it prospers, you too will prosper" (Jer. 29:7)—there is a link between person and place. Our well-being is linked to the place where we live, and sharing our perspective with our community and the larger country is an important part of living out the gospel.

Illustrating the Text

The American dream in creedal form

Bible: 1 Chronicles 4:10. A few years ago the prayer of Jabez was a craze in some Christian circles ("Oh, that you would bless me and enlarge my territory! Let your hand be with me, and keep me from harm so that I will be free from pain"; 1 Chron. 4:10), and all too often it was an effort to put the American dream into creedal form. Our psalmist brackets the blessings of marriage and children and prosperity with the fear of the Lord. Even in our world with its social and economic changes, our families are at the top of the list of blessings for which we ought to thank God, for without them, especially without the peace and prosperity they can bring, God's intended blessing is inhibited.

The family legacy of those who fear the Lord

Story: Daniel A. Poling. In our world where families are too often dysfunctional, this psalm gives us the profile of a "blessed" and productive family, whose head is one who "fears the LORD." As we see in "Teaching the Text," the psalm depicts a home where father and mother and children work together to realize and share the blessings the Lord provides (128:5), and the result is not only a happy home but also peace on Israel. At least three generations are in view here, and they contribute to the welfare of the country as a whole ("Peace be on Israel," 128:6). Poling, a great Christian leader of the twentieth century, editor of *Christian Herald* magazine, and president of the World's Christian Endeavor, tells the story of his grandfather, who was an itinerant preacher, traveling on horseback to preach the gospel. While he traveled, the grandmother stayed home with their children, where they worked the farm and provided the living that the grandfather did not earn as a circuit rider. That legacy was passed down to Poling's parents, and Poling put the Christian virtues of those two generations of faith into practice, trusting in God's promise that we find in another psalm, "I have never seen the righteous forsaken or their children begging bread" (Ps. 37:25).[7] It is the kind of spiritual legacy the psalmist celebrates.

"They Have Greatly Oppressed Me . . . , but They Have Not Gained the Victory over Me"

Big Idea

As the Lord of history, God turns Israel's and our past hardships into victories.

Key Themes

- We remember hardships, but we celebrate the fact that, by God's grace, they did not overcome us.
- One little word is the fulcrum of history.
- God's actions are an expression of his righteous character.

Understanding the Text

Psalms 124 and 129 have liturgical and thematic similarities, even sharing evidence of a community thanksgiving. The gist of Psalm 129 is that just as Yahweh's righteous character has assured Israel historically of his righteous judgment, so may he continue dispensing his covenantal character to his people in future years.

The Text in Context

Psalms 124 and 129 are different in that Psalm 124 raises the question, what if the Lord had not been on our side? And Psalm 129 presents the historical realities of Israel's experience of God's grace, giving the general picture that the Lord had been on Israel's side. The two poems accomplish this with a combination of beautiful metaphors and similes, and Psalm 129 declares the opposite truth of the apodosis in 124:3–5 (e.g., "They would have swallowed us alive"): "They have not gained the victory over me" (129:2b).

Outline/Structure

1. Israel's historical oppressors (129:1–4)
2. Israel's hopeful future (129:5–8)

Historical and Cultural Background

It is better to view "all who hate Zion" (129:5) as Israel's foreign enemies rather than internal foes, since the "many times" of the psalm (see the comments on 129:1) intends to cover Israel's historical conflicts generally. Most likely Psalm 129 was sung in the temple on an occasion of thanksgiving, perhaps as a capstone psalm of thanksgiving to celebrate deliverance from their Babylonian foe, and the priest and congregation engaged in a mutual blessing (129:8).

Interpretive Insights

129:1 *They have greatly oppressed me from my youth.* The first section of the psalm (129:1–4) is a general review of Israel's past, describing the historical oppression they have endured, but it still has not overcome them. The opening word in the Hebrew of verses 1 and 2 means "many times" (NIV: "greatly"), and it is placed at the front of the verse to emphasize the frequency. "My youth" is sometimes a metaphor for the exodus and wilderness era (Hosea 11:1; Jer. 2:2). The personal pronoun "me" at first seems to suggest an individual lament, but the address to the congregation makes it clear that this is a community lament. In Book 5 it is often the case that the individual psalms are spoken on behalf of the nation.

let Israel say. Like 124:1 and 118:2, this is a liturgical directive, inviting the congregation to respond.

129:2 *but they have not gained the victory over me.* The conjunction "yet" (NIV: "but") is the one little word that turns the battle tide in the direction of victory (see "Teaching the Text").

129:3 *Plowmen have plowed my back.* Verse 1a is a look at the dark horizon of Israel's history, and here the psalmist gives us a video picture of the cluttered landscape of the past. This metaphor speaks of the cruel and painful exploits of war. Compare Amos 1:3, where Damascus "threshed Gilead with sledges having iron teeth."

129:4 *But the LORD is righteous; he has cut me free from the cords of the wicked.* These words are a continuation of the metaphor of "the plowmen" in verse 3, and now the Lord has cut the ropes that tied the plows to the animals that pulled them, and they no longer plow Israel's back.[1] It is the equivalent of the declaration of verse 2b, "but they have not gained the victory over me." The action flows out of the Lord's righteous character, which is the source of our victory over evil.

129:5 *May all who hate Zion be turned back in shame.* The haters of Zion are obviously the external enemies of Israel. In the last section (129:5–8) the psalm uses jussive verbs ("let them") to issue four curses against Israel's enemies: (1) may Zion's haters be turned back and be ashamed (129:5); (2) may they be like the grass on the rooftop that withers before it can be harvested (129:6); (3) may their harvest be meager (129:7); and (4) may they not be able to engage in the harvester's blessing (129:8). They connect to the curses of Psalm 109 and apply to the present enemies. The point of the expression "be turned back in shame" is not that Israel's enemies may change their minds and be ashamed of their hatred of Zion but rather that the fact they did not succeed may shame them before their fellow Zion haters (see 6:11).

129:6 *May they be like grass on the roof, which withers before it can grow.* The grass cannot grow because the soil on the rooftop is too thin (see Jesus's parable of the sower in Matt. 13:1–9).

129:7 *a reaper cannot fill his hands with it, nor one who gathers fill his arms.* There are two pictures here. The first clause depicts the reaper who holds his gathered grain in one hand while he gathers with the other, and the second is that of a reaper who gathers grain and folds it in his garment (like folding it in one's apron). The English translations generally render the second clause similar to the NIV: "nor one who gathers fill his arms." But the noun that most English translations render as "arms" here means "fold of a garment" or "bosom," rendered beautifully by the Jerusalem Bible, "Roof-grass never yet filled reaper's arm or *binder's lap*."[2] The translation "arms" is probably intended to signify holding the grain (in one's garment) close to one's bosom (the Targum has "his shoulders").

129:8 *May those who pass by not say to them.* The curse concludes by praying that the enemies' harvest will be so desolate that they will not even be able to exchange harvest greetings.

The blessing of the LORD be on you; we bless you in the name of the LORD. This blessing is reflective of the harvesters' blessing in Ruth 2:4, where the first part is an expansion of Boaz's blessing on the harvesters, and the second half the harvesters' response. Some English translations (e.g., NIV, ESV) blend together these two blessings in the Ruth story as if they were a single blessing (see NJPS, which translates the blessing and response). Evidently here we have both blessings together, "The blessing of the LORD be on you" being that of the giver of the blessing, and "we bless you in the name of the LORD" being the response of those who are blessed.

Theological Insights

There is one little word in this psalm that signals the turning tide of history, the little word "yet" (129:2b; NIV: "but"). This word is like "the blast of trumpets, or the roll of kettledrums," as Spurgeon expresses it.[3] It is the psalmist's way of raising the banner of victory. And the poet reminds us that oppressors have dogged Israel over and over again ("from my youth"), "yet they have not prevailed against" them (ESV) (see the comments on 129:1). This little word incorporates the power and grace of God to turn Israel's misfortunes into victories, to transform the sins of God's people into forgiveness, and thus to turn the tide of history. The power, of course, was in neither the weapons of war nor the warriors who wielded them but in the "righteous" God who had waged his character, not war, against those forces. We could say that this word "yet/but" represents God's incomparable grace. Paul affirms God's intervening force in words that reflect God's covenantal commitment in Jesus Christ: "We are more than conquerors through him who loved us" (Rom. 8:37).

Teaching the Text

We may begin our sermon/lesson by observing that the psalmist makes a one-sentence review of Israel's history, a look at the dark horizon more than the detailed landscape: "They have greatly oppressed me from my youth" (129:1). It is a lament, and the biblical laments normally lead to an affirmation of faith, as here in verse 4, "But the LORD is righteous." Israel's worship often involved a review of the past, and so should ours, because it is a reminder of what God has done and how our hardships have not overwhelmed us. In our confessions we are generally pretty adept at reviewing the history of the church universal and its triumph by God's power, but it could be a great theological benefit to phrase our local history in our confessions, alongside our universal, and celebrate what God has done for his church in the place where we live and work and pray. This could especially be a good perspective on anniversary celebrations.

Our second point should be that the psalmist invites the whole congregation to join in the confession, and they not only repeat the confession of verse 1a but expand it in an affirmative direction. Verse 2b begins with one little word, "yet/but," which becomes the fulcrum on which the psalm turns in the positive direction: "*but* they have not gained the victory over me." And here, as we observed in "Interpretive Insights," the psalm gives us a cameo picture of the landscape of history, filling in the picture of verse 1a: "Plowmen have plowed my back and made their furrows long" (129:3).

If we choose to open up the subject of God's governance of history, which underlies this picture of history, we might entertain numerous questions: How does God govern the universe? How does he administer the details of our personal lives? What is the moral principle by which God governs? Some people think God's way is pretty helter-skelter, and many of us are sympathetic to that point of view, especially when our lives themselves become helter-skelter, and Romans 8:28 ("In all things God works for the good of those who love him") is all out of focus. It would seem that God doesn't really have any master plan, so he works by the trial-and-error method of governing our lives and the world. But here that one little word "but," like a flash of lightning, lights up the landscape, and "They have not gained the victory over me" is the equivalent of Paul's "If God is for us, who can be against us?" (Rom. 8:31).

Our third point introduces a series of curses on Israel's (and our) enemies (129:5–8). Here we may not feel so comfortable, but we need to understand the function of the curses. They are in essence a description of the reversal of fortunes for our enemies, all encrypted in the metaphor of the harvest. In our world these enemies may be personal, international, social, or physical. We may note that these enemies, hopefully, do not match the horrible treatment of Israel's enemies (129:3), but generally speaking, they are a reversal of the blessing of 128:2, something we do not seek.

Illustrating the Text

One little word

Story: Verse 2 of our psalm has one little word ("but") that functions as the thought fulcrum of the psalm, turning the subject from destruction to victory (see also Ps. 91, where the single word "surely/because," *ki*, functions as a "signpost" in that psalm). One little word can sometimes be the thing that devastates our ego and hopes, or it can be the thing that builds up our character and confidence. A high school English teacher once instructed a class to write a theme on their summer vacation. In the course of the essay one student wrote, "I really enjoyed myself." When she received the theme back, in red ink the teacher had written in the margin opposite this idiom, "illiterate!" with the comment, "One does not enjoy *oneself* but enjoys *something*." That one little word, "illiterate," was devastating to this student, and for years it virtually immobilized her writing skills. Thankfully, there are other instances when one little word can build up a person's courage and send them on their way to greater personal confidence and achievement. Or one little word—O the power of words!—can mark, as in this psalm, the turning tide of a nation's history: "*but* they have not gained the victory over me."

A new relationship, the product of the righteous God

Bible: **Amos and Jeremiah.** The Old Testament is the cradle in which the concept of righteousness was rocked to maturity. The prophets, who were preachers of righteousness, interpreted a righteous person as someone who had a right relationship with God. That is, righteousness is a relational term. Amos had seen people go to the temple with regularity to offer their sacrifices, but they couldn't wait till it was all over so they could go back into their workaday world to cheat and oppress their neighbor. Nothing had changed. They just refrained from doing it on the Sabbath and festival days. (See Amos 8.) Jeremiah, a century and a half later than Amos, saw the same kind of false pretense in the worshipers who came to the temple. They broke the Ten Commandments, and then came to the temple and felt they were secure. Their temple manners were different from their street behavior. (See Jer. 7:9–12.) What Amos and Jeremiah and other prophets called for was not merely a conscientious enactment of the ritual law but an enactment of a new relationship with God and with their neighbor. It is not just having our offenses revoked and their penalties canceled—it is the establishment of a new relationship to the law, a new relationship to the will of God, to the Lawmaker himself. That is, we do the will of God because we want to know God better and want to love him more. All of those dimensions are not covered by our psalm, but the basic one does find coverage here, that our victories—we should say our victorious lives!—flow out of the character of God, who has set us free from evil's machinations and established a new relationship with us (129:1–4).

"I Wait for the LORD, My Whole Being Waits"

Big Idea

We can call out to God from the depths of our sins, because we know that he is forgiveness and unfailing love.

Key Themes

- God is forgiveness.
- God is unfailing love.
- God's forgiveness and unfailing love are the foundation for hope.

Understanding the Text

Verses 1–3 easily fit the genre of an individual lament, and verses 4–6 are words of trust. Psalm 130 is the sixth of the early church's seven penitential psalms (Pss. 6; 32; 38; 51; 102; 130; 143). The message is essentially that the psalmist can cry out to God from the depths because he knows that Yahweh is a God of forgiveness and unfailing love.

The Text in Context

Psalm 130 is first in the last group of five Songs of Ascents. Quite appropriately it laments Israel's sins and assures them that Yahweh, by nature, is forgiveness and unfailing love (see the comments on 130:4). The centering psalm of this group, Psalm 132, does not by its title anchor this group in history like the other two centering psalms (Ps. 122, "of David"; and Ps. 127, "of Solomon"), but more importantly, the content of Psalm 132 functions in that way (see table 1 in the unit on Ps. 127). Israel prays that Yahweh will restore the Davidic dynasty (132:10–11) and restore Israel to their priestly role (132:9). Psalm 131 is a response to Psalm 130:7, admonishing Israel to hope in the Lord, and the last pair of psalms in the group pronounce a blessing on Israel as the renewed royal priesthood (Ps. 133) and position Israel at worship in God's presence in the temple (134:1–2). Psalm 134, the final psalm, issues one final blessing on God's people (134:3).

Outline/Structure

The personal pronouns are the key to the division of the psalm into four sections.

1. The "I-you" section: "*I* cry to *you*, LORD" (130:1–2)
2. The "you" section: "With *you* there is forgiveness," so that *you* may be feared (130:3–4)[1]
3. The "I" section: "*I* wait for the LORD, . . . and in his word *I* put my hope" (130:5–6)
4. The "you-he [the LORD]" section: "Israel, put *your* hope in the LORD. . . . *He* himself will redeem Israel from all their sins" (130:7–8)[2]

Historical and Cultural Background

Since there are no historical references in this psalm, its anchor in history is difficult to determine. The fact that it is part of the Pilgrim Psalter would indicate that it was composed in the postexilic period, or at least adapted for use in that time.[3]

Most English translations (KJV and ASV are exceptions) render the verb of verse 1 in the present tense ("I cry"). In fact, the imperative of verse 2, "Lord, *hear* my voice," implies that the psalmist's distress is still a present reality. That would incline the translator to render the verbs of verses 5 and 6 as present tense also (either the present or the past tense is possible in vv. 1 and 5–6), suggesting that the crisis has not passed, and this would tend to move the poem into the genre of an individual psalm of trust (see the sidebar "Psalms of Trust" in the unit on Ps. 16). Appealing to our interpretation of the Pilgrim Psalter as a collection of poems celebrating the return and restoration, we may view Psalm 130 as a celebration of Yahweh's forgiving nature, now attested by the miraculous events of the return from exile and the rebuilding of the temple (see "Additional Insights: Songs of Ascents, the Pilgrim Psalter [Psalms 120–34]," following the unit on Ps. 120).

Interpretive Insights

130:1 *Out of the depths I cry to you, LORD.* The metaphor "depths" refers to deep waters (69:2, 14). The psalmist's state of mortal danger seems to have been created by his own sins (130:3) and the sins of Israel (130:8).

130:2 *Lord, hear my voice.* The sentence begins with '*adonay* ("Lord," written in English translations with lowercase letters, rather than "LORD," written with small caps), a substitute for the tetragrammaton (*YHWH*, "LORD") that denotes divine mastery, whereas verse 1 ends with the term "my cry for mercy" (lit., "my supplications"), suggesting the picture of the servant standing before his master, pleading for mercy (see 123:2).[4] Psalm 86 also has an interesting combination of these two terms for God (see the comments on 86:2 and "Teaching the Text" in the unit on Ps. 86).

130:3 *If you, LORD, kept a record of sins, Lord, who could stand?* This is reminiscent of the conditional clause in 124:1 and 2 ("If the LORD had not been on our side"). Here, however, the main clause is a rhetorical question, "Lord, who could stand?" and the implied answer is "no one," whereas in Psalm 124 the question is answered by a statement of what might have happened. In both instances, however, the main clause describes a condition that did not and could not occur because of the Lord's help. Here the point of the question is that if the Lord dispatched punishment according to the strict standard of the law, then nobody could survive the enforcement of that standard.

Following the pattern of verse 1, where *YHWH* stands at the end of the first clause and is then followed by the substitute *'adonay*, in this sentence the first clause ends with the shortened form of *YHWH* (*Yah*) and is then followed by the substitute *'adonay* ("Lord, Master"). In other words, the picture of Master/servant in verses 1 and 2 is continued in verse 3.

130:4 *But with you there is forgiveness.* The noun "forgiveness" occurs only three times in the Hebrew Bible (Ps. 130:4; Dan. 9:9; Neh. 9:17), and here it has the definite article, which signifies that forgiveness (or, "the very essence of forgiveness")[5] is Yahweh's true nature. The word "unfailing love" (*hahesed*, 130:7) also has the definite article and carries the same signification: Yahweh's essence is unfailing love.

so that we can, with reverence, serve you. The forgiveness of sin increases one's sense of reverence and worship: "that you may be feared" (ESV). The Hebrew reads: "For with you is (the) forgiveness so that you may be feared."

130:5 *I wait for the LORD, my whole being waits.* The psalmist is waiting for Yahweh's forgiveness (see 40:1). Note the use of *'adonay* and *YHWH* in verses 5 and 6, the same pattern as we have seen in verses 1 and 2.

130:6 *more than watchmen wait for the morning.* The metaphor of the watchmen waiting for the morning encapsulates the emotional and physical intensity of wakefulness and watchfulness that the watchmen endured during the night (see "Teaching the Text" in the unit on Ps. 59; see also 127:1). The repetition is also characteristic of the literary style of the Songs of Ascents.[6]

130:7 *Israel, put your hope in the LORD.* This is a call to all Israel to hope in the Lord, or a direct address to the congregation. In light of the liturgical leads we have seen in 118:2; 124:1; and 129:1, these words are likely liturgical. This community, now poised in the hope as well as the reality of restoration, takes on a repentant spirit and seeks Yahweh's forgiveness as they hope in the future.

for with the LORD *is unfailing love and with him is full redemption.* Here is the assurance of the forgiveness they hoped for. See the comments on 130:4.

130:8 *He himself will redeem Israel from all their sins.* The idea behind the language is that of a people or person who is in captivity and waiting to be released.[7] Verse 3 raises the question, "If you, LORD, kept a record of sins, who could stand?" and verses 4–7 answer that question: God forgives, based on his "unfailing love." The psalm closes with the promise that the Lord will "redeem Israel from all their sins," the word "sins" forming an *inclusio.* The fact that the psalmist summons Israel to "put your hope in the LORD" (130:7) may suggest that, on Israel's journey back to their homeland, they are reassured of God's forgivenss that is a product of his unfailing love. Such a moment of repentance and hope on this journey reveals the new heart the Lord has given Israel.

Theological Insights

Two nouns in this psalm have the definite article, "forgiveness" and "unfailing love," making them as awkward in English as in Hebrew ("with you is *the forgiveness*" and "with the LORD is *the unfailing love*"). But the purpose of the definite article is to indicate that these qualities are God's very essence. It is equivalent to John's equation, "God is love" (1 John 4:8). That is, when we talk about God, we could say with confidence that "God is forgiveness" and "God is unfailing love." That, of course, does not mean that we can start with human forgiveness and human love and declare them divine and their human subjects divine. But it does mean that when these qualities are evident in our human associations, however deficient they may be, they are echoes of divine forgiveness and unfailing love (see "Illustrating the Text").

Teaching the Text

First, we may stress that the word "depths" (130:1) is a metaphor for the painful experiences of life, especially those that take us to ground zero of faith, to the furthest edge of endurance, to the rock bottom of our sin. But the suppliant's words are not absolute despair, because he writes them with the knowledge that God does not keep a record of our sins but is the forgiving God. When our experiences of life initiate a cry of distress from the depths of our despair, we can be sure that the forgiving God has joined us in the depths, and that he is there with us. We are not only crying out to God, but God is crying out to us, crying out for us, and based on Jesus's use of Psalm 22:1 on the cross, crying out with us. MacDonald formulates this truth in his beautiful saying "Never a cry of love went forth from human heart but it found some heavenly chord to fold it in" (see "Illustrating the Text").

Second, before we get too far into our sermon/lesson, we need to observe that Psalm 130 deals with the erroneous assumption that God is counting our sins, just waiting for us to make one of our characteristic blunders so he can carve another notch in his big stick—"If you, LORD, kept a record of sins, Lord, who could stand?" (130:3). Job at moments thought God was just waiting for him to sin so God could jump out and lunge at him: "What is mankind that you make so much of them, that you give them so much attention, that you examine them every morning and test them every moment?" (Job 7:17–18). Such a vindictive God would make life miserable and hopeless, but that's not the kind of God that God is.

And our third point takes shape in light of that: "If you, O LORD, should mark iniquities, O Lord, who could stand? *But with you there is forgiveness, that you may be feared*" (130:3 ESV).[8] As observed in the comments on verse 4 above, the nouns "forgiveness" and "unfailing love" in the Hebrew text of Psalm 130 have the definite article, suggesting that these qualities constitute God's essence, similar to John's statement that "God is love" (1 John 4:8).

Because the psalmist is so convinced of the Lord's forgiveness, he puts his feet down on the solid ground of God's grace and resolves: "I wait for the LORD, my whole being waits, and in his word I put my hope" (130:5). The two words "wait" and "hope" are a synonymous pair that occurs quite often in Isaiah and the Psalms. Waiting for the Lord is an *expectant* waiting; it is waiting in faith, based on God's character of forgiveness and unfailing love. In this hope we watch for the first rays of the morning light because the Lord is forgiveness and unfailing love. The morning will indeed come. God has heard our prayers, and with him is "plenteous redemption," as the King James Version so beautifully expresses it. The sleepless night of anxiety and the tossing bed of sins unrepented will turn into the bright rays of God's morning of forgiveness and unfailing love.

Illustrating the Text

Some heavenly chord

Quote: **George MacDonald.** "God is love," wrote John (1 John 4:8), and that describes God's essence. God is "(the) forgiveness" (Ps. 130:4) and "(the) unfailing love" (130:7), says the psalmist, and those nouns also define his essence. MacDonald's insightful statement should not surprise us, then: "Never a cry of love went forth from human heart but it found some heavenly chord to fold it in."[9] In effect, says MacDonald—and John's declaration underwrites

MacDonald's version of this truth—no cry of love (God's essence) is ever lost, but it reverberates with some chord in God's true being.

The depth is the height inverted.

Quote: P. T. Forsyth. Forsyth said of God's love, "The depth is simply the height inverted. . . . The cry is not only truly human, but divine as well. God is deeper than the deepest depth in man. He is holier than our deepest sin is deep. There is no depth so deep to us as when God reveals his holiness in dealing with our sin."[10]

Christ is in the depths with us.

Biography: John Wesley. Wesley, with deep emotion, heard Psalm 130 sung in St. Paul's Cathedral in London in May of 1738—it expressed precisely what his heart was doing, crying out from the depths. That very same night in a London meeting house he heard the reading of Luther's exposition of the Epistle to Galatians and, prepared by the reading of Psalm 130, he was converted to Christ.[11] We cry out from the depths, and we find that the Lord is already there in the depths with us, to raise us up, to restore us, to forgive us. It was "out of the depths" that Christ prayed for his crucifiers: "Father, forgive them, for they do not know what they are doing" (Luke 23:34).

"Like a Weaned Child
I Am Content"

Big Idea
We become our true selves only when we humble ourselves before God.

Key Themes
- Our sense of self-worth is not self-authenticating—it must come from a higher source.
- Pride begins in one's heart, sees the world through one's eyes, and engages in actions beyond its bloated competence.
- Quiet, confident pleasure in God's presence is the goal of the spiritual life.

Understanding the Text

This psalmic lullaby is one of the most beautiful psalms in the Psalter, the "outpouring of a mature faith," says Weiser,[1] and, Spurgeon, comparing it to all the other psalms that we may call gems, likens this one to a "pearl."[2] It is a psalm of trust that positions the psalmist and Israel in a spiritual state of contentment in God's presence.

The Text in Context

Psalm 131 constitutes a confession of trust in the presence of God (the "mother" is the symbol of God, as the weaned child is a symbol of the psalmist and Israel), a faith to which this community had been summoned by the prophet Haggai (see "Historical and Cultural Background"). It positions Israel theologically in a place of contentment in God's presence rather than in "great matters" (131:1), like temple reconstruction, and so aligns the people with David, whose portrait in the Psalter looks forward to the temple, especially as it represents God's presence (e.g., 23:6). So the psalm looks back to 130:7 and forward to the portrait of David and God's covenant with him outlined in Psalm 132. At the same time, Psalm 131 anticipates the renewal of Israel's priestly role anticipated in 132:9 and depicted in Psalm 133 and the final portrait of God's people at last in the "house of the LORD" ministering as the royal priesthood (Exod. 19:6) in the presence of the "Maker of heaven and earth" (Ps. 134:3). After so many centuries of oppression (Ps. 129) and a time of crying out to the Lord from the "depths" of their suffering and sins (Ps. 130), now Israel celebrates their spiritual maturity.

Outline/Structure

This brief poem falls into two parts that are determined by the addressee, first Yahweh, and second Israel.

1. To the Lord: Confession of trust in negative terms (131:1–2)
2. To Israel: Exhortation to hope in the Lord (131:3)

Historical and Cultural Background

Delitzsch connects this psalm to David's response to his wife Michal's disparaging remark about his behavior upon the arrival of the ark in Jerusalem (2 Sam. 6:21–22). Form critics are less concerned with historical setting and much more concentrated on how the psalm might have been used in temple worship or in the life of the community of Israel. I believe a combination of those perspectives is necessary for an adequate exposition of the Psalms, and this psalm is a good illustration of how these two perspectives blend together (see "Trends in Psalms Studies" in the introduction in vol. 1). First, Psalm 131 seems to be a response to the call of 130:7 for Israel to hope in the Lord, and it affirms that call in 131:3. We have already observed the call for a congregational response in 124:1 and 129:1 ("let Israel say"). This might very well have been a part of the Second Temple liturgy, invoking the congregation and Israel more generally to put their hope in the Lord rather than in the temple restoration project that, according to Haggai (2:1–9), had become disappointing to many. His prophetic oracle redirects the exiles' attention away from the mediocre edifice rising before their eyes and toward the all-important presence of God: "My Spirit remains among you" (Hag. 2:5). His contemporary Zechariah joined them; he assures Zerubbabel that it is "not by might nor by power, but by my Spirit" (Zech. 4:6), and he challenges the community: "Who dares despise the day of small things . . . ?" (4:10). I suggest that Psalm 131 deals with the event of Zerubbabel's laying the foundation of the temple that had evoked "a great shout of praise to the LORD" from the enthusiasts (Ezra 3:11) but so much weeping from the priests and Levites who had seen Solomon's temple (3:12). The "great matters" were, I suggest, the reconstruction efforts, especially the temple, which had the potential for so much acclaim and, at the same time, so much disillusionment. In accordance with the message of the prophets Haggai and

Zechariah, our psalmist has refocused attention from the "great matters" to the Lord's presence. The expectation is now shaped by hope in the Lord, as the psalmist and the community respond to the call of 130:7. The simile "like a weaned child with its mother" is a perfect description of a psalmist and community who now put their hope in the Lord's presence ("'I am with you,' declares the LORD"; Hag. 2:4) rather than great accomplishments that were destined for disappointing results.

Interpretive Insights

Title *Of David.* See the comments on the title for Psalm 122.

131:1 *My heart is not proud,* LORD. Verses 1 and 2 are addressed to Yahweh, whereas verse 3 is addressed to Israel. The verb "to be proud" expresses the condition of haughtiness, which is likely to lead a person to do evil.[3]

my eyes are not haughty. "Haughty eyes" are among the "seven" things that are an abomination to the Lord in Proverbs 6:16–17.

I do not concern myself with great matters. These are things that one either is not permitted to know or have or is incapable of attaining.[4] Schaefer notes three phases of pride: heart (which is the seat), eyes (which are the heart's windows to the world), and soul/self (which is the place of actualization; lit., "I do not walk among great things").[5] "Things too wonderful for me" likely carries the negative connotation of the same term in 119:18 (see the comments on 119:17–24), where the term refers to "things too difficult for me," reflecting the judicial problem of Deuteronomy 17:8 that must be appealed to a higher judge. The psalmist trusts the Lord like a weaned child and does not concern himself with the matters that are too difficult for him in this challenging era of Israel's history, and he (and the community) is trusting the Lord, a higher judge, to sort out those matters.

131:2 *But I have calmed and quieted myself.* The Hebrew expression behind "but" sometimes introduces an oath to affirm a fact or situation. While this is not an oath as such, the phrase gives it a sense of affirmation (asseveration), and older English translations have tried to duplicate that with the adverb "surely" (KJV, ASV), while later translations generally use an adversative "but," as does the NIV. However, since the affirmation here arises out of the disavowal statement of verse 1 ("My heart is not proud"), this expression calls for an affirmative term, like "surely" (KJV, ASV) or "truly/verily" (Delitzsch), rather than an adversative one.[6] The Jerusalem Bible has the correct idea: "Enough for me to keep my soul tranquil and quiet like a child in its mother's arms, as content as a child that has been weaned."

like a weaned child with its mother. The child no longer wants to be nursed by the mother but merely desires her nearness and affection. It is a mark of maturity.

131:3 *Israel, put your hope in the* LORD *both now and forevermore.* This is 130:7a verbatim, except "both now and forevermore," which also occurs in 121:8 and 125:2. The individual psalmist has now turned to the congregation and Israel at large, admonishing them to put their hope in the Lord rather than focusing on the "great matters" that have occupied them formerly, which they must leave to a higher judge.

Theological Insights

In his comments on this psalm, Spurgeon says: "Many through wishing to be great have failed to be good."[7] All of us have seen, and many have experienced, the wreckage along this heavily traveled highway. Israel's history, also cluttered with much debris, is an illustration of how dependence on power and material resources can become a travelogue of disaster. Yet, occasionally, and most gratefully, we see a picture of this nation trusting in God's presence to lead the way and to assure safe arrival and, further, to work out those problems that are too difficult for them to solve alone. Psalm 131 is such a picture. Here the psalmist has become the person the Lord intended him to be, trusting, calm, and content—and his hope for Israel is the same. "Unless you change and become like little children, you will never enter the kingdom of heaven" (Matt. 18:3). God mocks the proud but gives grace to the humble and oppressed (Prov. 3:34; James 4:6; 1 Pet. 5:5). Moreover, the suppliant (and this also represents the community of faith) has come to the place where he can sort out the problems he can solve and those he cannot.

Teaching the Text

Spurgeon calls Psalm 131 "one of the shortest Psalms to read, but one of the longest to learn."[8] That sums it up very well. We can read it in twenty-five seconds, but we probably have only begun to learn its lesson in twenty-five years.

Our first point should deal with the matter the psalmist introduces in the opening verse: "My heart is not proud, LORD, my eyes are not haughty; I do not concern myself with great matters or things too wonderful for me" (131:1). Under whatever label we are examining this statement, whether an exaggerated sense of power and self-worth that troubles the human spirit or other important projects of life ("great matters") that have replaced the truly vital ones (see "Historical and Cultural Background")—all sometime replacements for hope—true hope in the Lord is now the psalmist's mainstay. The psalmist has dealt with his prideful spirit and has weaned himself from its greedy, self-focused ways (131:1). He doesn't tell us *how* he came to that position, nor does he map out the road that led him from pride to humility, but he gives us imagery that hints at how *hard* the road has been, and how *satisfying* the destination. It's that of a child who has been weaned—and that comes with some crying and protesting—but when success comes, the child just enjoys being near his or her mother. She was once the symbol of need. Now she is the symbol of quiet, confident pleasure, and that is the message of the psalm: quiet, confident pleasure in God's presence. Once it was a give-me-what-you've-got relationship, but now it has become an I-just-love-to-be-in-your-presence bond.

Modern psychology claims that high self-esteem is good and low self-esteem is bad, and it's hard to argue with that. Self-esteem is not necessarily the same thing as pride, nor low-esteem the same as humility, even if we do confuse them sometimes. But there has been a major paradigm shift in our world along with new understanding of human personality. Once our society was God centered, but now it is human centered. The self has become the standard by which we define everything else; God and his will for the world and for our lives have been marginalized, or moved off the charts altogether. Yet, Judaism and Christianity insist that we have to become aware of the source of our self-esteem. Self-worth is not self-authenticating. When the only source is our human ability and accomplishments, and we bow to no higher authority, there is, as Augustine asserted, an innate disqualifier (see "Illustrating the Text"). We become our true selves only when we humble ourselves before the Lord. That's precisely what the psalmist has done (131:2).

Second, the dual idea of pride/humility gives us an opportunity to provide the ultimate example of humility in Jesus Christ. Paul expresses this mystery so graphically in Philippians 2:5–9. Humanly speaking, Christ was the only one who had a right to the highest view of his self-worth, but with him it was not a matter of right but a matter of revealing his true nature, and that was one of humility. Humility is knowing who we are, knowing what our capabilities are, and knowing where we stand. Christ was the Exemplar of self-knowledge and knowledge of his Father. Psalm 131 turns our eyes on our distorted selves and how we can be changed into what God wants to make of us.

Illustrating the Text

More is less, and less is more.

Church Fathers: In his book *The City of God*, Augustine writes:

> There is, then, a kind of lowliness which in some wonderful way causes the heart to be lifted up, and there is a kind of loftiness which makes the heart sink lower. It seems to be contradictory that loftiness should debase and lowliness exalt, but holy lowliness makes us bow to what is above us, and since there is nothing above God, the kind of lowliness that makes us close to God exalts

us. On the other hand, the kind of loftiness which is a defection by this very defection refuses this subjection to God and so falls down from Him who is supreme, and by falling comes to be lower.[9]

The crown of contentment

Literature: *Henry the Sixth*, **by William Shakespeare.** In Shakespeare's play, the king is asked, "But, if thou be a king, where is thy crown?" The king answers,

> My crown is in my heart, not on my head;
> not deck'd with diamonds and Indian stones,
> nor to be seen. My crown is call'd content;
> A crown it is that seldom kings enjoy.[10]

Our psalmist, citing another king, David, tells us he had "calmed and quieted" himself like "a weaned child with its mother" (Ps. 131:2). His crown could also be called content, and it was also in his heart, not on his head.

"I Will Not Enter My House or Go to My Bed . . . Till I Find a Place for the LORD"

Big Idea

Obedience to God's commands and trust in his promises intertwine to form the creed of the believing life.

Key Themes

- God's promises are the treble clef of faith, and the discipleship of obedience is the bass clef.
- God's promises are the continuing thread of divine grace.

Understanding the Text

Psalm 132 is a Zion song (see the beginning of "Understanding the Text" in the unit on Ps. 48) or a royal psalm, which deals with David and his dynasty (see the beginning of "Understanding the Text" in the unit on Ps. 18). The psalm reveals, in the language of an oath, David's resolve to find a place for the Lord and God's promises to bless his people.

The Text in Context

While not attributed to David, Psalm 132 is a prayer that God will remember his covenant with David, which, along with the four psalms with David in their titles, positions the Pilgrim Psalter in the Davidic covenant. The congregation prays for the restoration of the Davidic dynasty (132:10) and receives God's promise to fulfill their desire (132:17).

Psalm 132:8–10, with some minor differences, contains reflections of Solomon's prayer of dedication of the temple in 2 Chronicles 6:41–42. The occasion

We have to listen in on the psalms very carefully to hear their stories, which are often snippets of history, and, just as often, unadorned with such chronological connectors as we are used to in the biblical narratives (e.g., "when," "then," "at that time"). Here in Psalm 132 we have such a case: the location of the ark of the covenant in Kiriath Jearim and its transfer to Jerusalem (see "Historical and Cultural Background"). Verses 6–7 contain code language for these events. In our own historical setting, when we refer to "Gettysburg" or "the Boston Tea Party" or "9/11," our audience knows the story. So it is with "Ephrathah" and "fields of Jaar." The poet did not need to review the whole story, just give word hints.

The same is true with liturgy, which, generally speaking, the psalmists recorded not in full but in an abridged form. While this psalm may have been written in the preexilic era and adapted in the postexilic period for the Pilgrim Psalter (I am inclined to think it was written in the postexilic era), it preserves a congregational lead that signals that the procession is on its way to Jerusalem with the ark ("Let us go to his dwelling place . . ." [132:7]) and a snippet of the ancient ark liturgy that was used when they set out to move the ark from one place to another ("Arise, Lord," 132:8a; see Num. 10:35). While we cannot reconstruct the full liturgy from these samplings, we have a pretty good sense of the overlay of its use. First, it was used in Moses's day, then judging from the historical names, it was repeated in David's time, and it was most likely used again in the postexilic era to commemorate the restoration of temple worship (even though the ark tragically disappeared in the Babylonian destruction of the temple in 586 BC). (See also "The Text in Context" in the units on Pss. 46 and 47.)

would have required the movement of the ark from the temporary tent that David had prepared for it to the new temple edifice.

The procession that brought the ark from Kiriath Jearim to Jerusalem (132:6–9) is, on a smaller scale, reminiscent of Israel's procession from Egypt to Zion, which is depicted in Psalm 68.

Outline/Structure

1. The Psalmist's petition and David's oath (132:1–10)
   ("David" in verses 1 and 10 composes an *inclusio*.)
   a. The Petition (132:1)
   b. David's oath (132:2–5)
   c. The transfer of the ark in David's time (132:6–7)
   d. The liturgy of transfer (132:8–9)
   e. The final petition (132:10)
2. The Lord's oath and promise (132:11–18)
   (Again "David" in verses 11 and 17 forms an *inclusio*.)
   a. The Lord's oath (132:11–12)

b. Declaration of Zion as the Lord's dwelling and the promise of
   blessing (132:13–18)
   i. Declaration of Zion as the Lord's dwelling (132:13–14)
   ii. Promise of blessing (132:15–18)

Historical and Cultural Background

The background story of this psalm is threefold. First is the story of Israel as they depart from Sinai and move into the wilderness, with the ark leading the way. The expression "Arise, LORD" in verse 8 includes the first words from the liturgy that was used when the ark set out on a journey (Num. 10:35). Second is David's use of that liturgy in his own transfer of the ark from Kiriath Jearim to Jerusalem (132:7; see 2 Sam. 6). Third, judging from the postexilic setting of the Pilgrim Psalter, this psalm was either written or adapted for use in the postexilic era, probably the dedication of Zerubbabel's temple in 516 BC. Some prefer the time of Nehemiah,[1] although the procession of Nehemiah 12:27–43 is in regard to the dedication of the walls of Jerusalem.

As the center psalm of the last group of psalms in the Pilgrim Psalter (Pss. 130–34), this psalm centers the five-psalm unit, and the Pilgrim Psalter itself, on David's oath to find a place for the Lord (132:3–5), and the Lord's oath to David to assure his perpetual dynasty (132:11–12) (see table 1 in the unit on Ps. 127). It is most appropriate for this psalm to recall those reciprocal commitments that established the Davidic dynasty and made Jerusalem the place of the Lord's dwelling, especially in view of the exiles' return to Jerusalem and the hope of a revival of the Davidic monarchy, perhaps in the person of Zerubbabel, a descendant of David. This psalm was likely a temple celebration of those two integral hopes.

Some date the psalm to the time of Solomon ("your anointed one," 132:10) and point out that the literary style, which uses repetitions, does not engage the "step" technique that characterizes the other psalms in the Songs of Ascents. While the technique may not be as obvious as in other poems of the Pilgrim Psalter, it is certainly evident, nevertheless—for example,

"I will not enter my house" → "or go to my bed" (132:3);
"I will allow no sleep to my eyes" → "or slumber to my eyelids" (132:4);
"Let us go to his dwelling place," → "let us worship at his footstool" (132:7);
"May your priests be clothed with your righteousness" (132:9a) → "I will clothe her priests with salvation" (132:16a);
"May your faithful people sing for joy" (132:9b) → "and her faithful people will ever sing for joy" (132:16b).[2]

Interpretive Insights

132:1 LORD, *remember David and all his self-denial.* Since this psalm was most likely written for the generation of the return and restoration, the prayer is to the effect that the Lord might have regard for David's "afflictions" (NIV: "self-denial"). The NIV's "self-denial" is obviously supported by David's self-imposed renunciation of certain comforts in the oath of verses 3–5, but those were only part of David's "afflictions," and not the worst part. The implication is that because of them the Lord will bless this generation.[3]

132:2 *He swore an oath to the* LORD. In 2 Samuel 7 there is no reference to an oath. In telling the story, the psalmists are so intent on the reliability of David's promise to God and God's promise to David (see 132:11) that they have no reluctance to put them in terms of an oath (see also 89:35; 110:4).[4] See the sidebar "Oaths" in the unit on Psalm 7, and the sidebar "The Hebrew Oath" in the unit on Psalm 66.

132:3–5 *I will not.* These verses contain David's oath. The Hebrew oath consists of a conditional sentence (protasis), introduced by "if" or "if not," followed by the apodosis, which stipulates the curse if the condition is not observed. Normally the apodosis is missing, as it is here, which means that the conditional clause must be translated negatively if it is positive, and positively if it is negative (see table 1).

Table 1. The Oath in 132:3–5

Literal Text (Positive)	Translation (Negative)
If I enter the tent of my house,	I will not enter the tent of my house,
if I go up on my bed,	I will not go up on my bed,
if I allow sleep to my eyes,	I will not allow sleep to my eyes,
slumber to my eyelids,	slumber to my eyelids,
until I find a place for the LORD,	until I find a place for the LORD,
a dwelling place for the Mighty One of Jacob.	a dwelling place for the Mighty One of Jacob.

Note: All translations are the author's.

In this psalm, each time the conditional clause should be completed by "till I find a place for the LORD, a dwelling for the Mighty One of Jacob" (which is the end of the protasis).[5] The writer anchors this psalm in Israel's history in three ways: (1) the references to David's oath to the Lord and the Lord's to David, (2) the title for God as "the Mighty One of Jacob" (as well as the brief story of the finding and transferring of the ark from Kiriath Jearim to Jerusalem in verses 6–7), and (3) the historical names in verse 6.

David's oath not to dwell in his palace until he has found a place for the Lord reminds one of Uriah's solemn declaration that he will not enter his own house as long as his fellow warriors and the ark are camped in the open fields of battle (2 Sam. 11:11). Now David is represented as having that kind of integrity (which he certainly did not have in that story). The words of verse 4 are found almost verbatim in Proverbs 6:4.

132:6–7 *We heard it in Ephrathah . . . fields of Jaar.* "Ephrathah" is Bethlehem (Gen. 35:19; Ruth 4:11; Mic. 5:2), where David was anointed king (1 Sam. 16:1–13); the "fields of Jaar" is a reference to Kiriath Jearim, a town that goes under several different names (e.g., *Ba'ale Y*e*hudah,* 2 Sam. 6:2; 1 Chron. 13:6; NIV: "Baalah of Judah"), and the place where the ark was kept for twenty years after the Philistines returned it (1 Sam. 7:1). These two place names further anchor the psalm in Israel's history. The "we" alludes to those who assisted David in bringing the ark from Kiriath Jearim to Jerusalem and may serve doubly as a liturgical invitation to go to the sanctuary in Jerusalem.

his footstool. See the comments on 99:5, and "The Text in Context" in the unit on Psalm 110.

132:8–10 These words could be those of a priest, or those in the festal procession to bring the ark to Jerusalem. The NIV closes the quotation at the end of verse 9, but verse 10, with its petition on behalf of "your anointed one," could be considered the close of the quotation.

132:8 *Arise, Lord.* These are words of the prayer that was spoken when the ark was moved (Num. 10:35–36; NIV: "Rise up, Lord!"), and probably when it was returned to the sanctuary after battle (see "Teaching the Text" in the unit on Pss. 9–10).

your resting place. The term implies permanence, and in verses 13–14 it is identified as Zion, where Yahweh will be enthroned.

you and the ark of your might. The ark and Yahweh are distinguished, lest Yahweh be identified as the ark. The "ark of your might" alludes to the great miracles Yahweh performed when Israel took the ark into battle with them (78:61). This is the only mention of the ark in the Psalter, even though there are veiled references (e.g., 78:61).[6]

132:9 *May your priests be clothed with your righteousness.* While this may allude to the priestly garments, it probably goes beyond that to include the righteous behavior of the priests (see Isa. 11:5).

132:10 *For the sake of your servant David, do not reject your anointed one.* "Your servant David" and "your anointed one" may be two different persons, the latter a king of the Davidic line, or the governor Zerubbabel, a descendant of David (Ezra 3:2; Hag. 1:1), whom the people hoped would become king.

132:11 *The Lord swore an oath to David.* See the comments on 132:2. See also 89:3, 35, and table 1 in the unit on Psalm 89.

132:12 *If your sons keep my covenant.* This condition means that the continuation of David's line is dependent on their keeping the covenant, which is parallel to Yahweh's "statutes."

132:13–18 These verses are a climactic point in the psalm and introduce a comprehensive program—a virtual golden age, in fact—that includes Yahweh's reign from Zion (132:13–14) and the blessings his reign will entail: abundant prosperity, satisfying the poor with food,[7] an exemplary priesthood, a joyful people, the Davidic dynasty, and the defeat of David's enemies (132:15–18). While this is not the real picture of the postexilic community, it is their vision, and thus a messianic vision of the future age.

132:13 *the* LORD *has chosen Zion.* See Deuteronomy 12:4–7.

132:14 *my resting place.* See Isaiah 66:1. Verses 14–18 are the answer to the prayer of verses 8–10.

132:16 *I will clothe her priests with salvation, and her faithful people will ever sing for joy.* This statement represents the repetition that characterizes the Songs of Ascents (the priests are clothed in righteousness, 132:9), although Psalm 132 does not exhibit the anadiplosis as clearly as we see in the other Songs of Ascents. See "Additional Insights: Songs of Ascents, the Pilgrim Psalter (Psalms 120–34)," following the unit on Psalm 120.

132:18 *I will clothe his enemies with shame.* This is intended to draw a sharp contrast between the priests, clothed in "salvation," and Israel's enemies, clothed in "shame." Verses 15–18 paint an optimistic picture of Israel's future. The king's radiant crown further draws out the contrast.[8]

Theological Insights

This psalm teaches a lesson that is profoundly written in the lines and between the lines of Scripture: doing the will of God is the most imperative duty believers have to fulfill ("Thy will be done, on earth as it is in heaven") (see "Illustrating the Text" in the unit on Ps. 69). In fact, David's obedience to God's command to find a place for God had become a passion for him (see "Historical and Cultural Background"). And that is precisely what God's will should become for each one of us, our passion, and we should find no rest until we have fulfilled God's will for us personally and for his kingdom.

Teaching the Text

We can begin our sermon/lesson by making a comparison with Psalm 131, which gives us a description of the childlike faith that Jesus said all must have to enter the kingdom of God (Matt. 18:3). Psalm 132 presents an obedient faith that understands and acts on God's promises.[9] It is the same faith, but viewed from two different perspectives: that of Psalm 131 is trust, and that of Psalm 132 is obedience. We can't have one without the other. A childlike (trusting) faith will lead to obedience, and obedience arises out of trust. So the two perspectives are complementary.

First, we want to recognize that David "swore an oath"—that's how the psalmist expresses David's resolve—that he would find "a place for the LORD" (132:5). Presumably the psalmist has in mind David's purchase of Araunah's threshing floor (the future site of the temple) at the behest of the prophet Gad (2 Sam. 24:18–25), as well as his preparations for building the temple (1 Chron. 28:11–19; 29:1–5), although David himself would never see the finished edifice.

We may draw attention to the fact that when the people heard about the ark in Kiriath Jearim, they responded by going there to worship ("Let us go," 132:7), and then they followed that by doing something about the "ark in exile"—they moved it to Jerusalem (1 Sam. 7:1–2), using the ancient words of Moses in Numbers 10:35, "Arise, LORD." Peterson says: "Christians tramp well-worn paths: obedience has a history."[10] The grandstands of history are filled with those saints who passed the torch on to this generation, and who passed it on to us, and they are waiting to see how we are going to run our leg of the race (see "Illustrating the Text"). We might even draw on stories of our own Christian history to further illustrate this point (for example, Calvin's call to go to Geneva; see "Illustrating the Text" in the unit on Ps. 23).

Second, we may emphasize the truth that obedience is anchored in God's promises, and the psalmist is so sure of them that he uses the same language convention, an oath, to introduce them (132:11). God's promises were the thread that ran through Israel's history. The people had anticipated a place for the Lord from Moses's time (Deut. 12), and at last God's promises came true in David's and Solomon's time, and they were coming true again in the postexilic era. Peterson makes the perceptive observation that "obedience is not a stodgy plodding in the ruts of religion, it is a hopeful race toward God's promises."[11] It may be of some significance, however, to note that God's promises and Israel's obedience (and ours!) were interwoven: "If your sons keep my covenant and the statutes I teach them" (132:12). Here we are reading the treble clef of the divine perspective and the bass clef of the human perspective together. That's how we hear the harmony. On the treble clef, God's promises do not depend on us, nor are they based on our ability. Rather, they are the manifestation of God's grace and goodness. On the bass clef, the way we appropriate the promises is by obedience to God's commandments. It is not privilege without responsibility, but it is promises of grace (treble clef) with obedient discipleship (bass clef).

The picture of the impending new age of blessing (132:15–18) is to be taken not as a specific picture of our age but rather as a model of divine grace that shapes the age to come: prosperity, and enough for the poor; saving grace through God's ministering servants; the new reign of God through David's descendant in Jesus Christ; and the final defeat of God's enemies in this new kingdom.

Illustrating the Text

Watching from the bleachers of history

Bible: Hebrews 11–12. The writer to the Hebrews has caught a spiritual vision of the critical juncture of history's believers who were obedient and those to whom they bequeathed God's promises. It is the picture of a relay race, with the stands filled by the countless hosts of those who have already run the race and have passed the torch on to the next generation. The imperative question is whether or not this new community of believers will take the torch and run their leg successfully. The past generations are watching from the bleachers of eternity, gathered in hope. There is the righteous Abel, obedient Abraham, faithful Moses, hopeful Rahab, nameless martyrs, the destitute and ill-treated—of whom the world was not worthy—watching to see what the new generation will do when the torch is passed on to them. The race is not over, the victory has not been won, until the last runner has picked up the torch and run his or her leg. Only then will the heavenly hosts and the communion of saints burst into the hallelujah chorus: "Hallelujah! For the Lord our God the Almighty reigns. Let us rejoice and exult and give him the glory, for the marriage of the Lamb has come, and his Bride has made herself ready" (Rev. 19:6–7 RSV). "And all these, though well attested by their faith, did not receive what was promised, since God had foreseen something better for us, that apart from us they should not be made perfect" (Heb. 11:39–40 RSV). This is the "hopeful race toward God's promises."[12]

Clothed with God's righteousness

Hymn: "My Hope Is Built," by Edward Mote. An example of our idyllic picture of our relationship to God is found in 132:8–9. The Lord takes up his dwelling place in Israel and his priests are "clothed with [his] righteousness," the end product being the joy of God's people: "May your faithful people sing for joy." It is only when we are "clothed" in God's righteousness that we are fit for God's dwelling. Mote expressed that truth in his hymn "My Hope Is Built":

> When he shall come with trumpet sound,
> O may I then in him be found:
> dressed in his righteousness alone,
> faultless to stand before the throne.

To draw this point out further, the concept of "righteousness/righteous" prominent in Torah, Prophecy, the Psalms, and Wisdom literature, especially Job and Proverbs, moves up and down a nuanced scale. At the lower end of the scale is the application of the adjective "righteous" to balances, weights, and measures, implying a standard of fairness and justice. But even this mundane nuance is anchored in God's character and his saving acts in history: "Use honest [Heb. "righteous"] scales and honest weights, an honest ephah and an honest hin. *I am the* LORD *your God, who brought you out of Egypt*" (Lev. 19:36).[13]

Moving further up the scale, the person who practices justice toward one's neighbor is "righteous," suggesting that it is a character issue—not just a trait, but a character disposition—which expresses itself in caring for one's neighbor. This sense of the term can be seen in Deuteronomy 24:13, where returning a poor person's garment before sundown is viewed as *righteousness* (*ts^{e}daqa*): "Return their cloak by sunset so that your neighbor may sleep in it. Then they will thank you, and it will be regarded as a righteous act in the sight of the LORD your God." Johannes Pedersen comments on the meaning of the term, "Righteousness is thus the mutual acknowledgment of souls; but it is still more, viz. their mutual maintenance of each other's honour. The acknowledgment can never exclusively be a feeling or a mood, but it must manifest itself in action."[14]

Perhaps at the top of the scale is the fact that the priests are to be "clothed in *your* [Yahweh's] righteousness" (Ps. 132:9). While it certainly would be a stretch to insist that the psalmist is speaking of "imputed" righteousness (see Gen. 15:6; Ps. 106:30–31), it is *God's* righteousness nevertheless, however received. It is the imitation of God's character.

"How Good and Pleasant It Is When God's People Live Together in Unity!"

Big Idea

The unity of the worshiping people of God is infectious, affecting the whole community and resulting in the blessing of "life forevermore."

Key Themes

- Unity in worship prepares God's people for blessing.
- The unity of the people of God is not optional.
- God is not a one-child Father.

Understanding the Text

The genre of Psalm 133 is difficult to label. Perhaps "blessing" is the best we can do, even though it is not a blessing per se but more like a reflection on blessing, as is 132:14–18; the final clause announces that the Lord has "commanded" (NIV: "bestows"). The psalm gives us a picture of the worshiping community in unity ("how good and pleasant"; see the comments on 133:1), a picture rarely seen with such beauty and clarity.

The Text in Context

After Psalm 132 has painted the beautiful word picture of the return of the ark to Jerusalem and the impending new era of blessing, Psalm 133, with enviable brevity and noble beauty, declares that this new era is like the transference of Hermon's dew to Zion (the two psalms are to be read as a pair). And even the common citizen would know the implications of such a climate change for Zion, with its single source of water (Gihon Spring) and the resultant blessing of the vintage such a climate change would bring. See "Historical and Cultural Background."

Outline/Structure

1. The blessing of unity in worship (133:1)
2. The blessing of "life forevermore" under two similes (133:2–3)
   a. First simile: "Like precious oil . . . running down on Aaron's beard" (133:2)
   b. Second simile: Like "the dew of Hermon . . . falling on Mount Zion" (133:3a–b)
   c. The blessing of "life forevermore" (133:3c)

Historical and Cultural Background

Psalm 133 has been connected to three different occasions. Some say it celebrates David's coronation as king at Hebron, when all the tribes of Israel came to him, unified and acting together, to make David king. Others think Psalm 133 was written for an occasion when the Israelites met in Jerusalem for one of the pilgrimage festivals, of which there were three: the Feasts of Unleavened Bread, Weeks, and Tabernacles. Still others—I am of this opinion—think Psalm 133 celebrates Judah's return from Babylonian exile sometime around 538 BC.

While we have acknowledged that there is no strict chronological order in the Pilgrim Psalter, there is nevertheless an order that continues to bring us slowly to Mount Zion, with its new temple, and to the new era of blessing that the return from exile and restoration to the homeland represent.

We also need to recognize the importance of the dew in Israel. During the dry season, when there is no rain at all for about six months, the dew is the only precipitation the country has. And it is sufficient to produce a great harvest of grapes, which ripen in time for the Feast of Tabernacles in September/October. Talking about dew was talking about the grape harvest. So the spiritual meaning is that the dew, one of God's great blessings on the land, falls on the high mountain and on the low mountain. It falls everywhere. There is no discrimination with God. Unity is like that. When it settles down on a family, or a church, or a community, or a nation, it brings blessing, a rich harvest of joy.

Interpretive Insights

Title *Of David.* See the comments on the title for Psalm 122.

133:1 *How good and pleasant it is when God's people live together in unity!* The NIV's "live together" is the meaning of the almost verbatim expression in Deuteronomy 25:5; but since the same verb appears in Psalm 132:14 ("Here I will dwell [NIV: "sit enthroned"], for I have desired it"; but see the comments on 132:14), where it clearly refers to the Lord's dwelling in Zion (a religious nuance), contextually we ought to translate it "dwell" in the religious sense of the word. The psalmist is primarily speaking about worshiping together in unity, which is an appropriate declaration after Psalm 132 has given us the picture of the reestablishment of Zion as God's "dwelling" (132:13). There may very well be a political nuance also in the phrase "in unity" (Gen. 13:6; 36:7; Deut. 5:5), since the story of the ark's transfer to Jerusalem follows the narrative of the reunion of the country under David. This would then parallel the story of 2 Samuel 5–6, which relates how David made Jerusalem both his political and religious capital. To some degree, the unity of the country under David was being repeated in the return of the people to Zion.

133:2 *precious oil . . . running down on the beard, running down on Aaron's beard.* "Precious oil" ("good" oil) is oil that was perfumed with spices (Exod. 30:22–33). "The beard, running down on Aaron's beard" illustrates the "step" pattern of the Songs of Ascents.[1] The oil was poured on his head and naturally ran down on his beard. Just as Haggai's inquiry regarding consecrated meat and touching a dead body alludes to the priests' knowledge of the ritual law (Hag. 2:10–13), and thus their preparedness to reengage in the priestly ministry in the new temple, this reference to Aaron's anointing may be an allusion to the reconsecration of the priests for service in Zerubbabel's temple.

on the collar of his robe. Literally, "the mouth of his garments." This is a reference to the priestly garments (Exod. 28). While the Targum (Aramaic) renders "mouth" as "hem," thus making the oil much more effusive, the "mouth" (NIV: "collar") of the priest's garments was the hole in the garment for his head (Exod. 28:31–32).

133:3 *It is as if the dew of Hermon were falling on Mount Zion.* Hermon was the highest mountain in Israel, standing as a sentinel overlooking Galilee, and Galilee was known (and still is) for its heavy dew. This should not evoke a "mythic atmosphere,"[2] because it is a simile. In fact, the falling dew is one of the reasons Galilee is such a good place for vineyards. The heavy dew nourishes the grapes (and this is the dry season in Israel) and thus produces an abundant harvest for the festival of joy (Tabernacles) (see "Historical and Cultural Background"). Now imagine, says the psalmist, the dew of Hermon falling on Mount Zion, and we then will have some idea of the blessing of this new era of grace: "For there [Zion] the LORD bestows his blessing, even life forevermore." It is significant that this psalm ends with an announcement of "the blessing of life forevermore," reminding the reader of the description of the new era of blessing announced in 132:15–18.

Theological Insights

Sometimes a single word in the psalms conveys a message that runs like a thread through the text. We have such a word in this psalm: the threefold occurrence of the participle "descending" (133:2a, 2b, and 3a; NIV: "running down" and "falling on"). Kidner succinctly enunciates this message: "In short, true unity, like all good gifts, is from above; bestowed rather than contrived, a blessing far more than an achievement."[3] The biblical concept of blessing involves a superior giving favor to an inferior (Heb. 7:7), like Melchizedek blessing Abraham (Gen. 14:18–20). And that is precisely what blessing is, a gift from our superior God to his earthly underlings. Who would ever think of allocating Hermon's dew for Mount Zion! It describes a spiritual blessing, and as Zenger says, "This is not about meteorology or geography; this is theological topography."[4]

Teaching the Text

The theme of this psalm is unity, and that is where we should start our sermon/lesson. Old Testament Israel had a sense of community that we have lost in our Western culture. In fact, we have developed a popular religion in America. I suppose it could even be called a Christian cult. One of its tenets is that we can be private Christians, and we see it in church members who rarely set foot in God's house and those who prefer electronic media services to worshiping in community with God's people.

A second theological tenet of this religion of the masses (and it meshes with the first) is that we can relate to God without relating to fellow Christians. The assumption is that he is a God of the "only child." According to that thinking, God has just one child, me (but in truth, we may be just spoiled brats). And we think our private faith is something between our individual selves and God, and nobody else. Now, I want to say immediately that a personal relationship with Jesus Christ is primary. And I emphasize the word "personal." But this religion of the masses emphasizes a *private* relationship to God that needs no wider dimension. Obviously there are circumstances that isolate us from the community of believers, and then our relationship to God, by necessity, must be much more private than it would otherwise be. Yet, in normal circumstances, all believers in Jesus Christ are members of the church, and isolating ourselves from it is to our detriment and to the detriment of the community of faith (see 1 Cor. 12).

A third theological tenet of this popular religion is that every person must work out his or her own religious system, and no one has any right to tell someone else that he or she is wrong. Sadly, the church has often been an accomplice to this fallacious way of thinking, as Muggeridge has claimed (see "Illustrating the Text"). I admit there are some particulars of the faith that we have to work out for ourselves, for example, not *whether* we keep the Sabbath/Lord's Day, but *how* we keep it. Yet, Christianity, like Judaism, is fundamentally not a private religion but a communal one. Both have an individual component, but the corporate is foundational. One wonders to what extent Robert Bellah and his colleagues' conclusions were right in their follow-up to de Tocqueville's work (see "Illustrating the Text"), and if so, is a correctional course possible, and what would it look like?

There are a number of places in the Psalms where this sense of community vis-à-vis individual identity comes into focus. For example, in Psalm 25 David prays a very personal prayer, and then at the end he prays for Israel, "Redeem Israel, O God, out of all his troubles" (25:22 ESV). He knew that his personal redemption was incomplete until the Lord had also redeemed Israel. His personal identity was bound up in the community of faith to which he belonged. His personal identity was greatly damaged apart from it. Jesus sets forth both dimensions of our faith when he informs the rich young ruler that the greatest commandment is to "love the Lord your God with all your heart," and then he adds that the second is like it, "You shall love your neighbor as yourself. On these two commandments depend all the Law and the Prophets" (Matt. 22:36–40 ESV). It's the *second* great commandment, loving our neighbor as ourselves, that puts us into community with one another. It's this commandment that produces the "good and pleasant" state of being that our psalmist is speaking about, and it is not optional.

At this point we may speak about the two similes that the psalmist uses to describe this "good and pleasant" state of living in unity. First is the picture of Aaron as he was anointed high priest—the anointing oil on his head ran down his beard to the collar of his robe. The point of it is that the oil consecrated his whole being, symbolically speaking, not just his head. The unity of the church consecrates the whole church and anoints the whole body of Christ for service.

The second image is that the dew of Mount Hermon falls on the mountain(s) of Zion. The two mountains are located some hundred miles apart, so what does dew on high Hermon have to do with low Mount Zion? Or what do these two mountains have to do with brothers and sisters dwelling together in unity? The unity of the church applies to both high and low, and it affects every level of the church's life. Moreover, it applies to every aspect of the church's theological topography, Hermon's abundant dew for Zion's arid landscape. This psalm is a herald of divine blessing to come and a hint of heaven.

Illustrating the Text

Individualism versus community

Sociology: In the early nineteenth century, a French admirer of American society, Alexis de Tocqueville, traveled through America to discover the mores and "habits of the heart" that made America a unique new culture. In 1835 he published his *Democracy in America*, still a classic work on American culture. In that book he addressed one of those American traits he deeply admired: individualism. But along with his words of admiration were words of warning, to the effect that unless American individualism was accompanied by other balancing habits, it would eventually lead American society into fragmentation and social isolation.

In the twentieth century (1985) a highly respected sociologist, Robert Bellah, along with some colleagues, wrote a book, in a sense a follow-up of de Tocqueville's work, called *Habits of the Heart*. They argued that de Tocqueville's prediction has in fact come true, that we have not balanced our individualism with other compelling traits, particularly a sense of community, and that we have become a fragmented culture.[5]

A defense system against God's incursions

Quote: **Malcolm Muggeridge.** Psalm 133 is a window into "organized religion" in the postexilic era. The priesthood was returning to its central place in religion, represented here by Aaron's anointing as priest and the acclamation of unity in the restored community. Ironically—and this could not be far from the poet's mind—religion has sometimes played a reverse role in bringing the world to God. This potential of the church, or any other religious organization, to turn itself into a self-serving institution is always lurking and necessitates that the church keep a constant vigil to avoid this distortion of its mission. Muggeridge, an English satirist and devout Christian, says: "One of the most effective defensive systems against God's incursions has hitherto been organized religion. The various churches have provided a refuge for fugitives from God—his voice drowned in the chanting, his smell lost in the incense, his purpose obscured and confused in creeds, dogmas, dissertations and other priestly pronunciamentos."[6] This perspective on the church should not deter us from it but should draw us into the watches of the night to guard against this tragic process taking effect.

"Praise the LORD, All You Servants of the LORD Who Minister . . . in the House of the LORD"

Big Idea

The biblical protocol of blessing is that the superior blesses the inferior, which is an implied principle of this psalm.

Key Themes

- God's blessing is reciprocal: Israel blesses God, and God blesses Israel.
- When we humans "bless" God, he humbles himself to receive it.

Understanding the Text

Psalm 134 comes at the end of the Pilgrim Psalter as a final blessing on the people of God as the people of the exile depart from Jerusalem and the temple and return to their homes, blessed by the "Maker of heaven and earth" (134:3).

The Text in Context

Psalm 134, the final song of the Pilgrim Psalter, dismisses the pilgrims with a benediction, reminiscent of the priestly benediction (see the comments on 134:1). In Psalm 132 the pilgrims have arrived in Jerusalem and celebrated the restoration of worship in the temple, making it again the religious capital, much as David's transfer of the ark to Jerusalem had made that city the religious capital of David's unified country. In Psalm 133 they celebrated this new era of unity in their community life. Now they are ready to return to their homes. Psalm 134 incorporates a reciprocal blessing, as the unknown speaker (a priest or even the congregation itself) summons the "servants of the LORD" (134:1) to bless the Lord. The reciprocal blessing occurs in verse 3 when the priests, with language from the priestly benediction, give the people the Lord's blessing from Zion. The benediction is all the more valid and authoritative because it bears the imprimatur of the "Maker of heaven and earth," the Creator of life, the only one who can give the blessing of "life forevermore" (133:3).

While those "who stand [NIV: "minister"] . . . in the house of the Lord" could be the laity, the phrase "by night" certainly tips the clause in favor of the official ministers of the temple, since laypersons did not normally remain in the temple overnight (but compare Anna in Luke 2:36–38). The temple gates were normally locked at sunset (*y. Berakhot* 4.1). See "Historical and Cultural Background."

Outline/Structure

1. Invoking the "servants of the Lord" to bless the Lord (134:1–2)
2. The priestly blessing (134:3)

Historical and Cultural Background

The Mishnah tells us that in the second temple the priests kept watch at three places and the Levites at twenty-one (*Middot* 1.2). Certain nightly maintenance duties, such as keeping the lampstand burning (Exod. 27:21), stoking the fire on the altar of burnt offering (Lev. 6:9), and guarding the gates (1 Chron. 9:22–27, 33), were part of the officiants' duties. The Mishnah also records that an officiant visited each station during the night and greeted those on duty (*Middot* 1.1).[1]

Interpretive Insights

134:1 *Praise the Lord, all you servants of the Lord*.[2] To end the Pilgrim Psalter, whose distinctive character is blessing, the compiler appropriately places this song of blessing at the end. The poem begins with a call to the priests and Levites who keep the night watch in the temple to "bless the Lord" (NIV: "Praise the Lord") and ends with the Lord blessing the people. On "servants of the Lord," see "The Text in Context." The verb "minister" (lit., "stand") is used to describe the priestly and Levitical services in the temple (e.g., Deut. 10:8; 1 Chron. 23:30).

134:2 *Lift up your hands in the sanctuary and praise the Lord*. Lifting up the hands toward the sanctuary is a gesture of worship (63:4; 119:48). The noun "sanctuary" has no preposition (such as "to/toward"; NIV: "in"). If this is the holy of holies,[3] the priests lifted their hands "toward" the sanctuary rather than "in" the sanctuary, since only the high priest could go into the holy of holies. The NIV interpretation is obviously that the worshiper would be in the courts of the temple, which is normally the case.

134:3 *May the* LORD *bless you from Zion, he who is the Maker of heaven and earth.* The blessing in the first half of the verse also occurs in the ninth Song (128:5), and the ascription in the second half occurs also in the fifth (124:8) and the second (121:2). "May the LORD bless you" are the first words of the priestly benediction (Num. 6:24) and are evidently intended to invoke the priestly blessing. I take the position that the pilgrims have come to the temple to receive the priestly blessing before they disperse to their homes.

Teaching the Text

We may begin our sermon/lesson by explaining the meaning of "bless" in the Psalter. On one level the word is just a synonym for "praise." That's the way the NIV usually translates it. So here the pilgrims would simply enjoin the priests and Levites to "praise the Lord." Yet, that is not the basic level of "bless." Rather to "bless the Lord" is to recognize God in his superior position of power and greatness—that is, to attribute power and greatness to God.

To understand the problem with this definition, we must speak about the biblical protocol of blessing. The writer to the Hebrews makes a point of this while telling the story of Melchizedek's blessing of Abraham. Although Abraham in the covenantal program "had the promises," it was Melchizedek who blessed Abraham, thereby demonstrating his superiority, for "it is beyond dispute that the inferior is blessed by the superior" (Heb. 7:7 ESV). And this is where we can observe that the biblical protocol of God's people blessing God involves a certain demeanor, virtually irreverent: the inferior blesses the superior (see "Illustrating the Text"). In all of the ancient religions outside the Hebrew religion, the deity is always the giver of blessing, but never the receiver of it. The Old Testament gives hints along the way that God's eternal decrees include the humility of redemption. And we should recall that "when the set time had fully come, God sent his Son, born of a woman, born under the law, to redeem those under the law, that we might receive adoption to sonship" (Gal. 4:4–5). When Christians bless God, they not only acknowledge his greatness but acknowledge God's condescension in human flesh and our human condition. No word of praise more powerfully acclaims God's worth or more genuinely ennobles our humanity than "bless."

Illustrating the Text

The biblical protocol of blessing

Personal Testimony: A few years ago a former student called and asked if I would talk with a man in his congregation. This man took seriously the biblical protocol of blessing, that only the superior could bless the inferior, and since we humans are inferior, it is not appropriate for us to bless God. So he would not sing the hymns, lest he step out of line and assume that superior position of *blessing God*. As a result of my student's request, this man and I met for lunch one day, and I tried to explain to him that in the Old Testament this is one of the indicators of God's *self-humiliation* or his *condescension*. In fact, it is one of the hints that God would in time condescend to our human condition, even to go to the cross, a hint of the truth Paul taught in Philippians 2:5–11. Already in the Psalms we see this faint but nevertheless visible image of God's condescension to receive blessing from his inferior human creatures.

The psychosomatic dimension of worship

Literature: *The Screwtape Letters*, **by C. S. Lewis.** Another term of Psalm 134 is the summons in verse 2 to use one's hands in a gesture of worship, perhaps spoken also to the priests and Levites: "Lift up your hands to the holy place and bless the Lord!" (ESV). There is a psychosomatic dimension to worship, for the bodily gestures and the spirit of worship go together. Lifting up the hands was a gesture and symbol of lifting up their hearts. Sometimes we kneel to acknowledge our humility before the majestic God, even though some Protestants have moved away from such gestures, especially kneeling, because they identify it with an idolatry that worships the elements of the Eucharist and images of Christ and the saints. In the *Screwtape Letters*, Screwtape advises his understudy, Wormwood, on the matter of spontaneous prayers. Some well-meaning Christians, Screwtape insists, consider prepared prayers that are sometimes attended by certain bodily gestures and positions, like kneeling, less genuine. Speaking of those who take this position, Screwtape advises: "At the least, they can be persuaded that the bodily position makes no difference to their prayers; for they constantly forget, what you must always remember, that they are animals and that whatever their bodies do affects their souls."[4] Sometimes, especially when our souls are weary, our bodies take the lead in acting our way into a new condition of the soul.

"I Know That the LORD Is Great, That Our Lord Is Greater Than All Gods"

Big Idea
God's image as a personal God who acts on our behalf is sketched against the lifeless portrait of the idols of this world.

Key Themes
- The worship of lifeless idols is a hint of the helplessness and hopelessness of their human worshipers.
- The lifeless image of our idols is an inverse portrait of the image of God.

Understanding the Text

Like Psalms 105 and 106 and Psalms 111 and 112, Psalms 135 and 136 are twin psalms and are intended to be read together. There is some validity in calling Psalm 135 a "patchwork" psalm, because it draws on so many other Old Testament texts (see "Interpretive Insights" and table 1). The theme of the psalm is that Yahweh is a *living* God, not a lifeless one like the idols. This psalm is a historical hymn of praise.

The Text in Context

There is a difference of opinion on the extent of the Great Hallel. One tradition suggests that it includes the Songs of Ascents plus Psalms 135 and 136 (*b. Pesahim* 118a). Others identify it as the paired Psalms 135 and 136,[1] but the more common opinion restricts the Great Hallel to Psalm 136. The name *Great* Hallel is intended to distinguish it from the Egyptian Hallel (Pss. 113–18), to which it, however, is definitely oriented (see table 1).[2]

The significance of looking at Psalms 135 and 136 as parallel to the Egyptian Hallel is that the Egyptian Hallel celebrates the exodus from Egypt in Moses's day, while the Pilgrim Psalter celebrates the second exodus, the exodus from Babylonia. Like the companion Psalms 117 and 118, the twin Psalms 135 and 136 form the conclusion to the Pilgrim Psalter, and log the return from Babylonia to Jerusalem.[3] Table 1 illustrates the intertextuality of this capstone and the Egyptian Hallel (especially Ps. 115).

Table 1. Verbal Correspondences between Psalms 135–36 and the Egyptian Hallel (Pss. 113–18)

Psalm 135	Psalm 136	Psalm 113	Psalm 115	Psalm 116	Psalm 118
"Praise the Lord. Praise the name of the Lord; praise him, you servants of the Lord" (135:1) (the four calls to praise the Lord match the four calls to bless the Lord in vv. 19–20)	"Give thanks to the Lord for he is good; for his love endures forever" (136:1, etc.) (response 26 times)	"Praise the Lord. Praise the Lord, you his servants; praise the name of the Lord" (113:1) (the second and third clauses are reversed)			"Give thanks to the Lord for he is good; for his love endures forever" (118:1, 29)
"In the courts of the house of our God. Hallelujah" (135:2)				"In the courts of the house of the Lord, in your midst, Jerusalem. Hallelujah" (116:19)	
"All that the Lord desires he does in the heavens and the earth" (135:6)			"But our God is in the heavens, all that he desires he does" (115:3)		
"He smote the firstborn of Egypt" (135:8a)	"To him who smote the first-born of Egypt" (136:10) (a slight verbal change)				
"He smote many nations, and he killed strong ['atsumim] kings" (135:10)	"To him who smote great [gᵉdolim] kings" (136:17) (response) "And he killed powerful kings" (136:18) (response)				

Psalm 135	Psalm 136	Psalm 113	Psalm 115	Psalm 116	Psalm 118
"Sihon, the king of the Amorites" (135:11)	"Sihon, king of the Amorites" (136:19) (response)				
"And Og, the king of Bashan, and all the kingdoms of Canaan" (135:11)	"Og, the king of Bashan" (136:20) (response)				
"And he gave their lands (as) an inheritance, an inheritance to Israel his people" (135:12)	"And he gave their land for an inheritance," (response) "an inheritance to his servant Israel" (136:21)				
	"For his love endures forever" (136:26b) (refrain)				"His love endures forever" (118:29b) (last clause of Egyptian Hallel and the refrain in Ps. 136)
"The idols of the nations are silver and gold, the work of man's hands" (135:15)			"Their idols are silver and gold, the work of man's hands" (115:4)		
"They have a mouth but do not speak, they have eyes but do not see" (135:16)			"They have a mouth but do not speak, they have eyes but do not see" (115:5)		
"They have ears but do not hear [ya'azinu], a nose, [but] there is no breath in their mouth" (135:17)			"They have ears but do not hear [yishmᵉu], they have a nose but do not smell [yᵉrihun]" (115:6) (uses verb "to smell" rather than "breath")		

Psalm 135	Psalm 136	Psalm 113	Psalm 115	Psalm 116	Psalm 118
"Like them are those who make them, all who trust in them" (135:18)			"Like them are those who make them, all who trust in them" (115:8)		
"House of Israel, bless the Lord; house of Aaron, bless the Lord; house of Levi, bless the Lord; you who fear the Lord, bless the Lord" (135:19–20)			"Israel, trust in the Lord, he is their help and their shield; house of Aaron, trust in the Lord, he is their help and their shield; you who fear the Lord, trust in the Lord, he is their help and their shield" (115:9–11)		

Note: I have made some adjustments in the NIV translation to make the comparisons more easily recognizable.

Outline/Structure

Hallelujah (135:1a)

1. Introduction: Call to praise (135:1b–3)
2. God's greatness (135:4–18)
   a. God's election of Israel (135:4–5)
   b. God's wonders in creation (135:6–7)
   c. God's wonders in history: The plagues in Egypt and the conquest (135:8–12)
   d. God's eternal existence and deliverance of his people (135:13–14)
   e. Repudiation of idolatry (135:15–18)
3. Call to bless God (135:19–21b)[4]
   Hallelujah (135:21c)

Historical and Cultural Background

With Psalm 135 as a capstone to the Pilgrim Psalter, the review of God's actions in nature and history and the notice that Yahweh is dwelling in Zion (135:21) complete the picture of redemption, whose expanse begins in Egypt and culminates in Zion.

Interpretive Insights

135:1–3 *Praise the* Lord. "Hallelujah" (NIV: "Praise the Lord") begins and concludes this introduction (135:3) and then concludes the psalm itself (135:21), and it is also accompanied by two variants, "Praise the name of the Lord" (135:1b) and "Praise him, you servants of the Lord" (135:1c). The second variant forms a link to "servants of the Lord" in 134:1. The beginning of the Egyptian Hallel contains all three clauses of verse 1, thus hinting that this begins a conclusion to the long section of Book 5 that began with Psalm 113. The exception is that the two variants are interchanged in 135:1 (see 113:1). The address "servants of the Lord" bears only part of the definitive clause of 134:1, missing the phrase "by night": "who stand in the house of the Lord" (135:2, author's translation; see the comments on 134:1). Some identify these with the worshipers in the temple rather than the priests and Levites, as we identified them in our study of Psalm 134. However, given the proximity of this term's occurrence to the same phrase in 134:1, the two terms seem to be synonymous. That, of course, is not to ignore the congregational participation in Psalm 135, and especially the twenty-six occurrences of the response, "For his love endures forever," in Psalm 136 (ESV). The addressees in this case are standing in the "courts of the house of our God," a phrase that parallels "the house of the Lord" in the previous line (135:2). The court of the priests and the court of Israel were located outside the temple proper.

Four times the speaker uses the imperative "praise the Lord" ("hallelujah") to call the people to prayer (135:1a, 1b, 1c, and 3a), and once the speaker summons them to "sing praise" (135:3b). In the last two instances the psalmist gives two reasons for praise: the Lord is "good," and his name is "pleasant" (135:3). The two terms are virtually synonymous, and in 133:1 they together describe the state of God's people when they worship/dwell together in unity.

135:4–5 *Jacob to be his own, Israel to be his treasured possession.* Having cited God's "good" nature as a reason to praise the Lord (135:3),[5] now our psalmist resorts to God's acts in history that illustrate his goodness. Yahweh's election of Israel ("Jacob" is another name for Israel) as "his own" is further spelled out with the term "treasured possession," which means that Israel belongs to him and to no one else. This is a Deuteronomic term to describe Yahweh's election of Israel and the favored status that implies (Deut. 7:6; 14:2; 26:18).

I know that the Lord *is great, that our Lord is greater than all gods.* The personal pronoun "I" of verse 5 is evidently the leader of the congregation, most likely a priest or Levite, the one who spoke the calls to praise in verses 1–3. Already he introduces a comparison between Yahweh and "all gods," and in verses 15–18 he declares that these gods are nothing more than "silver and gold, made by human hands" (135:15), void of the human capabilities of speaking, seeing, hearing, and breathing (135:16–17). "I know that the LORD is great" may be an allusion to a liturgical formula, as seems to be the case in the acclamation of 40:16: "The LORD is great!" This acclamation virtually duplicates the acknowledgment of Moses's father-in-law, a non-Israelite, that Yahweh is the true God (Exod. 18:11). Zenger contends that this quotation, a confession of faith from a non-Israelite, is a virtual "universal acknowledgment of YHWH's divinity."[6] Here in this context of the new exodus and the restoration of the people of God, this is a most powerful acclamation.

135:6–7 *The* LORD *does whatever pleases him.* Our poet describes God's wonders in creation. The final thought of the previous psalm, "the Maker of heaven and earth" (134:3), is in the writer's mind as he describes Yahweh's actions in creation (the heavens and earth, the seas and deeps), uninhibited by other powers, especially the other gods who in verse 5 were demoted to an inferior status. God's actions are described in meteorological terms: he "makes clouds rise," "sends lightning with the rain," and "brings out the wind from his storehouses" (a slight variation of Jer. 10:13; see also Job 38:22). Verse 6 is an adaptation of 115:3 (see table 1). In Psalm 115 the psalmist has cited the skeptical nations who ask, "Where is their God?" and has answered them with the declaration, "*Our God is in heaven*; he does whatever pleases him" (115:2–3). Now, in our psalm, the declaration moves from a description of God's heavenly being to a description of his actions, both in heaven and on earth: "The LORD does whatever pleases him, *in the heavens and on the earth, in the seas and all their depths*" (135:6). Then follows the list of Yahweh's works in nature and his "signs and wonders" in Israel's history (135:9).[7]

135:8–12 *He struck down the firstborn of Egypt.* Here begins a list of God's "signs and wonders" in history, starting, not surprisingly, with the Egyptian plagues. The psalmist mentions only the tenth, which was the most decisive (Exod. 11). "Signs and wonders" in verse 9 is a summary of the plagues (see Ps. 105:27).[8]

Sihon . . . Og . . . and all the kings of Canaan. The second of God's wonders in history is the defeat of the Canaanite kings, Sihon of the Amorites and Og of Bashan (Num. 21), "and all the kings of Canaan," likely the thirty-one kings whom Joshua put to death (135:11; see Josh. 12:24). God is the subject of this chain of conquering events, because "the LORD does whatever pleases him" (135:6a). The historical events stretch all the way from the plagues of Egypt to the conquest of Canaan ("He gave their land as an inheritance, an inheritance to his people Israel"; 135:12).

135:13–14 *Your name,* LORD, *endures forever.* "Name" and "renown" in verse 13 (lit., "your remembrance") are synonymous, and the verse is an allusion to Moses at the burning bush and Yahweh's revelation of his name in Exodus 3:15: "This is my name forever, and thus I am to be remembered throughout all generations" (ESV). The freshness of Yahweh's name revelation to Moses is thus invoked in this era of the reconstitution of Israel as God's people. The following statement of the certainty of God's judgment and compassion on Israel is all the more poignant because of the appeal to Yahweh's self-revelation to Moses on the eve of the exodus. In the Hebrew, verse 14 is an exact duplicate of Deuteronomy 32:36, the song Moses sang to Israel on the verge of his death and on the brink of their entrance into Canaan. Thus Israel, on the brink of regaining their land, their "heritage" (135:12; NIV: "inheritance")—a second exodus, no less—hears Yahweh reassure them of his identity, as they also listen to strains of Moses's song before they enter Canaan. Just as the readers heard Moses's voice (Ps. 90) when the Davidic covenant had come under reexamination (Ps. 89), so the readers, some seventy years later, hear Moses's voice again as they are poised on the edge of this new "Canaan."

135:15–18 *The idols of the nations are silver and gold, made by human hands.* It is certainly no coincidence that the topic of idols is next in the psalmist's review, for idolatry was Israel's worst betrayal, and the golden calf incident was forever lodged in their guilt-ridden conscience. The inability of human hands to make their own gods had not changed.[9] While the artisanship of idol makers was well known, their products still could not replicate real gods, and their efforts essentially had a reverse effect, for "those who make them will be like them, and so will all who trust in them" (135:18).

135:19–21 *All you Israelites . . . house of Aaron . . . house of Levi . . . you who fear him, praise the LORD.* The four instances of the call to praise in verses 1–3 (*hal*e*lu-yah*, "Praise the LORD") are matched by four occurrences of the call to "bless the LORD" (*bar*a*ku*; NIV: "praise") in these final three verses. "All Israelites" seems to cover the three categories that follow: priests ("house of Aaron"), Levites, "you who fear" the Lord (135:19–20). In verse 9 the historical review begins with the plagues in Egypt and leads the reader through the conquest of Canaan, and now verse 21 concludes the psalm, like Psalm 134, in Zion, except in 134:3 the Creator of the world blesses his people from Zion, while Psalm 135 concludes with God's people blessing the Lord, the "dweller" of Jerusalem, from Zion. The Creator, now an occupant of Zion, has taken up residence among his people (compare the third part of the covenant formula, "and I will dwell in your midst"; see the sidebar "The Covenant Formula" in the unit on Ps. 79). And that deserves the final "hallelujah!" (NIV: "Praise the LORD!"; 135:21).

Theological Insights

The Psalms do not often inveigh against idolatry as do the prophets, but here our psalmist presents us with a classic disclaimer of idolatry: "Those who make them will be like them" (135:18). By so doing, he touches on one of the features of idols that was their obvious deficiency: they are wanting the necessary capacities that their worshipers most need (135:16–17). And worse still, their makers and worshipers will become like them: mute, blind, deaf, and dead! The puzzlement is why human beings would be attracted to such lifeless objects, especially when they have a God who does what he desires and acts on behalf of his people, as is witnessed by his actions in nature and history.

Teaching the Text

As preachers and teachers, we look to the text of Scripture to provide the content of our message, and sometimes the order of our message. Yet those two concerns are not necessarily coordinate. While our uncompromising insistence on preaching and teaching the message of the text is nonnegotiable, the order in which the text presents the message is not always the best order for our presentation. The outline I am suggesting for developing a sermon/lesson on Psalm 135 may best be arranged in a sequence that is not the order of the text. Since we might form our message on the idea of the two portraits of the deity in this psalm, we might find it more effective if we consider the portrait of idols/idolatry as our first point and then deal with the portrait of the true God as our second point. That contrast, in fact, is one of the major messages of this psalm. While we are inclined to speak about a *personal* God, that is not the way the Psalms speak about the Lord, even though they have other ways to describe him as personal. As pointed out in "Interpretive Insights," the description of idols in verses 15–18 is to the effect that they lack all of the personal attributes of human beings—that is, they are not personal, but our God is. In fact, the faculties of idols are deficient in all four categories: speaking, seeing, hearing, and breathing. The other side of that coin is that the psalmist makes the assumption that the true God has all of these faculties, and these are part of being made in the image of God. While the image is not defined in Genesis 1:26–27, the Creator, whose image we reflect, made the world by speaking ("God said"), he declared that it was good ("God saw"), and he gave his human creature the breath of life ("The Lord God . . . breathed into his nostrils the breath of life," Gen. 2:7). While there is no mention of hearing, the fact that God spoke in the first-person plural, "Let us make," assumes the hearing faculty—someone was listening. All of these are personal faculties of which the idols are deficient. So the assumption of the psalmist is that Yahweh is a personal God, and in no sense can the idols qualify as personal.

Second, we want to move to the portrait of the true God that is painted by our psalmist in such beautiful, even though sometimes subtle, words (see the comments on 135:4–5). The personal nature of God is presented in terms of his choosing Israel (135:4) and making them "his treasured possession" (135:4). Moreover, our poet continues to lay out the Lord's personal nature: all he desires he does (135:6); he opens his storehouses and provides rain, with its attendant natural phenomena (135:7); he miraculously delivered Israel from Egypt (135:8–9) and conquered the land of Canaan for their inheritance (135:10–12); he did all that because Israel is his "treasured possession," and Yahweh is a personal God and has all the faculties required to do what he desires. The combination of Israel as God's "treasured possession" (God's love) and God's ability to do as he pleases (God's election) signifies Israel's and our position in grace. As Horton states, at the cross God frees us to become his "treasured possession," releasing us from all other allegiances (see "Illustrating the Text"). This portrait of a personal God is in line with the God of the Old and New Testaments. And to bring the biblical message of a personal God home to humankind, God took upon himself our humanity and lived among us. While the message of verse 21, that Yahweh "dwells in Jerusalem," is a long way from the New Testament doctrine of the incarnation, it is nevertheless the message of "God with us."

Illustrating the Text

See also "Illustrating the Text" in the unit on Psalm 115.

The new cross

Quotes: A. W. Tozer and Michael Scott Horton. In 135:4 the psalmist speaks of Israel as the Lord's "treasured possession," meaning that Israel is the Lord's and no one else's. Horton quotes Tozer's assessment of Christianity in his day—it still applies—that makes it look like bargain-basement prices:

> All unannounced and most undetected there has come in modern times a new cross into popular evangelical circles. . . . This new evangelism employs the same language as the old, but its content is not the same and its emphasis is not as before. . . .
> The new cross does not slay the sinner; it redirects him. It gears him into a cleaner and holier way of living and saves his self-respect. To the self-assertive it says, "Come and assert yourself for Christ." To the egotist it says, "Come and do your boasting in the Lord." To the thrill-seeker it says, "Come and enjoy the thrill of the abundant Christian life."

Horton adds his comments: "Being 'bought with a price' (1 Cor. 7:23) means that we have become the property of someone else. At the cross, then, we were freed from slavery to sin—not to become 'in control' again, but to become the property of Jesus Christ, who frees us from other allegiances to be entirely his."[10]

God's "human deficiencies" perceived?

Bible: Job. Our psalmist makes the point that the Lord, unlike the idols, is a personal God. Somewhat in contrast, Job laments that God does not have the sensory capacity with which we humans are endowed, but Job thinks it would be a good idea if he did. In his desperate situation Job sees himself as the helpless victim of a God who has no regard for justice and no notion of how his defenseless victims feel (Job 9:22). Job is hemmed in on one side by the demarcations of death and on the other by a God he considers amoral, and his situation is made more intolerable by God's insufficient understanding of the human dilemma: "Do you have eyes of flesh? Do you see as a mortal sees? Are your days like those of a mortal or your years like those of a strong man?" (Job 10:4–5). The fact that Job sees the logic of God's having such a relationship to the world, of seeing it through human eyes, of feeling the depressing bewilderment of us humans, who are always looking death in the face—this is a spiritual insight that extends far beyond Job. Some have called it a vacuum. In fact, the Christ-shaped vacuum, as it has been called, existed in the Old Testament and was filled in the New. Jaroslav Pelikan writes that the disciples of Jesus in the first three or four centuries carried out their mission on the growing assumption that "there was no culture 'where a Christ is not expected' and that therefore, in his person and in his teaching, in his life and in his death, Jesus represented the divine answer to a question that had in fact been asked everywhere, the divine fulfillment of an aspiration that was universal."[11] The incarnation produced the historical and personal confirmation of God's sympathy with us (Heb. 4:15); and whether Job is right or wrong in his assessment of God's understanding of the human dilemma, God's assumption of human flesh in Jesus of Nazareth has filled the vacuum that Job sketches. Indeed, in his pencil sketches of the deficiencies of the spiritual cosmos, Job sketches the contours of the incarnation.

"Give Thanks to the LORD . . . Who Alone Does Great Wonders, His Love Endures Forever"

Big Idea

God's love is the underlying cause of creation and redemption.

Key Themes

- God's love, the moving power of history, stretches from creation through the expanse of time and just goes on and on.
- God's wonders include the saving events of history and even God's daily provisions of bread—all God's gifts are grace.

Understanding the Text

Psalm 136, called the Great Hallel, puts into a liturgical form the "great wonders" God has performed in creating the world and redeeming Israel. Psalm 135 closes by bidding all Israelites, priests, Levites, and God-fearers to "bless" the Lord from Zion, and Psalm 136 is the grand response to that call. Although the addressees of Psalm 136 are not identified, we can assume they are the congregation at large, on the analogy that when the glory of the Lord came down on Solomon's temple, the congregation responded, "He is good; his love endures forever" (2 Chron. 7:3). The theological infrastructure of the psalm is God's love that undergirds the "great wonders" of God's grace.

The Text in Context

The psalm has no title, encouraging the view that Psalms 135 and 136 form a pair of psalms that should be read together. In fact, the historical reviews in 135:8–12 and 136:10–22 are very similar, both of them concluding that the purpose of God's actions in history was to give Israel "an inheritance" (135:12; 136:21–22; compare 105:43–45). Moreover, in different terms, of course, both acknowledge Yahweh's compassionate actions on Israel's behalf: "For the LORD will vindicate his people and have compassion on his servants" (135:14), and "He remembered us in our low estate . . . and freed us from our enemies" (136:23–24). What Psalm 135 announces in general terms ("the LORD . . . will have compassion," 135:14), Psalm 136 announces with specificity (he "freed us from our enemies," 136:24). Verses 25–26 return to the topic of creation and pick up the theme of food in Genesis 1:29–30, rounding out the creation details that have included the earth and heavenly bodies and now, by implication, the plants for food.

While we cannot be sure that Psalm 136 concluded Book 5 at an earlier stage of development, it is quite evident that the formula "Give thanks to the LORD, for he is good; for his love endures forever" has been installed at strategic points in Psalms 107–36: at the beginning (107:1), with its alternate refrain (107:8, 15, 21, 31); at the beginning and end of the final psalm of the Egyptian Hallel (118:1, 29); and at the beginning of Psalm 136 (and internally at vv. 2, 3, and 26), with the repeated refrain ("His love endures forever"). The overarching design of this collection suggests an intentional editing. Zenger speaks of a composition arc that is visible particularly at 107:1; 118:1, 29; and 136:1, signifying the mode of thanksgiving for God's redeeming "love" (*hesed*).[1]

The correspondences between Psalms 135 and 136 and the Egyptian Hallel (Pss. 113–18) are covered in table 1 in the unit on Psalm 135.

Outline/Structure

1. Introduction: Call to give thanks (136:1–3)
2. God's wonders in creation (136:4–25)
   a. God's wonders in the creation of the world (136:4–9)
   b. God's wonders in the exodus (136:10–15)
   c. God's wonders in the wilderness and conquest (135:16–22)
   d. God's wonders in remembering Israel in their low estate (136:23–24)
   e. God's wonders in provision of sustenance (136:25)
3. Conclusion: Call to give thanks (136:26)

Historical and Cultural Background

Our working hypothesis is that the Pilgrim Psalter was designed to celebrate the return from exile and the restoration, even though it may have been reedited at a later date for use in the time of Ezra-Nehemiah. Psalms 135 and 136, as already stated, are the conclusion to that collection. Psalm

135 invoked the community of faith to bless the Lord, and Psalm 136 is the response to that invocation. We cannot determine when it might have been first used in the temple, but I am inclined toward the early days of the new temple (late sixth century BC).

Interpretive Insights

136:1–3 *Give thanks to the* LORD, *for he is good. His love endures forever.* The call to "give thanks" occurs three times in the beginning of this psalm (136:1–3) and once at the end (136:26), forming an *inclusio*.[2] Book 5 begins with this same call (107:1), and the twin psalms, Psalms 111 and 112, introduce the Egyptian Hallel with "I will give thanks to the LORD with all my heart" (111:1 NASB). It is a standard liturgical formula (see the comments on 135:4–5 and the first endnote there). Psalm 118, the concluding psalm of the Egyptian Hallel, begins with the call and the congregation's response (118:1–4) and ends with the same call to give thanks (118:26). Psalm 136 crowns this section of Book 5 with twenty-six occurrences of the response, while the call to give thanks has to be assumed before each stated proof. The extended pattern gives the sense of continuity ("forever") to Yahweh's love—it just goes on and on.

136:2 *Give thanks to the God of gods.* Even at this moment in Israel's history, when the people were at last turning toward monotheism, an element of henotheism still existed in the religion (135:5; see the sidebar "Yahweh and Other Gods in the Psalter" in the unit on Ps. 7).

136:4–9 *to him who alone does great wonders.* God's "great wonders" include his works of creation, historical deliverance, and compassionate care of Israel and humanity. In fact, the phrase "great wonders" in verse 4 is followed by a list of them through verse 25 (see "Outline/Structure"). The adverb "alone" that establishes Yahweh's uncontestable godship moves in a monotheistic direction.

who by his understanding made the heavens . . . spread out the earth. "Understanding" (136:5) suggests the marvelous design the Lord has impressed on the universe (Jer. 10:12; Prov. 3:19). "Who spread out the earth" is a present participle related to the noun "vault" in Genesis 1:6–8 (KJV: "firmament") and derives from a verb meaning "to beat out" (Exod. 39:3; NIV: "hammered out"). In Genesis 1:6–8 the "vault" is the canopy that one sees when looking at the sky and that is stretched out over the primordial waters. It was in this "vault" that God installed the heavenly luminaries ("to separate water from water"). But here it seems to be the earth, rather than the sky canopy, "stretched out" over the waters (seas), as if it had been laid on the waters (it is an optical, not a scientific, description).

who made the great lights . . . the sun . . . the moon and stars. Verse 7 mentions the "great lights," as if to continue the description of Genesis 1:14–19, and then verses 8 and 9 enumerate the lights: "the sun to govern the day" and "the moon and stars to govern the night." The language of creation here is more in line with that of Genesis 1, while the language of Psalm 104 is highly poetic. From verse 1 and continuing throughout the psalm, the call to give thanks should be understood before each line, as each new "wonder" is rehearsed.

136:10–15 *who struck down the firstborn of Egypt.* In these verses the psalmist mentions the highlights of the exodus narrative: the tenth plague (136:10), the exodus itself (136:11–12), the parting of the Red Sea (136:13), Israel's crossing of the sea (136:14), and the perishing of Pharaoh and his army in the sea (136:15). "Egypt" is the object of the participle "struck," giving the sense that Yahweh struck Egypt "in their firstborn" (struck them where it really hurt the most).

136:16–22 *who led his people through the wilderness . . . who struck down great kings.* The wilderness period receives summary attention (136:16–17), but the conquest is remembered with the major notices about the defeat of Sihon king of the Amorites and Og king of Bashan (136:18–19; see Num. 21). The fact that the eastern side of the Jordan is the object of the conquest is a bit perplexing.[3] However, Psalm 135:11 adds "and all the kings of Canaan," and Psalm 136 mentions that Yahweh "struck down great kings . . . and killed mighty kings" (136:17, 18) before mentioning Sihon and Og.

136:23–24 *He remembered us in our low estate.* This is most likely an allusion to the exile, and the fact that God remembers "us" in "our" state of humiliation (the only occurrences of the first person in the psalm) is among his "great wonders." The verb "remember" connotes more than a mental function. It implies a covenantal function. See "Illustrating the Text."

136:25–26 *Give thanks to the God of heaven.* This liturgy ends in a universal tone (cf. 118:29: "Give thanks to the LORD") and thus points back to the Creator in verses 5–9 and forward to the universal call to praise in the final verse of the Psalter (150:6).

Theological Insights

Since this is a psalm of thanksgiving, and such psalms are an acknowledgment of what God has done (see the sidebar "Psalms of Thanksgiving" in the unit on Pss. 9–10), Psalm 136 appropriately makes God the subject of the creative and redemptive acts that are commemorated. There is no question about God as subject of the creation narrative of Genesis 1, a story the psalmist is familiar with, but the historical accounts are not always so specific. The plague narrative (Exod. 7–12), for example, has a combination of grammatical subjects—sometimes the Lord is the cause of the plagues, sometimes Moses and Aaron, and sometimes no subject is specified at all.[4] Lest there be some misunderstanding, this psalm makes clear that the real Creator and Redeemer is Yahweh, even though the name *YHWH* appears only once in the psalm (136:1). Further, the moving power in history is stipulated in the refrain as "love" (*hesed*).

Teaching the Text

We may begin our sermon/lesson by observing that in the Psalms, and other literature as well, small words can be powerful forces, and in conjunction with other words, they can burst into poetry and narrative with truths that take center stage. Psalm 136 is such an instance. Not to minimize the impact of the rest of the language of the Psalms, there are two words in the refrain that demand the reader's attention and become more than supporting actors.

The first is the conjunction "for/because." It is the word that begins each of the twenty-six instances of the refrain, "*for/because* his love endures forever." The NIV has unfortunately left it untranslated.[5] While Yahweh's "great wonders" are the proofs of God's love (*hesed*), the divine infrastructure of those proofs is found in the refrain "because his love endures forever." In fact, God's actions in creation and history are motivated by his love—that is the cause. The conjunction "for/because" is the tether that binds the two parts of the whole together.

The second word is "love" (*hesed*; see the sidebar "*Hesed*—God's Love" in the unit on Ps. 36), which occurs only in the refrain, announcing the divine attribute that governs all God does. In fact, we made the point in our discussion of 130:4 that God's essence is described as "unfailing love" (with the article, *hahesed*). Moreover, the description of Yahweh given in Exodus 34:6 refers to Yahweh as "abounding in love and truth" (author's translation).

While the proofs of creation and history may not be so obvious in the catalogue of "great wonders," God's love, unnamed also in all other instances of this catalogue, clearly surfaces in Yahweh's remembrance of Israel "in our low estate" (136:23). "Remembered" is a verb of redemption. In "Illustrating the Text" I have outlined the beautiful pattern of "God remembered" laid out in the book of Genesis, marking significant poles of redeeming history. Also here we have the opportunity to speak about the golden thread of God's love that runs through all of the pieces of our lives, often unrecognized, but surfaces in obvious ways in our moments of crisis. The proofs we see in creation and history in the first half of these twenty-six verses have a deeper underlying cause, and that is God's love. The first half of verse 23, "He remembered us in our low estate," is the covenantal equivalent of "His love endures forever."

It is only natural that we connect this to the New Testament doctrine of the love of God. It is at the heart of God's self-commitment to Israel and to us, and in the New Testament message God's love takes center stage, becoming very personal in Jesus of Nazareth: "But God demonstrates his own love for us in this: While we were still sinners, Christ died for us" (Rom. 5:8). But already in the Old Testament it is the golden thread that the Great Designer has woven into the fabric of creation and history. On the basis of this psalm we could say that God created the world because he loved us, and he shapes the design of our personal and world history because he loves us. This may be an appropriate place to speak about Paul's principle of grace in Romans 8:28. Paul speaks of God's special life-design for those "who love him." Since God created the world because he loved us, it is not surprising that his attention to the details of our lives is undergirded also by his love, and that makes Romans 8:28 and Psalm 136:1 virtual equivalents.

Illustrating the Text

God remembered.

Bible: **Genesis.** The book of Genesis reveals a level of covenantal consciousness by saying three times, "God remembered," all at strategic theological points in the Genesis story—the Lord's covenant underwrites the narrative, much like the point the writer of Psalm 136 makes by his repeated line "because his love endures forever." The first mention of "God remembered" in Genesis grows out of the flood narrative as the story draws to a close, a story that could have ended the story of humankind had it not been that "God remembered" and spared humanity (in the persons of Noah and his family) and the animal world: "But God remembered Noah and all the wild animals and the livestock that were with him in the ark" (Gen. 8:1). The second grows out of the narrative of Sodom and Gomorrah, a theological capstone, a *note bene*, observing that the covenant relationship Abraham had with God was valid and effective, and making what could have been a rather random story an integral part of the story line of the Abrahamic covenant: "So when God destroyed the cities of the plain, he remembered Abraham, and he brought Lot out of the catastrophe that overthrew the cities where Lot had lived" (Gen. 19:29). The third instance grows out of the story of Jacob and his favored wife Rachel, when Rachel's barrenness could have cut off God's covenant line of succession, but "God remembered Rachel. . . . She became pregnant and gave birth to a son and said, 'God has taken away my disgrace.' She named him Joseph, and said, 'May the LORD add to me another son'" (Gen. 30:22–24). The point of this theme is to say that when God remembers, it is more than a mental function—it is the function of grace in action.

Our exile and God's remembering

Quote: **David Wolpe.** We could make a case that exile is one of the major paradigms of Scripture. In the book of Genesis alone it begins with Adam and Eve's expulsion from the garden, continues to Cain as a fugitive and wanderer on the earth, extends to Abraham's departure from his homeland and to Jacob's twenty years away from his family in the land of the east, and climaxes in Joseph's servitude in Egypt and his family's subsequent move there. The book of Exodus continues the story with the primal story of Israel's sojourn in Egypt. The theme climaxes later in the Old Testament with the exile of the northern tribes to Assyria in the eighth century and the Judeans to Babylonia in the sixth century, and in a sense that last exile became, geographically and spiritually, the diaspora. In the New Testament, 1 Peter is addressed to the "exiles scattered through the provinces," suggesting that the New Testament believers viewed themselves as being in exile.

Wolpe speaks about two kinds of exile, exile from the world and exile from the self.[6] Our modern world is a victim of both. Geographically we have seen people in Cuba, Europe, Asia, South America, and the Middle East—too many places to name—expelled from their homes, often with no place to go. Many times the forces behind these tragic displacements have been the tyranny of self-serving egomaniacs. At the same time our modern world has been victimized by the tyranny of self-serving individuals—we can include ourselves here—and we feel alienated from our world and from ourselves. In many instances our religious underpinnings have been swept away, and we have become exiled from God, which is the greatest tragedy of all. Although Psalm 136 does not speak of exile as such, exile, or the conditions that led to it, is nevertheless the atmosphere in which the psalm operates. Psalm 135 speaks of Israel's exile from God, which went under the name of idolatry (135:15–18) and was an alienation from God that parallels our own. Psalm 137 laments the exile itself and exhibits the awakening to reality that began in exile. Wolpe reminds us, "There is no homecoming until the pain of exile is sharp enough to disturb our nights and shadow our days."[7] Psalm 136 is a reminder, not so much of what Israel (and we in our modern circumstances) has done but of what the Lord has done, particularly that "he . . . remembered us in our low estate, *for his love endures forever*" (136:23 ESV). Let us hope heartily and pray fervently that this will be the outcome of our exile.

"By the Rivers of Babylon We Sat and Wept When We Remembered Zion"

Big Idea

Our "Babylon" perspective and our "Jerusalem" perspective can be mutually enriching.

Key Themes

- Lamenting is not an end in itself but a means to an end: the praise of God.
- God's faithfulness is written in and between the lines of our "Babylon" and "Jerusalem" perspectives.

Understanding the Text

"Stylistically," says Schaefer about Psalm 137, "the composition is a gem. It expresses unbridled emotion, from melancholy to nostalgia to rage."[1] As to genre, it is a community lament, expressing the sorrow of the Judeans while they were in Babylonian captivity and their resolve not to forget their beloved Jerusalem. It belongs also among the Zion songs (Pss. 46; 47; 48; 76; 84; 87; 122; and 137).

The Text in Context

The position of Psalm 137 between the conclusion following the Pilgrim Psalter (Psalms 135–36) and the final Davidic collection of psalms (Pss. 138–45) is a bit perplexing. It seems as lonely here as the exiles by the rivers of Babylon, unable to sing their joyful tunes of Zion. The psalm's lamentive tone is one of the last remnants of the exiles' sorrow preserved in the Psalter. It is a witness to the fact that Yahweh remembered Israel in their "low estate" and freed them from their enemies (136:23–24).

Outline/Structure

The occurrence of "Babylon" in verses 1 and 8 marks an *inclusio*, insisting that the psalmist can no more forget Babylon than he can forget Jerusalem. But the two cities stand at opposite ends of his memory spectrum and represent life's two emotional extremes ("we wept" and "songs of joy").

1. The lament (137:1–4)
   a. In Babylon: The memory of Zion with tears (137:1)
   b. In Babylon: The memory of harps on poplar trees (137:2)
   c. In Babylon: The memory of scornful captors (137:3)
   d. In Babylon: The memory of the Lord's songs "on heathen soil"[2] (137:4)
2. The oaths (137:5–6)
   a. The first oath: Never to forget Jerusalem (137:5)
   b. The second oath (a curse): Never to fail to make Jerusalem his highest joy (137:6)
3. The family betrayal and two negative "beatitudes" (137:7–9)
   a. The Edomite betrayal (137:7)
   b. The first negative "beatitude": Happy is the one who repays Babylon for what they did to Jerusalem (137:8)
   c. The second negative "beatitude": Happy is the one who dashes Babylon's infants against the rocks (137:9)

Historical and Cultural Background

There is no question that this psalm's scenes are from the memories of the Babylonian exiles. Jeremiah mentions three exiles (597, 586, and 582 BC; see Jer. 52:28–30). Since the Edomites join the cacophonous chorus of Jerusalem's captors and haters (137:7), the date of the psalm is probably later than the fall of the city of Jerusalem in 586 BC and after the return of the exiles in 537 BC.

This poem is a beautiful example of opposing memories that play against one another. The poet's mind flies at the speed of sound between two locations, Babylon and Jerusalem. At one moment he sees the rivers of Babylon, and rivers of tears, harps hanging on poplar trees, taunting captors, conflicting loyalties, family betrayal, infants dashed to pieces. At another moment the poet's mind flashes with Jerusalem's images, undescribed, but evoking the strongest joy and the deepest thoughts of retribution. But still no music, for Babylon's strange sights have muffled Jerusalem's familiar tunes.

Interpretive Insights

137:1 *By the rivers of Babylon we sat and wept when we remembered Zion.* Babylon had an elaborate system of engineered canals that distributed the water of the Tigris and Euphrates Rivers inland.[3] While not mentioned here, it is possible that the exiles worked on that canal system. Ezekiel, exiled in 597 BC, the same exile as King Jehoiachin, was by the canal Kebar (Ezek. 1:1). In the verses 1 and 3 the psalmist describes this place beside the river as "there" (*sham*), perhaps implying that he was now in a different place. The position that identifies the psalmist as having already returned with the exiles to Jerusalem seems correct.

137:2 *on the poplars we hung our harps.* (See the sidebar "Musical Instruments in Psalm 33" in the unit on Ps. 33.) Hanging their harps on the poplars (see the sidebar below) may suggest that they were trying to hide them, especially if they were, as political prisoners, working on the canals and should not have been spending their time playing the instruments. The demand of their captors does not necessarily suggest that the captors had heard the captives play and sing on the job (although that is possible), but perhaps they sang and played in their communal settings when they were not engaged in slave labor.

137:3 *Sing us one of the songs of Zion!* The tone of the demand is one of mockery, and it is intensified by the fact that their captors want them to sing "songs of joy." Psalms 46; 47; 48; 76; 84; 87; and 122 are Zion songs, but the Babylonians were probably using a general reference to songs sung in Zion.

137:4 *How can we sing the songs of the* LORD *while in a foreign land?* This question unveils a significant aspect of the exiles' life in Babylonia. Zion's songs were intended to be sung in Zion, so singing them outside Yahweh's land may have aroused certain religious objections among the captives. Goulder renders the phrase "in a foreign land" as "on heathen soil," which seems to be the idea.[4] We know that the Syrian general Naaman wanted to take Israelite soil back to Syria with him after he had been healed of his leprosy by Elisha so he could worship Yahweh in Syria on Yahweh's own soil (2 Kings 5:17). So the assumption is that a god must be worshiped on his own soil, and it would not be surprising to hear a similar reluctance expressed by the Judean exiles in Babylonia.

The Poplar Tree

The poplar tree ('*arabah* [sg.], '*arabim* [pl.]; *Populus euphratica* = Euphrates poplar), sometimes called the "willow," grows along river banks. On the same branch of the tree grow both elongated leaves and rounded leaves, giving the tree its name '*arabah* ("mixed"). It is one of the four species mentioned in Leviticus 23:39–40 that were used to celebrate the festival of Sukkot (Tabernacles).[a]

[a] Hareuveni, *Nature in Our Biblical Heritage*, 76–79.

137:5–6 *If I forget you, Jerusalem, may my right hand forget its skill.* There are two oaths here, the second reversed for literary effect (see the sidebar "Oaths" in the unit on Ps. 7). The form of the oath includes both the protasis, introduced by "if" ("if I forget you, Jerusalem"), and the stipulated curse in the apodosis (in case the oath was not kept, "may my right hand forget its skill"). The Hebrew simply says, "may my right hand forget" (how to do its tasks). The curse in the second oath is to the effect that the oath maker might lose his power of speech. While the grammatical person has changed from first plural ("we/our") to first singular ("I"), it applies to all in the community. Oaths are taken by individuals, not communities.

137:7 *Remember, LORD, what the Edomites did on the day Jerusalem fell.* The Edomites, descended from Esau, were thus ancestrally related to Israel, but they joined the Babylonians in their fight against Jerusalem in 586 BC (Lam. 4:21; Ezek. 25:12; 36:5; Obad. 10–14). The "day of Jerusalem" (NIV: "the day Jerusalem fell") means the day Jerusalem was captured by the Babylonians (the ninth of Av). "Tear it down" has the sense of exposing one's nakedness, and the additional phrase in verse 7c, "its foundations," implies that basic meaning of the verb.

137:8–9 *Daughter Babylon, doomed to destruction.* The participle "doomed" may be anticipatory, and if it is, it may imply that the psalm should be dated sometime between 586 and 539 BC, the latter year being the date of the Persian king Cyrus's capture of Babylon, although the city was not "destroyed." If we insist on taking the verb quite literally, then that reopens the case. There are two beatitudes (*'ashre*, "blessed"; NIV: "happy") in these last two verses, the first announcing the principle on which the Babylonians' punishment should be determined, *lex talionis* ("an eye for an eye"): "Happy is the one who repays you according to what you have done to us" (137:8b); and, more specifically, the second, representing the most cruel deed the Babylonians did to them, dashing their infants against the rocks (137:9). See "Theological Insights" (see also Isa. 13:16).

Theological Insights

Psalm 137, so beautiful of imagery and design, is often ruled an imprecatory psalm (see "Additional Insights: Imprecatory Psalms," following the unit on Ps. 34) and, even worse, ruled unutterable in some traditions of public worship. While our moral sensitivities may rightly turn us away from the psalm, at least verse 9, our modern sense of justice is often very selective and applies only where we decide to apply it. Even though I would not insist on a congregational recitation of verse 9, I would insist that we understand that the exiles are not taking matters into their own hands, even though they certainly hope the same fate will happen to their Babylonian enemies—and maybe that is just as merciless. Rather, in their view, and probably by the common moral code of the psalmist's world, this was the only thing that could even the score, even though the highest ethical plateau of the Hebrew Scriptures might turn this negative "beatitude" into a positive one (see Lev. 19:18). Whatever position we take on this psalm, we should heed Zenger's reminder that we listen to the whole choir of the Psalter: "The individual psalm is then 'only' a single voice within the many-voiced choir of the Psalter. This sharpens its distinctive individual profile, while relativizing shrill dissonances."[5]

Teaching the Text

A sermon/lesson on Psalm 137 may follow the lines of the two perspectives we have in this psalm. One is the perspective of the exiles on their exile in Babylon. The other is their perspective on the home in Jerusalem.

First, our "Babylon" perspective is one that most of us carry around with us wherever we go. It includes the painful and tragic events that are seared in our memories. Our psalmist provides an example of how we may lament over them, recalling the bitterness and the tears. Lamenting is good for the soul, and we can make that point unapologetically (see "The Anatomy of Lament" in the introduction in vol. 1; see also "A sacred sorrow" in "Illustrating the Text" in the unit on Ps. 3). The exiles' enemies, however, as happened in the Holocaust, tried to deplete their lament of its soul and replace it with a fake joy (see "Illustrating the Text"). We may also observe that lament is not an end in itself but the means to an end, and the laments of the Psalms illustrate the fact that praise and lament are not strangers but can work in tandem to enhance the brilliance of our "Jerusalem" perspective. That is demonstrated by the fact that the psalms of lament often incorporate words of praise before they are complete (see "From lament to praise" in "Illustrating the Text" in the unit on Ps. 30).

And that brings us to our second point: our "Jerusalem" perspective is the one that illuminates the darkness of our lives, the one that even casts our Babylon experiences in the light of hope. In fact, a sense of God's faithfulness is written in and between the lines of this psalm. While the returnees can still remember Babylon with all its sorrows, that experience made the memories of Jerusalem more brilliant and alluring. Our "Babylons" have a way of making our "Jerusalems" stand out more brightly. But it is a mutual interchange, and the low points instill a new determination to live out our oaths and our promises and revive the hopes that faded when we took our Jerusalem for granted. Against the memories of the rivers of Babylon, our thoughts of Jerusalem as our highest joy can be renewed. And the reason that we in our Jerusalem perspective can look back on our Babylon perspective at all is found in God's faithfulness, which is written in and between the lines of our everyday existence, especially when we walk through the valleys and discover that the Lord "remembered us in our low estate" (136:23).

Illustrating the Text

Depriving the victim of sadness

Quote: Elie Wiesel. When the Romans destroyed Jerusalem (AD 70) and later renamed it Aelia Capitolina, they forbade the Jews to come near the city except on one day a year, the ninth of Av, when the Jews mourned the destruction of Jerusalem. The purpose was to give the Jews an opportunity to see the ruins of the city and to give them even greater reason to weep. In a book of essays on the Holocaust, Elie Wiesel observes: "The German enemy went much farther: he deprived the victim of his sadness. The victims had to be and look happy."[6] And so it was when the Babylonians demanded the Jewish captives sing "songs of joy" (137:3)—they deprived the captives of their sadness: "How can we sing the songs of the LORD while in a foreign land?" (137:4).

"The Chorus of the Hebrew Slaves"

Personal Testimony: The Italian composer Giuseppe Verdi and his librettist Temistocle Solera composed an opera in Italian in 1841 called *Nabucco* based on a play by Auguste Anicet-Bourgeois and Francis Cornue, which tells the story of Nebuchadnezzar's conquest of Jerusalem and the exile of the Judeans to Babylonia. The opera contains one of the most famous choruses in Italian opera, "The Chorus of the Hebrew Slaves" ("Va, pensiero"), inspired by Psalm 137. Its pensive mood and haunting melody convey something of the depressive tone of Psalm 137. When I have come to the study of the exile in the Old Testament Survey class at Wheaton College, I have played this chorus for the class. Even those students who might not appreciate opera seem to be moved by it. The chorus replicates the nostalgia of the exiles as they contemplated their lost homeland: "By the rivers of Babylon we sat and wept when we remembered Zion" (137:1): "Oh, remembrance, so dear and so fatal!"[7]

"Do Not Abandon the Works of Your Hands"

Big Idea

We can be confident that God will complete his purpose for us, because his love endures forever.

Key Themes

- Our high God looks on the lowly.
- The Lord will complete the work he has begun in us.
- Our faith is underwritten by God's love.

Understanding the Text

Even though the psalmist speaks in the first-person singular, "I," in this psalm, he also speaks on behalf of the entire people of Israel, especially those returning from the Babylonian exile. Some Septuagint manuscripts add "of Haggai and Zechariah" to the title, with the view that it comes from the time of the restoration and the rebuilding of the temple. In form, it is an individual psalm of thanksgiving used corporately to celebrate Yahweh's "unfailing love" (*hesed*) and commemorate the fact that, although it was inappropriate for Israel to sing Yahweh's songs in a heathen land, it is most appropriate for the "kings of the earth" to sing Yahweh's praises on Israel's land (138:5).

The Text in Context

Psalm 138 geographically positions the final collection of Davidic psalms (Pss. 138–45) in Judea, and this psalm perhaps even in the temple court (138:2). The praise of the "kings of the earth," once they hear what the Lord has done (138:4), brings Yahweh's universal nature and universal worship to the surface, and this universal praise is a tacit acknowledgment of Yahweh's universal dominion.

Hossfeld proposes a concentric pattern for this final group of Davidic psalms, constituted by two framing psalms of praise (Psalms 138 and 145) and a center made up of four lament psalms (Psalms 140–43). The leftover psalms (Psalms 139 and 144) are harder to assign a genre to, but their content fits comfortably within the collection.

After the description of Israel's exile (Ps. 137), Psalm 138 is the answer to the Great Hallel that calls Israel to give thanks (the subject of "give thanks" is not specified, and we assume it was Israel, worshiping in the temple): "I will give you thanks [NIV: "I will praise you"] with all my heart" (138:1, author's translation); and, like 134:2, the location is the temple (138:2). Further, Psalm 138 is an affirmation that the God who created the world (136:4–9), redeemed Israel from Egypt (136:10–15), and delivered them from the kings of Canaan (136:16–22) also remembers them in their exile (136:23–24). Now, here in the temple (138:2), the service of thanksgiving has begun, and there is some reason to believe that the Davidic collection of Psalms 138–45 is intended to be an elongated service of thanksgiving (138:1, 2; 139:14; 140:13; 142:7; 145:10). Indeed this thanksgiving theme began in 107:1 and does not end until Psalm 145. The destination of the journey is indeed the temple, and the object is to give thanks to Yahweh. So the service of thanksgiving has begun, and it should be no surprise that the voice they hear in the temple is David's (Pss. 138–45), for that was his journey too.

Table 1. Common Motifs and Recurring Terms in the Final Davidic Collection (Pss. 138–45)

Common Motifs and Recurring Terms	Psalm 138	Psalm 139	Psalm 140	Psalm 141	Psalm 142	Psalm 143	Psalm 144	Psalm 145
	Framing psalm	Psalms of lament						Framing psalm
To/for David	Title	Title	Title	Title	Title	Title	Title	Title
David his servant						143:2, 12	144:10	
Temple / Yahweh's presence	138:2		140:13	141:2	142:3 (2x)	143:2, 7	144:12	
Yahweh's love	138:2, 8					143:8 12	144:2	
Yahweh's name	138:2		140:13		142:7	143:11	144:5	145:1, 2, 21
Yahweh's glory	138:5							145:5, 11, 12
Yahweh's salvation	138:7		140:7					145:19
Yahweh's greatness	138:2, 5							145:3, 6
Yahweh observes from afar	138:6	139:2						
Yahweh's right hand	138:7	139:10						

Common Motifs and Recurring Terms	Psalm 138	Psalm 139	Psalm 140	Psalm 141	Psalm 142	Psalm 143	Psalm 144	Psalm 145
	Framing psalm	Psalms of lament						Framing psalm
Yahweh's ways	138:5							145:17
Motif of the way		139:24				143:8		
Yahweh's works	138:8	139:14				143:5		145:4 (2x), 9, 10, 17
Yahweh/God as King	138:4a						144:1	145:1
Kings	138:4						144:10	
Enemies without	138:7	139:22				143:3, 9, 12		
Enemies within			140:1–5, 8–11		142:6	143:3, 9		
Yahweh preserves psalmist's life	138:7					143:11		
Musical praise	138:1, 5						144:9	
To give thanks	138:1, 2, 4	139:14	140:13		142:7			145:10
Hunting metaphors			140:5	141:9, 10	142:3			
"My spirit grows faint"					142:3	143:4		
"To trust" (bth) in Yahweh				141:8		143:8	144:2	
"To keep" (shmr) and "protect" (ntsr)			140:4	141:3		143:1		

Note: I am indebted to Hossfeld's information for a significant part of this table (Hossfeld and Zenger, *Psalms 3*, 532–33).
[a] All the kings praise Yahweh when they hear his decrees (*'imre-pika*). Yahweh's royalty is implied.

Outline/Structure

The "love" (*hesed*) of the Lord forms an *inclusio* ("your unfailing love," 138:2; "Your love, LORD, endures forever," 138:8), which puts the covenant watermark on the psalm.

1. Israel praises God (138:1–3)
   a. Giving thanks in the temple (138:1–2)
   b. Recalling past answers (138:3)
2. The kings of the earth praise God (138:4–6)

3. Prayer for salvation (138:7–8)
   a. Yahweh's presence and salvation (138:7)
   b. Yahweh's completion of his work (138:8)

Historical and Cultural Background

Solomon's prayer of dedication of the temple in 1 Kings 8 seems to be the template on which this psalm is composed, or there is a common source to both texts. Correspondences between these two texts are both verbal (see table 2) and thematic (see "Additional Insights: The Model of Historical Double-Tracking," following this unit).

Table 2. Shared Vocabulary between 1 Kings 8 and Psalm 138

Terms/Phrases	1 Kings 8	Psalm 138
"The glory of the LORD"	*"For the glory of the LORD filled* the house of the LORD" (8:11)	"And they will sing of the ways of the Lord, *for the glory of the LORD is great"* (138:5)
"The name"	"And it was in the heart of David my father to build a house *for the name of the LORD the God of Israel"* (8:16, 17, etc.)	"For you have magnified your word over *all of your name"* (138:5) "And I will give thanks to *your name"* (138:2)
"Give thanks"	"When your people are struck before the enemy when they sin against you, and they return to you *and give thanks to your name"* (8:33–34)	"And I will *give thanks to your name"* (138:2)
"With all their/ my heart"	"When they sin against you . . . so that their captors carry them away to the land of the enemy, far or near, . . . and they return to you *with all their heart* and mind" (8:23, 46, 48a)	"I will give thanks to you *with all my heart"* (138:1)
"Toward [*'el/ derek*] the temple / the house / this place"	"In the land of their enemies who exiled them, and they pray to you *toward* their land which you gave to their fathers, the city which you chose, and *the house* which I have built to your name" (8:29, 35, 38, 48b)	"I bow down *toward* [*'el*] *your holy temple"* (138:2a)

Note: All translations are the author's.

Interpretive Insights

Title *Of David.* This psalm has correspondences in other Davidic psalms, thus justifying the attribution to David.[1]

138:1 *I will praise you, LORD, with all my heart.* "I will praise you" is literally, "I will give thanks to you." The NIV frequently renders the verb "to give thanks" as "to praise," but they are not equivalents. Deuteronomy

6:5 is a more comprehensive description than "with all my heart" ("Love the Lord your God *with all your heart and with all your soul and with all your strength*"), but their meaning is essentially the same, indicating "all my being." In Solomon's dedicatory prayer for the new temple, he prays that if the people who have gone into exile turn back to the Lord "with all their heart and soul" (1 Kings 8:48), the Lord will hear their prayer and answer them. The tetragrammaton "Lord" (*YHWH*) appears in a few manuscripts, and the NIV has chosen to insert it here, but actually the Hebrew (MT) gives the sense in verses 1–3 that the Lord is unnamed, just as the "gods" are unnamed, until, of course, the "kings of the earth" hear the "words of your [the Lord's] mouth and acknowledge the Lord" (138:4, author's translation). I suggest that is the reason the psalmist makes the perplexing statement at the end of verse 2: "You have magnified Your word above all Your name" (NKJV). Since God's word in Exodus 34:6 is "love and truth [NIV: "faithfulness"]," and this is the parallel line to the cryptic statement at the end of verse 2, we may assume that the psalmist is acknowledging the revelation of Yahweh's name described there as greater than his name.[2]

before the "gods" I will sing your praise. In relation to Psalm 137, where Yahweh seems to be absent from Babylon, there is a tone of defiance here as the psalmist sings Yahweh's praises "before the 'gods'" and evidently before the "kings of the earth," including Babylon's king (138:4). The NIV's quotation marks around "gods" (Heb. *'elohim*) evidently suggests that they are nonexistent deities, such as we have in 135:15–18. Sometimes the term means "angels" who attend God's throne (29:1; 58:1, where the word is *'elim*). See the sidebar "Yahweh and Other Gods in the Psalter" in the unit on Psalm 7.

138:2 *I will bow down toward your holy temple . . . your unfailing love and your faithfulness.* The psalmist worships toward the temple (see table 2). While this may be descriptive of a physical position of worship that one would assume away from the temple, it is more particularly an ascription of the psalmist's devotion to God, stated in terms of his praise for God's "unfailing love" and "faithfulness." If the final psalm of the Pilgrim Psalter (Ps. 134) is a dismissal of the congregation to their homes and various locations in and outside of Jerusalem, as some have suggested, the psalmist may be located outside the city, although he could as well be located within the city, even in the temple court. The place where the laity worshiped was the court of the temple, which was not space within the temple structure but an extension of it to the east. So they would "bow down *toward*" the temple. Verse 2a is an exact equivalent of 5:8b ("I will bow down toward your holy temple").

for you have so exalted your solemn decree that it surpasses your fame. This is a difficult verse, the apparent meaning of which is that God has made his word (Torah) greater than his name (NIV: "fame"). That is, God's Torah reveals God to a degree that surpasses what can be known merely through his name. Given the strategic place of Psalm 119 in Book 5 and the fact that it unveils an era in which the Torah was assuming a central place in Judaism, we are not surprised to hear this elevation of the Torah. At the same time, it is not a "decree" as such, because the Hebrew for "word" is used as a synonym of the Torah in Psalm 119 (vv. 38, 41, 50, etc.; NIV: "promise").

138:3 *When I called, you answered me.* As noted above (see "Historical and Cultural Background"), the psalm seems to be written on the template of Solomon's prayer of dedication in 1 Kings 8, in which Solomon asks that when Israel is exiled to a foreign land and they repent of their sins and bow down toward their land and temple, then the Lord will hear from heaven and answer their prayer (1 Kings 8:49).[3] In that context, the unnamed event alluded to in the prayer ("when I called") would be the exile, and the answer ("you answered me") would allude to the return from exile. This illustrates God's "unfailing love" and "faithfulness" mentioned in verse 2, and what better setting to base God's response on than the covenant and the Sinai revelation? And this is precisely what our psalmist does when he cites in verse 2 Yahweh's two attributes revealed in Exodus 34:6: "The LORD, the LORD, the compassionate and gracious God, slow to anger, *abounding in love and faithfulness.*" Also, in keeping with the nature of the psalms of thanksgiving, God's deliverance is an accomplished fact. The answer, however, is by implication an answer not only to the psalmist's (and Israel's) prayer but also to Solomon's.

138:4 *May all the kings of the earth praise you, LORD.* Now the psalmist addresses the Lord by name, whereas he has referred to him as "you" in verses 1–3 (see the comments on 138:1).

138:6 *Though the LORD is exalted, he looks kindly on the lowly.* (See 136:23.) The noun "lowly" may allude to the exiles and may also be a general reference to those who are poor and humble. The last clause of the verse expands that idea, implying Yahweh's "high" place in heaven, from which he still, despite the distance, sees the lowly. The wonder is that the high God looks on those who are not highly esteemed, an expression of God's condescension. So he has regard for the "lowly" despite their condition and distance. The fact that the worshipers of Psalm 137 have concern about singing the Lord's songs in a heathen land may be a companion idea. That is, the psalmist, with the exile in view, suggests that the Lord himself has an issue with their place in a heathen land, but he still "sees them from afar."

138:7 *Though I walk in the midst of trouble.* The word "trouble" can have the meaning of the underworld (Sheol; see Jon. 2:3), but here it probably means simply any kind of trouble in this world. The whole psalm is a victory celebration for David, who has triumphed over his enemies, and verse 8 picks up the theme of Psalm 136, that God's love (*hesed*) has accomplished these blessings for David and Israel.

138:8 *The Lord will vindicate me; your love, Lord, endures forever.* The verb translated as "vindicate" also means "to complete" (ESV: "fulfill his purpose for me"). Since the psalm closes with a petition that Yahweh not "abandon the works of [his] hands" (138:8c), it would imply that his work on the psalmist (and Israel) is not yet complete, but they are confident that he will complete it, for his love "endures forever." The prayer that God not abandon them ("the works of your hands") elicits thoughts of the exile and other troubles double-tracked in Israel's historical experience (see "Additional Insights: The Model of Historical Double-Tracking," following this unit).

Theological Insights

The psalm is mostly an expression of the suppliant's (Israel's) gratitude, and verse 8 contains the only petition of the psalm. While this order, thanksgiving and petition, is not particularly sacrosanct for prayer, it is an order that we ought to practice often. Thanksgiving makes sure we are focused on God, while petition tends to focus on the petitioner. There is certainly nothing wrong with that, but it is all too easy to get lost in the petition and neglect our praise of God.

Teaching the Text

My suggestion is that the preacher/teacher use the ESV, NRSV, or another version that reflects the translation "complete" or "fulfill" for the verb in verse 8a (see the comments on 138:8): "The Lord will fulfill his purpose for me; your steadfast love, O Lord, endures forever. Do not forsake the work of your hands" (ESV). The middle line, which is the refrain of Psalm 136, and which is the basis of the psalmist's petition in verse 8a and c, is the foundation the psalmist's faith is built on.

So we may make our first point: we can be confident that God will fulfill his purpose for us, because his love endures forever. As long as God's love endures, his purposes for us endure. If there is any one theological tenet that connects the two Testaments, it is God's love (see "Teaching the Text" in the unit on Ps. 112). God's love is the heart of the covenant (*hesed*) and the heart of the gospel. At this point we could bring in Paul's assertion in 1 Corinthians 13 that "faith, hope and love" remain, but "the greatest of these is love" (1 Cor. 13:13). Paul's statement in Philippians 1:6 sounds the same confident note: "being confident of this, that he who began a good work in you will carry it on to completion until the day of Christ Jesus." God is constantly working to make us all that he intends us to be, and that is his will for us. His purpose for us, in fact, is determined and shaped by his love. So from one angle, we don't even have to ask him to do that, because it is part of the program of love that he has begun in us. Yet, it is most appropriate to ask God to do what he has determined in his eternal purposes to do, which is both an acknowledgment of his work and a word of confident faith that what God has purposed he will do. We should recognize that God's purposes for us are both corporate and individual. As for the individual perspective, Rabbi Zusya (see "Illustrating the Text") reminded his followers that God wants to make of each of us what he has purposed we should be, and that may be very different from what he wants to make of another person.

Our second point may look at this truth from another angle: we can petition God not to abandon us ("the works of your hands"), because he loves us. In the case of Psalm 138, the "works of your hands" refers to us human beings, to the psalmist personally and the restoration community more generally. This is the only petition in the psalm, and while our suppliant does not describe the nature of the work God is doing, given the context, it involves a reshaping of the individual and the community in this newly forming world that God is bringing into being. We may observe that in any era of history, however dramatic world events become, we must submit to God's reshaping grace, not to reshape us in the image of the world but to reshape us in God's image so that the changing world can see more clearly the God who redeems.

We might also mention that in the Old Testament world, at least up until the Persian period (last half of the sixth century BC), once a population had been exiled, they generally remained in the land of their captivity. Now the Lord was doing a good work of overwhelming proportions, having returned them to their land, and our psalmist prays that God will not abandon his work. The work of restoration also carried some pain, because it was a reshaping of individual lives and of the corporate people, and, moreover, there were enemies without and enemies within. We can transfer this lesson to the reshaping of our own lives and world. And we should be grateful for these reshaping pains, as Albrecht Dürer was grateful to Martin Luther for the reshaping work of Luther's teachings in his own personal life (see "Illustrating the Text").

Illustrating the Text

A truth that can change one's life

Biography: Albrecht Dürer. As the Psalter draws to a close, our psalmist, out of a deep sense of gratitude for God's answering David's prayers, echoes David and expresses his deep sense of thanksgiving that God has fulfilled his purposes for David and has looked "kindly on the lowly" (138:6a). Dürer, a

German humanist and artist, was a patron of the Renaissance, and his early art depicted his commitment to the Renaissance belief in humanity. But when he heard that one is saved by faith, his heart was possessed by gratitude, and he wanted to see Luther and paint his portrait "as a lasting memorial of the Christian man who has helped me out of great anxiety." That truth not only changed Dürer's art; it changed his life.[4]

They will not ask me why I was not Moses.

Quote: Rabbi Zusya. Our psalmist prays that God will not abandon the work of his hands (138:8). The psalmist seems to be asking the Lord for the same transformative work that Paul affirms in Philippians 1:6. A well-known Hasidic admonition encourages one to strive to be all that one can become but not more than that. A famous quip is attributed to Rabbi Zusya of Anipolye: "When I reach the true world, they will not ask me why I wasn't Moses. They will ask me why I wasn't Zusya."[5]

The Model of Historical Double-Tracking

The Psalms, especially Book 5, represent a view of history that structured events in parallelisms, much like Israel's poetry structured ideas using parallelism (see "The Text in Context" in the unit on Ps. 107). For example, there were two major stories of redemption, redemption from Egyptian bondage and redemption from Babylonian exile, with many similarities, and Jeremiah promises that the second story will be the trademark by which Israel's history will be known (Jer. 16:14–15). The Egyptian Hallel (Pss. 113–18) observes such a parallel notion, as it celebrates the exodus from Egypt, which becomes the precursor of the return from exile (see "Additional Insights: The Egyptian Hallel [Psalms 113–18]," following the unit on Ps. 113).

We have already observed the model of historical double-tracking in Psalm 132, which reflects the story of David's transfer of the ark to Jerusalem and also, on a parallel track, celebrates the life and worship of the new temple. Even though the ark had been captured by the Babylonians and was not part of Zerubbabel's temple, a recitation of the story of the ark's transfer would parallel the ancient transfer and, in a spiritual sense, become the "reality" in absentia. (In the rabbinic period the recitation of biblical texts ordering and describing the sacrifices became "substitutes" for sacrifice. The "additional service" [*musaf*] in the Sabbath liturgy added Numbers 28:1–8 and 9–10 to represent the sacrifices that were no longer made.) Psalm 138 is not as clear an example as Psalm 132, because the remnants of the historical narrative are not incorporated in the psalm. However, when we read 1 Kings 8 and Psalm 138 alongside each other, there are remarkable correspondences in theme and even in language. (See table 2 in the unit on Ps. 138.)

First, in terms of setting, the ideas of exile and restoration are set forth in Solomon's prayer, and though they are not mentioned in the psalm, Book 5 is set against that background, both exile and restoration being predicted in the 1 Kings 8 account (1 Kings 8:34, 46).

Second, several themes run through Solomon's prayer that are remembered briefly in Psalm 138. The main theme, of course, is the dedication of Solomon's temple (generally called "this house" in 1 Kings 8). Correspondingly, it is also quite plausible that Psalm 138 is set in the temple courts, for the psalmist says, "I will bow down toward your holy temple and will praise your name" (138:2); and the poet speaks of the "kings of the earth" responding to the "glory of the LORD" by singing Yahweh's praise (138:4), reflective of the glory of the

Lord that filled Solomon's temple (1 Kings 8:11; Ps. 138:5). Even the "name" theology of 1 Kings 8 is reflected in 138:2, and the exalted image of Yahweh in 138:6 is a reflection of Solomon's assertion that "the heavens, even the highest heaven, cannot contain" Yahweh (1 Kings 8:27). Yahweh's exalted portrait is further reflective of Solomon's petitions that Yahweh would "hear from heaven, [his] dwelling place" (1 Kings 8:30, 32, 34, 36, 39, 43, 45, 49). Nor is the note in 1 Kings 8:42, that the foreigner "will hear of [Yahweh's] great name," lost on our psalmist, for he too declares the hope that "all the kings of the earth" will praise Yahweh (138:4). The result is that our psalmist has built his psalm of thanksgiving out of materials that reflect the dedication of Solomon's temple, recognizing that history is repeating itself, and that validates this new age and this new event. Whether Psalm 138 is dependent on 1 Kings 8 may be debatable, but their common themes and language, at the least, suggest a common source.

While Psalm 138 does not celebrate the dedication of Zerubbabel's temple, it nevertheless, like so much of the Pilgrim Psalter, bears the watermark of Solomon's dedication of his temple, and as such, it celebrates the new temple and reminds this regathering community that the Lord has not abandoned the work of his hands (138:8c).

"You Have Searched Me, LORD, and You Know Me"

Big Idea

Our pursuit of God turns out, by grace, to be God's pursuit of us.

Key Themes

- God's providential care involves both love and restraint.
- There is no thing and no place outside the range of God's presence and knowledge.
- Sometimes our flight from God is our flight to him.

Understanding the Text

This lovely psalm, a hymn celebrating an intimate level of the divine-human relationship, belongs among other intimate psalms like Psalm 23. The "I"-"you" phrasing of the poem is very personal and does not merge into a corporate expression at any point; but in the setting of this final Davidic collection (Pss. 138–45), there is most likely a corporate voice-over that we are intended to hear, for Book 5, by the very nature of its setting in the postexilic experience, resounds within a reawakening community of faith and a new temple of worship (for "I" as the communal voice, see the sidebar "Reading Psalm 119" in the unit on Ps. 119 and the comments at the beginning of "Understanding the Text" in the unit on Ps. 140). While the psalm type has been considered a hymn since Gunkel's monumental work on the Psalms,[1] it is more likely a mixed genre, made up of elements of the hymn and the lament. Verses 19–22 certainly have a lamentive tone (compare the appeal of verse 19 with that in the laments of 17:13–14 and 74:22–23), whereas there are elements of the hymn (praise psalm), including rhetorical questions (139:7, 17); praise of Yahweh's greatness, thoughts, and works (139:14, 17); and references to creation (139:13, 15–16).[2]

The Text in Context

Psalms 138 and 139 share some linguistic features (see table 1 in the unit on Ps. 138). First, both are titled "to/for" David; second, Yahweh observes from afar (138:6; 139:2); third, Yahweh's right hand holds the psalmist (138:7; 139:10); fourth, the suppliant prays that Yahweh will not abandon the "works of [his] hands" (138:8), and these works are among the great wonders of creation (139:14); fifth, the psalmist's enemies are a problem in both psalms (138:7; 139:22); and sixth, the psalmist gives thanks to Yahweh (138:1, 2; 139:14).

If we consider Psalms 138–45 a response to the lament of Psalm 137, which mourns the absence of Yahweh in the exile, Psalm 138 is a redirection of the reader's attention from Babylon to the temple (138:2) and a virtual admission that even though Yahweh was not there, he recognizes (lit., "knows") them from afar (138:6). Yet, in anticipation of Psalm 139, the suppliant (on Israel's behalf) declares that the Lord preserves him even "in the midst of trouble" (138:7), which implies Yahweh's presence, even though it may be undetected. Then Psalm 139 enlarges on the double theme of God's presence/absence. That is, God was there in exile with Israel even when it seemed he was not.

Outline/Structure

The psalm is framed by four words or synonyms, forming an *inclusio*, and that frame shows that the psalmist intended for part 2 (139:19–24) to be an integral piece of the poem.

1. Praise of the Creator (139:1–18)
   (Frame [139:1–2]: Search, know, discern, thoughts)
   a. God's knowledge of human affairs (omniscience) (139:1–6)
   b. God's reach of humankind wherever they are (omnipresence) (139:7–12)
   c. God the Creator of humankind (139:13–18)
2. A prayer of supplication (139:19–24)
   a. A prayer regarding the wicked (139:19–22)
   b. A prayer regarding the psalmist (139:23–24)
   (Frame [139:23]: Search, know, test, thoughts)

Historical and Cultural Background

This splendid poem of literary and theological beauty, "one of the summits of Old Testament poetry,"[3] is part of the ongoing celebration of the return from exile, remembering God's long arm of love that has rescued Israel from captivity. As we saw in Psalm 137, Babylonia was the extremity of spiritual and emotional existence, where the singers of Zion could not find their pitch because they were in a heathen land (137:4). The imagery of 139:7–12 plays the same theme—the extremities of God's providence. In fact, the gist of this text is not that Israel fled from God to Babylonia, or any other place, to escape divine scrutiny, but rather that wherever they went, and under whatever circumstances, God's presence was there to guide them and hold them securely (139:10). Even in Psalm 137 they could not forget Jerusalem, and thus they could not forget their God. This text is much more a matter of God's haunting grace than of his haunting judgment. And it is in this context that the troubling curse of verses 19–22 must be viewed. Just as Psalm 137 closed with a beatitude on those who treat the Babylonians as they have treated the Judeans, this psalm closes with a virtual curse on those who hate God. Wilcock is correct in his assessment: "Psalm 139 would sit well alongside 137 in a hymn book for the new temple."[4]

Interpretive Insights

Title *For the director of music.* See the comments on the title for Psalm 4. *Of David.* See "The Nature of the Book" in the introduction in volume 1. *A psalm.* See "The Name of the Book" in the introduction in volume 1.

139:1 *You have searched me, LORD, and you know me.* The Lord's search of the psalmist involves a thorough and repeated investigation of his thoughts and deeds, and "You know me" is the result of that search. The verb "know" occurs six times in the psalm, with one occurrence of the noun "knowledge."[5]

139:2 *You know when I sit and when I rise.* "Sit" and "rise" denote all the psalmist's activities. It is similar to the expression in 121:8, "your going out and your coming in" (ESV), another comprehensive phrase for all the psalmist's activities. God knows everything about the psalmist.

you perceive my thoughts from afar. Psalm 138:6 has declared that God, even though he is "lofty," knows the psalmist "from afar" (see the comments on 138:6). That statement is very similar to 139:2, although here the verb is "understand" (*bin*); the verb "know" (*yada'*) occurs in verses 1, 2, 4, 6, 14, and 23, but they are virtual synonyms.

139:3 *You discern my going out and my lying down; you are familiar with all my ways.* The metaphors of "going out" and "lying down" allude to the daytime and nighttime activities of the suppliant, and the second clause sums up the thought.

139:4 *Before a word is on my tongue.* God knows what we are going to say before we say it (see "Theological Insights").

139:5 *You hem me in behind and before.* The verbal imagery is that the Lord lays a siege around the suppliant so that he cannot move in any direction.

you lay your hand upon me. The sense is that of restraint so that he cannot rise farther than the restraining hand. The oppressive hand of God and the saving hand are not identical, but in God's providence they sometimes seem indistinguishable.

139:6 *Such knowledge is too wonderful for me, too lofty for me to attain.* God's providential work described in verses 1–5—searching, perceiving, discerning, restraining—is overwhelming when our psalmist thinks about it, so overwhelming that he cannot comprehend it. The phrase "too lofty for me to attain" (lit., "it is too high, I am not able [to climb that high] to attain it") is almost a verbal equivalent, expressed positively, to Numbers 13:30, when Caleb, upon the report of the spies, challenges the Israelites to go up and take Canaan: "We are well able to take it" (author's translation).

139:7–10 *Where can I go from your Spirit?* Here begins a series of scenarios that show there is no place where the psalmist may flee from God's providential care, even though that care is sometimes more restraint than freedom. Both belong to divine providence. The point in verses 8–10 is that there is no place where the psalmist might flee that God is not present: the heavens (the highest point in the world), the depths (the deepest point), the dawn (the farthest point), the other side of the sea (the farthest navigable point). The presence of God is announced by the adverb "there" and "behold," and at each place where the psalmist entertains the Lord's absence, it is a great discovery, perhaps even a surprise, that God is "there" / "there you are!"

> "If I ascend to the heavens, *you are there*" (139:8a);
> "if I make my bed in Sheol, *there you are!*" (139:8b);
> "If I take the wings of the dawn (and) dwell on the other side of the
>   sea" (139:9),
>   "even *there* your hand will guide me" (139:10a);
>   "and [*there*] your right hand will take hold of me" (139:10b,
>   "there" is
> understood; author's translation).

The directional terms take the psalmist to the highest (heavens) and deepest (Sheol; NIV: "depths"; see the sidebar "Sheol" in the unit on Ps. 6) points of creation, to the east (dawn), and to the west (other side of the Mediterranean Sea). God's providential hand will find the psalmist wherever he is and will "guide" and "hold" him. In 138:7 God stretches forth his "right hand" to save the psalmist, and here God's "hand will guide" and his "right hand hold," both verbs normally having a saving nuance, which seems to be the meaning here. Kidner says, "Verse 10 appreciates that God's long arm is moved by love alone."[6] See Jeremiah 23:24 for that prophet's version of this truth.

139:11–12 *Surely the darkness will hide me.* Distance having failed to give the psalmist a place where God's presence is absent; he has one final alternative, darkness. He contemplates this alternative in verse 11, and in verse 12 it is turned to the opposite effect: the darkness is not dark to God, and the night shines like daylight, the reason being that "darkness is as light" to Yahweh. In the verb "will hide" (139:11) some commentators see an allusion to Genesis 3:15 ("bruise" your head; NIV: "crush"). While "will cover me" fits the context better, the Targum understands the verb "bruises me" in the sense of "overwhelms me."[7]

139:13–16 *For you created my inmost being.* These verses compare with Genesis 2:7 and 21–23 as anatomical descriptions of the creation of human beings. Even though not based on Genesis 2, this account is a bit more graphic than the Genesis story, but in the same literary category. The first line reads literally, "For you formed [*qnh*, also Prov. 8:22, "brought forth"] my kidneys." "Kidneys" were considered to be the seat of the emotions (see the comments on Ps. 7:9), and here they represent the internal organs as the poet begins to describe the prenatal development of the human body. The psalmist gives thanks (NIV: "I praise you") because he is "fearfully and wonderfully made," which is reflective of God's works of creation that are called "wonderful." The meaning of the verb is "to make wonderful," and the noun/adjective "wonderful" in the following clause ("your works are wonderful") is from the same root. The psalmist is very much aware of the "wonderful" works of creation, implying that they are beyond human understanding.

139:17–18 *How precious to me are your thoughts, God!* If there were any doubt of God's felicitous care of his human creatures at this point, the psalmist puts it to rest here by saying God thinks about us all the time. Just as his presence is an immeasurable reality, so are his thoughts about us: "They would outnumber the grains of sand" (139:18). If the genre of the psalm is lament rather than praise, then the psalmist is lamenting, like Job (Job 7:17–19), that God pays an inordinate amount of attention to him, and of such a kind that he would prefer no attention at all. In fact, the term "precious" can also have the sense of "rare." The HCSB picks up this negative strain of thought but does not quite espouse the Joban view: "God, how difficult Your thoughts are for me to comprehend; how vast their sum is!" (139:17).

139:19–20 *If only you, God, would slay the wicked! Away from me, you who are bloodthirsty!* Most English translations translate the first clause as a wish, "O that God would . . . !" The question for the interpreter is whether verses 19–20 express essentially the same thought as verses 21–22, "Do I not hate those who hate you, LORD?" I think Calvin is right to lean in that direction, suggesting that the psalmist will "advance in godliness and in the fear of [God's] name" if God would take vengeance on the wicked.[8] Hossfeld is inclined in the same direction.[9] It is the same spirit that closes Psalm 137 and pronounces a beatitude on those who dash the Babylonians' infants against the rocks.

139:21–22 *Do I not hate those who hate you,* LORD . . . ? These words "are calculated to put maximum distance between the poet and the wicked," says Schaefer.[10] While we are encouraged to hate the sin and love the sinner, this rhetorical question puts the psalmist at arm's length from that ideal. At the same time, the psalmist, I am confident, thought of himself as doing something quite extraordinary. He was in perfect alignment with God's way of thinking, with God's will, no less (see the comments on Ps. 5:5–6). The psalmist awaits the redeeming perspective of Jesus that we are to love our enemies (Matt. 5:43–48).

139:23–24 *Search me, God, and know my heart.* That is, if God has any problems with this psalmist who has tried to align himself with God's ways, then let God search him for any "offensive way" and lead him in the right way ("way everlasting").

Theological Insights

Wilcock calls Yahweh the "Already God": "I cannot utter a word without his knowing it already (v. 4); I cannot go anywhere without his being there already (v. 8); I cannot even be what I am without his having already made me thus in my mother's womb (v. 13)."[11] This is a good text in support of divine omnipresence and omniscience. God is everywhere, and God knows everything. Regarding omniscience, we may also recall Isaiah's striking way of describing God's answer to our prayers: "Before they call I will answer; while they are still speaking I will hear" (Isa. 65:24). While Isaiah is obviously speaking of God's certain efficiency to answer our prayers, he also is addressing God's certain efficiency in knowing our needs, thus implying his omniscience.

Teaching the Text

There are numerous ways the preacher/teacher can approach this psalm. One of them is suggested by Wilcock as focusing on the "Already God."[12] God is always ahead of us—"Before a word is on my tongue you, LORD, [already] know it completely" (139:4). That's an expression of God's great love as well as his omniscience. (See "Theological Insights.")

Another approach is one that Weiser follows in his commentary. While he labels the components of part 1 (139:1–18) as *omniscience* (all-knowing, 139:1–6), *omnipresence* (all-present, 139:7–12), and *omnificence* (all-creating,

139:13–16), with a conclusion in verses 17–18, he comments that the psalmist does not use those rather abstract terms but personalizes God's attributes.[13] The poem is couched in "I"-"you" language. Even the questions are so reality bearing that the reader would almost expect God to speak, but he never does—the questions are rhetorical. Yet the fact that God never speaks may be a literary effect intended by the poet to replicate the absence of God. But ironically, it is in his "absence" that we recognize his pervasive presence.

There is no more personal psalm in the entire Psalter than Psalm 139. We can acknowledge that while the sophisticated theological terms may not serve us well in the pulpit (we might even decide not to use them, depending on our audience), the realities do: God's presence, God's knowledge, and God's creation. Weiser's general observation is quite apropos: "The poet does not shape his thoughts impersonally in abstract theological definitions, but develops them in the sphere of his personal experience of the reality of God in which he sees his whole life to be embedded."[14] The psalmist is aware that while he prays, God knows his outer life ("when I sit and when I rise," 139:2a) and his inner life ("you perceive my thoughts," 139:2b), and that knowledge frees him to confess that sometimes he has entertained the thought of fleeing God's presence or hiding in the darkness, only to discover how wonderful is our knowledge of God (139:6), how wonderfully God has made us (139:14a), and how wonderful are his works (139:14b). And to install the crowning piece, this psalmist, lost in wonder, love, and grace, revels in the knowledge that God's thoughts about him—about us—are precious and immeasurable (139:17–18).

Moreover, when we find ourselves in a place that seems to be devoid of God's presence, we discover, perhaps to our surprise, that God is *there* (139:7–12), and not only *there* but even guiding us by his right hand. When we find ourselves in the darkest places of our lives, when human logic would insist that we can't see God's way and God can't see us, we discover that darkness is no obstacle for God's providential care—darkness is like light to him. God's pursuit is more one of love than of judgment. Weiser incisively comments on this delicate balance between escape from God and fleeing to him: "It is not at all the bad conscience of a sinner, . . . but the innate reaction of a man who trembles at the greatness of God."[15] Francis Thompson recognizes that in his famous poem "The Hound of Heaven," when at the end the "Hound of Heaven" says: "I am He Whom thou seekest! Thou dravest love from thee, who dravest Me."[16] The pursued, by his actions and attitudes, drove love away, not realizing that the driver of the Hound of Heaven was love itself. Our pursuit of God turns into God's pursuit of us, and that is the nature of grace. "Surely your goodness and love will follow [or "pursue"] me" (23:6; see "Teaching the Text" in the unit on Ps. 23).

Illustrating the Text

Where is God?

Story: The story is told about a Hasidic rabbi, Rabbi Yitzhak Meir, that when he was a little boy, his mother took him to see the Preacher of Koznitz. While there, someone said to the young lad, "Yitzhak Meir, I'll give you a gulden if you can tell me where God lives!" The boy replied, "And I'll give you two gulden if you tell me where He doesn't!"[17] This is the message of 139:4–12; we are the beneficiaries of this marvelous truth, and "such knowledge is too wonderful for me" (139:6).

When we flee from God, we only flee to him.

Prayer: In addition to my forty-year college teaching ministry, it has been my joy to serve in various pastoral roles in the church, and the following prayer of adoration is one that I crafted for use in the "Service of Witness to the Resurrection," drawing on the language of the first question and answer of the Heidelberg Catechism and Psalm 139.

> O gracious God, in life and in death we belong to You. Wherever we go, You are there; and even when we flee from You, we only flee to You, for You are everywhere. In Your presence we find rest when we are weary, and eternal rest when life is done. In faith we look to You and cling to our hope in Christ that does not fade with pain, or trouble, or time, or eternity. Amen.

"Such knowledge is beyond my understanding."

Science: The Jerusalem Bible translates verse 6, "Such knowledge is beyond my understanding, a height to which my mind cannot attain." Psalm 139 has the vastness of the world in view, but even more than that the vastness of God's presence—there is no place where God is not present. With our increasing understanding of the incomprehensible immensity of the universe, our view of the incomparable immensity of God's presence ought to increase proportionately. For example, the Hubble Space Telescope has revealed a galaxy thirteen billion light-years from the earth. Sam Storms figured out that if one traveled five hundred miles per hour nonstop, twenty-four-seven, it would take twenty quadrillion years to get there (that's fifteen zeroes after the twenty!).[18] This is overwhelming data about the universe and puts our understanding of the Creator in a daunting category of comprehension, which puts the truth of Paul's words resounding in a universe with, so far as we can tell, no limits: "For I am convinced that neither death nor life, neither angels nor demons, neither the present nor the future, nor any powers, neither height nor depth, nor anything else in all creation, will be able to separate us from the love of God that is in Christ Jesus our Lord" (Rom. 8:38–39).

God's claim on creation

Bible: 1 Peter 3:19–20. Psalm 139 puts God's claim on every nook and cranny of the universe. The New Testament counterpart is the words of Peter, who says that Christ even preached to the spirits in prison—that is, the unrighteous souls who did not obey the preaching of Noah (1 Pet. 3:19–20). When Christ announced the message of redemption to the cosmos, not even Sheol missed the proclamation that evil was defeated and death was conquered. Figuratively, Christ posted an official notice on the bulletin board of hell that the war was over and an unconditional surrender was demanded. This is God's world, and no other powers have a claim on it. So when the psalmist contemplated a hypothetical place of escape from the divine presence, he only discovered that God had already posted his claim of ownership everywhere. See also "Christ cries 'Mine!' over every square inch of the domain of our human life" in "Illustrating the Text" in the unit on Psalm 93.

"I Say to the LORD, 'You Are My God'"

Big Idea
Evil has its natural progression from thought to deed, but God's counterplan is that evil's final progression will lead to self-destruction.

Key Themes
- Evil deeds begin in our hearts.
- Evil hunts itself down and self-destructs.
- Because God is *our* God, he will hear us.

Understanding the Text

This psalm is an individual lament, decrying the internal opponents of the community in metaphors of war, the serpent's venom, and the hunter's traps. If we understand Psalm 139 to have, at least in part, a lamentive tone, then this lament follows logically. It is a prayer from beginning to end, and the subject sees himself as a victim of the malicious designs of the opponent(s), but most likely it is, like so many of the individual prayers of Book 5, intended to apply to the community as a whole. The postexilic period, a time of rebuilding the temple and community, was also a time of internal tensions, some quite hateful, as Psalm 140 attests. Despite the opposition, however, this strong community builder knows that God's ethical demands and standards of justice have not changed—God still is attentive to the cause of the poor and needy—and the righteous will dwell in Yahweh's presence (140:12–13).

The Text in Context

The presence of God that is so prevalent in the universe (139:7) is the place where the righteous will live (140:13). The reality they fled from was, ironically, the reality they sought. In the historical setting, it is an allusion to the temple.

Almost every line speaks of enemies, and this psalm has affinities to Psalm 120, which exposes the evils of Israel's captors (120:2–5). Now similar language exposes the internal enemies, which makes the situation all the more degrading. It is a reminder that the postexilic community did not represent a totally unified purpose.

Psalm 140 reflects a frequent usage of the second Davidic collection of Psalms 51–71 (Pss. 66–67 are not attributed to David). Psalms 54 and 58 are particularly similar, both lamenting the opposing forces that have risen up against David (54:3; 58:2–5), and 58:10–11 declares the triumph of the righteous and God's fair judgment as does 140:9–13. The composers of these "Davidic" psalms reconstruct the spirit and the themes and often employ the precise language of the earlier Davidic psalms,[1] thus justifying "to/for" David. And for Israel to hear the voice of David in this critical time of their history, especially as they embark on the experience of a new temple just as their royal patriarch embarked on the era of the first temple, was comparable to hearing the voice of Moses at the opening of Book 4 (Ps. 90) and at the conclusion of the Pilgrim Psalter (see the comments on 135:13–14). While David did not build the first temple, he was responsible for the plans and preparations, and much of the initial momentum. It is most interesting that the Psalter gives very little credit to Solomon for the first temple and virtually none for the second. Even though Psalm 138 reflects Solomon's dedicatory prayer from 1 Kings 8 and Psalm 127 is dedicated to Solomon, there is virtually no other positive hints of Solomon's involvement in temple building in the Psalter (see "Historical and Cultural Background" in the unit on Ps. 127). The credit belongs to David. Of course, the reason may very well be attributed to Solomon's departure from the true worship of Yahweh (see 1 Kings 11:1–13).

Paul quotes Psalm 140:3 in Romans 3:10–18 to make the point that sin is universal and deadly. Romans 12:20 echoes the words of Psalm 140:10 and 12. See also James 3:5–8 on the power of the tongue.

Outline/Structure

1. Prayer for deliverance from those who "stir up war" (140:1–3)
   Refrain: Protect me from the violent (140:1b)
2. Prayer for protection against those "who devise ways to trip my feet" (140:4–5)
   Refrain: Protect me from the violent (140:4b)
3. Prayer for mercy that the wicked's plans will not succeed (140:6–8)
4. Curses on the wicked (140:9–11)
   a. May their evil talk engulf them (140:9)
   b. May burning coals fall on them (140:10a)
   c. May they be thrown into the fire (140:10b)
   d. May slanderers not be established in the land (140:11a)
   e. May disaster hunt them down, just as they have tried to hunt down the psalmist (140:11b)

5. Affirmation of the Lord's justice, and blessing on the righteous (140:12–13)

Historical and Cultural Background

In addition to providing insights into Israel's faith and practice during the postexilic era, the psalms of Book 5 also open up vistas on the opposition that had developed within that community. Psalm 140 reveals no physical hand-to-hand combat among the compatriots, but the vicious language that individuals within the community lodge against the righteous (including our psalmist) is nothing short of social and religious warfare.

Interpretive Insights

Title *For the director of music. A psalm of David.* The title contains the same elements as the title of Psalm 139, although they follow another order: "To the choir master [NIV: "director of music"]; a psalm; to/for David." This order appears also in psalms in other Davidic collections (e.g., Pss. 13; 41; 51; 64; 65).

140:1–2 *Rescue me, LORD, from evildoers; protect me from the violent.* After Psalm 139 ends in the prayer that the Lord search the supplicant and "see if there is any offensive way in [him]," Psalm 140 begins with the petition for rescue from evil plans and violence of other individuals. The petition "Protect me from the violent" ("violent" = *'ish hamasim*) is used as a refrain in verses 1b and 4b (2b and 5b MT). The term "violent" refers to violence against other human beings, especially against the powerless. Sadly, the evil person often becomes the violent person. The four terms of this verse are in chiastic order. The "war" (lit., "wars") they stir up seems to be a war of words.

140:3–4 *They make their tongues as sharp as a serpent's . . . protect me from the violent.* The malicious talk ("tongues as sharp as a serpent's") suggests that this is opposition not from external enemies but from within the postexilic community. The phrase "poison of vipers" is similar to the phrase in 58:4. "*Selah*" occurs at the end of verses 3, 5, and 8, apparently marking the end of strophes.

140:5 *a snare . . . cords of their net . . . traps.* These are hunting metaphors describing the efforts of the psalmist's opposition to "trip" his feet (140:4). They are "the cry of a hunted soul,"[2] much as David was hunted by Saul (1 Sam. 17–31). The fact that there are three (some think four) hunting metaphors suggests the intensity of the opposition (see "Teaching the Text").

140:6–8 *You are my God.* See also 31:14. This confession is in line with the covenant formula whereby Yahweh commits himself to Israel as their God, calls them to confess him as their God, and promises to dwell in their midst (see the sidebar "The Covenant Formula" in the unit on Ps. 79 and "Theological Insights" in the unit on Ps. 99; see also 95:7 and "Theological Insights" in the unit on Ps. 118); and it is on the basis of that covenantal confession that the suppliant prays for mercy. It is both a personal and community affirmation of the Mosaic covenant.

Sovereign LORD. The direct address "Sovereign LORD" is the combination of the tetragrammaton (*YHWH*) and its substitute *'adonay* ("my master" or "Lord"), which implies the psalmist's acknowledgment of servanthood.[3] The statement in verse 7b sounds like the psalmist has had battlefield experience, and he transfers the metaphor of "surrounding his head" (probably with a full-body shield) to his troubled community and particularly to himself.

140:9–11 *Those who surround me proudly rear their heads; may the mischief of their lips engulf them.* The language of verse 9 is difficult. However, it appears that the metaphor of God protecting the psalmist's head in the day of battle is in play here in a negative way. The ESV (see also NRSV) catches that sense of the verse: "As for the head of those who surround me, let the mischief of their lips overwhelm them!"

May burning coals fall on them; may they be thrown into the fire. Verses 10–11 contain curses against the opponents. The first, that "burning coals" will fall on them, is reminiscent of the punishment of Sodom and Gomorrah (Gen. 19:24; see also Prov. 25:22), and the "miry pits" are allusive to the pits around the Dead Sea that pose great danger to travelers. The second, that disaster may "hunt down the violent" to push them into the pits, thus completes the metaphor (the NIV does not translate the final infinitive "to push").

140:12–13 *I know that the* LORD *secures justice for the poor . . . the needy.* Finally, the psalmist affirms his confidence ("I know") that the Lord acts justly for the poor and needy (140:12), and the theological extension of this confidence is that the righteous will give thanks to Yahweh's name and will live in his presence. God's "presence" is an allusion to the temple, and in the broader range of biblical theology it is the realized kingdom of God. David's passionate yearning was to dwell in the Lord's presence (27:4), and now he has finally arrived there, at least rhetorically, along with all the righteous, who are the poor and needy (see the sidebar "The Editing of Book 2" in the unit on Ps. 70).

Theological Insights

The nature of evil is a topic of interest in this psalm. In the first place, it is so intense and focused on its target as to employ multiple instruments of destruction in order to extinguish the righteous (140:4–5). At the same time, the psalmist engages in prayer, the most powerful and effective instrument of all, leaving the results to God. And the results, interestingly, are that the hunt for the righteous is turned into evil's hunt to chase down the violent and to push them into the miry pits. That is, evil is self-destructive. In Psalm 9, hunting metaphors also describe the self-destructive, self-devouring nature of evil: the nations fall into a pit they have dug and are caught in a net they themselves have hidden (see 9:1, 16; see also 7:15–16). It may very well be that this view of nature's innate reversible quality has become so ingrained in psalmic thought that it assists the psalmists' commitment of the evil situations and machinations they face to God. In any event, they take comfort—and so can we—from this theological notion.

Teaching the Text

We may begin our sermon/lesson by observing that this psalm represents a progression of evil. The process begins in the heart (140:2), is transmuted into malicious speech (140:3), and finally is carried forth in violent deeds ("hands of the wicked," 140:4). When we think about it, this is a pretty general pattern for the development of evil in the lives of individuals, corporations, and nations.

First, we may focus on our inner person—that is, who we really are—and how that shapes and determines our thoughts and eventually our actions. This is obviously hidden from those around us, but it is not hidden from God. The wicked connive their wicked schemes in their minds, but they cannot confine them to their thoughts, for they externalize and "stir up war every day" (140:2).

That final thought of verse 2 is a transition to the second level of the progression, which is putting those thoughts into words, described in verse 3 as having "tongues as sharp as a serpent's." The use of the tongue should not suggest that this is an innocent stage, for the malicious thoughts have already poisoned the perpetrator's speech. As James reminds us in his words of wisdom about the power of speech, a ship is driven by strong winds, but a small rudder steers the ship wherever the pilot wants it to go (James 3:3–6). Our tongue is the rudder of our ship, and that's where we have to be a brave and determined pilot as we control our direction by the rudder of our tongue.

Third, we may note that the suppliant's prayer in verse 4 lays open this third stage, that of the violent deeds committed by violent persons. And they are not only violent; the perpetrators also use devious means to trip up the righteous (see the comments on 140:5), setting traps along their path.

It is at this point that our psalmist confesses his faith: "You are my God" (see the comments on 140:6–8). Spurgeon remarks, "Because he is God he can hear us; because he is *our* God he will hear us."[4] And the psalmist concludes with the confident affirmation that the righteous will live in God's presence. For David that was the ultimate goal, to live in God's presence (e.g., 23:6).

So David's deepest longing, especially as represented in the first Davidic collection of Book 1, is realized in God's people.

Illustrating the Text

Prayer kindled by grace

Quote: P. T. Forsyth. Though our psalmist is very much aware of the machinations of the wicked—he was the object of them—he is nevertheless conscious of the grace of God that both motivates our prayers and provides the answers. He confesses, "You are my God," and for that reason he pleads for divine mercy (140:6). Why pray to a god who is not merciful? God's concern for the poor, for example, is not pity, but it is grace that is the true substance of his nature. Forsyth says, "So many of us pray because we are driven by need rather than kindled by grace."[5] And Forsyth further lays out the New Testament theology of prayer: "[In the New Testament] we are taught that only those things are perfected in God which He begins; that we seek only because He found; we beseech Him because He first besought us. If our prayer reaches or moves Him, it is because He first reached and moved us to pray."[6] While the destructive plans of evildoers may function as a cause for prayer, the primary force behind our approach to God is ultimately grace: "I know the LORD secures justice for the poor and upholds the cause of the needy" (140:12).

"I sought the LORD, and afterward I knew he moved my soul to seek him, seeking me."

Hymn: "I Sought the Lord, and Afterward I Knew." An anonymous hymn published in the *Pilgrim Hymnal* (1904) phrases this doctrine of prayer and personal salvation quite richly:

> I sought the Lord, and afterward I knew
> he moved my soul to seek him, seeking me;
> it was not I that found, O Savior true;
>   no, I was found of thee.
>
> Thou didst reach forth thy hand and mine enfold;
> I walked and sank not on the stormy sea;
> 'twas not so much that love on thee took hold
>   as thou, dear Lord, on me.
>
> I find, I walk, I love, but O the whole
> of love is but an answer, Lord, to thee!
> For thou wast long beforehand with my soul;
>   always thou lovedst me.[7]

"Do Not Let My Heart Be Drawn to What Is Evil So That I Take Part in Wicked Deeds"

Big Idea

Avoiding evil and its practices often involves disassociation from its practitioners and gracious engagement with reproving love.

Key Themes

- It is God's will to deliver us from evil, so we can pray for that with utmost confidence.
- Social relationships can tempt us to compromise our faith.
- Moral discipline in the community of faith must be undergirded by a robust sense of community and an unimpeachable spirit of love.

Understanding the Text

Psalms 140 and 141 should be read together and may have been written by the same person (they are certainly in the same spirit), especially since the two psalms share imagery and since the speaker reveals that the wicked of Psalm 140 have, in Psalm 141, changed their approach from sheer opposition to the socialization of their victims. Psalm 141 is an individual psalm of lament, containing a strong element of trust.

The Text in Context

As a member of the last Davidic collection, this psalm draws on earlier Davidic psalms.[1] Like Psalm 140, it opens a window onto the postexilic scene with the inner struggles of the community, represented by this individual's encounters with evildoers whose blatant opposition has moderated to a more attractive appeal. Table 1 indicates how these two psalms are in some respects a mirror image of each other.

Table 1. Corresponding Terms and Style in Psalms 140 and 141

Psalm 140	Psalm 141
"For the director of music. *A psalm of David*" (Title)	"*A psalm of David*" (Title)
"Rescue me, Lord [A], from evildoers [B]; from the violent [B′] protect me [A′]" (140:1) (chiastic structure)	"I call to you, Lord [A], come quickly to me [B]; hear me [B′] when I call to you [A′]" (141:1) (chiastic structure)
"Who devise *evil plans* in their *hearts*" (140:2)	"Do not let my *heart* be drawn to *what is evil* so that I take part in wicked deeds" (141:4)
"*Keep me safe*, Lord, from the hands of the wicked" (140:4)	"*Keep me safe* from the traps set by evildoers, from the snares they have laid for me" (141:9)
"*Keep me safe*, Lord, from the hands of the wicked; *protect me* from the violent" (140:4)	"Set a *guard* over my mouth, Lord, *keep watch* over the door of my lips" (141:3)
"The arrogant have hidden a *trap* [*pah*] for me; they have spread out the cords of their *net* [*reshet*] and have set snares [*moqᵉshim*] for me along my path" (140:5 [140:6 MT])	"Keep me safe from the *trap(s)* [*pah*] set by evildoers, from the *snares* [*moqᵉshot*] they have laid for me" (141:9) "Let the wicked fall into their own *nets* [*makmorim*]" (141:10)
"*Give ear to the voice* of my supplication" (140:6)	"*Give ear to my voice* when I call to you" (141:1)
"God the Lord" (140:7) (a rare combination)	"God the Lord" (141:8) (see "Interpretive Insights")
"May the mischief of *their lips* engulf them" (40:9b)	"Keep watch over the door of *my lips*" (141:3b)

Note: Some of the translations are the author's in order to better show the correspondences.

Outline/Structure

1. Petition that the Lord would hear the psalmist's prayer (141:1–2)
2. Prayer that the psalmist not become like the wicked (141:3–7)
3. Prayer that the psalmist escape the traps of the wicked (141:8–10)

Historical and Cultural Background

It is a challenge to pin Psalm 141 to a specific date in history. Some commentators have dated it to David's time, and the kind of opposition the psalmist faced could qualify for that time. If that is the case, it has been refitted for this postexilic collection. However, in view of the death-delivering effect of the exile that seems to be reflected in verse 7, it would most likely be after the exile, given the general context of the other psalms in this Davidic collection

(Pss. 138–45). See also the comments on 141:2 below and Kraus's proposal that the "righteous" may be described by this psalm.[2]

Interpretive Insights

141:1 *I call to you,* LORD, *come quickly to me; hear me when I call to you.* Note the chiastic order, just like the opening verse of 140 (see table 1). The psalmist is desperate for the Lord's help.

141:2 *May my prayer be set before you like incense; may the lifting up of my hands be like the evening sacrifice.* The terms "incense" and "sacrifice" are general terms for the incense and sacrifices offered in the temple (see Isa. 1:13). While this could be a request that prayer itself be accepted as a substitute for incense and sacrifice, it may also mean that his prayer would be "like" incense and sacrifice, even though the comparative element is missing from the Hebrew text. If this psalm was composed before the resumption of sacrifice, then it might suggest that the practice of prayer had already become a substitute for these rituals during the exile. That would mean the psalm was written soon after the return, because the altar was rebuilt and sacrifice resumed in the early years of the return (Ezra 3:1–6). Incense was offered morning and evening on the altar of incense in the temple as a symbol of the divine presence (Exod. 30:7–8), and it was a practice to pray in the temple or toward the temple with uplifted hands (Ps. 28:2; 1 Kings 8:22). The "evening sacrifice" was offered in the afternoon.

141:3–5 *Set a guard over my mouth.* The "guard" (in 39:1 a "muzzle") was used to prevent one from speaking evil words with one's mouth.

Do not let my heart be drawn to what is evil so that I take part in wicked deeds. These verses reflect two stages of the progression of evil that we saw in 140:2–3 ("heart" and "deeds") and illustrate how Psalms 140 and 141 are like hand in glove (see table 1). The wicked try to attract the speaker to their cause with "their delicacies," a temptation that he resists.

let him rebuke me—that is oil on my head. In contrast, he is willing to be rebuked "in love" (*hesed*; NIV: "that is a kindness") by the righteous (see Prov. 25:12). Those eating a sumptuous meal also anoint their heads with oil ("You prepare a table before me. . . . You anoint my head with oil," 23:5).

141:6 *Their rulers will be thrown down from the cliffs.* This verse is very difficult, and some commentators think the text is corrupt. I take it as a metaphor. Throwing from a cliff was a method of execution (see 2 Chron. 25:12). But are the judges (NIV: "rulers") thrown over the rocks (lit., "into the hands of the rocks") or are they falling (slipping) on the rocks? Hakham interprets it in the latter sense, suggesting hard-nosed judgments.[3] The NJPS seems to suggest that it is a prayer of judgment against the judges rather than a statement of fact: "May their judges slip on the rock, but let my words be heard, for they are sweet." While the grammar is difficult, the sense seems to be that the judges will or should meet a tragic fate.

and the wicked will learn that my words were well spoken. The NIV understands the subject of the verb (it is impersonal, "they heard") to be the wicked, suggesting some beneficial outcome from the tragic event described in the first half of the verse. It is possible that the implied subject is rather the judges (or "rulers"), which seems more plausible since they have just been mentioned by name.

141:7 *They will say, "As one plows and breaks up the earth, so our bones have been scattered at the mouth of the grave."* The textual difficulties continue in this verse. "They will say" is not in the Hebrew text. The Hebrew treats the statement as a simile because it is introduced with "as/just as": "Just as one . . ." Evidently the "plowing" and "breaking" are supposed to raise the image of scattering, as the plow scatters the stones in the soil, and thus reinforce the imagery of the second half of the verse ("Our bones have been scattered"). I take "grave" (Heb. "Sheol") as a metaphor for the exile, and the Jews who did not return in 537/536 BC are the scattered bones at the door of Sheol. It is reminiscent of Ezekiel 37.

141:8 *But my eyes are fixed on you, Sovereign LORD.* In the Hebrew text the substitute for the tetragrammaton (*'adonay*, "my master") and *YHWH* occur together (NIV: "Sovereign LORD") and are juxtaposed with "my eyes," suggesting the idea of 123:2, that the psalmist's eyes look to the Sovereign Lord as a servant looks to his master (see also 140:7).

in you I take refuge—do not give me over to death. Now the suppliant declares his refuge in God and prays that God not "pour" him out (NIV: "give me over") to death. He identifies with the exiles, who are considered to be on the verge of death.

141:9–10 *Keep me safe from the traps set by evildoers . . . Let the wicked fall into their own nets.* Having resisted the temptation to join the evildoers, now the psalmist prays that God keep him safe from their "traps," and may they fall in the traps themselves. While the Hebrew word for "one" or "only" in the middle of the last Hebrew line (141:10; left untranslated by the NIV) is difficult to translate, the sense of the clause is nevertheless clear: while the wicked will fall into their own traps, this righteous individual will clear all the hurdles and "pass by in safety." Although the second half of verse 10 is difficult, Allen's translation seems to deal with the difficulties quite satisfactorily: "May the wicked fall one and all into their own nets, while I myself escape."[4]

Theological Insights

Reproving love is one of the decided benefits of the community of faith. Our psalmist has come to recognize that fact and to submit to its gracious embrace

(141:5). It is one of the keys to the good life, and one of the spiritual disciplines that will keep us on the right path. In an earlier psalm we observed that moral accountability, or spiritual discipline, must be undergirded in the church by two conditions: a sturdy sense of community and an unimpeachable spirit of Christian love (see "But for the grace of God, there go I" in "Illustrating the Text" in the unit on Ps. 94). The outcome of these conditions will be the spirit of the psalmist: "Let a righteous man strike me—that is a kindness; let him rebuke me—that is oil on my head" (141:5). This love, reproving love, is the gracious voice of Isaiah's teacher as he walks behind God's people saying, "This is the way; walk in it" (Isa. 30:21).

Teaching the Text

We may concentrate on the topic of how believers are to deal with evil and evil persons. The Psalms have a lot to say on this subject, but Psalm 141 makes one of the clearest statements on the matter.

First, we may emphasize the plea in verse 4 that the suppliant's heart not "be drawn to what is evil so that [he takes] part in wicked deeds." This is the central idea of the psalm, a spiritual reflex to avoid the pattern of evil described in 140:2–5. Both psalms recognize how evil begins in our hearts (140:2; 141:4) and is objectified in our actions (140:4; 141:4b) (see table 1). An equivalent idea is found in the Lord's Prayer: "Lead us not into temptation, but deliver us from evil." We should not assume, however, that praying such a prayer implies that the Lord may lead us into temptation to do evil, but it is a prayer that expresses God's will for us in obverse terms. That is, we pray that God will not allow us to be tempted to do evil, because that is the posterior side of "Thy will be done."

A second point, and one our psalm is so keen on, is how to keep a holy distance from the temptation to do evil, especially when it is so attractively represented by evil's agents: "Do not let me eat their delicacies" (141:4d). C. S. Lewis phrases the question, "How ought we to behave in the presence of very bad people?" and he has in mind those "very bad people who are powerful, prosperous and impenitent" (see "Illustrating the Text").[5] The temptation here is to favor associations with people who are socially and politically powerful, and unfortunately, the temptation is inclined to favor our own ego and self-interests rather than God's. It is a turning away from God's glory to our own. We ought to be aware of Wilcock's wise counsel that "options are to be weighed, not counted!"[6] And much discernment is needed in this area of our lives.

The third point is a corrective to this personal inclination to yield to temptation; that is, we need to be open to reproof by those who love us (141:5).

Proverbs 27:6 sums it up: "Wounds from a friend can be trusted." The Jerusalem Bible expresses the thought well: "From one who loves, wounds are well-intentioned; from one who hates, kisses are ominous." This is the point at which our spiritual discipline is critical. To draw on the Lord's Prayer again, here in the process of learning how to deal with evil and its patronage, we must decide whether we really are sincere about the final ascription of the prayer: "Thine is the kingdom, and the power, and the glory, forever." Is it for God's glory (*soli Deo gloria*) that we live, or is it primarily for our own, and God's glory is merely secondary? What spiritual gymnastics do we use to justify putting our glory first and God's second?

Illustrating the Text

Behavior in the presence of very bad people

Quote: *Reflections on the Psalms,* by C. S. Lewis. In a chapter called "Connivance," Lewis raises the question, "How ought we to behave in the presence of very bad people? I will limit this by changing 'very bad people' to 'very bad people who are powerful, prosperous and impenitent.'"[7]

To begin his answer, Lewis makes this commendation: "But I am inclined to think a Christian would be wise to avoid, where he decently can, any meeting with people who are bullies, lascivious, cruel, dishonest, spiteful and so forth." And he continues: "Not because we are 'too good' for them. In a sense because we are not good enough. We are not good enough to cope with all the temptations, nor clever enough to cope with all the problems, which an evening spent in such society produces."[8]

Lewis suggests four approaches for the believer. One is silence, which can be a good refuge, but a person must be careful that it is not a retreat from the truth. It can implicitly put one in the prevailing camp. The second is disagreement, "done argumentatively not dictatorially." And the third is simple protest, which, in some situations, must be made for integrity's sake and for the sake of truth.[9] Fourth is avoidance altogether, which keys into his initial commendation; he remarks: "The Psalmists were not quite wrong when they described the good man as avoiding 'the seat of the scornful' and fearing to consort with the ungodly lest he should 'eat of' . . . 'such things as please them.'"[10] It may be that those who do not enjoy protest will be the most effective at it.

The principle of true piety

Quote: **John Calvin.** The writer of Psalm 141 meets Calvin's basic principle for true piety: "That no creature whatever be exalted by us beyond measure."[11] Our psalmist is so desirous of reaching this goal that he prays for self-restraint in his speech (141:3) and deeds (141:4) and even welcomes reproof in love to help him shape his spiritual life (141:5). His singular focus is that his eyes are fixed on the Sovereign Lord (141:8), with his ultimate disposition expressed in these words: "In you I take refuge." It is the penultimate state of the pious life, the state that merges so homogeneously with God's will that the psalmist could say, "I am for peace" (120:7).

"There Is No One at My Right Hand; No One Is Concerned for Me"

Big Idea

As we approach the "new Canaan" of our spiritual life, God must become "our portion," our permanent dwelling place where we enter into his presence.

Key Themes

- Like ancient Israel, the psalmist met great opposition as he faced the "new Canaan."
- Like the Levites, we must recognize God as our "portion," our spiritual dwelling place.

Understanding the Text

Psalm 142 is an individual lament that concludes with elements of a psalm of thanksgiving. If there is progression in time and circumstances in this Davidic collection—and I think there is—then the psalmist's enemies, who have been in hot pursuit of him, have finally achieved their purpose of catching him in their trap, and the suppliant is in true-to-life "prison" or metaphorically in circumstances that mimic incarceration, hoping to be freed (142:7).

The Text in Context

Psalm 142 has been called a "mosaic" of words and phrases from other Davidic psalms. While this psalm could come from an earlier time, it is possible that the psalmist has intentionally drawn on other Davidic sources so as to justify the title "of/to/for David," if that indeed was a concern for the writer. Psalm 86, for example, is composed of Davidic materials from other psalms, providing the only Davidic representative in Book 3. The writer of our psalm has even borrowed the historical note "in the cave" from Psalm 57, a psalm set in the days of Saul and David's conflict, perhaps to re-create an atmosphere of conflict for his psalm. Just as important, however, is the psalm's relationship to Psalm 116 (see table 1), and this is particularly interesting because Psalm 116 is not attributed to David. However, it occurs in the Egyptian Hallel, where it, like Psalm 142, celebrates the return from the Babylonian exile (see "Historical and Cultural Background" in the unit on Ps. 116).

Table 1. Echos of Earlier Psalms in Psalm 142

Psalm 142	Other Psalms
"In the cave" (142 title)	"In the cave" (57 title)
"I cry aloud to the Lord" (142:1)	"I sought the Lord" (77:1)
"I lift up my voice to the Lord for mercy" (142:1)	"To the Lord I cried for mercy" (30:8)
"I pour out before him" (142:2)	"I pour out my soul" (42:4) "Pour out your hearts to him" (62:8)
"My complaint" (sihi) (142:2)	"My complaint" (64:1)
"My spirit grows faint" (142:3)	"My spirit grew faint" (77:3)
"Land of the living" (142:5)	"Lands of the living" (116:9)
"I was brought low" (142:6; NIV: "I am in desperate need")	"I was brought low" (116:6)
"He [the Lord] will deal with you bountifully" (142:7; NIV: "because of your goodness to me")	"The Lord has dealt bountifully with you" (116:7; NIV: "The Lord has been good to you")

Note: Some of the translations are the author's in order to better show the correspondences.

Outline/Structure

This psalm begins with an announcement of what the suppliant is about to do. Then follow two laments, each introduced by "I cry to you, Lord." The psalm closes with a vow to give thanks to God, and the psalmist is joined in that service by the congregation, "the righteous."

1. First lament (142:1–4)
   a. "I cry aloud to the Lord": Lament and cry for mercy (142:1)
   b. Lament of his trouble (142:2)
   c. Lament of his growing weakness and hidden snare (142:3)
   d. Lament that there is no advocate (142:4)
2. Second lament (142:5–6)
   a. "I cry to you, Lord": Lament and confession of trust (142:5)
   b. Lament regarding his pursuers (142:6)
3. Petition and vow to praise (142:7)

Historical and Cultural Background

The Babylonian exile, while politically a humiliating defeat for Israel, was a time when some of the exiles in Babylonia fared very well economically. In fact, Ezra 2:68–69 mentions that some of the returnees gave huge sums of money for the restoration of the temple. At the same time, some of the returnees also encountered fierce opposition from those Jews who had remained in the land and from the Samaritans who had come to dominate Judah while the exiles were away (Ezra 5:7–17). Moreover, failing crops and famine exacerbated the lot of the returnees (Hag. 1:9–11). One can also expect that after seventy years had passed, many of the ancestral portions of land left unoccupied by the exiles had long been claimed by others; reclaiming their ancestral land was not quick and easy.

Interpretive Insights

Title maskil. See the comments on the title for Psalm 74.

When he was in the cave. This note connects this poem to Psalm 57, a Davidic psalm. See 1 Samuel 24:1 and 3, and "Historical and Cultural Background" in the unit on Psalm 57.

142:1 *I cry aloud to the* LORD. Here the worshiper informs us regarding what he is going to do, then in verses 2–5 he laments his troubling circumstances, and then in verse 6 he renews his lament in words that are almost a duplicate of verse 1a; and finally in verse 7 he makes his vow to praise the Lord and mentions that the righteous will join him in the service of thanksgiving to celebrate God's kindness to him. Due to the future sense of the verb "will gather about" in verse 7, I assume that the worshiper is still in prison (literally or figuratively) and vows to have a service of thanksgiving when he is released.

142:3–4 *it is you who watch over my way . . . people have hidden a snare for me.* The psalmist describes the hostile circumstances he faces and their effect on him ("My spirit grows faint") and he confesses that the Lord watches over him even though he faces "hidden" dangers.

there is no one at my right hand. In court the defense's witness would stand at the person's right hand (see 109:31; 110:5, and "Additional Insights: A Hypothesis on Psalm 109," following the unit on Ps. 109). The topic of hidden snares is raised (142:3), as it is also in 140:5 and 141:9, but this time the psalmist's oppressors have proved too strong for him (142:6c), and he complains that he is in prison (142:7).

I have no refuge; no one cares for my life. "I have no refuge" is literally, "Flight has perished [or "will perish"] from me." These clauses are echoes of Jeremiah: "Flight will perish from the shepherds" (Jer. 25:35 NASB); "no one cares" for Zion (Jer. 30:17).

142:5 *You are my refuge, my portion in the land of the living.* While the psalmist may have been a Levite, who had no landed portion in Canaan (Num. 18:20), he may also be using "portion" in a metaphorical sense, reflecting the idea that the Lord has become his "portion." There is also the possibility that this reflects a new attitude of the nonlanded people in the community who have been unable to reclaim their ancestral property. The opposition that is represented in these Davidic psalms may very well arise from the Jews who were not exiled to Babylonia, and now the returnees are encountering their hostility as they attempt to reclaim their ancestral properties.

The terms "portion" (see the comments on 16:5; see also 16:8 and 52:7) and "land of the living" (see the comments on 27:13; see also 116:9) are metaphors for Canaan, and now the psalmist, perhaps in the midst of the legal struggle, is downplaying the importance of the recovery of the land they left behind when they went into exile. He is elevating the relationship to the Lord as being more valuable than the land.

142:6-7 *Listen to my cry, for I am in desperate need; rescue me from those who pursue me.* The opposition has not only been verbal, a point Psalms 140 and 141 make, but it has also been physical ("who pursue me") and, it would

---

A Pictogram of Worship

Psalm 142 presents us with one of those many instances when two or three words (or a single figure, as in the ancient Egyptian hieroglyphics) paint a picture of something in real life. In the case of verse 7 of our psalm, two words paint the picture: "to give thanks" (NIV: "praise") and "to encircle" (NIV: "gather around"). The picture is the voluntary service of thanksgiving in the temple on the occasion of some important event (healing, deliverance, etc.). It can be an individual or congregational occasion. The worshiper makes a vow to give thanks for the Lord's kindness (as in 142:7b), and he or she invites family and friends to join in the celebration, represented here by the "righteous" who "encircle me" (see the verb's similar usage in Judg. 20:43). The pictogram of this second verb is that of the congregation "encircling" the altar as a ritual, a practice that is mentioned in Psalm 26:6-7. The event the psalmist celebrates, along with the congregation, is release from prison (142:7a),[a] which he expresses at the end of the poem, addressing God directly: "for you will deal bountifully with me" (NIV: "because of your goodness to me"). Most English translations render the Hebrew verb in this clause as an affirmation of God's goodness (e.g., NLT: "You are good"; cf. 116:7), and certainly it is, but the implication of the psalm is that the suppliant is not yet free from prison: "The righteous will encircle me when you deal with me bountifully" (142:7; author's translation). That is, it is still a work in progress.

[a] Kraus (*Psalms 60-150*, 532) draws attention to Leviticus 24:12 and Numbers 15:34 to suggest that the suppliant may have been incarcerated until the moment of God's verdict of innocence; or imprisonment could be a metaphor for helplessness (see 142:6).

seem, has resulted in the suppliant's imprisonment. Here the suppliant is speaking for himself and not for his community.

Set me free from my prison, that I may praise your name. Now comes the vow to "give thanks" (NIV: "praise") to Yahweh's name, and the picture that follows reflects the righteous joining the worshiper at the temple and the ritual encircling of the altar as 26:6–7 depicts (see the sidebar).[1]

Then the righteous will gather about me because of your goodness to me. These are other worshipers who have joined the suppliant in the thanksgiving service in the temple. See the sidebar.

Theological Insights

We have observed in "Interpretive Insights" (see the comments on 142:3–4) that in the ancient Israelite court the advocate for the defense stands at the right hand of the accused (see 109:6–20). Our psalmist laments the absence of such an advocate in verse 4a, "there is no one at my right hand." Quite likely this refers to the struggle of the exiles to regain the property that they had left behind when they went into exile. This, however, may also be an allusion to the fact that the Levites did not receive a landed inheritance in Canaan, for the Lord is their "portion" (Num. 18:20). In the second part of the psalm the suppliant completes the picture and confesses the Lord as "my portion in the land of the living" (see the comments on 142:5), as any devout Levite should do. With his pending legal case and, to complicate matters, no advocate to plead his cause, he lays claim to the really important relationship, his relationship not to the land but to the Lord.

Teaching the Text

We may stress in our sermon/lesson two centers of meaning for our psalm: (1) the psalmist's deep faith and deep anguish, and (2) the sense of approaching a "new Canaan."

First, quite clearly the worshiper's personal faith is visible in every line of the psalm. In the beginning, he is unapologetically honest with God about his trouble and his uninhibited anguish. The latter, in fact, is audible in his declaration, "I cry (aloud)" (*z'q*), which is used to open each lament (142:1a and 5a). Further, the suppliant calls on God out of circumstances where he has no one to come to his defense (142:4a) and where hidden traps are planted along his path (142:3). To deepen the anguish, he believes there is no one who cares for him (142:4b–c).

Second, the psalmist has the sense that he is emerging from a hostile land into a "new Canaan." Admittedly, this theme is a bit more subtle, but it is lying in wait to surprise the incisive reader. The terms that open up this story are "my portion" and "land of the living" in verse 5. After Joshua led Israel into Canaan, he assigned a "portion" to each family. That was their claim on God's promises, their stake in the faithful God. Yet, the Levites had no portion because the Lord was their portion (Num. 18:20). That means that God was everything to them. David, to whom the psalm is attributed, was not a Levite, yet God has become his "portion." And as representative of the whole community of faith, this would approach Moses's wish: "I wish that all the LORD's people were prophets" (Num. 11:29). The equivalent would be: "I wish that all the LORD's people were Levites," to whom God is their portion, to whom God is their permanent security, as the land was to Israel. Their "exodus" from Babylonia was no less than the new exodus from "Egypt," and their return to Judea no less than their entrance into the "new Canaan." This has powerful implications for our spiritual walk. Our goal is that God be our portion, our permanent security as we approach our spiritual "new Canaan," "the land of the living" (142:5c). There is a sense in which we as the community of believers continue to repeat this paradigm of exodus from Egypt and entry into the promised land. Martin Luther King Jr. illustrated that so well in his famous speech "I've Been to the Mountaintop," in which he compared himself to Moses and the civil rights movement to ancient Israel about to enter the land of Canaan: "He's allowed me to go up to the mountain. And I've looked over. And I've seen the Promised Land. I may not get there with you" (see "Illustrating the Text"). In the history of the church and the personal stories of our lives we repeat this Egypt-Canaan paradigm, not so much in the guise of Moses but in that of the people of Israel. See "Additional Insights: The Model of Historical Double-Tracking," following the unit on Psalm 138.

Illustrating the Text

"I've been to the mountaintop."

Famous Speech: The last speech by Dr. Martin Luther King Jr., entitled "I've Been to the Mountaintop," was delivered on April 3, 1968, at the Mason Temple in Memphis, Tennessee, the day before he was assassinated. In this address he implicitly compares himself to Moses ("I've been to the mountaintop") and the civil rights movement to the people of Israel on their way to Canaan, the promised land ("I may not get there with you"):

> Well, I don't know what will happen now. We've got some difficult days ahead. But it really doesn't matter with me now, because I've been to the mountaintop. And I don't mind. Like anybody, I would like to live—a long life; longevity has

its place. But I'm not concerned about that now. I just want to do God's will. And He's allowed me to go up to the mountain. And I've looked over. And I've seen the Promised Land. I may not get there with you. But I want you to know tonight, that we, as a people, will get to the Promised Land. So I'm happy, tonight. I'm not worried about anything. I'm not fearing any man. *Mine eyes have seen the glory of the coming of the Lord.*[2]

While Dr. King spoke of the experience of the American civil rights movement using the paradigm of wilderness-Canaan, a theological application of this paradigm, or the Egypt-wilderness-Canaan paradigm, can be used for many periods of church history and is also applicable to our personal spiritual experience. Egypt is the period of oppression or sin, the wilderness the period of wandering or searching for God, and Canaan the period of stabilizing our lives in God. It is not the end of the journey per se, but the place where we experience God's presence (Jerusalem) and enter into a personal relationship with him.

How God builds his house

Quote: *Mere Christianity*, by C. S. Lewis. While the Psalms are largely concerned about God's "dwelling place" as the temple, and Psalm 22:3 only hints at the advanced stage of God's indwelling, the story of the psalmist's journey of faith has a further extension, and Lewis borrows a parable from George MacDonald to tell of it:

> I find I must borrow yet another parable from George MacDonald. Imagine yourself as a living house. God comes in to rebuild that house. At first, perhaps, you can understand what He is doing. He is getting the drains right and stopping the leaks in the roof and so on: you knew that those jobs needed doing and so you are not surprised. But presently he starts knocking the house about in a way that hurts abominably and does not seem to make sense. What on earth is He up to? The explanation is that He is building quite a different house from the one you thought of—throwing out a new wing here, putting on an extra floor there, running up towers, making courtyards. You thought you were going to be made into a decent little cottage: but He is building a palace. He intends to come and live in it Himself.[3]

"Let the Morning Bring Me Word of Your Unfailing Love"

Big Idea

Great petitions grow out of great confessions, and great deliverance from trouble grows out of God's unfailing love.

Key Themes

- God's unfailing love is the renewing grace of every morning.
- Our thirst for God grows out of our meditation on what God has done.
- The confession of our depravity is the great confession of our sin.

Understanding the Text

One of the seven penitential psalms of the early church, Psalm 143 is a prayer of David (title and 143:2 and 12, "your servant") on Israel's behalf. In this final Davidic collection (Pss.138–45), David, Israel's great king, prays for his people, confesses their depravity, and seeks to know the way he should go. Psalm 143 is an individual lament.

The Text in Context

In Psalm 142 the suppliant prays to be rescued from "those who pursue me, for they are too strong for me" (142:6), and he locates himself in prison either emotionally or physically (142:7). In Psalm 143 he awaits his trial and prays that Yahweh not bring him "into judgment," confessing, most likely on behalf of the postexilic people, the depraved state of this people (143:2). The supppliant is in a state of despair (142:3; 143:4) and petitions God to bring him "out of trouble" (143:11), perhaps an allusion to his imprisonment (142:7). See table 1 in the unit on Psalm 138. For the connection between this psalm and Lamentations 3, see "Theological Insights."

Outline/Structure

The psalm is divided into two parts, the *selah* after verse 6 marking the division. Part 1 is about God, about the enemy, and about the psalmist. Note the regular occurrence of consequences and causes attached to the petitions (in italics).

1. A threefold petition (143:1–6)
   a. About God (143:1)
      i. "Lord, hear my prayer" (143:1a)
      ii. "Listen to my cry for mercy" (143:1b)
      iii. "*In your faithfulness and righteousness* [cause] come to my relief" (143:1c)
   b. About the psalmist (143:2)
      i. "Do not bring your servant into judgment" (143:2a)
      ii. "No one living is righteous before you" (143:2b)
   c. About the enemy (143:3–6)
      i. The enemy's hostility (143:3)
      ii. The effect of the enemy's hostility on the psalmist (143:4–5)
      iii. The psalmist's prayerful response to the enemy's hostility (143:6)
2. Multiple petitions with consequences and causes (143:7–12)
   a. "Answer me quickly, Lord; *my spirit fails* [consequence]" (143:7a–b)
   b. "Do not hide your face from me, *or I will be like those who go down to the pit* [consequence]" (143:7c–d)
   c. "Let the morning bring me word of your unfailing love, *for I have put my trust in you* [cause]" (143:8a–b)
   d. "Show me the way I should go, *for to you I entrust my life* [cause]" (143:8c–d)
   e. "Rescue me from my enemies, Lord, *for I hide myself in you* [cause]" (143:9a–b)
   f. "Teach me to do your will, *for you are my God* [cause]" (143:10a–b)
   g. "May your good Spirit lead me on level ground" (143:10:c–d) (no consequence or cause)
   h. Final fourfold petition and fourfold cause (143:11–12)
      i. "*For your name's sake* [cause], Lord, preserve my life" (143:11a)
      ii. "*In your righteousness* [cause], bring me out of trouble" (143:11b)
      iii. "*In your unfailing love* [cause], silence my enemies" (143:12a)
      iv. "Destroy all my foes, *for I am your servant* [cause]" (143:12b)

Historical and Cultural Background

The Septuagint (LXX) assigns this psalm to the time of Absalom's rebellion: "A Psalm of David when his son pursued him." In the context of our thesis regarding this last Davidic collection, and most of Book 5, for that matter, we see the conflict of the postexilic period reflected in Psalm 143 as it was in the previous psalm. The nature of the conflict, understandably, has a lot to do with how this new community should reconstitute itself, and the psalmist prays, "Teach me to do your will," and makes the great covenantal confession, "for you are my God" (143:10). We have already seen in Psalm 142 that the hostility has resulted in the worshiper's imprisonment, either physically or emotionally, and now he evidently awaits his trial (143:2) and prays for deliverance (143:11).

Interpretive Insights

143:1 *Lord, hear . . . listen . . . come.* The trifold petition implies the expedience of the psalmist's need (lit., "hear," "listen," "answer"). Part 2 also begins with a trifold petition ("Be quick" [NIV: "quickly"], "Answer me," "Do not hide your face"; 143:7).

143:2 *Do not bring your servant into judgment, for no one living is righteous before you.* This verse is likely the reason the early church considered this psalm among the seven penitential psalms. The thought is that no human being is righteous by God's standard (JB: "No one is virtuous by your standards"). Yet that is not to raise an objection to God's standards but rather to acknowledge that God is God and we are human, and God is superior to us in every way.

143:3 *The enemy . . . makes me dwell in the darkness like those long dead.* Except for the interchange of two words, this is a duplicate of Lamentations 3:6 (see "Theological Insights"). The suppliant feels that he is approaching death.

143:5–6 *I remember the days of long ago.* Remembering the past is a common feature of psalms that enter into a conversation with God, as does this one, and it is out of these remembrances that the worshiper's thirst for God grows.

143:7–10 *Answer me quickly, Lord.* Here begins part 2 (143:7–12). The intensity of the petition has grown exponentially, indicated by the fact that the psalmist begins with the imperative "Be quick" (NIV: "quickly") and that there are eleven petitions in part 2 (see "Outline/Structure").

my spirit fails . . . Teach me to do your will. For the second time the psalmist speaks of his languishing spirit (143:7; also in 143:4, using a synonym), and for the second time he expresses his fear that if God does not intervene, he will die (also 143:3). Yet he sees the first rays of morning light that beam God's "unfailing love" (*hesed*), like the unfailing dawn of day (143:8). In the broad daylight of this new day he petitions Yahweh, "Teach me to do your will," and he declares himself a member of God's covenant family by reference to the covenant formula, "for you are my God" (143:10; see "Theological Insights" in the unit on Ps. 118; see also the sidebar "The Covenant Formula" in the unit on Ps. 79).

143:11–12 *For your name's sake . . . in your righteousness . . . In your unfailing love . . . for I am your servant.* The term "(your) righteousness" in verses 1 and 11 and the term "your servant" in verses 2 and 12 form an *inclusio*. The suppliant appeals to Yahweh on the basis of three divine attributes—Yahweh's "name's sake" (see the sidebar "For His Name's Sake" in the unit on Ps. 23), Yahweh's "righteousness," and Yahweh's "unfailing love" (*hesed*)—after having confessed that he and this community are not righteous (143:2b). See "Theological Insights."

Theological Insights

When a psalmist quotes a key verse from another biblical setting, it often serves the purpose of opening up the historical and theological dimensions of the context of that quotation. I suggest this is the case with Psalm 142:3c–d. The speaker of Lamentations 3:1, the verse quoted here, identifies himself as "the man who has seen affliction by the rod of the LORD's wrath" (Lam. 3:1). The "man" in that poem is either an individual, likely a leader of the community, or the community itself—probably both—who laments the humiliating exile and confesses that his/their hope is still in God. In verse 3 of our psalm the psalmist cites the brief statement in Lamentations 3:6, "He makes me dwell in the darkness like those long dead," and mercifully shifts the subject from Yahweh, the subject of the Lamentations text, to the suppliant's enemy. It is a significant change, for now, in this postexilic climate, the idea of making Yahweh the perpetrator of the exile, as Lamentations does, has softened, and the enemy, probably internal, has become the pursuing agent. The psalmist, having referred to himself in the framing verses as "your servant" (143:2 and 12), and having identified himself by name in the title as "David," has succeeded in writing David's situation, either Saul's persecution or Absalom's rebellion (see "Historical and Cultural Background"), all over this psalm. But the most important feature is that David, rhetorically speaking, is addressing Yahweh for the sake of this suffering community. He prays for them, suffers with them (143:3, 9), reminisces with them (143:5), and, most of all, confesses with them that "no one living is righteous before" Yahweh (143:2), an admission of gigantic proportions. David, being the chief political figure in Israel's history, identifies with his people and is viewed as their vicarious suffering servant (see "Additional Insights: A Hypothesis on Psalm 109," following the unit on Ps. 109), much in the vein of Isaiah 53:4–6. The effect is that Israel is moved to trust in Yahweh and waits to hear his word of "unfailing love" (*hesed*, 143:8). It is the same divine attribute that "the man who has seen affliction" found "new every morning" (Lam. 3:22–23).

Teaching the Text

The terms of this psalm are gigantic, and we need to reflect that fact in our sermon/lesson. First, we may speak about the *great supplication* represented in this psalm, for there are a total of fourteen petitions in the poem (see "Outline/Structure"). Of them all, verse 10 is the most important one, "Teach me to do your will," for it is the prayer that God's kingdom will come, taught so powerfully in the Lord's Prayer: "Thy kingdom come, thy will be done, on earth as it is in heaven." We may emphasize that this petition is particularly revealing of the writer's desire to see the restoration succeed by doing the will of God. And that should be the desire of every pioneer of the gospel, to do God's will and thus to build his church and his kingdom. So important is God's will that we may need to engage in a special process of discernment, remembering MacDonald's words that God is easy to please but hard to satisfy (see both illustrations in "Illustrating the Text"). Our suppliant recognizes that only doing God's will can satisfy God and, we might add, satisfy ourselves.

The second feature of the psalm is the *great confession* that occurs in two parts. The first is the confession of verse 2: "No one living is righteous before you." I have made the point in "Theological Insights" that this is the confession of the psalmist on behalf of the new community that seeks to reconstitute itself on the basis of God's grace (*hesed*), and this is both a disclaimer of human righteousness and an acclamation of God's perfect character. It is the impeccable standard by which we are to measure ourselves. Calvin observes: "David intimates that any righteousness which the saints have is not perfect enough to abide God's scrutiny, and thus he declares that all are guilty before God"[1] (see also Isa. 64:6). It is a reminder that there is only one way for the believer to live, and that is, in Weiser's words, "to give himself wholly up to the grace of God."[2] And in that is our security that is renewed every morning (143:8).

The second part of this great confession is a standard element of the covenant formula that bound God to Israel and Israel to God and assured God's continuing presence with his people: "You are my God" (143:10). It is the acknowledgment of the covenant, the character of which is described by God's "unfailing love" (143:8 and 12). And the new covenant is founded on the same divine love (John 3:16).

The third feature of our psalm is the *great deliverance* that is supported by three divine attributes: God's name, righteousness, and unfailing love (*hesed*) (143:11–12). These underwrite the certainty of deliverance petitioned by the fourfold supplication of these closing verses (see "Outline/Structure"). It is no wonder that the worshiper, supported by God's character of such gigantic proportions, can still, in the midst of his trouble, say, "I have put my trust in you" (143:8).

Illustrating the Text

God is easy to please but hard to satisfy.

Quote: **George MacDonald.** Greville MacDonald, in his biography of his father, George MacDonald, recalls that his father once said, "God is not hard to please, but it is impossible to satisfy Him."[3] That is the reason we have to continue to petition God, "Teach me to do your will" (143:10). Only when we can confess, "I am your servant" (143:12), with absolute abandonment of our human will, will we come close to the kingdom of God, which is the equivalent of God's will being done on earth as it is in heaven. While our thirst for God "like a parched land" will draw us in that direction (42:1), only the absolute grace of God will make our will a facsimile of God's and therefore "satisfy" him.

A Clearness Committee

Applying the Text: We cannot lay on the Psalms our democratic way of doing things, but there are ways of discernment that, with some validity, we may lay alongside certain discernment processes endorsed by the Psalms. Psalm 143, for example, includes a prayer that God will teach the psalmist to do God's will, and we should not rule out the possibility that the Lord's instruction may involve the counsel of others. In fact, it may be suggested by the petition of verse 8b, "Show me the way I should go, for to you I entrust my life." The Quakers have taught us a lot about the process of spiritual discernment. When a person (focus person) is in need of clarity regarding decisions, such as ministry, marriage, a job, or retirement, he or she (or they, in the case of a couple) may ask the congregation (meeting) to appoint a clearness committee of three or four Friends to join in worship, listening, and loving concern, in order to assist the focus person in discerning God's will. They will meet several times to worship together, listen, reflect, and ask probing questions. Of course, this assumes a spirit of trust, teachability, and openness to others' counsel and the guidance of the Spirit. This process is designed to produce a decision that will be shared with the meeting.[4] This process could easily be adapted quite generally for those who need counsel for important decisions, and it can include prayer, Scripture study, probing questions, careful listening, and confident waiting in the presence of those we trust. Such a process can bring clarity to our discernment of God's will and prevent us from missing the voice of God's people in an important stage of life.

"Blessed Is the People Whose God Is the LORD"

Big Idea

God's bold actions on his people's behalf are subject, in the presence of humility and upon request, to bold repetition.

Key Themes

- Only in the spirit of humility can we boldly make our prayers to God.
- "Our loving God," not a God of brute power, is the God who acts.

Understanding the Text

Psalm 144 is, like Psalm 18, a royal psalm, and it celebrates the developing challenges and successes of the postexilic community. Just as David in Psalm 18 commemorated his victory over Saul by recalling God's theophany on Sinai—a powerful intervention—the psalmist uses language of Yahweh's decisive action on Sinai again, now in the new context of the restoration of God's people after exile, to petition God to act in the same decisive manner. "Do it again, Lord!"

The Text in Context

The four consecutive psalms of lament (Pss. 140–43) are over, and a new genre is inserted into the collection to petition Yahweh's personal intervention in the situation, just as he had intervened in Moses's day to raise up his people (144:5) and in David's day to bring Saul's persecution of David to an end (see the comments on 144:5–8). In Psalm 18, on which Psalm 144 is heavily dependent (see table 1), David celebrated Yahweh's entry into his conflict with Saul, bringing victory to David. Psalm 18 alludes to the theophany on Sinai and Yahweh's rescue at the Red Sea, applying that theophany to David's time, and our psalmist puts these historical statements in the form of petitions, asking God to do it again (see 144:5–8 in "Outline/Structure"). Even though our suppliant utilizes the language of warfare from Psalm 18, where it connoted battle engagement, in Psalm 144 it is likely metaphorical, referring to the verbal war that was going on in the restoration community.[1]

Table 1. Intertextuality of Psalm 144

Psalm 144	Other Psalms	2 Samuel 22
"*Blessed be* [NIV: "Praise be to"] the LORD *my Rock*" (144:1a)	"*Blessed be* [NIV: "Praise be to"] *my Rock!*" (18:46a)	"The LORD lives! *Blessed be my Rock*" (22:47a)
"Who *trains my hands* for war, my fingers *for battle*" (144:1b)	"He *trains my hands for battle*" (18:34a)	
"He is my gracious one [NIV: "my loving God"] and *my fortress*, *my stronghold* and *my deliverer*, *my shield*, *in whom I take refuge*, who subdues peoples under me" (144:2)		"The LORD is my rock, *my fortress and my deliverer*; my God is my rock, *in whom I take refuge*, *my shield* and the horn of my salvation. He is *my stronghold*, *my refuge* and my savior—from violent people you save me" (22:2–3)
"*Who subdues peoples under me*" (144:2b)	"*Who subdues nations under me*" (18:47b)	
"LORD, *what are human beings that you care for them, mere mortals that you think of them?*" (144:3)	"*What is mankind that you are mindful of them, human beings that you care for them?*" (8:4)	
"They are like a *breath*" (144:4a)	"Everyone is but a *breath*" (39:5c)	
"Their *days are like* a fleeting *shadow*" (144:4b)	"My *days are like* the evening *shadow*" (102:11a)	
"*Part* your *heavens*, LORD, *and come down*" (144:5a)	"He *parted* the *heavens and came down*" (18:9a)	"He *parted the heavens and came down*" (22:10a)
"*Touch the mountains*, so that *they smoke*" (144:5b)	"Who *touches the mountains, and they smoke*" (104:32b)	
"*Shoot* your *arrows* and rout them" (144:6b)	"He *shot* his *arrows* and scattered them [NIV: "the enemy"]" (18:14a)	
"*Reach down* your hand *from on high*; deliver me and rescue me" (144:7a)	"He *reached down from on high* and took hold of me" (18:16a)	"He *reached down from on high*" (22:17a)
"From the mighty *waters*" (144:7b)	"He drew me out of deep *waters*" (18:16b)	"He drew me out of *many waters*" (22:17b; NIV: "deep waters")
"From the hands of *foreigners*" (144:7b)	"*Foreigners* cower over [NIV: "before"] me" (18:44b)	
"I will *sing a new song* to you, my God" (144:9a)	"*Sing to him a new song*" (33:3a)	
"*On the ten-stringed harp* [NIV: "lyre"] I will *make music* to you" (144:9b)	"*Sing* [NIV: "*Make music*"] to him *on the ten-stringed harp* [NIV: "lyre"]" (33:2b)	

Psalm 144	Other Psalms	2 Samuel 22
"*Blessed* [*'ashre*] *is* the people *whose God is the* Lord" (144:15b)	"Blessed [*'ashre*; NIV] *is* the nation *whose God is the* Lord" (33:12a)	

Note: Some of the translations are the author's in order to better show the correspondences.

Outline/Structure

Part 1 (144:1–8) begins with "blessed" (*baruk*; NIV: "praise be"), and part 2 (144:9–15) concludes with a double occurrence of another term for "blessed" (*'ashre*) (see also 72:17, where the verbs for these two terms occur).

1. The blessing, the question, the answer, and the petitions (144:1–8)
   a. The blessing (144:1–2): "Blessed be [*baruk*; NIV: "Praise be to"] the Lord my Rock"
   b. The anthropological question (144:3)
   c. The anthropological answer (144:4)
   d. Petitions for God's intervention in light of human deficiency (144:5–8)
      Note the double refrain: "Deliver me and rescue me" (144:7b, 11a). The refrain concludes the first strophe (144:7–8) and begins the new song of the second strophe (144:10c–11).
2. The new song and the final blessing (144:9–15)
   a. Intent to sing the new song to God for David's deliverance (144:9–10b)
   b. The new song (144:10c–14)
   c. The double blessing (144:15)

Historical and Cultural Background

Psalm 18 celebrated Yahweh's deliverance of David from his conflict with Saul, and David drew on the picture of Yahweh's descent on Mount Sinai. In effect, David was saying the Lord had performed a comparable miracle in his deliverance of David, the servant of Yahweh, from Saul. Psalm 144 draws on Psalm 18 (see table 1 and "The Text in Context") within another historical context, that of the second exodus, the exodus from Babylonian exile, and the complex of developments that followed: the reconstitution of the community, restoration of sacrifice, and rebuilding the temple. It was not an easy era, but the conflict was largely verbal, not military as were Moses's and David's situations. Yet, for the psalmist, the conflict is so critical that it seems appropriate to draw on the language of Psalm 18, apply it to this time of social and religious upheaval and change, and say in effect, "Do it again,

Lord!" While David's citations of the theophany on Sinai were in the past tense, in Psalm 144 they are transmuted into a series of petitions (144:5–8), using the same theophanic language and beseeching Yahweh to repeat what he had done at Sinai and in the Saul-David conflict.

While verses 12–15 are considered by some scholars to be an addition to the original psalm that comprised only verses 1–11, this statement may be considered the answer to David's prayer, and he celebrates by singing a "new song." Essentially, the answer in this stanza, whether original or later (I lean toward original), represents a reversal of the curses pronounced against a disobedient Israel in Deuteronomy 28:15–68, including exile (Deut. 28:49–51). The clauses are verbless, leaving the reader to determine whether they are present, describing the new community; future, describing what the new community will become; or optative, conveying their hope for the future. The NJPS, for example, makes them present, while the NIV opts for the future, and the ESV for the optative sense. In view of the beatitude pronounced on this new community of faith in verse 15b, I would consider the clauses to describe the developing reality, a present condition of the restoration community that is becoming more precisely qualified for the terms of verses 12–15.

The highlight of the confession in verse 15 is twofold. First, the people for whom the blessings of verses 12–14 come true receive a benediction ("Blessed [*baruk*] is the people"). Second, the use of the word "blessed" (*'ashre*) in verse 15 to describe this people means they have developed a new character, and it can be expressed in no better way than describing them as "the people whose God is the LORD." That one clause sums up the first two parts of the covenant formula: "I will . . . be your God, and you will be my people" (Lev. 26:12; see the sidebar "The Covenant Formula" in the unit on Ps. 79). Thus the triumph of the divine plan to make Yahweh Israel's God and Israel Yahweh's people is the ultimate confession (see 33:12).

Interpretive Insights

Title *Of David.* A simple ascription "of/for David," such as in Psalm 138.

144:1 *Praise be to the LORD my Rock.* In this initial verse, Psalm 144, by its quotations from Psalm 18:46a and 34a, signals the fact that the poem is heavily dependent on Psalm 18, as well as other texts (see "The Text in Context" and table 1).

who trains my hands for war, my fingers for battle. The reference to Yahweh's equipping the speaker for war is a bit surprising in the postexilic period; although we already know the psalmist has serious enemies, they are generally described in terms of interpersonal conflict rather than warfare (see the hunting metaphors in table 1 in the unit on Ps. 138). In the larger context of this final Davidic collection, these are probably metaphors and not literal battle language.

144:2 *He is my loving God and my fortress.* Even though the Hebrew word *hesed* ("love") appears only here (*hasdi*) in the psalm, it is an abbreviation for the longer phrase "my loving God" (*'elohe hasdi*), which appears in Psalm 59:10 and 17 (59:11 and 18 MT; NIV: "my God on whom I can rely").[2] As a term of endearment in this context, comparable to calling someone "my love," it sets a tone for the psalm.

144:3 LORD, *what are human beings that you care for them . . . ?* (See the sidebar, "What Is Mankind?" in the unit on Ps. 8.) The verbs are different from those of 8:4, but the meaning is the same. It is the anthropological question "What is mankind?" asked in the context of God's love, the only context in which a complete answer is possible.

144:4 *They are like a breath; their days are like a fleeting shadow.* In this context of conflict and uncertainty, it is only natural to answer the question of verse 3 by citing the unsubstantial nature of human existence and its brevity, much like Ecclesiastes and Job (Eccles. 1:2; Job 7:16).

144:5–8 *Part your heavens,* LORD, *and come down.* The unsubstantial and fleeting nature of human life calls for a more substantial intervention into the psalmist's situation, no less than God's personal appearance, described in terms of his descent on Sinai (Exod. 19:18). Verse 5 picks up the language of Psalm 18:9, where David describes God's personal intervention to deliver him from the hands of Saul in terms of the Lord's personal descent on Mount Sinai. Only that kind of decisive intervention could resolve the conflicts of David's time and of the psalmist's time. Note that 144:7b–8, with only slight differences, is repeated in refrain-like style in 144:11, setting forth the major supplications for God's action.

rescue me from the mighty waters, from the hands of foreigners. As we have observed, David has described his deliverance from the hands of Saul in terms of God's descent on Sinai, and now he uses that language to petition Yahweh to do the same in this new situation. The "waters" are the Red Sea (18:16b; 144:7a), and the "hands of foreigners" are the Egyptians (18:44b; 144:7b). (See "The Text in Context.")

whose right hands are deceitful. Literally, "their right hand is the right hand of a lie." One lifted the right hand to swear an oath, and this expression suggests that these people swore false oaths (Deut. 32:40).

144:9–11 *I will sing a new song to you, my God.* These three verses contain the lesson the psalmist has learned from history: God "gives victory to kings, who delivers his servant David[3] from the deadly sword" (144:10, author's translation). A "new song" is a song of praise, sung in celebration of a new event in God's saving history.[4] In the light of David's deliverance the suppliant offers his petitions a second time, represented by the refrain (144:11). The description "whose mouths are full of lies, whose right hands are the right hand of lies" (author's translation) supports the idea that the conflict is verbal (see "Enemies within" in table 1 in the unit on Ps. 138).

144:12–15 *our sons in their youth will be like well-nurtured plants, and our daughters will be like pillars.* Note that verses 1–8 are a prayer addressed to Yahweh, and at verse 9 there is a shift to first person ("I will sing a new song," the psalmist's vow to worship in the temple), and then in verse 12 the first-person plural "our" dominates. David's prayer has been heard, and that is indicated by the fact that verses 12–14a represent the reversal of the curses of Deuteronomy 28:15–68, and the community is now represented by "our."

There is some doubt that these verses were an original part of the psalm. They are constituted by temporal blessings: sons like saplings well planted, daughters like well-carved pillars that are strong and beautiful, barns that are filled with an abundant harvest, sheep that reproduce prolifically, and oxen that are strong. While interpretations vary, verse 14b–c can be interpreted as a description of exile, and in view of the context of Psalms 138–45, I think this perspective is quite plausible. The "breaching of walls," "captivity,"[5] and "cry of distress in our streets" all hint at some tragic event that has the contours and proportions of exile (see "Historical and Cultural Background").

Blessed is the people whose God is the Lord. In the previous psalm the suppliant declared, "You are my God" (143:10), perhaps both for himself and for his community, and now the speaker in 144:15b pronounces "blessed" (*'ashre*) those people "whose God is the* Lord."

Theological Insights

The undergirding state of heart that this psalm represents is humility, particularly evident in two features of the psalm. One is the anthropological question of verse 3, "Lord, what are human beings that you care for them, mere mortals that you think of them?" It is posed in much the same spirit of humility as the same question in 8:4. Human beings are so small and, in the wider context of God's creation, seemingly quite insignificant. With that perspective in mind, why does God care for them so much? And the question demands an exclamation point as much as it does a question mark. The second feature is David's status as "servant" (144:10), although he was a king. There is no place in the spiritual palette for pride of status. The only way to come to God is in the spirit of humility, and that is the spirit that Christ modeled for us in his condescension to human weakness that led to the cross, a disposition that Paul introduces with these words: "In your relationships with one another, have the same mindset as Christ Jesus" (Phil. 2:5). Then he follows that with his incomparable statement on Christ's condescension (Phil. 2:6–11).

It is in the light of humility that the boldness of God's servants must originate and operate. That is the theological atmosphere of this psalm (see Heb. 4:16). And it is not coincidental that this setting of boldness in a picture of humility (see Prov. 25:11 for the metaphor) will eventuate in a total dependence on grace. The bold petition of 144:5, "Part your heavens, Lord, and come down," evokes the imagery of God's descent on Sinai in Moses's day and may also suggest Moses's humility, out of which his boldness in prayer arose, as noted in Numbers 12:3: "Now Moses was a very humble man, more humble than anyone else on the face of the earth."

Teaching the Text

To be faithful to the text, our sermon/lesson on Psalm 144 will need to reflect the fact that David's story is "retold" in bits and pieces, largely taken from Psalm 18, a victory psalm that celebrates David's triumph over Saul. David's victory was of such proportions that he described it in terms of the theophany on Sinai. That also implies how challenging his situation before Saul was—no less of a power could have achieved that victory.

First, we may point out that the appellations for God in verses 1 and 2 are followed by a description of God's actions, "trains my hands for war" and "subdues peoples under me." Yahweh is a God of action, and his names are not mere static titles, but they are incarnational—that is, they represent something about God's protective action in human history (see "Teaching the Text" in the unit on Ps. 91). While we do not want to press the point too far, the same feature about God is seen in Isaiah 7:14, "Immanuel," "God is with us."

Second, the psalmist moves from the all-sufficient God in verses 1 and 2 to the insignificance of humanity in verses 3–4: "What are human beings that you care for them?" The humility that called forth this question is manifested also in the phrase "his servant David" (144:10). The wonder of God's decisive action on humanity's behalf is an ongoing awe in the presence of God's ongoing actions in redeeming history. Spurgeon, in the spirit of the psalmist's awe, exults in this truth: "That he should make man the subject of election, the object of redemption, the child of eternal love, the darling of infallible providence, the next of kin to Deity, is indeed a matter requiring more than the two notes of exclamation found in this verse."[6]

In the presence of the omnipotent God the suppliant senses humanity's insignificance, as does David in Psalm 8:4. Here we may utilize the idea expressed in "Theological Insights" that it is only in the context of humility that boldness in God's presence is appropriate; and that is precisely what comes next in the poem, the suppliant's bold petition: "Part your heavens, LORD, and come down" (144:5). This is a call for God to act as decisively in the psalmist's situation as he acted at Sinai and as definitively as he intervened in David's conflict with Saul. In this context of God's incredible power, we need to see the aura in which God has acted. It was not out of brute power but out of his character as "my loving God" (see comments on 140:2). That is the basis of all God's saving actions, from the exodus to the cross.

Illustrating the Text

A bold humility in prayer

Quote: Martin Luther. The psalmist's bold humility in prayer (144:5) is illustrated by the story of Luther's letter to his dying friend Friedrich Myconius. In 1540 Luther received a farewell letter from him, written in a weak and trembling hand. Immediately Luther sent back this reply:

> I command thee in the name of God to live, because I still have need of thee in the work of reforming the church. . . . The Lord will not let me hear while I live that thou art dead, but will permit thee to survive me. For this I am praying. This is my will, and may my will be done, because I seek only to glorify the name of God.[7]

Knowing God's will and submitting to it are the essence of humility. Luther's prayer arose out of that spirit of humility, knowing that it was God's will to call him as leader of the Reformation and God's will that he submit to that call. Myconius did in fact survive, and he lived a few months longer than Luther. Our psalmist too summons God out of a spirit of humility, perhaps matching that of Moses, the most humble man in all the earth (Num. 12:3), and thus the boldest in prayer.

Forgiveness means putting oneself in the offender's place.

Quote: I Believe, by Helmut Thielicke. In his study of The Apostles' Creed, Thielicke asks, "What occurs when I forgive another person?" While forgetting the offense is all but impossible, the sympathetic approach is absolutely mandatory: "I myself step into the breach and say to myself, 'The same thing that made the other person mean, hateful, and guilty toward me is in my heart as well. . . . I take over the burden of his guilt and place it on my own heart just as though it were mine. . . . I'll put myself in your place. I'll share your burden.'"[8] Our psalmist references the story of Moses, who stood in the breach for Israel when they sinned by making the golden calf, and in that instance he was willing to accept the same punishment that their sin had merited (Exod. 32:32). Paul's wish that he "were cursed and cut off from Christ for the sake of [his] people" conveys a similar sentiment, but his wish is for their salvation. Both Moses and Paul, however, would have accepted Israel's punishment for their sin.

"Great Is the LORD and Most Worthy of Praise; His Greatness No One Can Fathom"

Big Idea

God's greatness and goodness manifest themselves in nature and human circumstances.

Key Themes

- God manifests his greatness and goodness in his works and deeds.
- God's grace moves along at an unhurried pace.

Understanding the Text

This last of the Davidic psalms in Book 5 may be classified among the psalms of the heavenly King (see the beginning of "Understanding the Text" in the unit on Ps. 45). Not only is Yahweh called "the King" in verse 1, but the entire psalm exalts him for his creating and reigning power.

The Text in Context

Modern Psalms scholarship has tended to treat the final Davidic psalms (Pss. 138–45) and the hallelujah psalms (Pss. 146–50) as the two concluding collections of the Psalter. However, rabbinic tradition includes Psalm 145 in the final collection (Pss. 145–50), which is called *Pesukei Dezimra* ("The Everyday Hallel"), and these six psalms are recited every morning before the reading of the Shema.[1] The psalm is an alphabetic acrostic poem (see the sidebar "The Alphabetic Acrostic Psalms" in the unit on Ps. 25), with the Hebrew letter *nun* missing (the LXX and the Psalms Scroll from Qumran supply a *nun* line). The

Babylonian Talmud (*Berakhot* 4b) explains the missing *nun* as an attempt to avoid mentioning Israel's fall (since the verb "to fall," *npl*, begins with a *nun*). The verb "fall," however, does occur in verse 14 ("the LORD upholds all who fall"); if that verb was too painful to hear, its use in a somewhat hidden form in verse 14, there referring to a social or emotional condition other than the exile, may have been quite enough for the poet. Book 5 certainly has its share of alphabetic acrostic psalms, in fact, four out of the eight that are contained in the Psalter (Pss. 111; 112; 119; 145). Attention has been drawn to the similarity of line beginnings in Psalm 145 to those of the acrostic Psalms 111 and 112 that begin this long section of poems about the exile and restoration.[2]

Psalm 145 has a twofold purpose here in this Davidic collection. First, it provides a conclusion to the psalms that set Israel's current history (the return and restoration) in the context of the exodus from Egypt and the entrance into Canaan (see "Additional Insights: The Model of Historical Double-Tracking," following the unit on Ps. 138). It does this by drawing on the psalms in this Davidic collection (see table 1 in the unit on Ps. 138). Second, it provides a bridge to the hallelujah psalms that follow (Pss. 146–50). Being a psalm of praise, what Spurgeon calls David's "crown jewel of praise,"[3] it is not a summons to praise but a model of what the universal praise of God looks like: the psalmist is praising, the generations of Israel are praising, Yahweh's works are praising, and all humanity is praising God (see "Illustrating the Text" in the unit on Ps. 150).

Outline/Structure

The following outline divides the psalm into two parts, the first dealing with the divine King's greatness, and the second with the divine King's goodness.

1. The God-King's greatness (145:1–6)
   a. Praising the God-King's greatness forever (145:1–2)
   b. The God-King's fathomless greatness extolled by endless generations (145:3–6)
2. The God-King's goodness (145:7–21)
   a. Praising the God-King with Moses (145:7–8)
   b. Praising the God-King with his creation (145:9–10)
   c. Praising the God-King's kingdom (145:11–13a)
   d. Praising the God-King, who supports the fallen and lifts up those who are bowed down (145:13b–16)
   e. Praising the God-King, who is righteous and faithful (145:17–21)

Historical and Cultural Background

This poem has several Aramaic terms, which are the stimulus for assigning the psalm to a late postexilic date. Hossfeld would assign it to the Persian period in the fourth century BC.[4] On that basis, it could as easily be assigned to an early postexilic date, because Aramaic had become the vernacular language for the Israelites in exile.

Interpretive Insights

Title *A psalm of praise. Of David.* This is the only psalm that has "praise" (*tᵉhillah*) in its title. The psalmists do call their compositions "praise" within the body of certain psalms (40:3; 100:4; 119:171, etc.; see also Neh. 12:46). The psalm also has the word "praise" in the final verse.

145:1 *I will exalt you, my God the King; I will praise your name for ever and ever.* This strong word of praise, addressed to "God the King," joins the four occurrences of the word "kingdom" (145:11, 12, 13 [2x]) to make this a psalm about Yahweh's kingdom reign. Verses 11–13, in which the fourfold occurrence is found, are the centerpiece of the psalm. The verb "bless" (NIV: "praise") with God's name as its object and the adverbial phrase "for ever and ever" occurs also in verse 21 to form an *inclusio*.

145:2 *Every day I will praise you and extol your name for ever and ever.* God's praise is endless, and the psalmist is a part of that endless chorus of praise.

145:3 *his greatness no one can fathom.* There are no boundaries to his greatness. "Greatness" may also mean God's great acts of redemption (2 Sam. 7:21–23), and the parallel terms "your works" and "mighty acts" in verse 4 reinforce that sense.

145:4 *One generation commends your works to another.* One generation's commendation of God's works to the next, and on and on, is a way to describe the endless praise of God mentioned in verse 2. The thirteen attributes (see Exod. 34:6–7), partially listed in verse 8, are part of the words of praise that one generation passes on to another (see the sidebar "The Thirteen Attributes of God" in the unit on Ps. 111).

145:5 *the glorious splendor of your majesty.* Here the Hebrew has a string of three synonymous terms that describe the awesome God: "beauty," "glory," and "splendor."

145:7–8 *They celebrate your abundant goodness.* From here to the end of the poem, the psalm, for the most part, is preoccupied with praise for God's goodness, introduced by "They celebrate your abundant goodness." This recalls the Lord's words to Moses in Exodus 33:19: "I will cause all my goodness to pass in front of you." And then follows God's self-revelation of his attributes in Exodus 34:6: "the compassionate and gracious God, slow to anger, abounding in love and faithfulness." Verse 8 of our psalm, "The LORD is gracious and compassionate, slow to anger and rich in love,"[5] is a close duplicate of Exodus 34:6 (the first two terms are interchanged so as to accommodate the letter *heth* [*hannun*, "gracious"], although there are other instances of the interchange, e.g., Neh. 9:31). The prophet Jonah prays to the Lord and confesses that he fled to Tarshish because he knew that God was "a gracious and compassionate God, slow to anger and abounding in love" (Jon. 4:2).

145:9 *The LORD is good to all; he has compassion on all he has made.* Behind this psalm is the story of creation, and the clause "He has compassaion on all he has made" (lit., "His compassion is on all his works") speaks of all Yahweh's created works.

145:12 *so that all people may know of your mighty acts.* Here "all people" and in verse 21 "all flesh" sound a universal note, which is not surprising in view of the fact that Israel's experience in Babylonia and the generous policy of Cyrus, plus the prophetic insistence that the gospel is for the whole world, likely have had the effect of broadening Israel's horizons, both geographically and theologically.

145:13 *Your kingdom is an everlasting kingdom.* The first two lines of this verse occur in Daniel 4:3. The NIV has added the third and fourth lines, which are not in the major Hebrew texts but do occur in the Septuagint and Syriac; they serve the purpose of supplying the missing letter *nun*: "Faithful [*ne'eman*] is the LORD in all his words, and gracious in all his works" (author's translation). However, given the predominant absence of these lines in the Masoretic texts, I would prefer to leave them out. The Babylonian Talmud does take note of the absence of the *nun* line (*Berakhot* 4b; see "The Text in Context").[6]

145:15–16 *The eyes of all look to you.* These verses represent a rephrasing of 104:27–28. The verb "look" has the sense of looking expectantly.

You open your hand and satisfy the desires of every living thing. Psalm 136:25 is close in meaning. The Lord's hand is "open," implying generosity, and we would also expect it to be full of good things for the taking. The last part of the sentence suggests that Yahweh's generosity is appropriately gauged to human need.

145:18 *The LORD is near to all who call on him . . . in truth.* "The LORD is near" is an allusion to the divine presence, and in this case, it may be the temple, as seems to be the case in Isaiah 55:6. To call on Yahweh "in truth" means there is consistency in the life of the worshiper and his or her profession of faith.[7]

145:21 *My mouth will speak in praise of the LORD.* This is a vow to "bless" the Lord, most likely, in the temple, and "all flesh" (NIV: "every creature") will join in praise. This psalm, and especially this verse, forms a bridge to the hallelujah psalms, where all Israel and all creation and humanity are summoned to praise the Lord.

Theological Insights

The Old Testament, especially the Psalms and the Prophets, presents a picture of the kingdom of God. In that world of kingdoms, the "kingdom of God" (the term "your kingdom" occurs twice in this psalm, 145:11 and 13; cf. 103:19) can hardly escape the connotation of a geographical realm, but of greater importance, it is the ideal social order, shaped by a righteous God. Yet, the concept is much broader than that, for it is the story of God's reigning and redeeming work in human history, and that is the thrust of Psalm 145. This poem accomplishes that by focusing on the King rather than the kingdom as a political realm: "I will exalt you, my God the King" (145:1). This can be seen in the psalm's organization around the God-King's greatness and goodness (see "Outline/Structure"). Indeed, we could say that in the ancient world, where absolute kingship was the rule, the king *was* the kingdom. That political philosophy dominated the biblical and the Western world until the Magna Carta in AD 1215. And this psalm is about praising the King, not the kingdom, for the King of Scripture *is* the kingdom. The general description of the kingdom in 144:12–15, given in terms of human benefits (without the "kingdom" label), is now drawn out in terms of God's worthiness of praise and adoration. The psalm is a complement to Psalms 144 and 146, and even more significantly, it pulls together strands of thought that are represented in the final Davidic Psalter (see table 1 in the unit on Ps. 138). The Psalter, rhetorically speaking, ends with the voice of David, who is never called "king" in this collection, only "servant," and now he joins his voice with the rest of the faithful, all humankind, and all God's works, to praise the real King, "my God."

This psalm is a precursor to the emphasis that Jesus puts on the kingdom of God in Luke 17:21 when he redefines the kingdom from a mere realm to be established in the future, to a present and personal reality: "the kingdom of God is *in your midst*." Jesus is doing something very similar to what our author is doing here. Jesus is defining the kingdom of God as God's personality and presence among his people. The phrase in Luke 17:21, translated by most modern English versions as "in your midst," occurs only one other time in the New Testament, and it is rendered by the KJV as "within you," making God's presence internal (compare Jer. 31:33 and the internalization of God's "law"), coinciding with John's teaching that Christ dwells *in us*. The point is that the kingdom of God is the heavenly King himself and the story about his reigning and redeeming work of love.

Teaching the Text

For our sermon/lesson, we may take our cue from the two major themes of praise that our psalm engages: God's greatness and God's goodness. First, "no one can fathom" God's greatness (145:3b), and that means it has no bounds. To drive home this point, the poet employs his rich vocabulary to speak about God's acts of creation and redemption: God's works (145:4, 9, 10, 17), God's power (145:4, 11), God's wonderful works (145:5), and God's awesome works, which include the animate and inanimate creation (145:6). Probably one of the surprising things about this psalm is that God has compassion on his works (145:9b, 17). Nor are Yahweh's works speechless (see 19:1), for all God's works give thanks to him (145:10a). God's power is not brute force, so "only in the case of Yahweh is there no danger that power might corrupt its wielder."[8]

The second theme is God's goodness. God's profile has many facets, but this second one really opens God's heart to us. God's goodness is introduced in verse 7, and verse 8 follows with a description in terms of the formula of grace, quoted from Exodus 34:6 (see the comments on 145:7–8). In Exodus 33:19 the Lord informs Moses, "I will cause all my goodness to pass in front of you, and I will proclaim my name, the LORD, in your presence." Then that proclamation of his name is accompanied by a character description: "The LORD, the LORD, the compassionate and gracious God, slow to anger, abounding in love and faithfulness" (Exod. 34:6). Since God is slow to anger, the corollary is that his grace moves along at a slow but steady pace (see "Illustrating the Text"). We can understand why the psalmist exclaims, "Great is the LORD and most worthy of praise" (145:3a). Spurgeon says, "Worship should be somewhat like its object—great praise for a great God."[9]

Illustrating the Text

Outward signs of inward grace

Biography: **George MacDonald.** In Rolland Hein's *The Harmony Within: The Spiritual Vision of George MacDonald*, he speaks of MacDonald's sacramental view of God and nature, which means that the world of nature and the circumstances that surround humanity "are invested by God with the potential to speak to him. . . . God in grace is continually shaping outward circumstances to man's inner needs."[10] Hein quotes from MacDonald's novel *Thomas Wingfold, Curate*: "All about us, in earth and air, wherever the eye or ear can reach, there is a power ever breathing itself forth in signs, now in wind-waft, a cloud, a sunset; a power that holds constant and sweetest relations with the dark and silent world within us. The same God who is in us, and upon whose tree we are the buds, if not yet the flower, also is all about us—inside the Spirit; outside, the Word. And the two are trying to meet in us."[11] When God had created the world and humankind, he glanced in wonder on his creation and saw that "it was very good" (Gen. 1:31). Our familiarity with that pronouncement tends to obscure its gigantic dimensions. Pronouncing the creation very good was equally a pronouncement of God's goodness. Our psalm declares that God's wonderful works "celebrate [his] abundant goodness and joyfully sing of [his] righteousness" (145:7). David says in another setting, "The heavens declare the glory of God" (19:1), which is to say, we see in God's works, both in nature and in our circumstances, *outward signs of an inward grace.*

The unhurried pace of grace

Fable: The corollary to the truth that God is "slow to anger" is that grace too moves along at a slow but steady pace. We can recall Aesop's fable of the hare and the tortoise. The hare, fast and witty, challenges the tortoise, slow and dull, to a race (this is not an allegory but a moral tale). On the way the hare decides that his rapid pace has put him far ahead of the tortoise, so he stops to take a nap. When he awakes, he resumes the race, confident that he will still cross the finish line well ahead of the tortoise, only to find that the tortoise has plodded steadily along and has finished the race ahead of him.[12] On the one hand, grace moves along at an unhurried, determined pace in our lives. On the other hand, sin seems to run on ahead, getting all the attention, pretending to outrun grace. But in the end, sin cannot outdistance grace.

Yet, what difference does it make in the final analysis of things? What difference does it make in a world where evil seems to have the advantage, where the greedy CEOs (thank God, there are some honest ones!) walk away with millions of dollars and leave their employees with subsistence wages and stockholders with a stack of worthless certificates? What difference does it make in a world where people snuff out the life of innocent unborn children like putting out a candle, where religious zealots take thousands of lives in one day and think they have done their god a favor? I think the answer is found in this moral lesson. Grace moves along at a tortoise's pace, sometimes so slowly that we don't even notice that something wonderful is happening in our lives. We pray for grace, and we make it through another hour. We pray for grace, and we come to the end of another day. We pray for grace, and then the next day begins and we inch along our way, dealing with life's snarls and snares and disappointments. And when we have gotten through them, we look back and realize we have moved along the road of life, however slowly, however agonizingly painfully, and we realize we moved in a strength not our own. God's grace is the permeating force, permeating the little and the big events, making our world tolerable—more than tolerable—making it joyful (145:7)! We are not overcome by our sins, because grace is there to forgive, to encourage, to strengthen. The one side of the coin is that God is "slow to anger," and the other side is that he is "rich in love" and grace (145:8).

"Blessed Are Those Whose Help Is the God of Jacob, Whose Hope Is in the Lord Their God"

Big Idea

Our help is also our hope: that God will set this world right.

Key Themes

- The believer's life should be continuous praise.
- God's kingdom is an upside-down kingdom compared to the kingdoms of this world.
- We who hope in God are blessed not by our own nature but by the nature of our faithful God-King.

Understanding the Text

Psalm 146 is a hymn celebrating the kingdom of "my God the King" as a fulfillment of the psalmist's vow in 145:21 to "speak in praise of the Lord."

The Text in Context

Psalms 145 and 146 are related in both theme and language.[1] In fact, Psalm 145 has set the tone for 146 in that it gives us a portrait of the real King, "my God the King" (145:1a), and alerts us to the fact that this God-King is different from earthly kings. He has all the "greatness" that a servant king could ever want or need—and indescribably more—for "his greatness no one can fathom" (145:3b). And his "abundant goodness" is beyond what any servant king could ever demonstrate—and unspeakably more—for he is "gracious and compassionate, slow to anger and boundlessly loving" (145:8, author's translation). And now, after a vow to speak in praise of this God-King, the Lord (145:21a), Psalm 146 engages this God-King in hymnic exaltation.

Outline/Structure

The following outline represents the arc that stretches from Psalm 145 to Psalm 146, with this outline reflecting the fact that Psalm 146 is a description of the kingdom of "my God the King" spoken of in 145:1. So Psalm 145 provides the principles of the God-King (e.g., 145:8), and Psalm 146 translates them into the specifics of the kingdom of God (especially 146:6–9).

1. The "hallelujah" opening (146:1–2)
2. The hymn (146:3–9)
    a. Warning against trusting human princes who cannot save (146:3–4)
    b. Royal actions of the God-King (146:5–9)
        i. Beatitude on those whose help is the "God of Jacob" (146:5)
        ii. The faithful God, Creator of heaven and earth (146:6)
        iii. The faithful Creator God, who upholds the oppressed and provides food to the hungry (146:7a–b)
        iv. The faithful Creator God, who liberates prisoners (146:7c)
        v. The faithful Creator God, who gives sight to the blind (146:8a)
        vi. The faithful Creator God, who supports those bowed down (146:8b)
        vii. The faithful Creator God, who loves the righteous (146:8c)
        viii. The faithful Creator God, who defends the disadvantaged (146:9a–b)
        ix. The faithful Creator God, who frustrates the ways of the wicked (146:9c)
3. The "hallelujah" closing (146:10)

Historical and Cultural Background

The historical context of our psalm could range from the return (ca. 536 BC) to the time of Ezra and Nehemiah in the middle of the fifth century BC, perhaps even later, but we have no biblical parallels to determine the later possibility. I have made a case for viewing these final collections of Book 5 as early postexilic (see "Additional Insights: The Egyptian Hallel [Psalms 113–18]," following the unit on Ps. 113), and Psalms 145 and 146 raise the question of kingship, which was one of the issues in the new community as it reconstituted itself as the renewed people of God. Although Zerubbabel was a descendent of David, he was appointed governor, not king, but that did not mean that the long monarchical tradition in Israel was dead. On the contrary, while it may have been dead politically, it revived as a spiritual kingdom and an eschatological hope. This final collection of Davidic psalms builds in that direction, and Psalm 145 with its servant king, David, presents that concept in submission to the God-King of Psalm 146. That takes place alongside the restoration of the sacrificial system and the reconstruction of the temple, and, we might conjecture, a revival of the temple liturgy, much like David's revision of temple worship (1 Chron. 23–29).

Interpretive Insights

146:1–2 *Praise the* LORD. *Praise the* LORD, *my soul.* These first two verses use the verb "praise" (*hll*) three times, once in the introductory call to praise, "Hallelujah" (NIV: "Praise the LORD"), and twice in the psalmist's own self-admonition to praise the Lord. The adverbial phrase "all my life" may be temporal (as NIV, or "while I live") or instrumental, "with my whole being" (104:33, author's translation). Since the final word of verse 2 (NIV: "as long as I live"), parallel to "all my life," signifies a period of existence, the temporal is a better option.

146:3–4 *Do not put your trust in princes, in human beings, who cannot save.* Turning to the congregation, the speaker now bids them not to trust in those human leaders who cannot save them, calling attention to the fact that they will die and their plans and thoughts will perish with them (146:4; see also 118:8–9). The thoughts of Genesis 2:7 and 3:19 are reflected in verse 4.

146:5 *Blessed are those whose help is the God of Jacob, whose hope is in the* LORD *their God.* This beatitude begins with the Hebrew word *'ashre* ("blessed"; see 1:1), which is used in the praise of human beings, not God. Proverbs 31:28 uses the verbal form to praise the virtuous woman (see also 144:15).

146:6 *He is the Maker of heaven and earth, the sea, and everything in them—he remains faithful forever.* This verse follows upon the beatitude of verse 5, describing the God of Jacob and his faithful way of dealing with those "whose help is the God of Jacob" (146:5a), and now our psalmist identifies this God as "the Maker of heaven and earth." That is to say, his help will be more than adequate. The chain of participles that describes Yahweh's actions as faithful toward his people presents a portrait that stands in stark contrast to the "princes" of that world, and ours. They are descriptors of God's character, the portrait of earthly kings turned upside down, much like Jesus's Beatitudes, which, by their description of kingdom citizens, turn upside down the common idea of earthly kingdoms. With this description of God's kingdom (146:6–9) we can better understand why those whose help and hope are in the Lord are "blessed" (*'ashre*, 146:5a). The final phrase of this verse, "He keeps faith forever" (NIV: "He remains faithful forever"), is a qualifier, along with Yahweh's creative role, in all of the descriptors that follow (see "Outline/Structure").

146:7–8a *The Lord sets prisoners free.* The description of Yahweh's redeeming work is very similar to that described in Isaiah 61:1–3. See also Luke 4:16–21.

146:8b *the Lord loves the righteous.* Yahweh's love for the righteous is the reason for his gracious and faithful actions just enumerated in verses 7–8a.

146:9 *The Lord watches over the foreigner and sustains the fatherless and the widow.* Here we have a description of the Lord's concern for the disenfranchised. The Psalms testify that the Lord's engagement with the lower ranks of society is a characterizing trait of his sovereign rule (see the following verse).

146:10 *The Lord reigns forever, your God, O Zion, for all generations.* This may be a congregational response, as "Praise the Lord, my soul" in verse 1 appears to be. The verb "reigns" (*mlk*) puts the psalm in the category of the kingship of Yahweh psalms (Pss. 93; 96; 97; 99; see the sidebar "'The Lord Reigns': Psalms of the Heavenly King" in the unit on Ps. 93). Not surprisingly, the God adored in this psalm is the God of Zion, where his earthly throne is located.

Praise the Lord. The "hallelujah" opening and the "hallelujah" closing (NIV: "Praise the Lord") form an *inclusio*.

Theological Insights

Psalms 145 and 146 stand in a complementary relationship, identifiable most visibly in the phrase of 145:1, "my God the King," and the clause of 146:10, "The Lord reigns forever." We made the point in our discussion of Psalm 145 (see "Theological Insights" in the unit on Ps. 145) that the kingdom of God is the story of God's reigning and redeeming work of love. The story is essentially the narrative about God's greatness and goodness, translating Yahweh's greatness into Yahweh's creative power, "Maker of heaven and earth" (146:6a–b), and divine goodness into the form of Yahweh's actions on behalf of his people (146:6c–9).

Teaching the Text

As we build our sermon/lesson on Psalm 146, we need to keep in mind that this psalm deals with the reign of God. Interestingly, that detail comes at the end of the psalm (146:10). We, of course, should have anticipated this undergirding theme of the psalm by reading Psalm 145, especially 145:1 and 21 (see "The Text in Context"). This is an illustration of the interpretive principle of Psalms studies, that some psalms more than others must be interpreted in their context. They cannot be interpreted as stand-alone psalms but have to be interpreted in relationship to their neighboring psalms. The key that alerts the reader to this fact here is that this group of psalms is linked together by "hallelujah" (NIV: "Praise the LORD").

Getting to the heart of the psalm, we may make our first point: earthly rulers die, but God reigns forever. Obviously we formulate this statement from two ideas of the psalm that are not in proximity but are intended to be understood as companion ideas (146:3–4 and 10). This is the theological backbone of the psalm. We ourselves observe this reality, at least the temporal limitation of earthly leaders, but the other reality is one that comes not from our personal observation but from biblical revelation, that God reigns forever. It is not an avowal that we cannot trust human leaders, but it is a contrast between earthly leaders whose plans perish with them when they die and the God who reigns forever (146:10)—that is, a contrast between the temporal and the eternal.

Second, after establishing this truth, obvious enough to all of us but so easy to forget, our psalmist concentrates, as the psalmists normally do, on the realities of this world. That is one thing that makes the Psalms so powerfully effective in our lives: they deal with the world we live in, with all of its joys and disappointments and frustrations. In this instance, we observe that God, the Creator of heaven and earth, "loves the righteous" (146:8c), and he shows that in the way he governs and orders his world: he upholds the oppressed, gives food to the hungry, sets prisoners free, gives sight to the blind, lifts up those who are overburdened, watches over the foreigner, and sustains the fatherless and the widow (146:7–9). Here we see the front end of the equation, the pain of our human situation, but we also see the other end, what God can do about our human situation. Here is where the help and hope of verse 5 are so powerfully promising. As our Helper, God can change our circumstances; as our hope, he can give us the strength to wait on him to do it.

It is also very important that, in relation to this help and hope, we speak about the nature of the kingdom of God. The sum of our help and our hope is that God changes the painful realities of our human existence into what they ought to be. It is the view of the world as we know it turned upside down. We might compare this picture with Jesus's Beatitudes, which inform us that the kingdom of God, unlike the kingdoms of this world, is a state of being where the mourners are comforted, the meek are the heirs of the earth, those hungry for righteousness are filled, the merciful receive mercy, the pure in heart look on God's face, the peacemakers are God's children, and the persecuted are in charge of the kingdom (Matt. 5:1–10). It's the world we know turned upside down, or we should say, at last turned right-side up. This transformation can happen only by the power of the one who is the "Maker of heaven and earth"—that's the kind of power that is required. Those who put their trust in God will find that their help and their hope are realized in him.

If there be any doubt that God will turn his people's misfortunes into blessing and ignore the ways of the wicked, our psalmist leaves us with the assurance that the other side of the coin of blessing is God's frustration of the wicked peoples' ways. The Psalms do not ignore this truth, nor can we. When God—our help and our hope—sets our world right, it means that our world had been set wrong.

Illustrating the Text

Soli Deo gloria!

Quote: **John Calvin.** Human piety reaches its highest level when we truly and perfectly exalt the Lord and serve him, and the measurement of our piety is the degree to which we exalt God and acknowledge that he is our help and our hope (146:5). Calvin describes Christian piety in these terms: "The true definition of piety is, when the true God is perfectly served, and when he alone is so exalted, that no creature obscures his divinity; and, accordingly, if we would not have true piety entirely destroyed amongst us, we must hold by this principle, That no creature whatever be exalted by us beyond measure."[2] This means that true piety is giving God all the glory, *soli Deo gloria* ("to God alone be the glory"). And he deserves the glory because he is "Maker of heaven and earth" and "upholds the cause of the oppressed" (146:6–7). He has the power to effect his will and the heart to enact it in human affairs.

From the caricature to God's real world

Biography: **Evelyn Waugh.** After he spent his youth attracted to the ritual of the Roman Catholic Church, the British writer Evelyn Waugh attended Lancing College, which had been established in 1848 by Nathaniel Woodard. A subscriber to the Oxford Movement, Woodard had wanted to provide a sound Church of England education for the professional classes. There Waugh met a young instructor whose thriving zeal for agnosticism deeply affected Waugh and led him away from his Anglo-Catholic leanings. Subsequently Waugh's path followed the way of debauchery and agnosticism until, influenced by several literary figures and converts to the Catholic faith, he too converted and was received into the communion of the Catholic Church on September 29, 1930. Waugh "had found an island of sanity in a raving world, a light beyond the shadows and depth beyond the shallows."[3] Waugh himself describes his conversion as moving from a world of caricature to the real world: "Conversion is like stepping across the chimney piece out of a Looking-Glass world, where everything is an absurd caricature, into the real world God made; and then begins the delicious process of exploring it limitlessly."[4]

This world as we fallen humans see it is not the *real* world as God intends it, but it is a caricature of that world. Psalm 146, especially, helps us to understand what that *real* world looks like, as do also Jesus's Beatitudes (Matt. 5:1–12). Paul described it similarly, "Old things are passed away; behold, all things are become new" (2 Cor. 5:17 KJV).

"The LORD Delights in Those Who Fear Him, Who Put Their Hope in His Unfailing Love"

Big Idea

The Creator God builds up, binds up, and raises up those who "hope in his unfailing love."

Key Themes

- God's love (*hesed*), not brute force, is the power behind God's incomparable greatness.
- God's word runs swiftly to help the humble.
- Sometimes we are unjust to God's mercy by trying, by our own efforts, to make our kingdom work succeed.

Understanding the Text

Psalm 147 is a hymn that calls for grateful praise of the Lord, who "builds up Jerusalem." The suppliant declares that the God who "builds up Jerusalem" is the Creator who knows the number of the stars and calls them by name, the physician who "heals the brokenhearted and binds up their wounds" (147:3), and the God who sustains the humble. Being the Creator of the world, he is certainly adequate for his responsibilities of healer and sustainer.

The Text in Context

Psalm 147 draws heavily on Psalm 104, a psalm of creation, and to some extent on Psalm 33, a psalm that blesses the nation "whose God is the LORD, the people he chose for his inheritance" (33:12), a theme that resounds at the close of our psalm (147:19–20). Moreover, this psalm's proximity to Psalm

146 is not accidental, for the two psalms share vocabulary and may have been written by the same author (see table 1).

Table 1. Shared Vocabulary between Psalms 146 and 147

Psalm 146	Psalm 147
"*Praise the LORD*" (146:1a, 10c)	"*Praise the LORD*" (147:1a, 20c)
"I will *sing* praise to *my God*" (146:2b)	"How good it is to *sing* praises to *our God*" (147:1b)
"Maker of *heaven* and *earth*" (146:6a)	"He covers the *sky* with clouds; he supplies the *earth* with rain" (147:8a–b)
"Who executes *justice* [*mishpat*] to the oppressed" (NIV: "He upholds the cause of the oppressed") (146:7a)	"He has revealed his word to Jacob, his laws and *decrees* [*mishpatim*] to Israel" (147:19)
"And gives *food* to the hungry" (146:7b)	"He provides *food* for the cattle" (147:9a)
"[The LORD] *sustains* the fatherless and the widow" (146:8b)	"The LORD *sustains* the humble" (147:6a)
"He frustrates the ways of the *wicked*" (146:8c)	"[He] casts the *wicked* to the ground" (147:6b)
"The LORD reigns forever, *your God, O Zion*, for all generations" (146:10)	"Extol the LORD, Jerusalem; praise *your God, Zion*" (147:12)

Outline/Structure

Three verses (147:1, 7, and 12) contain exhortations to praise the Lord and thus mark the beginning of the three divisions of the psalm.

Hallelujah ("Praise the LORD") (147:1a)
1. Praise of the Lord's incomparable greatness as builder of Jerusalem (147:1b–6)
   a. Commendation of singing praise to the Lord (147:1b–c)
   b. The Lord as builder of Jerusalem (147:2a)
   c. The Lord as gatherer of the exiles (147:2b)
   d. The Lord as physician (147:3)
   e. The Lord as Creator (147:4)
   f. The Lord as possessing powerful and limitless understanding (147:5)
   g. The Lord as sustainer of the humble and vanquisher of the wicked (147:6)
2. Praise of the Lord's incomparable greatness as ruler of the universe (147:7–11)
   a. Call to praise (147:7)
   b. The Lord as giver of rain and provider of food for the animals (147:8–9)

c. The Lord's pleasure in those who fear him and who hope in his unfailing love (147:10–11)

3. Praise of the Lord's incomparable greatness as giver of the Torah (147:12–20b)
   a. Call to praise (147:12)
   b. The Lord's provision of security, blessing, peace, and food (147:13–14)
   c. The Lord's sending of his word (147:15–18)
   d. The Lord's unique revelation of his word to Israel (147:19–20b)
   Hallelujah ("Praise the LORD") (147:20c)

Historical and Cultural Background

Goulder takes the words "the bars of your gates" and "blesses your people within you" (147:13) to allude to Nehemiah's rebuilding the gates and walls of Jerusalem in 445 BC (Neh. 7:1–5) and the repopulation of the city (Neh. 11:1–2), respectively, and so he dates the psalm in the time of Nehemiah.[1] In that case, the reference to the "exiles" in verse 2 would be a backward glance at the return (537/536 BC).

Interpretive Insights

147:1 *Praise the* LORD. See table 1.

How good . . . how pleasant and fitting to praise him! The Hebrew clauses begin with the word *ki*, which can have several different meanings: temporal ("when"), nominal ("that"), exclamatory ("how," as in the NIV), emphatic ("indeed"), causative ("for/because"), and deictic ("truly"). In conjunction with the "good" and "pleasant" the deictic interpretation seems preferable.[2] The term "fitting" also occurs in 33:1, where the ESV translates it as "Praise *befits* the upright."

147:2–3 *The* LORD *builds up Jerusalem; he gathers the exiles of Israel.* See Isaiah 56:8; 11:12. If the time is that of Nehemiah in the middle of the fifth century, then the psalmist is conflating the renewal of the city of Jerusalem and the return of the exiles, which would not be surprising, since the return of the exiles brought new people and new resources to the city. Healing the brokenhearted and binding up wounds were part of the work of building up Jerusalem.

147:4–6 *He determines the number of the stars and calls them each by name.* God's creative activity and his providential care of sustaining the creation and humankind, juxtaposed here, are a single piece in creation theology (here note numbering the stars and sustaining the humble). The allusion is to God's creating work, which goes beyond even the Genesis narrative—the

Lord has a personal relationship with the stars and "calls them each by name" (147:4; see Isa. 40:26). God's naming the various entities that he created in Genesis 1 and man's naming of the animals in Genesis 2:19–20 imply authority over the creation, and the same idea is implied here. Moreover, it logically follows that, with such an incredibly vast knowledge, "his understanding has no limit" (Ps. 147:5). The one who builds up Jerusalem is the Creator of the world and the protector of the humble: he builds up Jerusalem, binds up the wounds of the brokenhearted, and raises up the humble. But be assured, he also "casts the wicked to the ground" (147:6).

147:7–9 *Sing to the* LORD *with grateful praise.* The call to praise of verse 1 is renewed, and now we see that the harp accompanies the singing (see the sidebar "Musical Instruments in Psalm 33" in the unit on Ps. 33). The topic of praise is God's provision of rain, which waters the grass that in turn provides food for the cattle and the ravens (see Job 38:41).

147:10–11 *His pleasure is not in the strength of the horse, nor his delight in the legs of the warrior.* As beautifully amazing as is the system of nature that God puts into operation, and as delightfully entertaining as is human athletic prowess (lit., "the thighs of man"; NIV: "the legs of the warrior"), the Lord's delight is in "those who fear him, who put their hope in his unfailing love [*hesed*]." This is reminiscent of Psalm 8, where the psalmist acclaims the beauty of the world and then is gratefully amazed that God has made humankind "a little lower than God" (NIV: "a little lower than the angels"; see comments on 8:5) and even put the created world—what a marvel!—under humankind's control (8:3–9). The sum of the matter in Psalm 8 is that however beautiful and magnificent is God's world, his human creatures surpass it by far, and God has endowed them with that unique status by making them in his image ("a little lower than God"). In Psalm 8 the psalmist is the one who delights in God's beautiful world, whereas here it is the Lord who would be expected to delight in the wonders of his creation, but instead he delights in the members of his human creation who fear him and hope in his unfailing love.

147:12–20 In the Hebrew text verses 12–20 compose a strophe. In the Septuagint these verses form an entire psalm of its own, which begins with "Alleluia. Of Haggai and Zechariah." The table below compares the numbering of the psalms in this section in the Hebrew text (MT) and the Septuagint (LXX):

MT	LXX
146	145
147:1–11	146
147:12–20	147
148	148
149	149
150	150

147:12–14 *Extol the* Lord, *Jerusalem; praise your God, Zion.* Now the psalm returns to the topic of Jerusalem, which was introduced in verse 2, where the Lord is called the builder-up of Jerusalem, and the topic continues through verse 14. The Lord "strengthens the bars of your gates and blesses your people within you" (147:13). Nehemiah was the human agent of this work, but the Lord was the real agent. He also brought peace to the city and supplied the people with the "finest of wheat" (147:14). The prayer of 122:6–9 has been answered. See Isaiah 54 for the eschatological picture of Jerusalem as a city of many children, a place of peace, and a fortified city.

147:15–20 *He sends his command to the earth; his word runs swiftly.* Now the psalmist turns again to God's providence in the natural world, a topic he deals with in verses 4–6 and 8–9. But there no intermediate agent of providence is evident—the Lord is the subject—whereas here we have the intermediate agent specified. Two words are employed as the name of the agent: God's "command" (*'imrah,* 147:15) and God's "word" (*dabar,* 147:15, 18, 19). In Psalm 119 both of these expressions are used as synonyms of the Torah (*'imrah,* 119:38, 41, 50, etc.; *dabar,* 119:9, 16, 17, etc.). This is the divine word that God sends forth, as in Isaiah 45:23 and 55:11, to accomplish his purpose (also Ps. 107:20); in fact, this word does not return to God until it accomplishes the purpose he sent it to do. The snow, frost, and hail of verses 16–17 are evidently figures for God's control of the cycle of nature, and the clause "He sends his word and melts them" (147:18) further affirms divine providence. We should note that the Torah was becoming the central focus of Judaism during this time, a fact illustrated in the middle of the fifth century by Ezra's reading of the Torah to the congregation (Neh. 8:1–8).

The purpose of the divine word in these verses is the providential control of nature, including snow, frost, and hail, and God sends forth his word and melts them (147:16–18). The final two verses (147:19–20b) explain that God's control of nature by his word distinguishes Israel from all other nations in that God has revealed this to Israel in his "laws and decrees." And that calls forth the final "hallelujah" (NIV: "Praise the Lord").

Theological Insights

This psalm is a full-bodied description of God's incomparable greatness, citing God's greatness as one who builds up Jerusalem and gathers the exiles, who rules the universe, and who gives his Torah to Israel (see "Outline/Structure"). While God's pleasure could easily be concentrated in the wonders of his creation (the "strength of the horse" and the "legs of the warrior," 147:10), he delights instead "in those who fear him, who put their hope in his unfailing love" (147:11)—that is, his people. And that is the marvel, much like God's wonderment in his human creation rather than the "glory" of the natural order, celebrated by Psalm 8. Humanity's status as "a little lower than God" (8:5, author's translation) means that God built his grand design into the nature of humanity, just as God's revelation of his "laws and decrees to Israel" marks the unique relationship he has with his people (147:19–20). And to add the capstone to this portrait of God's incomparable greatness, he who "determines the number of the stars and calls them each by name" is not diminished by condescending to build up Jerusalem (147:2), to heal the brokenhearted (147:3), to care for the earth (147:15–18), and to give his Torah to Israel (147:19–20). Spurgeon says of this psalm, "The God of Israel is set forth in his peculiarity of glory as caring for the sorrowing, the insignificant, and forgotten. The poet finds a singular joy in extolling one who is so singularly gracious."[3]

Teaching the Text

We could take a number of approaches to this psalm as we prepare our sermon/lesson. It is so rich with power and grace. In fact, we might use this idea to develop our sermon/lesson.

First, to get the theme out on the table, we can use Allen's statement: "Yahweh's power is harnessed to his grace."[4] This captures a major truth in the Psalter, and one that we would do well to understand. While God is incomparable in power, he does not operate by brute force, but grace is the energizer of his power. This theme is illustrated by the fact that the builder-up of Jerusalem strengthens the bars and gates (147:10, 13a)—yes, indeed—but the motive behind it is to bless his people. As I pointed out in the "Interpretive Insights" (see the comments on 147:4–6), God's creating activity and his providential care are a single piece in the theology of the Psalms and the theology of the Bible as a whole. We can sum that up by saying that whatever our personal and corporate needs may be, God's engine of power can and will deliver his decrees of grace, because it is powered by grace. To use another analogy, grace is always the first and last entries in God's glossary of operations.

Second, we can emphasize God's condescension to our human need as this truth is spelled out in the psalm. Spurgeon makes a lovely statement to sum up this point: "From stars to sighs is a deep descent! From worlds to wounds is a distance which only infinite compassion can bridge. Yet he who acts a surgeon's part with wounded hearts, marshals the heavenly host, and reads the muster roll of suns and the majestic system."[5] It is related to our first point, but all of our three points are interrelated. A Jewish saying affirms the theology of this psalm: "Wherever you find the Lord's might, you find his humility" (b. Megillah 31a). Divine grace is always condescending.

Third, the little clause in verse 15 is quite a precious picture of God's providential care: "His word runs swiftly." Amid our anxious waiting and nervous uncertainty, we have this assurance that God is sending his word out as his emissary to do his bidding, and it moves swiftly to do the Sender's work on our behalf. Calvin speaks of how he sometimes was unjust to God's mercy because he expended so much anxious toil to proclaim it (see "Illustrating the Text"). We need to remember that we are God's instruments in the work of grace, but we do not determine the success or outcome—God does.

Illustrating the Text

When we are unjust to God's mercy

Quote: **John Calvin.** Calvin was not inclined to talk about himself in his writings, but occasionally he unveiled his personal apprehensions. Once he wrote of his anxiety: "The thought repeatedly recurs to me that I am in danger of being unjust to God's mercy by laboring with so much anxiety to assert it, as if it were doubtful or obscure."[6] Our psalmist reminds us that God "sends his command to the earth; his word runs swiftly" (147:15). God is in full control of his word, and it accomplishes his will, which is a reminder that sometimes our effort to proclaim it is counterproductive because it is so fraught with anxious labor that is forgetful that it is God's word, not ours, and that God is the energizer, and we are not. That is not to suggest that our preparation should be effortless or slovenly, but it should be prompted and guided by trust in the power of God, who sends his word forth and it accomplishes his purpose.

The Healer of Shattered Hearts

Theological Book: *The Healer of Shattered Hearts*, **by David Wolpe.** Our psalmist presents a picture of God under two professions: the builder of Jerusalem and the healer of broken hearts (147:2–3). Jerusalem and the temple had been destroyed, and innumerable shattered hearts (NIV: "brokenhearted") were produced by these tragedies. While the return and the rebuilding of the temple were reasons for great joy, it was not an easy time but a time marked by much suffering and opposition to this movement of rebuilding. This psalm asserts and affirms that the Lord was personally involved in that time and place as the builder-up of Jerusalem and the healer of shattered hearts (147:2–3). Wolpe, in his book *The Healer of Shattered Hearts*, takes up the task of introducing the God of the Hebrew Scriptures, who is "personal and universal" and "whose majesty is tempered by familiarity."[7] The wide span between the descriptors "personal" and "universal" would imply an unapproachable God, until we recognize that he is "personal" and his character "tempered by familiarity." The New Testament revelation is replete with that message (John 1:1–5).

"Praise the LORD from the Heavens. . . . Praise the LORD from the Earth"

Big Idea
The praise of God is the newly discovered power of God's suffering people.

Key Themes
- The power of the faithful is found not in their own resources but in the power of the praise of God.
- We are privileged to pray to God, who is our "next of kin."

Understanding the Text

Psalm 148 is, like all the psalms in the Hallelujah Psalter (Pss. 146–50), enclosed in the single word "hallelujah" (NIV: "Praise the LORD"). This standard *inclusio* is intended to state the theme of Psalms 146–50, mark them as a chorus of universal praise, and install the final title of the Psalter, "Praises" (*Tehillim*). This is a hymn in praise of God the Creator of heaven and earth and all that is in them.

The Text in Context

Psalm 148 is the center psalm of the Hallelujah Psalter (Pss. 146–50), recalling some details from Genesis 1. It is related to Psalm 147 (147:9–20) by the hint of Torah ("decree"), applied here to God's command to creation (148:5–6; compare 147:19–20),[1] and by its shared term with the Torah, implicating Torah as God's instrument of providential care of his creation. Psalm 148 closes with a note on the power of praise in the life of Israel and anticipates the statement on the power of praise in 149:5–9.

Outline/Structure

In addition to being encompassed with "hallelujah" (NIV: "Praise the LORD"), thus giving it the mood of praise, this psalm begins each of its two parts with a call to praise, addressing first the heavenly beings (148:1b–2) and then the earthly beings and created things (148:7). Indeed, the praise of earth is probably intended to be an antiphonal response to the praise of heaven.

Hallelujah ("Praise the LORD") (148:1a)
Strophe 1: Call to the heavenly beings to praise the Lord (148:1b–6)
    a. General call to the heavens to praise (148:1b–c)
    b. Call to angels and heavenly host to praise (148:2)
    c. Call to sun, moon, and stars to praise (148:3)
    d. Call to the highest heavens and upper waters to praise (148:4)
    e. General call to heavenly beings to praise because the Lord created them (148:5)
    f. Concluding word of affirmation (148:6)
Strophe 2: Call to the earthly beings and created things to praise the Lord (148:7–14b)
    a. Call to earthly beings to praise (148:7a)
    b. Call to the sea creatures and ocean depths to praise (148:7b)
    c. Call to the meteorological conditions to praise (148:8)
    d. Call to the mountains and hills, fruit trees and cedars to praise (148:9)
    e. Call to wild animals and all cattle, creeping animals and birds to praise (148:10)
    f. Call to kings, princes, rulers, and other human beings to praise (148:11–12)
    g. General call to praise (148:13)
    h. Concluding word of affirmation (148:14a–b)
Hallelujah ("Praise the LORD") (148:14c)

Historical and Cultural Background

The historical situation of this psalm must be surmised on the basis of the Hallelujah Psalter, which might be dated to the period of Ezra and Nehemiah (middle of the fifth century BC). The absence of military language (see the comments on 149:6–9) in this collection might suggest the time of the restoration when military solutions were out of the question, and evidently out of the mind of the Jewish people. Psalm 146:3 definitely puts no confidence in human princes who might make (military?) plans; when they die, the plans die with them and so leave their followers in the lurch. I have proposed that the theological notion that was beginning to be advanced at that time was that the praise of God was the best option for Israel's future (see the comments on 148:14 and "Theological Insights").

Interpretive Insights

148:1b–6 The call to praise in 148:1b, "Praise the LORD from the heavens," is spoken to the heavenly beings and created things, which will be named one by one in verses 2–4. This strophe calls for praise of the Lord "from the heavens," distinguishing it from the second strophe, which calls for praise of the Lord "from the earth" (148:7).

148:2–4 *Praise him, all his angels; praise him, all his heavenly hosts.* This strophe (148:1b–6) is studded with praise language. The declarative "Praise him" occurs seven times (excluding the "hallelujah" [NIV: "Praise the LORD"] at the beginning of the psalm [148:1a]). Once the jussive "Let them praise the name of the LORD" occurs, followed by the reason: "at his command they were created" (148:5). The "angels" are those beings that serve God and do his bidding (103:20–21), and the "heavenly hosts" are either the stars or the heavenly "armies" (see NLT; cf. the name "LORD of Hosts" [see the comments on 84:1]; see also Job 38:7) who also serve God, and they are all among the created beings, but they are not mentioned in Genesis 1. Yet, the sun, moon, stars (Gen. 1:14–19), "the highest heavens" (lit., "the heavens of the heavens," Deut. 10:14), and the "waters above the skies" (Gen. 1:6–8) are works of the created order named in Genesis 1.

148:5–6 *at his command they were created . . . a decree that will never pass away.* The phrase "at his command" (the Hebrew of this clause reads, "for he commanded and they were created") points to the jussive verbs in Genesis 1 ("and let there be"), which carry an imperative force. The "decree that will never pass away" (lit., "will not transgress") may allude to Genesis 1:14: "and let them serve as signs to mark sacred times, and days and years." That cycle of nature will continue without interruption.

148:7–14b In this second strophe the poet turns from the heavens to the earth and its inhabitants and natural phenomena.

148:7 *Praise the LORD from the earth.* The phrase "from the earth" distinguishes this strophe from the first ("from the heavens," 148:1).

you great sea creatures and all ocean depths. The "sea creatures" (*tanninim*) are likely those referred to in Genesis 1:21, and the "ocean depths" are the deepest waters of the oceans, corresponding to the "waters above the skies" in verse 4. Genesis refers to these two entities as "the waters that were under the expanse" and "the waters that were above the expanse" (Gen. 1:7 ESV).

148:8–12 *lightning and hail . . . mountains . . . fruit trees and all cedars . . . wild animals.* Our poet has created his own categories of created beings and things: "lightning and hail" and "stormy winds" represent the meteorological phenomena (148:8); "mountains" and "hills" represent the earth (148:9a; Gen. 1:9–10); "fruit trees" and "cedars" represent all vegetation (148:9b; Gen. 1:11–12); "wild animals and all cattle" represent wild beasts and domesticated animals (148:10a; Gen. 1:20–23); "small creatures and flying birds" represent the remaining creatures of the created order (148:10b; Gen. 1:20, 24–25); "kings," "nations," "princes," and "all rulers" represent the ruling class of humankind (148:11); and "young men and women, old men and children" represent all humanity (148:12; Gen. 1:26–28). The call to praise in verse 7, "Praise the LORD from the earth," applies to all of the created things and beings in verses 7–12.

148:13 *Let them praise the name of the* LORD. The call to praise in verse 7 and this jussive call to praise form an *inclusio* for the strophe.

148:14 *And he has raised up for his people a horn.* The assumption is that during the exile Israel had lost their "horn," which Delitzsch identifies as "its comeliness and its defensive and offensive power"[2] (see also 75:4; 89:17, 24; 92:10). Indeed, "horn" is a metaphor for power and strength, and that is what Israel lost during their captivity. The real "horn" or power of the people, however, is now newly discovered, raised up by Yahweh himself, and that is "the praise of all his faithful servants."[3] This phrase is in apposition to "horn" in the first part of the verse. Understandably, the military option was not viable in their restoration context, and they have emerged from exile to realize the power of praise, which is the same as recognizing that it is Yahweh who brings victory to his people, not their weapons and horses (20:7). Similarly, in 149:6, if we read the "and" appositionally,[4] then we render the verse thus: "May the high praises of God be in their throat, *even* [appositional use of the conjunction] a two-edged sword in their hands" (author's translation). Thus the psalmist is commending praise as the "weapon" of choice. This is a significant theological note. Israel's "horn" (power) in the past failed them, and they went into exile. Now they have emerged to discover the power of praise. The writer(s) of this final Hallelujah Psalter is a theologian of merit, and he recognizes that the Lord has raised up this "horn," that is, "the praise of all his faithful servants." This is a gift of grace from Yahweh to his people, who are "close to his heart" ('*am-qᵉrobo*; lit., "a people his near relative"). The term "near relative" or "close (to him)" (*qarob*) is used in Leviticus 10:3 to describe the Aaronic priests and their special relationship to Yahweh. Naomi uses this term to refer to Boaz as their "next of kin" (NIV: "close relative") who has the right of redemption (Ruth 2:20). It is used in Deuteronomy 4:7 and Psalm 145:18 to describe Yahweh's nearness to his people. The significance of this statement is that the covenant relationship is still in effect.

Theological Insights

The theological thought that closes this psalm is that Israel, depleted of military resources and political reserves, has a new, or at least rediscovered, power ("horn") to rely on. This principle, that Israel's victories come not by military power but by the Lord's, is translated in this psalm into the metaphor of the "horn" that the Lord is raising up for Israel (see 148:14), and the new "horn" is the praise of God. This theological thought belongs to a complex of other expressions in a similar vein, particularly Deuteronomy 17:16 (also Pss. 20:7–8; 33:16–19; 1 Sam. 17:47; 2 Chron. 20:15, 22). The doctrine that God can and will do his work apart from the work of human helpers grows out of a more deeply rooted theology in the Old Testament. First, God is sovereign, and he rules over all the forces of nature and humanity. The ultimate proof of his sovereignty is that he does not need any outside help to do his work. And that brings us to the second observation: God has chosen to empower our praise of him as the force that accomplishes his will in the world. It is both a reminder of the inadequacy of our human resources and a reminder that the real power in the universe is operative in our relationship with God, endowed by him and powered by him. The fact that God chooses to use human beings and the forces of nature to accomplish his will is an expression of grace, not need. As Lewis says, God has chosen to need us. Further, here is the union of praise "from the heavens" (148:1) and praise "from the earth" (148:7), and when these unite, that is the ultimate power ("horn") to bring about God's purposes in the universe, and he has put this power of praise into the hands of his "faithful servants" (148:14). Praise the Lord!

Teaching the Text

We should approach this psalm with fear and trembling, because it brings us into the presence of God, not visibly but audibly, and God is everywhere, in his heavenly creation and his earthly creation. We might observe that, looking at the Psalter from one angle, this is the objective of the entire book, to call all Israel and all humankind to praise the Lord. The name itself, "Praises" (*Tehillim*), incorporates that purpose. But this "hallelujah edition" of Book 5, and especially the Hallelujah Psalter (Pss. 146–50), is intended to be a unique presentation of that theme.

First then, we need to recognize that the enclosing hallelujahs signal universal praise, and the contents of the psalm fill out that universal perspective: "from the heavens" (148:1) and "from the earth" (148:7). The Psalter from time to time has sermonized on the theme of praise, generally based on God's creation and redemption of the world and on his providential care. We saw the works of providence particularly emphasized in Psalm 147. In Psalm 148 there is a shift from providence to creation, creation of the heavenly beings and planets, and creation of the earthly beings. Thus we hear the praise of God from both realms of the created order, and as suggested above, their praise seems to be antiphonal (see "Outline/Structure"). Heaven and earth are in perfect harmony as they praise their Creator, reminding us of the Lord's Prayer: "Thy will be done, on earth as it is in heaven." Earth has finally acquired heaven's perfect pitch.

Second—and for this point we have to appeal to the context—the psalm reflects Israel's world where their power ("horn") has, by implication, been lost. Now in this period of restoration from exile, powerless and totally dependent on God's power, they have become conscious of a newly discovered, mystical power that God has "raised up" for them, the power of praise (see the comments on 148:14). As I have contended in "Theological Insights," this is the equivalent of the truth, variously revealed, that God's people, his covenant people, his "next of kin" (*qarob*, 148:14), must know that they cannot depend on their own resources for their salvation, but they must depend on God's. The word picture that *qarob* calls forth is illustrated in Ruth 3:12, where Boaz is called the *go'el* ("redeemer"). This means that Boaz has the right and the responsibility of raising up offspring for the widowed Ruth. The two words "redeemer" (*go'el*) and "next of kin" (*qarob*, 148:14; Ruth 3:12; NIV: "another who is more closely related [than I]") occur in synonymous relationship in Ruth 3:12. Without pressing the nuance of "redeemer" too severely, there is some justification for transferring the social nuances of that word to Yahweh—the Lord has the right to redeem his people. The reason is that he is their "next of kin," for they are created in his image.

Their reliance on their own resources is what has brought them into the humiliation of the exile, but at the same time, their "next of kin" relationship to God is the grace that has brought them to this time of restoration. The "next of kin" relationship has its source in God's own covenant making: "What other nation is so great as to have their gods near [*qᵉrobim*] to them the way the Lord our God is near us whenever we pray to him?" (Deut. 4:7). The parallels in our own lives are quite striking. Sadly, it is in the humiliation our sins have caused, as it was in Israel's, that we finally recognize that our real source of power is God, and God alone, and that he is our Redeemer because of that unique relationship we have to him, with which we had nothing to do: "It is he who made us, and we are his" (Ps. 100:3).

Third—and this is the mystical element about Israel's faith and ours—God has so ordered the world that the ultimate resource, the "weapon" of choice, is the praise of God. To engage in praise reminds us of our powerlessness. Praise is similar to the prophetic word that the Lord sent forth to accomplish his purposes (Isa. 40:8; 45:23), except this word is entrusted to human beings.

All of our weapons of military might and human plotting and scheming are of no worth when the kingdom of God is the reality we seek. That is not to say that our human efforts are totally worthless—certainly not. But it is to assert that they are not decisive. They are only catalysts in the building of the kingdom, and they would not even deserve that name except for the grace of God that empowers even our catalytic efforts. Ultimately and decisively, "Our help is in the name of the LORD, who made heaven and earth" (Ps. 124:8 KJV).

The mystical dimension of this psalm, that praise is faith's power, or as 149:6–9 would suggest, our "weapon" of choice, is demonstrated in the eschatological hallelujah chorus of Revelation 19:1–8. It is the nuptial song of redemption when Christ and his church are united in the eternal matrimony of grace (Rev. 19:7). And the appropriate instrument of celebration, the only one, is praise. Delitzsch expresses it so beautifully:

> The call to praise proceeds rather from the wish that all creatures, by becoming after their own manner an echo and reflection of the divine glory, may participate in the joy at the glory which God has bestowed upon His people after their deep humiliation . . . that the way through suffering to glory which the church is traversing, has not only the glorifying of God in itself, but by means of this glorifying, the glorifying of God in all creatures and by all creatures, too, as its final aim, and that these, finally transformed (glorified) in the likeness of transformed (glorified) humanity, will become the bright mirror of the divine doxa and an embodied hymn of a thousand voices.[5]

It is the declarative praise of God, with its multiple hallelujahs and ascriptions of blessing of God's name, or the declarative praise of the saints who have walked through this world waving their banner of faith (Heb. 11) and living out the precepts of their God. It is the praise to which this psalm calls us. When our talking praise and our walking praise become identical, the kingdom will come. John describes that day in Revelation 19 when the multivoiced chorus of heaven (the four living creatures) and earth (the twenty-four elders) join together in the eschatological hallelujah chorus announcing that the kingdom of God has come, there symbolized in the "wedding supper of the Lamb" (Rev. 19:9). The faithful should give witness to this marvelous truth, and the skeptical would do well also to give it their sober attention.

Illustrating the Text

There is joy in knowing that God does not need us.

Biography: **Lilias Trotter.** Trotter, missionary to the Muslims of Algiers, during her declining health, wrote, "It is very wonderful to watch these horizons unfold—Long ago—fifty years or more in the past, it was a joy to think that

God needed me: Now it is a far deeper joy to feel & see that He does not need me—that He has it all in hand!"[6] She also contemplates this topic in her diary: "[God] needs that helplessness as truly as the negative pole is needed to complete the electric circuit & set free the power. And so when one can only lie like sort of a log, unable to even frame the prayers one would like to pray, His Spirit will find the way through that lowest point which He so strangely needs, & lift them up to the Throne."[7]

In Psalm 148, Israel, now recovering from the humiliation of conquest and exile, at last recognizes their helplessness and ironically confesses that they had the weapons of victory all along, the power of praise (148:14). It is then that God's power is made perfect in weakness (cf. 2 Cor. 12:9).

The irony of desire unmatched by reality

Film: *Amadeus.* We see a lot of ironies in the world. One person tries very hard to achieve fame and fails, while another makes no attempt at all and succeeds. In the movie *Amadeus*, the composer Salieri has the desire to write great music but does not succeed—at least, not like Mozart—while Mozart hardly tries, and he writes some of the world's greatest music. It is an irony.

An irony is an illogical outcome of a logical action. History has many ironies. Putting the irony into words is easy. It's understanding it that's hard, understanding why what we expect doesn't happen and what we don't expect does. If we were all honest with ourselves, each one of us could probably name at least one situation in our own lives that could be called an irony. We aimed in one direction and tried so hard to succeed but never achieved our goal. In this psalm, Israel at last recognizes that their own history contains an irony: they have possessed the path to victory all along, the "horn for his people, praise for all his saints."

"May the Praise of God Be . . . a Double-Edged Sword in Their Hands"

Big Idea

Our spiritual weaponry is not of this world, but it has the power to demolish the strongholds of evil.

Key Themes

- The praise of God has an inherent power to accomplish God's will.
- Our spiritual strategy is to trust in God rather than our own resources.

Understanding the Text

The penultimate psalm in the Hallelujah Psalter is a hymn, composed for the purpose of celebrating the miraculous events that have transpired in the postexilic age. When one considers that Cyrus, a non-Israelite, issued the decree that permitted Israel to return to their homeland and rebuild their temple, without Israel's help—no battle fought, no arsenals exhausted—it is a reminder of the power of praise and prayer, which is the theme of this hymn.

The Text in Context

Psalm 149 has links to other closing psalms of Book 5 and to Isaiah 61, verifying the shared theology, which includes God's delight in his people, the kingship of Yahweh, the praise of the faithful, the good news to the poor, and divine vengeance reserved for Israel's enemies.

Table 1. Intertextuality of Psalm 149

Psalm 149	Other Texts
"Sing to the Lord a new song" (149:1a)	"I will sing a new song to you, my God" (144:9a)
"For the Lord takes delight in his people" (149:4a)	"The Lord delights in those who fear him" (147:11)
"Let the people of Zion be glad in their King" (149:2b)	"I will exalt you, my God the King" (145:1a)
"Let his faithful people [hasidim] rejoice in this honor" (149:5a) "This is the glory to all his faithful people [lᵉkol-hasidaw]" (149:9b)	"The praise [tᵉhillah] of all his faithful servants [lᵉkol-hasidaw]" (148:14)
"He crowns the humble ['anawim]" (149:4b)	"Because the Lord has anointed me to proclaim good news to the poor ['anawim]" (Isa. 61:1b)
"For the Lord delights [rotseh, ptc.]" (149:4a)	"To proclaim the year of the Lord's favor [ratson, noun]" (Isa. 61:2a)
"To inflict vengeance [nᵉqamah] on the nations" (149:7a)	"And the day of vengeance [naqam] of our God" (Isa. 61:2b)
"To carry out the sentence [mishpat] written against them" (149:9a)	"For I, the Lord, love justice [mishpat]" (Isa. 61:8a)

Outline/Structure

The poem divides into two parts, each beginning with a call to praise.

> Hallelujah ("Praise the Lord") (149:1a)
> 1. A new song of victory for God's faithful (149:1b–4)
>   a. Call to sing God's praise in the congregation (149:1b–c)
>   b. Call to rejoice in Israel's Maker and King (149:2)
>   c. Description of the musical celebration (149:3)
>   d. Reason for the new song of praise (149:4)
> 2. Renewed call to praise and the effect of the praise of God (149:5–9b)
>   a. A call for the faithful to rejoice (149:5)
>   b. The praise of God as the agent of judgment (149:6–9b)
>   Hallelujah ("Praise the Lord") (149:9c)

Historical and Cultural Background

This psalm belongs to the postexilic time of restoration, most likely that of Ezra and Nehemiah in the middle of the fifth century BC. The community is described as the "humble," probably an allusion to their political (oppression), economic (impoverishment), and spiritual state (meekness). See "Historical and Cultural Background," "Theological Insights," and the comments on 148:14 in the unit on Psalm 148.

Interpretive Insights

149:1 *Sing to the LORD a new song.* A "new song" sometimes designates a song celebrating new works of Yahweh (see the comments on 33:3). In this case the new works may be the return from exile and the restoration in general, including Ezra's and Nehemiah's restorative efforts. Significant, however, is the fact that Psalm 149 prepares the way, whichever time period may be the case.

the assembly of his faithful people. The "assembly" is most likely the worshiping community, or the larger Jewish community that would include the worshiping community. The "faithful people" (*hasidim*) are those individuals who keep the Torah. During the Maccabean period (second century BC) the *hasidim* were those who were faithful to the Torah, but this is too early for that definition, even though, in light of the emphasis on Torah, they might be among those who represent the incipient movement to Torah piety that eventually became the Hasidaeans of the Maccabean times.

149:2 *Let Israel rejoice in their Maker.* In 146:6 the Lord is called "the Maker of heaven and earth," but here he is the "Maker" of Israel, in the sense that he brought Israel into existence. The participle "Maker" is plural but obviously intended as a singular referring to Yahweh. This may be the plural of honor, such as *'adonaw* ("his Lord") or *'elohaw* ("his God"), both of which are plural and refer to the singular God.[1]

let the people of Zion be glad in their King. In verse 2 "rejoice" and "be glad" set the tone for the psalm. It is a psalm of joy or celebration, and the object of their joy is "their King," or Yahweh himself. Very likely we ought to see the full circle that takes us from the rebellious "kings of the earth" of Psalm 2, near the beginning of the book, to this penultimate psalm that calls Israel to "be glad in their King." This psalm represents the earthly congregation celebrating the Lord's ultimate accession to his heavenly throne; the "assembly of his faithful people" (149:1) and his heavenly sanctuary have at last become one (150:1).

149:3 *with timbrel and harp.* The "timbrel" was a small drum, similar to our tambourine but without the jingles. It was often played by women and accompanied by dancing (Exod. 15:20; 1 Sam. 18:6), but men played the instrument too (Ps. 81:2). It also appears, accompanied by dancing, among the praise instruments of Psalm 150:4.[2] The terms "timbrel" and "dancing" are the instruments of celebration at the Red Sea (Exod. 15:20) and here suggest that Israel is positioned on the cusp of a victory comparable to that miracle.

149:4 *For the LORD takes delight in his people; he crowns the humble with victory.* To crown the humble with victory is an irony, certainly not what we would expect. This affirmation comes close to the Deuteronomic declaration that God's election of Israel is understood only as an expression of his love for them (Deut. 7:7–8). By now the righteous people in Israel are virtually synonymous with the "humble" or "poor." The word can also be understood as "oppressed," and perhaps a combination of those nuances is the proper understanding of the term in this context. They are the "oppressed" who have returned from exile, where they have been refined from mere economic poverty to spiritual poverty (see the comments on 37:11; see also Matt. 5:5). And God's defensive posture toward them is a confirmation of his covenant loyalty (see, e.g., Deut. 15:4; 24:10–15). Most likely, in parallel with "his people," the "humble" are the entire community of Israel. Verse 4b is a famous line in the KJV: "He will beautify the meek with salvation." The Hebrew verb rendered by the NIV as "crowns" is generally rendered "adorn/clothe," and the word "beauty" seems to be a derivative. The NJPS translation reads: "He adorns the lowly with victory." See "Illustrating the Text."

149:5 *Let his faithful people rejoice in this honor and sing for joy on their beds.* This constitutes a second call to praise, and Gunkel observes that often in the Psalms a new call to praise signals a new part of the poem, as seems to be the case here, thus dividing the psalm into two parts.[3] "This honor" is evidently the Lord's delight in Israel ("the humble"). The term "faithful" (*hasidim*) forms an *inclusio* for this strophe (148:5 and 9).

149:6–9 *May the praise of God be in their mouths and a double-edged sword in their hands.* In view of the nonmilitary climate that prevailed in the restoration community, I view the "double-edged sword" as appositional (see the comments on 148:14). That is, the "double-edged" sword is synonymous with the "praise of God." As the verse stands in most English translations, the sense of the verse is an "ambidextrous" praising the Lord with one's mouth and wielding the sword in one's hand. There is the possibility that the psalmist is speaking of an eschatological day of vengeance, which was certainly part of Israel's long-term vision of the future. Yet, since the returning community had spent seventy years in exile and now was a defeated and humiliated people who had returned to their homeland through the intervention of a pagan king (Isa. 44:28)—as it turned out, a king the Lord had taken by the hand to direct his conquests (Isa. 45:1–4)—one wonders if this community would be brash enough to propose such a bold program of vengeance on their enemies at this particular time.

Theological Insights

I have laid out an interpretation of Psalm 149:5–9 that is in line with a rather strong strand of Old Testament theology and is in keeping with the political-theological context of this collection of psalms: that God's power, not military might, is the ultimate source of our defense. Whatever we think about the doctrine of trusting in God's saving power rather than our own resources, we have to admit that our own methods and resources sometimes— often, I would say—are so fraught with deficiencies and selfish motives that they are inherently self-destructive. While the Old Testament does not carve out a place for conscientious objectors as such, it is certainly accurate to say that the theology of the Hebrew Bible makes a place for those who would commit their cause so wholly to God that they can appeal to the mystical power of prayer and praise. And who can measure the outcomes and sort out the returns! In fact, Jehoshaphat's story in 2 Chronicles 20:15–24 is an episode in that direction, and there have been unnumbered cases in history when believers could not account for the incredible results of prayer, unassisted by human effort, except to say that "this is the glory of all [God's] faithful people" (149:9). See "God's work is perceptible only to those who believe" in "Illustrating the Text" in the unit on Psalm 53.

Teaching the Text

I suggest that we begin our sermon/lesson on Psalm 149 with verse 4. First, we can start with the KJV, "He will beautify the meek with salvation," and give another translation or two, like the NJPS, "He adorns the lowly with victory." The idea of verse 4, of course, is the surprise that the "meek/lowly" should take on such beauty and such victory ("salvation" is sometimes used in this sense), especially since they are the impoverished and disenfranchised, the "oppressed," no less. Thus, before our poet has introduced the weaponry issue, he has already informed us that the Lord will bestow on the "humble" a beauty that is entirely out of character for them since their lot in life is sorely depressed. Here we may also comment on the fact that God's clothing the meek with victory (salvation) may very well be a reflection of God's clothing Adam and Eve after their sin in Eden (Gen. 3:21; a verbal synonym is used here). The harp and lyre, instruments in the eschatological symphony of praise (Ps. 150:3, 4), were invented by descendants of Cain (Gen. 4:21). Both of these allusions thus create an undercurrent of meaning that reveals God's reversal of evil. And if we take Revelation 18:22 as an exclusionary note, describing the final state of the judgment of the world ("Babylon"), we may, as Reardon suggests, understand even the musical instruments to have been redeemed and preserved only for heaven.[4]

Second, having heard what the Lord will do for the humble, the new program that the psalmist introduces in verse 6, the power of praise, comes as no surprise: "May the praise of God be in their mouths." Since the Lord initiates a change of status for the lowly, it logically follows that the psalmist is speaking of a spiritual program, a mystical one, we might say, like that recorded in 2 Chronicles 20:15–24. The praise of God has an inherent power that is comparable to a "two-edged sword" in their hand. We have to be careful that we don't disavow this kind of spiritual "warfare" before we have some experience with it. Paul, for example, knew that believers have an arsenal of weapons that, shockingly, have this inherent power to counteract the evil forces of this world: "For the weapons of our warfare are not of the flesh but have divine power to destroy strongholds" (2 Cor. 10:4 ESV). And he insisted in his letter to the Ephesian church that "our struggle is not against flesh and blood, but against the rulers, against the authorities, against the powers of this dark world and against the spiritual forces of evil in the heavenly realms" (Eph. 6:12), and he admonishes these Christians to "put on the full armor of God" (Eph. 6:11). Behind the words of verses 6–9 we have the doctrine of God's power to bring about outcomes that we, with our natural instincts, would think were possible only if we were armed with the best weaponry humans can develop.

We need to recognize and acknowledge, of course, that we are not preaching/teaching about pacifism—that is another matter (see "Praise the Lord! And pass the ammunition" in "Illustrating the Text"). Rather, we are speaking about our ability to depend on God to change the circumstances of our lives, even the political and moral circumstances of our world. In fact, in the biblical sense of the word, vengeance is not ours to inflict on others anyway (Deut. 32:35). The question is, how do we engage our world in order to change the circumstances that oppose God's will and at the same time wield our spiritual weapons to bring about the divine will? This requires a faith that trusts when events are turning against us, and trust is a spiritual discipline that has to be sharpened and polished again and again. To put it another way, it means, how do we "seek first his kingdom and his righteousness" (Matt. 6:33) and let God supply all of the other resources needed to enable that pursuit?

Illustrating the Text

An egregious interpretation of the Psalms

Church History: The history of this psalm's interpretation contains a lesson in how not to interpret a psalm. Just as the Protestant Reformation was finding its feet, Thomas Münzer in Germany used Psalm 149 to stir up the Peasants' Revolt in 1524–25, in which one hundred thousand peasants were killed. Almost a century later, Caspar Scloppius wrote a book called *Classicum Belli Sacri*, in which he put forth the concept of holy war and used Psalm 149 as justification, thus helping to ignite the Thirty Years' War (1618–48), a bloody era between Roman Catholics and Protestants in Europe.

Praise the Lord! And pass the ammunition.

History: There is a story—some say legendary, but others claim to have verification—about a chaplain on the USS *New Orleans* on the day of the Japanese attack on Pearl Harbor in December of 1941. One version of the story is that the chaplain was asked to say a prayer, and he said, "Praise the Lord! And pass the ammunition," and proceeded to man one of the guns himself. Another version of the story, perhaps more plausible, is that the electricity on the ship was partly disabled, and the men had to move the ammunition to the gunners by bucket brigade. When the men were getting weary, the chaplain, part of the brigade himself, called back down the line, "Praise the Lord! And pass the ammunition." Frank Loesser wrote a popular song by that title to celebrate this story and this type of heroism.

Verses 6–9 of Psalm 149, as it is traditionally interpreted, represent a mixture of the power of praise and the power of the sword. If we look at that through the eyes of the Old Testament, it is not a theological contradiction, nor is the combination objectionable to the New Testament believer, if we accept a just war theory. But that issue is not the reason I have interpreted the military language as a metaphor for the power of praise (see "Theological Insights"). Rather, this newly reconstituted community had been miraculously released from the Babylonian exile and sent home to rebuild their temple. Whatever glimmers of vengeance were still harbored in their hearts were prudently kept repressed; and a new faith in Yahweh to bring salvation, as he had already done, began to engage their weary spirits. So for the psalmist, it was just "Praise the Lord," and that was also the ammunition.

Seek first his kingdom.

Bible: Matthew 6:33. There is an irony in 149:4, "He crowns the humble with victory" (see the comments on 149:4). The "humble" are the powerless and defenseless, and the fact that the Lord adorns them with "victory" is precisely the unexpected outcome of their vulnerable condition. Psalm 37:11, a close associate of our text, informs us that the "humble" (or "meek") will inherit the earth (see also Matt. 5:5). The inheritance is the very thing they had not sought, and the thing they had certainly not expected. By the time of the postexilic period, the "humble" were virtually synonymous with the "righteous," and they had learned the lesson through exile and numerous other hardships that human power is useless in bringing about the kingdom of God. Indeed, the very thing their vulnerability had lost them, the land, was precisely the bequest they had received. In 37:11 it was the "earth" or "land" (both can translate the same Hebrew word), and here it was the land lost to their Babylonian foe and regained by a stroke of Cyrus's pen (see Deut. 17:16). This "miracle" of history was evidence that God's power superseded military might, and thus their faith in the power of praise ("a double-edged sword in their hands," 149:6) to "inflict vengeance on the nations" (149:7) was both affirmed and strengthened (see the comments on 149:6–9). The meek are those who know, on the one hand, that they are pilgrims and strangers in this world but, on the other hand, that this world belongs to them. Jesus's message of Matthew 6:33 pulsates through this psalm: "But seek first his kingdom and his righteousness, and all these things will be given to you as well."

"Let Everything That Has Breath Praise the LORD"

Big Idea
The history of redemption is a parable of praise that climaxes in the universal chorus of all humanity praising the Lord.

Key Themes
- Human history and the human family are bounded with praise.
- The story of redemption is the story of praise.

Understanding the Text

Psalm 150 is a hymn or psalm of praise. The only verb used in the psalm is the verb "praise," used thirteen times. The ten occurrences of the imperative *hallᵉlu/hallᵉluhu* ("praise / praise him") are code language to say that this is the perfect "hallelujah," the perfect praise, which includes the heavenly sanctuary, the full orchestra of redeeming history, and the voices of all humanity from the beginning to the end of time. Psalm 150 is the hallelujah chorus of the Psalter.

The Text in Context

Psalm 149 was a call to the "faithful" (*hasidim*) to praise the Lord, and Psalm 150 follows as a call to "everything that has breath" to praise the Lord. The writers of the Psalter, especially David, have anticipated and longed to enter the presence of God, here represented by the sanctuary. Now this awesome book of praises (*tᵉhillim*) closes with a call to praise God in his heavenly sanctuary ("his holy place" [NIV: "his sanctuary"] and "his mighty heavens," 150:1). Given the journey of the Psalter's speakers into the presence of God (e.g., "that I may dwell in the house of the LORD all the days of my life," 27:4), there could be no more appropriate place to bring the book to a close than the sanctuary, and the heavenly sanctuary at that.

We should also note that the pattern to close each book with a doxology is the editorial feature the editor(s) of the book is following, and rather than a verse or two, he makes this doxology a collection of five psalms of praise, thus signaling its climactic effect.

Outline/Structure

As with the other psalms of the Hallelujah Psalter, Psalm 150 begins and ends with the burst of "hallelujah" (NIV: "Praise the Lord"). And distinctly, this psalm has the praise verb *hallᵉlu/hallᵉluhu* ("praise / praise him") at the beginning and in the middle of every verse, except the last (150:6), and there it occurs twice at the end of the verse, issuing the universal call for "everything that has breath" to praise the Lord. This psalm is the concentrated praise of Yahweh with no distractions. Its absolute focus is on Yahweh and Yahweh alone.

Hallelujah ("Praise the Lord") (150:1a)
1. Praise God, the sovereign King (150:1b–2)
   a. Praise Yahweh in his heavenly sanctuary (150:1b–c)
   b. Reasons for praise: Yahweh's power and greatness (150:2)
2. Praise Yahweh's sovereign reign (150:3–5)
   a. Praise Yahweh at his coronation (150:3)
   b. Praise Yahweh at the return of his presence (150:4)
   c. Praise Yahweh at the day of judgment and salvation (150:5)
3. Universal call to praise Yahweh (150:6a)
   Hallelujah ("Praise the Lord") (150:6b)

Historical and Cultural Background

No historical events or persons are mentioned by name in this psalm. Yet it contains the history of redemption in code language. As is often the case with the Psalms—and poetry in general, for that matter—words and phrases are intended to summon mental and emotional images with which readers are familiar and to unfold their mental and emotional dimensions. This psalm codes Yahweh's royal coronation, his reign, and the return of his presence to the temple, all couched in the language of praise. So as Israel praises God, they are also telling their story of redemption (see "Interpretive Insights"), and as their story of redemption unfolds, they are praising God.

Interpretive Insights

150:1 *Praise the Lord.* The psalm, like all of the hallelujah psalms in this final collection (Pss. 146–50), begins and ends with "hallelujah," or "Praise the LORD." In fact, our writer begins every line except verse 6 with "praise (the LORD)." It has a staccato effect, and Spurgeon comments that "his sentences are very short, for he is in haste to utter his next *Hallelujah*, and his next, and his next."[1]

Praise God in his sanctuary; praise him in his mighty heavens. While the phrase "his sanctuary" can mean the Jerusalem sanctuary, the implication is that it is God's heavenly sanctuary that is in view, since it is parallel to "his mighty heaven" (see 11:4 for another use of this term as the heavenly sanctuary).[2] Ezekiel 1 and 10 picture God's throne above the "firmament" (see Ezek. 1:26 KJV). The divine name "God" (*'el*) evokes the universal theme of the psalm. The shortened form of the tetragrammaton (*yah*) appears only in verses 1 and 6, forming an *inclusio*.

150:2 *Praise him for his acts of power; praise him for his surpassing greatness.* Verse 1 having established Yahweh's place in the universe, verse 2 appeals to his "acts of power" and "his surpassing greatness" (lit., "abundance of his greatness") as the reason for praise, the only verse in this psalm that gives reasons for praising God. In fact, the reasons for praise are one of the distinctives of a hymn. God's "acts of power" are his redeeming acts in history. So the psalm has moved from creation to redemption, the wide arch of salvation history. This is illustrated in the Revelation of John, where the 144,000, who have Christ's and the Father's names written on their foreheads, sing a "new song" that no one else can learn except those who have been redeemed from the earth (Rev. 14:3).

150:3 *Praise him with the sounding of the trumpet.* "The sounding of the trumpet,"[3] among other things, signals the crowning of a new king (2 Sam. 15:10; 1 Kings 1:34, 39, 41; 2 Kings 9:13). It also announces the rule of Yahweh in 47:5 and 98:6, and here, like other terms, conjures up such a scene in the minds of the psalmist and worshipers. Although Yahweh is not mentioned by name in verses 2–5, he is announced with the sound of the trumpet, as Yahweh's appearance is announced in Exodus 19:16 and 19, and he appears in verse 6—it is the coronation.

praise him with the harp and lyre. The "harp" (*nebel*) was a handheld stringed instrument, and the "lyre" (*kinnor*) was probably a small stringed instrument. These were the two instruments the Levites used to accompany the singing of psalms (1 Chron. 15:16; 16:5; 25:6).[4] So we see that after the heavenly King is announced, the Levitical music begins, most probably in the heavenly court, and the music is accompanied by dancing. These images suggest a great festival or a major service of thanksgiving (Ps. 30:11; see also Rev. 19:6–8).

150:4 *praise him with timbrel and dancing.* Here the instruments and dancing allude to the return of the ark to Jerusalem (2 Sam. 6; 1 Chron. 15). In code language the terms of this verse, "timbrel" and "dancing," reflect Yahweh's coming to the sanctuary, or abiding among his people, language that describes David's bringing the ark to Jerusalem (2 Sam. 6:5, 14). "Timbrel" and "dancing" are also mentioned as means of celebrating the crossing of the Red Sea (Exod. 15:20), which calls to mind Yahweh's great act of redemption. The reflective language of this psalm is an example of the conflation of events and ideas in the Psalms. It should bring to mind thoughts of both David's transfer of the ark to Jerusalem and the victory at the Red Sea.

praise him with the strings and pipe. The nature of these two instruments is unknown. The Targum renders the first as "flutes" (*halilin*) and the second as "pipes" (*'abubin*); the latter (*'ugab*) is also found in Genesis 4:21 together with the "lyre" (*kinnor*).

150:5 *praise him with the clash of cymbals, praise him with resounding cymbals.* "Cymbals" are mentioned in Chronicles, but this is the only time they are referred to in the Psalter. They were likely percussion instruments, as our modern cymbals are, and were struck together, giving a clashing sound, which is represented by the word "resounding" (*t⁽e⁾ru'ah*). This final word in the Hebrew of verse 5 is sometimes used to announce war, the religious festivals, or even the day of Yahweh (Zeph. 1:16: "a day of trumpet and *battle cry* [*t⁽e⁾ru'ah*]"). If that is the nuance, then the images of the final day of judgment and salvation herald its arrival, and the worshipers are praising Yahweh for the reality.

150:6 *Let everything that has breath praise the* Lord. "Everything that has breath" refers to human beings, an echo of Genesis 2:7, where God breathes the "breath" of life into Adam. Thus this is a summons to all human flesh to join in the celebration of Yahweh's coronation and reign.

Theological Insights

Zenger insists that Psalm 150 "gives the Psalter an *overall interpretation;* as the closing psalm, it makes the preceding individual psalms a polyphony of praise for and to YHWH, the King of Israel and of the world."[5] We might call it a parable encoded in musical language. In fact, in keeping with the idea that a "new song" marks a momentous event, this may be the "new song" that the psalmist summons Israel to sing (149:1). The musical instruments, by their allusions to certain momentous events in Israel's history, tell the story of redeeming grace: the trumpet announces Yahweh's coronation as King (150:3); timbrel and dancing reveal that Yahweh has entered into his sanctuary, for which all Israel and the world have waited (150:4); and the cymbals announce the long-awaited day of judgment and salvation—justice at last (150:5) (see "Interpretive Insights"). Then all humans who have populated this world, and all who ever will, join their voices to the instrumental praise and sing in unison

Number Symbolism

In later Jewish tradition the study of numbers and their significance (called "gematria") came to prominence as a favorite way to hear and send a coded message in literature. While I have insisted from time to time that certain incipient tendencies in that direction are detectable in the Psalms,[a] Psalm 150 seems to move beyond the incipient stage of this practice and provide a sample of a rather advanced practice. Zenger summarizes these code messages that can be detected in Psalm 150:

1. The imperative "praise" occurs ten times, ten being the number of completion and perfection, which may correspond to the ten "words" (commandments) of the Decalogue and the ten words God spoke in Genesis 1 to create the world.

2. The two framing hallelujahs and the ten occurrences of *hall*e*lu/hall*e*luhu* give us the number twelve, which equals the number of the tribes of Israel. In a symbolic sense, all Is-

rael, past, present, and future, gathers at this moment of time to offer ultimate praise to God.

3. The number of musical instruments listed in the psalm is seven, which is the perfect number, suggesting that this musical offering of praise is the perfect offering.

4. The total number of times the verb praise (*hll*) occurs is thirteen (this includes the jussive verb of verse 6a), which may point to the thirteen attributes found in Exodus 34:6–7 (although Zenger is less convinced about this one).[b]

These data may have implications for dating this psalm, especially if we knew when number symbolism became a conscious and developed instrument of Jewish thought. Even without that knowledge, we can say that the incipient form of the practice already appears elsewhere in the Psalms, and it can be seen in its developing form here.

[a] See the comments on 25:22; "Teaching the Text" in the unit on Psalm 26; "The Text in Context" in the unit on Psalm 47; "Theological Insights" in the unit on Psalm 68; and "Teaching the Text" in the unit on Psalm 89.
[b] Hossfeld and Zenger, *Psalms 3*, 657–58. I am greatly indebted to Zenger for his intriguing interpretation of Psalm 150, an interpretation that reflects the hermeneutical character of the Psalms. See also the sidebar "The Thirteen Attributes of God" in the unit on Psalm 111.

the ultimate and absolute "hallelujah." Psalm 150 crowns the entire book with praise, justifying the Jewish title of the book as the "Book of Praises" (*Seper Tehillim*), and most of all, affirming Yahweh as Lord of all humanity.

Teaching the Text

As we begin our sermon/lesson on Psalm 150, we might compare our study of the Psalms to climbing a mountain, with peaks and crevices that both assist and challenge our ascent. The mountain peak, however, is often in view—representing our entrance into God's presence—even though in some phases of the effort we lose sight of that highest point. Psalm 150 represents the highest peak, and from there we can get a glimpse of the world that no other position would offer. Spurgeon uses the analogy of a river: "The flow of the broad river of the Book of Psalms ends in a cataract of praise."[6]

Developing the message of this psalm will require us to use the same climbing gear and techniques we have acquired along the way. First, the psalm, like all the others in the Hallelujah Psalter, is bounded by the imperative "hallelujah" (NIV: "Praise the LORD"). As an *inclusio*, that gives the content of the poem the tone of praise. This little word that has become part of our universal worship language occurs in only two books of the Bible: the Psalms and the Revelation of John (chap. 19). In Revelation 19 it occurs four times as part of the announcement that the Lord's eternal kingdom has finally become a reality, and John's placement of the term at that juncture is obviously based on his knowledge of the Psalter (see "Additional Insights: The Hallelujahs of Books 4 and 5," following the unit on Ps. 104). As we see in the broad scheme of this collection, the placement of "hallelujah" before and after each psalm symbolically puts all of life and faith in the context of praise. Although lament often charts the path to praise, praise is the proper mode of life and the spiritual engine that propels us to our destination of living in God's presence (see "Theological Insights" in the unit on Ps. 148). And once we have reached our destination, praise is itself the life of God's people. We can make an application by pointing out how praising God for the good things of life and the good people of our world instills an aura of happiness and well-being in our human existence. Also in "Illustrating the Text," note the midrashic story of the creation's recognition that only one thing was missing when creation was finished, and that was the praise of God for his mighty and marvelous works.

Second—and this will be the challenge—the terms of the psalm are coded with language that leads us through the history of the Lord's redemption of his people. Verse 3a, with its "shofar" (NIV: "trumpet"), announces the coronation of Israel's real King (2 Sam. 15:10; 1 Kings 1:34; 2 Kings 9:13; also Pss. 45:1; 149:2), while the "harp and lyre" of verse 3b accompany the glory of the Lord as it fills the temple (2 Chron. 5:12–14); verse 4a, with its "timbrel" and "dancing," signals Yahweh's entry into his sanctuary (Ps. 149:3); the "strings and pipes" of verse 4b signal a great festival (Pss. 96:9; 114:7); the "cymbals" of verse 5 announce the prophetic day of the Lord (Zeph. 1:16); and in verse 6 "everything that has breath," recalling Genesis 2:7, points to the climactic praise of all humanity. This swell of praise by the whole human family puts a universal impression on God's saving work in Israel's history.[7]

We might note that no heavenly beings or nonhuman parts of creation are involved as they are in 148:1–6, only the human family, the crown of God's creation, the object of God's redeeming love. This, of course, illustrates the idea that praise is the real crown of the created order, because the Creator, and only the Creator, is worthy of praise (see "Illustrating the Text"). "To give the least particle of his honour to another is shameful treason; to refuse to render it to him is heartless robbery," says Spurgeon.[8] It would also be quite appropriate to refer to John's declaration about the redeemed church in Revelation 14:3: "No one could learn the song except the 144,000 who had been redeemed from the earth." So when the book of Psalms reaches the pinnacle of praise, we have reached the end of the psalmists' pilgrimage to the sanctuary of God, which is our pilgrimage too, and together we sing the song of the redeemed in the heavenly temple of God's presence. "Hallelujah" is not a fermata of praise, sustaining one eternal note, but it is a symphony of numerous themes, living and manifold, that develop the single theme introduced in the overture of redeeming grace: "Praise the LORD!"

Illustrating the Text

Praise is the crown of the story of redeeming grace.

Story: There is a Jewish legend that says that when God had created humankind, his highest form of creation, he turned to the angels and asked what they thought of the world he had created. They answered, "Only one thing is lacking. It is the sound of praise to the Creator." So "God created music, the voice of birds, the whispering wind, the murmuring ocean, and planted melody in the hearts of men."[9] While we certainly don't believe God forgot anything in the creation, this legend draws our attention to the fact that praise is the crown of the created order. And that is the thrust of Psalm 150. Praise is the crown of the Psalter and the crown of the story of redeeming grace.

The language of praise is incredibly rich.

Language: In the Psalms the praise of God is intended to be the language that expresses who God is and what he has done, and no one word or one language can fully do that. Even when we utilize the full vocabulary of declarative praise, we still have not exhausted God's eternal worth. One English-speaking missionary spoke about his language study, saying that he could say things in Spanish that he could not say in English, and when he had learned the native Guatemalan language of his intended ministry group, he found that he could say things in that language that he could not say in Spanish. And as even the amateur linguist can attest, the story goes on and on and illustrates the capability, as well as the incapability, of human language. That observation can be applied to the language of praise. We mortals cannot yet comprehend how incredibly rich and expressive will be the language of praise when the redeemed church joins its multiple voices—and we may also assume, its multiple "languages"—of praise in the ultimate "hallelujah" of Revelation

19. In fact, one wonders if "hallelujah," the term of ultimate praise, was not an effort on the psalmist's part to serve the climactic purpose of praise in the Psalter. If I may venture in a little gematria (see the sidebar), I note that "hallelujah" (NIV: "Praise the LORD") appears at the beginning and end of Psalm 150, while the verb occurs with other objects ten times, and once with another subject ("everything that has breath," 150:6a), making a total of thirteen occurrences, one short of a double perfect seven. Perhaps our psalmist/editor recognized that this final psalm of praise is still slightly deficient of the ultimate praise of which the Lord is worthy and the history of redeeming grace awaits the eternal moment. Christians would say that the deficit is supplied when heaven and earth combine their voices in the ultimate praise of the Sovereign King of the universe, "Hallelujah! For the Lord our God the Almighty reigns" (Rev. 19:6 ESV).

Notes

Psalm 73

1. See Bullock, *Encountering*, 77–79.
2. Hossfeld and Zenger, *Psalms 2*, 224–26.
3. See Bullock, *Encountering*, 200–212.
4. Using Scott's list of wisdom vocabulary (*Way of Wisdom*, 121–22; also Bullock, *Encountering*, 204), the common wisdom terms are quite replete: "understand" (*bin*, 73:17); "stupid" (*ba'ar*, 73:22; NIV: "senseless"); "to think" (*hshb*, 73:16; NIV: "tried"); "to desire" (*hpts*, 73:25); "to know," "knowledge" (*yd'*, 73:11a; *de'ah*, 73:11b [NIV: "know"]); "to rebuke" (*ykh*, 73:14; NIV: "punishments"); "heart" (*lebab*, 73:7 [NIV: "imaginations"], 13); "trouble" (*'amal*, 73:5; NIV: "burdens"); "counsel" (*'etsah*, 73:24); "wicked" (*r'sha'im*, 73:3).
5. Hossfeld and Zenger, *Psalms 2*, 225–26.
6. Walter Brueggemann and Miller, "Psalm 73," 45–56, esp. 63.
7. For the prophetic elements of the Asaph psalms, see 50:7–15, 17b–23; 75:2–5; 81:6–16; for the historical, see 74:1; 77:20; 78:52; 79:13; 80:1.
8. See Bullock, *Encountering*, 76–79.
9. The rhetorical voice of the Psalms is like the voice of an excellent choir when the individual voices become the corporate voice of the choir. A good choir director will emphasize that it is not the individual voices that should be heard but the sum total of the individual voices that make up the "choral" voice. The titles of the psalms, especially "to/for David," are among the individual voices that blend into the rhetorical voice of the Psalms, as well as the placement of psalms within the book, plus the distinctive and interrelated vocabulary of the psalms. All of these are contributors to the rhetorical voice. The difference between the choir and the

Psalms, however, is that we have to be concerned about two "listenings": the individual voices—which is primary—and then the blend of those voices in order to hear the rhetorical voice.

10. Hakham, *Psalms*, 2:130.
11. Hakham, *Psalms*, 2:130n4.
12. Anderson, *Psalms 73–150*, 533–34.
13. Hakham, *Psalms*, 2:137.
14. In private correspondence John Walton suggests that the word "glory" is an adverb rather than a noun. In this case it would refer to an anticipated acquittal by God (*lqh*) "honorably" (see 18:16, where the verb "took" [*lqh*] is used similarly). The following question, "Whom have I in heaven but you?" (73:25a), sounds very much like Job's contention that he had a "witness . . . in heaven" (Job 16:19).
15. Anderson, *Psalms 73–150*, 535–36. See also von Rad's statement on the afterlife in *Old Testament Theology*, 406–7.
16. Anderson, *Psalms 73–150*, 529.
17. Gregory the Great, *Pastoral Care*, 114–15.
18. Lewis, *Letters to an American Lady*, 22.

Psalm 74

1. Hossfeld and Zenger, *Psalms 2*, 250.
2. Hossfeld and Zenger, *Psalms 2*, 242.
3. For instance, Hilber, "Psalms," 380.
4. Hakham, *Psalms*, 1:242.
5. Kraus, *Psalms 1–59*, 25; Bullock, *Encountering*, 28.
6. Hilber, "Psalms," 244.
7. Hossfeld and Zenger, *Psalms 2*, 244 (and n. 12); see Psalms 44:9, 23 (44:10, 24 MT); 60:1, 10 (60:3, 12) (60:10 [60:12] =108:11 [108:12]); 77:7 (77:8); 89:38 (89:39); Lamentations 2:7; 3:17, 31.

8. Israel as the sheep of God's pasture is also found in Psalms 79:13; 95:7; 100:3; Jeremiah 23:1; Ezekiel 34:31.

9. Hakham, *Psalms*, 2:145.

10. Anderson, *Psalms 73–150*, 539.

11. Hakham, *Psalms*, 2:148.

12. See Bullock, *Encountering*, 77–79.

13. Hossfeld and Zenger, *Psalms 2*, 247.

14. In Hebrew the pronoun is already incorporated in the verb form, so the preceding pronoun is for emphasis, like our English "you *yourself* heard."

15. Hakham, *Psalms*, 2:150.

16. Hilber, "Psalms," 381–83.

17. Hossfeld and Zenger, *Psalms 2*, 249.

18. See 25:11; 31:3; 44:22; 106:8; 109:21; 143:11.

19. Goldingay, *Psalms*, 2:436.

20. C. J. H. Wright, *God I Don't Understand*, 50–51.

21. Selderhuis, *John Calvin*, 162.

22. Wolpe, *Healer of Shattered Hearts*, 158.

Psalm 75

1. See Goldingay, *Psalms*, 2:440, for a comparison of Hannah's Song and Psalm 75.

2. Hilber, "Psalms," 383.

3. Hakham, *Psalms*, 2:158.

4. Anderson, *Psalms 1–72*, 107.

5. Anderson, *Psalms 73–150*, 549.

6. The verb "established" (root *tkn*) is a variant of the Hebrew verb *kun*. It also means "to measure" (Isa. 40:12; NIV: "marked off") (Hakham, *Psalms*, 2:159).

7. The ESV has rendered the final word of the sentence as "lifting up" (Hiphil infinitive) and made that the subject ("mountains" and "lifting up" are the same form in Hebrew, *harim*; 75:7 MT). A preferable way to deal with this problem is to take the word "desert" (*midbar*) as an absolute rather than a construct form, as some Hebrew manuscripts do, leaving the final word to be read as "mountains" (LXX [74:7] has "desert mountains," *erēmōn oreōn*). The term "mountain" (*harim*) is a wordplay on the verb "lift up" (75:4, 5 [75:5, 6 MT], *tarimu*; 75:7 [75:8], *yarim*). The result would be a reference to the four directions, from which arrogance should not come, translating the conjunction (*ki*), following a negative clause, as "on the contrary/but." That is also appropriate for all three occurrences of this word at the beginning of verses 6, 7, and 8 (vv. 7, 8, 9 MT).

8. Quoted in Bainton, *Here I Stand*, 48.

9. Lewis, *Mere Christianity*, 33–34.

10. Littell, *German Phoenix*, xv.

Psalm 76

1. Tate, *Psalms 51–100*, 263.

2. Goldingay, *Psalms*, 2:449.

3. Hakham, *Psalms*, 2:165.

4. Calvin, *Psalms*, 2:201.

5. Goldingay, *Psalms*, 2:454–55.

6. Spurgeon, *Treasury of David*, 2:304.

7. Note that Joel 3:10 is a reversal of Isaiah's picture of peace (Isa. 2:4).

8. Augustine's description of evil as the absence of good may provide an analogy, for in a metaphorical sense we can look at darkness as an absence of light (Gen. 1:1–5), and God is totally light, and "in him there is no darkness at all" (1 John 1:5). In the words of Psalm 139, "darkness is as light to you" (139:12). The evidence for this divine attribute is God's majesty that outstrips that of nature, and his way of putting the warring human spirit to rest (Ps. 76:4–6). We might make the point that Christianity, despite the international strife it has too often experienced, and sometimes even created (God have mercy on us!), is still the religion of the Prince of Peace (Luke 2:14; cf. Isa. 9:6), and that should affect our conduct both personally as believers and internationally as a nation of the world.

9. George MacDonald, *Thomas Wingfold, Curate*, 3:247.

10. Potok, *The Chosen*, 249.

Psalm 77

1. Tate, *Psalms 51–100*, 271.

2. On the compositional arc, see "The Text in Context" in the unit on Psalm 74.

3. Ezekiel ruminated about this matter and recorded the reactions of the community (Ezek. 18:2, 25; 33:10, 17, 20; see also Zech. 1:2–6).

4. Hakham (*Psalms*, 1:306 [and n. 1]) mentions favorably the proposal that "Jeduthun" is a musical instrument named after the family of Jeduthun that either made it or played it.

5. Hakham, *Psalms*, 2:173.

6. J. Kselman believes verses 8–9 are a commentary on Exodus 34:6 (cited by Tate, *Psalms 51–100*, 273). For Exodus 34:6, see also Psalms 86:15; 103:8–12; 145:8. For a comparison of the literary similarities between 77:16–19 and Exodus 15:11–13, see Jefferson, "Psalm LXXVII."

7. Wallace, *Ben-Hur*, 325.

8. Miller, "On Rejoicing in God," 177.

9. George MacDonald, *Princess and the Goblin*, ch. 22.

10. Bunyan, *Grace Abounding*, §202.

Psalm 78

1. Weiser, *Psalms*, 538.

2. For a detailed comparison of Psalms 77–79 and their interrelationships and the position of Psalm 78 in the Asaph collection, see Hossfeld and Zenger, *Psalms 2*, 293–94.

3. E.g., Anderson, *Psalms 73–150*, 568.

4. Goldingay, *Psalms*, 2:499.

5. Wilcock, *Psalms 73–150*, 28.

6. The use of the divine name is, as a rule, determined by the context, and sometimes the writer chooses to use a substitute name (*'adonay*) so as not

to associate the covenant name with a subject that seems either inappropriate of Yahweh or disrespectful of Yahweh. Perhaps the common noun for God used in verse 65,'*adonay* ("Lord"), rather than the tetragrammaton (*YHWH*, "LORD"), is in deference to the violent actions used to describe God's reaction. The tetragrammaton, in fact, occurs only twice in the psalm (78:4 and 21), the second occurrence also in a context of God's anger, but certainly not so radical as the metaphor of verse 65.

7. See Davidson, *Vitality of Worship*, 254.

8. Weiser, *Psalms*, 543.

9. For further thoughts on God's self-humiliation, see "Theological Insights" in the unit on Psalm 108; "Teaching the Text" in the unit on Psalm 24; and "Illustrating the Text" in the unit on Psalm 134.

10. Lewis, *Magician's Nephew*, 121.

11. Chesterton, *Orthodoxy*, 137–38.

12. Weiser, *Psalms*, 542.

13. George MacDonald, *Maiden's Bequest*, 125.

Psalm 79

1. Hossfeld and Zenger, *Psalms 2*, 303.

2. Jeremiah gives the number 3,023, while 2 Kings 24:14 gives 10,000. Jeremiah's figure may not have included women and children, while the Kings account seems to be limited to officers, soldiers, skilled workers, and artisans.

3. Tate, *Psalms 51–100*, 299.

4. Thielicke, *I Believe*, 116.

5. C. J. H. Wright, *God I Don't Understand*, 50–51 (emphasis in original).

6. Newton, *Select Letters*, xii.

7. Dr. M. A. C. Warren, quoted in C. F. D. Moule, *Meaning of Hope*, 11.

Psalm 80

1. The idea was proposed by earlier scholars (e.g., Delitzsch, *Psalms*, 2:438) but developed more fully by Otto Eissfeldt, "Psalm 80," 78. Supporting this date is the idea that Benjamin seems to have been wholly occupied by the northern kingdom only during the Syro-Ephraimite War (Hosea 5:8), implied here by the position of "Benjamin" between the two entities of the northern kingdom, "Ephraim and Manasseh" (Ps. 80:2).

2. The image of God's smoking anger also appears in Psalm 74:1 and Lamentations 3:44 (in the latter verse God covers himself with a "cloud" rather than "smoke").

3. See Hakham, *Psalms*, 2:226. Tate renders the phrase "tears by the keg" (Tate, *Psalms 51–100*, 304).

4. The conjunction before the verb "pluck" is conjunctive and implies a continuous activity by passersby (Hakham, *Psalms*, 2:229).

5. C. H. Dodd associates the subject of the psalm with corporate Israel and proposes that God's "man at your right hand" and the "son of man" whom God strengthens (80:17) may provide

justification for the fusion of the two figures in Mark 14:62 (*According to the Scriptures*, 101–2). Also Hill, "Son of Man," gives a persuasive argument for a messianic interpretation of verse 17.

6. Weiser, *Psalms*, 550.

7. Weiser, *Psalms*, 550.

8. Mauriac, foreword to *Night*, x–xi.

9. Augustine, *Confessions*, 146–47.

10. George MacDonald, *Vicar's Daughter*, 530.

Psalm 81

1. Gerstenberger, *Psalms, Part 2*, 108.

2. In the Jewish tradition, the psalms for each day are:

First day	Psalm 24	Creation of the world
Second day	Psalm 48	Mount of God
Third day	Psalm 82	God's judgment of the world and reward and punishment
Fourth day	Psalm 94	God's judgment of the world and reward and punishment
Fifth day	Psalm 81	God's judgment of the world and reward and punishment
Sixth day	Psalm 93	End of days
Seventh day	Psalm 92	End of days

The list is given in the Mishnah (*Tamid* 7.4). The summaries are Hakham's (*Psalms*, 2:245).

3. See *m. Rosh Hashanah* 33b–34a.

4. The fact that "language" (*s⁰pat*) is in a construct form would suggest that an absolute noun, rather than a clause, would follow. Even though a bit unusual, we do have another example in Isaiah 29:1 (ESV): "the city [*qiryat*] where David encamped." See Hakham, *Psalms*, 2:237.

5. Tate, *Psalms 51–100*, 319–20.

6. Schaefer, *Psalms*, 200.

7. Schaefer, *Psalms*, 201.

8. Kennedy, *For Preachers*, 26.

9. Chesterton, *Orthodoxy*, 95.

Psalm 82

1. *ANET*, 68; Pope, *El in the Ugaritic Texts*, 47–49.

2. Hossfeld and Zenger, *Psalms 2*, 334.

3. Hebrew incorporates the personal pronoun in the verb form itself so that the personal pronoun is not necessary (although not completely analogous, compare our English imperative in which the subject is implied, e.g., "go!" [you]), but when added often signals an emphatic meaning, as here: "I *myself* thought."

4. Psalms 50:14; 73:11; 77:10; 78:35, 56; 82:6; 83:18.

5. Becky Schlikerman, "Quadriplegic Immigrant Dies after Chicago-Area Hospital Returned Home to Mexico," Chicago Tribune, January 4, 2012, http://www.chicagotribune.com/lifestyles/health/ct-met-quelino-death-20120104-story.html.

6. Barnhouse, *Let Me Illustrate*, 177–80.

Additional Insights, pp. 81–82

1. See Wilson's discussion of "Henotheism and Monotheism" (Wilson, *Psalms*, 1:507–9).

2. Ross, *Commentary on the Psalms*, 2:718–19.

Psalm 83

1. See Goldingay, *Psalms*, 2:574, for thematic parallels.

2. Hossfeld and Zenger, *Psalms 2*, 345.

3. This is an adaptation of Goldingay's outline, *Psalms*, 2:572–73.

4. Hakham, *Psalms*, 2:254.

5. Hakham, *Psalms*, 2:256.

6. Hakham, *Psalms*, 2:258.

7. Reardon, *Christ in the Psalms*, 164.

8. Reardon, *Christ in the Psalms*, 164.

9. Hossfeld and Zenger, *Psalms 2*, 346.

10. Hossfeld and Zenger, *Psalms 2*, 346.

11. Quoted in Bouwsma, *John Calvin*, 89.

Psalm 84

1. Spurgeon, *Treasury of David*, 2:432.

2. Wilcock, *Psalms 73–150*, 47.

3. Hilber, "Psalms," 390.

4. Hakham, *Psalms*, 2:265.

5. Kidner, *Psalms 73–150*, 304.

6. Hakham, *Psalms*, 2:268.

7. Kidner, *Psalms 73–150*, 303.

8. N. T. Wright, *Case for the Psalms*, 91.

9. Chesterton, *Orthodoxy*, 72.

10. Spurgeon, *Treasury of David*, 2:432.

11. Prothero, *Psalms in Human Life*, 59–61.

12. N. T. Wright, *Case for the Psalms*, 178–79.

Psalm 85

1. Hilber, "Psalms," 393.

2. Kidner, *Psalms 73–150*, 308.

3. There are many excellent word studies. Among those that are based on the Hebrew text is Jenni and Westermann, eds., *Theological Lexicon of the Old Testament*, and Prévost, *Short Dictionary of the Psalms*; also dictionaries, such as Longman and Enns, eds., *Dictionary of the Old Testament*, and Ryken, Wilhoit, and Longman, eds., *Dictionary of Biblical Imagery*.

4. Quoted in Bainton, *Here I Stand*, 178.

Psalm 86

1. Hossfeld and Zenger, *Psalms 2*, 370–71.

2. Schaefer, *Psalms*, 212.

3. Brueggemann, *Message of the Psalms*, 62.

4. Kidner, *Psalms 73–150*, 312.

5. Schaefer, *Psalms*, 212.

6. Augustine, *Confessions* 7.7.

7. Bunyan, *Pilgrim's Progress*, § 246.

8. Sandburg, *Abraham Lincoln*, 434.

Additional Insights, p. 111

1. Wilson, *Hebrew Psalter*, 211.

2. Hossfeld and Zenger, *Psalms 2*, 369, 371.

Psalm 87

1. Waltner, *Psalms*, 424.

2. Hossfeld and Zenger, *Psalms 2*, 386–87.

3. Hilber, "Psalms," 395.

4. Hakham, *Psalms*, 2:298.

5. Delitzsch, *Psalms*, 2:21.

6. These three points are from Maclaren, *Psalms*, 1:474–75.

7. Augustine, *City of God* 11.1; see also 10.7.

8. Wilcock, *Psalms 73–150*, 58–59.

Psalm 88

1. Schaefer, *Psalms*, 216.

2. Hossfeld and Zenger, *Psalms 2*, 394.

3. Wilcock, *Psalms 73–150*, 63.

4. Wilcock, *Psalms 73–150*, 60–61.

5. Reardon, *Christ in the Psalms*, 174.

6. Anderson, *Psalms 73–150*, 628.

7. See Gruber's translation of Rashi's commentary on the Psalms, 88:4.

8. Koehler and Baumgartner, *Lexicon*, 2:1443.

9. Lewis, *Letters to an American Lady*, 81.

Psalm 89

1. Kidner, *Psalms 73–150*, 319.

2. See "The Structure and Composition of the Psalter" in the introduction in vol. 1; "The Text in Context" in the unit on Psalm 2; and the sidebar "The Editing of Book 2" in the unit on Psalm 70.

3. Hakham, *Psalms*, 2:314.

4. Hakham, *Psalms*, 2:314.

5. Hossfeld and Zenger, *Psalms 2*, 405–6.

6. In fact, the combination of *hesed* and *'emet* (or its synomyn *'emunah* or *ne'emenet*) occurs seven times in the psalm (89:1, 2, 14, 24, 28, 33, 49 [89:2, 3, 15, 25, 29, 34, 50]), perhaps as a hint at God's oath (*sheba'*, "seven," is related to the word *sh'bu'ah*, "oath"). See Hakham, *Psalms*, 2:342n66c.

7. Kidner, *Psalms 73–150*, 319.

Psalm 90

1. VanGemeren, "Psalms," 687–88.

2. Hakham, *Psalms*, 2:345.

3. Hossfeld and Zenger, *Psalms 2*, 422.

4. Anderson, *Psalms 73–150*, 652.

5. The NIV evidently understands the word "their length" (*rahbam*) as "their best" or "the best of them" (*rabam*, see the critical note in Stutt-

gartensia on 90:10). However, "their length" makes good sense; it seems to fit the sense of the verse, and it also avoids amending the text.

6. Weiser, *Psalms*, 601.

7. Weiser, *Psalms*, 600.

8. Lewis, *Weight of Glory*, 26.

Psalm 91

1. Hossfeld and Zenger, *Psalms 2*, 429.

2. Stec suggests a date between the fourth and sixth centuries AD (*Targum of the Psalms*, preface).

3. VanGemeren, "Psalms," 696; see also his reflection "The Ways of Wisdom and Folly," in "Psalms," 84–89.

4. Hossfeld and Zenger, *Psalms 2*, 430.

5. Schaefer, *Psalms*, 228.

6. Hilber, "Psalms," 399.

7. Marvin E. Tate (*Psalms 51–100*, 446, 448–49) has proposed a similar solution.

8. Edman, *Not Somehow, but Triumphantly!*, preface.

9. Edman himself mentions some of these in the introduction to his book *Not Somehow, but Triumphantly!*

Psalm 92

1. Also Bullock, *Encountering*, 152–63.

2. Hossfeld and Zenger, *Psalms 3*, 461.

3. Weiser, *Psalms*, 615.

4. Rockness, *Passion for the Impossible*, 83; Trotter's quote of Ruskin's words.

5. Quoted in Rockness, *Passion for the Impossible*, 84.

6. Quoted in Rockness, *Passion for the Impossible*, 88.

7. Quoted in Rockness, *Passion for the Impossible*, 154–55.

8. Poling, *Faith Is Power*, 81–88, quote on 82.

Psalm 93

1. Tate, *Psalms 51–100*, 474.

2. Tate, *Psalms 51–100*, 479. Howard gives a tenth-century date, while Tate simply dates it preexilic. I would prefer an exilic date close to the time of Psalm 89, although the psalm could be preexilic and the editor of Book 4 has adapted it to the times and the tragedy of the Babylonian exile.

3. Howard, *Structure of Psalms 93–100*, 48–55.

4. Goldingay, *Psalms*, 3:66, 67.

5. See also Robertson's helpful discussion of *YHWH malak* in *Flow of the Psalms*, 153–54n12.

6. Spurgeon, *Treasury of David*, 3:134 (on Ps. 93).

7. Tate, *Psalms 51–100*, 477.

8. Delitzsch, *Psalms*, 3:75–76.

9. See Bullock, *Encountering*, 190–95.

10. Calvin, *Psalms*, 4:47; Delitzsch, *Psalms*, 3:34.

11. See Silverman, *Rabbinic Stories*, 73–76.

12. Stoddart, *Psalms for Every Day*, 230–31, quoting from the *British Weekly*, January 12, 1939.

13. Kuyper, "Sphere Sovereignty," 26.

Psalm 94

1. Tate, *Psalms 51–100*, 477, cites two papers read by David M. Howard Jr. at the Evangelical Theological Society, San Diego, CA, November 16, 1989: "Psalms 93–94" and "Psalms 90–94 and the Editing of the Psalter."

2. Anderson, *Psalms 73–150*, 671.

3. Hossfeld and Zenger, *Psalms 2*, 454.

4. Hossfeld and Zenger, *Psalms 2*, 390.

5. Waltner, *Psalms*, 459.

Psalm 95

1. Goldingay, *Psalms*, 3:93.

2. Waltner, *Psalms*, 465.

3. *Venite, exultemus Domino*, in The Book of Common Prayer (1789).

Psalm 96

1. Wilcock, *Psalms 73–150*, 96.

2. Hakham, *Psalms*, 2:405.

3. Calvin, *Psalms*, 4:55.

4. Calvin, *Psalms*, 4:55.

5. Sandburg, *Abraham Lincoln*, 247–48.

6. Introduction, in Newton, *Select Letters*, vii.

Psalm 97

1. Tate, *Psalms 51–100*, 520.

2. Hakham, *Psalms*, 2:416.

3. Hakham, *Psalms*, 2:416.

4. Calvin, *Psalms*, 4:68.

5. Weiser, *Psalms*, 635.

6. Chesterton, *Orthodoxy*, 160.

7. Calvin, *Psalms*, 4:60.

8. Lewis, *Psalms*, 56. In his poem "Ode to Duty," Wordsworth says to Duty:

Stern Lawgiver! yet thou dost wear
The Godhead's most benignant grace;
Nor know we anything so fair
As is the smile upon thy face.

9. Calvin, *Psalms*, 4:60.

10. Quoted in William, *Gospel of Luke*, 186.

11. George MacDonald, *Paul Faber, Surgeon*, chap. 5.

Psalm 98

1. Reardon, *Christ in the Psalms*, 193.

2. Goldingay, *Psalms*, 3:123–24.

3. Waltner, *Psalms*, 479.

4. Quoted in Rockness, *Passion for the Impossible*, 18.

Psalm 99

1. Delitzsch, *Psalms*, 4:99.
2. Kraus, *Psalms 60–150*, 268–69.
3. See Delitzsch's discussion and translation, *Psalms*, 4:98, 100.
4. Hossfeld and Zenger, *Psalms 2*, 491.
5. Another example of the use of an older formula as an instrument of renewal is the covenant formula ("I will be your God, and you will be my people, and I will dwell in your midst"). See the sidebar "The Covenant Formula" in the unit on Psalm 79.
6. See Ross, *Holiness to the LORD*, 351–57.
7. Otto, *Idea of the Holy*, 56–57.
8. Luther, *Lectures on Romans*, 38, quoting Augustine, *City of God* 4.4.
9. Wolpe, *Healer of Shattered Hearts*, 19.

Psalm 100

1. See Zenger's reasons for this conclusion in Hossfeld and Zenger, *Psalms 2*, 494–95.
2. An excellent resource on the English Reformation is Hughes, *Theology of the English Reformers*.
3. Otto, *Idea of the Holy*, xiii, n. 1.
4. Patterson, *God's Prayer Book*, 239.

Additional Insights, pp. 212–13

1. Hossfeld and Zenger, *Psalms 2*, 496.

Psalm 101

1. Mays, *Psalms*, 321. Mays gives no citation in Luther's writings, but the closest statement I have been able to find is on Luther's commentary on Psalm 101: "There David, who was a king and had to keep servants at his court, cites himself as an example of the way a pious king or prince should treat his personnel" (*Luther's Works*, 13:147).
2. See Hilber, "Psalms," 406–7.
3. Hakham, *Psalms*, 3:2.
4. Kraus, *Psalms 60–150*, 279.
5. Hakham, *Psalms*, 3:5.
6. Waltner, *Psalms*, 491.
7. Mays, *Psalms*, 322.
8. C. J. H. Wright, *Old Testament Ethics*, 38–42.
9. Mays, *Psalms*, 322. See also Glen Tinder's stimulating article "Can We Be Good without God?"
10. Quoted in Horton, *Putting Amazing Back into Grace*, 14.
11. This story comes from my own "folk lore" memory, and I have not found the written source, even though I have looked through the delightful book about Brother Bryan of Birmingham, *Religion in Shoes* by Hunter Blakely.
12. Delitzsch, *Psalms*, 4:107.

Psalm 102

1. Hakham, *Psalms*, 3:21.
2. Hakham, *Psalms*, 3:8n2b.
3. Hakham, *Psalms*, 3:11.
4. Anderson, *Psalms 73–150*, 706–7.
5. The response of the nations to Israel's miraculous return from exile is a frequent theme in Isaiah 40–55: see 41:5; 42:4, 10–13; 43:9–13; 45:5–6, 22–23; 49:6–7, 22–23; 51:4–5; 52:15; 55:4–5.
6. Twain, *Innocents Abroad*, 337.
7. Kuitert, *I Have My Doubts*, 97.

Psalm 103

1. Weiser, *Psalms*, 657.
2. Kidner, *Psalms 73–150*, 364.
3. Waltner, *Psalms*, 497.
4. E.g., Waltner, *Psalms*, 498.
5. See the editor's note in Calvin, *Psalms*, 4:129–30n2.
6. Calvin, *Psalms*, 4:126.
7. Perowne, *Psalms*, 2:226.
8. Hakham, *Psalms*, 3:23.
9. Delitzsch, *Psalms*, 3:120.
10. Delitzsch, *Psalms*, 3:121.
11. In regard to the older Aramaic possessive word endings found in verses 3–5, 2 Kings 4:1–7 shares the same pattern endings, but in the Kings text the Masoretes have supplied the later Hebrew pronominal endings in the margin, while here in verses 3–5 they are the longer forms unchanged.
Perowne does not believe the Kings passage points in the direction of a late date for the psalm, and he refers to the same phenomenon in Psalms 116:7, 19; 135:9; 137:6; and Jeremiah 11:15, observing that these forms do not occur in the David psalms but likely come from a time when Aramaic was influencing the language (Perowne, *Psalms*, 2:225). The logical time, of course, would be the Babylonian exile, when the exiles most likely began speaking Aramaic as a second language, if not a first.
12. Kidner, *Psalms 73–150*, 366.
13. For 103:14a, see Job 11:11 and 28:23; for 103:14b, see Job 7:7; Psalms 78:39; 89:48. For 103:16b, see Job 7:10.
14. Kidner, *Psalms 73–150*, 367.
15. Delitzsch's explanation for "mighty ones" (*gibbore-koah*) is that "they are called *gibborim* [Heb.] as in Joel iv. [iii.] 11, and in fact *gibbore-koah* [Heb.], as the strong to whom belongs strength unequalled. Their life endowed with heroic strength is spent entirely—an example for mortals—in an obedient execution of the word of God" (Delitzsch, *Psalms*, 3:124).
16. Perowne, *Psalms*, 2:229.
17. Waltner, *Psalms*, 498.
18. Von Rad, *Old Testament Theology*, 1:369–70.
19. Osbeck, *Amazing Grace*, 332.

Psalm 104

1. See Hilber, "Psalms," 393, 409.
2. Hossfeld and Zenger, *Psalms 3*, 58.
3. Hakham, *Psalms*, 3:45.
4. Delitzsch, *Psalms*, 4:136.
5. Calvin, *Psalms*, 4:146.
6. Perowne, *Psalms*, 2:233.
7. Perowne, *Psalms*, 2:233.
8. Selderhuis, *John Calvin*, 129.
9. Entry from Oct. 27, 1923, quoted in Rockness, *Passion for the Impossible*, 297. See also Rockness's chapter "With All Our Helplessness (1925–1926)," in *Passion for the Impossible*, 298–310.

Additional Insights, pp. 245–47

1. *Yah*, the shortened form of *YHWH*, occurs for the first time in the Hebrew Bible in the Song of the Sea (Exod. 15:2; also 17:16), celebrating Israel's victory at the Red Sea, and the song concludes with the declaration "The LORD reigns for ever and ever" (Exod. 15:18), reminding us of the kingship of Yahweh psalms.
2. Eric Zenger, "The Function of the 'Hallelujahs' in the Redaction of the Psalter," in Hossfeld and Zenger, *Psalms 3*, 39–41. Note also his table of their distribution on p. 40.
3. The pattern of "hallelujah" in Psalms 104–18 does not warrant the Septuagint displacement of "hallelujah" from the end of Psalm 104 to the beginning of Psalm 105.
4. Robertson, *Flow of the Psalms*, 197.

Psalm 105

1. Kraus, *Psalms 60–150*, 308; see also "The Anatomy of Praise" in the introduction in vol. 1.
2. See "Encountering Theology and History in the Psalms," in Bullock, *Encountering*, 100–118.
3. See Hossfeld and Zenger, *Psalms 3*, 75, citing Gosse, "Le quatrième livre," 249.
4. Hossfeld and Zenger, *Psalms 3*, 75–76.
5. This is an adaptation of Hakham's outline, *Psalms*, 3:54.
6. Wilcock, *Psalms 73–150*, 129.
7. Kraus, *Psalms 60–150*, 311.
8. Ross, *Psalms*, 3:269.
9. Allen, *Psalms 101–150*, 41. See also Kraus, *Psalms 60–150*, 309.
10. Weiser, *Psalms*, 675.
11. Westminster Shorter Catechism, Q & A 11.
12. Waltner, *Psalms*, 511.
13. Allen, *Psalms 101–150*, 43.
14. Augustine, *Confessions* 7.10.
15. Pollock, *Moody*, 17.
16. Weiser, *Psalms*, 424.

Psalm 106

1. The seven sins of the wilderness generation are (1) rebellion at the Red Sea (106:7–12), (2) demand for meat (106:13–15), (3) the Levitical rebellion of Dathan and Abiram (106:16–18), (4) the golden calf (106:19–23), (5) refusal to enter the promised land (106:24–27), (6) apostasy at Baal of Peor (106:28–31), and (7) testing God at Meribah (106:32–33).
2. See "The Text in Context" in the unit on Psalm 105. Here we have a study in the history of the text illustrated outside the Psalter, rather than inside, as is the case with Psalms 14 and 53 (see table 1 in the unit on Ps. 53).
3. Hossfeld and Zenger, *Psalms 3*, 87.
4. Anderson, *Psalms 73–150*, 738.
5. The term "Red Sea" (which translates the Heb. *yam sup*, "sea of reeds," perhaps papyrus reeds) comes from the Septuagint translation (*erythra thalassa*) of the Hebrew term, and the Septuagint was followed by the Vulgate (Latin) and by most English translations. While the term is used of a wide range of locations, including the Gulf of Aqaba (1 Kings 9:26–28), generally it is understood to designate an area in the delta (e.g., the Bitter Lakes) where the Israelites crossed "the sea" (Exod. 15:4). See Hoerth, *Archaeology*, 167–68; Kitchen, *On the Reliability*, 261–63; D. Matthew Smith, "Red Sea, Reed Sea," *NIDB* 4:750–51.
6. See also 2 Kings 16:3; 17:17; Jeremiah 7:30–32; Ezekiel 20:31. Shanks ("Human Sacrifice") raises the question whether human sacrifices in the Bible were of infants or more mature persons (Isaac is called a "lad" [*na'ar*], likely a teenager, Gen. 22:5).
7. Hodge, *Systematic Theology*, 1:537, quoted in Whyte, *Shorter Catechism*, 20.
8. *Starck's Prayer Book*.
9. Charles Williams, a British journalist and theologian, says of the church: "There are always three degrees of consciousness, all infinitely divisible: (1) the old self on the old way; (2) the old self on the new way; (3) the new self on the new way. The second group is the largest, at all times and in all places" (*He Came Down*, 119).

Psalm 107

1. Hossfeld and Zenger, *Psalms 3*, 101.
2. Schaefer, *Psalms*, 267.
3. Waltner, *Psalms*, 527.
4. Hossfeld and Zenger, *Psalms 3*, 105.
5. See Zenger for the intertextual references in Job (Hossfeld and Zenger, *Psalms 3*, 106).
6. Fortified ancient cities generally had two sets of gates, normally made of wood but covered or barred with bronze plates (Hossfeld and Zenger, *Psalms 3*, 106).
7. Hossfeld and Zenger, *Psalms 3*, 105.
8. Waltner, *Psalms*, 524.
9. Hossfeld and Zenger, *Psalms 3*, 105.
10. *Works of the Rev. John Newton*, 1:99.

11. The Carthusians are a Catholic order of monks and nuns that was established in Chartruse, France, by Saint Bruno in AD 1084.

12. Bainton, *Here I Stand*, 181.

Psalm 108

1. Jenkins, "Retribution in the Canonical Psalter," 42.

2. Haplography (writing once) is the omission of a double letter, word, phrase, or line by error. The Greek (LXX) and Syriac both restore the double occurrence of the clause, "My heart is steadfast," thus suggesting that either they had a manuscript that included both, as in 57:7, or they realized it had been omitted inadvertently, so they corrected the text.

3. Kirkpatrick, *Psalms*, 647.

4. Pagolu, *Religion of the Patriarchs*, 54.

5. Augustine, *Confessions*, 155.

6. Calvin, *Institutes of the Christian Religion* 2.2.11 (1:268–69).

Psalm 109

1. See Hossfeld and Zenger, *Psalms 3*, 128.

2. Zenger (Hossfeld and Zenger, *Psalms 3*, 128) gives this scheme for a petition:

opening petition (109:1, "do not remain silent"), with reason for it;
central petition (109:21, "deliver me"), with reason for it;
renewed petition (109:26, "save me"), with reason for it;
assurance of being heard in the form of a vow (109:30, "I will greatly extol").

3. Waltner, *Psalms*, 530.

4. E.g., Hossfeld and Zenger, *Psalms 3*, 129–30; Kraus, *Psalms 60–150*, 330; Goldingay, *Psalms*, 3:279–84.

5. With slight changes, this is Waltner's outline (*Psalms*, 531).

6. Psalms 108–10; 122; 124; 131; 133; and 138–45 are all Davidic psalms.

7. Hakham, *Psalms*, 3:123.

8. Kraus, *Psalms 60–150*, 340.

9. Beale and Carson, eds., *Use of the Old Testament*, 530.

10. Hakham, *Psalms*, 3:124.

11. Hakham, *Psalms*, 3:130.

12. Wolpe, *Healer of Shattered Hearts*, 21.

13. Wolpe, *Healer of Shattered Hearts*, 30.

Additional Insights, pp. 290–91

1. Jenkins, "Retribution in the Canonical Psalter," ch. 5, p. 23.

2. See endnote 9 in the unit on Psalm 34; "The Text in Context" in the unit on Psalm 41; and the sidebar "The Editing of Book 2" in the unit on Psalm 70.

Psalm 110

1. See "Additional Insights: Messianic Psalms," following the unit on Psalm 8.

2. Hakham, *Psalms*, 3:134.

3. "Your troops will be willing" (*nᵉdabot*) is a verbless clause (lit., "your people [are] offerings"), a grammatical equivalent of "I am prayer" (NIV: "I am a man of prayer") in 109:4.

4. See Ross, *Psalms*, 3:350–53.

5. Reardon, *Christ in the Psalms*, 217.

6. Reardon, *Christ in the Psalms*, 218.

7. Lewis, *Letters to an American Lady*, 20.

Psalm 111

1. See the sidebar "The Alphabetic Acrostic Psalms" in the unit on Psalm 25.

2. Hossfeld and Zenger, *Psalms 3*, 162.

3. Hossfeld and Zenger, *Psalms 3*, 170–72.

4. The noun "precepts" does not occur in 111:10b but has its referent in "all who do *them*" (NIV: "all who follow his precepts"), thus completing the *inclusio*.

5. See the sidebar "Psalms of Thanksgiving" in the unit on Psalms 9–10; "Teaching the Text" in the unit on Psalm 100; and the comments on 106:1.

6. Hossfeld and Zenger, *Psalms 3*, 166.

7. Hossfeld and Zenger, *Psalms 3*, 164.

8. Hossfeld and Zenger, *Psalms 3*, 164.

9. Silverman, *Rabbinic Stories*, 127–28.

Psalm 112

1. Goldingay, *Psalms*, 3:309.

2. Wilcock, *Psalms 73–150*, 172.

3. Hossfeld and Zenger, *Psalms 3*, 183.

4. Hakham, *Psalms*, 3:150.

5. Verse 9 begins with two finite verbs, a verbal hendiadys (*pizzar*, "he scatters freely," and *natan*, "he gives/distributes"), and the first verb modifies the second, "he freely distributes." See Ross, *Introducing Biblical Hebrew*, 409.

6. Wenham, *Psalms as Torah*, 161; see also his helpful discussion of this topic on pp. 158–65.

7. George MacDonald, *What's Mine's Mine*, vol. 1, chap. 5.

8. This was an occasion when Lewis was out of town and could not answer his American friend's letter, so his wife, Joy Davidman, answered on his behalf (Lewis, *Letters to an American Lady*, 73).

9. Williams, *He Came Down*, 89.

10. O'Connor, *Prayer Journal*, 3.

Psalm 113

1. Kirkpatrick, *Psalms*, 677.

2. Psalms 41:13 (41:14 MT), *mehaʿolam wᵉʿad haʿolam*; 72:19, *lᵉʿolam*; 89:52 (89:53), *lᵉʿolam*; 106:48, *min-haʿolam wᵉʿad haʿolam*; 145:21, *lᵉʿolam waʿed*. Note *ʿolam* ("forever" or "everlasting") occurs in all instances.

3. Kirkpatrick, *Psalms*, 678.

4. Kirkpatrick, *Psalms*, 679.

5. Hossfeld and Zenger, *Psalms 3*, 182. See 90:13, 16; 102:14, 28; 105:25; 119:91 (ESV: "for all things are your servants"); 134:1; 135:1, 14.

6. Sayers, *Letters to a Diminished Church*, 12.

7. Sifton and Stern, *No Ordinary Men*, 52; letter quoted from *Dietrich Bonhoeffer Werke*, 13:272–73.

Additional Insights, pp. 322–23

1. Millgram, *Jewish Worship*, 210–11.

2. Mays, "Place of the Torah-Psalms," 11.

3. Hossfeld and Zenger, *Psalms 3*, 178–79.

Psalm 114

1. Exodus 19:18 uses the verb *hrd*, "to tremble" (in fear). Since the sense here is that of joy, this is an example of how the Psalms often reinterpret historical events.

2. Weiser, *Psalms*, 711.

3. Weiser, *Psalms*, 712.

4. The generic name for God, *'elohim*, is a plural noun that can means "gods," but when used of Israel's God it is singular, "God."

5. Richard Bewes, "Nothing Can Go Wrong: John Stott is Here," in C. J. H. Wright, ed., *Portraits of a Radical Disciple*, 87.

Psalm 115

1. Hakham, *Psalms*, 3:168n4a.

2. See Beale, *We Become*.

3. Hakham, *Psalms*, 3:168.

4. Kidner, *Psalms 73–150*, 405.

5. Lewis, *Mere Christianity*, 191.

6. Mulholland, *Praying like Jesus*, 29–31.

Psalm 116

1. Hossfeld and Zenger, *Psalms 3*, 216.

2. Wilcock, *Psalms 73–150*, 186.

3. Gerstenberger, *Psalms, Part 2*, 292.

4. Hossfeld and Zenger, *Psalms 3*, 217.

5. The NIV's "as my mother did" is a loose rendering of "son of your handmaid." See also 86:16, where the same phrase occurs.

6. Wilcock, *Psalms 73–150*, 187.

7. The four Servant Songs of Isaiah are Isaiah 42:1–4; 49:1–6; 50:4–9; 52:13–53:12. The corporate interpretation, that Israel in its prophetic role is the Lord's servant, does not exclude the messianic interpretation. In fact, the servant may be both Israel and the personal Messiah. See Bullock, *Prophetic Books*, 188–90.

8. Hossfeld and Zenger, *Psalms 3*, 216, citing Janowski, "Dankbarkeit."

9. Newton, *Select Letters*, No. 26, 163.

10. Quoted in Rockness, *Passion for the Impossible*, 211.

Psalm 117

1. Kidner, *Psalms 73–150*, 412.

2. Delitzsch, *Psalms*, 3:221.

3. Mays, *Psalms*, 372.

4. George MacDonald, *Maiden's Bequest*, 169.

Psalm 118

1. Wilcock, *Psalms 73–150*, 191.

2. The metaphor is used particularly to suggest family assistance ("helper of the fatherless," 10:14) and assistance in battle (e.g., 27:9), that is, a helper in time of distress and danger.

3. Hakham, *Psalms*, 3:201.

4. The psalmist may, on the ground level of meaning, refer to a real stone that was rejected as the cornerstone of the new temple, but it symbolized Israel, and it is the reversal of the builders' decision to reject the stone. It is a parable of God's choice of Israel, as related in Deuteronomy 7.

5. Augustine, *Confessions* 5.8.

6. H. C. G. Moule, *Romans*, 233.

7. Quoted in Wolpe, *Healer of Shattered Hearts*, 42.

Psalm 119

1. See the sidebar "The Alphabetic Acrostic Psalms" in the unit on Psalm 25.

2. Wenham, *Psalms as Torah*, 83. Gerstenberger calls it a "Portrait of a Confessor," which sums up quite well the general purpose of the poem (*Psalms, Part 2*, 315). See also Bullock, *Encountering*, 213–26.

3. One suggestion is that the word *tob* ("good") is another word for law.

4. Kaufmann, "Biblical Age," 76.

5. Kaufmann, "Biblical Age," 78.

6. Hossfeld and Zenger, *Psalms 3*, 263.

7. This is the earmark of the new covenant promulgated by Jeremiah (Jer. 31:31–34) and also found in other key texts (Deut. 6:6; Isa. 51:7; Ps. 37:31; Prov. 3:3; 7:3).

8. Kirkpatrick, *Psalms*, 707.

9. See "Teaching the Text" in the units on Psalms 89 and 113; see also table 1 in the unit on Psalm 89, and "Theological Insights" in the unit on Psalm 116.

10. Note also that in 19:13 (19:14 MT) David uses the word *zedim* for "willful sins" as he does in 119:51.

11. The metaphor "in/to the dust" sometimes implies death (Ps. 22:29; Isa. 29:4; Dan. 12:2) (Hakham, *Psalms*, 3:220). The NIV translates it as humiliation, "I am laid low in the dust," unless the translators intend by this expression to suggest death.

12. Koehler and Baumgartner, *Lexicon*, 1:257–60.

13. Hakham, *Psalms*, 3:230.

14. Goldingay, *Psalms*, 3:402.

15. The Deuteronomic idea of seeking/calling upon God with all one's heart (Deut. 11:13; 13:3) signals total devotion to Yahweh's will. It is used in Psalm 119 in the sense of seeking Yahweh with all one's heart (119:2, 10, 58, 145) and keeping the Torah with all one's heart (119:34, 69).

16. The Piel form of the verb that the NIV translates as "bind" ('*iwwu*ᵉ*duni*; root '*ud*) does not appear elsewhere in the Hebrew Bible. "Ropes" is the tip-off for the NIV translators and seems the logical implication. Hakham (*Psalms*, 3:234–35) renders it "surrounded" on the basis of an Ethiopic word, but "ropes" do not "surround" so much as they "bind."

17. See comments on Psalm 51:17 and the note there for a discussion of unintentional sins and sins with a "high hand."

18. In 119:69 the NIV keeps the literal use of *sheqer* ("lie[s]"), "with lies," whereas in 119:78 and 86b the NIV translators render this word as "without cause." For example, verse 78 is literally, "they afflict me (with) lies," and verse 86b, "they pursue me with lies; help me!" The usual term for "without cause" is *hinnam*, which occurs in 69:4 (69:5 MT); 109:3; and 119:161. "With lie(s)" is a more aggressive term than "without cause" and paints the situation as aggressive, which is the point. It is not his innocence (which is assumed—"lies") but the hostile attacks of his opponents that are so hurtful.

19. Hossfeld and Zenger, *Psalms 3*, 275.

20. The NIV makes the question "how long?" of verse 84 apply to the psalmist's affliction, whereas the Hebrew regards the length of the psalmist's life: "How many are the days of your servant?"

21. Kirkpatrick, *Psalms*, 718; see also Hakham, *Psalms*, 3:244; and Rashi (Gruber, *Rashi's Commentary*, 681).

22. Kidner, *Psalms 73–150*, 426–27.

23. The particle *ki* means "because" or "for," but it can also carry the sense of "indeed," as it does in Psalm 103:14: "Indeed [*ki*] he knows our desires" (author's translation).

24. This is a light or lamp one would carry, not a lamppost.

25. Hakham, *Psalms*, 3:254n92b.

26. The NIV's translation of verse 121 obscures the Torah word in that verse. The adjective "righteous" is evidently intended to translate the Torah word "judgment" (*mishpat*).

27. For example, verse 122 is not the middle verse of the psalm, where we might expect some deviation from the pattern in order to get our attention.

28. See Wilcock, *Psalms 73–150*, 215.

29. Some commentators have observed that "peace" (*shalom*) appears only in verse 165 in Psalm 119, and that if one combines the initial letters of every other word of verse 165 (*sh-l-w-m*), it spells *shalom* (Hakham, *Psalms*, 3:278n146).

30. Hakham, *Psalms*, 3:276.

31. Wilcock, *Psalms 73–150*, 217.

32. The rabbis took the "seven" to refer to the blessings recited before and after the Shema: three in the morning (two before and one after) and four in the evening (two before and two after) (Hakham, *Psalms*, 3:277n145). This practice, however, may be later than the psalm.

33. Manton, *Sermons*.

34. Aitken, *John Newton*, 347. Aitken quotes William Jay, a friend of Newton's, who visited Newton before his death and heard him say these words.

35. Schaefer, *Psalms*, 291.

36. Hillenbrand, *Unbroken*, 188–89.

37. Anghelatos, "A Bible for Eight Pounds of Potatoes."

Psalm 120

1. Schaefer, *Psalms*, 298.

2. See Hossfeld and Zenger, *Psalms 3*, 303–5, for the comparative merits of these two options.

3. Schaefer, *Psalms*, 297.

4. See Tosefta *Sukkah* 4.7–9 (Neusner, *Tosefta*); see also Bullock, *Encountering*, 79.

5. Kidner, *Psalms 73–150*, 430.

6. Perowne, *Psalms*, 2:370.

7. Koehler and Baumgartner, *Lexicon*, 2:1239 (see the meaning of root 1of *rmh*).

8. Rasmussen, *NIV Atlas*, 245, 241; Block, *Book of Ezekiel*, 2:432–36.

9. Peterson, *Long Obedience*, 15.

10. Dallas Willard, Wheaton College Chapel address, November 2, 2001.

11. Peterson, *Long Obedience*, 14.

12. Jones, *Abundant Living*, 1–82.

Additional Insights, pp. 378–80

1. Hakham, *Psalms*, 3:286–87.

2. Liebreich, "Songs of Ascents."

3. See Neusner, *Sifré to Numbers*, 191–99; and *Midrash Rabbah on Numbers* 11.5–7.

4. Goldingay, *Psalms*, 3:448–49.

5. Hakham lists these literary "ascents" at the beginning of his discussion of each of the Songs of Ascents (*Psalms*, 3:287–368). See also Delitzsch, *Psalms*, 3, on 125:5; 129:8; and 134:3.

Psalm 121

1. Hakham, *Psalms*, 3:293.

2. Liebreich, "Songs of Ascents."

3. Hakham, *Psalms*, 3:295. In ancient times epilepsy was associated with the moon. See Stol, *Epilepsy in Babylonia*, 121–30.

4. Wilcock, *Psalms 73–150*, 223.

5. Hakham, *Psalms*, 3:294.

6. Peterson, *Long Obedience*, 39.

7. N. T. Wright, *Case for the Psalms*, 91.

Psalm 122

1. Hakham, *Psalms*, 3:302.

2. See Hakham, *Psalms*, 3:302, for the dating options implied by the "David" references.

3. Speaking of the psalm's usage in the Second Temple period, the Jerusalem Talmud (*Bikkurim* 3.2) says the pilgrims used to say this psalm as they made their journey to Jerusalem, "I was glad when they said unto me, 'Let us go to the house of the LORD.'"

4. Hakham, *Psalms*, 3:298.

5. E.g., 2 Samuel 8:15; 15:2, 6; 1 Kings 3:28; Isaiah 16:5; Jeremiah 21:12, and this may be a continuation of the office of the judges of Israel (see Anderson, *Psalms 73–150*, 856).

6. Goulder, *Psalms of the Return*, 47.

7. Hossfeld and Zenger, *Psalms 3*, 334. See also "Jerusalem," in Douglas, ed., *New Bible Dictionary*, 566–73.

8. See the quotation by Archbishop of Canterbury William Temple in "Illustrating the Text" in the unit on Psalm 48.

9. Peterson, *Long Obedience*, 56.

10. Peterson, *Long Obedience*, 52.

11. Moore, *Life Lessons*, 193.

12. George MacDonald, *Paul Faber, Surgeon*, chap. 15.

Psalm 123

1. Delitzsch, *Psalms*, 3:280.

2. See Mendelsohn, "Slavery in the OT."

3. The participle "who sits enthroned" (*hayyo-sheᵇbi*) is an archaic form (see also 113:5, *hammagbhii*; "note the archaic *i* ending in both forms). The definite article *ha* functions as a vocative ("*you* who sits enthroned," rather than "*he* who sits enthroned").

4. Surprisingly, the Songs of Ascents contain few prayers, and those that do occur are brief (120:2; 123:3–4; 125:4; 130:1–4; 131:1–2; 132:1, 8–10). The reason for this may be that the entire collection is a blessing on the psalmist and community, couched in various forms, and thus they are more recipients of the blessing than active intercessors in prayer.

5. Weiser, *Psalms*, 752.

6. *B. Berakhot* 28b.

7. Pierre, "Alice Frazier."

8. Barclay, *Gospel of Matthew*, 1:203.

Psalm 124

1. Goulder, *Psalms of the Return*, 52.

2. Goulder's hypothesis is that the fifteen Songs of Ascents were sung at the fifteen services of the Feast of Tabernacles, one in each service (Goulder, *Psalms of the Return*, 108–9). Psalm 120, according to his hypothesis, was the psalm for the evening of the fifteenth (Tabernacles, seventh month [Tishri], days 15–21 [Deut. 16:13–15], plus an eighth celebration: Lev. 23:39; Neh. 8:18), and all the even-numbered psalms were for the morning service, with the odd numbers for the evening, coinciding with

the two night psalms (Ps. 130, sundown song on the nineteenth/twentieth; and Ps. 134, sundown song on the twenty-first/twenty-second).

3. Kidner, *Psalms 73–150*, 437.

4. Psalm 124 in *Scottish Psalter, 1929*.

Psalm 125

1. Hakham, *Psalms*, 3:314–15.

2. The word "peace" (*shalom*) appears eight times in the Pilgrim Psalter: 120:6, 7; 122:6, 7, 8; 125:5; 128:6; 147:14.

3. Spurgeon, *Treasury of David*, 7:59.

4. Quoted in Lewis, *Letters to an American Lady*, 70–71.

5. Quoted in Bouwsma, *John Calvin*, 74.

6. Peterson, *Long Obedience*, 82.

7. Lewis, *Letters to an American Lady*, 70–71. Walter Hooper, in a footnote on this letter in *The Collected Letters of C. S. Lewis* (3:930n42), notes that the quotation of Augustine is difficult to locate and may be a paraphrase of something similar that Augustine wrote in his *Homilies on the Psalms*.

Psalm 126

1. See Hakham, *Psalms*, 3:318, for a list.

2. Hossfeld and Zenger, *Psalms 3*, 367.

3. The infinitive, in English as well as Hebrew, is like a weather vane. It has no force (tense) of its own but depends on the force and directions of the winds (context) to determine whether it is past, present, or future. In this case, the Hebrew infinitive *shub* can mean "restores" (future) or "restored" (past). The cue comes from the past tense of the verb "to be" ("we were like"), and the combination of the adverb "then" (*'az*) in verse 2, plus the future (imperfect, "fill"), which gives a past sense (see Exod. 15:1).

4. Glueck, *Rivers in the Desert*, 92–93.

5. Glueck, *Rivers in the Desert*, 93–94.

6. See Hossfeld and Zenger, *Psalms 3*, 378.

7. Hossfeld and Zenger, *Psalms 3*, 378.

8. Weiser, *Psalms*, 760.

9. Chesterton, *Orthodoxy*, 159–60; see also "Illustrating the Text" in the unit on Psalm 21, and "Teaching the Text" in the unit on Psalm 97.

10. Bernanos, *Diary of a Country Priest*, 272.

11. Augustine, *Confessions* 9.1.

12. Barnhouse, *Let Me Illustrate*, 132–33.

Psalm 127

1. Hossfeld and Zenger, *Psalms 3*, 384.

2. See Jeremiah 1:11–12 for the use of the verb "stand watch" (*shoqed*). Of course, the psalm has a more general application to the building of a family house, particularly in view of the mention of children in 127:3–6.

3. See "Additional Insights: Songs of Ascents, the Pilgrim Psalter (Psalms 120–34)," following the unit on Psalm 120; see also Hakham, *Psalms*, 3:322.

4. Quoted in Studdert-Kennedy, *The Word and the Work*, 33.

5. Stoddart, *Psalms for Every Day*, 322.

6. Luther, "A Mighty Fortress Is Our God."

Psalm 128

1. Hossfeld and Zenger, *Psalms 3*, 399.

2. Goulder (*Psalms of the Return*, 68–73) places it on the template of Nehemiah 11:1–2 and 7:26–33, proposing that it was a blessing on those who took up residence in the city as a defense force, even though Jerusalem is not mentioned in the psalm. I think the psalm is a bit more optimistic about the times or the impending time of peace that the suppliant prays for, and the belligerence of opposition of Nehemiah's time is not evident in the poem.

3. Jerusalem occurs in the Pilgrim Psalter in 122:2, 3, 6; 125:2; 128:5 (2x); and Zion occurs in 125:1; 126:1; 128:5; 129:5; 132:13; 133:3; and 134:3.

4. Hossfeld and Zenger, *Psalms 3*, 397.

5. Weiser, *Psalms*, 768.

6. Hossfeld and Zenger, *Psalms 3*, 403–4.

7. Poling, *Faith Is Power*, 95–100.

Psalm 129

1. Hakham, *Psalms*, 3:333.

2. See also Allen, *Psalms 101–150*, 187.

3. Spurgeon, *Treasury of David*, 7:109.

Psalm 130

1. See the comments on 130:4.

2. Hossfeld and Zenger, *Psalms 3*, 423.

3. Goulder's proposal that the historical template is Nehemiah 13:15–22, which deals with the desecration of the Sabbath in Nehemiah's Jerusalem (ca. 445 BC), is not very convincing since there is no hint of such a concern in Psalm 130 (see Goulder, *Psalms of the Return*, 80–85).

4. Hakham, *Psalms*, 3:338n2c.

5. Hossfeld and Zenger, *Psalms 3*, 435.

6. See Hakham, *Psalms*, 3:337, for a list of the "ascents" (repetitions).

7. Hakham, *Psalms*, 3:340.

8. This is one of those places in the NIV where you might want to switch to another translation, as I have done with verse 4, or use a different translation altogether for the basis of your sermon/lesson. The reason is that the NIV's rendering of the verb at the end of the verse ("to fear") as first-person plural ("we") has no textual basis and changes the perspective of the psalm from personal to corporate. While that would not be surprising in the Pilgrim Psalter, it is out of character with this psalm because the conclusion (130:7–8) is an admonition to Israel to "hope in the LORD," whereas a change of perspective from personal to corporate would normally require the corporate "I" or the introduction of the first common plural ("we").

9. George MacDonald, *Paul Faber, Surgeon*, chap. 7.

10. Forsyth, *Cure of Souls*, 128, quoted in Peterson, *Long Obedience*, 128.

11. Ker, *Psalms in History and Biography*, 162.

Psalm 131

1. Weiser, *Psalms*, 776.

2. Spurgeon, *Treasury of David*, 7:91.

3. Three nominal phrases (lit. "high-heartedness") also express this idea: "a high heart" (*gobah-leb*), "a great heart" (*godel-leb*), and "an elevated heart" (*rum-leb*) (Deut. 8:14; Isa. 9:9 [9:8 MT]; Hosea 13:6; 2 Chron. 26:16; Prov. 16:5) (Hakham, *Psalms*, 3:343).

4. Hakham, *Psalms*, 3:343.

5. Schaefer, *Psalms*, 312.

6. Delitzsch, *Psalms*, 3:305, 306.

7. Spurgeon, *Treasury of David*, 7:91.

8. Spurgeon, *Treasury of David*, 7:91.

9. Augustine, *City of God*, 310.

10. Shakespeare, *Henry the Sixth*, act 3, scene 1.

Psalm 132

1. For example, Wilcock, *Psalms 73–150*, 242–43; Goulder, *Psalms of the Return*, 90–101.

2. See Hakham, *Psalms*, 3:346, for a complete list.

3. "Afflictions" is a Piel verbal noun (pl.) that includes his physical as well as his emotional afflictions (in 1 Kings 2:26, Solomon says that Abiathar, David's high priest, was "afflicted with all that David was afflicted with"; thus he spared his life, though he was not one of Solomon's supporters).

4. Goulder, *Psalms of the Return*, 93.

5. Verse 3, conditional clause: "If ['*im*] I go under the roof of my house [translation: "I will not go under the roof of my house"] until I find a place for the LORD, a dwelling for the Mighty One of Jacob"; verse 4, conditional clause: "If ['*im*] I go to my bed [translation: "I will not go to my bed"] until . . ."; verse 5, conditional clause: "If ['*im*] I allow sleep to my eyes or slumber to my eyelids [translation: "I will not allow sleep to my eyes or slumber to my eyelids"] until . . . " (author's translations). The curse is missing from each of these sentences, which necessitates the negative translation.

6. The NIV has "ark of his might" in 78:61, but the term "ark" (*'aron*) in 132:8 is an allusion. See the comments on 78:61.

7. See 145:15–16 for the idea that a good king makes provision for the poor.

8. See 2 Samuel 1:10; 2 Kings 11:12; Psalm 89:39 for the crown as part of the royal accoutrements.

9. I am drawing upon the stimulating discussion of this psalm by Peterson, *Long Obedience*, 169–71.

10. Peterson, *Long Obedience*, 166.

11. Peterson, *Long Obedience*, 168.

12. Peterson, *Long Obedience*, 168.

13. This lower end of the scale, righteousness as a standard of fairness and justice, is also found in Isaiah 1:21, 27; 5:7; Ezekiel 18:5, etc.

14. Pedersen, *Israel*, 345.

Psalm 133

1. See Hakham, *Psalms*, 3:359, for the list of "ascents."

2. Hossfeld and Zenger, *Psalms 3*, 481.

3. Kidner, *Psalms 73–150*, 453.

4. Kidner, *Psalms 73–150*, 453.

5. Summarized by Peck, *Different Drum*, 26–27.

6. Muggeridge, *Jesus Rediscovered*, 42.

Psalm 134

1. Delitzsch reconstructs the activities of the night vigil (*Psalms*, 3:321–22).

2. While both Psalms 133 and 134 begin with "behold" (*hinneh*; the NIV does not translate the word in either case), this is the only place in the Hebrew Bible where this word introduces a command.

3. See Hakham, *Psalms*, 3:363.

4. Lewis, *Screwtape Letters*, 33–34.

Psalm 135

1. Hakham, *Psalms*, 3:369.

2. See Hossfeld and Zenger, *Psalms 3*, 495, for a list of intertextual references.

3. See "Book 5 as a Major Thanksgiving Celebration" in chapter 8 of Bullock, *Encountering*, revised edition (forthcoming).

4. An adaptation of Hakham's outline, *Psalms*, 3:369.

5. "Give thanks to the LORD, for he is good, for his love endures forever" was a liturgical response made by the officiants and worshipers in the temple (1 Chron. 16:34; 2 Chron. 5:11–14; 7:1–3; 10:21; Ezra 3:11); and it occurs in the following psalms: 100:4–5; 106:1; 107:1; 118:1–4, 29. Note that it begins Book 5 (107:1), concludes the Egyptian Hallel (118:1–4, 29), and occurs here in a slightly alternate and abbreviated form ("*Praise the LORD* [*Yah*] for he is good") in 135:3.

6. Hossfeld and Zenger, *Psalms 3*, 497.

7. In Deuteronomy 6:22; 26:8; 29:3; and 34:11 the paired phrase, "signs and wonders" (*'otot umopᵉtim*) refers to the plagues of Egypt.

8. Of particular interest also is the direct address to Egypt, probably to make the statement more personal and thus more indicting of Egypt. The Hebrew term *bᵉtokeki* is a poetic form of *bᵉtokek* = "in(to) your midst." The same term occurs with a direct address to Jerusalem in 116:19.

9. The language implies that the idols are not "doers" as is Yahweh, who "does" (root '*sh*) whatever he desires (135:6), but they are the product of human doers, "*made* by human hands" (135:15, root '*sh*, "to do/make").

10. Horton, *Putting Amazing Back into Grace*, 110–11, quoting Tozer, *Best of Tozer*, 175.

11. Pelikan, *Jesus through the Centuries*, 34. He quotes Ignatius, *Ephesians* 10.1; 1.2.

Psalm 136

1. Hossfeld and Zenger, *Psalms 3*, 244.

2. The NIV has unfortunately left untranslated the Hebrew word *ki* ("for," "because") before each response, thus missing the fact that the response provides the reason that we should give thanks. While Yahweh's "great wonders" are the stated reason for giving thanks, the underlying reason is "because his love endures forever." The *ki* is the tether that binds the two parts of the whole together. It cannot stand alone, because God's love is the underwriting factor of both creation and history—"because his love endures forever."

3. Citing the work of Christian Macholz ("Psalm 136"), Zenger favorably views his proposal that Psalm 136 was written after the Pentateuch as we know it was finished (Zenger's date is ca. 400 BC), since the Pentateuch does not mention the western conquest (Hossfeld and Zenger, *Psalms 3*, 503–4). But we should not expect this psalm or any other, for that matter, to recite the whole picture of the conquest.

4. In the Exodus narrative, sometimes Moses or Aaron seems to cause the plagues (e.g., "So they [Moses and Aaron] took soot from a furnace. . . . Moses tossed it into the air, and festering boils broke out on people and animals," Exod. 9:10; and sometimes the Lord is the cause (e.g., "Tomorrow the LORD will do this in the land," Exod. 9:5; "But the LORD hardened Pharaoh's heart," Exod. 10:20); and sometimes no cause is specified (e.g., "Yet Pharaoh's heart became hard," Exod. 7:13). With the tenth plague, however, there is no ambiguity about its cause: "At midnight the LORD struck down all the firstborn in Egypt, from the firstborn of Pharaoh, who sat on the throne, to the firstborn of the prisoner, who was in the dungeon, and the firstborn of all the livestock as well" (Exod. 12:29). While the plague narrative seems not to formalize Yahweh as the cause of all events and developments (although the writer was probably convinced of that), our psalmist evidently wants to leave no doubt about the cause-effect nature of God's creating and redeeming acts.

5. The fact that the NIV has unfortunately left the word *ki* untranslated (also JB, NLT, HCSB, and NJPS) means that it has missed the fact that the response provides the deeper underlying reason that we give thanks: "His [Yahweh's] love endures forever."

6. Wolpe, *Healer of Shattered Hearts*, 121.

7. Wolpe, *Healer of Shattered Hearts*, 129; I am indebted to Wolpe's stimulating discussion of

Notes to Pages 458–485

this topic in his chapter titled "The Two Exiles" (pp. 119–38).

Psalm 137

1. Schaefer, *Psalms*, 322.
2. Goulder's phrase (*Psalms of the Return*, 228).
3. Block, *Book of Ezekiel*, 1:84.
4. Goulder, *Psalms of the Return*, 228.
5. Hossfeld and Zenger, *Psalms 3*, 513.
6. Quoted in Fleischner, *Auschwitz*, 409.
7. Quoted in Seymour, "Power and Seduction," 13.

Psalm 138

1. Compare 138:1a to 9:1a and 111:1a; 138:2a to 5:7b; 138:5a to 18:21a ("ways of the LORD" as God's laws); 138:3a to 20:9b and 86:7 (juxtaposition of calling on God and being answered); 138:7 to 21:8 (God's right hand).
2. See Hakham, *Psalms*, 3:395.
3. If the psalm is composed after Solomon's prayer in 1 Kings 8, which we are assuming, this has implications for the date of the writing of the book of Kings (a single book that has been divided into two books because it had to be written on two scrolls). Since Kings knows nothing of the rebuilding of the temple, and the psalm presupposes the second temple, 1 Kings 8 would predate the construction (520–516 BC).
4. Bainton, *Here I Stand*, 99–100.
5. Holtz, *Back to the Sources*, 390.

Psalm 139

1. Gunkel, *Introduction to Psalms*.
2. Allen, *Psalms 101–150*, 323.
3. Kidner, *Psalms 73–150*, 464.
4. Wilcock, *Psalms 73–150*, 259.
5. Schaefer, *Psalms*, 325.
6. Kidner, *Psalms 73–150*, 464.
7. Stec, *Targum of the Psalms*, 233n9.
8. Calvin, *Psalms*, 3:220.
9. Hossfeld and Zenger, *Psalms 3*, 543, quoting Buysch, *Der letzte Davidpsalter*, 122.
10. Schaefer, *Psalms*, 326.
11. Wilcock, *Psalms 73–150*, 259–60.
12. Wilcock, *Psalms 73–150*, 259–60.
13. Weiser, *Psalms*, 802–6.
14. Weiser, *Psalms*, 801–2.
15. Weiser, *Psalms*, 803.
16. Francis Thompson, "The Hound of Heaven," 56. See "Illustrating the Text" in the unit on Psalm 23.
17. Silverman, *Rabbinic Stories*, 21.
18. Storms, *More Precious than Gold*, 191.

Psalm 140

1. Compare 59:2, which opens with a prayer for deliverance, with 140:1; compare 61:7 (61:8 MT) with 140:1b (140:2b) and 4b (5b) (the *nun* in the verb *tints^ereni*, "protect me," is unassimilated, as it is in 61:8 MT); compare 56:6a (56:7a MT) and 59:3b (59:4b) with 140:2 (140:3b) (use of same verb, *yaguru*, "to stir up war"); compare 52:2–4 and 64:3 with 140:3a (slanderer's words are as sharp as a "serpent's tongue"); compare 55:3c (55:4c MT) with 140:10a (140:11a) (the verb "topple," *mot*; NIV: "bring down" / "fall on"); compare 58:4a (58:5a MT) with 140:3b (140:4b); compare 69:22 (69:23 MT) with 140:5 (140:6) ("snare," *pah*, and "trap[s]," *moqesh*, occur in 69:22). See Goulder, *Psalms of the Return*, 251.
2. Spurgeon, *Treasury of David*, 7:293.
3. The two divine names are in the reverse order of their normal occurrence ("LORD, my Lord," rather than "my Lord, LORD"); but when the tetragrammaton is joined to *'adonay*, the tetragrammaton usually is given the vowels of *'elohim* and translated "GOD" in small caps. It may be that the reverse order here is in deference to the order of the divine names in 140:6a (140:7a MT): "LORD . . .God [*'eli*]." The tetragrammaton, which occurs first in 140:7a (140:8a MT), is pointed with the vowels of *'elohim* and pronounced the same.
4. Spurgeon, *Treasury of David*, 7:296.
5. Forsyth, *Soul of Prayer*, 45.
6. Forsyth, *Soul of Prayer*, 13.
7. Anonymous hymn, "d," no. 163, in Routley, *Rejoice in the Lord*.

Psalm 141

1. For example, "Come quickly to me" (40:13 and 70:5; 141:1a); "I call" to God (57:2; 141:1b); "the lifting up of my hands" (63:4; 141:2b); "my eyes are fixed on you" (25:15; 141:8); "in you I take refuge" (57:1; 141:8b).
2. Kraus, *Psalms 60–150*, 527–29.
3. Hakham, *Psalms*, 3:423.
4. Allen, *Psalms 101–150*, 270.
5. Lewis, *Psalms*, 68.
6. Wilcock, *Psalms 73–150*, 265.
7. Lewis, *Psalms*, 68.
8. Lewis, *Psalms*, 71.
9. Lewis, *Psalms*, 73.
10. Lewis, *Psalms*, 74.
11. Calvin, *Psalms*, 4:65.

Psalm 142

1. Hakham, *Psalms*, 3:430.
2. For the complete text of Dr. King's speech, see "Top 100 Speeches," *American Rhetoric*, http://www.americanrhetoric.com/speeches/mlkihaveadream.htm.
3. Lewis, *Mere Christianity*, 173.

Psalm 143

1. Calvin, *Psalms*, 3:250.
2. Weiser, *Psalms*, 819.

3. Greville MacDonald, *Reminiscences of a Specialist*, 15, 31, quoted in Hein, *Harmony Within*.

4. See Friends General Conference, "Some Guidelines for Clearness," accessed February 28, 2017, https://www.fgcquaker.org/sites/default/files/attachments/Guidelines%20for%20Clearness%20for%20a%20Leading%20or%20Ministry.pdf.

Psalm 144

1. Hossfeld and Zenger, *Psalms 3*, 586.

2. See the discussion of Book 5 in "The Structure and Composition of the Psalter" in the introduction in volume 1.

3. See the comments on the title ("servant of the LORD") for Psalm 18.

4. See Psalms 33:3 (see also the comments on 33:3); 40:3; 96:1; 98:1; 144:9; 149:1; Isaiah 42:10; Revelation 5:9; and 14:3.

5. The feminine participle is "going out" (*yotse't*; see Ezek. 12:4 for the sense of exile), even though it may mean miscarriage.

6. Spurgeon, *Treasury of David*, 7:356.

7. Quoted in Marshall, *John Doe, Disciple,* 154.

8. Thielicke, *I Believe*, 116.

Psalm 145

1. Hakham, *Psalms*, 3:450; see *b. Shabbat* 118b and *Soferim* 18.1.

2. Hossfeld and Zenger, *Psalms 3*, 602–3, citing the work of Franz (*Der barmherzige und gnädige Gott*, 253).

3. Spurgeon, *Treasury of David*, 7:375.

4. Hossfeld and Zenger, *Psalms 3*, 597.

5. See also Psalms 86:15; 103:8; Joel 2:13; Jonah 4:2; Nehemiah 9:17.

6. Goulder insists that the addition to verse 13 overloads the verse and leaves the second half of the verse without a connecting *waw* ("and"), and thus he maintains the Masoretic Text (Goulder, *Psalms of the Return*, 281).

7. Goldingay, *Psalms*, 3:704.

8. Anderson, *Psalms 73–150*, 939.

9. Spurgeon, *Treasury of David*, 7:376.

10. Hein, *Harmony Within*, 45.

11. George MacDonald, *Thomas Wingfold, Curate*, vol. 3, ch. 15, quoted in Hein, *Harmony Within*, 45–46.

12. *Aesop's Fables*, 23.

Psalm 146

1. "Wait" (root *sbr*): 145:15a ("the eyes of all look [root *sbr*] to you") and 146:5b ("whose hope

[root *sbr*] is in the LORD"); "[you] give them their food": 145:15b and 146:7b; "lifts up all who are bowed down": 145:14b and 146:8; "your kingdom is an everlasting kingdom": 145:13a and 146:10.

2. Calvin, *Psalms*, 4:65.

3. Pearce, *Literary Converts*, 163. See chapter 14, "Waugh and Waste Land," 146–65.

4. Quoted in Pearce, *Literary Converts*, 164.

Psalm 147

1. Goulder, *Psalms of the Return*, 289.

2. Hossfeld and Zenger, *Psalms 3*, 623.

3. Spurgeon, *Treasury of David*, 7:414.

4. Allen, *Psalms 101–150*, 310.

5. Spurgeon, *Treasury of David*, 7:415.

6. Quoted in Bouwsma, *John Calvin*, 32.

7. Wolpe, *Healer of Shattered Hearts*, 15.

Psalm 148

1. Hossfeld and Zenger, *Psalms 3*, 639.

2. Delitzsch, *Psalms*, 3:409.

3. See also Kirkpatrick, *Psalms*, 827.

4. See Waltke and O'Connor, *Biblical Hebrew Syntax*, 39.2.4, for the epexegetical use of the conjunction *waw*. One of their examples is Deuteronomy 32:28: "They are a nation without sense, *that is*, there is no discernment in them." See also Psalm 76:3.

5. Delitzsch, *Psalms*, 3:406.

6. Quoted in Rockness, *Passion for the Impossible*, 304.

7. Quoted in Rockness, *Passion for the Impossible*, 298.

Psalm 149

1. See Hakham, *Psalms*, 3:491n2.

2. See Braun, *Music*, 29–30.

3. Gunkel, *Introduction to Psalms*, 23.

4. Reardon, *Christ in the Psalms*, 301–2.

Psalm 150

1. Spurgeon, *Treasury of David*, 7:465.

2. Hossfeld and Zenger, *Psalms 3*, 658.

3. See the comments on 47:5; 81:3; 98:6.

4. Hossfeld and Zenger, *Psalms 3*, 660.

5. Hossfeld and Zenger, *Psalms 3*, 657.

6. Spurgeon, *Treasury of David*, 7:414 (on Ps. 147:1).

7. Hossfeld and Zenger, *Psalms 3*, 659–60.

8. Spurgeon, *Treasury of David*, 7:463 (on Ps. 150:1).

9. Silverman, *Rabbinic Stories*, 52.

Bibliography

Recommended Resources

Anderson, A. A. *Psalms 73–150*. Vol. 2 of *The Book of Psalms*. New Century Bible. Grand Rapids: Eerdmans, 1972.

Bullock, C. Hassell. *Encountering the Book of Psalms*. Grand Rapids: Baker Academic, 2001 (revised edition forthcoming).

———. *Psalms*. Vol. 1, *Psalms 1–72*. Teach the Text Commentary Series. Grand Rapids: Baker Books, 2015.

Craigie, Peter C. *Psalms 1–50*. Word Biblical Commentary 19. Waco: Word, 1983.

Goldingay, John. *Psalms*. 3 vols. Baker Commentary on the Old Testament Wisdom and Psalms. Grand Rapids: Baker Academic, 2006.

Hakham, Amos. *The Bible: Psalms with the Jerusalem Commentary*. 3 vols. Jerusalem Commentary. Jerusalem: Mosad Harav Kook, 2003.

Holladay, William L. *The Psalms through Three Thousand Years: Prayerbook of a Cloud of Witnesses*. Minneapolis: Fortress, 1993.

Kidner, Derek. *Psalms 1–72*. Tyndale Old Testament Commentaries. Downers Grove, IL: InterVarsity, 1975.

———. *Psalms 73–150*. Tyndale Old Testament Commentaries 14b. Downers Grove, IL: InterVarsity, 1975.

Bibliography

Aesop's Fables. Illustrated by Heidi Holder. New York: Viking Penguin, 1981.

Aitken, Jonathan. *John Newton: From Disgrace to Amazing Grace*. Wheaton: Crossway, 2007.

Allen, Leslie C. *Psalms 101–150*. Word Biblical Commentary 21. Waco: Word, 1983.

Anderson, A. A. *Psalms 1–72*. Vol. 1 of *The Book of Psalms*. New Century Bible. Grand Rapids: Eerdmans, 1972.

———. *Psalms 73–150*. Vol. 2 of *The Book of Psalms*. New Century Bible. Grand Rapids: Eerdmans, 1972.

Anghelatos, Miltos. "A Bible for Eight Pounds of Potatoes: The Testimony of Miltos Anghelatos." In *God's Word in a Young World*, by Nigel Sylvester. London: Scripture Union, 1985.

Augustine. *The City of God*. An abridged version from the translation by Gerald G. Walsh, Demetrius B. Zema, Grace Monahan, and Daniel J. Homan. Edited by Vernon J. Bourke. New York: Doubleday, 1958.

———. *The Confessions of St. Augustine*. Translated by Rex Warner. New York: New American Library, 1963.

Bainton, Roland H. *Here I Stand: A Life of Martin Luther*. Nashville: Abingdon, 1950.

Barclay, William. *The Gospel of Luke*. Rev. ed. Louisville: Westminster John Knox, 1975.

———. *The Gospel of Matthew*. Rev. ed. 2 vols. Louisville: Westminster John Knox, 1975.

Barnhouse, Donald Grey. *Let Me Illustrate: Stories, Anecdotes, Illustrations*. Westwood, NJ: Revell, 1967.

Beale, G. K. *We Become like What We Worship: A Biblical Theology of Idolatry*. Downers Grove, IL: InterVarsity, 2008.

Beale, G. K., and D. A. Carson, eds. *Commentary on the New Testament Use of the Old Testament*. Grand Rapids: Baker Academic, 2007.

Bernanos, George. *The Diary of a Country Priest*. Translated by Pamela Morris. New York: Macmillan, 1937.

Blakely, Hunter B. *Religion in Shoes: Brother Bryan of Birmingham*. Richmond: John Knox, 1953.

Block, Daniel L. *The Book of Ezekiel*. 2 vols. New International Commentary on the Old Testament. Grand Rapids: Eerdmans, 1997.

Bonhoeffer, Dietrich. *Dietrich Bonhoeffer Werke*. 17 vols. Gütersloh: Chr. Kaiser, 1986–99.

Bouwsma, William J. *John Calvin: A Sixteenth-Century Portrait*. New York: Oxford, 1988.

Braun, Joachim. *Music in Ancient Israel/Palestine*. Translated by Douglas W. Stott. Grand Rapids: Eerdmans, 2002.

Brueggemann, Walter. *The Message of the Psalms*. Minneapolis: Augsburg, 1984.

Brueggemann, Walter, and Patrick D. Miller. "Psalm 73 as a Canonical Marker," *Journal for the Study of the Old Testament* 72 (1996): 45–56.

Bullock, C. Hassell. *Encountering the Book of Psalms: A Literary and Theological Introduction*. Grand Rapids: Baker Academic, 2001 (revised edition forthcoming).

———. *An Introduction to the Old Testament Poetic Books*. Rev. ed. Chicago: Moody, 2007.

———. *An Introduction to the Old Testament Prophetic Books*. Updated ed. Chicago: Moody, 2007.

———. *Psalms*. Vol. 1, *Psalms 1–72*. Teach the Text Commentary Series. Grand Rapids: Baker Books, 2015.

Bunyan, John. *Grace Abounding to the Chief of Sinners*. 1905. Reprint, Project Gutenberg, 2013, http://www.gutenberg.org/ebooks/654.

———. *The Pilgrim's Progress from This World to That Which Is to Come*. Reprint, Project Gutenberg, 2008, http://www.gutenberg.org/ebooks/131.

Buysch, Christoph. *Der letzte Davidpsalter: Interpretation, Komposition und Funktion der Psalmengruppe Ps 138–145*. Stuttgarter biblische Beiträge 63. Stuttgart: Katholisches Bibelwerk, 2009.

Calvin, John. *Commentary on the Book of Psalms*. 5 vols. 1845–49. Reprint, Grand Rapids: Baker, 1979.

———. *Institutes of the Christian Religion*. 2 vols. Edited by John T. McNeill. Translated by Ford Lewis Battles. Library of Christian Classics 20. Philadelphia: Westminster, 1960.

Chesterton, Gilbert K. *Orthodoxy*. Garden City, NY: Image, 1959.

Coverdale, Miles. The Psalter. Edited by W. S. Peterson and Valerie Macys. http://www.synaxis.info/psalter/5_english/c_psalms/CoverdalePsalms.pdf.

Craigie, Peter C. *Psalms 1–50*. Word Biblical Commentary 19. Waco: Word, 1983.

Davidson, Robert. *The Vitality of Worship: A Commentary on the Book of Psalms*. Grand Rapids: Eerdmans, 1998.

Delitzsch, Franz. *Biblical Commentary on the Psalms*. 3 vols. London: Hodder & Stoughton, 1888–94.

Dodd, C. H. *According to the Scriptures*. London: Nisbet, 1952.

Douglas, J. D., ed. *New Bible Dictionary*. 2nd ed. Leicester, UK: Inter-Varsity, 1982.

Edman, V. Raymond. *Not Somehow, but Triumphantly!* Grand Rapids: Zondervan, 1965.

Eissfeldt, O. "Psalm 80." In *Geschichte und Altes Testament: Albrecht Alt zum 70. Geburtstag dargebracht*, edited by W. F. Albright et al., 65–78. Tübingen: J. C. B. Mohr, 1953.

Fleischner, Eva, ed. *Auschwitz: Beginning of a New Era? Reflections on the Holocaust*. New York: KTAV, 1977.

Forsyth, P. T. *The Cure of Souls*. Grand Rapids: Eerdmans, 1971.

———. *The Soul of Prayer*. 1916. Reprint, Vancouver: Regent College Publishing, 2002.

Franz, Matthias. *Der barmherzige und gnädige Gott: Die Gnadenrede vom Sinai (Exodus 34, 6–7) und ihre Parallelen im Alten Testament und seiner Umwelt*. Beiträge zur Wissenschaft vom Alten und Neuen Testament 160. Stuttgart: Kohlhammer, 2003.

Geller, Stephen A. "Myth and Syntax in Psalm 93." In *Mishneh Todah*, edited by N. S. Fox et al., 321–32. Winona Lake, IN: Eisenbrauns, 2009.

Gerstenberger, Erhard S. *Psalms, Part 2, and Lamentations*. Forms of the Old Testament Literature 15. Grand Rapids: Eerdmans, 2001.

Glueck, Nelson. *Rivers in the Desert: A History of the Negev*. New York: Norton, 1968.

Goldingay, John. *Psalms*. 3 vols. Baker Commentary on the Old Testament Wisdom and Psalms. Grand Rapids: Baker Academic, 2006–8.

Gosse, Bernard. "Le quatrième livre du Psautier, Psaumes 90–106, comme réponse à l'échec de la royauté davidique." *Biblische Zeitschrift* 46 (2002): 239–52.

Goulder, Michael D. *The Psalms of the Return (Book V, Psalms 107–150).* Journal for the Study of the Old Testament Supplement 258. Sheffield: Sheffield Academic, 1998.

———. "The Songs of Ascents and Nehemiah," *JSOT* 75 (1997): 43–58.

Gregory the Great. *Pastoral Care.* Translated by Henry David. Ancient Christian Writers. New York: Paulist, 1950.

Gruber, Mayer I. *Rashi's Commentary on the Psalms.* Brill Reference Library of Judaism 18. Leiden: Brill, 2004.

Gunkel, Hermann. *Introduction to Psalms: The Genres of the Religious Lyric of Israel.* Translated by James D. Nogalski. Macon, GA: Mercer University Press, 1998.

———. *The Psalms: A Form-Critical Introduction.* Philadelphia: Fortress, 1967.

Hakham, Amos. *The Bible: Psalms with the Jerusalem Commentary.* 3 vols. Jerusalem Commentary. Jerusalem: Mosad Harav Kook, 2003.

Hareuveni, Nogah. *Nature in Our Biblical Heritage.* Translated by Helen Frenkley. Lod, Israel: Neot Kedumim, 1980.

———. *Tree and Shrub in Our Biblical Heritage.* Translated by Helen Frenkley. Kiryat Ono, Israel: Neot Kedumim, 1984.

Hein, Rolland. *The Harmony Within: The Spiritual Vision of George MacDonald.* Grand Rapids: Christian University Press, 1982.

Hertz, J. H., ed. *The Pentateuch and Haftorahs.* 2nd ed. London: Soncino, 1965.

Hilber, John H. W. "Psalms." In *Zondervan Illustrated Bible Backgrounds Commentary: Old Testament,* edited by John W. Walton, 5:316–463. 5 vols. Grand Rapids: Zondervan, 2009.

Hill, David. "Son of Man in Psalm 80 v. 17." *Novum Testamentum* 15 (1973): 261–69.

Hillenbrand, Laura. *Unbroken: A World War II Story of Survival, Resilience, and Redemption.* New York: Random House, 2010.

Hodge, Charles. *Systematic Theology.* 3 vols. New York: Scribner, Armstrong, 1873.

Hoerth, Alfred J. *Archaeology and the Old Testament.* Grand Rapids: Baker, 1998.

Holladay, William L. *The Psalms through Three Thousand Years: Prayerbook of a Cloud of Witnesses.* Minneapolis: Fortress, 1993.

Holtz, Barry W., ed. *Back to the Sources: Reading the Classic Jewish Texts.* New York: Summit Books, 1984.

Horton, Michael Scott. *Putting Amazing Back into Grace: An Introduction to Reformed Theology.* Nashville: Thomas Nelson, 1991.

Hossfeld, Frank-Lothar, and Erich Zenger. *Psalms 2: A Commentary on Psalms 51–100.* Hermeneia. Minneapolis: Fortress, 2005.

———. *Psalms 3: A Commentary on Psalms 101–151.* Hermeneia. Minneapolis: Fortress, 2011.

Howard, David M., Jr. *The Structure of Psalms 93–100.* Winona Lake, IN: Eisenbrauns, 1997.

Hughes, Philip Edgecumbe. *Theology of the English Reformers.* London: Hodder & Stoughton, 1965.

Janowski, Bernd. "Dankbarkeit: Ein anthropologischer Grundbegriff im Spiegel der toda-Psalmen." In *Ritual und Poesie: Formen und Orte religiöser Dichtung im Alten Orient, im Judentum und im Christentum,* edited by Eric Zenger, 91–136. Herders Biblische Studien 36. Freiburg: Herder, 2003.

Jefferson, H. "Psalm LXXVII." *Vetus Testamentum* 13 (1963): 87–91.

Jenkins, Steffen G. "Retribution in the Canonical Psalter." PhD diss., Trinity College Bristol, 2015.

Jenni, Ernst, and Claus Westermann, eds. *Theological Lexicon of the Old Testament.* Translated by Mark E. Biddle. 3 vols. Peabody, MA: Hendrickson, 1997.

Jones, E. Stanley. *Abundant Living.* London: Hodder & Soughton, 1946.

Kaufmann, Yehezkel. "The Biblical Age." In *Great Ages and Ideas of the Jewish People,* edited by Leo W. Schwarz, 3–92. New York: Random House, 1956.

Kennedy, Gerald. *For Preachers and Other Sinners.* New York: Harper & Row, 1960.

Ker, John. *The Psalms in History and Biography.* Edinburgh: Andrew Elliot, 1888.

Kidner, Derek. *Psalms 1–72.* Tyndale Old Testament Commentaries. Downers Grove, IL: InterVarsity, 1975.

———. *Psalms 73–150.* Tyndale Old Testament Commentaries 14b. Downers Grove, IL: InterVarsity, 1975.

Kirkpatrick, Alexander Francis. *The Book of Psalms.* 1902. Reprint, Grand Rapids: Baker, 1982.

Kitchen, K. A. *On the Reliability of the Old Testament.* Grand Rapids: Eerdmans, 2003.

Koehler, Ludwig, and Walter Baumgartner. *The Hebrew and Aramaic Lexicon of the Old*

Testament. Study ed. 2 vols. Leiden: Brill, 2001.

Kraus, Hans-Joachim. *Psalms 1–59: A Continental Commentary.* Translated by Hilton C. Oswald. Minneapolis: Augsburg, 1988.

———. *Psalms 60–150: A Continental Commentary.* Translated by Hilton C. Oswald. Minneapolis: Fortress, 2000.

Kuitert, H. M. *I Have My Doubts: How to Become a Christian Without Being a Fundamentalist.* Translated by John Bowden. London: SCM Press, 1993.

Kuyper, Abraham. "Sphere Sovereignty." Translated by George Kamps. Inaugural Address, Free University of Amsterdam, October 20, 1880. http://www.reformationalpublishing project.com/pdf_books/Scanned_Books_ PDF/SphereSovereignty_English.pdf.

Lewis, C. S. *The Collected Letters of C. S. Lewis.* Vol. 3, *Narnia, Cambridge and Joy 1950–1963.* Edited by Walter Hooper. New York: HarperCollins, 2007.

———. *Letters to an American Lady.* Edited by Clyde S. Kilby. Grand Rapids: Eerdmans, 1967.

———. *The Magician's Nephew.* New York: Macmillan, 1955.

———. *Mere Christianity.* Westwood, NJ: Barbour, 1952.

———. *Reflections on the Psalms.* London: Geoffrey Bles, 1958.

———. *The Screwtape Letters.* 1942. Reprint, West Chicago, IL: Lord and King, 1976.

———. *The Weight of Glory and Other Addresses.* New York: HarperCollins, 2001.

Liebreich, Leon J. "The Songs of Ascents and the Priestly Blessing." *Journal of Biblical Literature* 74 (1955): 33–36.

Littell, Franklin Hamlin. *The German Phoenix.* Garden City, NY: Doubleday, 1960.

Longman, Tremper, III, and Peter Enns, eds. *Dictionary of the Old Testament: Wisdom, Poetry and Writings.* Downers Grove, IL: InterVarsity, 2008.

Luther, Martin. *Lectures on Romans.* Translated by Wilhelm Pauck. Library of Christian Classics 15. Philadelphia: Westminster, 1961.

———. *Luther's Works.* Vol. 13, *Select Psalms II.* Edited by Jaroslav Pelikan. St. Louis: Concordia, 1956.

———. "A Mighty Fortress Is Our God." Translated by Frederick H. Hedge. In *Trinity Hymnal,* no. 92. Atlanta: Great Commission Publications, 1990.

Lynch, Thomas Toke. "God's Help Sure." In *The New Laudes Domini: A Selection of Spiritual Songs, Ancient and Modern for Use in Baptist Churches,* no. 939. New York: Century, 1892.

MacDonald, George. *The Maiden's Bequest.* Edited by Michael R. Phillips. Minneapolis: Bethany House, 1985.

———. *Paul Faber, Surgeon.* Reprint of the 1900 edition, Project Gutenberg, 2004. http:// www.gutenberg.org/ebooks/12387.

———. *The Princess and the Goblin.* Reprint, Project Gutenberg, 2008, http://www.guten berg.org/ebooks/708.

———. *Thomas Wingfold, Curate.* Three vols. Reprint, Project Gutenberg, 2004. http:// www.gutenberg.org/ebooks/5976.

———. *The Vicar's Daughter.* Colorado Springs: Victor, 1997.

———. *What's Mine's Mine.* Three vols. Reprint, Project Gutenberg, 2012. http://www.guten berg.org/ebooks/5969.

MacDonald, Greville. *Reminiscences of a Specialist.* London: George Allen & Unwin, 1932.

Macholz, Christian. "Psalm 136: Exegetische Beobachtungen mit methodologischen Seitenblicken," in *Mincha: Festgabe für Rolf Rendtorff zum 75. Geburstag,* edited by Erhard Blum, 177–86. Neukirchen-Vluyn: Neukirchener Verlag, 2000.

Maclaren, Alexander. *Expositions of Holy Scripture: Psalms.* 2 vols. Edited by W. Robertson Nicoll. New York: A. C. Armstrong and Son, 1903.

Manton, Thomas. *One Hundred and Ninety Sermons on the Hundred and Nineteenth Psalm.* 3 vols. Reprint, London: Banner of Truth, 1990.

Marshall, Peter. *John Doe, Disciple: Sermons for the Young in Spirit.* Edited and with introductions by Catherine Marshall. Carmel, NY: Guideposts, 1963.

Matheson, George. "Make Me a Captive, Lord," In *The Hymnary of the United Church of Canada,* no. 313. Toronto: United Church Publishing House, 1930.

Mauriac, François. Foreword to *Night,* by Elie Wiesel. Translated by Stella Rodway. Toronto: Bantam, 1960.

Mays, James Luther. "The Place of the Torah-Psalms in the Psalter." *Journal of Biblical Literature* 106 (1987): 3–12.

———. *Psalms.* Interpretation. Louisville: John Knox, 1994.

Mendelsohn, I. "Slavery in the OT." In *The Interpreter's Dictionary of the Bible,* edited by

George Arthur Buttrick, 4:383–91. 5 vols. Nashville: Abingdon, 1962.

Miller, Donald G. "On Rejoicing in God: A Sermon on Habakkuk 3:17–19." *Interpreter* 2 (1948): 173–79.

Millgram, Abraham E. *Jewish Worship*. Philadelphia: Jewish Publication Society, 1971.

Moore, Pam Rosewell. *Life Lessons from the Hiding Place: Discovering the Heart of Corrie ten Boom*. Grand Rapids: Chosen, 2003.

Mote, Edward. "My Hope Is Built." In *Hymns for Praise and Worship*, no. 427. Nappanee, IN: Evangel Press, 1984.

Moule, C. F. D. *The Meaning of Hope*. Philadelphia: Fortress, 1963.

Moule, H. C. G. *The Epistle of Paul to the Romans*. 3rd ed. London: Hodder & Stoughton, 1896.

Mowinckel, Sigmund. *The Psalms in Israel's Worship*. Translated by D. R. Ap-Thomas. 2 vols. Oxford: Blackwell, 1962.

Muggeridge, Malcolm. *Jesus Rediscovered*. Glasgow: Collins, 1969.

Mulholland, James. *Praying like Jesus: The Lord's Prayer in a Culture of Prosperity*. San Francisco: HarperSanFrancisco, 2001.

Neusner, Jacob. *Sifré to Numbers: An American Translation and Explanation*. 2 vols. Atlanta: Scholars Press, 1986.

———. *The Tosefta*. 2 vols. Peabody, MA: Hendrickson, 2002.

Newton, John. *Select Letters of John Newton*. Edinburgh: The Banner of Truth Trust, 1960.

———. *The Works of the Rev. John Newton*. 6 vols. New York: Robert Carter, 1944.

North, Frank Mason. "Where Cross the Crowded Ways of Life." In *The Covenant Hymnal*, no. 538. Chicago: Covenant Press, 1973.

O'Connor, Flannery. *A Prayer Journal*. New York: Farrar, Straus & Giroux, 2013.

Oden, Thomas C. *Pastoral Counsel*. New York: Crossroad, 1989.

Osbeck, Kenneth W. *Amazing Grace: 366 Inspiring Hymn Stories for Daily Devotions*. Grand Rapids: Kregel, 1990.

Otto, Rudolf. *The Idea of the Holy*. 2nd ed. Translated by John W. Harvey. London: Oxford, 1950.

Pagolu, Augustine. *The Religion of the Patriarchs*. Journal for the Study of the Old Testament Supplement 277. Leiden: Brill, 1998.

Patterson, Ben. *God's Prayer Book: The Power and Pleasure of Praying the Psalms*. Carol Stream, IL: Tyndale, 2008.

Pearce, Joseph. *Literary Converts: Spiritual Inspiration in an Age of Unbelief*. San Francisco: Ignatius, 1999.

Peck, M. Scott. *The Different Drum: Community-Making and Peace*. New York: Simon and Schuster, 1987.

Pedersen, Johannes. *Israel: Its Life and Culture I–II*. London: Oxford University Press, 1926.

Pelikan, Jaroslav. *Jesus through the Centuries*. New York: Harper & Row, 1985.

Perowne, J. J. Stewart. *The Book of Psalms*. 2 vols. London: George Bell, 1883.

Petersen, Allan Rosengren. *The Royal God: Enthronement Festivals in Ancient Israel and Ugarit*. Sheffield: JSOT Press, 1998.

Peterson, Eugene H. *A Long Obedience in the Same Direction: Discipleship in an Instant Society*. Downers Grove, IL: InterVarsity, 1980.

Pierre, Robert E. "Alice Frazier, at 81; Southerner Hugged Queen Elizabeth II." *Washington Post*. March 20, 2005.

Poling, Daniel A. *Faith Is Power—For You*. New York: Greenberg, 1950.

Pollock, John. *Moody: The Biography*. Chicago: Moody, 1983.

Pope, Marvin H. *El in the Ugaritic Texts*. Leiden: Brill, 1955.

Potok, Chaim. *The Chosen*. Greenwich, CT: Fawcett, 1967.

Prévost, Jean-Pierre. *A Short Dictionary of the Psalms*. Translated by Mary Misrahi. Collegeville, MN: Liturgical Press, 1997.

Prothero, Rowland E. *The Psalms in Human Life*. New York: Dutton, 1905.

Rassmussen, Carl G. *Zondervan NIV Atlas of the Bible*. Grand Rapids: Zondervan, 1989.

Reardon, Patrick Henry. *Christ in the Psalms*. Ben Lombon, CA: Conciliar Press, 2000.

Robertson, O. Palmer. *The Flow of the Psalms: Discovering Their Structure and Theology*. Phillipsburg, NJ: P&R Publishing, 2015.

Rockness, Miriam Huffman. *A Passion for the Impossible: The Life of Lilias Trotter*. Grand Rapids: Discovery House, 2003.

Ross, Allen P. *A Commentary on the Psalms*. 3 vols. Grand Rapids: Kregel, 2011–16.

———. *Holiness to the LORD: A Guide to the Exposition of the Book of Leviticus*. Grand Rapids: Baker Academic, 2002.

———. *Introducing Biblical Hebrew*. Grand Rapids: Baker Academic, 2001.

Routley, Erik. *Rejoice in the Lord: A Hymn Companion to the Scriptures*. Grand Rapids: Eerdmans, 1985.

Ryken, Leland, James C. Wilhoit, and Tremper Longman III, eds. *Dictionary of Biblical Imagery*. Downers Grove, IL: InterVarsity, 1998.

Sandburg, Carl. *Abraham Lincoln: The War Years (1861–1864)*. New York: Dell, 1954.

Sayers, Dorothy L. *Letters to a Diminished Church: Passionate Arguments for the Relevance of Christian Doctrine*. Nashville: Thomas Nelson, 2004.

Schaefer, Konrad. *Psalms*. Berit Olam: Studies in Hebrew Narrative and Poetry. Collegeville, MN: Liturgical Press, 2001.

Scott, R. B. Y. *The Way of Wisdom in the Old Testament*. New York: Macmillan, 1971.

The Scottish Psalter, 1929. London: Oxford University Press, 1929.

Selderhuis, Herman J. *John Calvin: A Pilgrim's Life*. Downers Grove, IL: InterVarsity, 2009.

Seymour, Michael. "Power and Seduction in Babylon: Verdi's *Nabucco*." In *Seduction and Power: Antiquity in the Visual and Performing Arts*, edited by Silke Knippschild and Marta García Morcillo, 9–20. London: Bloomsbury, 2013.

Shanks, Hershel. "Human Sacrifice to an Ammonite God?" First Person. *Biblical Archaeology Review* 40:5 (September/October 2014): 6, 57.

Sifton, Elisabeth, and Fritz Stern. *No Ordinary Men: Dietrich Bonhoeffer and Hans von Dohnanyi, Resisters against Hitler in Church and State*. New York: New York Review Books, 2013.

Silverman, William B. *Rabbinic Stories for Christian Ministers and Teachers*. New York: Abingdon, 1958.

Spurgeon, C. H. *The Treasury of David*. 3 vols. Reprint, Peabody, MA: Hendrickson, 2011.

Starck, Johann. *Starck's Prayer Book*. Translated and edited by W. H. T. Dau. St. Louis: Concordia, 1921.

Stec, David M. *The Targum of the Psalms*. Collegeville, MN: Liturgical Press, 2004.

Stoddart, Jane T. *The Psalms for Every Day*. London: Hodder & Stoughton, 1939.

Stol, M. *Epilepsy in Babylonia*. Groningen: Styx, 1993.

Storms, Sam. *More Precious than Gold: 50 Daily Meditations on the Psalms*. Wheaton: Crossway, 2009.

Studdert-Kennedy, G. A. *The Word and the Work*. London: Hodder & Stoughton, 1965.

Stuhlmueller, Carroll. *Psalms 2: 73–150*. Old Testament Message. Collegeville, MN: Liturgical Press, 1983.

Tate, Marvin E. *Psalms 51–100*. Word Biblical Commentary 20. Dallas: Word, 1990.

Thielicke, Helmut. *I Believe: The Christian's Creed*. Translated by John W. Doberstein and H. George Anderson. Philadelphia: Fortress, 1968.

Thompson, Francis. "The Hound of Heaven." In *Selected Poems of Francis Thompson*, 51–56. New York: John Lane, 1908.

Tinder, Glen. "Can We Be Good without God? On the Political Meaning of Christianity." *Atlantic Monthly*, December 1989, 69–85.

Tozer, A. W. *The Best of Tozer*. Grand Rapids: Baker, 1980.

Twain, Mark. *The Innocents Abroad*. New York: Penguin, 1966.

VanGemeren, Willem, ed. *New International Dictionary of Old Testament Theology and Exegesis*. 5 vols. Grand Rapids: Zondervan, 1997.

———. "Psalms." In *The Expositor's Bible Commentary*. Rev. ed. Edited by Tremper Longman III and David E. Garland. Grand Rapids: Zondervan, 2008.

von Rad, Gerhard. *Old Testament Theology*. 2 vols. Translated by D. M. G. Stalker. New York: Harper & Row, 1962, 1965.

Walker, Winifred. *All the Plants of the Bible*. New York: Harper, 1957.

Wallace, Lew. *Ben-Hur: A Tale of the Christ*. New York: Harper, 1880.

Waltke, Bruce K., and M. O'Connor. *An Introduction to Biblical Hebrew Syntax*. Winona Lake, IN: Eisenbrauns, 1990.

Waltner, James H. *Psalms*. Believers Church Bible Commentary. Scottdale, PA: Herald, 2006.

Watts, J. D. W. "Yahweh Malak Psalms." *Theologische Zeitschrift* 21 (1965): 341–48.

Weiser, Artur. *The Psalms: A Commentary*. Old Testament Library. Philadelphia: Westminster, 1962.

Wenham, Gordon J. *Psalms as Torah: Reading Biblical Song Ethically*. Grand Rapids: Baker Academic, 2012.

Whyte, Alexander. *The Shorter Catechism*. Reprint, Edinburgh: T&T Clark, 1949.

Wilcock, Michael. *The Message of Psalms 73–150: Songs for the People of God*. The Bible Speaks Today. Downers Grove, IL: InterVarsity, 2002.

Williams, Charles. *He Came Down from Heaven*. 1938. Reprint, Grand Rapids: Eerdmans, 1984.

Wilson, Gerald Henry. *The Editing of the Hebrew Psalter*. Chico, CA: Scholars Press, 1985.

———. *Psalms*. Vol. 1. NIV Application Commentary. Grand Rapids: Zondervan, 2002.

Wolpe, David J. *The Healer of Shattered Hearts: A Jewish View of God*. New York: Penguin, 1990.

Wordsworth, William. "Ode to Duty." In *The Complete Poetical Works of William Wordsworth*, 213. London: Macmillan, 1983.

Wright, Christopher J. H. *The God I Don't Understand: Reflections on Tough Questions of Faith*. Grand Rapids: Zondervan, 2008.

———. *Old Testament Ethics for the People of God*. Downers Grove, IL: InterVarsity, 2004.

———, ed. *Portraits of a Radical Disciple: Recollections of John Stott's Life and Ministry*. Downers Grove, IL: InterVarsity, 2011.

Wright, N. T. *The Case for the Psalms: Why They Are Essential*. New York: HarperCollins, 2013.

Contributors

General Editors
Mark L. Strauss
John H. Walton

Series Development
Jack Kuhatschek
Brian Vos

Project Editor
James Korsmo

Interior Design
Brian Brunsting

Cover Direction
Paula Gibson
Michael Cook

Index

Aaron, 200, 461, 464
  house of, 323, 331, 333, 349,
    351, 475
Aaronic priesthood, 293–94
abiding in Christ, 95, 96
Abiram, 260
abortion on demand, 218
Abraham, 159, 195, 249–50,
    252–53, 346, 484
Absalom, 534, 535
absence, of God's promise, 366
accountability, 169, 522
acrostic structure, 308
'adonay, 110, 136, 295, 296, 326
adversity and deliverance, 64
agapē love, 218
Alexander the Great, 202
Allen, Leslie C., 567
"all flesh," 550
Almighty, shadow of, 144
alphabetic acrostic, 301, 357, 547
"Already God," 508
Amalek, 86
Amen, 132, 262
Ammon, Ammonites, 53, 62,
    84, 86
anadiplosis 379, 428, 455
Anderson, A. A., 5, 6
angels, 82, 145, 147, 148, 571
anger of God, 43, 61
anguish of the grave, 339, 342
anointing, 152
anthology style, of a psalm, 337
anthropopathism, 45
Antiochus Epiphanes, 10
anxiety, 8
Apostles' Creed, the, 386, 545

Aramaic, 549
ark of Noah, 484
ark of the covenant, 46, 177,
    199–200, 250, 261, 445, 451,
    452, 454, 465, 459, 587
armor of God, 582
arrogant, 3, 4, 361, 363
arrows, 373
Asaph psalms, 1, 9, 11, 67, 76, 84
ash heap, 309, 318
assembly of God, 76, 579
assurance, 147
Assyria, 60, 85, 86
Aten (Egyptian sun god), 237
Augustine, 65, 66, 117–18, 202,
    280, 356, 410, 417, 448–49,
    594
awakening
  from dark night of exile, 331
  from sleep, 5

Baal, 260
Babel, 92
Babylonian exile, 19, 32, 34,
    130, 170, 178, 188, 269, 339,
    487–91, 527
  return from, 98, 191, 193, 208,
    213, 261, 269, 271, 302, 303,
    310, 322, 374, 379–80, 384,
    401, 413, 460, 480, 501
Babylonians, 3, 166
Baka, Valley of, 93–94
barrenness, 315–16, 322
Baumgartner, Walter, 123, 361
Beatitudes, 377
believer, character of, 310–12
benediction, 344, 465

benefits, 229, 231
Benjamin (tribe), 42, 61, 63, 595
blessed, 91, 93–94, 95, 259, 262,
    302, 310–11, 359, 540, 541,
    543
blessing, 61, 429, 434, 456, 467
  on all who fear the LORD, 427
  biblical protocol of, 467–68
  of God, 309, 467, 550
  of Israel, 381
  on the one God disciplines,
    166, 169
  of posterity, 312, 333
  on postexilic community, 373
  from superior to inferior, 462
  of unity, 459–61
Blessing of Moses, 135, 136,
    138, 379
Boaz, 434
boldness, 545
bones, burn like glowing embers,
    221, 222
Book of Common Prayer, The,
    173, 209, 210
boundary, 239
bowlful of tears, 62, 66
broom bush, 374
Brueggemann, Walter, 2
Bunyan, John, 38, 110
burning coals, 373, 515
burning thorns, 352
burnt offerings, 378

Calvin, John, 15, 16, 27, 88,
    161, 179, 188, 210, 241, 243,
    280–81, 456, 507, 568
  liturgy of, 403, 405

on peaceful life, 410
on piety, 523–24, 560
Canaan, 528
Canaanites, 261, 474
cattle, 572
cave, 526, 527
cedar tree, 153, 154, 572
chains, 340
chaos, symbolized by sea, 160
character, 306, 311
chariot, 238
cherubim, 199, 200, 238
Chesterton, G. K., 49–50, 73–74, 188, 416
children
    as a blessing, 426–31
    as heritage from the Lord, 422, 429
    security of, 224
choral voice, of the psalms, 593
Chrysostom, 281
church
    as body of Christ, 272–73
    local history of, 435
    on pilgrimage through this evil world, 16
citadels, 391
citizenship, 113, 116–18
cloud, 185, 200, 252
comfort, 363
coming of the Lord, 184
command of God, 566, 571
community, 169
    and individual, 273, 462–63
community lament, 9, 83, 98, 119, 125, 134, 276, 395, 486
community repentance, 51
community thanksgiving, 353, 400, 432
confession of faith, 174
confession of sin, 52
conquest of Canaan, 45, 317, 474, 482
contentment, 93, 95, 449
cords of death, 338, 339, 342
cornerstone, 352, 601
corporate prayer, 175–76
Court of Israel, 373
Court of the Women, 373
covenant, 35, 213, 454
covenant formula, 54, 170, 174, 207, 210, 327, 352–53, 354, 475, 515, 535, 536, 541, 598
creation, 52, 136, 174, 234–42, 480, 481, 504, 507, 573–74
    boundaries of, 13
    frustration of, 180
    goodness of, 553
    observant of redemption, 326, 328
    serves the Creator, 364
    as wonderful, 504, 507, 509

crying out, 120, 123, 269, 270, 271, 351, 529
cup of God's wrath, 20
cup of salvation, 340
curse on the ground, 422
Cush, 115
cymbals, 588, 590
Cyrus, 212, 271, 377, 489, 577
    decree of, 167, 193, 414

dancing, 115, 579, 587, 590
darkness, 121, 122, 144, 270, 311, 490, 507, 509
Dathan, 260
David
    afflictions of, 453
    conflict with Saul, 526, 527, 538, 540, 544, 545
    coronation of, 460
    kingly office of, 292
    as man of prayer, 285
    oath of, 452, 453, 456
    passion against his enemies, 290–91
    plans for the first temple, 513
    prayers for his people, 532, 535
    as prototype for "poor and needy," 111
    rest of, 160, 339
    as the righteous individual, 303
    as shepherd, 46
    as suffering servant, 105–7, 291, 535, 543
    victory over enemies, 302
Davidic covenant, 126, 128–29, 200, 452, 455, 475
    endurance of, 129
    failure of, 3, 33, 91, 98, 125, 129, 135, 159, 171, 212, 294
Davidic psalms, 214, 215, 228, 276, 284, 492, 513, 518, 525, 547
dawn of day, 534
day of judgment, 588
day of salvation, 101
days of creation, 235–36
death, 122, 137, 289, 534
    as sleep, 136
deceit, 216, 542
deceitful tongue, 373, 375
decree(s), 262–63, 362, 369, 569, 571
Delitzsch, Franz, 142, 160, 161, 229, 240, 346, 395, 445, 572, 575, 598
deliverance, 64, 327, 341, 497, 536–37
depths, 439, 441, 443
despair, 441
destiny, 376
Deuteronomy, 135

dew, 460–63
director of music, 505, 514
discernment, 522, 537
discipline, 166, 169
disobedience, of wilderness generation, 170, 171, 173
divine kingship, 171
Dodd, C. H., 595
domesticated animals, 572
doorkeeper, 94
double-edged sword, 580, 582
double heart, 109
doubt, 109
dove, 13
doxology, 262, 586
dust, 136, 230, 232, 309, 318, 320, 601
dwelling in God's presence, 95, 96
dwelling place, 5, 95, 96, 135, 136, 138–39

eagle, 228
earth, 20, 27, 95, 180, 194, 326
Eden, 91
Edom, Edomites, 53, 62, 86, 278, 487, 489
Egyptian bondage, 40, 44, 70, 339, 501, 542
Egyptian Hallel, 246, 247, 268, 303, 305, 309, 315, 322–23, 324, 326, 342, 344, 347, 348, 351, 353, 358, 359, 408, 469–72, 473, 526
Egypt-wilderness-Canaan paradigm, 530–31
'elohim, 2, 11, 142, 144, 157, 275, 326, 601
Elohistic Psalter, 11, 25, 77, 83, 142, 157, 275
enemies, 85, 223, 433, 455
English Reformers, 173, 175
envy, 6
Ephraim, 40, 42, 61
Ephrathah, 451, 454
escape, from dangers of exile, 396–97
Esther, 85
eternal life, 123, 124
Ethan the Ezrahite, 128
Ethiopia, 115
euthanasia, 218
everlasting ruins, 12, 16
"Everyday Hallel, the" 547
every nation, tribe, people and language, 346–47
evil, 14, 288, 515–16
    as absence of God, 594

hating of, 187, 189
progression of, 516, 520
reversal of, 581
self-destruction of, 516
evildoers, 365, 408, 410, 518
exile, 131, 485, 535
  restoration from, 114–15, 213,
    225, 246, 266, 339, 341, 460,
    499, 564
  See also Babylonian exile
exodus, 34, 35, 52, 69, 114, 158,
  178, 200, 246, 252, 325, 330,
  367, 469, 482, 530
Ezra, 299, 380, 556, 570, 578, 579

faithfulness, 101, 103, 572–73,
  579
fatherless, 77, 166, 285, 558
fear of the LORD, 28, 30, 137,
  179, 196, 213, 223, 302, 305,
  333, 363, 427, 428–29
Feast of Tabernacles, 68, 69, 389,
  460, 603
Feast of Trumpets, 68, 69
Feast of Unleavened Bread, 460
Feast of Water-Drawing, 378
Feast of Weeks, 460
feathers, 144
festive psalms, 171
fire
  with God's presence, 185
  in wilderness wanderings, 252
firstborn, striking down of (tenth
  plague), 45, 251–52, 474, 482
first commandment, 70
flowing streams, 272
food, 239–40, 305, 480
foolish and wise, 13
foot, slipping of, 168, 383
footprints of God, 35, 37
footstool, 199–200, 295
"for/because" (conjunction), 483
forgetting, 41
forgiveness of sins, 54, 55, 99–
  100, 103–4, 198, 201–2, 228,
  440, 441, 442
forgiving others, 55, 264
form criticism, 68, 330
Forsyth, P. T., 443, 517
fortress, 144, 542

gatekeepers, 128, 349, 352
gates of Jerusalem, 114, 390
gates of the righteous, 352
gates of the temple, 207
Genevan Psalter, 210
gentiles, 225, 346
gifts of God, 422
Gilead, 278
gittith, 68, 92
Glueck, Nelson, 413

God
  anger of, 100, 173
  attributes of, 229, 508–9
  as avenger, 165, 168
  as awesome, 30
  builds up Jerusalem, 562,
    564–65, 568
  character of, 132, 224, 225,
    306–7, 312
  chooses the weak and insignifi-
    cant, 355
  compassion of, 141–42, 227–
    30, 305, 306, 312, 480, 550
  condescension of, 320, 497, 567
  constancy of, 269–70
  control over evil, 45
  covenant faithfulness, 102, 207
  covenant remembrance, 193,
    195, 250, 261, 305, 482, 483,
    484–85
  as Creator, 172, 211, 224, 364,
    474, 511, 564–65, 590–91
  crowns the humble with vic-
    tory, 579–80, 583
  does whatever he pleases, 332,
    474, 477, 499
  dwells in the midst of his
    people, 135, 138–39, 143,
    327, 354, 531
  dwells in Zion, 26, 460–61,
    475, 477
  election of Israel, 167
  enthroned in heaven, 396,
    397–98
  eternity of, 224
  as exalted, 201–2, 277, 279
  faithfulness of, 128, 130, 131–
    32, 193, 246, 332, 345–46,
    354, 362–63, 490–91, 558
  as Father, 210–11, 230, 232
  fulfills purposes in us, 498
  generosity of, 550
  glory of, 100, 186, 523
  goodness of, 2–3, 98, 101, 108,
    154, 207, 340, 353, 480, 549,
    552–53, 555
  grace of, 54, 263–64, 479
  greater than all gods, 179, 186,
    473, 481
  greatness of, 473–74, 549, 552,
    555, 558, 566, 587
  great wonders of, 481–82, 483
  as helper, 351, 559–60
  as hidden, 130
  holds on to us, 88
  holiness of, 35, 162, 187,
    197–203, 277
  and human actions, 56–57
  on Israel's side, 400–402,
    432–36
  of Jacob, 326, 557

  as judge, 76, 78, 168–69, 194,
    195
  justice of, 19, 199, 201–2,
    217–18, 366
  keeps his promises, 253
  kingship of, 157, 171, 204,
    212–13, 223, 555–56
  knowledge of, 505–6, 509, 510
  as light, 29–30
  looks kindly on the lowly, 497
  love of, 46, 130, 131–32, 137,
    145, 146, 154, 168–69, 193,
    204, 207, 215, 217–18, 229,
    232, 246, 259, 267, 268, 287,
    332, 345, 347, 351, 353, 354,
    369, 441, 443, 480, 483, 498,
    558, 559
  as Master Architect, 355, 423
  as Master Teacher, 361
  as merciful, 44
  mighty acts of, 13, 34, 35, 40,
    114, 178, 193, 230, 270, 271,
    304, 416
  as mother, 444, 448
  nearness of, 369, 550, 551
  as object of history, 15
  omnificence of, 508
  omnipotence of, 544
  omnipresence of, 508
  omniscience of, 508
  as only hope, 278
  as portion, 528, 529
  power of, 567, 580–81, 587
  presence of, 5, 6, 94, 237,
    326–28, 406, 410, 504, 509,
    510, 512, 515, 573, 589
  promises of, 132
  protection of, 143, 146, 406
  provision of, 422
  reign of peace, 29
  rescue of Israel, 354
  righteousness of, 103, 186, 535
  as rock, 541
  as savior, 54
  self revelation of, 29
  as shepherd, 33, 36, 59, 62,
    64–65, 172, 208
  silence of, 83, 85, 284
  as slow to anger, 553–54
  sovereignty of, 28–29, 30, 84,
    161, 163, 164, 168, 184, 202,
    242, 318–19, 320, 423, 436,
    573
  stoops to see the earth, 317–19
  strength of, 179, 250
  as subject of history, 15
  swears an oath, 28, 173, 296,
    454
  takes delight in his people,
    579–80
  tests Israel, 70

thirteen attributes of, 229, 304, 305, 549, 589
and time, 135, 136, 138
unfailing love of, 35, 100, 102, 167, 168, 272, 286, 441, 442, 496–97, 534–35
as warrior, 46
will not forsake the afflicted, 27
wisdom of, 239
gods, 75–79, 81–82, 108, 171, 210
golden calf incident, 135, 260, 330
Goldingay, John, 14, 27, 195, 308, 379
goodness, 64–65, 153, 217–18
gospel, 209–10
Goulder, Michael D., 401, 488, 564, 603, 604
grace, 46, 54, 71–72, 139, 146, 148, 174, 375, 517, 536, 553–54, 567
gratitude, 498
grave, 521. *See also* Sheol
great assembly, 81
Great Commission, 209, 253
great confession, 536
Great Hallel, 268, 469, 479, 493
great lights, 481
great wonders, 481–82, 483, 504
Greene, W. B., Jr., 45
Gunkel, Hermann, 503, 580

Haggai, 444, 445, 492
Hagrites, 86
Hakham, Amos, 222, 295, 334, 361, 362, 520
Hallel. *See* Egyptian Hallel; "Everyday Hallel"; Great Hallel; Passover Hallel
hallelujah, 240–41, 245–47, 252, 303, 310, 316, 317, 330, 344, 473, 547, 585, 586, 591–92
Hallelujah Psalter, 241, 247, 569, 570, 572, 577, 590
hallelujah redaction, the, 303, 317
hand of God, 506
Hannah, 18, 316, 318, 322
happiness, 203, 430
"happy mother of children," 316, 318, 322, 340
harp, 68, 151, 152, 193, 276, 488, 579, 581, 587, 590
harvesters' blessing, 434
Hasidaeans, 579
Hasmonean era, 299
hear/listen, 71–72
heart, 306
as divided, 109
not proud, 446–47
as perverse, 216

hearts, as steadfast, 311
heaven and earth, unite in praise to God, 573–74
heavenly hosts, 571
heavens, 180, 506
"he comes" (clause), 180–82, 191
hedonism, 139
Heidelberg Catechism, 175, 386, 510
help from the LORD, 277, 383, 402, 403–5
Heman the Ezrahite, 120
heritage, 422, 424–25
Hermon's dew, 459, 461–63
hesed, 35, 122, 130, 229, 230, 232, 247, 259, 267, 270, 272, 276, 286, 288, 312, 314, 332, 345, 347, 348–49, 355, 363, 365, 366, 369, 440, 483, 494, 498, 534–35, 536
hidden things, 41
highest heavens, 571
Hilary of Tours, 423
hills, 572
historical double-tracking, 498, 501–2, 548
historical psalms, 39, 248
history
irony of, 576
purpose of, 254–55
holiness, 103, 162, 191, 201, 215
holy splendor, 295–96
honey, 365
hope, 58, 224, 440, 442, 447, 604
horns, 19, 20, 21, 152, 352, 572–73, 574
Hossfeld, Frank-Lothar, 9, 33, 111, 127, 249, 492, 507–8, 549
house of the LORD, 389–91, 444
Howard, David M., Jr., 158, 164
"how long?" (phrase), 12, 14, 16, 53
human effort, and God's enabling, 422–23
human help, as worthless, 278–80
humanity
and creation, 565
insignificance of, 542, 543–44
a little lower than God, 565, 567
in praise of God, 588
human plans, as futile, 165–67
humiliation, 318, 601
humility, 78–79, 110, 280–81, 320, 447–48, 543, 544–45, 581, 583
hunting metaphors, 144, 514, 516
Hymenaeus and Alexander, 410
hypocrisy, 306

idols, idolatry, 3, 46, 179, 186, 323, 330, 359, 475–76
becoming like them, 332–35, 476
as lifeless, 332–33, 476
manufacturing of, 258
mockery of, 332
image of God, 174, 175, 333–34, 565, 574
imitation of God, 217, 312, 313, 320
imprecatory psalms, 282, 285, 288, 291, 489
imprisonment, 532, 534
incarnation, 188, 280
incense, 520
individualism, and community, 462–64
individual lament, 119, 220, 276, 512, 525, 532
individual psalm of trust, 395, 439. *See also* psalms of trust
inheritance, 11, 166, 475, 480
iniquity, 4
injustice, 122, 164–65, 168
innocence, of psalmist, 2, 4
insecurity, 410–11
intertextuality of psalms, 106, 337, 349, 470, 539, 578
intimacy with God, 145
irony, 576
Ishmael, 373
Ishmaelites, 86
Israel
all, 349, 351, 475
complaint of, 43
disobedience of, 46–47
in Egypt, 251–52
election of, 473, 477
and Gentiles, 346
insignificance of, 354–55
as a parable, 254
rebellion of, 259–61, 263–64
as sheep, 11
sin of, 257–58
spiritual maturity of, 445, 446–47
stubbornness of, 71
testing God, 42, 44, 70
as treasured possession, 473, 477
unbelief of, 44
vow of faithfulness, 63
in the wilderness, 363
as Yahweh's congregation, 11
Israel (as name for postexilic community), 407
Israel (northern kingdom), 25, 407
"I"-"you" phrasing, 503

Jeduthun, 34
Jenni, Ernst, 123
Jerusalem, 114, 389, 390–92, 393–94, 428, 487
  blessing on, 430
  eschatological picture of, 566
  fall of, 14–17, 32, 85, 130, 144, 489
  as home, 490
  personification of, 220–21, 223
  rebuilding of, 562, 564–65, 568
Jesus Christ
  Beatitudes of, 377, 559
  condescension of, 544
  death of, 484
  humiliation of, 48–49
  humility of, 448
  as image of God, 334
  interpretation of the psalms, 299–300
  lineage through David, 130
  messianic rule, 294
  personal relationship with, 462
  priestly office, 293
  reconciling work, 103
  as true temple, 96
Job, 22, 119, 122, 223, 311, 478, 507
Jonah, 550
Jordan River, 325, 326
Joseph, 61, 69, 250–51, 254, 255, 263, 270
Joshua, conquest of land, 45
Joshua (high priest), 299
journey from Babylon to Judah, 383
joy, 95, 154–55, 172, 187, 188, 204, 208, 209, 211, 240, 392, 415–17
Judah, as God's sanctuary, 325
Judah (southern kingdom), 25, 407
Judah (tribe), 40, 42, 46
Judaism, emergence of, 303, 310, 359
judges, the, 77, 81, 520–21
judgment, 76, 167, 168–69, 195, 200, 282
justice, 6, 21–22, 77, 78, 81, 129, 168, 185, 199, 214, 215, 307, 375, 458, 515

Kaufmann, Yehezkel, 359
Kedar, 373–74, 376
Kidner, Derek, 93, 108, 125, 227, 346, 364, 373, 462, 506
kidneys, 507
king
  as shepherd, 172
  suffering of, 105–6

kingdom of God, 101–2, 231, 393, 515, 536, 537, 550, 551, 556, 557, 559–60, 575
kings of the earth, acknowledge the LORD, 28, 30, 492, 496, 497, 572
Kiriath Jearim, 451, 452, 454, 456
Kirkpatrick, Alexander Francis, 276, 363
"know" (verb), 505
knowing God, 145
Knox, John, 210, 404
Koehler, Ludwig, 123, 361
Korah, 128, 260, 402
Korah psalms, 91, 93, 94, 112–13, 119
Kraus, Hans-Joachim, 199, 285, 520

lament, 15, 57
  clad in joy, 412
  as good for the soul, 490
  See also psalms of lament
Lamentations, 119, 535
land of the living, 339, 341, 528, 529, 530
Last Supper, 342
law, 166
laws and decrees, 566–67
Leah, 40, 42
Leviathan, 13, 239
Levites, 373, 475
  portion of, 2, 5, 529, 530
Lewis, C. S., 8, 22, 49–50, 124, 138, 139–40, 188, 298, 335, 411, 468, 522, 523, 531, 573
lex talionis, 289
Liebreich, Leon J., 378, 381, 409
lies, 602
life
  brevity of, 138, 152, 224–25, 228, 231, 232, 542
  vanishes away, 221, 222
life after death, 120
life of praise, 242–43
lifting up hands, 466, 468
light, 29–30, 187, 237–38, 365
lightning, 238, 572
lilies, 61
lion, 12, 145
listening, 41
liturgy, 451
locust, 44
long life, 146
LORD Almighty, 93
  reign of, 157–63, 179–80, 181, 184, 185, 186, 188–89, 199, 202, 248–49, 558
lordship, and servanthood, 109
Lord's house, 153

Lord's Prayer, 55, 101, 133, 522–23, 536, 574
love, 215, 218, 338, 341–42
  for each other, 313
  for enemies, 508
  and faithfulness, 100–102
  for God, 430, 463, 496
  for neighbor, 430, 463
  as solution to envy, 6, 8
Luther, Martin, 22, 103–4, 146, 149, 210, 214, 274, 423–24, 499–500, 545
lying lips, 373, 375
lyre, 68, 151, 581, 587, 590

Maccabeans, 294, 299, 579
MacDonald, George, 31, 37–38, 50, 66, 189–90, 209, 313–14, 347, 392, 394, 442–43, 531, 536, 537, 552
Maker of heaven and earth, 383, 384, 385–86, 402–5, 445, 465–66, 467, 474, 557, 560, 579
Manasseh (tribe of), 61, 278
manna, 43, 260, 305
Manton, Thomas, 369
Marduk, 76, 92
Mary's Song, 188
maskil, 11, 39
Masoretes, 61, 151, 207, 277, 383, 598
Massah, 173, 261
master, 396
Master/servant picture, 440
maturity, in Second Temple period, 368
Mays, James Luther, 217–18, 323, 598
meek, the, 581, 584
Melchizedek, 186, 246, 292–93, 296, 297, 299, 462, 467
mercy, 396–97
  cry for, 440
Meribah, 173, 261
Meshek, 373–74, 376
Messiah, 63, 299–300
metaphor, 36–37
Michal, 445
Midian, 86
"Mighty Fortress Is Our God, A" (Luther), 146, 149, 424–25
mighty heavens, 585, 587
mighty ones, 231, 598
Miller, Donald G., 37
Miller, Patrick, 2
Moab, Moabites, 53, 62, 84, 86, 278
mockery, 4
monotheism, 323, 359, 481
moon, 239, 382–83, 482

morality, 217–18
mortality, and sin, 139
Mosaic covenant, 105, 130, 159, 193, 217–18, 305
Moses, 134, 136, 154, 158, 200, 317, 326, 475
    Blessing of, 135, 136, 138, 379
    disobedience of, 261
    humility of, 544, 545
    prayer of, 82, 260, 262–63, 264, 366–67
Most High, 77, 84, 87, 115, 144, 147, 186–87
mother, as symbol of God, 444, 448
mountains, 26, 238–39, 325, 383, 385, 407, 572
Mount Bashan, 383
Mount Gilboa, 42
Mount Sinai, 325, 540–41, 542, 544, 545
Mount Zion, 11, 26, 383, 407, 460
Muggeridge, Malcolm, 124, 462, 464
music, 152, 581

Naaman, 488
name of God, 12, 14, 54, 88, 474–75, 535
names of God, 92, 144
"name" theology, 54, 84, 502
Nathan, 125
nations, 53–54, 56, 78, 85, 87, 179–80, 181, 351, 572
    fear of the LORD, 225
    salvation of, 207–8, 345–46
    taunting by, 332
    taunting of, 336
    trembling of, 199
Nebuchadnezzar, 10, 14
needy, 580
Nehemiah era, 380, 416–17, 556, 564, 566, 570, 578, 579
Neo-Assyrian period, 85
new birth, 117–18
new Canaan, 529–30
new community, 541
new covenant, 368, 369
new exodus, 200, 246, 266, 322, 353, 530
new heavens and new earth, 225
new Jerusalem, 215
new life, from restoration, 339
New Moon, 68, 69
new song, 177, 178, 180, 192, 193, 541, 542, 579, 588
new temple, 323, 460
Newton, John, 58, 116–17, 182–83, 273–74, 342–43, 369
next generation, 225

next of kin, 572, 574
Noachian covenant, 13
Noah, 484

northern tribes, 35
number symbolism, 589

oaths, 365, 453, 489
obedience, 428, 456–57
ocean depths, 571
"of/for David" (superscription), 389, 401, 525, 541
Og of Bashan, 474, 482
oil, 152, 461
"Old One Hundredth" (Psalm 100), 210
olive shoots, 428
one generation, passes heritage to the next, 424, 549
oppression, 433–35. 580, 581
owl, 222

pacifism, 582
palm tree, 152, 153, 154
pantheon of gods, 81
parable, 41
parable of the vine, 138
parallelism, 501
parched ground, 272
Passover Hallel, 315
Passover seder, 315, 342, 415
patriarchs, 249, 250, 262
peace, 29, 103, 373, 374, 389, 391, 406, 408–9, 410
Pedersen, Johannes, 458
penitential psalms, 532, 534
Perowne, J. J. Stewart, 229, 241–42, 598
Petersen, Allan Rosengren, 159
Peterson, Eugene, 375, 385, 392, 409, 411, 456
Petra, 278
Pharaoh, perishing of, 482
Philistia, 115, 278
Phinehas, 258, 260–61
piety, 523–24, 560
pilgrimage, 93, 94–96, 97, 373, 375, 400
Pilgrim Psalter, 247, 378, 427, 451, 465, 472, 480
    centering effect of, 419–20
    See also Songs of Ascent
Pilgrim's Progress (Bunyan), 110, 376
pillar of cloud, 200
pillars, 543
pipes, 588
plagues in Egypt, 69, 251–52, 304, 474, 482, 605
plagues in the wilderness, 260

plants, 239
plenteous redemption, 441, 442
plowmen, 433–37
Poling, Daniel A., 155, 431
poor and needy, 106, 107, 111, 284, 286–88, 309, 311, 313, 317–19, 322, 515
poplar tree, 488
portion, 2, 5, 362, 528, 529, 530
posterity, 312, 333, 427
powerless, 397, 514
praise, 242, 402, 467, 495, 549, 557, 585, 591
    befits the upright, 564
    as crown of created order, 591
    as double-edged sword, 580, 582
    as fitting, 564
    as weapon, 574–75
praise the LORD, 231–32, 237, 258, 303, 310, 317, 345, 473, 558
prayer, 209, 262–63, 269, 298, 307, 368
prayer of David, 106, 107, 111, 532
prayer of Jabez, 430
precepts of God, 305–6, 307
pride, 3, 165, 446–48
priesthood, 260–61, 296, 444
priest-king, 292, 296, 297, 299–300
priestly benediction, 378–79, 381, 408, 465–66, 467
priests, 454, 455, 458, 461
princes, 557, 570, 572
prison, 529
prisoners, 270
prodigal, return of, 198
prosperity, 5, 427–30, 456
    of the wicked, 3–4
providence, 252–54, 319, 505, 506, 564, 566, 568, 569, 573–74
Psalms
    editing of, 111
    five books of, 214
    rhetorical voice of, 593
psalms of creation, 234, 562
psalms of lament, 256, 538. See also community lament; individual lament
psalms of praise, 248, 256
psalm of thanksgiving, 150, 208, 248, 256, 259, 266–67, 287, 302, 337, 339, 348, 482
psalms of the heavenly king, 157, 159, 161, 161, 170, 179, 187, 194, 197, 204, 208, 212, 249
psalms of trust, 141, 144
    individual, 395, 439
pure in heart, 3
putting God to the test, 42, 44

quail, 260, 305
quieted, 446, 449
"quotation" theory, 282

Rachel, 40, 42, 484
Rachel to Leah transition, 40, 46, 48, 61
Rahab, 114
ram's horn, 68, 194
Rashi, 121
Reardon, Patrick Henry, 87, 194, 296, 581
rebuke, 238–39, 520
recognition theme, 84, 86
redeemed, four categories of, 269–73
redeemer, 574
redemption, 243, 272, 328, 441, 472, 483–85, 501
Red Sea, 34, 35, 158, 325, 326, 482, 542, 599
reeds, sea of, 599
refuge, 144, 145, 521, 527–28
remembering, 10, 13, 14, 34, 37, 40, 44, 361, 483–85 534
Renaissance, 500
repentance, as prayer and practice, 264–65
reproving love, 521–22
rest, 170, 173, 339, 341
resurrection, 123
return from exile. See Babylonian exile: return from
reverence, 440
revival, 63, 100
righteous, 309, 311, 366, 520, 534
righteousness, 101, 103, 104, 129, 167, 185, 229, 307, 437, 458
righteousness and peace will kiss, 100–102
right hand of God, 12, 295, 297, 354
right hand of the accused, 284, 285, 288, 527
right-hand side, 382, 386
rivers, 160
rivers of Babylon, 487–88, 490
Robertson, O. Palmer, 246, 248
rock of salvation, 172
rod, Babylonian control as, 408
root, 62
Rosh Hashanah, 69
royal psalms, 292, 450, 538. See also psalms of the heavenly king
rulers, 572
Ruth, 434

Saadyah Gaon, 378
Sabbath, 150, 151, 171, 240
sacred space, 91

sacrifice, 520
Salem, 26
salvation
    new era of, 178
    waiting for, 368
    of the world, 212–13, 225
salvation history, 195
Samuel, 200
Sanballat and Tobiah, 352, 401
sanctuary, 4–5, 7, 12, 36, 587
Saul, persecution of David, 538
scepter, 295, 407
Schaefer, Konrad, 108, 144, 267, 370, 446, 486, 508
school setting, of postexilic community, 358, 360
Scottish Psalter, 210
sea, 160, 180, 194, 271, 272
sea trade, 268
second exodus, 178, 330, 469, 475, 540–41
second temple, 179, 466. See also temple: reconstruction of
Second Temple period, 368, 373, 389, 445
secret sins, 136
security, 409–10
seeking/calling, 602
selah, 90, 514, 533
self-esteem, 448
Sennacherib, 25–26
Septuagint, 534, 565
Sermon on the Mount, 321, 322–23, 377, 393
serpent, 145
servanthood, 109, 515
servant of the LORD, 340–41, 360
servants of the LORD, 319, 320, 384, 465, 466, 473
servitude, 396, 397
seven (number), 368, 589
shadow of the Almighty, 144
shalom, 373, 391, 394, 408, 409, 410, 602
Shechem, 277–78
sheep, 11
shelter of the Most High, 143
Shema, 547, 602
Sheol, 108, 122, 332, 402, 497, 506, 511, 521
Shepherd of Israel, 59, 61, 62, 64–65
shepherd theme, 33
Sheshbazzar, 294
shield, 92, 94
Shiloh, tabernacle at, 46
shout for joy, 206
sickness, 121
signs and wonders in Egypt, 44, 605
Sihon of the Amorites, 474, 482

silence
    in awe of God's judgments, 26
    follows God's acts of grace, 30
sin, 259
    ranking the severity of, 230
    record of, 440, 442
singing, 215
singing of psalms, 587
singing praise, 473, 496
sing to the LORD, 193
slander, 4, 216
slave-master relationship, 396, 397
sleep, as death, 136
slothfulness, 423
smoke, 61
Sodom and Gomorrah, 484, 515
Solomon, 421, 513
    prayer at dedication of temple, 175–76, 450, 495, 496, 497, 501–2
Song of Deborah, 86
Song of Mary, 18
Song of Moses (Deuteronomy), 134, 165, 362
Song of Moses (Exodus), 36, 158, 599
Songs of Ascent, 245, 247, 372, 374, 378–80, 381, 384, 408–9, 419, 428, 603
songs of joy, 415, 488, 491
son of David, 293
son of man, 63, 595
Sons of Korah, 93
soul, 276
Sovereign LORD (direct address), 515, 521
sowing tears and reaping joy, 415
sparrow, 93
spies in Canaan, 260
spiritual disciplines, 522
spiritual warfare, 582
Spurgeon, Charles, 28, 90, 97, 160, 409, 435, 444, 447, 516, 544, 548, 552, 567, 587, 590, 591
stars, 482, 565
statutes, 41, 69, 160–61, 162, 200, 360, 362, 454
steadfast, 276
step parallelism, 379, 401, 428, 452
streams in the Negev, 413–14, 415
strength to strength, 94, 96
strings and pipes, 588, 590
submission to God's will, 55, 133
suffering, 226, 255, 319–20, 339, 363
suffering servant, 105–7, 291, 363, 535
Sukkoth, 277–78
sun, 239, 382, 386, 482

sun and shield, 94
superiority complex, 48
surely (’ak), 2, 5, 6–7, 144, 147

table of nations, 87
Tate, Marvin E., 69
teaching, 41
teaching, teachers, 41, 361, 364
temple, 10, 53, 91, 95, 128, 215
  courts of, 93, 179, 207
  gates of, 207
  reconstruction of, 100, 138,
    167, 193, 412, 445
  See also new temple; second
    temple; Zerubbabel's temple
temptation, 522
ten (number), 589
Ten Commandments, 78, 359
ten-stringed instrument, 151
terracing, 379
terror of night, 144
testimony, 41
thank offering, 206, 271, 323,
  337, 340
thanksgiving, 172, 206, 207, 259,
  493, 498, 527, 529
theophany, 180, 185, 538, 541
Thielicke, Helmut, 55, 72, 545
thirteen attributes of God, 229,
  304, 305, 549, 589
Thompson, Francis, 509
thorn in the flesh, 354
throne of God, 160, 162, 185, 231
thrones for judgment, 390, 392
thrones of the house of David,
  389, 390
thunder, 35
timbrel, 68, 579, 587–88, 590
time, 135, 136, 138
Titus (general), 10, 85
"today," 171, 173
to/for David (psalm title), 513,
  593
tongue, 516
Torah, 160–61, 166, 200, 302,
  317, 358, 365, 370
  center place in developing Ju-
    daism, 303, 305–6, 323, 359,
    368, 496–97, 566
  opposition to, 361
  written on hearts, 368–69
Torah psalms, 317, 358
tourists, vs. pilgrims, 374–76
traps, 521
travel, dangers of, 382
Trotter, Lilias, 155, 196, 243–44,
  343, 575–76
trouble, 497–98
  and sorrow, 137
trumpet, 194, 587, 590

trust, 7, 41, 43, 109, 141, 147, 400
  in the LORD, 311, 333, 339, 397
  in princes, 557
truth, 276
twelve (number), 589
Tyre, 86, 87, 115, 268, 277

unfailing love. See God, unfailing
  love of
unity, of worshiping community,
  459–63
universal praise of God, 548
universal salvation, 195, 206, 208,
  212–13
upright, 309, 366–67, 408
Uriah, 453

VanGemeren, Willem, 135
vengeance, 168, 582, 583, 584
vindication, 194, 498
vine metaphor, 62
violence, 3, 514
von Rad, Gerhard, 232
vows, 27, 28, 340

wadis, 403
waiting, 442
Wallace, Lew, 37
Waltner, James H., 173, 231
Walton, John, 593
war, 374, 514, 541
"watch over / keep" (verb), 381,
  384
water, from the rock struck by
  Moses, 326–27
way of falsehood, 361
way of holiness, 103
way of truth, 361
weak, 77
wealth and riches, 311
weaned child, 444–49
weariness, 96
wedding blessing, 426
wedding supper of the Lamb, 101
Weiser, Artur, 48, 64, 139, 227,
  252, 254, 255, 408, 415, 444,
  536
Wenham, Gordon J., 313
Wesley, John, 183, 443
Westminster Shorter Catechism,
  253, 262
"what if" psalm, 403
"why?" (question), 10, 14
wicked, 94, 154, 165–67, 168,
  312, 313, 433
widows, 166, 221, 285, 289, 558
Wilcock, Michael, 118, 119, 177,
  250, 308, 340, 348, 367, 369,
  505, 508, 522
wild animals, 382, 385, 572

wilderness, 40, 43, 269
wilderness generation, 170, 171,
  173, 256–58, 599
wilderness wanderings, 252
Willard, Dallas, 375
Williams, Charles, 599
will of God, 535, 536, 537
winds, 232, 238, 271, 572
wine, 19
wineskin, 363
wings of an eagle, 142, 144
winter, 13
wisdom psalms, 1, 143, 308
Wolpe, David, 16–17, 288–89,
  356, 485, 568
wonderful deeds, 230, 270, 271
"wonderful things" (pl’), 360
word of God, runs swiftly, 566,
  568
work, 423, 426–27
world
  beauty of, 565
  as vertical and horizontal, 219
worship, 7, 154–55, 172, 186,
  206, 207, 341, 391–92, 440,
  528
  restored in the temple, 465
  in unity, 461
wrath of God, 20, 130, 135, 137
wrath of man, 27, 28–29, 30
Wright, Christopher J. H., 15,
  56, 57
Wright, N.   92, 96, 97, 386–87

"yet/but" (c   ne ion), 435–37
YHWH (et   ammaton), 63,
  142, 44, 147, 275, 277, 295,
  296, 39
Yom Kippur, 16–17
youth, 296, 360

Zechariah, 445–46, 492
Zenger, Erich, 9, 33, 84, 87, 111,
  127, 267, 273, 282, 302, 305,
  309, 323, 337, 345, 359, 363,
  419, 426, 429, 430, 462, 474,
  480, 490, 588, 589
Zerubbabel, 445, 452, 556
Zerubbabel's temple, 100, 326,
  331, 338, 452, 501
Zion, 114–16, 186, 199, 221,
  388, 428
Zion songs, 112, 386–87, 406,
  412–13, 450, 486, 488